ETURN

Publications of the Bureau of Business and Economic Research
University of California

❖

Previously published in this series:

A TREATISE ON WAR INFLATION
by William Fellner (1942)

BREAD AND DEMOCRACY IN GERMANY
by Alexander Gerschenkron (1943)

THE ECONOMICS OF THE PACIFIC COAST PETROLEUM INDUSTRY
PART 1: MARKET STRUCTURE
by Joe S. Bain (1944)

LAND TENURE PROBLEMS IN THE SANTA FE RAILROAD GRANT AREA
by Sanford A. Mosk (1944)

NATIONAL POWER AND THE STRUCTURE OF FOREIGN TRADE
by Albert O. Hirschmann (1945)

THE ECONOMICS OF THE PACIFIC COAST PETROLEUM INDUSTRY
PART 2: PRICE BEHAVIOR AND COMPETITION
by Joe S. Bain (1945)

CALIFORNIA BUSINESS CYCLES
by Frank L. Kidner (1946)

MONETARY POLICIES AND FULL EMPLOYMENT
by William Fellner (1946, 1947)

THE ECONOMICS OF THE PACIFIC COAST PETROLEUM INDUSTRY
PART 3: PUBLIC POLICY TOWARD COMPETITION AND PRICING
by Joe S. Bain (1947)

THE STRUCTURE OF TRANSCONTINENTAL RAILROAD RATES
by Stuart Daggett and John F. Carter (1947)

THE CHANGING COMPETITIVE STRUCTURE OF THE WHOLESALE
GROCERY TRADE: A CASE STUDY OF THE LOS ANGELES
MARKET, 1920–1946
by Ralph Cassady, Jr. and Wylie L. Jones (1949)

TAXING MUNICIPAL BOND INCOME
by Lyle C. Fitch (1950)

CRISIS IN BRITAIN

Publications of the
Bureau of Business and Economic Research
University of California

CRISIS IN BRITAIN

*Plans and Achievements of
the Labour Government*

BY ROBERT A. BRADY

UNIVERSITY OF CALIFORNIA PRESS
BERKELEY AND LOS ANGELES
CAMBRIDGE UNIVERSITY PRESS · LONDON
1950

UNIVERSITY OF CALIFORNIA PRESS
BERKELEY AND LOS ANGELES
CALIFORNIA

◇

CAMBRIDGE UNIVERSITY PRESS
LONDON, ENGLAND

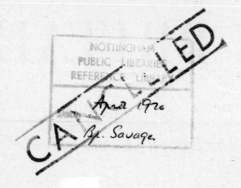

PRINTED IN THE UNITED STATES OF AMERICA
BY THE UNIVERSITY OF CALIFORNIA PRESS

TO HOPE

WHO UNDERSTANDS THE NEED OF
SOME IRON IN ONE'S SOUL

Preface

THIS STUDY was begun in January, 1948, and was financed by a generous grant from the Bureau of Business and Economic Research of the University of California. Some eight months were spent in England, mostly in London, but with occasional side trips into various industrial districts of South Wales, the Midlands, and Scotland. An intensive examination was made of the background and content of the more important laws passed by the Labour government, which, their sponsors believe, will lead, directly or indirectly, to the Socialist commonwealth of the future. This book is a report on the findings of that investigation.

Two subjects dominated the study throughout: the nature and meaning of the Labour party's "middle-way Socialism," and the content and future possibilities of the British version of economic planning. Since Labour experts share the proverbial British penchant for a piecemeal and empirical approach to all problems—however long-standing or immediate and insistent—to such an extent that it is virtually impossible to generalize about either their Socialism or their planning except within the reference of the specific program, there was no escape from the procedure suggested by this approach. In so proceeding to review each separate program in some detail the risk had to be run that the forest would be lost for the trees, and this risk was made doubly hazardous by the simple fact that every policy looking toward fulfillment of long-run objectives was necessarily complicated by the unusual conditions surrounding an inescapable postwar struggle for sheer national economic survival.

Yet the difficulty of obtaining by such seemingly roundabout methods an adequate and sure grasp of the larger trend of events in Labour Britain is fully matched by the American need for understanding both the conditions which gave rise to the reforms undertaken and the long-run implications of such parts of the dimly outlined program as have thus far been revealed. That Labour spokesmen—not to mention most of Labour's official opposition—see little or nothing which may justly be termed radical in either the details of the Labour program or in the general ideas which lie behind each separate proposal, is a point commonly missed by American observers. The British Labour leaders see themselves not as innovators, but as modest fulfillers of past trends rooted both in British history and in the doctrines of Western European Enlightenment. In this self-portrait they are the residuary legatees of Ricardo, Bentham, and John Stuart Mill, of Francis Place, Chadwick, and Shaftesbury, of Cartwright, the People's Charter and the great reform bills of 1832 and 1867, of Disraeli, Gladstone, and Lloyd George, and of William Morris, Hyndman, Keir Hardie, George Bernard Shaw, and the Webbs. They see Socialism, in short, as nothing more than the permeation of tried-and-true democratic ideas and practices through the whole of the power structures of modern society, and themselves as playing in all this merely the role of midwives in the accouchement of an old society giving birth, by wholly natural processes, to a new.

This new society they hold to be not only natural, in the philosophic sense, but thoroughly practical, for it is to provide a "middle way" between the excesses of both East and West—between Russian communism with its legacy of violence, and American capitalism with its tendency to reaction. They see in this not only a far safer course for the future, but also the road to a middle ground where the seemingly irreconcilable conflicts of the vast and swiftly spreading cold war may ultimately be resolved in peace. Whether Attlee's Government is thus engaged in *the* noble experiment of modern times, each must judge for himself. But in judging he had best also realize that upon the success or failure of British recovery and reform under Labour auspices depends much which is of vital importance for American democracy. The die has already been cast for far-reaching changes which affect plans for unification of Western Europe, for breakup or consolidation of the British Commonwealth of Nations and the role to be played therein by the great colonial powers, and for general economic recovery in Europe without danger to democratic institutions. Upon the adequacies or inadequacies of the British experiment may very well rest much of our own chance of success in achieving full employment in a society where the dominating view of democratic polity shows but little disposition to compromise very far with the social and economic planning emphasis underlying the conception of the Welfare State, which now commands so much popular support abroad.

Perhaps this book may help somewhat to give a more realistic picture of this British experiment in democracy. So far as it may, its virtues will largely be a result of assistance given by a host of British experts—far too numerous to mention here. Many of them could not be identified by name in any case, for they occupy official positions in various ministries and administrative bodies where their opinions, even though given on a purely personal basis, might still be construed as official statements of policy. This includes at least one or more persons in each of the government agencies whose policies are discussed in the following chapters, who read, criticized, and amended appropriate sections of the manuscript on condition that they remain anonymous. In respecting this request, it is a pleasure, however, to acknowledge with gratitude their indispensable aid, while wholly absolving them from any direct responsibility for any of the views expressed.

To those whose positions permit me to thank them publicly, I wish especially to mention the following: For countless suggestions regarding persons to consult on various problems, both inside and outside government circles, Max Nicholson, of the offices of the Lord President of the Council; for special assistance in obtaining and reviewing documents, Maurice Orbach (Labour M.P.), the library staffs of the London School of Economics, the Fabian Society, and Political and Economic Planning, the research staff of the Labour Party (Transport House) and of the Co-operative Wholesale Society (C.W.S.), the Reference Division of the British Library of Information in London, the staff of the British Library of Information in San Francisco, the research staffs of the Iron and Steel Federation and the British Gas Council, and various members of the firm of industrial consultants, Urwick, Orr & Partners; and for reading one or more chapters of the manuscript, Robert Hall of the Cabinet offices, D. L. Burn and Francois Lafitte of the *London Times*, Barbara Ward of the *Economist*, Rita Hindon of the Fabian Colonial Bureau, George Walworth of the C.W.S. (Manchester), Professor Harold Laski of the London School of Economics, Frank Hellings of Blakeney and Marsden Pobble, Ian Mikardo (Labour M.P.), Professor Sargant Florence of the University of Birmingham, and Professor Charles Mowat of the University of California at Los Angeles. An especial debt is owed to Kay Graw, student at the London School of Economics, and Mark Daniels, research associate of the Medical Research Council, for performing the disagreeable task of handling the distribution and collection of manuscript read by these and other British experts who consented to review for errors of omission and commission. Irwin Anderson of the staff of the American Embassy in London gave assistance in innumerable ways.

Among my colleagues at the University of California I am especially grateful to Professor Frank Kidner, Director of the Bureau of Business and Economic Research, whose close and sympathetic attention to countless details, financial and otherwise, is largely responsible for early publication of this study. I am also grateful for the criticisms and suggestions of the committee appointed by the Bureau of Business and Economic Research to review the manuscript under the chairmanship of Professor Leonard Crum. Professor John Condliffe has made several helpful suggestions. Above all, I am most deeply indebted to Edward Bryant, research assistant throughout the conduct of this study. Mr. Bryant collected much of the material, kept all of it in impeccable order under the most unfavorable circumstances of virtual noncoöperation by the author, and has been throughout a constant source of stimulation and suggestion. Finally, it is a pleasure to acknowledge the assistance in making countless small improvements in style and manner of presentation which was given by the staff of the University of California Press, particularly John Gildersleeve, which may well prove of major importance when the tallies have all been made.

It is perhaps important to concede that however much help I may have received from these and other sources, the faults of summary and interpretation are mine alone. Not even my wife, Mildred Edie, who has had a very great deal to say of value about what is written here, seems disposed to deny me this dubious honor.

Throughout the following text special applications of British law to Scotland and North Ireland have usually been omitted. Unless otherwise noted, all *Hansard* references are to the daily *Hansard*, not the bound volume, where the paging arrangement is somewhat different. With exception of brief references in the first and last chapters to subsequent events, the narrative is brought down to, but not past, July 1, 1949.

Robert A. Brady

Berkeley, California
January 3, 1950

Contents

CHAPTER I

"Third Force" Socialism

Before a crowded and tense House, Mr. Attlee unfolded a grim picture of Britain's economic
position. He made it clear that many of Britain's difficulties arose from the vast effort for
war purposes and the enormous burden this had placed upon the British economy. The war
that Britain had helped to win had fundamentally disrupted the post-war economic system,
and it was clear that, to a large extent, the solution to Britain's economic problems could
only come by the efforts and sacrifices of the British people themselves ... But Mr. Attlee
stressed that Britain's situation was part of a world problem which would ultimately have
to be solved on a world-wide scale.—British Information Services, August 6, 1947.

FROM THE MOMENT of its coming to power the British Labour government has had to contend not only with issues that were legacies of two
world wars, but with many of the still unsolved problems that had led
to those wars. It has been compelled to divide its forces in order to
battle for national economic survival in the international sphere and,
at the same time, struggle for wide-ranging social and economic revolution at home. The first task involves a web of interdependent issues
which is coextensive with virtually the entire range of economic policy-
making decisions by all parties and interests through the nation, and is
further complicated by the fact that very nearly everywhere, and with
almost every facet of such policy, success at home depends upon a
world economic situation over which Britain can exercise at best only
a very limited and highly tentative influence. The second is no less complex or vital; it reaches to the central ideological conflicts, and their
attendant cultural values, which lie at the heart of not only British but
all Western civilization.

Since the collapse of the Axis, the resolution of each task has been
hanging in precarious balance. But the worst lies in the simple fact that
while success on either front requires a clearly visualized set of goals,
the best of broadly conceived logistical stratagems, and a capacity for
singular, sustained, and Herculean efforts, both must be tackled at once.
Neither struggle can be won—indeed, has any chance of being won—
unless some degree of success crowns efforts in the other field at the
same time. So far as the Labour party is concerned, the two struggles
are indissolubly linked at a thousand points—are, in fact, but two aspects of a single struggle for survival of the British people.

That this is the Labour view there can be no question. In the party's reckoning it provided the clue to victory at the polls in 1945; it held the key to the elections of 1950; and it contains the secret to the future of the Labour party for many generations to come. But in so viewing the matter, the Labour party does not stand wholly alone. The vital connection between economic and social issues is well known to the Liberal and Conservative parties—not to mention parties further to the left. A glance through the more recent publications of the Conservative Political Centre,[1] for example, shows that the moral of the story is grasped in some dim sense even by Labour's most bitter Parliamentary opposition. If even the parties of the right, as subsequent chapters will detail, must make major concessions to the popular demand for wide-ranging social change as a condition to obtaining any mass support at all, then the Labour party must reach even more widely and change even more fundamentally if it is to survive as a political force. The time may come when it may appear that its major political weakness was not that it has gone as far as it has in this direction, but that it did not go far enough at a time when to hesitate was not merely to lose ground, but also to risk giving way entirely to a strong movement from either the far left or the far right.

It is especially necessary to emphasize this close connection between economic recovery in Britain and drastic social reform—a connection which Britain shares with practically all the rest of the postwar world— since it is generally either not understood in the United States, or being understood it is frequently opposed and decried as the source of nameless abominations. Not even, for example, the large comprehensive *Report of the ECA Mission to the United Kingdom*[2] troubles to take note of the social side of the British recovery program. It is passed over as though it were either irrelevant, or at best a nuisance and a handicap to be endured as a condition to getting on with more important matters. American journals and newspapers, with minor exceptions, reflect a similar view. Yet such an attitude is unquestionably a mistake so serious that it may lead not only to a complete misorientation of American

[1] See, e.g., the pamphlets, *Conservative Social and Industrial Reform 1800 to 1945* (Dec. 1947), and David Clarke, *The Conservative Faith in a Modern Age.* Foreword by R. A. Butler, M.P. (April 1947). Butler is one of the three or four most important leaders of the Conservative party. Similar arguments run through *The Industrial Charter: A Statement of Conservative Industrial Policy* (1947), and *The Agricultural Charter: A Statement of Conservative Agricultural Policy* (1948), published by the closely allied Conservative and Unionist Central Office.

[2] (London, Dec. 31, 1948.) 3 vols. Vol. I: "The Highlights"; Vol. II: "Supporting Facts"; Vol. III: "Statistical Supplement." (Hereafter referred to as *ECA Report*).

foreign policy—including the results hoped for from extension of Marshall Plan aid[3]—but also to a simple failure to understand the nature of the *Realpolitik* which limits the range of choices open to the Labour party, the goals and steps which divide it from its opposition, or, even the chances of success or failure on the more narrowly circumscribed issues of short-run planning for immediate postwar recovery, irrespective of the political position of the sponsoring party.

THE ECONOMIC FRONT: RECOVERY AND SURVIVAL

The battle for economic recovery must be understood before the issues of social reconstruction can be grasped. Here the mood is grim. The analogy savors of Dunkirk, and it is frequently drawn. At Dunkirk, it will be remembered, the British managed a hairbreadth escape under appalling circumstances from what appeared to be a logistically impossible situation. Its aftermath saw the beginning of a protracted uphill fight, long alone and unaided, from what seemed a hopelessly vulnerable position. Allies were found eventually, but aid came only in the nick of time, and at first in driblets so small that each successive renewal seemed just barely enough to stave off overshadowing and total catastrophe. Even then, only the military folly of the Nazi assault on the heartland of Asia, combined with the mounting scale of the American offensive, came barely in time to rescue England at the final brink.

By these accidents of good fortune, Britain was saved, but the question remained whether or not it was, for her at least, a Pyrrhic victory. Habit reinforced by the irreducible facts of her exhaustion carried over into the postwar reconstruction phase the phraseology and the attendant mood of "her finest hour." Political talk is that of battle, of ineluctable crisis, of struggle against insuperable odds, of possible defeat, and of heroic effort to stave off impending disaster. Each tactical victory is achieved to face a more formidable situation still; each driblet of outside aid in the form of loans, special trade agreements, and finally of the European Recovery Program (ERP), has come just in the nick of time, and its coming is greeted as the provider of still another breathing spell for the long, difficult, and trying uphill pull that lies ahead.

It seems gratuitous to offer examples to illustrate the mood. Every

---

[3] See, e.g., Barbara Ward, *The West at Bay* (London, 1948), particularly pt. iv: "Western Association," and Seymour Harris, *The European Recovery Program* (Cambridge, 1948), particularly "Concluding Remarks," pp. 272–275, and "Postscript on the First Six Months of the ECA," pp. 297–300. Of interest also is the pamphlet by John Kenneth Galbraith, *Beyond the Marshall Plan*, Planning Pamphlets, no. 67 (Washington, National Planning Association, 1948), pp. 9–27 in particular.

daily newspaper carries something of the lengthening record of grim declamation, gloomy forebodings, and records of partial failures to balance each partial success. There are not lacking strong and encouraging words, but behind even the most sprightly there is some indication that hope drags with leaden feet. In the 1948 *Economic Survey*,[4] for example, after recording notable gains, the conclusion is drawn that "our situation is therefore such that, without further substantial external aid, we can have no hope of recovering equilibrium at a reasonable standard of life within the next few years." The *Survey* closed with the warning that "if that aid is offered, on the scale indicated by the Paris Conference, under the Marshall Plan we shall still have to exert the utmost economy in our overseas expenditure."

When the aid was forthcoming a few days later, the Chancellor hastened to warn the public that it provided no lasting solution for any of the major problems confronting the country. Picking up the refrain a member of the Opposition noted that were the objectives and "targets" discussed in the white paper achieved, and these achievements further buttressed by continued Marshall Plan aid, there would still be left a £100,000,000 shortage in the critical overseas balance. A colleague rose to plead for unity with these dolorous words: "If in these darkening days, with so many dangers, we continue to fight together, we may all go down together, and if Britain falls there will fall with her the freedom of the world she saved."[5]

A year later, when hope had been somewhat revived by visible proofs that Britain was entering "upon the fifth post-war financial year with tremendous achievements to our credit,"[6] still a most heavy task lay ahead before the British future could be assured. Most formidable of all was the "deficit on dollar account, amounting over the year to no less than £423 million for the sterling area as a whole" (£360,000,000 for Britain alone).[7] Even more dangerous for the Labour government, however, was the shock given to the country by presentation of a budget which offered no tax relief and held out no prospect of

[4] Chancellor of the Exchequer, *Economic Survey for 1948*, Cmd. 7344 (London, HMSO, 1948).

[5] Col. Stanley and Harold Macmillan in a budget debate as reported in the *Daily Telegraph*, April 14, 1948.

[6] "... not only have we ... travelled a long way on the road to economic recovery, but we have, in addition, carried through, and paid and provided for, the greatest programme of social services ever undertaken in any country in so short a period of time, while at the same time surpassing all previous records for exports and capital investment at home." The Chancellor of the Exchequer (Sir Stafford Cripps), reporting on the *Financial and Economic Statement* (Budget) for 1949–50, *Hansard*, Vol. 463, col. 2108.

[7] *Ibid.*, col. 2077.

decline in the gigantic defense costs; which anticipated slowing down the vital export drive to a snail's pace; which required a tapering off of food subsidies that inevitably threatened the wage stabilization program and with it the prospect of maintaining an effective brake on inflation; which indicated a decline of the anticipated annual increase in production from an encouraging 12 per cent for the previous year to a mere 2½ per cent for the following year, and with this, what may very well prove to be a politically disastrous tapering off of the whole vast and highly popular social security program; and which held out many other prospects that seemed to dash the rosier hopes of both enemies and supporters for some easily foreseeable lifting of the seemingly endless burdens of the postwar era. The general reaction was quickly reflected in the first real political setback received by the Government when the voters went to the polls in the rural and urban district council elections during the following week.[8]

Thus the Labour party, in formulating its election program for the 1950 elections, does not exaggerate when it speaks of the "tremendous fight ahead"[9] before victory can be won on the economic front—and clearly without success here there is waning hope of further substantial gains at the polls. The long-sustained austerity mood is in keeping with the stern realities. These are a heritage which any British government would have found on its doorstep on V-E day, and they are most formidable indeed. Partly they trace back to the temporary, but crippling, losses of the Second World War. Partly they are the product of long-run adverse changes in both domestic and world conditions antedating the war. And partly they involve continuing postwar handicaps of a kind that are only partly subject to manipulation and control by the British themselves.

War losses and damage have been detailed at great length in numerous places, most notably in the *ECA Report*. Outstanding is the loss of "Over $18.1 billion worth of capital assets . . . as a direct result of the struggle in which she took part. Bomb damage to buildings, equipment and machinery, and shipping losses account for about $9.9 billion of this total. An even greater loss came through so-called 'disinvestment'— the reduction in value due to inability to repair and maintain physical

---

[8] The results of the elections during the week ending April 10, 1949 for 3,062 seats on over 500 rural and urban district councils showed net gains of 265 seats for the Conservatives, and 159 net losses for the Labour party. *Home Affairs Survey*, April 20, 1949, p. 9.

[9] *Labour Believes in Britain*, [for consideration at the Annual Conference of the Labour Party at Whitsun, 1949,] (National Executive Committee of the Labour Party, April, 1949), p. 6.

equipment] ... if new capital were formed in the United Kingdom at the pre-war rate, it would take seven years to make good the physical damage that was suffered between 1939 and 1945."[10]

In physical terms this meant loss of nearly half of her merchant marine of some 18,000,000 tons carrying capacity, destruction or damage to nearly one-third (4,000,000 out of 12,000,000) of all the houses in Britain, badly run-down industrial plant and transport facilities, etc. In addition Britain "lost gold and foreign investments and ... incurred new debt to an extent which implies a worsening of our pre-war capital position in relation to the rest of the world by nearly £6,000 millions" including "the full United States and Canadian credits the need for which has arisen from the war" before the granting of Marshall aid.[11] In the place of prewar overseas investments of some £3,700,000,000, around one-third or one-half of which had been liquidated by sale or destroyed by enemy action, were to be found "overseas debts totalling £2,879,000,000 to cover war purchases and the cost of maintaining military forces."[12]

Meanwhile, the war had saddled the country with a vast public debt, the interest upon which currently absorbs something like a sixth of the national budget,[13] a postwar defense program which is set at a level that absorbs something like 11 per cent of the entire national income,[14] and a budget of overseas military, occupation, relief, and allied costs which at the present time is running at the rate of approximately £200,000,-000 per annum.[15]

Paralleling huge overseas expenditures went not only loss of overseas investments, but loss of overseas banking income, numerous other overseas invisible sources of income—particularly from the merchant

[10] *ECA Report*, Vol. I, p. 11. Table 60, Vol. III, p. 57, gives a slightly different total. Total domestic loss of capital for the interval 1940–1947 is estimated at £4,650,000,000 (the £ is converted into dollars at the rate of £1 = $4.00), and net capital formation in 1938 is given as £616,000,000 (all figures in 1948 prices).

[11] *Economic Survey for 1947*, Cmd. 7046, p. 11.

[12] Francis Williams, *Socialist Britain* (New York, 1949), p. 12.

[13] For the fiscal year 1947–48 "the cost of interest on National Debt and other Consolidated Fund services, including £23 million for sinking funds, was £542 million, against the estimate of £534 million." Total expenditure for the same period was £3,176,000,000. Sir Stafford Cripps, in *Hansard*, Vol. 453, col. 2083.

[14] The "gross cost of the Services" absorbed 7 per cent of national income in 1938, 49 per cent in 1945, and 11 per cent in 1947. *Economic Survey for 1947*, p. 31. The Budget estimates for 1949–50 calls for an increase of Defence expenditure from £753,000,000 to £760,000,000 (the 1947–48 figure was £854,000,000), and no decrease is anticipated for an indefinite period of time. "So far as Defence is concerned, we obviously cannot look for any marked reduction for some years, unless there is a complete change in the international situation." Cripps, in *Hansard*, Vol. 453, col. 2089.

[15] Williams, *op. cit.*, p. 13.

marine,[16] and, most important of all, loss of overseas markets. As for visible trade, many branch plants and overseas distribution and sales outlets had been closed down or sold, and inability of those left open to supply buyers over a long period of time had entrenched American competitors and local interests. It is difficult to weigh and appraise the importance of the drastic curtailment of these contacts which had been built up through several decades of continuous business operation but it is, no doubt, of enormous significance to a country whose economic strength has rested so heavily on trading and financial operations.

Britain has long been dependent upon a net surplus of visible and invisible items for large and absolutely indispensable imports of basic raw materials. According to Williams,[17] before the war "Nearly three-quarters of all the food she ate came from abroad, 55 per cent of her meat, 75 per cent of her wheat, 85 per cent of her butter, all her tea, cocoa, and coffee, three-quarters of her sugar. Every year more than 20,000,000 tons of imported food had to be brought across the seas and unloaded at her docks. Moreover, with the single exception of coal,[18] the raw materials upon which her major industries depended were largely or wholly imported; all the cotton, all the rubber, five-sixths of the wool, practically all the petroleum, two-thirds of the iron ore, most of the timber. Altogether, nearly 25 per cent of her entire national income, or, in other words, a quarter of the combined value of all the goods and services produced by her people, went in paying for imports of one kind or another."

Excepting only foodstuffs, where a heavily subsidized program had served materially to increase home production,[19] the war increased rather than diminished this dependence upon foreign raw materials. Population meanwhile has increased by some four million since 1939. Furthermore, there is no possibility of considerably increasing exports of goods—at the very time when adverse trade balances throw virtually the entire cost of payments upon visible exports—without correspondingly increasing imports. And here Britain faces the additional diffi-

---

[16] "In the decade before the war Britain averaged about £224 million a year on net invisibles. In 1946, she had a *negative* balance on invisibles of £168 million, and by 1947 this negative balance had increased to £192 million." *ECA Report*, Vol. I, p. 4. See also Vol. I, chart 4, p. 3, and Vol. III, table 23, p. 22.

[17] Williams, *op. cit.*, pp. 11–12.

[18] "Exports of coal, which amounted to 54.9 million tons in 1930 and 35.9 million tons in 1938, fell to 5.1 million tons in 1941 and 3.3 million tons in 1945." *British Fuel & Power Industries*, PEP Report (London, 1948), p. 27, and table, p. 224. The "target" for coal exports for the end of 1949 was set at 155 per cent of 1938. *Hansard*, Vol. 463, col. 2068.

[19] Possibly, however, only at a considerable net increase in the cost of home-grown foodstuffs.

culty that the average price of imports relative to the average price of exports has been rising since before the war. According to the *ECA Report*,[20] the terms of trade, "expressed as volume of exports required to purchase a given volume of imports," has risen from 100 (taken as base) for 1938 to 121 for the first quarter of 1948. "Britain's deficit in 1946 was higher by £136 million than it would have been had export and import prices remained at their 1938 levels. In 1947, the amount attributable to price changes was more than twice as great as in 1946. Price increases accounted for about four-fifths of the trade deficit in each of these postwar years."[21]

There are many other aspects of the heritage from the war which render the British task of postwar economic recovery onerous. But the picture looks no less gloomy when placed in the perspective of long-run changes affecting Britain's domestic economy and international economic position. Dependence on overseas raw materials has not been accompanied by a rising capacity to compete on advantageous terms in international markets. Ever since the end of the First World War, Britain had experienced a more or less continuous decline "in the amounts by which . . . net earnings on invisibles exceeded her trade deficit"; during the thirties the net over-all "deficit in the balance of payments ran at the rate of £27 million per year."[22] This is all the more interesting in light of the fact that the adverse terms of trade had throughout this period been generally speaking much lower than before the First World War, and that after 1929 terms of trade had moved strongly in her favor.[23]

What had happened over the years since Britain began to lose her preëminence as the major industrial country of the world,[24] was a change in the structure of her exports which saw Britain losing out on more and more of the mass-produced lines to German, American, Japanese, and other competitors. This decline in one major field, that of textiles, was absolute, large scale, and catastrophic. Whereas, for example, she was exporting 6,791,000,000 square yards of cotton piece goods in 1913 on the eve of the First World War, there had been a more or less steady decline until she was exporting only 1,369,000,000

---

[20] Vol. III, table 2B, p. 2.

[21] *Ibid.*, I, p. 5.

[22] *Ibid.*, I, p. 3.

[23] Using 1938 as a base (100) the terms of trade between 1836 and 1913 had never dropped below 141; in 1921–1925 they had dropped to 112; by 1929 they had risen to 121, but had dropped in 1933 to 97. *Ibid.*, III, table 2B, p. 2.

[24] Between 1881–1885 and 1931–1935 the percentage share of the United Kingdom in world exports of manufactured goods had declined from 38.1 to 18.4. *Ibid.*, table 3, p. 3.

square yards in 1938.[25] In 1938–39 her production had dropped below that of both Japan and India, and her exports were exceeded by those of Japan by 50 per cent.[26]

But it was only a little less true in other major mass-production lines. A few major exceptions to the contrary (e.g., chemicals), one by one Britain lost the lead to her newer, more modern, and more enterprising overseas competitors in iron and steel products, many lines of machinery, cheaper woolens and rayon products, various lines of manufactured foods, etc. Part of this loss was the result of a shift to the production of higher quality products, but most of it was due to growing technical backwardness which had already become general by the time of the First World War in large segments of her industrial system. Between the two world wars Britain never staged an effective or sustained industrial recovery similar to that of the United States during the twenties, or to that of Germany with her "rationalization movement" after 1925. Recovery had scarcely begun before there occurred the crippling setback of the general strike in 1926, brought about in part by the increased cost of living which followed the revaluation of the pound in the preceding year, and three years later came the onset of the long drawn-out general depression from which only the defense program offered any surcease in the late thirties. Gross capital formation over this twenty-year interval necessarily remained at low levels.

Except as they may be dealt with briefly in the following chapters, it would lead this study too far afield to inquire into the scale and the industrial incidence of this technical retardation,[27] the causes and conditions of its existence,[28] its effects upon costs and prices both at home and abroad, and the reasons why it persisted up to the eve of the Second World War. Suffice it to say that over the vast range of her raw materials and older manufacturing industries, in the freight handling sections of her entire rail transport system and most of her docks and harbors, and throughout virtually the whole of her wholesale and retail distribution system (excepting primarily the coöperative movement) Britain was in arrears, and that this technical retardation was paralleled on the one side by the swift proliferation of an efficiency-inhibiting

[25] *Ibid.*, table 18A, p. 17. See also chapter xiii following.
[26] Respectively, production: United Kingdom 3.4 billion sq. yds., Japan 4.0, India 4.2; exports: United Kingdom 1.6, Japan 2.4, and India 0.2. *Ibid.*, table 18B, p. 17.
[27] For such a comparison on a statistical basis see the careful and exhaustive study by Rostas.
[28] A very suggestive and highly provocative analysis of pre-First World War technical retardation in Britain is contained in chapter iv: "The Case of England," in Thorstein Veblen, *Imperial Germany and the Industrial Revolution* (New York, 1915).

growth of closely interwoven trade association and cartel controls the effects of which upon production were generally of a restrictionist character, and on the other—in the face of chronic mass unemployment—by a wide-ranging and deeply rooted aversion to job-destroying technical change in trade-union circles. Along with this, compared with either German or American practice, went little attention to industrial research, scientific management, standardization in the field of consumer goods, or technical rationalization on an industry-wide basis.[29]

World conditions following the Second World War were no more favorable. In contrast with the situation following the Napoleonic wars, defeat of the Axis did not find either a Britain with huge supplies of cheap goods available for sale on the Continent, or a Continent ready and able to buy. Exhaustion, depletion of resources, and bankruptcy on the Continent exceeded that of Britain herself. Furthermore, recovery in Europe was greatly hampered by the fact that the whole of Western Europe was now largely cut off from trade with Eastern Europe by the existence of an "iron curtain" which split the continent in two, by losses of overseas markets, merchant marine, and investment resources, which were even more severe than those of Britain, and by the necessity of meeting these losses by resorting to the same import-restricting and export-promoting tactics which the British were already finding so relentless an imperative. Added to these were the crippling effects of the politically inflammable social wars in Germany, France, and Italy, which so divided the parties as badly to lame economic recovery, the enormous costs of attempting to hold on to overseas colonies—most notably Indonesia, Viet Nam, Burma, and Malaya—deeply infected with the spirit and technics of revolt against European imperialism, and the triumph of the Communists in China and the removal of this vast subcontinent from the manipulative controls of the older industrial countries.

Especially important was the drastic curtailment of the east-west traffic between the manufacturing centers of the Baltic and North seas areas and the raw-materials producing areas (just beginning to industrialize) which constituted their natural hinterlands lying to the east and southeast. This reorientation worked a hardship on Britain in com-

---

[29] "The recovery of industrial Germany in four years from a situation not far removed from catastrophic collapse is contrasted with the continuance of acute depression in the British basic industries," is the conclusion reached by Walter Meakin, Labour Correspondent for the *Daily News*, in a book described on its jacket as "The first full and non-technical description of 'rationalisation' by which German Industry has been transformed." *The New Industrial Revolution, or How British Industry Can Be Saved* (London, 1928).

mon with all northwestern industrial Europe. And in addition to that, where formerly Britain sat astride the most important trade lanes of the world, she now appeared on the edge of a vastly altered pattern of world-girdling traffic lines. In this dilemma the loss of India and Burma from her own Empire meant a curtailment of what had long been regarded as her more or less exclusive trading areas. In the reorientation to the West she was faced by the gigantic industrial strength of the United States, upon whose aid she felt her own recovery depended, but where closer trade relations were severely inhibited by the large and growing dollar deficit. Furthermore, the need for American support compelled her to submit to the American demand for equal access to markets, raw materials, and investment opportunities in her own imperial domains,[30] and she was compelled to shape her plans on the assumption that the United States was prepared to favor large-scale reconstruction and even further extension (along certain lines at least) of industrial capacity both in the areas of her former allies and in those of her former enemies—most notably Germany and Japan.

These superficial observations scarcely indicate the full scale, or outline all the leading ramifications, of the altered postwar international situation which complicated the problem of recovery in Britain. Indeed, they barely scratch the surface. But further elaboration would serve only to underscore the central fact that prewar, war, and postwar conditions, both at home and abroad, combined to lay an especially heavy premium upon the need for a drastic, fundamental, and comprehensive overhauling of the British industrial system. This she must do as a condition to anything beyond mere temporary recovery to prewar depression levels, and it was doubly required wherever plans anticipated reaching beyond these levels to new standards of wealth and welfare for her whole population.

The Social Front: The Welfare State

The Webbs, who have done more to shape the thinking of the Labour party intellectuals than any other pair of writers in Britain, in writing their first general "indictment" of the system as a whole, and attempting to interpret in its proper historical setting the full implications of the catastrophe of the First World War, found that "just as the Sumerian, the Egyptian, the Greek, the Roman and the Christian medieval civilizations have passed away, our present capitalist civilization, as

[30] See, e.g., *ECA Report*, II, sections on "Strategic Materials."

mortal as its predecessors, is dissolving before our eyes, not only in that 'septic dissolution' diagnosed by the Dean of St. Paul's, brought upon us by war, and curable by genuine peace, but in that slower changing of the epochs which war may hasten, but which neither we nor anything else can hinder."[31]

As portrayed by the Webbs, by every major token—ranging from the vast tragic scourge of war and economic depression over to the simpler workaday facts of loss of personal freedom for the vast mass of the working population, and the wholesale erosion of even the more humble virtues of hearth and home—the system stood condemned. All these evils were inherent in capitalist society. Viewing the matter from the larger perspective of world history, they saw the huge productive po- tentialities of the industrial system for improving the welfare of the human race to have been paced in England only by the relentless de- struction which the system of private ownership and management had wrought on the lives and hopes of millions of those who toiled within its factory gates. Disease, malnutrition, squalor, fear of unemploy- ment, uncertainty about the future, deadly factory routines, lack of amenities during leisure hours, illiteracy, vice, crime—all, in fact, of the manifest evils of unrelieved and hopeless poverty dogged the steps, when indeed it did not saturate the lives, of the average workman from the cradle to the grave. The entire lives of millions of craftsmen, whose skills had long made England the envy of the world, were spent in vast reeking slums—slums which, in the wake of the factories, slowly erupted into the decaying countryside surrounding the great industrial centers like monstrous malignant growths, and from which large dere- lict segments were cut off to leave resident populations stranded in huge depressed areas whenever the impersonal calculus of profits and loss shifted mines and mills to distant and more favorable locations.[32] How- ever hard the lot of the men, these conditions bore more heavily still upon the women and the children.[33]

There is no need to retrace the story here, nor to attempt to determine how much is fact and how much fiction. These conditions have given

[31] Sidney and Beatrice Webb, *The Decay of Capitalist Civilization* (New York, 1923), pp. 231, ix.

[32] An excellent, vivid, and very precisely outlined sketch of such derelict areas is given in the magnificent study by the West Midland Group in *Conurbation, A Survey of Birmingham and the Black Country* (London, 1948). See, in particular, plates 8 and 9 on "Surface Utili- sation." The best recent survey of the whole problem of the depressed areas is to be found in the *Report of the Royal Commission on the Distribution of the Industrial Population* [com- monly referred to as the *Barlow Report*], Cmd. 6153 (HMSO, 1940).

[33] E.g., Wal Hannington, *The Problem of the Distressed Areas* (London, 1937), chapter vi, "The Tragedy of the Youth."

rise to countless investigations, governmental and private, and huge masses of detail have been catalogued into an immense continuing record. The impact of the First World War, combined with the long drawn-out depression which afflicted Britain between the two world wars—reaching its nadir during the thirties[34]—found the country on the eve of the Second World War with a social legacy for which there are few good parallels in the annals of modern industrial countries. This was true despite a century and a quarter of significant and widening attention to the problem which had resulted in an impressive mass of remedial legislation. From the days of the Philosophical Radicals, whose legislative maneuvering under the leadership of Francis Place led to the repeal of the Anti-Combination laws during the first quarter of the nineteenth century, the movement had gone ahead. Extension of the franchise—beginning with minor concessions in the Reform Bill of 1832, subsequently widened in 1867 and 1884, and finally enlarged to include all adults over twenty-one in the acts of 1918 and 1928—was paralleled by a wide range of factory legislation, poor-law reform, housing legislation, laws relating to proper sanitation, provision for educational facilities, land-tenure reform, social security measures culminating in the pioneering National Health Insurance Act of 1911, etc.

Impressive as this record may be—and in many respects Britain led the world along these lines—it is difficult to avoid the conclusion that, relative to the times at least, there had been astonishingly little net change for the better. Over three-quarters of a century, to be sure, real wages had risen[35] along with the passage of remedial legislation, but the combination of the mass unemployment of the thirties with the prospects of the Second World War following as a natural consequence of the breakdown of the economic society of the West, made the gains seem small indeed. A leading Labour party spokesman, Emanuel Shin-

---

[34] "The decisive characteristic of the economic situation which persisted during the whole of the period between the two wars was the existence of mass unemployment . . . In the troughs of the depressions there were from two and a half to three million unemployed amongst the insured workers. At the peak points of the booms there were still a million." John Strachey, *A Programme for Progress* (London, 1940), p. 15.

[35] "Starting from 100 in 1859, the index, which allows for unemployment, rose to 132 in 1875; fell to 121 in 1879; rose to 179 in 1900; fell to 169 in 1914; rose to 202 in 1920; and after various post-war oscillations had recovered to 202 in 1933." Douglas Jay, *The Socialist Case* (London, 1946), p. 34; based on data taken from the first edition of *Introduction to the Study of Prices*, by Sir Walter Layton and Geoffrey Crowther. According to G. D. H. Cole, there was a fall of money wages from an index of around 160 in 1920 to 100 in 1924, from which floor they had not recovered as late as 1936. Meanwhile the cost of living had fallen from 100 in 1924 to something over 90 by the latter date. Real wages on this showing could not have recovered to the figure cited by Jay. See the charts, p. 238 in *The Condition of Britain* (London, 1937).

well, found that the condition of the people of Britain in 1936 could be
illustrated by the simple fact that, "taking the country as a whole, 52
per cent of those who presented themselves at the recruiting offices were
declared medically unfit, while 68 per cent of those who volunteered
from some industrial areas were in like case."[36] Looking back over a
long life devoted to relieving the plight of the poor, Beatrice Webb
wrote in 1938 that "confronted with this dismal tragedy of mass unemployment, with its constantly increasing core of manufactured para-
sitism, it is futile to suggest that the recommendations of the minority
report of the Poor Law Commission of 1906–9, even if fully implemented, would or could prevent mass destitution of the able-bodied,"[37]
even though that report summarized virtually the whole program of
reform for which the long record of previous remedial legislation had
paved the way, and which the Webbs had hitherto felt would constitute
the first decisive step in the direction of the social democracy of the
future.

But labor and other radical groups were not alone in their belief
that something must be done. Irrespective of the motives which lay behind the Conservative support of reform proposals, and however vigorously they may at various times have fought to delay or emasculate
proposals for change, from the days of Disraeli on even they had been
led ineluctably to permit the passage of remedial legislation as a
means of insuring the *status quo* against the political disorders that
might arise from mounting social unrest. More recently an attempt has
been made by the Conservative party to lay claim to the leading remedial acts of the last century and a half,[38] and during the war the
Conservative-dominated Coalition government sponsored a wide range
of investigations designed to supply the factual background for a vast
extension of postwar social reform which went so far as to include a
type of national planning that would insure full employment on an
enduring basis.[39]

Without attempting to evaluate here the comparative merits of these
plans and counterplans, it is possible to say with certainty that all
parties were agreed (1) that the country could not return to the eco-

[36] E. Shinwell, *The Britain I Want* (London, 1943), p. 46.
[37] *Our Partnership* (London, 1948), p. 487.
[38] Charles E. Bellairs, *Conservative Social and Industrial Reform 1800–1945* (Conservative Political Centre, 1947).
[39] See, in particular, the two "social security" Beveridge reports, summarized in chapter
viii following, and the three reports—Barlow, Scott, and Uthwatt—having to do with town
and country planning, summarized in chapter x following.

nomic and social *status quo ante* the Second World War without risking the most disastrous consequences, (2) that the changes which must be made in the conditions of the lower income classes must be far-reaching and fundamental, and (3) that the issues underlying the anticipated social changes were inextricably interwoven with the economic problems of postwar recovery and future prosperity. Whatever hesitancy there may have been on this score was gradually dispelled as the war dragged on, for it became increasingly clear that this world-wide conflict was largely, if not primarily, a social war. If any lingering doubts remained on V-E day, they were laid to rest as Britain's leaders watched the steady spread of the social wars in Central Europe and Asia, and as the record of growing unrest in other more backward and colonial regions began to crowd the columns of the daily newspapers.

Thus it seems obvious that no party—of the right, the left, or anywhere in between—could have avoided the necessity of coupling fundamental social reform to programs for recovery and other long-range economic plans. But this alone does not explain the peculiar dilemma faced by the Labour party when it assumed the duties of the government in power in the autumn of 1945. The reform program of the British Labour party was committed to the advance of socialism,[40] and this was utterly anathema to its official opposition. But it was committed also to a special type of socialism—one which seemed designed under the given historical circumstances not to simplify its task of changeover from a capitalist society, but to complicate it at very nearly every turn.

Externally, it was caught in the mounting ideological warfare between the United States and the Soviet Union, and its particular tissue of compromises was bound to reassure and make firm allies with neither, while adding to the suspicions of both. To the United States, this rather New Dealish socialism quickly became not a bulwark against, but rather a doormat—when not, indeed, a doorman—for the expansion of Russian communism. It was therefore suspect to some degree or other at every twist and turn of policy formation. To the Soviet Union it was viewed as no more than a thin disguise for a still

---

[40] "The Labour Party is a Socialist Party, and proud of it. Its ultimate purpose at home is the establishment of the Socialist Commonwealth of Great Britain." *Let Us Face the Future* (London, 1945), the program for the British Labour party, on the basis of which they won the elections in 1945. Looking forward to the 1950 elections, the position was reaffirmed: "At the last General Election they decided that Britain should be rebuilt as a socialist nation. To this end we seek freedom from the enslaving material bonds of capitalism." *Labour Believes in Britain.*

regnant Tory economic and social system. Hence it was not to be defended as a socialist weakling, but doubly damned as a socialist imposture.

Neither line of interpretation might have appeared, or at least would most certainly have been differently slanted, but for certain seeming accidents of postwar history. In America the untimely death of President Roosevelt had left the "economic Royalists," whom he had once so roundly scored, in virtually complete control as an incident to the staffing felt necessary in Washington while fighting an all-out war. Throughout his four terms, Roosevelt—even long after he had almost wholly abandoned reform at home—had stood for New Deal reformism, and the great similarity between his earlier domestic program and that which was soon launched by the Labour party (barring possibly certain of the nationalization schemes) might have meant that his immense prestige in America would have been used to give a sympathetic interpretation of British gradualist socialism to the American people. With his death this possibility was removed.

By one of the strangest ironies of history, when Roosevelt died, Winston Churchill remained for Americans as the authentic Voice of Britain; it was he, and not his successors in office, who interpreted the new government, which he heartily despised. And he interpreted it with matchless oratory, by use of a colorful and vivid invective which was ideally designed to appeal to popular American sentiments, and with benefit of a keen understanding of the wide sweep around the ideological circle from radical New Dealism to reactionary Toryism which had taken place in the United States over the intervening years and under the very shadow of the New Deal leadership itself. The fact that he was a great and honored war leader, that his name had long been associated with that of Roosevelt, and that he had come to stand, willy-nilly, as one of the great defenders of democratic institutions and ideas, meant that what he said was difficult for his American opponents to refute.

Still, when Churchill delivered his spectacular Fulton, Missouri, speech, the average American was doubtful and hesitant. But while he hesitated, and while political reaction took Churchill's word that British socialism was in reality no more nor less than a transmission belt for communism, events abroad seemed thoroughly to bear out this prophecy. As fate would have it, reformist types of socialism very similar to that which had won out in the British general elections had also appeared in Czechoslovakia, Hungary, and Roumania, and one by one these gave way to outright Communist systems. With the *coup d'état* in Czechoslovakia the case seemed complete. Henceforward, no effort on the part of the British Labour party to free itself from the incubus of this suspicion was or could be successful. To the easily convinced, the Labour government was attempting to accomplish in Britain what had foredoomed democracy in Czechoslovakia, and was bound, accordingly, soon to find itself in the predicament of Lady Macbeth: though technically guiltless, it would then find that the more it tried to cleanse itself of the red taint by purges and solemn declarations of libertarian faith,[41] the more would blood appear to stain its hands.

Conversely, the proof to the Soviet Union that the Labour party was no more than a sort of tea and treacle version of the same old Tory system was not long in putting in an appearance. The acid test for them was Greece, where the Russians saw, or thought they saw, not a Labour government attempting belatedly to find some way of withdrawing from the imperialist commitments of the supplanted regime, but an active carrying out of the very same program on behalf of which these specific commitments had been made, and with benefit of the same complacent rationalizations for which the British had long been notorious. What was the British lifeline to the East except the umbilical cord of Empire, and a pipeline for Arabian oil? Meanwhile, British Labour dilly-dallied until it had no choice but to abandon its original plans for nationalizing the heavy industries of the Ruhr. In going along, however reluctantly, with the American proposal for reintroducing the very same German free enterprise system which had once so loyally supported Hitler, the Russians saw merely betrayal of both socialism and the purposes for which the war had been fought.[42] By easy steps,

---

[41] Practically no publicity reaching the general American public, for example, was ever given to a resolution by the National Executive Committee of the Labour party in 1946, in which it declared that "It is clear that the temporary Communist talk of working-class unity behind the Labour Party is merely a clumsy camouflage for their real aim of breaking up the Labour Movement so as to increase their own chances of establishing a party dictatorship." Pursuant thereto, Harold Laski, on behalf of the National Executive, wrote a pamphlet called *The Secret Battalion*, issued by the Labour party, in which he declared of the Communists that "They act like a secret battalion of paratroopers within the brigade whose discipline they have accepted. They meet secretly to propose their own line of action; they have one set of rules to regulate their conduct to one another, and a different set of rules to be observed towards those who are not in the battalion" and its alpha and omega of political tactics and working class morality comes to rest in the central fact of its "subservient devotion to the dictatorship of the Communist Party in Moscow," pp. 12, 15. A more recent statement of the same position is found in the T.U.C. pamphlet, *The Tactics of Disruption: Communist Methods Exposed* (T.U.C., 1949).

[42] E.g., "In November, 1942, British and American military authorities announced that all heavy industry would be handed to German Trustees, the question of ownership being left for the Germans to decide once a West German Government had been set up. This effec-

each effort after that of the British partially to reconstruct the disintegrating Empire in the Far East, and to consolidate Western Europe for purposes of rehabilitation and recovery came to appear as a fulfillment of the worst Russian suspicions. In the Marshall Plan and the North Atlantic Pact they were then prepared to see the fine Italian hand of Churchill, and henceforward it was Churchill's voice—not that of Bevin or Attlee—which the Russians heard whenever Downing Street spoke.

When doubt arose in either the American or the Russian council chambers about the real meaning of British "socialism," close scrutiny of the Labour party's internal policies clarified nothing. On the contrary, these policies frequently appeared, when viewed through the appropriate lenses, to be of such a character as to support the worst suspicions previously held. To cite a late example, in 1948 the purge of Communists from the Labour party, the Trades Union Congress (T.U.C.), and government offices meant for the Russians what the nationalization of the iron and steel industry meant for the Americans. The justifications offered for each action by the British did little or nothing to allay further suspicion. The purge was explained by Bevin and others in terms almost identical with those of the Un-American Activities Committee in Washington, and this added to the Russian belief that Whitehall had become a side street to Pennsylvania Ave. The iron and steel nationalization was unaccompanied by any plan for modernization, and thus, lacking any seeming technical justification, appeared to Washington to be merely nationalization for socialism's sake. Fear of Russia has kept the British defense budget up to the astronomical figure of roughly £750,000,000, or nearly a quarter of her entire national budget and almost 10 per cent of her national income, and American fear of "Socialist advance," typified by the iron and steel nationalization, very nearly cost Britain her vitally necessary ERP aid. (A similar action with respect to another major British industry might very well cut it off entirely.)

But the implications for Britain of her middle position in this widening ideological warfare does not end with the imposition of crushing military burdens and a Hobson's choice with respect to ERP. Externally, British Empire holdings (along with those of all the other European powers) are in process of rapid liquidation. India, Burma,

---

tively killed all hope of nationalisation, because the anti-Socialist parties in Western Germany as a whole are in a strong majority. Ownership remains, therefore, in the hands of the magnates who brought Hitler into power, and if things continue as they are, will do so in the future." *Labour Research*, Feb., 1949, p. 35.

and Ceylon, Britain has had to set free. One of the major dominions, South Africa, has, under the Malan government, parted company with Britain on a mixture of ideological and economic grounds. Others are drifting into the American orbit (most notably Canada) or the Russian orbit (e.g., Hongkong and Malaya). As the Accra, Gold Coast, and Durban, South Africa, disturbances of recent times have indicated, unrest in Britain's African possessions is increasingly directed at the sanctions underlying the whole principle of empire.[43] The past anti-imperialist position of the Labour party, which was in many respects very emphatic, serves only to add fuel to the flames, and the fact that any failure to offer wide-ranging and fundamental concessions may at any moment serve to throw disappointed radical or nationalist senti-ment in the colonies in the direction taken either by the Malan govern-ment (extreme nationalism) or by the Russians, makes the situation more precarious still. Finally, none of these problems are made any simpler by the aggressive belief held in powerful American circles that "this is our century"—just as the "eighteenth and the nineteenth centuries belonged to the British"—and that consequently American adventurers, pioneers, colonizers, and businessmen are the natural residuary legatees of the decline and fall of the British Empire.

But like the countless woes of Job, the tribulations arising from the unavoidable interlinkage of economic and social issues do not end with the posing of such vexatious external issues. Internally, as pointed out above, all plans, attempts, and hopes of technical modernization must immediately come to grips with a vast, closely interwoven, politi-cally conscious network of private monopoly and cartel-like controls the policies of which are shaped by a mentality which is dominated by financial and trading interests. This attitude is in strong contrast with both German and American monopoly controls where large-scale in-dustries play far more important roles. It is not only restrictionist—engaged in what a witty Oxford professor referred to as "profitable ossification"—but also it is unusually conservative in technical matters; it is shot through and through with nepotism,[44] and it is firmly rooted in both Parliament and the British administrative system.[45] When the

[43] For detail on the Accra affair, see chapter xiv following.

[44] See, e.g., any recent issue of Burke's *Peerage, The Stock Exchange Official Yearbook,* or *The Directory of Directors.*

[45] Much has been made of this point in the pre-war Labour party literature. See, e.g., Ernest Davies, *"National" Capitalism* (London, 1939) ; also Simon Haxey, *Tory M.P.* (Lon-don, 1939). This is also a favorite theme for the pro-Marxist publication, *Labour Research,* which, while very critical of the Labour government, nevertheless goes all out in its support on this point. An interesting example is given in an article entitled "Jobs For the Boys" in

Government acts in Britain it is the civil service which makes top administrative policy decisions (immediately below the minister in question). The colonial, foreign, and military services are manned largely by persons drawn from Opposition ranks; in many leading offices, perhaps most notably the Board of Trade, the situation is only slightly less true at home. While the analogy is certainly inexact, there is plenty of evidence for any orderly and systematic investigator to find which will suggest that comparison with the role played by the higher echelons of the German civil service in the effective nullification of the government's program during the interregnum of the Weimar Republic[46] would not be entirely misleading. At the legislative level lobbying in the American sense plays a far less significant role in Britain than in America, simply because the lobbyist in America is usually outside attempting to influence legislators, whereas in Britain he is ordinarily inside helping to make the laws. Analogously, in the upper ranks of the civil service the placing of relatives and social—particularly "school-tie"—companions, friends, and the right people in general, in paying governmental career offices has been accepted as entirely fitting and proper, time out of mind. Even in the lower and formally entirely professional civil service ranks social criteria play an extraordinarily significant role.[47]

---

the issue of Feb., 1949, giving detail on the various government and private corporate jobs held by a number of leading Conservatives in Parliament and offered as a reply to the common Opposition jibe that the newly nationalized industries are intended by the Government to "give jobs to the boys" in the Labour party.

[46] All suggestion of such a comparison will meet typically with hot and indignant rejection in Labour party circles. Yet upon pointed and detailed questioning, it will also usually be admitted that virtually the whole of the British foreign service, most of the nontechnical staff of the Ministry of Food, the Board of Trade, and the newly nationalized corporations, are drawn from social layers largely if not wholly unsympathetic with the central doctrinal position of the Labour party wherever it involves significant departures from the past; furthermore, that this is only a little less true of the other more important government offices. But the reply will typically be that this is irrelevant, because the British civil servant is (1) technically competent, (2) patriotic, and (3) puts duty above party loyalty. Which may very well be so, but the argument employed is usually an adaptation of the one developed in James Burnham, *The Managerial Revolution* (New York, 1941), and this work will be cited more frequently in this context than any other. Only occasionally will it appear, as in Rita Hinden's pamphlet for the Fabian Colonial Bureau, *Socialists and the Empire*, that this situation can lead to virtually total nullification of the Government's plans; see, e.g., pp. 23 and 25. To describe the mode of handling much of the Ministry of Food's distribution scheme as "sabotage of the Government's program" would be to misconstrue only in part. But the misconstruction would lie in the fact that it is run in most details by industry people who maintain their industry affiliations, and that these are in large part not consonant with objectives set by the Government. But such also is the fundamental problem of the development councils, for which see chapter xiii following.

[47] For example, one of the leading experts at Ruskin College in Oxford—probably the leading "labour college" in Britain, and an intellectual clearing house for the Labour education program—gave as one of the principal reasons why even lower income people in Britain would not send their children to the County Council Schools if they could possibly

But such direct and simple nullification, whether conscious or not, and however much there may be, is the least of the handicaps created by the carry-overs from Britain's once compelling social caste system. Sex and occupation are still identified with status. England is preëminently a man's country, and such institutions as "housekeeping money"—where the wife regularly receives a definite and more or less fixed sum which is conventionalized in most communities—makes it difficult, when not wholly impossible, to make a direct appeal to female progressives whenever a proposal may involve serious departures from past habits, customs, loyalties, and hopes which are rooted in the socially inferior status of women.[48] In middle-class circles, to which the Labour party is compelled by force of circumstances to make a strong appeal for support, "there is much public expression of snobbery, disdainful comments about the 'working class' or the 'lower classes.' And within some sections, at least, of the working class ranks there is a bitterness towards the middle class that beggars description."[49] One even finds hostility among loyal Labor Party supporters for those middle-class members of the Party and Government who have attained some

---

avoid it when it was hoped that the boys (girls are rarely included in such a conversation for in Britain only upper class women have careers) might enter the government service is that they would never afterward shake off colloquial accents, and so handicapped it was virtually impossible for them to occupy any except lower paid positions. This judgment was given as one with which there seemed no possible dispute so far as the military services (excepting possibly a few of the newer branches), the Foreign Office, the Colonial Office, and the older and more prized positions in both national and local governmental departments are concerned. With the shrinkage of the Empire, and the increased necessity for younger sons and other poor relations of the "cousinhood" to seek gainful employment as a result of steeply graduated income taxes, this pressure for the granting of socially acceptable governmental jobs to the clientele of the Government's official Opposition has tended to increase, and no doubt contributes much to the bitterness expressed whenever Labour supporters are handed the paying and socially attractive positions.

[48] An experiment conducted in one of the mining districts, with a view to providing incentives for increased output, placed a wide range of hitherto unobtainable durable goods in the stores where mining wives shopped. The object was to stimulate miners to work harder to earn money with which to buy the new goods. The experiment was a total failure. The reasons given the writer upon making inquiry were the following: (1) the expenditure had to come out of the husband's money to help the wife out with tasks for which she had already been given the money with which she was expected to "make do"; (2) the wife did not know (typically) what the husband earned, and hence whether or not he could afford the purchase; (3) the husband would not purchase the goods for fear of the social pressure brought to bear upon him by labor companions who would then be pressured by their wives for similar purchases; (4) once the fixed sum incorporated in "housekeeping money" was upped, it stayed there, and the man would have to continue to work harder; (5) it was this sort of thing which led to family quarrels, breakup of families, etc.

[49] Best reflected in the Yorkshire, Glasgow, and South Wales districts, and with respect to the vindictive Trades Disputes Act passed by the Conservative government following the disastrous General Strike of 1926. Repeal of the act was one of the first steps taken by the new Labour government in 1946. The debates on the repeal reflect the heat which the act engendered on both sides. Of interest in this connection is the elaborate justification of the act in the pamphlet *All You Want to Know About the Trades Disputes Act* (Conservative Party, 1946).

prominence . . . Perhaps the most serious charge against British society and those governing groups which have dominated it in the past is the toleration of a shocking wastage of first rate ability. It is difficult to believe that any controls developed by a democratic state could prove as repressive of individual development as did the social structure of Britain."[50]

To wide layers of the middle and upper classes servants are a psychological and social, as well as an economic, necessity. Instead, for example, of changing the depressing, badly arranged and poorly equipped scullery into a modern kitchen (and it is often easily possible to do so), the tendency is to keep the maid and let the kitchen go. So also for the countless doormen, butlers, lackeys, flunkeys, coachmen, scrubwomen, governesses, private tutors, instructors, and porters, in private homes and government offices. The attitude that maintains these mostly obsolete jobs and functions which exist only to wait on the whims of the upper and middle classes, also resists any movement to cut down on what has been established in the past as a socially acceptable ratio of clerks in stores, waiters in restaurants, secretaries and flunkies in the countless private clubs, hawkers and miscellaneous street venders, staffs of now largely functionless charitable, humanitarian and purely "social" bureaus, clubs and organizations, the great numbers of almost equally functionless real estate and rent dealers, petty advocates, and in general all the vast wasteful carry-over from a social system which is rapidly becoming defunct, and an economic organization which is still largely grounded in an archaic regime of handicraft, small-scale production, and petty trading.

Much of this servile and servant class is emotionally attached to the political platforms of Labour's most bitter opposition. In attempting to woo adherents from those whose training and tradition incline them to speak of the gentlefolk with complacently servile pride, the Labour party faces the hazard of alienating votes by any action designed to shift them away from their currently wasteful occupations (from the point of view of national production), or to thin out necessary, but overmanned occupations by various man-power conservation measures. Still more does it risk, in so doing, the votes of many members of the middle and upper classes who might otherwise be inclined to sympathize with the Labour cause. To most of these persons disturbance of caste, or status, means destruction at once of both social standing and

[50] H. H. Wilson, "Some Impressions of Labor England in 1948," *New Century* (Fall, 1948), pp. 3–5, 28–34.

jobs. Yet the man power and resources tied up in full- and part-time disposable occupations of a servile, semiservile, purely ceremonial, or otherwise partly or wholly superfluous character, is very great indeed.[51]

Avoiding further detail, it is evident that the social problems facing any postwar British government were no less formidable than the economic. That the two must be dealt with together seemed in many respects to compound in a sort of geometric progression the difficulty of solving the problems of each. Yet there were many factors on the favorable side. War-weariness, set against the background of the depression of the thirties, created a favorable climate for fundamental change. Leading Labour leaders had acquired a good deal of valuable experience in top wartime administrative posts. Wartime experiments in planning had made possible not only a prodigious war production effort, but also a maintenance, and in some respects an improvement (most notably in food consumption) of mass standards of living. Many of these changes were definitely of a socialist character, and there was not, consequently, "likely to be the same difficulty in continuing or perpetuating many of these changes as there would have been had the changes been initiated in peace time with strong opposition from the Tory Party."[52] Despite the colossal economic losses, British man-power casualties had been very small[53]—it is not at all uncommon, for example, to hear in Britain the Second World War referred to as "the easy war."

There were many other factors which were especially favorable to the Labour government upon which the mantle of power had fallen. Not the least of these was its dramatic and overwhelming Parliamentary victory at the polls[54] and the fact that this vote included both the great majority of the young and politically aware war veterans, and a greatly broadened following in middle-class ranks. That this could happen in face of the great concessions to socialist principles that both the practi-

---

[51] For a partial and inadequate classification, see appendix 1, table 1.

[52] John Parker, *Labour Marches On* (London, 1947). See also, J. E. D. Hall, *Labour's First Year* (London, 1947).

[53] "A rough comparison in the report (Ministry of Pensions, Oct. 16, 1948) of the casualties (deaths and wounded) in the two world wars puts them at 600,000 for the 1939–45 war and 2,500,000 for the 1914–18 war." *Home Affairs Survey*, Oct. 26, 1948, p. 36.

[54] ". . . on July 26 the country abruptly woke up to the fact that a revolution had taken place. The results showed that the Labour candidates had swept the polls like a tidal wave and brought the Labour Party to Westminster with a majority of 148 over all other Parties and groups combined. In under a half century this young Party had increased its representation in the House from two to 395 seats, 79 divisions voted Labour for the first time in their history and the Conservative Party, with years of power behind it, had lost 181 seats." Hall, *op. cit.*, p. 1.

cally defunct Liberal party[55] and the still mighty Conservative party—in its turn led by one of the most popular and politically shrewd war heroes in Britain's entire history—were prepared to make in order to obtain rank-and-file support, gives some measure of the popular belief in the imperative need for a radically new approach to the problems of peace.

How did the Labour party propose to meet this challenge on its chosen grounds? There are three aspects to this question. First, what set of interests dominates the selection of the issues contained in the program? Second, what underlying point of view, or theory, or social philosophy guides the larger outlines of the program and shapes it in terms of what broad social objectives? And third, how did the specific platform contained in the 1945 election manifesto, *Let Us Face the Future*, express the influence of these interests and ideas in a definite plan of action to meet the peculiarly difficult problem of postwar Britain?

The Trade Unions and the Labour Party

The Labour party's greatest support comes from the Trades Union Congress, as may be shown in terms of its origin and development, in terms of organizational linkages, and in terms of actual representation in Parliament, and without cognizance of this there can be no understanding of its current political maneuvering. With respect to origins, though "Keir Hardie the Lanarkshire miner who formed the I.L.P.[56] and the Labour Party, had radicalism in his bones," the party, which on his initiative the Trades Union Congress founded, had from its earliest beginnings[57] "no definite programme; its Parliamentary members were for the most part solid Trade Unionists of little imagination, who thought, as far as they thought at all, that the unemployed should

---

[55] How far the Liberal Party was prepared to go may be seen by examining its pamphlet, *Liberal Policy* (London, Liberal Publications Dept., 1947).

[56] I.L.P. = Independent Labour Party. "In 1893, the year of the great Coal Strike, the Independent Labour Party was formed at Bradford, absorbing a number of local bodies. The I.L.P. soon became the most influential Socialist Society, and at once began to press in the Trades Union Congress the demand for Labour political action, which is visualized as the principal means to the attainment of Socialism." G. D. H. Cole, *The British Labour Movement*, A Historical Introduction for Classes and Study Groups, Syllabus Series No. 1 (Labor Research Dept., 1922), p. 16. The I.L.P. still exists as a small fraction party. In the 1945 General Election it polled 46,679 votes out of a total of 24,968,286 votes cast, or less than ⅕ of 1 per cent. Margaret Cole, *The General Election 1945 and After*, Fabian Research Series, No. 102, March, 1945, p. 3.

[57] "In 1899, the Trades Union Congress voted in favour of forming a Labour Representation Committee. This was formed in 1900, on the basis of a Trade Union–Socialist alliance, and at the General Election of that year it returned two Members, of whom Keir Hardie was one. The L.R.C. assumed the name of the 'Labour Party' in 1906." Cole, *The British Labour Movement*.

be more kindly treated, but could not envisage any drastic change at all," being even "horrified by Victor Grayson's loud and tactless demands that unemployment itself should be abolished"[58] when the issue was raised before the First World War.

So far, furthermore, as the Labour party may properly be regarded as the political *alter ego* of the T.U.C.,[59] it is important to note that the latter is a rather loose confederation which is dominated at its annual meetings, and during the fifty-one weeks in the year when it is governed by its General Council, by a small group of giant unions centered in transport, mining, and the heavy metallurgical and engineering industries.[60] These unions in turn are closely knit bureaucracies which are effectively run by small inside cliques of more or less coöptatively recruited labor politicians, and whose power tends to be further consolidated by the fixed policy of promoting further amalgamation on both local and national levels.[61]

Most of the trade unions are affiliated to the T.U.C., and the trade unions dominate Labour party membership. As appendix 2 shows, at the time of the general elections in 1945, 85 per cent of trade union membership (6,671,120 out of 7,803,000) were affiliated with the T.U.C., and 82 per cent of the Labour party's membership (2,150,369 out of 3,038,697) came from the trade unions. Membership in a trade union, as a matter of fact, is required when the appropriate unions exist, as a condition to membership in the Labour party.[62] Furthermore,

---

[58] "James Keir Hardie" in Margaret Cole, *Makers of the Labour Movement* (London, 1948), pp. 203, 219.

[59] "The Trades Unions are the voice of the organised workers. They find their political expression in and through the Labour Party, which they effectively control. Seventy-five per cent of the votes at last year's Annual Conference of the Labour Party were cast by Trades Unions." Harold Campbell, *Wanting and Working*, (Coop-Union and Co-operative Party, May, 1947), p. 8.

[60] In 1945, 72 unions falling under these classifications out of 192 affiliated with the T.U.C. fell into the 6 out of 18 main groups into which the membership is divided, and possessed 3,594,777 out of 6,671,120 members on the T.U.C.'s registers. Better than half of these fell into four main unions: Transport and General Workers Union, Amalgamated Engineering Union, National Union of Mineworkers, and the National Union of Railwaymen. See N. Barou, *British Trade Unions* (London, 1947), Appendix II, p. 239 and Appendix IV, pp. 243–4. In 1947, of the 19 trade groups into which the T.U.C. was then organized, the previously mentioned 6 held 15 out of 33 representatives on the General Council of the T.U.C. *Rules and Standing Orders, Trades Union Congress*, Revised and Operative from Jan. 1st, 1947 (T.U.C., 1947), p. 5.

[61] For a "List of Leading Amalgamations (1930–August 1946)" see Barou, *op. cit.*, Appendix III, pp. 240–242.

[62] "All men and women being British subjects over sixteen years of age, who accept and conform to the programme, policy and principles of the Labour Party and not connected with political or other organisations deemed ineligible for affiliation to the Party. *Those who are eligible must be members of their appropriate union, and contribute to the political funds of the union.* This stipulation does not affect housewives and others who have no appropriate trade union." Sara Barker, *How the Labour Party Works*, with a Foreword by Morgan Phillips (Labour Party, n.d. [1947?]), pp. 3–4. Italics mine.

the trade unions nominate directly twelve out of the twenty-five members of the Labour party's governing body, the National Executive Committee.[63]

But these data do not adequately reflect the real strength of the T.U.C. in Labour party councils. For one thing, the membership of the consumers coöperatives is considerably larger than that of all trade unions combined (in 1945, 9,400,000 as against 7,803,000 for the trade unions), and the number of members of coöperatives in the Co-operative party is greater than the entire membership of the Labour party (7,511,072 as against 3,038,697). But the membership of the consumers coöperatives is overwhelmingly dominated by trade unionists; the two movements have grown in strength and importance as though they were but two aspects of a common movement,[64] and they are commonly so described. The discrepancy in numbers of party members is accounted for by the difference between the broad national emphasis of the Labour party as against the narrow, specialized emphasis of Co-operative party and the fact that for all practical purposes the latter acts through its affiliated membership as an agent of the former.[65]

Organizational connections between the T.U.C. and the Labour party reflect a like picture. At the top level, policy is coördinated by each of the three main groups—T.U.C., Co-operative Union,[66] and the Labour party—appointing six representatives to the National Council of Labour, whose objects are "to consult on matters of common interest, where necessary, in an emergency to take united action, and to make pronouncements on matters of national policy where there is agreement."[67] The secretaries of the three organizations serve in rotation as secretaries of the National Council of Labour. Moving from the top down through the various layers of the political organization of the

---

[63] *Ibid.*, p. 11.

[64] For a compact summary of this growth relationship from 1873 on, see chap. xxii of G. D. H. Cole, *A Century of Cooperation* (London, 1944), pp. 370–374.

[65] See, e.g., J. Bailey, *The Co-operative Party, An Outline of Organisation* (London, n.d.). Of the 393 Labour party members elected to Parliament in 1945, only 23 directly represented the coöps. As a rule, Coöp candidates are only put up for election in those constituencies where, by agreement with the Labour party, they have either the stronger candidate or the Coöp appeal has greater vote-giving strength.

[66] "The Co-operative Union is of central importance to the whole co-operative movement, influencing not only its trading activities but also its educational, social and political life" and serves, in effect, as a top policy coördinating body for (a) the membership of the coöperative movement as a whole and (b) relationships between its affiliated organizations and all other bodies with which it comes in contact—economic, political and otherwise. See, A. M. Carr-Saunders, P. Sargent Florence and Robert Peers, *Consumers' Cooperation in Great Britain* (London, 1942), chapter xii, "The Co-operative Union," pp. 201–213.

[67] J. Bailey, *op. cit.*, p. 19.

Labour party, it will be discovered that similar liaisons, sometimes formal, sometimes informal, are maintained between the three groups at all levels.

Nevertheless, in all this machinery the T.U.C. is clearly the dominant group. As for the coöperatives, representing as they do consumer interest, a very large percentage of their actual contacts are with the wives of trade unionists, and it has proved very difficult to organize political action directly around this strictly economic concern. It is only when the consumer is allied with the more compactly organized and politically conscious producer and wage earner that it has been possible to breathe much life into the Co-operative party's political activities. Liaison between the Labour and Co-operative parties has been formalized in two agreements, first in 1937, and later at Brighton in 1946. This last agreement (1) set up a liaison policy-making committee made up of six representatives from each body, (2) established a liaison National Organisation Committee "to consider political organisation and allied problems of concern to the two parties," (3) arranged for "an exchange of Minutes of the two National Executives," and (4) provided rules for coördinating political activities at national and local levels so that in effect all candidates put up by one party are endorsed by the other. All candidates nominated by the Co-operative party, however, must be acceptable to the Labour party and run under its banner.[08]

Partly because of this agreement, and partly because of the very great widening of the Labour party's middle-class basis of appeal consequent upon the decline of the Liberal party, there is considerably less of a tendency to draw Parliamentary candidates exclusively from trade-union circles. Speaking of the 1945 elections, for example, "The proportion of M.P.'s who are Trade Union or other paid officials has dropped from about 50 to 20%; and the number of those whose candidatures were financed by Trade Unions is only about 119, with 23 financed by the Co-operative organisations. Nearly two-thirds of the whole membership was financed in one way or another, by Divisional Labour Parties"[09] which draw some or most of their money from trade-union circles.

The fact that increasingly large numbers of Labour's Parliamentary

---

[08] Jack Bailey, *Facing the Future Together: The Co-op Labour Agreement Explained* (London, Co-operative Party, n.d.), pp. 9-12 gives the actual draft of the agreement. The author is secretary of the Co-operative party.

[09] Margaret Cole, *The General Election 1945 and After*, p. 19.

candidates are "chosen and paid for by local workers within the constituencies for which they stand, and that paid servants of organisations play a much smaller part than they did in the past" leads Margaret Cole to conclude that "Nobody can possibly contend now that the Party in Parliament is 'dominated' by Trade Union or any other salaried officials, though the number of Trade Unionists in Parliament" after the 1945 elections was probably a total of 231 out of 393 elected on the Labour ticket, "including those who are members of such non-manual organisations as the National Union of Journalists and the Association of Scientific Workers." Of these, including officials, some one hundred and fifty "come from manual working occupations."[70]

In summary, to say that the T.U.C. dominates the Labour party involves no poetic license. Whatever doubt there might be on this score would be laid to rest by observation of the manner in which the annual conferences of the Labour party, which is the real "fountain of authority,"[71] cater to the trade-union vote. Here the system of block voting, whereby the vote of an individual delegate is weighted in terms of the membership of the organizations he represents, throws the balance of power unmistakably in the hands of those in a position to swing the three to six largest national trades unions.[72] The National Executive of the Labour party reflects in its membership over the years the same trade-union emphasis, as does also the general congruence between the platforms and resolutions of the annual conferences of the Labour party and the annual congress of the trade unions.

Outlook and Theory of the Labour Party

Until well after the First World War the congruence between the platforms and resolutions of the Labour party and the T.U.C. were so

---

[70] Of these, 39 are miners, 35 are transport and general workers, 29 are railway workers and 20 are distributive workers. Of the professions, 44 are lawyers, 49 university and school teachers, 26 are journalists, and 15 are doctors, dentists, etc. There are 21 Labour women M.P.'s, eight of whom are "working housewives." "There are 18 who describe themselves as company directors or business men, 4 each of farmers and owners of small shops, and 16 who are managers or technical men—a group hitherto almost unrepresented." Loc. cit.

[71] Barker, op. cit., p. 10.

[72] This is further accentuated by a method of representation which permits double, and in many cases at least, triple or quadruple counting of the same membership. Thus, there is "one delegate for each 5,000 members or part thereof" of (1) trade unions and other affiliated bodies, of which the trade unions are overwhelmingly the most important, and (2) Constituency Labour parties (or trades councils acting as such), which are largely, and in most cases completely, dominated by the trade unions already represented through their own "Affiliated Trade Union." The same holds also for federations of Constituency Labour parties, each of which has an extra delegate. In addition, there is one delegate for each "Central Labour Party (Or Trades Council Acting As Such)," once again largely dominated by the trade unions.

close,[73] that the Labour party appears to be but little more than the political expression of the sentiments and practical proposals advanced by the T.U.C. After the reorganization of the Labour party in 1918, a difference appears, but it consists essentially of less of a departure from the T.U.C. than in a broadening of the Labour party to consider issues previously not given much serious attention by that body. Part of this departure may be due to the influence of the coöperatives, though this remains definitely minor down to the present time. Most of it, however, is due to the infiltration of middle-class persons and intellectuals drawn from various sources, and mostly brought into active contact with the party through the intermediation of the Fabian Society.

As for the ideas of the T.U.C., a close survey of its annual reports will show a remarkable degree of continuity throughout. New ideas, issues, and interests have obtruded from time to time, but the main emphasis has clearly been centered around the strategy and tactics of business unionism—narrow trade union gains and union careerism. It has fought in detail for the political planks of the Chartist movement, the economic gains of better wages, shorter hours, and improved working conditions, and the social objectives of the minimum program of national ownership of certain basic public utilities and the provision of general social security aids. It has been organized largely on a craft-union basis; craft interests have tended to dominate even after the establishment of large national unions and extensive amalgamation between and among closely related crafts.

The rank and file in the member unions of the T.U.C. have been primarily concerned with short-run gains. They are accustomed to a type of hard bargaining with employers which does not necessarily draw any line between private, coöperative,[74] or public employers— even under a Labour government;[75] they tend to be highly suspicious

---

[73] The T.U.C. was organized in 1868, following a meeting held in St. Martin's Hall, London, the year before. The regular *Reports* begin with the fifth annual Trades Union Congress held in Leeds, 1873. The *Reports* of the annual conferences of the Labour party begin with the first meeting of the predecessor body, The Labour Representation Committee, in 1901.

[74] There have been at various times severely strained relationships existing between the Co-operative Wholesale Society and various affiliated organizations—particularly in the manufacturing fields—and the trade unions. Since the General Strike of 1926 there has existed a joint committee between the Co-operative Union and the General Council of the T.U.C. "to formulate proposals intended to promote closer harmony between the two movements and to prevent the repetition of events which occurred during the national strike of 1926" when many workers employed in the coöperative movement went out on strike. Carr-Saunders et al., *op. cit.*, p. 354.

[75] As illustrated in appendix 3 of strikes occuring since 1945, which includes a number of rather spectacular strikes directed against the government, most notable of which was the London dock strike of 1948.

of copartnership schemes—even when promoted at times by top officials—which involve continuous friendly working relationships with
employers.[76] The membership is rarely "production minded" since appeals for increased output are likely to be suspected as disguises for
the speedup;[77] in general the rank and file are either indifferent to
socialist appeals, or interpret these in terms of short-run, immediate,
tangible gains which do not at the moment necessarily run counter to
the main tenets and sanctions which lie at the foundation of capitalist
society. The rank and file of British trade unionists are very religious;[78]
very practical in their demands; antitheoretical; insular, and suspicious of foreigners and intellectuals; jealous of male prerogatives and
suspicious of women's rights proposals;[79] sensitive to station, status,
and the "good manners" of the self-conscious social inferior.[80]

The dominant personalities (mostly older men) in the leadership of
the current British trade-union movement are men like Arthur Deakin
of the transport workers, Sir Will Lawther of the miners, or Foreign
Minister Ernest Bevin; shrewd, hard driving, essentially opportunistic,
earthy, practical, and contemptuous of ideas, ideologies, theories, and

[76] Thus scientific management techniques, such as are known in the U. S., have made very
little headway in Britain with either employers or trade unions; labor relations departments
and institutes are practically unknown, aside from the Whitley Councils in the civil service;
such conferences and committees as have been set up are primarily a product of Second
World War experience, are primarily centered around "grievances," and rarely go beyond
the shop or plant level of consultation. More recent efforts of top T.U.C. leaders to whip up
rank and file support for copartnership schemes under the development council program
(see footnote 77 following) appear to have been almost a total failure.

[77] So far as organized labor is concerned, this is the Achilles' heel of the plan put forward
by Sir Stafford Cripps for the 80 per cent of industry not to be nationalized under the Labour
government, but instead to be brought under the device of the development council. But it
is only a little less true, as the experience of the National Coal Board and the Transport
Board have already demonstrated, even within the newly nationalized industries. Many
aspects of trade union policy operate to a like end, not the least of which is craft union
fractioning of work. See, e.g., A. S. J. Baster, *The Little Less: An Essay in the Political
Economy of Restrictionism* (London, 1947), chapter entitled "Working Less."

[78] Since the days of the great Tory evangelists, Charles and John Wesley, the "chapel
churches" have dominated wide layers of the laboring classes of Britain with their essentially
quietist and middle class virtues of industry, frugality, piety, and dread of revolutionary
sentiments. See, e.g., Frederick C. Dietz, *Political and Social History of England*, pp. 450–
454. Meanwhile, the highly significant Workers Education movement—according to Margaret
Cole, *The General Election 1945*, over 100 Labour M.P.'s came through some form of adult
education—has been heavily influenced throughout its history by Tory humanitarian reformism. Especially interesting in this connection is the book, F. A. Iremonger, *William
Temple: Archbishop of Canterbury* (Oxford, 1948).

[79] For example, the Labour party, while approving in principle, has never been willing to
commit itself on "equal pay for equal work" by women largely because of the general
hostility expressed by the rank and file of the more important trade unions.

[80] Most pubs, for example, have a workman's entrance, and a "Gentleman's" or white-
collared man's entrance. Even dressed up, a workman would never think of going to the
wrong entrance. In factory committees, workmen, as with menials, are usually addressed by
their first names, whilst they address the employer by his last name, as "Sir," or, if he has a
title, by the title. British "manners" are the etiquette of status in relationships between
inferior and superior.

social philosophies. Aside from trade-union matters of immediate practical interest, the one thing they readily comprehend is the coöperative movement. The sense of alliance, however, for both the T.U.C. and the coöperatives, is tentative and thin. "Production for use and not for profit," a Co-operative Union pamphlet[81] points out, "is a Socialist *cliché*, which, perhaps half unconsciously, recognises the importance of the consumer," and the Labour party, dominated as it is by the producer outlook, "does not always see clearly the logic of this professed aim." The coöps, on the other hand, stand for the "sovereignty of the consumer," and Stanley Jevons, not a Keir Hardie—not to mention a Karl Marx—is their prophet.[82]

The T.U.C. "represents less than 15 per cent of the whole population," and any major trade union, "could (in times of shortage and crisis) hold the community up to ransom," but the coöps represent "all the people," and "the specific role of the Co-operative Movement in politics is the advocacy of a libertarian socialism, based on the classlessness of consumer sovereignty . . ." It seeks to maximize the freedoms of man in society, and a leading object is "to demand that society should be so organised and governed as to provide for the maximum degree of free and voluntary association."[83] In other words, the coöperatives are in favor of planning, socialism, and, under some circumstances, nationalization, yet "it may . . . be regarded as the possible middle way between *laisser faire* liberalism and rigid planning on a compulsory basis, and in this aspect it has a strong claim to the allegiance of all those who believe that some form of economic planning is necessary, in the interests of order and justice, but who dislike the element of coercion in other systems which are offered for their approval."[84]

This term "middle way"—once given wide circulation in the United States in a eulogy of the Swedish coöperatives written by Marquis

---

[81] *Wanting and Working.*

[82] Before the presidency of J. T. W. Mitchell (1874–1895) the coöperatives "had been largely influenced by the doctrine of the Labour Theory of Value" but "with Mitchell this influence was consciously countered and finally defeated . . . the Rochdale Co-operators, he said in his Presidential address to Congress (1892), did not start with capital or labour, but with consumption; use was the basis of all values. He, therefore, anticipated the economists—Jevons, Marshall, and the Robbins school of economic thought." *Ibid.*

[83] *Ibid.* This is also the theme of the official biography of the Co-Operative Wholesale Society; Percy Redfern, *The New History of the C.W.S.* (Manchester, C.W.S., 1938).

[84] Carr-Saunders, et al., *op. cit.*, p. 534. Coöperating in the writing of this book was John Jewkes, author of the recent bitterly invective *Ordeal by Planning* (London, 1948). This statement of planning is also essentially congruent with that formulated by Prof. James Meade, of the London School of Economics in his *Planning and the Price Mechanism* (London, 1948).

Childs,[85] but which has also been claimed by a leading spokesman of the Conservatives as a term most appropriately designating the general Conservative program[86]—has gradually crept into the Labour patois, and has, along with the equally ambiguous term, "Third Force," come to be accepted in Labour circles as a reasonably good way of summarizing the direction and emphasis of the Labour party. In terms of practical politics, it means a middle way between the Conservatives and the Mosleyite Fascists to the right of them, and the syndicalist (Guild Socialist) and Communist and other Marxist groups to the left of them. It is not, that is to say, centered, in any definite and clear-cut sense of the term, around the formulae of a "Co-operative" dominated society.

Nor, conversely, is it centered around the idea of worker ownership and control of industry. This program, long associated in British labor history with the syndicalist propaganda of the Guild Socialists,[87] has—along with other versions of the same idea—been completely sidetracked for the concept of the governmentally owned "autonomous public corporation" which is to be set up to manage whatever properties a socialist society desires to transfer to public ownership.[88] Here the state, not the workers, are the owners, and management does not even include representatives of the trade unions. Although some, or conceivably even all, of the directors of such corporations might be drawn from working-class and professional ranks, appointment is to be solely on the basis of technical qualifications, and trade-union appointees must first resign all trade-union offices before accepting jobs. The trade unions are to bargain and otherwise deal with the new managements in

[85] Marquis Childs, *Sweden: The Middle Way* (New York, 1936).

[86] Harold Macmillan, *The Middle Way* (London, 1939). The paper cover shows the middle way half way between a bundle of fasces (the symbol of Italian Fascism) and the hammer and sickle. It was given out by the Westminster book club of the Conservative Political Centre as the best extant statement of the whole general Conservative position, and as the source of practically all the constructive ideas which the Labour party has claimed credit for since their rise to power in 1945.

[87] Guild Socialism has always been opposed to "Municipal and State Socialism" under which ownership of industry passes directly into the hands of public bodies. A. R. Orage, in his classic *National Guilds: An Inquiry into the Wage System and the Way Out* (London, 1914), writes, *"Both are equally committed to the exploitation of the wage system, to the aggrandisement of the municipal investor.* State Socialism is state capitalism, with the private capitalist better protected than when he was dependent upon voluntary effort." (P. 21.) Italics in the original.

[88] As viewed by Herbert Morrison, its leading spokesman in Labour government circles, the public corporation is the solution for the desired "combination of public ownership, public accountability, and business management for public ends." See his *Socialisation and Transport* (London, 1933), pp. 149–212. The most elaborate case for this device has been given in W. A. Robson, *Public Enterprise: Developments in Social Ownership and Control in Great Britain* (London, 1937).

capacities similar to those which they have followed vis-a-vis private employers in the past. In effect, for the syndicalist idea has been substituted a Labour version of the Burnham thesis of management by disinterested professional experts.[89] This idea has been applied by the Labour government to both nationalized industries and those to be left indefinitely or permanently in the hands of private enterprise.[90]

Is there a theory—a philosophy—for this "middle way"? Apparently not.[91] Clearly there is no single compact, widely known book—no Bible or Koran, no *Das Kapital* or *Mein Kampf*—which contains the central doctrine, or theory, or corpus of principles, or conscious *Weltanschauung*, or clearly formulated organon of aims and objectives. There exists, of course, a vast medley of pamphlets, brochures, editorial statements, speeches, and booklets emanating from Labour party headquarters and from the numerous organizations associated with it. These have been supplemented by numerous books written by Labour party spokesmen on various aspects of policy. None of these lays authoritative claim to being an officially recognized expression of the logic, general theory, or broad social philosophy underlying the central theses of the Labour party, nor are they referred to by Labour spokesmen as such.[92] On the contrary, it is a well-accepted cliché of British

[89] Burnham, *The Managerial Revolution*. The one point at which Labour party spokesmen appear to be in disagreement with Burnham, is that while Burnham believes that expert and professional-minded management is gradually superseding private and special-interest minded management within the framework of capitalist society, the Labour people believe there must at some time take place a *formal* shift in ownership *title*. But with this difference, disagreement almost wholly disappears. Numerous conferences with Labour spokesmen in Britain on this specific point showed no serious disagreement. The Labour government, in a figure employed by one leading spokesman, is merely playing midwife to somewhat speed up and ease a process of natural birth.

[90] There is this difference, that although a member of a trade union may be appointed to a management position in a nationalized industry, he may be appointed only to an advisory position with respect to private industry under the "self-government in industry" program of the development council.

[91] When this question was submitted by the author in 1948, three different Labour-government ministers answered it with emphatic negatives. One suggested that so far as there might be said to exist either a "theory or a Philosophy" it was to be found in Beatrice Webb's *Our Partnership*, which closes its narrative with 1912. There had been, this minister said, "No new ideas in the Labour Party since that time."

[92] There are two partial exceptions to this generalization: George Bernard Shaw, ed., *Fabian Essays in Socialism* (London, 1889) and Douglas Jay, *The Socialist Case* (London, 1946). For the first, see pp. 36–37 below. In a foreword to the latter, written in November, 1946, Prime Minister Attlee commends this book "to all those interested in the present British experiment in democratic socialism." Yet while "It is the aim of *The Socialist Case* to set out the basic philosophic arguments for collective management of our economic resources" it is directed to the demonstration "that the economic scramble of laissez-faire cannot achieve a distribution of wealth in accordance with the needs of the common people." This position is, or course, no longer held by Socialists alone; all Keynesians, for example, accept this fundamental proposition. Aside from one or two persons who made quite laudatory references to Jay's book, however, few could be found during my stay in England during 1948 who would agree that this book was in any respect an authoritative statement of either Labour "theory" or "philosophy."

Labour party propaganda that it subscribes to the British way, which means to proceed "undogmatically." This is virtually always regarded as being synonmous with the practical, the empirical and the experimental approach; and it has specifically been termed a procedure which is unregimented and democratic because it is held to be free of any definite commitment to any clear-cut theory.

May a theory, nevertheless, be inferred? It seems not. What is to be found in Britain at the moment is a highly unstable set of compromises which seem to be related to one another in the immediate postwar period in somewhat the following fashion: The principal substance of the program is derived mainly from the separately evolved programs of the T.U.C. and the Co-operative Union in which the former has played the dominating role. So far as the T.U.C. is concerned, this has come to mean primarily three things: (1) the usual run of trade-union demands relating to hours, wages, working conditions, and the like, now supplemented by advocacy of means for preventing unemployment; (2) the demand for "Public Ownership and control of natural resources and of services" consisting of four features, "(a) Nationalisation of land, mines, and minerals; (b) Nationalisation of railways; (c) The extension of State and municipal enterprise for the provision of social necessities and services; (d) Proper provision for the adequate participation of the workers in the control and management of public services and industries";[93] and (3) a full social security program. So far as the coöperatives are concerned, the T.U.C. program is opposed on 2, d above, and extended in terms of a hope for more emphasis upon voluntary action, which means less state direction, and continued expansion of the coöperative form of consumer dominated production and distribution.

To the hard kernel or central substance of the program, there are to be added certain real extensions and certain propaganda which are mostly of the order, as one Labour party spokesman put the matter, of the frosting on the cake. This consists of a number of elements drawn from a variety of sources. One of these is Christian Socialist in its inspiration. As indicated above, this is partly traceable to the Evangelical movement, partly to writers such as Maurice, Kingsley, and Carlyle, and partly to the crusading Christian humanitarianism of such almost legendary Tory reformers as Chadwick and Shaftesbury. Currently it receives its best, most vigorous, and most liberal interpretation

---

[93] *Rules and Standing Orders, T.U.C.*, pp. 3–4.

in the speeches and writings of Prime Minister Clement Attlee and Sir Stafford Cripps.[94]

Far less important is the influence traceable directly or primarily to Marxist sources of inspiration. Of three such parties, one, the Social Democratic Federation (SDF), passed out of existence entirely in 1948, a second, the Independent Labour Party (far less Marxian) has long since ceased to have any influence, and the third, the Communist party, exists as a minor group represented in Parliament by only two M.P.'s.

Somewhat more important is an intermediate group within the Labour party, difficult to define, commonly referred to as the Keep Left Group. Centered more or less around the *New Statesman and Nation*,[95] it has served primarily as a gad-fly in the hopes of needling the Labour government into following internationally an independent course between the United States and the Soviet Union, and into a more vigorous prosecution of internal technical modernization and social reform. On the fringe this group has partly overlapped, and been somewhat influenced by, the group sometimes referred to as the "Nenni telegram group,"[96] who favor a closer coöperation with other socialist movements on the Continent and, generally, a more conciliatory attitude toward the U.S.S.R. Never strong, the Nenni Group has been almost wholly dissolved by the Labour party (one of its members, J. Platts-Mills, was expelled from the party), and the Keep Left Group has tended to fall apart of its own accord.[97]

Still more important, finally, is the Fabian Society. But it is difficult to say just what the nature of the influence on the Labour party of the Fabian Society is now or has been in the past. The society, as Herbert Morrison once said, has never had a program of its own, and has always

[94] Typical is the following: "I have myself always regarded Socialism and Christianity as synonymous, and I am convinced that all we are seeking to do by way of organisation and planning must be carried out—if we are to succeed—in the light and under the guidance of our Socialist and Christian principles." Stafford Cripps, *Democracy Alive: A Selection of Recent Speeches* (London, 1946), p. 63.

[95] Their position has been set forth in a New Statesman Pamphlet, *Keep Left*, by a Group of Members of Parliament (15 in number), published in May, 1947.

[96] Signers of the "Nenni telegram" sent on the eve of the 1948 Italian elections to Nenni, leader of the left-wing faction in the Italian labor movement, and favoring collaboration with the Italian Communist party.

[97] This judgment may require some considerable modification. Expulsion of several members of the Nenni Group, and disciplining of remaining members of the two groups, has been only partially successful. On various leading programs—most notably those associated with foreign policy—dissidence has been growing. Furthermore, it has received considerable support from the growing dissatisfaction in certain trade union circles—especially strong in the more radical mining and heavy industrial regions of South Wales, Scotland, Yorkshire, and the waterfronts of the larger ports—with the conduct, policies, and management of the nationalized industries.

operated more as a forum for discussion and debate than as an exponent of any given doctrine or set of ideas. Yet it must, nevertheless, have actually exercised a very considerable, though mostly indirect, influence in party councils. This seems to have been primarily a result of the life and labors of Sidney and Beatrice Webb, and a word must be added on the effect of the work of this remarkable pair of writers, thinkers, and agitators on the shaping of Labour party policies.

Broadly speaking, the program of the Fabians under the direction of the Webbs may, without undue distortion of the facts, be said to constitute more or less a straight-line projection of Benthamite utilitarianism as it left the hands of John Stuart Mill. Cole believes that the first clear-cut statement of this program found in *Fabian Essays* of 1889,[98] contains the clearest "exposition of what has been called 'English Socialism'—a conception of Socialism which fits in with the English tradition, and shows the Socialist doctrine as the logical outcome of the Benthamite utilitarian philosophy which provided the main driving force of nineteenth-century social reform."[99] What marked off this "English Socialism" from other brands of socialism?

As with Marx, the broad foundation was evolutionary,[100] but instead of basing their system of thought on the Hegelian dialectical triad, with its overtly revolutionary implications, the Webbs and their confreres evolved the concept of the gradualist approach. In this view there existed in the background of history a vastly potent demiurgos of progress. In his 1889 essay, Sidney Webb spoke of "the irresistible momentum of the ideas which Socialism denotes . . . The main stream which has borne European society towards Socialism during the past 100 years is the irresistible progress of Democracy."[101] Theory and practice alike were bent and shaped by the overpowering thrust of this elemental coercive moral force[102]—which, in the final analysis, nothing

---

[98] George Bernard Shaw, ed., *Fabian Essays in Socialism*, by G. Bernard Shaw, Sidney Webb, William Clarke, Sydney Olivier, Annie Besant, Graham Wallis, and Hubert Bland (London, 1889) ; reissued with a new Foreword by G. Bernard Shaw (London, 1948).

[99] G. D. H. Cole, *The Fabian Society, Past and Present*, Tract Series No. 258 (Rev. ed.; Fabian Publications, 1946), p. 16. In an earlier Fabian Tract, No. 168, being No. 4 of the Fabian Biographical Series, *John Stuart Mill* (1913), the author writes that had Mill "Lived another ten years he would almost certainly have been amongst the founders of the Fabian Society."

[100] Marx originally planned to dedicate *Das Kapital* to Charles Darwin.

[101] *Fabian Essays*, pp. 30, 33.

[102] Following the heresies of the Philosophic Radicals, the "nest of singing birds" at the Lakes, De Quincey, Coleridge, Robert Owen and Carlyle "came Maurice, Kingsley, Ruskin, and others who dared to impeach the current middle class cult; until finally, through Comte and John Stuart Mill, Darwin and Herbert Spencer, the conception of the Social Organism has at last penetrated to the minds though not yet to the books, even of our professors of Political Economy. Meanwhile, caring for none of these things, the practical man had been

could resist because, given everywhere unconscious expression in the form of a prepotent *Zeitgeist,* it must gradually suffuse all conscious action until it would result in an "irresistible glide into collectivist Socialism."[103]

But if this irresistible glide could not be forestalled by its reactionary enemies, yet its approach could be more widely heralded and its speed accelerated by its progressive friends. The mode was the Fabian way:[104] consciously to permeate all layers of society, upper, middle, and lower, with detailed knowledge of why the irresistible could not be foresworn, diverted, or explained away, and how it must of necessity work itself out, fanwise, in the detailed affairs of men until it came ultimately to envelop the whole of the social organism. But there might be a moment of final taking over. Hence, the motto of the Fabian Society has been: "For the right moment you must wait, as Fabius did; but when the right moment comes you must strike hard, or your waiting will have been vain and fruitless."

Neither the Webbs nor any of the leading figures in the Fabian movement have ever departed from the position expressed in that motto. But there has been a double and enormously important, shift of emphasis with regard to tactics. The first was slow and gradual, and in the apprehension of the Webbs at least, in thorough keeping with the Fabian approach. It consisted of a gradual abandonment of permeation of circles previously dominated by the Conservative and Liberal parties—with the turning point coming at the time of the failure of the Liberals in 1911 to carry out effectively the minimum program contained in the recommendations of the minority report of the Poor Law Commission, which had been written largely by Beatrice Webb[105]—for

---

irresistibly driven in the same direction." Hence a vast mass of early remedial legislation, operating essentially without benefit of theory, but unfolding, like an Aristotelian entelechy, out of the inner essence of the spirit of the English and French Enlightenment, and into the full flower of an emerging Democratic Socialism. *Ibid.,* p. 46.

[103] "Thirty years ago Herbert Spencer demonstrated the incompatibility of full private property in land with the modern democratic State; and almost every economist now preaches the same doctrine. The Radical is rapidly arriving, from practical experience, at similar conclusions; and the steady increase of the government regulation of private enterprise, the growth of municipal administration, and the rapid shifting of the burden of taxation directly to rent and interest, mark in treble lines the statesman's unconscious abandonment of the old Individualism, and our irresistible glide into collectivist Socialism." *Ibid.,* p. 60.

[104] "The Fabian Society was named... after a certain Roman general, Quintus Fabius Maximus Cunctator—which means 'the Delayer.' This may appear an odd way of naming a Society which has stood throughout its existence for Socialism" but it meant not "rushing in where more timorous angels fear to tread" but rather "biding their time, as Fabius did against Hannibal, from whom he saved Rome." Cole, *The Fabian Society.*

[105] How vital a role the failure played in the thinking of the Webbs is revealed in *Our Partnership,* pp. 477–491.

open support of a greatly activized Labour party whose program was to be based directly upon the achievement of goals foreseen in the "Democratic Socialism" of the future.

The high tide of this identification came with the drafting of the Labour party's new constitution by the Webbs (mostly by Sydney) in 1918. Thereafter, a second shift occurred, stimulated by the disastrous failure of the first and second Labour governments (1924 and 1929-1931), and the betrayal of Labour by the defection of the party's titular leader, Ramsay MacDonald, in the formation of the Conservative-dominated National government of the thirties. Bit by bit the Webbs became disillusioned with the whole Fabian tactical approach. There are few recantations in political literature to be compared with that of this pair as it has been outlined by Beatrice Webb in 1938.[106] It meant a confession of the failure of a central tenet of a lifetime of research, writing, and agitation, and their final, though reluctant, abandonment of tactical procedures which they had helped develop.

Thereafter events, rather than policies, began slowly but cumulatively to breathe new life into what seemed a hopelessly shattered Labour party. Most important of these events were the repressive Trades Disputes Act of 1927, the long continuation of the depression of the thirties, the terrible fright given democratic elements in the country by the successive episodes of the Abyssinian War, the Spanish Civil War, the Munich and Berechtsgaden appeasements—which seemed both logical developments of Conservative foreign policy, and bound to lead to the total destruction of popular democracy abroad—and finally the outbreak of the Second World War. So far as the Fabian Society was concerned, the gradual decline of the influence of the Webbs was partly offset by the incorporation in 1939 of the New Fabian Research Group made up of "such men as Attlee, Cripps, Dalton, Arthur Henderson, Bevin and Pritt,"[107] and it was this group which the events of the war helped to consolidate into the leadership of the Labour party.[108]

Meanwhile, there occurred the "Keynesian Revolution," and broadly speaking it is probably correct to say that the part previously played by the Webbs in top Labour party strategy has been taken over by the

---

[106] *Ibid.*, pp. 488–490. See also the closing chapter of Vol. II of their *Soviet Communism: A New Civilisation* (N.Y., 1935). A contributing factor, of course, was old age, which gradually compelled the Webbs to assume less active roles.

[107] Cole, *The Fabian Society*, p. 10.

[108] Every important top official of the Labour government has at one time or another been actively associated with the work of the Fabian Society, and most of them—as, e.g., Cripps, Morrison, Bevin, Dalton, Attlee, Tomlinson, Griffiths—have been the authors of one or more Fabian pamphlets.

proponents of some version or other of the Keynesian stratagems. In sharp contrast to the Webbs of the *Decay of Capitalist Civilization,* and of the last chapter of *Our Partnership,* it is now not difficult for an ardent Labour party leader to adopt the Keynesian shift in emphasis, and to find himself in so doing in line—as did Keynes himself— with both the dominant trend in received orthodox economic thought and with the programs of the T.U.C. and the Co-operative Union, and still to see himself ensconced among the residuary legatees of the past Fabian movement. Yet this outlook is also wholly lacking in the emphasis which could, and did, lead to the disillusionment of the Webbs with the gradualist approach. In short—with due apologies for adjectival limitations—the Labour "new look" is essentially short range in its approach, opportunistic in its maneuvers, vague—and generally impatient with discussion—about long-run objectives, practical and realistic (unphilosophical) regarding the details of its specific program, and humanitarian-reformist in such value judgments as its spokesmen may on occasion be willing to make. It does not desire seriously to disturb the *status quo* unless and until the champions of the here-and-now maintain an obdurate and irrational resistance to what it feels to be an unequivocal common sense change for the better—a change which it believes all honest and patriotic citizens must ultimately concede entirely on its own merits, once the appropriate facts have been assembled, and once the inherent logic of the new position has been adequately unraveled. To paraphrase: "You shall know the Truth, and the Truth shall make you vote Labour." It appears, in effect, essentially as a British version of the American New Deal program as it was visualized by President Roosevelt in the heyday of his interest in the domestic scene.[109]

THE 1945 PROGRAM: LET US FACE THE FUTURE

It was against this larger background and with benefit of such an outlook, that the Labour party formulated its 1945 manifesto, *Let Us Face the Future.* In the forthcoming election, they said, "the effective choice

[109] Thus even the question of whether all, only a part, or even very little, of capitalism is to be liquidated is held in abeyance. Socialism thus becomes an enlightened, humanitarian common sense which attempts to reshape the institutions of the present so as to give a larger and fuller life to all. It remains suspicious of private property only so long as it results in (1) the evils and wastes of *laissez faire,* (2) the collusive and restrictive devices of cartels and monopolies, or (3) as it serves to perpetuate serious inequities in the distribution of wealth and income. This is the central core of the program incorporated in the Working Party reports and the subsequent Development Councils. See Chaps. xii and xiii following. Planning, consequently, consists of the setting of targets, and the hope that all will bend their efforts and wills to seeing that—seconded and led by a Government willing to employ manipulative aids at will—they are achieved.

of the people . . . will be between the Conservative Party, standing for the protection of the 'rights' of private economic interest, and the Labour Party, allied with the great Trade Union and Co-operative Movements, standing for the wise organisation and use of the economic assets of the nation for the public good. Those are the two main parties; and here is the fundamental issue which has to be settled."[110] But of just what did this "fundamental issue" consist? The aims, it said, are "good food, in plenty, useful work for all, and comfortable labour-saving homes that take full advantage of the resources of modern science and productive industry. It wants a high and rising standard of living, security for all against a rainy day, an educational system that will give every boy and girl a chance to develop the best that is in them." The over-all difference between itself and other parties is not between the felt need for "a tremendous overhaul, a great programme of modernisation and re-equipment of its homes, its factories and machinery, its schools, its social services," for "all parties say so." The difference is only that "the Labour Party means it."

Specifically this means (1) "Jobs for All," or a program for full employment which includes the establishment of a National Investment Board and nationalization of the Bank of England;[111] (2) "Industry in the Service of the Nation" to be effected by (*a*) nationalizing fuel and power, inland transport, iron and steel, (*b*) public supervision of monopolies and cartels, (*c*) a program for increasing the export trade, (*d*) price and materials-priorities controls, and (*e*) some reorganization of government departments; (3) substantial aids to, and some degree or other of national land planning for, agriculture; (4) a greatly extended housing and building program, and considerable extension of town and country planning; (5) further expansion of educational and recreational facilities; (6) a broad social security program, including health and social insurance; and (7) a program for promoting peace abroad and for aiding Empire development.

Thus far, and aside from the nationalization program—and then primarily with respect to the iron and steel industry—the Labour party was apparently not in serious disagreement with either the Liberal or Conservative parties.[112] The sentiments were essentially the same, and the planks in the rival platforms showed no other sharp differences in

[110] *Let Us Face The Future*, p. 12.

[111] These several planks in the Labour program are outlined in more detail in the following chapters.

[112] A further partial exception was the fact that the Labour party was committed to self-governing status for India.

principle. In fact, there was so little difference that one feels at times compelled to accept the judgment of the Labour party that the primary difference lay in the belief that they meant what they said whereas the other parties did not, and that the voters endorsed this belief.

As the program unfolded after Labour came into power, this impression was further reenforced by many striking facts. For example, with the partial exceptions of transport and steel, all of the nationalization, or seminationalization programs were based squarely on findings, and in large part on recommendations, which had been made by Conservative-dominated fact-finding and special investigating committees. This was true of the Bank of England (MacMillan report), coal (Reid report), gas (Heyworth report), electricity (McGowan report), town and country planning (Barlow, Scott, and Uthwatt reports), and social security (Beveridge report). Even the nationalization of the iron and steel industry seems to have been mainly the nationalization of a plan for reorganizing the industry which had been advanced by the Iron and Steel Federation itself.

Externally, with the exception of the conferring of dominion status on India, both foreign and colonial policies are, and have consistently been, indistinguishable from those previously pursued by Conservative governments. The Groundnuts Scheme (see chapter xi following) was based on a report submitted by the giant Unilever combine, and the reorganization of cable and wireless upon recommendations submitted by the company taken over. Internally, the development council plan evolved by Sir Stafford Cripps is a slightly altered version of the formulae of capital-labor copartnership which had once been actively sponsored by the Federation of British Industries and other giant business groups, and is based on the coöperatively minded concept of self-government in business. To cap it all, the top planning machinery evolved by the Labour government represents a relatively minor adaptation of wartime controls to somewhat altered peacetime circumstances.

Yet there were some differences in emphasis. Among these, two stand out. First, the range and extent of the proposed nationalization program. Second, the highly transitional character of the general social reform program. The first involved little by way of a fundamental difference of principle until iron and steel nationalization came up, and the question arose whether this was an augury of what was eventually to come in the form of future expansion of public ownership should the

Labour government stay in office. The second seemed to rest its case on the achieving of immediate gains in a context where the Labour government became—despite all reassuring disclaimers to the contrary—suspect of securing these gains only for the purpose of employing each new victory as a means of wresting still further concessions from its political and economic adversaries in the future. Is there here more confusion, only bungling, or a real constrictor encroachment?

It is, then, with these two main issues that any attempt to understand the nature, scope, and content of the Labour government's plans for achieving "Democratic Socialism" must come to grips. It is here that fundamental departures from past trends, and from the plans of current adversaries—if any there be—must be discovered and analyzed, and it is in this context that we may discover possible lines of further change in Labour party plans for the more distant future.

CHAPTER II

The Bank of England

...the Bank of England with its financial powers must be brought under public ownership, and the operations of the other banks harmonised with industrial needs ... A National Investment Board will determine social priorities and promote better timing in private investment.—*Let Us Face the Future: A Declaration of Labour Policy for the Consideration of the Nation* (1945).

It would take a very nervous heart to register a flutter at what is contained in the Bill. Nothing could well be more moderate. The proposal of the Chancellor of the Exchequer is plain: "I will aggravate my voice so that I will roar you as gently as any sucking dove; I will roar you as 'twer any nightingale."—*The Economist*, October 13, 1945.

WHEN Chancellor of the Exchequer Hugh Dalton proposed that "the Old Man of the Treasury and the Old Lady of Threadneedle Street should be legally married" to avoid any further "danger of their living in sin,"[1] the Opposition was disarmed by the mildness of the implementing bill, and both friends and foes were puzzled by its trappings. If the bill for nationalizing the Bank of England was, as its sponsor claimed it to be, truly "a streamlined Socialist Statute,"[2] and if this model statute forecast the manner in which the Labour party intended to fulfill the mandate given it by the general electorate in the preceding summer, had business-as-usual anything to fear? Was the lion of socialism preparing to lie down with the lamb of conservatism with only the genial reservation that contract terms be defined and fraternal etiquette observed?

Or was there more than met the eye? Winston Churchill, leader of the Opposition, apparently thought not, for he did not even attend the second reading of the bill. To the few doubting Thomases Dalton spoke in reassuring language and with a dulcet voice. He reminded the followers of the former Prime Minister that Churchill had recently stated that "the national ownership of the Bank of England does not, in my opinion, raise any matter of principle. . . . There are important examples in the United States and in our Dominions of central banking institutions."[3] Furthermore, Dalton went on to say, all were concerned with a "united Empire Policy," and the Government was concerned

[1] *Hansard*, Vol. 415, col. 47.
[2] *Ibid.*, col. 43.
[3] *Hansard*, Vol. 413, col. 93.

here with "a united Empire Policy on the organization of Central Banks."[4] When all was said and done, "There are two different lines of argument, reinforcing each other, but distinct, which may be used in support of this Bill. The first is that this Bill, in effect, brings the law in relation to the facts as they have gradually evolved over the years. It brings the antiquated and outmoded constitution of the past into a form which fits the practical realities of the present. That is one line of argument, we make the law fit the facts. The second line of argument is even more important. It is that by this Bill we ensure a smooth and efficient growth of our financial and banking system, in order to meet the new needs of the future."[5]

It would seem difficult for even the diehards to find fault with such a mild sentiment as this. The Opposition could accept it as trivial, or jeer that the mountain of socialism had labored only to bring forth a mere mouth for the legal-minded puritan. But when Dalton went on to say that "this Government have a mandate, an emphatic mandate, for a five year plan of economic development . . . and this Bill is one of the foundations,"[6] the issue ceased to be merely a question of enacting a formal change in the legal status of the Bank of England, and became a problem of the nature of the plan for the future for which the nationalized Bank was to constitute such an important foundation stone.

Yet, so far as anybody knew, aside from certain broad objectives for which nationalization was regarded as a precondition, no such plan existed. Until it did, it was quite impossible to divine the meaning of Dalton's phrase. The bill either had to be debated on its merits—where differences were easily reconciled— or analyzed and contested in terms of the edifice which socialist architects were constructing out of institutional building stones such as the Bank of England. But no blueprints were to be seen; it wasn't even certain that the architects had yet sat down to their task. Thus, at first, there was little for argument to come to grips with, and that little consisted entirely of a series of rather vague and contradictory utterances from Labour spokesmen in the past.

FRAGMENTS OF A LABOUR FINANCIAL PROGRAM

Labour's concern with the problem of finance stems mostly from the decade of the thirties. Neither its official spokesmen nor any of its advisory or tutelary groups, including the Fabian Society, had, except for

---

[4] *Ibid.*, Vol. 415, col. 46.
[5] *Loc. cit.*
[6] *Ibid.*, cols. 46, 47.

certain of the milder conventional left-wing declamations, anything to say on the money question before the First World War.[7] The policy program drafted by Sidney Webb for the reorganized Labour party in 1918, *Labour and the New Social Order*, proposes extension of the Postal Savings System and nationalization of life insurance, but otherwise ignores financial problems and institutions entirely.

The first formal step was taken at the thirty-first annual conference of the Labour party at Scarborough in 1931, when F. W. Pethick-Lawrence moved a resolution that "this Conference ... reaffirms its view that the banking and credit system of the country cannot continue to be left in private hands, and demands that it shall be brought under public control. It further recommends the formation of a national investment board with statutory powers in relation to both home and foreign investment."[8] The motion was carried, but two amendments, (1) that after "public" the words "ownership, and" be inserted, and (2) that the words "credit system" be followed by "including the Bank of England and the Joint-Stock Banks," were rejected.

The next year a resolution was carried which accepted the full import of these amendments. Dalton's original proposal at this conference was "that the Bank of England should be brought under public ownership and control, and that the Governor of the Bank of England should be appointed by the Government and be subject to the general direction of a Minister of Cabinet rank who should be responsible to the House of Commons for banking and credit policy, the day-to-day business of the Bank being caried on by the Governor and his staff."[9] To this E. F. Wise moved the following amendment: "After 'Bank of England' insert 'and the Joint Stock Banks' and after 'Governor and his staff' add 'the Banking system should be managed with a view to utilising available capital and credit resources in accordance with a Socialist plan for the development of industry and international trade; and the redistribution of purchasing power; and with this same object in view,

---

[7] Only one mention of money—a parenthetical reference by Bernard Shaw on "monetization of silver" (p. 191)—appears in the 1889 *Fabian Essays*. Subsequent interest prior to 1918 is confined almost wholly to concern over peoples' savings banks, and similar supplementary financial aids to the impecunious. See, e.g., Sidney Webb, *How to Pay for the War* (Fabian Society, 1916), on extension of Post Office Banking facilities. There is no frontal attack on financial institutions comparable to those upon land, transport, mining, heavy industries, and even distribution. The same holds for the Labour party and its precursor organizations.

[8] *Report of the Thirty-first Annual Conference of the Labour Party* (Scarborough, 1931), pp. 187–188.

[9] *Report of the Thirty-second Annual Conference of the Labour Party* (Leicester, 1932), p. 182.

power should be taken to nationalise or control the other finance, acceptance and banking houses.' "[10]

The resolution and the first part of the amendement ("After ... power") were carried. Not, however, without opposition from Mr. Ernest Bevin, who wished the amendment to be rejected on the grounds of its impracticality. The reply given by Sir Stafford Cripps is interesting in the light of subsequent events. "This Amendment," he said, "raises perhaps the most important issue that is going to come before the Conference. The issue is whether we intend, immediately upon coming to power, to seize the power of finance ... My own view is that it will be impossible for a Socialist Party to carry through Socialism so long as the Joint Stock Banks remain under private control. I believe we shall be making a profound mistake if we are so timid as to withdraw from the position we took last year."[11]

If "timid" is an apt choice among words, then Labour's timidity followed its usual gradualist tactics, for it took nearly a decade for the sentiments expressed in the amendments to be completely by-passed. Nevertheless, while a Labour party brochure in 1935 reaffirmed the need for nationalizing the Bank of England, the idea of control had already been substituted for that of ownership and direction of commercial banking and investment by the state. "The Labour Party proposes," it said, "... the setting up of a National Investment Board which, acting in co-operation with the Nationalised Bank of England, the Board of the National Banking Corporation and the economic planning authorities will control the flow of investment in the national market."[12] The phraseology of nationalization is carefully avoided when speaking of savings and investment institutions. Subsequent statements dropped ever more snugly into the academically secure cachements of the Keynesian monetary control theory.[13] By the time of the outbreak of the war the argument had become almost wholly Keynesian, and nationalization of the Bank of England was justified, as it was at the time of its enactment, almost entirely as an act belatedly

[10] *Ibid.*, p. 188.

[11] *Ibid.*, p. 192. Only the first part of the amendment was carried. On this the vote was— For: 2,241,000; Against: 984,000.

[12] *Labour's Financial Policy* (London, Labour Publications Dept., 1935), p. 15.

[13] See, e.g., The Labour party brochure, Douglas Jay, *The Nation's Wealth at the Nation's Service* (London, 1938) ; *Full Employment and Financial Policy*. A Report of the National Executive Committee of the Labour Party to be presented to the Annual Conference to be held in London from May 29th to June 2nd, 1944; the subsequent review of Labour's first Parliamentary achievements in the financial field in a pamphlet prepared for the 1946 Bournemouth Conference, *Financing Labour's Plan;* and *The Bank of England and the Nation*. Labour Discussion Series, no. 3 (London, 1946).

to baptize as a public institution an infant which had now grown to giant proportions and was hoary with age.

In the debates preceding the nationalization of the Bank of England two general lines of argument, accordingly, are to be found. The first is clearly socialist and is grounded in the belief that the financial power of the private banking system, being but part and parcel of the capitalist system, must, with the constrictor advance on that system by socialist gradualism, become public property. More than that, the strategic nature of the position held by private banking and finance in capitalist society required that this strategic height be taken immediately upon Labour's assumption of power. While this argument has never wholly disappeared from Labour literature, what remains of it has been greatly modified by the second line of argument and in some respects has become almost wholly subordinate to it.

This second line of argument, which for purposes of convenience may be termed Keynesian, begins by accepting the fact of the strategic position of the banks in the shaping of national economic policy, but posits its acceptance on the assumption that public direction of the private banking system could, and should, be reconciled with the requirements of public welfare in general, and in particular with the measures which need to be taken to maintain full employment—always the dominating concern of the Keynesians. So far as financial matters are concerned, the transition from the first to the second position in Labour circles has been gradual, but it was well-nigh complete by the time of Labour's victory in 1945. To be sure, the stigmata of the earlier emphasis have never been wholly obliterated, and there are current grumblings among the back benches which threaten a return to the more purely socialist argument. But the tone is in the minor key, and its dissent is scarcely audible.

The most widely circulated blend of the two lines of argument is found in the writing of Douglas Jay, the Oxford economist who became the Parliamentary Secretary[14] to the Chancellor of the Exchequer, Sir Stafford Cripps, when the latter became virtual economic dictator through the creation of the coördinative Ministry of Economic Affairs.[15] Unemployment, he argues, is a "now familiar disease of capitalism . . . one important cause" of which "is the private credit and banking monopoly, which controls the volume of money and repeatedly refuses to

---

[14] "Parliamentary" in fact, but called "Economic Secretary to the Treasury."

[15] In September, 1947, Cripps became Chancellor and for the first time combined this position with that of Minister for Economic Affairs.

create sufficient purchasing power for the system as a whole to work at full capacity." This monopoly power is unfriendly to labor, and it employs criteria in its policy formation which may be inconsistent with those favored by the government. "The part played by the Bank of England in the manipulation of the 1931 crisis, and the ejection of the Labour Government from office, is now well-known ... Not quite so well-known is the fact that throughout the post-war period the Bank has used its power of granting foreign loans to pursue a foreign policy frequently in conflict with that of the Government of the day."[16]

The first charge, that there exists a "private credit and banking monopoly" in England, has received a good deal of attention at times—particularly during the thirties. Ernest Davies, Labour M.P., in a widely circulated book called *"National" Capitalism*,[17] has detailed the case at length. It is a case, however, which relates primarily to the so-called "Big Five" commercial banks,[18] and would appear to have been valuable primarily as an argument for the nationalization of commercial banking. Although there have been repeated charges that the Bank of England is so closely allied with the Big Five and with industry that it must of necessity heed the voice of a master other than the government when private interests and the government are in conflict, yet it would seem that this would always be so whenever any private banking interests assume policy-making powers which rightly belong to the government, the exercise of which may at critical moments actually defeat the carrying out of governmental policy.

Ignoring "ancient history," there is adequate evidence, it is argued, to show that the Bank has on numerous occasions shown a marked degree of irresponsibility to the government. For example, "During the 1914–18 War ... a Governor showed an almost arrogant independence of the Chancellory and, as Lord Beaverbrook has described, opposed

---

[16] Douglas Jay, *The Nation's Wealth*. The general theoretical setting for Jay's financial arguments is to be found in his book *The Socialist Case*, written in 1937, and revised in 1946 with a Foreword by Prime Minister C. R. Attlee who says of it that "these arguments are unanswerable."

[17] Published for the Left Book Club with the subtitle: *The Government's Record as Protector of Private Monopoly* (Gollancz, 1939).

[18] The Big Five are: Midland, Westminster, National Provincial, Lloyds, and Barclays. See, in particular, *ibid.*, pp. 293–301. He finds that three qualifications determine selection of their directors: family connections, commercial affiliations, and political positions. "No fewer than 67 of 150 directors of the Big Five are titled gentlemen." Eton and Harrow turned out 40 of 71 banking directors who went to public school, Oxford and Cambridge 43 of the 47 who went to a university. "The 150 bank directors of the Big Five share among them 1,036 directorships of which but 162 are of other banking firms or institutions, such as discount houses." 88 insurance directorships are held by bank directors. Their industrial, commercial, transport, financial, etc. directorships are scattered through the powerful concerns. A large percentage of these directors are Lords.

the Chancellor on important matters, and ultimately proved incapable of action at a critical moment. In 1920, Mr. Montagu Norman (now Lord Norman) began his remarkable reign as Governor. While it is perhaps too much to agree with one writer (Paul Einzig, *Montagu Norman*, 1932) that 'He has carried out work . . . properly within the province of a Prime Minister,' yet great influence cannot be denied him during his term of office, especially in the years 1920 to 1931.'[19]

Four examples, to which a fifth may be added, are generally given of the way in which the Bank of England may put partisan concern above the public interest. First is the Bank's role in effecting return to the gold standard in 1925. This now appears to have been a mistake in judgment with which the Treasury concurred, rather than an evidence of sabotage of governmental policy. Second is the Bank's loan to the defunct Austrian Kredit Anstalt Bank in 1931, which began a series of events resulting in the international crisis of that year. A by-product of this crisis was the dissolution of the second Labour government. Labour spokesmen believe the Bank of England greatly aided the Opposition by insisting that the Government make dangerous economy cuts as a condition to the receipt of emergency credits from France and America. Third is the transfer, on instructions from the Bank for International Settlements, of Czech gold held by the Bank of England to the Nazis after they had over-run Czechoslovakia. The fourth, and more general example, is the restrictionist policy pursued by the Bank of England generally throughout the depression of the thirties.

The fifth example which might be added is reflected in the Keynesian argument that the orientation of credit policy at the initiative of the central bank in terms of international exchange rates and bank reserve ratios should be changed to concentrate on the maintenance of full employment. Since the first and the last two of these examples are matters not so much of contests between the Treasury and the Bank of England as of mutual mistakes, or at least of differences in practical applications of theory for which both share the blame, the case for nationalizing the Bank of England would seem, in effect, to rest on two grounds. The first is that when differences of interpretation do arise, the view of the government should, as a matter of course, dominate Bank policy. The second is that it should not, under any circumstances, be technically possible, as intimated in the third and fourth examples cited above, for the Bank actually to sabotage governmental policy.

---

[19] *The Bank of England and the Nation*, p. 13.

The difficulty with so summarizing the Labour argument is that the first ground, more or less by common agreement, meant merely the substitution of the formalities of *de jure* for the realities of *de facto*. Douglas Jay to the contrary notwithstanding, both Labour and the Conservatives seemed to agree on this point. Speaking for the Government, Dalton said that "The Bank does recognise that, in all matters of major policy, the Treasury has the last word, and has loyally carried out this arrangement; decisions taken by the Treasury have been put into operation by the Bank."[20] Summing up the Conservative case a year later, Quintin Hogg repeated a like sentiment. "The Bank of England," he wrote, "has been for many years subject to the Treasury on all matters of major importance, and this modest purchase of shares by the Government in fact confers no additional power either on the public or on the Government."[21]

As for the second ground, the transfer of Czech gold would have to be ruled out since such transfer was actually consistent with the appeasement policies then being pursued by the Chamberlain government. Although this decision by the Bank of England was, in the Labour view at least, inconsistent with the national welfare, it was nevertheless in keeping with contemporary governmental outlook, and hence we are left with the belief that it was the part the Bank of England played in turning out the second Labour government which the existing Labour government feared and could not risk having repeated. At any rate, it was the fear of sabotage of a Labour government which dominated the discussions in Labour party councils in the fall of 1945.

The belief persisted, that is to say, that although the Bank of England might appear to have been following the Treasury in all clearly outlined particulars in the past, it was doing so largely because there existed between the then-existing government and the Bank of England a community of interests and outlooks which would not be found to exist when a Labour government took over. Moreover, a private institution placed in the strategic position of the Bank of England surely possessed among its powers of administration numerous methods, in sum enormously effective, of dragging its feet even while appearing faithfully and loyally to be carrying out Treasury directives. It seems to have been taken for granted in Labour circles that this not only could happen, but was bound to happen when the bank was asked to implement policies of a Government with which it was out of sympathy

[20] *Hansard*, Vol. 415, cols. 190–191.
[21] Quintin Hogg, *The Case for Conservatism* (London, 1947), p. 154.

against the opposition of organized business interests to which its directing and administrative personnel were closely bound both by a multitude of private, personal interests and by a common social outlook.

This interpretation of the Labour position on nationalization of the Bank of England is amply reinforced by an examination of the arguments presented. Invariably they turn less on what the Bank has done in the past and more on what it might do in the future. More than that, it is not a matter of what it might do under any circumstances, but only what it might do under certain specific circumstances, namely, when the government was proposing measures with which the banking and business community in general were out of sympathy and might oppose vigorously.

That this is the heart of the Labour position is entirely evident from the records. Yet it is also difficult to square this conclusion with the equally evident fact that when the position is spelled out it refers primarily not to the Bank of England, which Labour proposes to nationalize, but to the private joint-stock and commercial banks, which it had by that time dropped out of the category of businesses ripe for socialization. This becomes all the more difficult to understand when it is realized that the typical conjecture on the capacity of these and other large scale and monopolistically organized private financial institutions effectively to sabotage the government runs largely in terms of their ability to do this against the wishes and despite the public character and responsibility of the Bank of England itself.

The arguments of Davies are representative. They take on additional significance by virtue of the very important role which he played in actually shaping up the Labour party's financial program, and in carrying through the nationalization of the Bank of England. Suppose, he says, that the interests of the private banks "were in opposition. The Bank of England, following a policy of expansion, might be faced with the Banks calling in loans, or refusing additional credits, or not taking up Government loans just at the time when it was desirable that they should do so. When the Bank of England increased credit, the Banks might decrease it. They would do so by ignoring the increase in their deposits at the Bank—that is, they might not increase their loans or buy Government securities. This is a dangerous weapon in the hands of the Joint Stock Banks which could seriously embarrass a Labour Government if used against it."[22]

---

[22] *"National" Capitalism*, p. 289.

Specifically, the private banks might (1) refuse "to lend freely when the Bank of England was making credit readily available" and "industry might lack working capital"; (2) refuse "to lend in those directions in which the Government was most anxious to see credit advanced," as in the current export industries, or those just being or about to be, nationalized; (3) counteract "the expansion policy of the Bank of England by calling in loans," or follow an expansionist policy when the Government was seeking contraction; (4) refuse to assist certain types of operations, such as those involved in reorganization schemes as visualized in the socialized sectors; (5) refuse to take up, or "go even further and sell" government stocks against the government's interest; (6) make funds available for speculation in commodities, shares, or other lines of activities where such speculation was harmful to governmental objectives; or, finally, (7) it could promote export of capital when capital's flight from the homeland might, in effect, wreck the government's whole financial program.[23] And so, *ad infinitum.*

Davies' examples follow a discussion of the various mistakes made in these very same particulars by the Popular Front government of Leon Blum in France during the middle thirties, and the over-all conclusion is that a future Labour government must be prepared "to meet the possibility of active opposition from capitalist interests" by taking "control of the financial machine at the first sign of sabotage . . . If the Joint Stock Banks show signs of failing to co-operate with the Government's monetary policy there would have to be no hesitation to bring them under public ownership."[24]

The gravamen of Davies argument has not seriously, nor at any important point, been altered by subsequent discussion in top Labour party circles. It points to the conclusion that the Bank of England must be immediately nationalized, and that a sword of Damocles must be held constantly over the head of the private banker. Thus nationalization of the Bank of England is unimportant taken by itself, but tremendously significant if it augurs further unilateral action against opposition certain to develop in the future if the program being pursued by Labour continues the process of liquidation of the leading capitalist strongholds.

But this "if" involves the entire problem of Labour's intentions, and these, while superficially of a very simple and straightforward character, have, in practice, become very difficult to make out. If a further

[23] *Ibid.*, pp. 289–292.
[24] *Ibid.*, p. 301.

"if" may be risked, and it turns out that the Labour party's socialism is, in effect, to begin and end with a program centering on the achievement of full employment—modified by special ameliorative legislation for badly distressed areas, and for aid to the more sadly underprivileged amongst the sick, the lame, and the halt—then the weakness of the Conservative opposition to the nationalization act would become entirely explicable. For then, the Opposition argues, this is not only a program with which the Conservatives are in agreement, but is in fact their own. Thus it would appear that the sin of Labour is reduced to the tepid indiscretion of plagiarism. It is pink-hued plagiarism, to be sure, and naturally less palatable to persons of sensitive taste having this peculiar chromatic aversion than it would otherwise be. But that is all. *The Industrial Charter* of the Conservative party accepts nationalization of the Bank of England on the score of need of proper endorsement of proper themes.[25] The only real evil the Tories see in the act is not that of nationalization, *per se*, but of "the powers of the Bank to give directives to the commercial banks."[26] Even this does not define their area of disagreement or agreement, for if directives need to be given to private banks in pursuance of the goal of full employment it would be, they hold, only because the Government had not made adequately clear the steps which it feels must be taken at any given time "to ensure that the demand for goods and services is always maintained at a level which will offer jobs to all who are willing to work."[27] It is not the goal, they say in effect, but the steps by which the goal is to be achieved[28] which are in dispute.

If, in other words, the steps taken from the time of nationalization of the Bank of England are designed to aid and to coöperate with business, organized business and the Conservative party are prepared to go along. Not, of course, that this would mean approval of further nationalization—at least when introduced by Socialist—and never, of course, could there be any concessions to the heresies of socialist doctrine. But

[25] *The Industrial Charter: A Statement of Conservative Industrial Policy* (Conservative and Unionist Central Office, 1947), being the "declaration of the Conservative attitude towards industry ... drawn up by a Committee appointed as a result of a resolution moved at the Blackpool Conference of the Party in October, 1946." p. 3.

[26] *Ibid.*, p. 25.

[27] *Ibid.*, p. 16.

[28] In December of 1947 the Conservative Political Centre published a brochure, *Conservative Social and Industrial Reform 1800 to 1945*, in which they find that "Conservatives fought and won the battle against *laissez faire*, under which the worker was regarded as a commodity to be bought or sold in the open market" and that they evolved a State which "has increasingly concerned itself with the improvement of the social conditions of the people and the protection of the individual from exploitation." This includes both measures for achieving full employment and planning. See p. 57, and section iv: "The Four-Year Plan," pp. 45–55.

wherever, and in whatever sectors, business was given aid and encouragement, Conservatives could give their approval. If this could include the financial community, so much the better.

Whether any such assurances were ever given to the Opposition there is no way of telling. But so far as the true history may be inferred from the record, it was not necessary that any such an offer be tendered. General like-mindedness on matters such as these does not require definition of the area of agreement, and if there be something further in Labour's financial program which indicates need for the Tories to worry for their future, it does not spring readily to the eye.[29] The bill of particulars, in fact, appears actually in large part to have been written by spokesmen for the Opposition itself. Whether or not this picture is just may be judged by examining so much of the record as may be supported from publicly available data.

THE BANK OF ENGLAND ACT, 1946

By act of Parliament on December 19, 1945,[30] confirmed by the issuance of the *Bank of England Charter*,[31] dated March 1, 1946, the vesting date, the Bank of England became public property. Both documents are short, and easy to summarize. The first section provides for the exchange of former bank stock through a nominee of the Treasury, for government stock at the rate of four shares of par value stocks earning 3 per cent for one share of par value bank stock earning (as an

[29] Thus the problem of technical rationalization of the over-all postwar financial machinery does not appear seriously to have concerned the government. This seems a curious omission in view of Dalton's earlier castigation of the City on these very same grounds. In 1935 he wrote, "Our network of financial institutions, a large part of which is concentrated in the City of London, is a historical growth. British finance is not a planned system, and if it were now to be intelligently planned afresh from the beginning, it would bear little resemblance to its present form. It is full of unnecessary complication. It is incoherent, without proper contact between some of its essential parts, for example, between the Bank of England and the Joint Stock Banks. It is lopsided, providing better facilities for the investment of capital abroad than at home, and very poor facilities for certain classes of home investment, for example, in small businesses. As an agency for the supply of new capital on long terms, it is wasteful and needlessly expensive. For the supply of short term credit at home, it is passive and unenterprising, though it lent recklessly to Germany. For credits of intermediate length it makes hardly any provision. It permits many opportunities for swindling both inside and outside the law. It is honey-combed with nepotism, and with patronage based on family and business connections. There are too many soft jobs for influential people, too many multiple directorships, carrying fat fees without real functions, too many 'guinea-pigs,' paid simply to 'give their names' and so to attract custom. The City is unrationalised to an astonishing degree. If rationalisation is necessary in British industry it is no less necessary in British finance." Hugh Dalton, *Practical Socialism* (London, 1935), pp. 190–191.

[30] Royal Assent was given on February 14, 1946 (9 & 10 Geo. 6, Chap. 27). The full title reads: "An Act to bring the capital stock of the Bank of England into public ownership and bring the Bank under public control, to make provision with respect to the relations between the Treasury, the Bank of England and other banks and for purposes connected with the matters aforesaid." (References to this act hereafter will be to Bank of England Act.)

[31] Cmd. 6752. (Hereafter referred to as Charter.)

average over the preceding 23 years) 12 per cent. The second section calls for the establishment of a Court of Directors, made up of the governor, the deputy governor, and 16 directors of the Bank, all to be appointed by His Majesty on the initiative of the Chancellor of the Exchequer. Subsequent sections and a second schedule define the functions of the managing directorate and its relations to the Treasury. Section four defines the duty of the Treasury in issuing general instructions to the Bank and the Bank's responsibility in carrying out its duties. The Charter repeals the acts of 1694 and 1892,[32] and defines the qualifications and terms for office and certain management details, but does not enlarge the legal authority or functions of the Bank.

Aside from the dispute over nationalization *per se,* only two issues gave rise to controversy. Both were settled on the Opposition's terms. The first had to do with the rate of compensation for former stockholders. Here Dalton, as initiator of the bill and Chancellor of the Exchequer, made an offer which was so generous that it left the Opposition virtually speechless. "The Bank of England stock," he said, "had maintained an unchanged dividend of 12 per cent over the past 23 years, since 1922. This Bill, therefore, provides that the stockholders shall receive a suitable quantity of a new 3 per cent Government Stock, so as to assure to them the same income as they get now, at least until the year 1966, when the Treasury will have the right to redeem this new stock at par. To have offered terms less favorable than these would, in my view, have been unfair to the stockholders of whom there are some 17,000. The Bank stock is fairly widely distributed; 10,000 out of the 17,000 stockholders hold less than £500 of Bank stock. The average holding of all the 17,000 is £850. On the other hand, to have offered better terms than these would, in my view, have been unfair to the community . . . I do not believe any impartial body of arbitrators, or any court, would sustain the claim of the stockholders to better terms than are provided in this Bill. Under Clause I (4) the Bank will pay to the Treasury each year, in lieu of dividends hitherto paid on the Bank stock, the sum of £1,746,360. That is equal to the amount of dividends hitherto paid for the last 22 years on an unchanging quantity of Bank Stock; and it will, in future, be paid over by the Bank to the Treasury in place of being paid out to the shareholders."[33]

[32] The Bank of England Act of 1694 was the original Charter granted by William and Mary for the establishment of the "Governor and Company of the Bank of England." The 1892 act spelled out somewhat more in detail the regulations governing "the internal affairs of the Bank of England."

[33] *Hansard,* Vol. 415, cols. 48–49.

Some dismay was expressed from the Government's supporters. Captain Poole thought that "the Chancellor of the Exchequer has been unduly generous . . . The Hon. Member . . . brought us up to 1697, the date of the formation of the Bank when its capital was a little over £1,000,000. From then up to 1782 the capital rose to just over £11,000,000. In 1816 . . . that capital of £11,500,000, by one stroke of the pen and by a little manipulation, became . . . £14,500,000 the figure at which it stands to-day—a 25 per cent appreciation of the Bank's stock. Therefore, what the stockholders of the Bank of the Bank of England have been receiving for the past 20 years has not been interest of 12 per cent, but interest approximating more closely to 15 per cent, and in return for the actual subscribed capital of £11,500,000 the Government are giving £58,000,000."[34]

Pargiter expressed a similar sentiment and suggested an alternative: "A better way than that of giving nearly £58,000,000 for £14,500,000— even accepting the latter figure—would have been to distribute those reserves as profit, not as capital appreciation. Then by that excellent remedy of Excess Profits Tax, consumer tax, and so forth, the Chancellor could very well have collected a large portion of it . . . I regard 12 per cent on a gilt-edged security as not a proper return but an excessive return."[35] Even this comparatively mild suggestion was brushed aside by the Commons leadership. The *coup de grace* to the dissentients was given by disposal of the final suggestion by Paton that the hidden reserves—the existence of which Dalton did not deny and which he refused to divulge after having made the cheery comment that the "terms of transfer of the Bank's stock are, in my view, on the one hand, fair to the shareholders, and on the other hand, undoubtedly a good bargain for the state"[36]—of the Bank of England "are very largely the product of special privileges accorded to the Bank of England" and would there not, accordingly, be "complete justification for returning to the nation what the nation has thus accorded." No one picked up the cue.

With minor, and wholly unimportant, exceptions, the Opposition and the business circles for which they spoke were satisfied, if not actually delighted, with the deal. *The Economist* has summarized this reaction so accurately that it is worth quoting almost in full:

There are few surprises in the Bank of England nationalisation Bill, and with one exception, they are pleasant ones. From the City point of view . . . this is plainly nationalisation in its most palatable—or least unpalatable—form. The

---

[34] *Ibid.*, cols. 137–138.   [35] *Ibid.*, col. 76.   [36] *Ibid.*, col. 47.

stockholder, certainly has no legitimate ground for complaint. He is to receive, as expected, a four-to-one allotment of Government stock, to provide him with the same annual income as his holdings of Bank stock has in fact produced annually for the past twenty-two years. The market had assumed that this income would be assured by a 3 per cent stock analogous to Local Loans, which are redeemable at Government option at any time: Bank stock, at 388½ on Tuesday, was, allowing for accrued interest, roughly ¾ of a point below parity with Locals at 97⅜. In fact the 12 per cent return to Bank stockholders is guaranteed for a further 20 years and the new 3 per cent stock—redeemable by Government option only after April 5, 1966—therefore has a slight advantage over Local Loans during that period. Subsequent movements of the two stocks have registered this difference. On Thursday (when there was something of a reaction from first thoughts) Bank stock was cited at 392 and Local Loans at 97⁵⁄₁₆. These prices are equivalent to a premium ¾ of a point for the new Government stock over Local Loans, reckoning per £100 of stock."[37]

To which the *Economist* adds the laconic remark, "This is obviously satisfactory."

The second subject of controversy was also settled on terms which are largely if not wholly satisfactory to the Opposition. This had to do with Section 4 (3) of the act, which reads: "The Bank, if they think it necessary in the public interest, may request information from and make recommendations to bankers, and may, if so authorised by the Treasury, issue directions to any banker for the purpose of securing that effect is given to any such request or recommendation." Considering the fact that Section 4 (1) specifies that "the Treasury may from time to time give such directions to the Bank as, after consultation with the Governor of the Bank, they think necessary in the public interest"— without which it is hard to see how nationalizing the Bank could have had any meaning at all—the question was raised whether or not Section 4 (3) did not, in effect, give the Treasury, first, the right to gather information of a private character from the private banks, and second, to issue instructions to them on the ordinary conduct of their private business affairs.

Since by this time the Labour government had given up the idea of nationalizing these very same private banks, it might seem that the Tories would have been satisfied to let this rather mild right of search and counsel go by with a sigh of relief that no more had been forthcoming. Nevertheless, they did at first protest, and protest vigorously. The result was a formulation which proved almost wholly satisfactory to all except a few die-hards. Two riders were attached to Section 4 (3)

[37] *Economist*, Oct. 13, 1945, p. 532.

which provided some reassurance. They read, "Provided that:—(a) no such request or recommendations shall be made with respect to the affairs of any particular customer of a banker; and (b) before author-ising the issue of any such directions the Treasury shall give the banker concerned, or such person as appears to them to represent him, an op-portunity of making representations with respect thereto."

Even then, although in asking for information or making recom-mendations and giving directions "the Treasury certify that it is neces-sary in the public interest," and that the data obtained shall be kept secret, the information comes under the Official Secrets acts of 1911 and 1939, and cannot be made known to the public or to Parliament. Furthermore, as the *Economist* correctly observed, "the Treasury is empowered to give directions to the Bank—but only after consultation with it at the highest level. Subject to these directions, the Bank, as now, is free to conduct its affairs according to its own judgment of what is in the national interest, and will not in any case be subjected to day-to-day interference . . . There is power here to interfere with the busi-ness of the banks in any way whatever that the Bank and Treasury consider to be in the national interest . . . But the section contains one important safeguard. The whole initiative in this matter is placed upon the Bank. The Bank cannot 'Direct' the banks without Treasury sanc-tion, but the Treasury cannot direct the banks at all unless the Bank agrees."[38]

While "this safeguard" might be regarded as inadequate by some, the *Economist* felt that still "it is hard to see what better one could be devised," and proof that this was also the judgment of the banking community was given when it was "officially stated that the members of the Clearing Bankers' Association after learning the terms of the Bill have assured the Chancellor—through Lord Catto—that he 'can count upon the co-operation of the banking community.' "[39]

One final doubt remained concerning the intentions of the Govern-ment, and this was decorously laid at rest. If the bank's powers, duties, and prerogatives are to remain substantially as they were before, much if not everything depends upon the makeup of the bank's directorial personnel. "But it is plain," the *Economist* pointed out, "that the present Government does not contemplate revolutionary changes in

---

[38] *Loc. cit.*

[39] *Loc. cit.* Too much, however, cannot be made of these safeguards. Real power lies in the appointment of directors, and with this, nominal safeguards such as these may well turn out to be a mere matter of legal etiquette.

personnel, and is certainly not intending to recommend 'political' appointments to the Court. The recommendations of Lord Catto[40]—and his willingness to serve—as the first Crown appointee are sufficient proof of that. And the decision to retain an effective Court of Directors at all—instead of replacing it, as the Australians have done, by a panel of advisers—shows that the basic merits of the present system are recognized."[41] Nor have subsequent reappointments and new appointments to the court been of such character as to create much unrest in City circles.[42] One appointment only has come from Labour circles, that of George Gibson, formerly a Chairman of the T.U.C.[43] There have been no appointments from financially experienced Labour or other government circles, such as the coöperatives or the Post Office.[44]

Aside from their more ordinary business interests, the members of the Court of Directors have held a wide variety of offices and performed many top-flight duties in the past in connection with the conduct of prewar, war, and postwar government activities. If any clearcut change is evident in the business complexion of the membership at all, it would seem to be a somewhat lessened emphasis on recruitment from strictly banking and financial circles, and a somewhat greater dependence on personnel drawn from general industrial and commercial circles.

[40] Former Governor of the Bank of England. Among other connections Lord Catto was Chairman and Managing Director of Andrew Ule and Co., Ltd., Calcutta; Director of the London firm of Ule, Catto and Co., Ltd., since 1919; a managing Director of Morgan Grenfell and Co., Ltd.; Director (Extraordinary) of the Royal Bank of Scotland; Director of the Mercantile Bank of India, Ltd.; Director of the Royal Exchange Assurance; Director of the Union Castle Mail SS. Co., Ltd. He was succeeded in October, 1948, by C. E. Cobbold, former Deputy-Governor, trained under the Montagu Norman regime. His appointment, as it was put by *The Times* (Oct. 15, 1948), will give "The City . . . a special sense of satisfaction" with a long family tradition of banking behind him. He had, said the *Daily Telegraph* (Oct. 20, 1948), "in a comparatively short time established a golden reputation" in City circles.

[41] *Economist*, Oct. 13, 1945, p. 532. A similar sentiment was expressed by *The Banker* for November, 1945 in an article on "Banking under Legal Control."

[42] Among the directorships in private business held by appointees to the Court in 1947 and 1948 are the following: *Banking:* Lazard Brothers, Whitehall Trust, Bank of England and South America, Hambros Bank, Hongkong and Shanghai Bank, Mercantile Credit; *Insurance:* Royal Exchange, Provident Mutual Life, Alliance, Northern; *Industrial:* Cierva Autogiro, Union Courtaulds, A Reyrolle, Bren Mfg., Jowett Cars; *Public Utilities:* British Power and Light, Chinese Central Railways; *Commercial:* Jardin Matteson, British and Chinese Corp., Chambers Wharf and Cold Stores, Hudson's Bay Fur Co.

[43] Gibson resigned on December 15, 1948, after giving evidence before the Lynsky Tribunal, and in connection with charges leveled against him having to do with lobbying and bribery. He was succeeded by Sir M. Chester, also a T.U.C. official.

[44] This seems especially strange when it is recalled that the Post Office was by all odds the largest Savings Bank in Great Britain—its Annual Account of $10,121,241,273.68—and the coöperatives, one of the three main groups making up the Labour party, had a central bank (C.W.S. Bank) which in 1946 possessed resources of $1,038,503,988 and had a turnover of $5,338,383,864 (*The People's Yearbook* [Manchester, C.W.S., 1948], p. 130), making it a more important financial institution than any one of the Big Five private joint stock banks, and closer liaison and integration were among Labour's avowed objectives.

Thus, despite the queasiness of the Opposition over the technical heresy of nationalization in the banking field *per se*,[45] the City seems to have been well satisfied that no real change was anticipated in the normal functioning of the Bank, nor in the policies which were to be pursued by it. One opinion, offered independently by officials in the Bank of England, the Treasury, and banking circles, is worth mentioning. Although none of the commentators was willing to be quoted directly, they all concurred in a view which may be paraphrased as follows: There is and probably will continue to be less publicity on the bank's actual operations, less direct responsibility to Parliament and less questioning in Parliament, and possibly somewhat less publicity regarding the operations—so far as they affect the Bank—or the Treasury itself.

There were scheduled to be, however, some further changes in machinery. These were soon forthcoming in the shape of the Borrowing (Control and Guarantees) Act, and the Exchange Control Act. The first was directed primarily to the problem of channelizing savings into preferred or otherwise neglected investments. The second was established to implement the government's control over international exchange. Both were satisfactory, at the time of their introduction and subsequently, both to the Opposition in general and to the City in particular.

CONTROL OVER INVESTMENTS

In seeking control over savings and investment, Labour theorists appear to have abandoned all socialist measures which are not consistent with the new orthodoxy of the Keynesian financial therapy for underemployment of economic resources. The point of departure is the famous 1931 report of the Macmillan committee. Two evils, as viewed by Labour's theorists, were uncovered by the investigators at that time. The first was that of "scandals and frauds" in the conduct of the stock exchanges and the traffic in new capital issues. The second was the failure of investment policy so to be directed that it prevents depressions and insures full employment.

Labour seeks, wrote Douglas Jay, a cure for these evils in a financial policy which would "control . . . the nation's savings in the interest of the whole community. The individual would be safeguarded against

---

[45] This seems actually to have disturbed the Opposition far less than they let on, for they conceded, as Churchill put it, that not only does "National Ownership of the Bank of England" not "raise any matter of principle" but also "There are important examples in the United States and in our Dominions of central banking institutions" similarly owned and operated. See *Hansard*, Vol. 415, col. 93.

exploitation, and the nation's capital would be scientifically invested."[46] Under current circumstances the individual's savings are invested via "one of the most scandalous of all the institutions thrown up by private capitalism," the London Stock Exchange, "centre and focus of the City," which "has been likened by the great economist, J. M. Keynes, to a 'casino' in which the rich speculator's attempt to guess the winner determines which industry shall obtain a share of the nation's savings." The result is that "savings are misinvested, and the small investor continually robbed!" Furthermore, "traffic in new capital issues, so vital for the nation's economic life is the most indefensibly conducted by all." Privileged insiders with "influential connections, bring out the issues in an atmosphere of mystery and suspicion . . . huge profits are made" and "afterwards the public finds itself left with shares which are inexplicably but steadily falling."[47]

Oddly enough, this argument does not lead to a proposal for nationalizing the Stock Exchange nor any existing financial institutions other than the Bank of England. It leads to the demand that there be set up, instead, a National Investment Board which would have the function of so directing savings and investments of existing institutions as to maintain full employment. This is not the first time that such a proposal has been made by Labour spokesmen, but Jay's formulation in 1938 seems to have been accepted subsequently without important variation. His proposals take on added interest since his elevation to the position of Parliamentary Secretary to the Treasury, where he has played a singular role in formulation of Labour's whole financial program. His statement is, consequently, worth reproducing in full. To the question of how the Board would work, Jay writes:

It would begin by consolidating in its own hands the powers of control that have actually been developed in the hands of the Treasury, the Bank of England, the Stock Exchange Committee, and other bodies in the last ten years. These include:—

a) The Foreign Transactions Advisory Committee's power to veto or approve loans to foreign countries and purchases of foreign securities.

[46] *The Nation's Wealth*, p. 5.
[47] *Loc. cit.* He goes on to say, "The Macmillan Committee found that some £117,000,000 was subscribed for the shares and debentures of 284 companies in 1928, and that at May 31, 1931, their market value was £66,000,000, showing a depreciation of 47 per cent. Some 70 of the companies had been wound up, and 36 were of no ascertainable value. By 1934 some 40 per cent of the 1928–29 companies were out of business." Unfortunately, this does not prove scandalous behavior in the issuance of stocks, nor in stock exchange transactions. What it proves is that a depression occurred, and that some of the more recently floated issues were among its victims. This is not an argument for curing scandalous behavior, but for preventing a depression.

This Committee is under the control of the Treasury, and it now avowedly takes political factors into consideration in making its decisions. The existing Committee might, in the first instance, be made a subcommittee of the National Investment Board, and it would doubtless work in close co-operation with that other successful State enterprise, the Export Credits Guarantee Department, now directly controlled by the Board of Trade.

b) The Bank of England's supervision of Government and Municipal issues.

Already the Bank, on the initiative of the Treasury, has assumed an 'advisory' control over trustee issues. All important Municipal issues are priced and timed on the advice of the Bank so as to prevent a competitive forcing up of rates. This is an important part of the new technique of controlling interest rates which Labour wishes to develop. These powers could be regularised and handed over to the National Investment Board, to be exercised in harmony with the general economic plan.

c) The Stock Exchange Committee's power to grant 'permission to deal.'

This power to admit new securities to quotation on the Stock Exchange is of the utmost importance. For a security not dealt in on the Stock Exchange is not easily marketable, and therefore does not command so high a price. In many cases, therefore, a new issue will not be made at all if "permision to deal' is refused. Yet this crucial power is at present exercised on no clearly defined principles, and by a purely private body—the Stock Exchange Commision— which does not even possess a Royal Charter.

It would be a simple and logical step, which many in the City would welcome, to make the Stock Exchange Committee also a sub-committee of the National Investment Board, and to place upon it a certain quota of Treasury or Board of Trade representatives. This would have the added advantage of bringing the Stock Exchange Committee's other important powers under public control and into harmony with the general economic plan.

d) Another increasingly important avenue for the investment of small savings is the Unit Trust movement.

This movement has on the whole performed a useful function in enabling the small middle-class saver to "spread" his risk over many industrial securities. When the further legal safeguards urged by the recent Board of Trade Committee on Unit Trusts are enacted the Unit Trusts could play an important and beneficial part in the planned investment of the nation's savings. It is possible that the National Investment Board might be made trustee for all Unit Trusts, instead of the banks and insurance companies which act as such at present. At any rate legislation regularising the position of the Unit Trusts is urgent.[48]

Contacts might be established through additional subcommittees with insurance companies and building societies. The board would "supervise the flotation of Government-guaranteed or Government-

---

[48] Jay, *The Nation's Wealth*, pp. 7–8. A unit trust scheme is defined by the Investment (Control and Guarantees) Bill, Cmd. 6726, p. 6 as "any arrangements made for the purpose, or having the effect, of providing facilities for the participation by persons, as beneficiaries under a trust, in profits or income arising from the acquisition, holding, management or disposal of securities or any other property whatsoever."

favoured industrial loans." It might "go further than this and itself issue big Government-guaranteed loans for public development, including housing, electrification, transport, agriculture," etc. The interest of the board in protecting the small investor might be supplemented by reforms in existing company laws, and by compelling publication of more adequate data on the actual financial standing of large corporations for the perusal of the untutored layman.[49]

At first glance, Jay's set of specifications may appear to call for quite formidable changes in the existing financial machinery. But closer examination will show that what he is suggesting falls under two main categories; "tidying" up the less respectable fringes and practices of the securities market, and channelizing the general flow of investment funds. The enabling act is the Borrowing (Control and Guarantees) Act of 1946,[50] which took under the government's wing the two new finance corporations which had recently been set up, and which had been sponsored, if his own statements made in the House of Lords are to be taken at their face value, not by the Government, but by none other than Lord Catto, Governor of the Bank of England, himself.[51] Its purpose was stated by the Office of Information to be "to give the Government power to control and direct the flow of new investment, and if necessary to stimulate that flow. It provides therefore for regulation by the Treasury of the borrowing and raising of money by the issue of shares whether within the country or by Overseas Governments where the securities are to be registered here. It also empowers the Treasury to guarantee loans for purposes of industrial reconstruction and development provided such loans are expedient in the public interest."[52]

A subsequent memorandum issued by the Chancellor of the Exchequer interpreted this to mean, (1) regulation of "the borrowing of money and the raising of money by the issue of securities," and (2) the making of "provision for the guarantee of loans in appropriate cases

---

[49] "There is no reason why big privately-owned companies should not give to the public the same sort of information as is given, for instance, by the Co-operative Wholesale Society." *Ibid.*, p. 9.

[50] The full title reads: "An Act to provide for the regulation of the borrowing and raising of money, the issue of securities, and the circulation of offers of securities for subscription, sale or exchange, to enable the Treasury to guarantee loans in certain circumstances, and for purposes connected with the matters aforesaid." It is dated July 12, 1946. 9 & 10 Geo. 6, Chap. 58.

[51] "... the Lord's debate on the second reading of the Bank Bill was on the whole a mediocre affair ... Only two new facts emerged—both from Lord Catto. The first ... is that he himself, not the Government, was the sponsor of the new Finance Corporations." *Economist*, Jan. 26, 1944, p. 144.

[52] Central Office of Information, Reference Division, *Summary of Legislation in the United Kingdom, Aug. 1945–Aug. 1947*, No. R. 1448 (London, Aug., 1947).

for the reconstruction or development of an industry or part of an industry in Great Britain." This was necessary because, since "It is the policy of His Majesty's Government to establish and maintain a proper balance between the economic resources of the community and the demands upon them," it is important that a system of priorities be established "for those projects of capital development which are of the greatest importance for the national interest" and so that no national resources, human or material will be "wasted in idleness."[53]

The coverage of the act was not designed to include all borrowing by private individuals, partnerships and corporations, or public bodies in the ordinary course of business—broadly interpreted—but only when it involved the capitalizing of profits or reserves, amalgamations and mergers of existing corporations, reissues and new issues of corporate securities, and borrowing outside of England. The machinery for effecting the purposes of the act involved some old institutions and some new facilities. In the memorandum cited above it was stated that "the Capital Issues Committee will be continued. Subject to directions from the Treasury, it will deal with individual applications for permission to borrow. The Public Works Loan Board will also be continued. But the important duties of these authorities in controlling and assisting the flow of new investment, and of the Finance Corporation for Industry and the Industrial and Commercial Finance Corporation in providing financial assistance to industry, must be effectively linked with the operations of the Bank of England and with the planning by His Majesty's Government of the investment programme as a whole."

Finance, savings, and investment were to be planned on a national scale. "With this end in view His Majesty's Government have decided to set up a National Investment Council. The Chairman will be the Chancellor of the Exchequer. The members of the Council will include the Governor of the Bank of England, the Chairman of the London Stock Exchange, the Chairman of the Capital Issues Committee and the Public Works Loan Board, and a number of other persons chosen for their wide knowledge and experience of financial, economic and industrial questions. This Council will assist the Government in so organising and, when necessary, stimulating investment as to promote full employment."[54]

The Capital Issues Committee is an advisory body stemming from

[53] *Memorandum and Draft of Order to be made under Clause 1 of the Bill*, Cmd. 6726 (Jan., 1946).
[54] *Loc. cit.*

the prewar period. It was originally known as the Foreign Transactions (Advisory) Committee, appointed by the Chancellor of the Exchequer in 1936, and it had the duty of coördinating the long-term financial relationships of the Treasury, the Bank of England, the Stock Exchange, and the general business community. Behind its establishment lay a long series of discussions regarding the export of capital and Britain's international exchange position, centering in large part around the return to the gold standard in 1925, its abandonment six years later, and the exhaustive report of the Macmillan Committee on Finance and Industry in 1931. The first intimation of a government need to set an embargo on capital issues came in 1932 when the Chancellor of the Exchequer requested the suspension of new issues while it was engaged in attempting its big reconversion of war loans.

With the outset of the war the name was changed to Capital Issues Committee, having as its primary purpose that of assisting the Treasury in its interpretation of the Defense (Finance) Regulations of 1939. Regulation no. 6 of this act forbids an issue of capital and a public offer of securities for sale unless the consent of the Treasury has been given. The Emergency Powers Act of 1939, under which the Defense (Finance) Regulations were established, was extended by the Labour government for a period of five years in the Supplies and Services (Transitional Powers) Act of 1945. Thus the Capital Issues Committee becomes an advisory body of semiofficial standing on a war emergency basis to assist the government in carrying through its postwar financial control measures.

The first step in redefining the purposes of the Capital Issues Committee in assisting the government to carry through postwar reconstruction plans came with the issuance in May, 1945, some two months before the general elections, of *Capital Issues Control: Memorandum of Guidance to the Capital Issues Committee,*[55] which reaffirmed the principle of maintenance of over-all controls, gave an outline of the somewhat widened categories of stocks which could now be issued, and defined the general nature of the appropriate investment priorities which would guide its decisions.

With change of government it became evident that sooner or later

---

[55] Cmd. 6645. A prefatory note states that the purpose of the memorandum is "... to set out the principles which will until further notice govern the grant of Treasury consent to new issues of capital" and the first Clause states that the "objects of the control are to ensure" the order of priority and the timing of issue of capital "according to their relative importance in the general national interest, having regard, particularly, to current Government policy in respect of physical investment."

there must come reconsideration along each of these lines. Faced with "serious changes in the balance of payments position and the consequent need for internal economic adjustments" it was decided late in 1947 that "substantial modifications must be made. The main objectives are: (*a*) to reduce the total demands of capital projects upon man-power and upon steel, coal and other materials in order that the requirements of the export industries and other vital purposes may be met; (*b*) to ensure that there is a concentration of effort on completing as rapidly as possible the more important schemes."[56]

Under these instructions the Capital Issues Committee must pass upon the price at which new issues are to be put out, the marketing arrangements of placings, underwriting arrangements, and the treatment given different classes of shareholders. The stock exchange refuses to list any stock unless these requirements, as determined by the Capital Issues Committee, are complied with. Thus the committee becomes a body for assisting the exchange to comply with Treasury directives. Further to promote this collaboration, an Issuing Houses Association, made up of some fifty-two issuing firms, was established in 1946 to provide a recognized channel of communication between these firms and the Treasury, the Bank of England, the National Investment Council, and the finance corporations.

There are two of these finance corporations. The first, the Industrial and Commercial Finance Corporation, was established to provide intermediate credit for the small borrower. The second, the Finance Corporation for Industry, was created to assist primarily those long-run adjustments and industrial reorganization and reconstruction schemes of the postwar period which involve capital requirements on a scale or under conditions which would "put them out of court" in the ordinary investment channels. Both are institutions established by the Churchill government on the initiative, as indicated above, of Lord Catto, Governor of the Bank of England.

The Industrial and Commercial Finance Corporation (I.C.F.C.) came into existence on February 20, 1945, as a privately owned bankers' agency for the purpose of aiding certain classes of small bor-

---

[56] *Capital Issues Control: Special Memorandum to the Capital Issues Committee, Presented by the Chancellor of the Exchequer to Parliament by Command of His Majesty,* Cmd. 7281 (Dec., 1947). In April, 1949, a superseding memorandum added two new priorities: (1) "the development of technical advances and new projects contributing to industrial progress" and (2) "projects which will yield marked and immediate reductions in costs." *Times,* April 16, 1949. This memorandum reflects the Government's growing concern over failure of cost-reducing technical nationalization.

rowers who previously had experienced difficulty in securing loans which were too "long" for ordinary bank credit, or too "short" for the regular issues market. There are two main classes of such advances. One is made up of well-secured loans at rates varying between 4 and 4.55 per cent, which are repayable on an installment basis over periods ranging up to 20 years. The other consists of the provision of risk capital by purchase of ordinary shares or notes which contain an option permitting conversion into shares.

The I.C.F.C. thus appears as a banker devised, banker owned, banker controlled, and managerially autonomous—in the *patois*, "independent"—financial institution which enjoys both government sponsorship and the security of a governmental guarantee against certain classified types of losses peculiar to the type of loan which this institution is devised to extend.[57] Via the I.C.F.C. the member banks are here engaged in entering certain small and hitherto neglected areas for the conduct of profitable financial operations.

The I.C.F.C. was established to handle the unusual small loan; the Finance Corporation for Industry (F.C.I.) was organized to handle the unusual large loan. The F.C.I. was launched as a going concern with the announcement of the composition of its Board of Directors in May, 1945. It appeared as a private limited company owned jointly by a number of insurance companies, trust companies, and the Bank of England. The first was to contribute 40 per cent of the authorized capital of £25,000,000; the joint stock banks and the Bank of England 30 per cent each. Resources at the end of the first year of business were about a million pounds, mostly made up of deposits from the clearing houses and the Scottish banks.

The scale of business operations, over-all, is small. At the end of the first year of business (June, 1946) total loans and shares at cost were £254,000. One year later, they had reached the figure of £1,862,051. During the first year the principal assistance provided was extended to gas turbine production, chemicals, diesel engineering, and prefabricated housing. An outstanding example was the financing of Petrocarbon, Ltd. to develop the "Caterole" process, where the F.I.C. agreed to take up half of an issue of £1,800,000 of notes repayable by September, 1954. The other half was taken up by member banks. The first

[57] I.C.F.C. is a commercial organization. Its resources of £45,000,000 were subscribed by the London clearing banks, the Scottish banks, and The Bank of England. Its operations are purely commercial and small scale. In 1947–1948 applications for loans "were little more than one-half the average rate of the preceding year." *Times*, Dec. 13, 1948.

big venture came with the "arrangement to provide £35,000,000 for the Steel Company of Wales, Ltd."[58]

While the financing of the Steel Company of Wales points to the possibility of future operations on a much larger scale, still the over-all possibilities seem to be comparatively small. It has been pointed out, for example, that while the participation of British commercial banks in these institutions provides somewhat of a break with banking traditions in England in the past—traditions which prevented commercial banks, in sharp contradistinction with continental practice, particularly in Germany, from participating in the financing of fixed capital—the break, nevertheless, is comparatively small. Were the banks to participate in these activities to the maximum, the rates of advances to deposits for the United Kingdom would not exceed about 3 per cent. This is surely a new adventure on a modest scale, particularly when the government virtually guarantees the two institutions against loss.

Neither the I.C.F.C. nor the F.C.I. are to engage in the ordinary run of banking business. Fears that the latter corporation might do so were refuted by its chairman by the statement that "there have been several instances in which your Directors having declined business on the grounds that, in their view, the applicants should attempt to find their money through the usual channels have subsequently observed that the money has been provided in this way."[59] The rule is coöperation between the F.C.I. and the City. Viewed as "a mechanism for mobilising the credit resources of the City in order to finance schemes of post-war modernisation and re-equipment which could not be handled appropriately through the normal financial channels," it sometimes acts alone, and sometimes it "has been associated with one or more of the Issuing Houses of the City." In any event, the role of the government is to see that if the issues involve matters of national import, the credit extensions receive government guarantee. In the first year of business, one such loan, involving a sum of £210,000, was placed in default, directors of the F.C.I. being "unanimous in the view that the Corporation is equitably entitled to compensation from the Government."[60]

Curious as this picture of the timidity of the once-vaunted and supposedly intrepid managers of risk and venture capital may seem, the

[58] Finance Corporation for Industry, Ltd., *Note of Chairman's Speech at the Second Annual General Meeting* (1947). It is interesting that this financing in the South Wales steel industry is in keeping with reorganization proposals of the industry which provides the principal opposition to the Government's proposals for nationalization of the steel industry as a whole.

[59] *Loc. cit.*

[60] *Loc. cit.*

reflection it casts on the Labour party's machinery for guiding the flow of investment capital is more curious still. Gone wholly is the talk of fraud and corruption. Gone also is the grand array of financial machinery and controls for reorganizing the economy of a socialized state. In its place is coöperation with the City on the City's terms, by use of the City's financial machinery, and with the resources of the government marshaled to see that even these small-scale efforts involve the institutions making the City's decisions for the City's purposes in no risk to themselves.

The view underlying Labour's support of these Tory-dominated institutions was, of course, that the purposes for which such loans were to be extended were to be in the national interest. This meant that it was in the national interest to revive small business and reorganize large business, provided that the line of economic activity was consistent with these purposes and the risks were not unduly high. The revival of small business seems to derive its justification largely, if not indeed solely, from the belief that numerous small concerns actively competing against each other are economically advantageous, not from any principled idea of scientific organization of sectors of the economy, or of the nature and justification of the specific activities of the individual concerns—except, of course, that such activities must not be inconsistent with national objectives. It caters, in other words, to the classical Marshallian dogmas of free competition as they may be modified by the helping hand of a paternal state.

The reorganization of major industries follows a variation on the first pattern, that of government aid to industries prepared to define their functions under the formula of self-government in business in such a way as to include modernizing to achieve reasonably high levels of efficiency. It was with the purpose, apparently, of effecting at once these two ends, and of bringing them into harmony with an over-all plan of national development that the National Investment Council was established. Under their terms of reference, the council is "to assist the government in so organising and, when necessary, stimulating investment as to promote full employment."

Here, at last, was to be a real financial coördinating agency whose function would be to draw together all the interests, institutions, and resources of the entire economy. "The planning of the investment programme as a whole" was essential, and it "must, therefore be continuously guided by the Government and must be related to other

Government plans for the use of the country's economic resources."[61] The National Investment Council was the chosen instrument. But the council exists in name only. Meeting originally on a monthly basis, not for the purpose of planning, but to advise Dalton when he was Chancellor of the Exchequer, it has since been allowed to perish by the time-honored process of obsolescence through disuse. Investigation in 1948 failed to turn up anybody in financial circles who could even remember when it had last met.[62]

With two exceptions, this summarizes the nature and the fate of the machinery conjured or adopted for the purpose of carrying into effect the reforms sketched by Jay. Neither of the two exceptions involves any generically new devices or ideas, and neither is designed to upset the *status quo*. The first, dealing with control of the foreign exchanges, is an inevitable consequence of the application of Keynesian doctrines to the peculiarities of postwar conditions in Britain. The second, consisting of a series of physical controls over materials, construction, and manpower, involves nothing more than an extension into postwar times of priorities systems evolved during the war.

EXCHANGE CONTROL

The Exchange Control Act of 1947[63] "was introduced to give the Government power to supervise the whole range of foreign payments, since the financial position of the country makes it essential that capital investment abroad should serve the national interest exclusively. Under the bill therefore:

i) dealing in gold and foreign currency except with authorised dealers (principally banks) is restricted. Gold and most foreign currency must be sold to them; and they in turn must buy and sell from the Exchange Equalisation Account;

ii) payments to persons outside the sterling area, without Treasury permis-

---

[61] Cmd. 6726.

[62] Total capital investment (gross capital formation) in 1948 was estimated to be running at the rate of roughly £2,000,000,000, or approximately 20 per cent of national income. This, said Sir Stafford Cripps was "not altogether unsatisfactory"—a characterization which seems very strange until it is realized that this figure includes depreciation and maintenance. *Home Economic Survey*, Oct. 26, 1948, pp. 15–16, and Nov. 16, 1948. In an article in *Lloyd's Bank Review*, quoted in the *Times*, June 6, 1948, Mr. S. P. Chambers, Finance Director of Imperial Chemicals, suggests that, "outside of one or two specially favoured branches of industry, the amount spent on capital formation is almost certainly less than what is necessary to replace worn-out equipment at to-day's prices." This suggests an over-all lack of any net new capital formation at all!

[63] The full title reads: "An Act to confer powers, and impose duties and restrictions, in relation to gold, currency, payments, securities, debts, and the import, export, transfer and settlement of property, and for purposes connected with the matters aforesaid." It became law on March 11, 1947. 10 & 11 Geo. 6, Chap. 14.

sion (except for certain approved classes of payment, which the banks can handle without formality) is forbidden;

iii) the existing control over the issue and transfer of securities where non-residents are concerned is maintained; and a new control over foreign and bearer securities is introduced;

iv) the present controls over import and export of currency are maintained; and the necessary powers to ensure that exports are properly paid for are provided;

v) regulations are made concerning the prompt collection of debts, the control of foreign subsidiaries and ancillary matters; and

vi) persons wishing to leave the United Kingdom will be subject to new forms of Government control.[64]

Little, if anything, need be added to this summary for present purposes. The act was devised in such a way that under it virtually any move or measure deemed essential by the authorities may be carried out internally without being nullified by uncontrolled movements of goods and funds through international channels. Appendix 4 gives a picture of the general structure of the controls as they existed early in 1949.

Thus protected, the Labour government has attempted to minimize imports and to maximize exports with a view to securing a favorable over-all balance without unduly drawing down gold reserves or sacrificing further foreign investment and other important overseas interests. Success then depends upon the ability of the government so to manage the internal economy as to secure the maximum exportable surplus, and this in turn depends upon the ability to obtain maximum production of approved types of output. Such maximum production, finally, is contingent upon the success of the government in obtaining full employment of economic resources, and the appropriate division of these resources among alternative employments.

The first need not detain us here except as it involves compliance with the general intention to hold the internal standard of living at a constant or very slowly advancing rate in order, given full employment, to maximize the exportable surplus, and so to guide the flow of investment funds that they enhance still further the capacity to export. In this situation, the maximization of exports becomes the peacetime equivalent of the wartime object of maximizing the output of military supplies, and the plans of the Labour government in thus effecting this substitution have not yet gone beyond extension of wartime controls.

[64] *Summary of Legislation*, p. 15.

Next to the Exchange Control Act, the most important measure for extending these controls has been the Supplies and Services (Transitional Powers) Act of 1945, under which the government is able on a day-to-day basis to control output and prices of all types of consumer and producer goods, manipulate distribution shares of various income classes, and to some degree or another determine the total volume of savings.

Thus, aside from the cases cited above, no new machinery has been devised, and no new controls have been set up, for securing the permanently balanced economy at the level of full employment which Labour's theoreticians have set as the goal of their financial policies. Nevertheless, it cannot be gainsaid that the Labour government is in a position more or less fully to coördinate finance with any over-all and long-view planning of the economy as a whole—if and when any such planning may be forthcoming—without the necessity, at least at the outset, of creating any more new financial machinery at all.

That this is so may readily be seen by surveying briefly the machinery, over which it possesses complete control, or which it may, by means now at its disposal, bend more or less readily to its will. Under the Foreign Exchange Act it is in a position to control gold movements, the inward and outward flow of investment funds, and the balance of payments. It is in a position, that is to say, partially to insulate the national economy from the more random vagaries of international price changes and goods movements. By its direct control over the Bank of England, it may now coördinate management of the public debt with control over the supply of money, short-term credit, and the level of interest rates. This may be implemented by adding the power to give instructions to the joint stock banks in particular, and to the City in general, to regulate rediscount policy and to control open-market operations.

Long term credit and investment control possesses a rather elaborate machinery. Through the Capital Issues Committee it is able to influence, if not actually to veto, the amount, terms, times of issuance, and prices at which private investment securities are listed on the stock exchange. Through its power to supervise the issuance of government and municipal securities it may add public to private finance. Furthermore, it can guide the supply of special types of large issues for reorganization purposes through its control over F.C.I., of small borrowings through I.C.F.C., and of agriculture through the Agricultural

Mortgage Corporation.[65] Supplementary controls are implied in the establishment of special machinery—such as the Film Finance Corporation recently devised for aiding the domestic movie industry—for supplying funds for activities deemed of special importance to the national economy and as a consequence of the government's close supervision of unit trust schemes. Finally, the government controls the Public Works Loan Board, and the Treasury serves as financial advisor to the various government corporations set up under the several nationalization acts and falling under the auspices of the Colonial Office (Overseas Development Corporation) and the Food Ministry (e.g., the African Groundnuts Scheme for developing tropical estates to supply Britain with edible oils from peanuts).

Similarly, the government can exercise some indirect control over savings through its management of the Postal Savings System; direct control over prices of all rationed goods, indirect price control over unrationed goods, and by its system of subsidies and bulk buying may hold down market prices of certain classes of rationed and unrationed consumer goods, and over income through wage control, taxes, and other internal revenue controls, and import duties controls.[66] Supplementary to all such controls is the government's capacity under extension of wartime authority to establish materials priorities for the more important raw supplies such as metals, lumber, fuel and power, for all industries, and man-power supply by a combination of its powers to allocate labor directly and to determine the amount and location of housing and supplementary living facilities.

[65] "Formed to raise money by the issue of debentures, debenture stock, or other securities constituting a general charge on the undertaking and assets, and to apply same (a) in making advances on 1st. mortgages of agricultural or horticultural properties in Great Britain up to $\frac{2}{3}$ of value of each property the advances to be repayable within 60 years by equal yearly or $\frac{1}{2}$ yearly installments, and (b) in making advances under Improvement of Land Acts 1864 and 1899; also to raise money on loan from His Majesty's Government not exceeding in the aggregate £2,500,000 [as provided by Agriculture (Misc. Provisions) Act 1944]. The Government's sanction is required to any alteration in the Memorandum and Articles of Association. Capital-Authorised and issued £750,000 shares of £1 fully paid; held by various banks. While any of the Government loans remains outstanding the memorandum of Association limits the dividend to a non-cumulative $3\frac{1}{2}$ per cent. per annum. In a liquidation, available assets will be applied to repaying the Government loan and share Capital ratably, and assets then remaining will belong to the shareholders." *Stock Exchange Year Book* (1947), pp. 2092–2093. See also below, chapter xi, footnote 46.

[66] "A *Survey of National Savings* based on interviews with 2,268 adults was conducted in Feb., 1948 by Social Surveys Ltd." It brought out that, "Generally speaking it is the smaller holdings which are most likely to have decreased, and the larger holdings which are most likely to have been increased. Clearly the existing concentration of National Savings is being further accentuated." *Home Affairs Survey*, Sept. 11, 1948, p. 9. This would seem to bear out one of the most frequently repeated trade union complaints that despite the steepness of income tax graduation, the over-all incidence of postwar governmental controls bears most heavily on the lower income brackets.

This listing does not by any manner of means exhaust the repertory of powers lying at the government's disposal if it chooses to plan finance with reference to, and in keeping with, some over-all plan for the long-run development of the economy as a whole. (It may, for example, directly influence the uses made of accumulated resources in the hands of the insurance companies.) But far more important is the sheer pre-ponderating weight of governmental expenditures. Two sets of data are particularly important in this connection. The first is the secular rate of growth in the ratio of total government expenditures to national in-come, for which the relevant data is given in table 11, appendix 10. What these data show is that "government expenditure amounted to roughly one-sixteenth of the national income in the first year (1907–8); the corresponding proportion for the middle years was a little under one-fifth (1924–5); and for the year just ended (1948–9, not shown, but reflected in the Budget estimates for 1949–50) it was roughly one-third (or nearly two-fifths if outlays 'below the line' are included)." Al-though, to avoid misunderstanding, these data "must not be read as implying an outright withdrawal from the means of welfare available to the population; what it measures—and that only very roughly—is a transferance of purchasing power out of the stream of private incomes and into the stream that flows through the Exchequer and, by way of Government expenditure, back into personal incomes again . . ."[67]

During this interval between 1907–08 and 1949–50 the na-tional debt has grown from some £700,000,000 to approximately £25,000,000,000 (end of March, 1949), or some thirty-five fold. What these figures show is that the Labour government—just as would any contemporary British government—sits astride a vastly increased per-centage of the flow of national income, and that this percentage is now so large that it possesses a power to force virtually any phase or aspect of the national economic system into compliance with governmental directives without benefit of additional enabling legislation.

Almost equally important is the government's direct control over in-vestment. As appendix 10, table 5, based upon special, although fairly exhaustive (better than 95 per cent of the estimated total), "categories of investment which can be clearly distinguished and for which it has been possible to make fairly detailed estimates," as reported in the *Economic Survey for 1949*, shows, over one-third (£705,800,000 out of £1,995,400,000) of all investment in 1949 was made directly by the

---

[67] *Midland Bank Review*, May, 1949, pp. 1–2.

national or local governments and nearly another third (£584,800,000 out of £1,995,400,000) was made by industries and services in which the government plays a large, and in some respects a predominant role (e.g. housing). Should the iron and steel industry be nationalized in 1950 the category of wholly private investment would drop (on 1949 figures) from slightly more than one-third of the total to somewhat less than one-third (from £704,800,000 to £654,800,000). This does not exaggerate the central government's direct influence over investment. For one thing, expenditures of local government authorities are, at least for the most important items, largely if not wholly under the control of the national government. For another, the enormous purchases made by the government from private enterprise, for both operating and investment purposes, puts it in a position to determine which companies in what locations shall be expanded or contracted.

This domination of investment by the national government is, of course, very considerably enhanced by the new nationalization legislation. What is significant, however, is that an indirect but comprehensive control of investment is now possible as a mere by-product of the government's direct control of its own investment, without benefit of any supporting legislation.

There are two other factors which enhance the government's capacity to shape the national finances as it chooses. One is the number of workers employed by the government. Appendix 1, table 2, is a compilation of estimates made by a Labour M.P. of the total number of persons who would be employed by public concerns in 1950 if the separate categories at that time should remain as they were in the latest year of estimate at the time at which he wrote. His total of 6,040,194 is very nearly one-third of the total number of gainfully employed persons in that year. Although it may be doubtful whether these categories will remain very stable (particularly "Armed Forces," which is already 300,000 below his figure), and whether the coöperative movement should be included as a public concern at all, from the subsequent evidence it seems that the total figure for 1950 will not be far from his estimate. The second factor is the Government's direct influence over the trade unions and top trade-union strategy. So long as it may be able to command the latter height, its capacity to enforce its decisions is certain to be enhanced.

The result of all this is that the Government is now able to give real meaning to its program for planned investment and planning for full employment, of which one reads so much in Labour literature. Should this program become anything more than a mere general statement of objectives, clearly the Bank of England would play a very important— indeed, an absolutely strategic—role in its implementation. The other financial machinery at the government's disposal would have to follow its lead. That is if in reality there is any plan, for obviously all this can have no particular meaning unless there exists some over-all coördinating scheme which is to show how the several parts, categories, and controls are so to be meshed as to achieve the objectives laid down.

But here is the nub of the matter: Do such plans exist? The fact that one is not to be located does not prove that one does not exist, nor does the probability that one does not exist necessarily establish the point that piecemeal action may not eventually be made to add up to something which might well serve as the equivalent of a national plan. It is possible, but highly improbable, that a piecemeal plan will have to serve unless somewhere along the way there appears clear evidence that the plan is to do something more than merely "tidy up" previously existing financial controls the better to proceed along entirely conventional lines to achieve no more than the full employment advocated by Beveridge and Keynes.

Should this latter possibility actually come wholly to dominate—as may very well already be so—then it would also be true that subsequent nationalization measures would appear as little, if anything, more than a mere extension of the public utility concept—long since sanctified in capitalist society by government ownership and management of streets, highways, postal and similar services—to natural monopolies which may no longer be left to private enterprise without unduly cramping the full realization of the potentialities in other fields of that same private enterprise itself. In this event, two general conclusions would follow. First, that neither the nationalization of the Bank of England nor much of the other domestic or foreign investment-control machinery was very important. And second, that it was highly doubtful whether this disjointed planning could solve the fundamental and wholly inescapable problem of thorough overhaul of Britain's industrial system.

This latter holds the key both to Britain's possibility of attaining a high level of national prosperity, and the future political fortunes of the Labour party itself. The greater part of the Labour government's program is presumably addressed more or less directly to this subject. It remains to be seen with what degree of probable success.

CHAPTER III

Fuel and Power: Coal

It is my duty to warn the House that the existing position contains the elements of industrial disaster. In this context I speak without a trace of partisanship. The drift from the industry is appalling. The natural wastage cannot be overtaken by orthodox treatment. Relations between owners and men, generally speaking, are soured and embittered, and the efficiency of the industry relative to that of our Continental and other competitors is distinctly backward ... We contemplate a complete modernisation of the industry.—Emanuel Shinwell, Minister of Fuel and Power.

NATIONALIZATION of coal, said Shinwell in opening debate on the bill, involves no question of principle. Had not Churchill made this clear when he stated that "the principle of nationalisation is accepted by all, provided proper compensation is paid?"[1] Even the Mining Association had given up its opposition when they had declared that "while they preferred private rather than public ownership nevertheless because of the result of the General Election and the acceptance by Parliament of the contents of the Gracious Speech they did not propose to continue their opposition to the principle of nationalisation of the coal industry."[2]

As spokesman for the Conservative Opposition, Anthony Eden was prepared to accept this proposition. Indeed, he reminded the Government benches that "in the past, the Conservative Party and the Liberal Party had had a responsibility for Measures of nationalisation which had been put through in this country."[3] The Post Office and the BBC were cited as examples. Others might have been added, such as the London Passenger Transport Board, the Port of London Authority, and the Central Electricity Board. The issue, Eden went on to say, was clearly not nationalization, *per se*, but whether or not nationalization was the best solution of the problem of coal, and—should even this be conceded—whether or not the bill in question was adequate for the purpose. Upon this ground the Opposition took a determined stand. "The Socialists," Colonel Lancaster wrote later, "like the eighteenth century ship's doctor, had only one medicine bottle for all ills, and that

---

[1] *Hansard*, Vol. 392, col. 921, cited by Shinwell, in *Hansard*, Vol. 418, col. 701.
[2] *Loc. cit.*
[3] *Ibid.*, col. 717.

was labelled 'Nationalisation.' "[4] This nostrum, the Opposition said, was bad for mining, and the bill itself was full of holes and was unworkable.

Yet upon one matter there was general agreement. The coal industry was in lamentable shape. While few would go so far, as one M.P. put it, as to say that "the industry had been gradually dying for the last 21 years," still heroic measures were required if it was to be placed on an efficient production basis in time. There had been enough of investigations, recommendations, and reports. For twenty years Parliament had been seeking to "devise a remedy . . . yet every treatment prescribed to cure the malady, whether by the Sankey, Samuel or Coal Reorganization Commissions, has resulted in failure."[5] It was time to cease arguing and begin acting. The "vast majority of our pits," Shinwell said, "are unworthy of a great industrial nation."[6] The report of the Reid committee, set up by the preceding Conservative-dominated Coalition Government for the purpose of making a thorough study of the coal industry, had detailed the picture at great length and, on the technical side at least, in a most authoritative manner.[7] It showed conclusively that what the industry needed was speedy and drastic reorganization on the largest possible scale.

THE CRITICAL CONDITION OF THE COAL INDUSTRY

There has been an enormous literature on the troubles of the British coal industry, but in the main there is agreement on the essential facts. Coal is a "wasting asset" of limited but unusual importance in British industry, there has been a steady and inescapable deterioration of the geological conditions under which extraction must take place, and these limited and deteriorating resources are being even more rapidly exhausted by wasteful methods of extraction and use. The industry is technologically backward and organizationally obsolete compared either with best methods or with practice abroad, and this generalization holds for virtually all steps in extraction and processing from the coal face to delivery to ultimate consumers. Working conditions are bad, accident and health hazards in certain areas (particularly Wales) are relatively high, and personnel relations have been deteriorating

---

[4] C. G. Lancaster, *Facts and Ideas: Colonel Lancaster Talks with You About Coal* (Conservative Political Centre, Feb., 1948), p. 13.

[5] *Hansard*, Vol. 418, col. 703.

[6] *Ibid.*, col. 702.

[7] *Coal Mining: Report of the Technical Advisory Committee*, Cmd. 6610 [hereafter referred to as the *Reid Report*] (March, 1945).

steadily since the First World War. Unemployment has been chronic, recruitment has become increasingly difficult, there has been a flight of miners from the industry, and the average age of miners is rising. And all this concurrent with Britain's relative, and in some respects absolute, decline as an industrial nation, and her growing relative dependence upon this failing resource in the years of her decline.

In the coal industry Britain thus faces a sort of scissors crisis; she must lean on it most heavily at the time when the support it can give is weakening most rapidly. Upon her capacity to reverse this trend depends much, if not most, of her ability to effect any sort of lasting recovery. Without some measure of success in the battle of coal no sort of favorable existence in the future is possible. Hence it will be necessary briefly to review the major problems which must be considered in making any plans for reorganization.

Resources.—British coal reserves have been inadequately surveyed, geological data is incomplete, and estimates of reserves vary widely. Best informed sources, however, estimate the known and probable reserves of usable coal in veins over 18 inches thick and down to 4,000 feet in depth to be in the neighborhood of "about two hundred years' supply, assuming an average consumption of about 200 million tons per annum."[8] It is believed by some that future discoveries will somewhat increase available reserves, though it is worth noting that in the past the general tendency has been to overestimate future discoveries.[9] There appears, for example, no justification for the Coal Board's own estimate that "Britain's ascertained workable coal reserves ensure production for at least 540 years at the rate of 250 million tons a year."[10]

When combined with the fact that it is probably true that "the relative proportions of different types of coal mined can remain stable for ascertained workable reserves of 33,000 million tons,"[11] the data on total reserves might be cause for considerable short-term complacency, but the picture varies considerably from district to district, and every-

---

[8] *The British Fuel and Power Industries: A Report by PEP* [hereafter referred to as *PEP Report*] (London, 1947), p. 61. This report is based upon regional survey reports of the Ministry of Fuel and Power made in 1945. The estimates of the Reid committee, *op. cit.*, p. 118, are in essential agreement.

[9] Thus the best known and most widely accepted previous estimate, that of the Royal Commission in 1901, placed the proved reserves at about 100,000,000,000 tons and the "concealed and unproved coal" at 40,000,000,000 tons. While these estimates did not include several subsequent discoveries, they were still more than three times as high as they should have been.

[10] *Notes on the British Coal-Mining Industry and the National Coal Board* [mimeographed] (National Coal Board, n.d.).

[11] *Loc. cit.*

where geological conditions are less and less favorable. With respect to the first, for example, "In Cumberland practically all the landward coal is exhausted and all that remains is the undersea areas. New pits of great depth are necessary. The field is considerably cut up with faults . . . In Lancashire, the easiest and most accessible coal has been extracted and a great reconstruction programme is necessary if the remainder is to be got at reasonable cost. The virgin areas that remain are very deep, entailing considerable expenditure for new sinkings . . . In Durham the reserves of high-class coking and gas coals . . . have reached a dangerous level."[12] As coal reserves in certain areas decline or are exhausted entire industries and their attached working cadres must move.

Throughout Britain the geological conditions under which coal must be mined are already very bad and are steadily getting worse. "The average depth at which British coal seams are being worked (950 feet) is nearly three times that of the average depth of American workings (350 feet); while about 55 per cent of British coal is cut from seams less than four feet deep, compared with 25 per cent of American coal. In the U.S.A. the seams are usually more level and the coal itself of good quality and relatively clean. Roofs generally need less support and floors are steadier; firedamp, water and spontaneous combustion are met less frequently."[13] In some areas water flow has become so serious that entire fields, such as those at South Staffordshire and the Nailsea Basin of Bristol, have had to be permanently abandoned.[14]

Methods of extraction have wasted much of the available reserve. The Haldane report, for example, estimated that in the Midland mining district there were some 10,000 acres of "thick coal," having an average thickness of 24 feet, lying more than 1,200 feet deep, and constituting a resource of 288,000,000 tons "of which 115,000,000 will not be won" because of the weight of the superincumbent strata, the character of the coal, and the methods of extraction. This loss of 40 per cent of resources is stretched to 60 per cent at 2,000 feet. Possibly half of this total loss is due to leaving behind barriers "to protect one colliery area from being inundated by water from another colliery." The total loss to the contrary as a whole from barriers has been estimated at between 3,500,000,000 and 4,000,000,000 tons. The other

---

[12] *Hansard*, Vol. 418, cols. 704–705.

[13] *Home Affairs Survey*, April 11, 1947, p. 17.

[14] See, e.g., the *Final Report of the Coal Conservation Committee* [Haldane Report] (Jan. 23, 1918) for a good early summary of this problem.

half of this loss is largely the result of the manner in which the coal
fields have been split up into independent property holdings, and is
thus to be regarded as preventable loss.

It is easy, however, to exaggerate these factors. A survey by the Fuel
Research Board in 1946 found that the various classes of coals[15] were
being produced at rates roughly proportionate to total reserves, and
that in the main the same held for both the leading uses of the coal and
the rates of exhaustion—with the exceptions noted above—from the
leading districts.[16] Furthermore, notwithstanding geological conditions,
PEP has estimated that over the next hundred years "in the country as
a whole the majority of the seams worked . . . will be between 3 ft. and
5 ft. in thickness, and the overall increase in ash content should not be
serious" though "more elaborate coal preparation or the designing of
appliances to use lower-grade fuels efficiently will eventually become
necessary."[17] Thus for another century at least, the principal coal beds
to be worked are adaptable to modern methods of mechanized extraction, although costs of such mining in the different regions are still not
really known.

Technological backwardness.—"Before the 1914–18 War," the
Reid committee found, "the OMS (Output per Man-Shift) in Britain
compared favourably with that of practically all the major coal-
producing countries other than the United States."[18] But by the middle
thirties Britain had fallen far behind, as table 1 shows.[19] Despite rapid
mechanization at the face of the seam, and the development of many
new large-scale and modern-type mines in a few preferred locations
(e.g. Fife), the British rate of improvement was at the bottom. Although the actual level of output was higher in Britain than in France
and Belgium, according to the I.L.O. *Report on World Coal Mining
Industry*, yet between 1913 and 1936 the latter had shown an increase
in OMS of 22.4 per cent and 50.6 per cent respectively, and the
U.S.S.R. had shown an increase of 72.1 per cent in the nine-year interval 1927–1936.[20] The comparison with the United States was even
more telling. In 1913 the American OMS, including strip mined coal,

---

[15] There are several methods of classifying coals. The one used by the Fuel Research Board
is based upon physical, not chemical, characteristics of coal. The classification runs from
very hard coal (anthracite) through the various degrees of low-volatile, high-caking coals
to high-volatile and noncaking coals.

[16] *Rapid Survey of Coal Reserves and Production*, Fuel Research Survey Paper, no. 56
(Fuel Research Board, 1946).

[17] *PEP Report*, p. 63.

[18] *Ibid.*, p. 29.

[19] *Loc. cit.*

[20] (International Labor Office, 1938.)

was over-all, in the bituminous industry, 3.22 tons, but in 1939 it was 4.69 tons, or approximately four times the British rate.

While better geological conditions and the inclusion of strip mining output might account in part for the superior American production, this was decidedly not so in the Ruhr and Holland, where natural conditions were no more favorable than in Britain. Their mining operations were based on newly developed German methods, and their superior output was clearly a product of this reorganization and modernization. The reorganization of the Dutch mines was particularly

TABLE 1
COAL OUTPUT PER MAN-SHIFT

Country	Basic year	OMS in basic year	OMS in 1936	Increase
		cwt.	cwt.	per cent
Poland.....................	1927	23.44	36.20	54
Holland...................	1925	16.48	35.94	118
The Ruhr.................	1925	18.62	33.66	81
Britain...................	1927	20.62	23.54	14

interesting for it demonstrated in detail the full extent of British backwardness and, at the same time, showed the potentialities which modernization might realize in heightened productivity.[21] Further, experimentation abroad had demonstrated that adverse geological conditions did not so much retard modernization as define the conditions which technical replanning of mining operations had to take as a point of departure. Even in the United States, as one expert concluded after a visit to America, high OMS "is mainly due to differences in their mining methods which are vastly superior to ours."[22] Surely, if, "in American mines it was not so much the good conditions which produced the high output per man, but taking advantage of these conditions, and adapting machines"[23] then a similar approach might bring analogous results for British mining.

A first requirement was that the system of leaseholds common in Britain should be abandoned and mining experts left free to plan

---

[21] See, e.g., the *Reid Report* on Holland, paragraphs 69–116, and the Fabian pamphlet, James Griffiths, *Dutch State Coal Mines*, Research Series No. 84 (n.p., n.d.). Griffiths is now Minister of Insurance.

[22] Sir William Firth, "Why Welsh Mining Experts Should See U. S. Pits," *Western Mail*, May 10, 1944. This position has been contested by other British mine reports.

[23] T. Lester, commenting on a paper by Dr. Wheeler, "American Systems of Mining," delivered to the Staffordshire and Warwickshire Institute of Mining Engineers, as reported in *Iron and Trades Review*, July 28, 1944.

operations on the basis of the coal fields taken as a whole. The case for doing this in coal is very nearly as clear as it is in petroleum extraction, where unified development of the underground pool has long been standard practice. On the Continent the fact that "ownership of the mineral has always been vested in the State, which has exercised control and supervision over the orderly extraction of the seams to ensure proper regard for the conservation of the national resources,"[24] has tended to favor unified development of coal fields. The reverse has been true in Britain. "In Britain . . . the ownership of the mineral was, until recent years, in the hands of many owners. When, therefore, a mine was to be sunk it was often necessary to obtain leases from a number of different owners, each wanting his coal to be worked quickly, so that he could draw his royalty. Even where a single landowner held the mineral rights of an area which an undertaking wished to work, he sometimes pursued a deliberate policy of granting leases for comparatively small areas, with the intention of increasing his royalty receipts by having several undertakings working his coal simultaneously."[25]

This dispersal of ownership has meant a large number of comparatively small and inefficient mines. In 1943 there were some 966 mines in Britain producing less than 50,000 tons annually, and accounting for only about 10 per cent of the total output. "The 816 mines producing more than 50,000 tons annually, which cover 90 per cent of the total output of the country, are owned by 353 separate undertakings with an average annual output in 1943 of 228,000 tons per mine. Many of these mines are of comparatively small size, and may already be producing at full capacity in relation to the size of the leasehold. But there are many others which are capable of a large increase above their present output."[26] This situation had not been altered by the nationalization of coal royalties in 1938. "There are mines on the point of exhausting their reserves; mines which should be closed down altogether and their reserves worked from adjoining collieries; mines where the remaining reserves can, under no scheme of reconstruction, be worked profitably; mines between which valuable coal has been sterilised to form barriers; and mines which, for a period of their reconstruction, will have to be completely closed down . . . There are undertakings which have a lease of coal that could be worked to better advantage by

---

[24] *Reid Report*, p. 30.
[25] *Loc. cit.*
[26] *Ibid.*, p. 122.

another undertaking; and undertakings whose mines are widely spread through a district, and even among several districts."[27]

A first requirement, then, is a complete reorganization of mining on the basis of large-scale pit operations spaced to permit unified development on a coal-field basis. With this goes a complete overhauling of mine operations below and above ground. The method of working should be shifted wherever possible from the longwall advancing system to either the room and pillar (the usual American method, though it tends to leave a larger percentage of coal underground) or longwall retreating system. Mechanization means the introduction of "the longwall coal cutter; the heading coal cutter—both shortwall and arcwall; percussive machines and picks; power boring machines, mechanical loaders for headings, room, drifts, and scourings; electric trucks for coal cutters, materials, and men; conveyor-belt, chain and shaker; mechanical shovels and slushers for dirt handling; mechanical dirt stowers; shuttle cars; locomotives; large mine cars."[28] Though much had been done along these lines in the larger and more modern mines, there was still room for vast extension of these methods.

In its discussion of technical reorganization particular emphasis was laid by the Reid committee on the backward condition of underground haulage. The "tonnage of coal handled per haulage worker in British mines," the report pointed out, "is the low figure of approximately five tons per shift, compared with 20–25 tons in Holland, and upwards of 50 tons in the United States."[29] Whereas haulage workers made up only some 5 per cent of the total employment in American coal mining, in Britain the comparative figure was nearly 20 per cent. The Reid committee estimated that if British underground haulage were made as efficient as the Dutch this change alone would raise the underground OMS from an average of 30 hundredweight per shift to 40 hundredweight.

Reorganizing the more backward of existing mines in keeping with best technical methods could effect an approximate 100 per cent increase in output, as shown in table 2, compiled from data supplied by the Reid committee on the basis of studies of sample mines. Should such reorganization be accompanied by gradual closing down of small-scale and inefficient collieries, and concentration of manpower in the

---

[27] *Ibid.*, p. 137. See also table 2.
[28] Presidential address to the Midland Institute of Mining Engineers, Sheffield, October 25, 1944, cited in Harold Wilson, *New Deal for Coal* (Contact Press, 1945), p. 164. Wilson is now president of the Board of Trade.
[29] *Reid Report*, p. 66.

modernized and large-scale pits, and by new developments of large-scale and completely modernized pits of the types now being planned,[30] it is possible that in many mines a further increase of 25 to 50 per cent might be realized.

The methods of coal distribution require a similar overhauling. Storage facilities at most collieries are inadequate, so that many small mines ship out single wagon loads at a time, or ship by truck. Numerous

TABLE 2

INCREASE IN OUTPUT OF COAL EFFECTED BY REORGANIZATION OF MINES

Location of reorganization scheme	Before change			After change			Increase in OMS
	Daily output	Number employees	OMS	Daily output	Number employees	OMS	
	tons		cwt.	tons		cwt.	per cent
Scotland............	950	830	21	1,600	700	40	90
Durham I...........	847	841	20.2	2,574	841	60	197
Durham II..........	1,470	1,334	23.8	3,488	1,098	63.6	169
Cumberland........	460	466	19	900	193	86	353
Northumberland....	1,150	.....	28	1,500	.....	60	115
Lancashire.........	3,000	2,089	22.5	4,000	.....	35	36
Yorkshire I.........	3,000	2,370	27	4,700	2,296	41.2	49
Yorkshire II........	2,500	2,232	23.2	5,000	2,240	45	94
Nottinghamshire I...	1,930	1,613	32	2,400	.....	46	43
North Staffordshire.	3,200	2,405	26	6,400	1,998	60	131
South Wales II......	1,270	1,298	20	1,838	803	40	100

and small haulages from the collieries is paralleled by inadequate storage space at the marketing end, so that the average small merchant—and there are over 30,000 private traders, including some 5,000 to 6,000 barrow hawkers[31]—and the numerous small branches of the larger merchants[32] require many small deliveries. Most of these local depots are unmechanized, coal is shoveled out of railway wagons, and later into lorries, by hand. There is an unnecessarily large offering of sizes and varieties of coal to be kept on hand; merchants' price lists are said to show around forty varieties of coal. Merchants, factors (believed now to be wholly unnecessary in coal distribution as a whole), and

[30] See, e.g., the plans for the Frances and Rothes collieries and the surface Benarty mine, published by the Scottish Division, Fife and Clackmannan Area, of the National Coal Board.

[31] *Nationalisation of Coal*, Labour Discussion Series, No. 7 (Labour Publications Dept., 1946).

[32] "In 1943, larger merchants alone operated some 27,000 branches at depots; nearly half these branches handled less than 20 tons a week (11½ per cent. of the total tonnage), and only 6 per cent. handled over 100 tons a week (40 per cent. of total tonnage)." *Ibid.*, pp. 10–11.

collieries are in the habit of buying from individual mines and mercantile centers over wide areas—not infrequently all over England—without regard to distance or to crosshauling; much equipment, consumer and industrial alike, is equipped to take only a given size of a specific quality of coal; there appears to be great duplication and overlapping of haulage facilities between the railroads and coal hauliers, etc.[33]

While the Reid committee did not deal with the problem of retail distribution at all, such evidence as is available appears to show that disorganization and inefficiency here is as great as in colliery production. Reorganization of distribution, however, extends far beyond wholesaling and retailing organization and practices to include transportation, manufacture of heating and other coal-using facilities, and the whole general problem of more efficient use of coal through improved by-product utilization on the one hand, and the transformation of the heat and energy derived from coal into gas and electricity on the other.

Working conditions, health and occupation hazards, and morale.— However obsolete the technology of British mining and coal distribution may be, there can be no doubt that the human relations prevailing throughout the industry are worse. The data run the gamut of ailments: working conditions are bad, health is poor, accident rates are high, the incidence of occupational diseases is high—particularly in certain districts, for example, South Wales and Durham—management is frequently poorly trained and inefficient and where efficient it is circumscribed by a mentality shaped by protracted limitation to the single objective of getting out coal and producing profits for the owners, nepotism is common, and the general heritage of management-labor relations is one of bitter, uncompromising and well-nigh universal hostility and hatred. It is wholly impossible adequately to summarize the record in short space, or to measure its precise implications for production. Its seriousness can, to a limited extent, be seen in the record of high absenteeism and unauthorized stoppages, and the picture of a charged atmosphere which may at almost any moment result in large-scale strikes and lockouts.

Figures computed by the Ministry of Fuel and Power[34] showed that the number of shifts that were lost through absenteeism crept up gradually from 6.4 per cent weekly in 1938 to 12.4 per cent in 1943.

[33] See, e.g., H. Norman Smith, *Your Coal and You*, Fabian Tract Series No. 259, pp. 4–11.
[34] Ministry of Fuel and Power, *Statistical Digest from 1938*, Cmd. 6538 (1944), table 7, p. 9.

Voluntary absenteeism constitutes about two-fifths of the total, and in 1943, a war year of major and generally recognized national emergency decreased national production of coal by almost 5 per cent. More important, this absenteeism is highest underground; particularly among workers at the coal face. Since it is the output of the latter that determines mine production as a whole, this is a particularly serious situation. Furthermore, it is a type of absenteeism which has been growing under peacetime conditions of high and relatively full employment.[35]

TABLE 3

NUMBER OF PERSONS KILLED AND INJURED (DISABLED FOR MORE THAN THREE DAYS) PER 1,000 PERSONS EMPLOYED IN BRITISH MINES

Year	Underground workers	Surface workers	Underground and surface workers
1938	194	64	165
1939	202	69	171
1940	225	82	192
1941	263	90	221
1942	273	93	229
1943	287	92	239

SOURCE: Ministry of Fuel and Power, *Statistical Digest, 1944*, Cmd. 6639, p. 28.

The principal cause of involuntary absenteeism appears to be the high accident-frequency and accident-severity rate. Table 3 scarcely requires elaboration. Undoubtedly the wartime presence of large numbers of untrained and youthful recruits brought in from the outside (the so-called "Bevin boys") and the longer working hours had a good deal to do with the increased rate. But even after making due allowance for these factors, the situation is admittedly serious, and is further aggravated by the loss of effective manpower through occupational diseases, and a shortage of workers caused by the fear of incurring these diseases. The validity of this fear may be illustrated by a case report by Margot Heinemann which is particularly interesting, since, though it is admittedly an extreme example, yet it has received extraordinarily wide circulation since the Labour government came into power. It is worth repeating in full.

[35] See, *ibid.*, table 8 where a sample study showed the effect of preholiday and postholiday voluntary absenteeism in 1943 among coal-face workers. The per cent of lost time through voluntary absenteeism runs 5.82 on Sunday and Monday before a holiday, declines gradually to 3.53 on Friday, and then rises sharply to 6.71 on Saturday. During the postholiday week, the rate for Sunday and Monday was 20.43, Tuesday 24.15, Wednesday 10.29, Thursday 5.41, Friday 5.81, and Saturday 13.78. Postwar figures show a similar pattern.

There is a true story, reported to me with full names and details by a miners' agent in West Wales, which serves to sum up the worst tragedies of mining life. In March, 1930, at a large colliery in the anthracite area, employing 1,200 men, a Soccer team was selected for the championship matches. The men chosen were all employed as colliers—strong young men at the summit of their strength and skill. The agent happened to keep the list of the team among his papers. Here is the condition of these eleven men in 1943:

Goalkeeper. Age, thirty-seven. Buried in 1939 under a fall of roof, injured spine and fractured pelvis. For weeks his life was in danger. He is alive to-day, but will never be able to work again.

Right Back. Age, forty-one. Total incapacity due to silicosis.

Left Back. Age, thirty-four. Buried by a fall in 1934. Fractured leg and shoulder. Only able to perform light work on the surface.

Right Half. Age, fifty-two. Partial incapacity due to silicosis.

Centre Half. Age, forty-two. Total incapacity due to silicosis.

Left Half. Age, forty. Total incapacity due to silicosis.

Right Wing. Age, forty. Total incapacity due to silicosis.

Inside Right. An exceptionally good workman and very strong, he was always willing to work in the wettest places. At the age of twenty-five he contracted rheumatic fever and died.

Centre Forward. Age, forty-two. Total incapacity due to silicosis.

Inside Left. Age, thirty-three. Partial incapacity due to silicosis.

Left Wing. Age, thirty-six. Buried by fall of roof. Injured his spine and will never be able to work below ground again.[36]

While this story is no doubt unusual,—a critic refers to it as "exceptionally biased reporting"—similar tales will be heard in almost any colliery field. They supply, however, only the more poignant detail on a much wider canvas of the misery and neglect which plagues large sections of the industry. In addition to the major occupational diseases of pneumoconiosis and nystagmus (an eye disease resulting from bad lighting of underground operations) there are the common ailments of "beat knee," "beat hand," and "beat elbow" from working in cramped quarters at the coal face, rheumatism, respiratory ailments from bad ventilation, and a wide variety of skin diseases. A common complaint is that it is necessary to travel long distances underground on foot. A half mile walk to and from the coal face underground is common, and distances over one mile are not infrequent, particularly in the older mines. The Samuel Commission found one mine in which the distance travelled on foot was "4,305 yards, in one direction, which occupied some 61 minutes, i.e., over two hours travelling time each day under-

---

[36] Margot Heinemann, *Britain's Coal* (Gollancz, 1944), p. 64. This story is reproduced in full by Harold Wilson, *op. cit.*, pp. 42–44.

ground."[37] While this seems to be true only in the older mines, the fact that "in 1945 nearly 50 per cent of total output came from pits over fifty years old"[38] indicates that the complaint has widespread justification.

Housing conditions, particularly in the smaller and more isolated villages where most of the older collieries are located, are deplorable. The Sankey report, in 1919, spoke of "houses in some districts which are a reproach to our civilization. No judicial language is sufficiently strong or sufficiently severe to apply to their condemnation."[39] Yet on the eve of nationalization a quarter of a century later housing conditions in most mining districts had not materially improved. In 1945 a miner with 30 years experience, mostly underground, wrote of "the massed greyness of the average colliery street" which "looks like a long stone wall with doors set in at regular intervals . . . It is quite the accepted thing to be married ten or twelve years and still exist in one room up and one down, never having a home of your own."[40] Most of these houses do not have running hot and cold water, bathrooms and inside lavatories, or heat and ventilation. Where pit-head baths are not installed, and this is still the typical condition in the smaller mines,[41] miners "come away from a pit like a horde of, well, rather doubtful looking characters . . . all black" and looking like "a lot of wild men" to do their "bathing in the living room" with all the confusion and disorder this means for the women and the children.[42]

The picture ramifies until it embraces most aspects of the miner's working and leisure life, and the hardships are quite apparently as great or greater for the women and the children as for the men. Nor, with occasional significant exceptions, have conditions been growing better in recent years. It appears in general to be true that the social side of the industry has been stagnating since the outbreak of the First

---

[37] *Report of the Royal Commission on the Coal Industry* (1925) [commonly referred to as the *Samuel Report*], p. 271. See also B. L. Coombes, *Miners Day* (Penguin, 1945).

[38] *Home Affairs Weekly*, April 11, 1947, p. 16.

[39] *Coal Industry Commission Reports and Minutes of Evidence* (1919) [commonly referred to as the *Sankey Report*], p. ix.

[40] Coombes, *op. cit.*, p. 74.

[41] By 1943 there were 379 baths, accommodating 460,092 or 65 per cent of all miners, "built or in the course of construction." These were primarily concentrated in the larger mines. Cmd. 6538, p. 50.

[42] "A further point to be borne in mind is the undesirable moral effect on miners' children, which may sometimes result from the practice of general bathing in the living room; the effect on their health of being frequently exposed to a steamy atmosphere; the many cases of young children falling into tubs of scalding water; and the offensive smell of the drying clothes in the cramped accommodation of a miner's home." Testimony of Dr. J. S. Haldane, President of the Institution of Mining Engineers and Chairman of the Health Advisory Committee of the Secretary for Mines. *Samuel Report*, p. 206.

World War. Overtopping all other maladies, and appearing partly as cause, partly as effect of poor conditions in the mining industry is the record of low wages and unemployment.

In 1938, at a time when wages in the coal industry had begun to rise slowly from their depression depths to a level approaching that of the early twenties, "a survey, made by the Economics and Statistics Directorate of the Ministry of Fuel and Power, and given by the Minister in the House of Commons, showed that . . . coal occupied the eighty-first

TABLE 4

AVERAGE WEEKLY EARNINGS (CASH AND ALLOWANCES) OF
MINERS, 1938–1945

Year	Cash earnings			Value of allowances in kind	
	£	s.	d.	s.	d.
1938	2	15	9	2	2
1939	2	19	6	2	3
1940	3	8	8	2	6
1941	4	0	0	2	9
1942	4	13	2	3	0
1943	5	0	0	3	3
1944	5	9	4	3	8
1945	5	12	8	4	3

SOURCE: *PEP Report*, p. 85.

highest place in a 'ladder' of nearly a hundred industries, so far as average adult male earnings were concerned" making this "most dangerous industry where men worked in darkness . . . one of the dirtiest and hardest of occupations" one of the lowest paid industries in Britain.[43] Table 4 gives the record of "average weekly cash earnings and value of allowances in kind of wage-earners (all ages)" for the ensuing period. Even these figures exaggerate the miner's income, since against these earnings must be offset certain "deductions for tools, explosives, sick clubs, accident insurance, welfare payments, etc."[44] and it is possible

[43] Harold Wilson, *op. cit.*, p. 38.

[44] *Ibid.*, p. 16. In a large colliery in Fife visited by the writer in the summer of 1948—before the new social insurance levies had been initiated—an example was given of a typical miner working five regular shifts at the face who received an average weekly wage of £5 15s. From this were deducted 5d. for medical insurance, 2s. for health insurance, 10d. for unemployment insurance, 2d. for the Miners' Home, 2d. for the Mining Association, 1d. for Ambulance Service, 1d. for the Welfare Institute, and 1d. each (voluntary) for the Red Cross and the local Bond Fund. These deductions total 3s. 1d., and 11s. are deducted for income tax, making a total weekly deduction of 14s. 11d. Additional costs of 6d. for soap and 2d. for his lamp bring the sum to 15s. 7d. Against this he gets a packed lunch and tea for 6d., free baths (formerly costing 6 to 9d. per day), and coal at pithead cost.

that on the average these were more than double the total allowances in kind (mostly coal for home use).

Before increases brought about by war preparation in 1939, British mining wages were among the lowest of the major coal mining countries. The 1938 I.L.O. *Report on the Coal Mining Industry* gave the figures shown in table 5 on average earnings for various coal-mining countries for the year 1936.

TABLE 5

AVERAGE EARNINGS IN 1936 IN COAL MINING. EXPRESSED IN A
COMMON CURRENCY (GOLD SWISS FRANCS)

Country	Per hour (underground)	Per man-shift (underground and surface)
U. S. A. (Bituminous)	2.44	12.40 (1933)
Netherlands	1.39 [a]	10.21
France	1.22	8.71
Germany: Ruhr	1.20	9.05
Upper Silesia	0.97	7.32
Great Britain	1.06	7.88
Czechoslovakia	0.86	6.12
Poland	0.67	5.06
Belgium	0.57 [a]	4.18 [a]
Japan	0.18	1.69
Canada	....	13.86 (1935)

SOURCE: Cited by Heinemann, *Britain's Coal*, p. 44.
[a] Averages include an estimate of nonmoney earnings.

Subsequent wage increases, as indicated by table 4, do not appear greatly to have increased the relative status of the miner within Britain, though they may then have compared more favorably with the Continent. They do appear, however, somewhat to have bettered his absolute status by putting a floor under his earnings in the form of a minimum wage. Nevertheless, such improvement as he has experienced seems more to be a product of steadier employment than betterment in rates. The prewar employment record is appalling. The data given in table 6 scarcely require elaboration. What is shown for the years between wars is a state of chronic unemployment which is partially, but never fully, relieved by wastage from the industry.

The net product of such conditions, long sustained as they have been, is a mood of bitter and uncompromising warfare. In its details it is involuted, tortuous, and difficult to follow, and very complicated and deceptive in its manifestations. Disputes are rarely what they seem, and all issues in dispute between managers and men are cast into the framework of local conditions where a long tradition of hostility—centered around personalities, peculiarities of pit conditions, and a thousand and one aspects of social life and working experience—frequently renders even the questions at stake largely obscure, if not, indeed, wholly inexplicable to the outside observer. One will gain

TABLE 6

NUMBERS INSURED AND UNEMPLOYED IN THE COAL INDUSTRY

Year	Persons insured[a]	Total unemployed	Unemployment rate
	thousands	thousands	per cent
1923	1267	39	3
1924	1259	72	6
1925	1233	198	16
1926	1226	...	..
1927	1199	221	18
1928	1116	252	23
1929	1075	177	16
1930	1069	219	20
1931	1047	298	28
1932	1045	355	34
1933	1024	339	33
1934	982	281	28
1935	939	241	25
1936	896	199	22
1937	868	130	15
1938	858	133	16

SOURCE: Wilson, *New Deal for Coal*, p. 17.
[a] The figures cover all persons aged 16 and over to 1927 and all persons aged 16-64 thereafter.

more of a feeling for these intangibles by reading, for example, such a novel as *Charity Main*,[45] than by perusing any amount of the vast statistical outpouring on the problems of the industry.

In its larger outlines, however, the story can be told in the record of strikes and lockouts. How bad the record is may be seen by perusing the data given in table 7, which shows that nearly half the time lost in all strikes and lockouts in British industry are attributable to coal mining alone. This record speaks for itself. But there is another record which is less eloquent in a statistical way, but which virtually all authorities agree is equally significant, and that is the slow and cumulative growth of more or less subconscious habits of sabotage—"sabo-

[45] Mark Benney, *Charity Main: A Coalfield Chronicle* (London, 1946). See, in particular, chapter ix, "The Sack."

tage" because it is in truth a definite, widespread and general withdrawal of efficiency, and subconscious because it has become so deeply ingrained in the habit patterns of the average worker and in the tactical maneuvers of trade union officials, that restriction is virtually second nature. As such, furthermore, it appears in part as a reflection of, and reaction to, technical backwardness, managerial slovenliness, and excessive concern over making quick returns for the owners. "Nearly every manager with whom I have spoken," writes the author of *Charity Main*, "has admitted that the underground layout of his pit, after twenty years of snatch working and 'quality grading,' has become an unmanageable honeycomb of ill-kept roads such as to make efficient underground transport impossible. Ventilation is bad, lighting is worse, and research to improve these and other technical deficiencies almost non-existent." Above-ground operations and office routines are conducted in a similar manner. The inevitable result of such indifference on the part of management towards improvement or efficiency of output is that it shall be reflected in a similar attitude on the part of the men. When this attitude becomes set in an environment of unrelieved hostility between managers and men, sabotage soon becomes elevated to a canon of virtue.

Flight from the industry.—A further result of these conditions is a slow but cumulative wastage of man power attached to the coal-mining industry. This has been particularly true in certain of the so-called depressed areas, most notably South Wales.[46] But to some degree or other, it is true of the entire industry. Those who can leave the industry have, in increasing numbers, been leaving mining villages in search of employment elsewhere, and recruitment of new, and in particular younger, workers has become steadily more difficult.

Higher wages and better working conditions during and following the war and the later advent of nationalization have done something to offset this tendency,[47] but it remains still as a critical problem. For example, three separate coal fields—suggested by staff members of the National Coal Board as typical of conditions ranging from bad to good—were visited by the writer in 1948 and in one only could be found miners who would permit their own children to go into the mines if any other possible alternative could be found at all. In one South Wales mine

---

[46] "During the depression South Wales lost 400,000 men from the countryside who went to seek work elsewhere." Davis, in *Hansard*, Vol. 418, col. 737. Many of these men came from the mining villages.

[47] See pp. 124–125 following.

TABLE 7

DISPUTES IN THE COAL MINING INDUSTRY, 1926–1939

Year	All disputes		No. involved (gross)[a]		No. of men involved in coal as of total disputes	Working days lost by disputes		Working days lost by miners as percentage of all man-days lost
	All industries	Coal mining	All industries	Coal mining industry		All industries	Coal miners	
1926	323	1	2,751,300	1,050,000	38.2	162,233,000	145,200,000	89.5
1927	308	110	114,200	73,000	63.9	1,174,000	688,000	58.6
1928	302	97	124,400	83,200	66.1	1,388,000	452,000	32.6
1929	431	153	533,800	78,500	14.7	8,287,000	576,000	7.0
1930	422	150	308,700	148,600	48.1	4,399,000	663,000	15.1
1931	420	147	491,800	281,000	57.1	6,983,000	2,848,000	40.8
1932	389	111	382,000	52,400	13.7	6,488,000	287,000	4.4
1933	357	112	138,100	72,300	52.4	1,072,000	446,000	41.6
1934	471	143	134,100	73,300	54.7	959,000	364,500	38.0
1935	553	217	279,000	199,700	71.6	1,955,000	1,368,000	70.0
1936	818	270	322,400	181,800	56.4	1,829,000	852,000	46.6
1937	1,129	457	610,200	392,500	64.3	3,413,000	1,496,000	43.8
1938	875	363	275,300	173,600	63.1	1,334,000	697,000	52.2
1939	940	404	337,300	205,800	61.0	1,356,000	565,000	41.7

SOURCE: Wilson, *New Deal for Coal,* pp. 36–37.
[a] Including those employed in more than one dispute.

there had not been a single application for a job from a man under twenty years of age in two years. In a central Yorkshire area a Labour party organizer with over twenty years organizing experience in this field, and herself wife of a miner with forty-two years experience underground and mother of thirteen children, including four sons in the mines, gave it as her opinion that none of the miners in that region would think of allowing their sons to go into the pits if they could do anything at all to prevent it.[48] The women—mothers, wives, and sweethearts—felt even more strongly on the matter. The Coal Board has found that in many districts school teachers and ministers of the gospel advise boys against going into the mines, and girls against becoming miners' wives. Part of this is now due, of course, to the possibility of obtaining other employment elsewhere; but most of it is due to conditions in the mines and the mining villages—including the bitter legacy in the memories of the long-resident mining population.[49]

Such success as the Coal Board has had in reversing the trend has come only in part from betterment of conditions, and promises of still further improvement. It is the housing shortage, rather than any actions or promises of the Coal Board, which has kept the younger men in the mines. Miners get priority on new housing, and lack of living quarters elsewhere makes it impossible for the younger generation to leave for other jobs. Since most of the smaller mining villages provide few, if any, other occupational outlets, there is nothing for most of the younger men to do but to go into the mines. This pressure, which will last as long as the housing shortage is acute, but not longer, has been somewhat reinforced by special inducements to remain in the mining industry, including extra food allowances and exemption from military service. These, however, are conceded to be of short-term potency only. Sooner or later they will lose their capacity to retard flight from the industry unless a vast, comprehensive, and far-reaching overhauling of the industry is effected which is at once coextensive with the entire range of the technological, sociological, and morale issues involved.

The critical need for coal production in Britain.—"In Peace and War alike," Lloyd George said in a now famous address before a Miners' Conference during the First World War, "King Coal is the paramount

---

[48] "The recruitment of younger men to the mines...offers a major problem in modern conditions, since today so large a proportion as 43% of the men employed are over forty years of age." C. G. Lancaster, *Facts and Ideas About Coal* (London, Conservative Political Centre, 1948). Colonel Lancaster was the leading opponent of nationalization.

[49] For details of this picture see the Forster Committee, *First Interim Report* (H.M.S.O., 1942), p. 20, and remarks by Seymour Cocks in *Hansard*, Vol. 392, col. 796.

Lord of Industry. Not only does it enter into every article of consumption and utility, but it is our real international coinage. When we bring goods, raw materials, and food from abroad, we pay in diamonds—only they are black."[50] Coal is the primary—almost the sole—energy source for all British industry, transport, communication, and household heating and cooking, it is the principal source of raw material for many of the newer branches of the chemicals industry,[51] and it has been in the past a very important export commodity. Table 8 is, accordingly, very interesting, for it provides a rather crude picture of Britain's central

TABLE 8

ANNUAL PRODUCTION AND CONSUMPTION OF COAL
(in million tons)

Year	Production	Consumption		Manpower
		Inland	Export[a]	
1913..............	287	193	94	1,017,000
1938..............	227	181	46	782,000
1946..............	189	180	9	697,000

SOURCE: *Labour and Industry in Britain,* V (1947): 185.
[a] Includes bunkers.

industrial dilemma. The downward trend in coal production since 1913 has been more or less continuous, and while fuel economies have largely, if not wholly, offset tonnage declines in internal consumption, nothing has been able to prevent the decline of the relative importance of coal in the export trade.

By rough estimate, were it possible to achieve a return of exports to the 1938 level it would mean in current value terms a contribution to the favorable balance of trade of approximately £100,000,000, or about one-fifth of the trade deficit being incurred at the time of the coming of the Marshall Plan in the summer of 1948. Even more important, however, is the effect of the shortage of fuel on the British export drive in manufactures, and its lack precludes even the discussion of possibilities of maintaining or increasing the domestic standard of living. The shortage of coal in 1947 was clearly the major limiting factor in the over-all national postwar reconstruction effort. Since 1947 industrial reorganization has assumed the more important role.

[50] Cited in James Griffiths, *Coal, Between Two Wars,* with a Foreword by Will Lawther, President of the Mineworkers' Federation of Great Britain (Labour Party, n.d.), p. 7.
[51] See chapter v following.

Thus the picture presented by coal upon the Labour government's advent to power was that of an industry disorganized and failing at the very time when on its health and vigor depended both British production and the success of the export drive, and through these, the possibility of molding the national economy along lines which would promote rising national prosperity in the socialist commonwealth of the future. This made quick, significant and comprehensive action necessary, with no other alternative than a further deterioration of British economy with its consequence of disastrous Labour government failure. The action chosen was nationalization.

The Case for Nationalization

But why nationalization? A first, and overwhelmingly important reason why this solution should have been sought by the Labour party is that it had long been a leading plank in the party platform. The party was committed, in short, so completely and absolutely to seeking this solution that virtually any other action would have been unthinkable. Yet, although nationalization in one form or another, and applied to one industry or another, had been featured in Labour party discussions from the earliest days of its activities, and a Labour M.P. had in 1913 presented, at the request of the Miners' Federation, a bill for nationalization of mines, its official interest in coal nationalization goes back only to the First World War. At the sixteenth annual conference of the Labour party, in 1917, the first clear-cut statement of this principle was made in a resolution "that the Government should at once take over all coal and other mines, work them as a national enterprise, and appropriate to the nation all rents and way leaves."[52]

The real campaign, however, was launched in 1920 when, following publication of the Sankey Commission report, there began what was known as the "Mines for the Nation" campaign, constituting a joint effort of the executive committee of the Miners' Federation, the parliamentary committee of the Trades Union Congress, and the executive committee of the Labour party. A nation-wide propaganda campaign in favor of nationalization of the mines was undertaken, and was financed to the amount of £4,500 contributed in equal proportions by the three bodies. This led to a series of ninety-six demonstrations organized

---

[52] *Report of the Sixteenth Annual Conference of the Labour Party* (Manchester, 1917), p. 117. The first T.U.C. reference to nationalization of coal came in 1890. See "President's Address," by William Matkin, in *Report of the Twenty-third Annual Trades Union Congress* (Liverpool, 1896), p. 28.

in conjunction with the local trade union and Labour forces in most of
the cities and large towns throughout the country. The following resolution, approved by the joint committee, was submitted and adopted at
every demonstration.

This Meeting declares:—

1) That the coal of the country forms an obvious necessity to national life,
and that its ownership should therefore be vested in the community.

2) That the Mines, Machinery, and other means for the production and distribution of Coal, being essential to the industry should also be owned by the
country.

3) That the direction and conduct of the Coal-mining industry, being of vital
importance to the workers in the industry and the Coal-consuming public,
should be under the control of the National District and Pit Committee, representative of the national Government and the various classes of workers, including those engaged in the managing, technical, commercial and manual processes.

4) That the objects to be sought by National Ownership and Joint Control on
the lines indicated are:—

a) To provide the maximum output of the Coal consistent with the provision of adequate protection for the workers engaged in this most dangerous
employment.

b) The introduction of labour-saving appliances on the widest possible
scale.

c) A more economic working of Coal mines consequent on the elimination
of the interests of private land and royalty ownership.

d) The remuneration of the workers in this industry on a scale commen-
surate with the dangers endured and sufficient to provide a healthy natural
life for all concerned.

e) The coordination of the distributive machinery of the trade by the
elimination of existing private interests and the substitution of municipal
and co-operative supplies at prices sufficient to cover costs of production and
distribution.

This meeting therefore calls upon the government to bring forward legislation for the National Ownership of Coal Mines and Minerals on the lines indicated, and in accordance with the recommendations of the Majority Report
of the Coal Industry Commission.[53]

In conjunction with the demonstrations, literature stating the miners'
case for nationalization was distributed on a scale that has probably
never been equaled in the history of the labor movement. A series of
twelve leaflets dealing with various aspects of the problem was drafted
and printed, and in the course of five weeks editions totaling 15,000,000
leaflets had been printed and circulated in an organized house-to-house

[53] "Report of the Executive Committee," in *Report of the Twentieth Annual Conference
of the Labour Party* (Scarborough, 1920), p. 7.

distribution in all parts of the country. New editions of *Facts from the Coal Commission* and *Further Facts from the Coal Commission,* originally published by the Miners' Federation and the Labour Research Department, were distributed. Other pamphlets were circulated in large numbers.[54]

The arguments set forth in the 1920 resolution were repeated with monotonous regularity in subsequent Labour party congresses. From congress to congress the only variation was to be found in the shifting of emphasis upon one or another of the three basic demands contained in the 1920 declaration: (1) Nationalization of royalties; (2) nationalization of collieries; and (3) workers' participation in control of whatever administrative machinery should be established under nationalization. The first of these demands was met by the nationalization of royalties under the Conservative government in 1938. The third was destined to be more or less completely sidetracked by both the Conservative and Labour parties, though the effect of doing so was to leave a very bitter taste in the mouths of the miners when nationalization of collieries was finally brought about.

How completely the second demand had come to dominate Labour party inner councils can be seen from the statement of the 1945 platform declaration, *Let Us Face the Future,* which limited itself to the following statement on coal: "For a quarter of a century the coal industry, producing Britain's most precious national raw material, has been floundering chaotically under the ownership of many hundreds of independent companies. Amalgamation under public ownership will bring great economies in operation and make it possible to modernise production methods and to raise safety standards in every colliery in the country."[55] The goal, that is to say, had shifted from nationalization to achieve socialist and workers' control over a basic industry, to nationalization in order better to effect technical rationalization. Not, of course, that the former excludes the latter, but that the latter may very well be conducted in such a way as to ignore, if not actually exclude, much of the former.

This shift in emphasis is consistent with a second reason for Labour's insistence upon nationalization, namely the fact that the various government investigating committees, from the days of the Sankey Commis-

---

[54] Among others, 50,000 copies each of a 32-page pamphlet *The Mines for the Nation,* being reprints of articles on the nationalisation of the mines written by members of the Coal Commission, and an 8-page pamphlet, *Workers' Control in the Coal Mining Industry,* were circulated.

[55] *Let Us Face the Future,* p. 6.

sion to the end of the Second World War, had been unable to find any
other effective alternative to the disorganized conditions which had so
long plagued the industry. Most of them had sought to avoid this way
of putting the matter. The Samuel Commission rejected nationalization because it found "no scheme that will withstand criticism," and
because "we perceive grave economic dangers; and we find no advantages which cannot be attained as readily, or more readily, in other
ways," and confined itself to recommending amalgamations of existing
mining properties and the establishment of a National Fuel and Power
Committee whose role it would be to "exercise functions that would be
advisory and not executive" on a continuous basis, and for the purpose
of effecting technical reorganization of the industry by a step-by-step
procedure.[56]

Without reorganization of the industry, satisfactory solution of
problems of wages, hours, and working conditions on an enduring basis
were clearly impossible. In part the great strike of 1926 resulted from
this failure. In partial recognition of this fact, the Coal Mines Act of
1930 hoped to solve the problems of bad labor relations by establishing
a National Wages Board, supplemented by a Joint Standing Consultative Committee "representing the two national federations of owners
and men"; of profitability by a system of coördination in markets
centered around joint selling schemes with power to fix prices over wide
areas; and of disorganization by the setting up of a Coal Mines Reorganisation Commission with power to encourage and, under certain
circumstances, actively to promote amalgamations. Though subsequently reinforced by supplementary legislation, the total effect of
these measures was to leave the industry substantially unchanged with
respect to the leading problems which had given rise to the legislation.

Such was substantially the picture when the war broke out in 1939.
Upon failure of the industry to respond to the mounting demands made
upon it by the conduct of war, the government proceeded in 1942 to
take over general management of the industry along lines which were
highly reminiscent of the recommendations of the 1919 Sankey report.
A sort of partial nationalization was carried out in keeping with recommendations made in a white paper, Coal (Cmd. 6364, 1942). This
small, compact report is of considerable interest since both its declared
objectives and proposed machinery of organization were to exercise a
great deal of influence on the legislation which Labour was to shape

[56] Samuel Report. See, in particular, pp. 29, 30, and 73.

some three years later for thoroughgoing nationalized control of the industry for peacetime purposes.

The government was "to take full control over the operation of all coal mines and the allocation of the coal raised." In the discharge of his duties the responsible Minister was to

be assisted by a Controller-General, who will have as his chief officers:—

i) A Production Director, responsible for efficiency and volume of production.

ii) A Labour Director, responsible for welfare, safety, health and working conditions of coal-miners, and allocation of labour.

iii) A Services Director, responsible for distribution and allocation of coal.

iv) A Finance Director, responsible for all financial arrangements, including advice on coal prices.[57]

The Minister was to form a National Coal Board which would meet under his chairmanship, and be representative of the regional coal boards to be set up under its auspices, pit managers and technicians, and coal distribution and consumption. The functions of the Board were to consider:

i) the general planning of production, including the allocation of district and regional targets;

ii) the best means of securing the highest efficiency of the coal-mining industry and any improvement in machinery or methods of operation whereby output may be increased;

iii) the provision of supplies, equipment and materials for the conduct of mining operations;

iv) matters relating to the maintenance of man-power and labor productivity, including the enrolment of new entrants and the instruction, training and advancement of boys and youths;

v) all matters affecting the welfare of the mine-workers, including housing, transport and feeding facilities; and

vi) questions of health and safety and, in particular, such occupational diseases as silicosis and nystagmus, with a view to providing all possible preventive measures, clinical treatment and rehabilitation.[58]

The regional coal boards were to "advise the Controller on matters concerning output and the means of achieving maximum production" and were to be made up of appointed representatives of "coal-owners, miners, managers and technical staff." Under this arrangement the powers of the Controller were far-reaching indeed. "With the advice of the Regional Coal Board, the Controller will have, and exercise, full

[57] *Coal*, Cmd. 6364, p. 5.
[58] *Ibid.*, pp. 5–6.

and undivided responsibility for the policy and general conduct of mining operations in his Region. With the assistance of his staff, he will exercise general supervision over all the mines in the Region; and this supervision will be sufficiently close to enable him to give such directions as will ensure the most efficient operation of the industry, treated as a whole, in the Region, including directions as to concentration, grouping of pits, and other necessary matters relating to mining operations. At the same time, it is undesirable that the Controllers should be burdened with the details of day-to-day management of the pits. This will be left, as it is to-day, in the hands of the managers, who will continue to be the servants of the owners, though subject to removal at the instance of the Controller, should he deem that course necessary."[59]

Wage problems only were excluded from the purview of the Controller. Thus, with the exception of the clause relating to the residuary authority of the owners, and the fact that ownership claims on net income remained undisturbed, the white paper confirmed the view of the Sankey Commission that the industry must be unified on a national basis. Subsequent history of war control seemed also to bear out the further majority conclusion of the Sankey Commission that effective reorganization without change of ownership was assured of little chance of success. The final judgment of the Sankey Commission, delivered in 1919, might well be taken as a summary of the cause of the failure in the Second World War significantly to improve either technical or human conditions in the mines, when it said, "any system of bureaucratic control of capitalist enterprise—which is sometimes mistaken for the very different proposition of public ownership and administration—is apt to be irksome and irritating, alike to those whose profits are controlled and to the consumer; and however preferable to the absence of any regulation whatever, to combine, in fact, the drawbacks of both systems with the full advantages of neither."[60]

The fact that the suggestions of government commissions for solving the problem of coal after the First World War were the products of the thinking of the Conservative party provided the Labour party with its third, and ultimately most weighty, reason for insisting on the nationalization of the industry. The commissions, Labour leaders held, were merely reflecting in their recommendations the desires of the mine owners, and it was the expression of these desires which had already brought the mines into their lamentable condition. Water could not rise

[59] *Loc. cit.*
[60] *Sankey Report, Reports and Minutes of Evidence,* Vol. I, p. xix.

above its source; no more could the recommendations of the mine-owners be better than the quality of ownership and management which had created the chaos of which it was now imperative to rid the industry.

There were two closely related lines of reasoning behind this view. The first and less sophisticated was the popular and widely held opinion among miners all over England that the owners were making fantastically high dividends out of a process which meant simultaneously the gutting of natural resources and the bleeding white of a labor force which it neglected and rendered everywhere derelict. The high profits meant rich living for an idle and irresponsible few at the expense of the ruination of hundreds of mines and millions of men. "Every miner," said Will Lawther, president of the Mineworkers' Federation of Great Britain, "loathes his industry because of its owners."[61] Replying to Anthony Eden, spokesman for the Opposition in debate on the nationalization bill, a Labour M.P. summarized the view when he said, "May I say to the House and to him, that I believe that private ownership itself, by its 'get rich quick' policy in the late nineteenth century, coupled with an almost complete disregard of human feelings, has done more to bring this Bill before this House today than anything else . . . Many of the non-working and non-mining directors," he went on to say, "are concerned only with getting a good dividend. I could recite from my own knowledge the names of companies that paid for years dividends of 10, 15, 20 or 30 per cent and never put a single penny piece to a reserve fund. They wanted to take it all out in dividends. When the depression came, they were on their hands and knees, asking for help to keep the pits going. What have managers said to me time after time when I have been in their pits? 'I know it wants doing but I cannot get the capital. The Boards are not prepared to give it to me. They say they are not concerned about long-term policy.' "[62]

Table 9 gives Harold Wilson's data on profits earned within the industry.[63] These data, of course, are given as submitted by the industry for wage-ascertainment purposes and are not believed by the miners to represent the real profits earned. Furthermore, they undoubtedly include funds ploughed back into the industry; in some fields investment during the thirties was quite heavy. Nevertheless, this record of earnings, which (after 1938) are also exclusive of the £4,430,000 set aside annually as royalty earnings under the royalties nationalization meas-

---

[61] Quoted by Harold Wilson, op. cit., p. 154.
[62] Hansard, Vol. 418, cols. 773–776.
[63] Op. cit., p. 211.

ure of 1938, is quite remarkable for an industry which (when taken as a whole) was suffering from so many crippling disabilities of so many different kinds—technical, economic, social—throughout the entire period covered by the data given in the table.

TABLE 9

Total Credit Balance of the Coal Industry 1920–1943[a] as Returned for Wage Ascertainment Purposes

Year	Total profit	Profit per ton disposable commercially	
	thousands of pounds	s.	d.
1920	34,092	3	4
1921	......	..	..
1922	10,357	0	11¾
1923	26,149	2	2
1924	13,336	1	2
1925	2,858[b]	0	3¼[b]
1926	......	..	..
1927	−5,378	−0	5¾
1928	−9,778	−0	11
1929	4,238	0	4½
1930	3,782	0	4½
1931	2,811	0	3½
1932	1,493	0	2
1933	2,178	0	2¾
1934	4,128	0	5
1935	5,204	0	6¼
1936	9,812	0	11½
1937	13,347	1	2¾
1938	13,594	1	4
1939	16,944	1	7½
1940	15,806	1	7
1941	16,150	1	9¼
1942	10,223[c]	1	1½[c]
1943	11,758[c]	1	4[c]

Source: Wilson, New Deal for Coal, p. 211.
[a] Based on returns covering approximately 97 of the industry.
[b] After subvention.
[c] Subject to additions to bring it up to the guaranteed profit.

The more sophisticated version of the Labour case against the plans of the owners takes this profits record as a point of departure, and argues, in effect, that both the history of the industry and the more specific of the mineowners' proposals for therapy center in three major types of change, no one, or combination, of which is adequate for purposes of meeting the problems which the industry faced at the end of the war. The three suggested types of change are (1) proposals for mollifying labor with respect to wages, working conditions, and aspects of social security, (2) price-fixing arrangements, and (3) amalgamation of collieries.

The history of efforts along these lines, the argument runs, is one of self-evident failure. The various proposals, of which the two most important and most recent were the Foot Plan,[64] and the program put forward by the Tory Reform Committee[65] have all been examples of "too little and too late."

The policy of the industry on the first point, Labour argues, has always been to make the minimum concessions possible to labor, with the result that now only by acceding to labor's maximum demands can its resentment be quieted. As for prices, it has been the industry's practice to resort primarily to regional and interregional cartel-like measures, which, so far as they affect costs at all, tend to fix prices at a level which will make the most inefficient and marginal business profitable. The result is to freeze the existing uneconomic patterns of company organization, colliery operation, and coal distribution—the very things which are in need of being unfrozen, and completely shaken up from top to bottom—instead of improving them. More than that, after resorting to such devices, the industry expects a continuation of the extensive subsidies received from the government during the war; subsidies which were used for stabilizing dividends and not for revamping operations. Finally, the owners are prepared to suggest combination but have a record of resisting amalgamation unless it enables them to exercise monopolistic powers over the industry to the detriment of both labor and the consumer. What the industry, when needled into action by events, has attempted to do, in short, is to do the wrong things and to do them with the wrong ends in mind.

It is not necessary here to review the evidence for and against these arguments. In general, the only pronounced changes in the industry which might be claimed to meet the problem of technological obsolescence were always subsumed under plans for achieving amalgamation. Actual amalgamation had, of course, made some rather rapid strides. One estimate finds that twenty-five coal combines could, on the eve of nationalization, "account for an annual output of 124 million tons, or about 65% of the total output of coal in this country, about 18% being

---

[64] *Plan for Coal: A Report to the Colliery Owners* (London, 1945).
[65] Quintin Hogg, Col. Lancaster and Peter Thorneycroft, eds., *Forward by the Right: A National Policy for Coal* (Tory Reform Committee, 1944).

produced by the two largest combines alone."[66] But amalgamation, while accompanied in some outstanding cases (e.g. Powell-Dufferin, Amalgamated Anthracite, Fife Coal Co.) by measures of technical rationalization, served mainly as a point of departure for more effective efforts to exercise monopolistic controls. Hence the fact that industry and Conservative proposals placed such heavy emphasis on amalgamations tended to condemn their plans, rather than to recommend them, in Labour's eyes.

Of the two major plans emanating from the employer side, the one issued by the Tory Reform Committee is the more important and comprehensive in its avowed intentions. It contains a set of proposals which are almost identical in their general intention with those which underlay the government's plan when taking over the operation of the coal mines in 1942.[67] It differed in only two important particulars. First, there was to be a miner's charter, and, second, the government was to possess power to make amalgamations compulsory. The charter was to guarantee a "minimum based on five days a week of 7½ hours a day" for a minimum regular labor force, improved piecework systems, arbitration machinery for handling disputes, and improved pit production committees. The amalgamations proposals required submission to the Coal Commission by the various coal regions of schemes which, when approved by reorganization committees—themselves to be representative of the Mining Association and the Miners' Federation—would be put into operation by the industry on its own initiative. Failing that, they were to be effected under direction by a regional controller.[68] The Reid report, issued just a year later, might be considered, as in actuality the Conservative leaders in Parliament did look upon it, as a mere spelling out in detail of the technical implications of the Conservative party's *Forward By the Right* pamphlet.

Nevertheless, even this proposal was unacceptable to the Mining Association, and the recommendations of their own Foot report served to give notice that such changes as might occur in the mining industry in the future would be made on their own terms, and at their own convenience; above all, there could be no truck with compulsory amalgamations. And so after a quarter of a century of agitation for change,

---

[66] Heinemann, *op. cit.*, p. 175. See also pp. 120–123 for a schematic outline of three of the larger combines, and pp. 176–195 for an itemization of the holdings, number of employees, and political interests of the 25 combines producing over 2,000,000 tons of coal a year.

[67] See above, pp. 100–102.

[68] Hogg, *op. cit.* See, in particular, recommendations 14–21 on the labor charter, and 4–11 on amalgamations.

mounting from all sides, the future was to be left to the policy determination of a few large collieries serving the interests of indifferent
absentee owners and accepting the guidance of bankers and other financial interests!

At least this was the picture as Labour saw it at the end of the war,[69]
and so it came about that when debate opened on January 29, 1946,
on the second reading of the Coal Industry Nationalisation Bill the
mineowners' suggestions were impatiently swept aside. "As a matter
of fact," said W. Foster, Parliamentary Secretary to the Ministry of
Fuel and Power, "the Foot Report and the Reid Report are 20 years too
late, and the Foot Report is the death-bed repentance of the mineowners. They have allowed this industry to drift into its present position. Now we are faced with the problem of reorganising it from top
to bottom."[70] "I can hardly recall a Session of Parliament," said Shinwell in opening the debate, "in that period [the past 20 years] without
either a coal Debate or a coal crisis, yet every treatment prescribed to
cure the malady, whether by the Sankey, Samuel or Coal Reorganization Commissions, has resulted in failure. Nor should we forget that a
Conservative Government nationalised the royalties, which it was
thought would achieve amalgamations, thus promoting reorganisation.
Yet all these devices have proved fruitless, as indeed would the proposals of Mr. Robert Foot or the Tory Reform Committee, for the
reason that private interests within the industry, with a few honourable
exceptions, will not move unless they are forced, that vast sums are
required to meet the cost of reconstruction and that no comprehensive
method of reorganization is possible without cutting across a great mass
of private interests and privileges."[71]

Though they make fascinating reading, it is not necessary to summarize here in detail the arguments on the proposed bill. In the main
the facts on the condition of the industry as detailed in the Reid report
were taken as definitive, though in the course of the debates a wealth
of supplementary and elaborative data were added. The over-all picture was that of a vital industry which was in an alarming state of
disorganization, and whose continued deterioration—despite notable
technical advances in various mines—carried with it the most disastrous implications for the postwar economy of Britain. Drastic and

---

[69] See, e.g., Harold Wilson, op. cit., pp. 166–169 on "The Quality of Management," pp.
169–181, "The Technical Revolution and the Directoral Organisation of the Industry," and
pp. 184–186, "Private Versus Communal Interests."

[70] Hansard, Vol. 418, col. 885.

[71] Ibid., cols. 703–704.

thoroughgoing reorganization was needed. The miners were bitter and wholly unprepared to accept any solution except nationalization.[72] For better or for worse, the political necessities of the situation did not permit any other solution or any attempt to find an alternative. The miner's "status in the nation's economy was on a par with that of the lowest class in the Hindu caste system;"[73] he must be helped out of this deplorable situation or he would, like a blind and angry Sampson, pull down the edifice of British economy and destroy himself in the process.

Furthermore, the scale of reorganization required to meet the needs of the situation could only be carried out on a national basis, and as such involved capital investment far beyond the resources of the mineowners. The government, Shinwell said, proposes "to make advances up to £150 million for the first five years, for the purpose of capital expenditure, and for the provision of working capital."[74] The public could not be expected to put up the necessary funds in the form of government subsidies or guarantees only to get a cartelized industry in return.[75] But even more important, without nationalization even technical reorganization would do no good, for it was absolutely necessary to instill a sense of coöperation and copartnership in the minds of labor, and the starting point for this was nationalization itself. "The managements and the miners in the main will decide whether this new and hopeful chapter is to end well or ill." To "miners and managements," but "particularly to the miners," Morrison felt he must say, "emancipate yourself from the understandable inhibitions created by the past, emancipate yourselves from the mentality thrust upon you by a crude capitalism" and learn "to become co-operators and partners in a great and worthy adventure for the common good."[76] Nationaliza-

[72] "The demand for the nationalization of the mining industry has been born out of almost a century of struggle between the miners and the mineowners for a decent standard of life, with the result that bitterness has entered the soul of the miner and he is now determined that this struggle must end by a change in the ownership of the industry. It can only end in this way because the bitterness which is in the soul of the miner makes it impossible to reconcile his struggle with the interests of a privately-owned industry. The miner has made up his mind about this, and so did the electors at the last General Election." W. Foster, in *Hansard*, Vol. 418, cols. 892–893.

[73] C. F. Grey, *ibid.*, col. 753.

[74] *Ibid.*, col. 711.

[75] "Is the private capitalist going to put millions into the British mining industry? I do not think so. I think he will be very slow coming forward. The queue will not be a long one to put money into the British mining industry. The money would have to be got from the State or be State guaranteed. What happens then? (Hon. Members: "Ah.") What would private enterprise, of which the Conservative Party is so proud, do then? It begins to get where some of it has been getting too often. It begins to join the poor law queue. It begins to feel it cannot be enterprising without having the State behind it. If the State is going to be behind it and provide the financial guarantees, then let the State own the show." Herbert Morrison, Lord President of the Council, summing up for the Government, *ibid.*, col. 966.

[76] *Ibid.*, col. 972.

tion, in short, was *the* indispensable prerequisite to fundamental change in the organization of the coal industry.

Was there, in the final analysis, any other way open at all? Labour thought not. The answer was found, they held, in the fact that the mine-owners actually had put forth no real case against nationalization. The argument of the Opposition "proved to be nothing more than a damp squib," said Foster, "there was so little opposition to the principle of the Bill, and so few points made by Hon. Members opposite, that I have had great difficulty in finding any argument to refer to in speaking this afternoon."[77] At least they had no constructive solution to offer,[78] and it is hard to see what alternative they could put forward.[79]

The Opposition did, however, have a great deal of criticism to offer. Quite aside from the issue of nationalization as such—which, as Eden had confirmed, was not the issue at stake—the question was whether or not this solution was the best solution for the admittedly sick industry which British coal mining had become. Two general sets of arguments were forthcoming. The first related to the application of the principle of nationalization to coal. The second, conceding the in-evitability of nationalization on political grounds, centered around a series of specific criticisms of the bill as presented.

The first set involved three principal points. Of these, the leading argument, detailed at great length by Colonel Lancaster for the Opposi-tion, was that nationalization of such an industry as coal could only mean an unbearable bureaucratization which would ramify *ad nau-seum*.[80] Next, the industry would be further unsettled by reorganization precisely at the time when it would complicate reconstruction to the maximum.[81] And the result, finally, would be not socialism but "a closed industrial system of State Capitalism."[82]

Except for the first of these three points—a stock argument out of a conventional laissez-faire position which could not be too vigorously pushed by opponents who were prepared themselves to offer in substi-

[77] *Ibid.*, cols. 886, 888.

[78] "... it is evidently the technique of the Opposition to avoid at all costs themselves ad-vancing a positive and constructive policy. I do not say that the Opposition is obliged to do so; they are an Opposition, and they are perfectly entitled to oppose and attack. Neverthe-less, throughout this Debate they have been unable to put forward a positive policy of their own, and they have not done it" Herbert Morrison, *ibid.*, col. 960.

[79] The Tory *Industrial Charter* (Conservative and Unionist Central Office, 1947) seems to bear out this judgment when it says that "Rather than proposing complete denationalisation of the coal industry we would examine and modify the methods by which the Socialists will have tried to run it." p. 25.

[80] See his argument, *Hansard*, Vol. 418, cols. 753–759.

[81] The best statement of this position is that in C. G. Lancaster, *Facts and Ideas*.

[82] Harold Macmillan, in *Hansard*, Vol. 418, col. 957.

tute nothing other than amalgamation, cartel controls, and state aid to the industry—this first set of contentions does not appear to have been advanced with much enthusiasm. Not so, however, the second set. If, on grounds of *Realpolitik,* nationalization must be conceded as inescapable, there was a great deal to say about the bill proposed. Superficially, much heat appears to have been generated in this aspect of the debates, and many of the clauses were bitterly disputed in the eighteen days of proceedings of Standing Committee C, the committee to which all bills are referred for recommendations as to revision. Yet seen in broad perspective, only two matters in controversy stood out in bold relief.

The first of these had to do with the makeup and organization of the Coal Board itself. The second, and, to the Opposition, much more important point, was the rate of compensation. The importance of both can be more readily grasped, and the implications for long-run policy more easily visualized, through an examination of the bill as it finally emerged from the legislative mill.

The Coal Industry Nationalization Act, 1946

The bill to nationalize the coal industry was introduced in December and became law on July 12, 1946.[83] The vesting day, when the newly established Coal Board was to take over, was given as January 1, 1947. The act begins by establishing a

National Coal Board which shall, on and after the primary vesting date, be charged with the duties of:

a) working and getting the coal in Great Britain, to the exclusion (save as in this Act provided) of any other person;

b) securing the efficient development of the coal-mining industry; and

c) making supplies of coal available, of such qualities and sizes, in such quantities and at such prices, as may seem to them best calculated to further the public interest in all respects, including the avoidance of any undue or unreasonable preference or advantage.[84]

The Coal Board was to be a body corporate which would consist of the chairman and eight other members, all of whom "shall be appointed by the Minister of Fuel and Power from amongst persons appearing to him to be qualified as having had experience of, and having shown capacity in, industrial, commercial or financial matters,

[83] The full title reads: "An Act to establish public ownership and control of the coal-mining industry and certain allied activities; and for purposes connected therewith." 9 & 10 George 6, Chap. 59. It is a rather lengthy document, consisting of 65 clauses and 55 pages of text, supplemented by three schedules which fill 23 pages.

[84] *Coal Act*, Clause 1, p. 1.

applied science, administration, or the organisation of workers."[85] In
formulation and review of policy, the board is to be assisted by two
advisory consumers' councils, to be known, respectively, as the Industrial Coal Consumers' Council, the members of which are likewise to
be appointed by the Minister from persons broadly representative of
industrial and domestic distributors and users, and the Domestic Coal
Consumers' Council, representing various classes of ultimate consumers.[86] The Miners' Welfare Commission is to be reconstituted as a
ten-man commission, appointed by and responsible to the Minister,
with "power to act as agent of the Board with respect to any matter
relating to the health or welfare of persons in the employment of the
Board."[87]

To the Coal Board, as outlined in the first schedule,[88] some coal mining assets are "to be transferred without option," some "at option of
the Board or of owners," and some "at option of the Board or of owners
subject to arbitration in the case of objection." Broadly speaking, the
first included all worked and unworked coal deposits, other minerals
which could be worked only in conjunction with coal deposits, and all
collieries, coke ovens, manufacturing plants, power-generating facilities, and colliery properties in transport, storage, merchandising, office,
and other equipment used primarily in connection with colliery production. The second group of assets included stores, supplies, facilities,
housing, farming properties, and other assets which the board might
find useful in conducting its operations, or which former owners—finding such holdings remaining as truncated remnants after transfer of
the first type of assets—might find it desirable for the board to take
over. The third class consisted of ancillary properties, e.g., facilities
for loading and storage, brick and manufacturing plants. These were
similar to properties in the second group, except that their disposal
might involve issues of policy which would make arbitration necessary.
Only one set of activities formerly engaged in by colliery owners which
could seriously affect the problem of supplying adequate amounts of
low-cost fuel was excluded. That was coal distribution.

The procedure to be followed in granting compensation for properties so transferred was adequately summarized by Shinwell in opening debate on the bill in Parliament, when he said that compensation

[85] *Ibid.*, Clause 2, p. 3.
[86] *Ibid.*, Clause 4, pp. 4–6.
[87] *Ibid.*, Clause 40, pp. 40–41.
[88] "Assets to be Transferred to the Board," pp. 56–62.

will be "settled in three stages and the amounts will be determined by an impartial body at each stage. There is also provision for impartial arbitration at the final and most important stage where the individual colliery concern is most directly affected. First of all, there is the global sum which is to be determined by the tribunal working under the agreed terms of reference set out in the White Paper. The global sum will be divided up by a Central Valuation Board into district allocations which, in their turn, are divided up among the individual undertakings within each valuation district. The only way to complete the division among the various undertakings is to value them, add up the total values, and scale them all up and down in due proportion so that the total then agrees with the global sum."[89]

The method of arriving at the global sum is as follows: "Those assets which are at present taken into account in district wage ascertainments will be priced by a special Tribunal, which will adopt much the same procedure as that used for coal royalties. This Tribunal has to decide two things—first, the net yearly revenue that the owners might reasonably be expected to earn in future if the mines were left in their hands; and secondly, the number of years' purchase to be applied. The Tribunal will then multiply the maintainable annual revenue by the number of years to arrive at a global sum of compensation."[90] This global sum will then be divided among individual holders as indicated by Shinwell, and paid in government stock issued by the Treasury.[91] Ancillary properties were to be separately evaluated, but by a similar method.

The remainder of the clauses of the act concern primarily details which elaborate the means of implementing compensation and the organization and functioning of the prospective Coal Board. In the short run, the problem of compensation was the most important issue in controversy simply because this property transfer was the heart of the formal act of nationalization. But this was a once-for-all problem; once settled, there was no returning to it. It was no less important an issue because of this fact, however, and it illustrates again the essentially businesslike approach of the Labour government.

But a businesslike approach does not necessarily mean that everybody is satisfied. The principle adopted was that of a "willing buyer to a willing seller." Not all Government supporters were satisfied with

[89] *Hansard*, Vol. 418, cols. 709–710.
[90] *Nationalisation of Coal*, p. 2.
[91] *Coal Act*, Clause 23, pp. 30–31.

the bargain. One Labour M.P. felt that the willing seller was being paid a very high price for a dying industry.[92] Another feared that the industry might be paid "a going concern price for a white elephant."[93] A third pointed out that in the twenty-year interval from 1893 to 1913, some "£332,000,000 was paid in profits and royalties, although the capital invested in the industry was only estimated at £130,000,000" and commented that "two and a half times the invested capital in profits in 20 years is not bad going."[94] Another, finally, believed that the Foot report showed that the owners were "prepared to sell their out-of-date and inefficient plant to the community . . . for immediate payment of a high price and in cash" whereas, "on a dispassionate examination of the facts and figures" he marveled "at the generosity of His Majesty's Government . . . In fact," he went on to say, "I am inclined to think the mineowners ought to be penalized for the inefficient manner in which they have administered this national asset, this real wealth of Britain."[95]

The Opposition, on the contrary, insisted that the formula of a willing seller to a willing buyer was a mockery, since the buyer was not willing either to sell or to take the price offered. Dalton, for the Government, felt that the latter point was answered by the fact that the City in general approved of the terms of compensation,[96] and on several occasions the point was made that the Mining Association had accepted the global method and therewith the principles underlying the value determination.[97]

Without going into details on the methods applied, suffice it to say that the total arrived at for the global sum came out to £164,660,000, and that this was then equated to 1946 salable output to arrive at a compensation figure of 18s. 5d. per ton. Claims were then put forward on a district basis against this sum, the total running to £270,160,000, ranging from a low of 13s. 4d. per ton for Bristol to 91s. 3d. for South Derbyshire, and averaging 30s. 1d. per ton—or better than 50 per cent above the government figure.[98] Since the global sum cannot be exceeded the claims must be scaled down and readjusted among districts so that they add up to a sum not to exceed that amount, a result which, since the claims are presumably based upon what mineowners believe to be

[92] John R. Thomas, in *Hansard*, Vol. 418, col. 947.
[93] George Brown, *ibid.*, col. 771.
[94] F. Fairhurst, *ibid.*, col. 741.
[95] C. R. Hobson, *ibid.*, cols. 786–787.
[96] Hugh Dalton, Chancellor of the Exchequer, *ibid.*, col. 815.
[97] *Ibid.*, cols. 791–794, and cols. 813–814 where the statement is disputed.
[98] *Daily Telegraph and Morning Post*, April 23, 1948.

market values, is not too far short of the guess made during the debates that compensation would average about 50 per cent of such value.[99]

Since, however, under the conditions prevailing at the end of the war, market values of individual colliery securities were to a considerable degree determined by cartel pricing policies permitted, when not in fact consolidated, by government wartime price regulations, and since coal properties were being quoted at prevailing levels partly because of the anticipation of valuation at a higher figure—not to mention Government subsidies—no very serious injustice appears to have been done the owners by Labour's application of fair value on the willing seller to willing buyer footing. The mildness of the stock market reaction, and of commentary in the financial and Opposition press seems to bear out this conclusion.

More serious in the long run, however, was the matter of the organization and functioning of the Coal Board. Discussion of the Coal Board, both in the course of debate on the bill and since its establishment, has been highly critical, and criticism has been forthcoming, frequently on identical points, from both the right and the left. Five points have been underscored: The board has been accused of (1) undue and unworkable centralization of authority, (2) being so organized with relation to the Ministry of Fuel and Power that it is difficult, if not impossible, adequately and quickly to locate and place responsibility for making policy decisions, (3) adopting an unworkable principle of functional organization which fractions executive responsibility at every level and makes interfunctional coördination difficult at all levels, (4) inability to arouse a sense of coöperation and responsibility among the miners because of lack of any means of securing worker representation above the pit level, and (5) selecting for key offices former colliery operators who are unable, by training and general background, to run the coal mines in a manner very much different from that which has prevailed in the past. To these as a sixth point

[99] *Hansard*, Vol. 418, col. 814. By the middle of 1949 the district valuations (21 districts) had been announced by the Central Valuation Board, and it was estimated that two more years would be required before the amounts to be received are likely to be known. Meanwhile favorable district valuations (especially South Wales and Scotland) had the effect of enhancing prices of colliery shares of companies resident in those areas, and of lowering prices where the valuations were less favorable (Yorkshire, Durham, Notts, and Derbyshire). "Considering, however, the extent of the rise in prices of colliery shares as a whole over the past three years, the adjustments conceived to be called for in the light of the awards were mostly small. A big element of surprise has been the prospect that the ancillary assets of the undertakings might provide sums—outside the amount of the so-called global compensation—which in particular cases might be substantial. The Central Board's allocations do not throw any light whatever on the relative importance of these assets." *Times*, Feb. 4, 1949.

might be added that the board is able to operate indefinitely without adequate control and check from Parliament.

The last point need not detain us here, since it is a criticism that relates not only to the Coal Board, but to the device of the independent public corporation which the Labour government, under the tutelage of Herbert Morrison, has chosen for all its nationalized undertakings, and is best understood in the context of a comparison and contrast of its several applications. The criticisms fall into two categories, the first three criticisms having to do mainly with principles of management and the discharge of executive responsibility, and the last two being concerned primarily with the problem of labor morale. The two sets of criticism, however, are very closely related to each other, and in the aggregate they constitute such a weighty argument for change that it is probable that they will force a general reorganization of the whole system of control and operation. They have been particularly emphasized in the criticism of Colonel Lancaster, spokesman of the Opposition, who submitted his suggestions to Shinwell in great detail.

The act left the Coal Board with the power to implement its authority by any method it saw fit, subject only to approval of the Minister of Fuel and Power. The method chosen[100] is shown in chart 1. The board is made up of a chairman, a deputy chairman and seven functional directors, there being a separate director for each subsidiary department: Finance, Labour, Legal, Manpower and Welfare, Marketing, Production and Scientific Work. The chairman is, as the name implies, a chairman of a committee called the National Coal Board, and not a manager who is assisted by a series of functional division heads. The board discharges its functions in detail through the instrumentality of regional, or divisional, boards, there being one such board for each of the eight chief coal divisions of Britain. (See map 1.) These regional boards are patterned after the National Coal Board, to which they are responsible, as are also the forty-eight area offices which are responsible to them. The National Coal Board may issue instructions to the divisional boards, and the divisional boards in turn to the regional offices, but delegation by functions in the line of authority is less from the board and more from the functional head—i.e., Finance, Labour, etc.—downward. Substantially the same rule holds from the area offices down to the collieries themselves.

[100] For a description of the steps taken to get the Coal Board organized before vesting day, see National Coal Board, *Annual Report and Statement of Accounts for the Year Ended 31st December, 1946* (London, 1948).

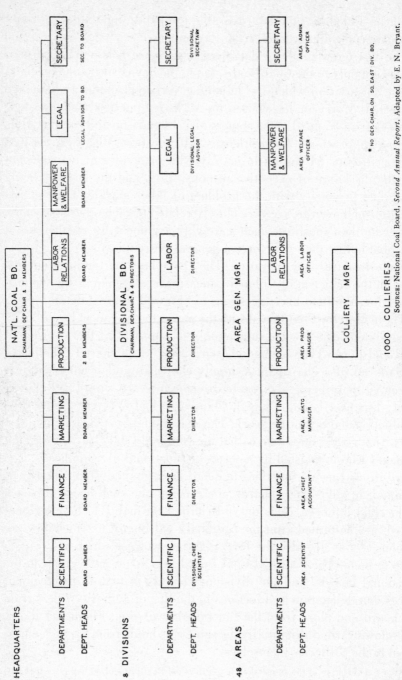

Chart 1. Organization of the National Coal Board.

SOURCE: National Coal Board, *Second Annual Report*. Adapted by E. N. Bryant.

HEADQUARTERS

NAT'L. COAL BD.
CHAIRMAN, DEP CHAIR & 7 MEMBERS

DEPARTMENTS	SCIENTIFIC	FINANCE	MARKETING	PRODUCTION	LABOR RELATIONS	MANPOWER & WELFARE	LEGAL	SECRETARY
DEPT. HEADS	BOARD MEMBER	BOARD MEMBER	BOARD MEMBER	2 BD. MEMBERS	BOARD MEMBER	BOARD MEMBER	LEGAL ADVISOR TO BD.	SEC. TO BOARD

8 DIVISIONS

DIVISIONAL BD.
CHAIRMAN, DEP.CHAIR.* & 4 DIRECTORS

DEPARTMENTS	SCIENTIFIC	FINANCE	MARKETING	PRODUCTION	LABOR	LEGAL	SECRETARY
DEPT. HEADS	DIVISIONAL CHIEF SCIENTIST	DIRECTOR	DIRECTOR	DIRECTOR	DIRECTOR	DIVISIONAL LEGAL ADVISOR	DIVISIONAL SECRETARY

48 AREAS

AREA GEN. MGR.

DEPARTMENTS	SCIENTIFIC	FINANCE	MARKETING	PRODUCTION	LABOR RELATIONS	MANPOWER & WELFARE	SECRETARY
DEPT. HEADS	AREA SCIENTIST	AREA CHIEF ACCOUNTANT	AREA MKTG MANAGER	AREA PROD MANAGER	AREA LABOR OFFICER	AREA WELFARE OFFICER	AREA ADMIN OFFICER

COLLIERY MGR.

1000 COLLIERIES

* NO DEP. CHAIR. ON SO. EAST DIV. BD.

The system of organization, consequently, is that of a pyramid of functionally organized committees (called boards at the upper two levels) lacking definite responsibility to a single executive authority at each level. Since there are no clean-cut principles of delegation of authority from one level to the other, every policy issue in dispute at the level below may be remanded for decision at the level above. At each higher level it is either decided by the functional officer, acting independently of his compatriots at that level, or is referred to the next higher committee or board. The tendency, consequently, is to combine lack of coördination at each level—the common fault of all functional organization—with undue centralization. Since all policy decisions tend to go upward under such a system every issue must be carefully defined and fully documented with the appropriate data, and the result of this emphasis is to require masses of reports, investigations, and paper work.

More than that, when each level is managed not as a coördinative function subject to executive decision, the most trivial issue may be remanded step by step all the way to the top. This situation is further complicated by the fact that at the two upper levels neither the board nor the functional authority above appoints the board or functionary below. On the contrary, all members of the National Coal Board and of the eight divisional boards, are appointed by the Minister of Fuel and Power and are, in the final analysis, responsible only to him. Thus at the two upper levels there is necessarily a question mark placed behind every decision of every officer, and this question mark can never be entirely removed until the Minister has spoken. One result is that technically a regional board is in a position to by-pass the national board. This situation is still further complicated because it is not clear from the act whether the board can formulate policy at all. The Minister may make regulations respecting appointments, procedure, and many other matters, and it is also presumably possible for the two advisory consumer councils completely to by-pass the board by making their recommendations directly to the Minister without prior consultation.

Thus the act combined three bad principles of organization: unduly high degree of centralization, failure adequately to delegate authority at each level, and functional control. This situation has subsequently been partially overcome by two changes. One change has been to constitute the chairman, vice-chairman and one board member without

DIVISIONAL H.Q.

1. EDINBURGH
2. NEWCASTLE UPON TYNE
3. SHEFFIELD
4. MANCHESTER
5. ARNOLD
6. DUDLEY
7. CARDIFF
8. RICHBOROUGH

COALFIELDS

SCOTTISH

NORTHERN

NORTH EASTERN

NORTH WESTERN

EAST MIDLAND

WEST MIDLAND

SOUTH WESTERN

SOUTH EASTERN

Source: National Coal Board. Adapted by E. N. Bryant.

Map 1. National Coal Board divisions.

portfolio into a policy committee acting for the board as a whole; a second has been to elevate the area general manager from a position of *primus inter pares* to one where all the area specialists are definitely responsible to him, and so that he becomes, consequently, "clearly responsible for all that happens in his area."[101] Far more than this, however, seems to be necessary, as seems subsequently to have been recognized by the establishment of an investigating committee to make recommendations for improving the efficiency of the board.

The second set of criticisms is more difficult to appraise. Clearly the problem of morale was a sort of cumulatively spreading, implacable, and cancerous growth that required swift surgical action. But merely to nationalize, as the Liberal leader, Major Lloyd George (former Minister of Fuel and Power) pointed out in a remarkable statement, will have but little psychological effect on the miner unless he sees a decided change in management. "On the date when the State takes over the mines what will be the effect on him," he asked. "He will go to the same pit and get the same lamp from the same man; he will go into the same cage, will probably be lowered by the same man, and when he gets to the bottom, he will, if he is in certain parts of the country, see the same expression on the face of the pony. He will see the same manager, the same deputy, the old roadway, the same coalface, and, on the Friday, he will probably be paid by the same man. But because the boss is different, it is said, it will make all the difference. I thought that one of the difficulties in private industry was that the boss was so remote, but here you are getting the one who will be much more remote, and I am not at all sure that he will be quite as good as the previous boss."[102]

This was a remarkably accurate forecast of what was to follow vesting day. The sit-down strikes at Grimethorpe and Waleswood, insignificant in themselves, became immensely important as symptomatic of the feeling of the miners that changeover might mean a distinction without difference so far as relations between management and men were concerned. "The same old faces" was a common comment among miners, indicating doubt that management was any more sympathetic than it had been before, and it was paired with the complaint that remoteness of the decision-making authority from the workplace made prompt settlement of disputes even more difficult than it had been before. Two sets of events appear to have still further worsened the

---

[101] *Economist*, May 22, 1948, p. 847.
[102] *Hansard*, Vol. 418, col. 879.

effect. The first was the principle, incorporated in the act, of no direct miner representation on the control boards or authorities above the pit level.[103] The second was the selection of leading colliery owners to fill top policy-making offices. The first chairman of the board was Lord Hyndley, not only a leading colliery owner, but a man whose experience was entirely in the sales and finance aspects of coal mining, and who was known in the trade as a sales-minded, not a production-minded, man. Since technical modernization and morale improvement were the two major problems which gave rise to the Labour solution of nationalization for the problem of coal, the net result of the Coal Board's manner of interpreting its authority seems to have been greatly to handicap its capacity to move quickly to the necessary solutions.

ACHIEVEMENTS AND PROBLEMS OF THE COAL BOARD

The principal properties taken over by the Coal Board on vesting day consisted of:

1400 collieries—of which 400 are "small mines owned by the Board but operated by private concerns under license from the Board"—with "their stocks of products and stores, their plant and equipment—waterworks, power stations, etc."

30 manufactured-fuel and briquetting plants, "of which 10 were not transferred under the Nationalisation Act but were bought from the Ministry of Fuel and Power."

55 coke ovens, producing "over two-fifths of the country's 'hard coke,' i.e., other than gas coke" along with tar-distillation plants, benzol-recovery, sulphuric-acid, and pyrites-recovery plants.

85 brick works and pipe works.

225,000 acres of farm land, freehold and leasehold, and in addition, sports grounds, undeveloped housing land, and the land on which colliery buildings, sidings, etc. stand.

[103] The National Consultative Council was established with 27 members, "six appointed by the Board, nine by the National Union of Mineworkers, nine by the National Association of Colliery Managers, and three by the National Association of Colliery Overmen, Deputies, and Shotfirers. Divisional councils were to be set up with 20 members and area councils with 12 members, appointed by the same organizations in varying proportions. Then there were to be colliery consultative committees, consisting of the colliery manager, as chairman, the area agent and colliery lodge secretary of the miners' union, and the mining agent as *ex-officio* members, two underground officials and one surface official appointed by the manager, one deputy elected by the deputies by secret ballot, and six elected representatives of the five main grades of workers (including face-workers).... The committees discuss everything connected with the pit—reconstruction projects, details of the production, amenities, welfare, absenteeism, training, transport, equipment, and a hundred other subjects." Nevertheless, it was primarily a management-dominated device of a purely advisory sort and "Interest does not often appear to extend beyond the committee to the bulk of the men. The continued large number of unofficial strikes and high rate of absenteeism show this. Indeed the problem of securing the interest and coöperation of the workers as a whole is the most difficult the committees have to contend with." *Times,* Jan. 15, 1949.

141,000 houses, of which 86,000 are freehold. "In addition there are more than 2,000 farmhouses and agricultural cottages. Some colliery villages with their village halls, schools, etc. are owned entirely by the Board."
Other buildings include the Board's "own offices, ships, hotels, swimming baths, a cinema and a slaughter house."
Miscellaneous assets "vary from private railways, wharves and coal-selling depots to retail milk rounds, a holiday camp, and a cycle track."[104]

That the Board should have taken over this vast array of properties, improvised a workable organization (the task of building an organization to take over the mines had been begun with the appointment of the members of the National Coal Board on July 15, 1946), and shown both an increase in output from 188,618,900 tons to 196,587,100[105] tons and an increase in recruitment which raised the mining manpower from an annual average of 696,660 to 711,380[106] in a single year and at an operating loss of only £6,187,300[107] is surely no small achievement in view of the circumstances under which it began operations. These circumstances were certainly not favorable. Not only the conditions of the mines, the state of workers' morale, and the self-imposed handicaps of an organizational character outlined above, but all other circumstances, were very nearly as inauspicious as possible when it began operations. Distributed coal stocks were at an all-time low of 8,500,000 tons when it took over on January 1, and on January 23, barely three weeks later, it faced one of the most severe winters in British history. The combination of heavy snow and freezing lasted until near the middle of March. In many places pit production suffered; in some areas it was difficult to get the miners to and from work. Rail movements of coal were slowed up, and in some places brought to a standstill. At one time 12,800 railway wagons loaded with coal could not be moved in the East Midlands division alone. Canals in many parts of the country were frozen for five weeks. Power and gas supplies were curtailed for both industrial and domestic use, with the result that many industries operated on severely limited rations. Exports were temporarily eliminated almost entirely.

Nor was this all. Labour believed, rightly or wrongly, that it was politically impossible and socially undesirable to resist the miners'

---

[104] National Coal Board, *Annual Report and Statement of Accounts, for the Year Ended 31st December, 1947* (London, 1948). This is the second annual report (the first since taking over) of the Coal Board and is an extremely thorough, well-organized, frank and readable report of some 255 pages. It will be referred to hereafter as *2d An. Report.*
[105] *Ibid.*, table, pp. 214–215.
[106] *Ibid.*, table, pp. 232–233.
[107] *Ibid.*, balance sheet statement, p. 146.

demands for the five-day week, a concession which the board found had meant a production loss of some 14,000,000 tons of coal.[108] A further estimated loss of 1,652,000 tons was incurred through stoppages caused by disputes, resulting in some 1,635 unofficial strikes, most of which arose over situations that had been inherited from the past.[109] Colliery costs—as a result of wage adjustments and other changes and improvements involved in beginning the long, slow about-face toward bettering work conditions and improving relations between manage-

TABLE 10

DEFICIT SHOWN BY COLLIERIES AND ANCILLARY OPERATIONS, 1947

Colliery losses	9,203,905
Ancillary profits [a]	3,016,605
Operation loss	6,187,300

Other Transactions

Loss on imported coal	1,697,992
Provision for compensation for loss of office	406,192
Other income	156,177
Interest and interim income payable	15,120,586
Net deficit	23,255,586

SOURCE: *Economist*, July 17, 1948, p. 113. Compiled from *2d An. Report*.
[a] Profits on ancillary activities such as brickworks, coke ovens, etc.

ment and men—were increased by some 4s. 3d. per ton.[110] Because of the general fuel shortage it was found necessary to keep open many small, inefficient, and unprofitable firms, although the board might have been able to save a very large sum by closing them.[111] Largely as a result of the fuel crisis, coal had to be imported and sold at a loss, the loss being debited to the Coal Board to the amount of £1,697,992.

There were additional and miscellaneous handicaps of a minor character. But on the acid tests of getting more coal from the mines and more men back into them, the board's operations during its first year were on the favorable side of the ledger. Financially, the picture is somewhat less bright. The net deficit of £23,255,586 was made up as shown in table 10.

As table 11 shows, operating costs varied a great deal from area to area, ranging from a profit of £7,510,621 for the East Midlands to a loss of £10,741,405 for the Southwest (Wales) areas. The average loss

[108] *Ibid.*, table, p. 121.
[109] *Ibid.*, table, p. 17.
[110] *Ibid.*, table, p. 123.
[111] *Ibid.*, p. 84.

of one shilling per ton might easily have been made up had not the Minister of Fuel and Power scaled down proposed increases in price submitted by the board. Gains in wages and other items to labor over the year were estimated at £62,000,000, a figure which was alone nearly three times the annual deficit. Even as matters stood, during six months of the year, including the first four months of the fuel crisis, the board was able to show a small profit on its colliery operations.[112]

TABLE 11

OPERATING COSTS, PROFITS, LOSSES, AND WAGES BY MINING DIVISIONS, 1947

Division	Costs per ton		Profit or loss		Total profit or loss	Average weekly earnings (including allowances in kind)	
	s.	d.	s.	d.	£	s.	d.
Scottish	38	9.4	1	5.0	1,574,097	137	10
Northern	45	3.4	−4	10.8	−8,795,131	142	3
Northeast	38	7.6	..	3.9	623,022	137	3
Northwest	46	10.0	−2	4.5	−1,570,675	132	8
E. Midlands	33	0.4	4	4.0	7,510,621	155	6
W. Midlands	37	9.4	3	2.7	2,686,092	133	0
Southwest	52	11.7	−9	7.0	−10,741,405	128	5
Southeast	52	11.9	−7	1.6	−490,526	139	5
Average	51	3.0	1	0.0	−9,203,905	138	9

SOURCE: *Times*, July 15, 1948. Compiled from *2d An. Report*.

Such were the extenuating circumstances, and such the more important of the immediately calculable results. But these alone do not give an adequate picture. The board was charged with the duty of getting not small, but large results, and not with appearing to break even, but of effecting an overhauling of operations from coal face to coal consumer which with due regard to improving economic and social conditions for the miners would increase efficiency and reduce prices. The deficit was as low as it was mainly because prices had been increased as much as they had. A deficit could have been turned into a profit by increasing the prices still further, but it would have been a wholly illusory gain so far as the nation's total economy was concerned. The far more important question was what the board had done by way of beginning the essential reorganization and what its plans were for the future.

[112] If exports reached 16,000,000 tons, it was estimated that 1948 might show a net profit of £5,000,000. *Times*, Nov. 9, 1948. But where profits are shown, the amount shown is largely a matter of the way the accounting is set up.

Superficially, a good deal was accomplished. Seventeen of the smaller and less-efficient pits and two drift mines, employing 2,680 men, were closed, and 2,136 men transferred to other collieries. Some 550 short-term projects "were begun and about 340 of them were completed. In carrying them out nearly 1,500 conveyors were installed in the mines during the year, and 32 locomotives were put to work underground. In this way the number of conveyors installed was increased by 16 per cent, and the number of locomotives by 55 per cent." The board estimated "that as a result of the purely technical measures, that is introduction of machinery and reorganization of pits, there was an increase in coal production of 3.5 million tons during 1947."[113] First steps were undertaken on long-term plans for more fundamental change. The act had authorized the expenditure of £150,000,000 for this purpose. By the end of 1947 the board had begun work on projects totaling £36,000,000, had approved schemes involving £22,700,000 and had actually expanded £2,900,000. Some of these schemes are very impressive indeed,[114] although practically all of them were inherited from plans of the now superseded private enterprise. Few new plans are in evidence, although it is a bit early to expect many to be worked out, for such operational plans take time.

A good deal was undertaken which had long-run implications, but which is less easy to summarize. Among these are such changes as the regrouping of mining areas; beginning the work of reducing to the minimum rail cross-hauling; grading of coals and reduction of dirt and slate content (particularly from open-cast mining); the attempt to forecast demand by domestic and foreign consumers, by regions, industries, and types of coal; improving marketing and distribution of coal; and promoting research on mining operations and fuel utilization. These are all compactly and intelligently summarized in the second annual report, and they give the impression of both solid achievement and a determination to get ahead with the job of technical reorganization.

On the personnel and welfare side of its activities, the board has also some notable achievements. Absenteeism, one of the best general indications of human relations in industry, is down from an annual average of 15.95 for 1946 to 12.43 for 1947, and there is fairly clear indication of what might be a possible beginning of a secular trend

[113] *2d An. Report*, pp. 40–41.

[114] For a detailed summary, "Reconstruction Schemes and New Collieries," see pp. 111–115 of the *2d An. Report*.

downward.[115] Recruitment of former miners from other industries showed marked increases (28,960 as against 19,817), indicating that mining had acquired drawing power against other industries,[116] and from residential training centers (15,865 as against 4,835), indicating a higher level of technical competence among the new entrants. There was also some increase in the employment of juveniles under eighteen (14,654 as against 12,691), and this may indicate a reversal of the former trend of the younger generation away from the mines—particularly so, since this increase took place in face of the raising of the school age from fourteen to sixteen.[117]

Viewing the first year of operations, the board shows no inclination to overstate its achievement. Nor, to its very great credit, does it show a tendency to gloss over the more obvious of its shortcomings and failures. Yet there is much to question when answers do not—perhaps cannot, for they go back to fundamentals—spring readily to the eye. Questions of principle cannot be answered favorably by reference to passing successes, nor unfavorably by citation of short-term failures and inadequacies. Such answers come only with long-term success or ultimate failure. Yet answers may be seen—or at least apprehended—in the dim outlines of the environmental conditions and the premises which make up the general background against which the parade of the present takes place, and which will, unattended, come ultimately to exercise a coercively shaping and compelling influence on the conduct of day-by-day events. In general the fault seems to lie, not in the way coal was nationalized, but in the absence of any thought for a general system of coördination.

Four possible weaknesses stand out. They are based upon broad considerations and are here offered for whatever they may be worth. First, it is difficult to escape the conclusion that there is actually not very much planning, anywhere within the industry, of a type which sees its detailed solutions linked to those of the other industries with which its fortunes are interlocked, and to other activities of the communities concerned. Other agencies, to be sure, such as the Ministry of Town and Country Planning, are charged with carrying forward such joint

---

[115] *Ibid.*, table, pp. 236–237. Absenteeism is still, however, above the prewar level. Hugh Gaitskell has expressed the belief that absenteeism is largely responsibe for the fact that production was up by only 50,000 tons a week in 1948, whereas it was necessary to increase it by 250,000 tons. *Times*, Nov. 22, 1948.

[116] This trend was reversed in the latter part of 1948, when recruitment not only began to fall off, but the industry began to suffer net manpower losses. *Times*, Nov. 10, 1948.

[117] *2d An. Report*, table, p. 47.

programming, yet there seems to exist no plan, or machinery for improvising a plan; nothing but bits and pieces. This might not matter if it were not that the coal act calls for a fundamental and far-reaching reorganization of the coal pits, the coal regions, and all phases and aspects of coal distribution and use throughout the entire country.[118]

Can the planning necessary to carry through the reorganization of coal on such a basis as this take place without some effective planning of relationships with other industries? The answer is obviously, "No." Yet—aside from some more or less unrelated *ad hoc* committees, improvised commissions and liaison research and advisory agencies of one sort or another—none of the necessary machinery for such planning exists, and no planning is taking place. Scarcely a reference to this problem appears in the report. Yet it is *the* central problem to be faced the instant one's eyes rise above the level of emergency measures taken to solve emergency problems.

A second weakness has already been dealt with above, and lies in the awkward and cumbersome organization of the Coal Board. A number of proposals for reorganization have been forthcoming. A leading Opposition critic, Colonel Lancaster, believes that since "The National Coal Board has created an organization which . . . is too highly centralized, and this elaborate administrative superstructure has damped initiative and enterprise, deprived local management of the stimulus of responsibility, slowed down decisions, and caused confusion and antagonism," there must occur a drastic simplification. The cure would be to create complete executive autonomy within twenty-one districts, by setting up in each an autonomous mining corporation which would be "an entity created by Parliament, and not by the Coal Board itself," with the areas being "industrial concerns in their own right." Their boards "would presumably not be appointed by the National Coal Board itself, but by the Minister." To do something of this sort, he feels, is now "essential if the industry, and with it the whole of our national economy, is not to break down."[119]

A somewhat similar argument was advanced by Sir Charles Reid, author of the Reid report, following his resignation from the Coal

---

[118] "The essentials of a national plan," according to E. H. Browne, chief mining engineer of the National Coal Board, are "(a) the allocation of production between the coalfields, the determination of the extent and rate of reconstruction work, the allocation of capital expenditure, and, where necessary, the redistribution of labour; and (b) the preparation of a coordinated scheme of reconstruction in accordance with (a)." The right kind of a plan should lay out a program of development covering all phases and aspects of mining, fuel distribution and use, and it should look ahead at least 15 years. *Times,* Aug. 27, 1948.

[119] As summarized in the *Times,* Nov. 24, 1948.

Board in the summer of 1948. Finding the Coal Board's decisions to be based primarily on the basis of "expediency rather than of principle," and feeling that the size of the various divisional undertakings was too great to "be adequately managed, technically reconstructed, and brought into economic daylight by boards so ill equipped in commercial and industrial experience" he proposed that "these great undertakings . . . be decentralized and re-formed into manageable entities." In place of the present eight regional divisions he would put twenty-six corporations, each of which "should be managed by a board consisting of a managing director, who would have full executive power, a general mining manager, and a sales manager." There would also be some part-time members, all appointments would be made by the National Coal Board in London, and each corporation, subject to general policy directives from London, would constitute an otherwise independent and autonomous unit. Properly organized, he believes, to carry through the necessary reconstruction, it will be possible in time "approximately to double the present output per manshift."[120]

Meanwhile, the Coal Board's own investigating committee (Burrows committee) has proposed a number of additional changes, mostly of a minor nature in connection with some clarification and simplification of the line of command, but its report is almost wholly lacking in suggestions for major change. It concludes with the obvious truism that "a sound scheme of organization does not in itself ensure efficiency" since "this can only come gradually as individuals engaged in management acquire the habit of working together and as suitable people are found or developed for the various posts."[121] Here, as elsewhere, the reaction of the board shows some indications of consciousness of the need for change, but in the main it appears, even to sympathetic critics who know it well, to be an overstaffed, unintegrated, and generally torpid body which even in the first year of normal functioning was in great danger of running afoul of all the well-known illnesses and shortcomings of excessively bureaucratic organization. During the first year its administrative and nonindustrial staff increased by 4,412 persons.[122] Many reasons are given for this increase, and some of them are quite persuasive. Nevertheless, the feeling is widespread among persons qualified to know that the board has shown a tendency to enlarge staffs without benefit of adequate definition of the functions to be performed,

[120] "The Problem of Coal," a series of four long articles in the *Times*, Nov. 21, 22, 23, and 24, 1948.
[121] *Home Affairs Survey*, Nov. 30, 1948, pp. 17–19.
[122] *2d An. Report*, table, p. 33.

to expand greatly the amount of paper work at all levels,[123] to establish new and poorly defined functions for which people have been recruited who possess little by way of special qualifications, and to send running around the country miscellaneous staff members on numerous, duplicative, and more or less unrelated missions. And so *ad infinitum*.

All this might be passed off as relatively unimportant, or a mere by-product of short-term readjustments were it not that it does not appear to the board actually to be much of a problem. The board seems to suffer from what has been dubbed "Coal Board mentality"—a general mixture of caution and complacency which permits it, for example, to move along in a slow and leisurely manner to technical reorganization; to gloss over such problems as that of coal distribution by what appears to be the improvisation of a complex and unwieldy machinery which not only uses, but seems to consolidate and perpetuate much of the present inefficient, disorganized, and thoroughly out-of-date apparatus of prenationalization days; to pour capital for reconstruction into areas such as South Wales out of proportion to prospects of technical improvement even when modified by considerations of population stability and the supply of housing and service facilities; and in general even to follow as a principle the old cartel pricing policies of prenationalization days. All such lines of policy implementation, of course, require independent evaluation, and there is no doubt a great deal to be said on both sides of the question in each case.

The general effect is for the board to set an unnecessarily slow and snail-like pace when great speed is required, to fail to see that all this is a reflection not only of difficulties which are inherent in the situations faced, but also of bad organization and the outlook of the Government itself, and in this mood to fail adequately to understand the need—if the preëminent and overwhelmingly important problem of morale among the miners is to be solved at all—of a complete revision of personnel policies and of the manner of interpreting policies to the miners. If the miner faces, as mine experts and miners both appear to agree, only, or primarily, nonproduction-minded people at the top policy levels, and narrowly production-minded people inherited from the old, hard-driving, and get-rich-quick days of the past at the lower levels, then the problem of morale remains insoluble.

[123] All persons at all levels outside the offices of the National Coal Board in Hobart House (London) interviewed during 1948 in three major mining areas made this same point. The estimated proportions of increase over the year in the number of reports, size and scope of the detail to be recorded, and amount of time required varied from three-fold to five-fold. Reference here is only to comments made by persons favorable to the nationalization act.

The problem of morale does in truth seem insoluble without a radical and far-reaching change in the Coal Board's approach to the problem. The early increase of output during the severe winter of 1947—an increase of over a million tons for the period of the worst freezeup—appears to have been misunderstood. It was, no doubt, a combination of new enthusiasm for nationalization and a spiritual rising to the occasion of a national emergency. Yet the fact that the early production rise was not sustained is highly significant. The Grimethorpe strike, which remained unsolved throughout 1947, was a far better expression of the second thoughts of the miners than most Coal Board people are inclined to think.[124] It was precisely because, as Major Lloyd George had prophesied, the miners saw in managerial positions nothing but "the same old faces," and that, apart from the pit committees (and to a limited extent even there), there was little sense of active copartnership with the Coal Board, or of power seriously to affect basic policy higher up, that the Grimethorpe strikers could hold out in defiance of special committees, the Coal Board, and even their own trade union.

Even this, however, is not the board's most important weakness. Overshadowing it is the fact that in general the Board's means of handling the problem of educating the miners to their new rights and responsibilities is awkward, largely negative, careless, disorganized, and amateurish. The Oxford summer school for miners, where some 450 miners, trade union leaders, and technical experts from mining areas all over the country meet with representatives of the Coal Board each summer for exchange of views and a close-knit analysis of various problems besetting the industry, is a major step in the right direction. But relatively little beside general, highly repetitive, and not very illuminating or persuasive exhortation reaches the rank and file. Even this little has come through a complicated network of cross jurisdictions, countermanded orders, bickering, confusing restrictions, and so on, in top Coal Board offices, and is rarely backed by a program which is sufficiently specific to make the reader or listener feel that it constitutes a compelling need for action.

---

[124] In January, 1946 the National Union of Mineworkers drew up a "miners' charter" containing a series of demands which mine reorganization was to concede. Several of these have gone into effect. Others, such as the two weeks' holiday with pay, have been refused. (*Times*, Dec. 18, 1949.) Too much has been made out of differences of opinion over details of this sort. But one impression rises unmistakably out of the disputes: the Coal Board is regarded by rank and file with considerably more doubt and suspicion than is at all reconcilable with the urgent need to secure the large increase in output which the miners have within their capacity to offer. That the initiative in the resolution of this problem must of necessity come from the Coal Board itself cannot possibly be escaped—irrespective of the merits of any specific dispute—by blaming the miners.

Thus it comes about that the almost total lack of responsibility, which widely placed observers find general among the miners, is a result as well as a cause of the Coal Board's failure to arouse more than a spark of early enthusiasm. Instead of seeing this, the tendency in board circles is to blame the miners instead of themselves. The case of the Wales-wood mine offers a good example. This sit-down strike occurred primarily, not for the reasons debated in public by the board and the strikers, but because of failure to realize, or realizing, to find an answer to, the fact that the closing down of the mine meant a wage reduction for the miners. The problem was not met and not diagnosed as seen by the men. It does not matter whether or not the men were in the right—on the main issue, which was the closing down of the mine and transfer of personnel to a nearby mine, they were clearly and unequivocally in the wrong. What does matter is the fact that the representatives of the Coal Board did not see the problem that faced the men, and that the miners felt that it did not see because it had neither the eyes to see, nor the desire to interpret sympathetically what it might have seen.

None of these four major weaknesses are incurable. They are serious only so long as the board fails to see and plan for their elimination. It is not, in other words, the existence of these problems, but the lack of self-criticism which may prove to be the board's great weakness. If the board continues in the future to balance its books, and to secure some slight increases in productivity, it will, on present showing, feel itself a success. But it may, on the contrary, be true that by the same token it will have proved a major failure, for the issue is increased production— not grudgingly, at a snail's pace, and in the dim vistas of time, but willingly, on a big scale, and with maximum speed, if Britain is to survive and Labour's program is not to end in disaster.

And this for three reasons. First, because coal is the center, foundation, and point of departure for the reorganization of the fuel and power economy of Britain, and because without this reorganization Britain cannot solve many of the more fundamental of the critical problems facing it during these early postwar years. Second, because failure to galvanize the miners into action in the Labour show-piece of the coal industry, where opportunity to do so was, and still is, golden, will mean a falling off of labor enthusiasm for reorganizing production methods in other nationalized industries, and for measures to improve morale in industries not to be nationalized. And third, because such failure means also the decline of political following in the critically important ranks of its current middle-class and professional supporters; should this situation eventuate it might easily exercise a chilling effect on much of their enthusiasm for the new order.

A real plan, the Coal Board has intimated on several occasions, is in the making. But if it comes with the ebbing of the tide it will already be too late. Britain cannot afford any significant loss of production, or pass up any legitimate means of enhancing efficiency, without suffering disaster. At this juncture the Coal Board is caught in a cul-de-sac of its own making; what lies ahead is no more nor less than an unexampled opportunity to make or break the whole of Labour's postwar program.

CHAPTER IV

Fuel and Power: Electricity and Gas

The great waste of fuel must be apparent to the most cursory observer; and the uses to which Fire is employed are so very extensive, and the expense for Fuel makes so consider-able an article in the list of necessaries that the importance of the subject cannot be denied. And with regard to the Economy of Fuel, it has this in particular to recommend it, that whatever is saved by an individual is at the same time a positive saving to the whole com-munity.—Count Rumford, *Essays*.

IN 1865 JEVONS nearly created a panic when he estimated that the coal resources of England "would be exhausted within 110 years from the year 1861."[1] Fear led to a wave of enthusiasm for conservation "which made fuel economy a fashion"[2] and resulted in numerous investigations to discover new coal reserves and to find ways and means of making better uses of available fuels. Much was done in the interim, but it was not until 1942, when England was no longer the industrial leader of the world but deeply involved in a bitter and exhausting struggle for survival, that concern over these vital problems led to the establishment of an authority charged with facing the issues in all their complex ramifications. The Ministry of Fuel and Power, said Shinwell in the opening debate on the Electricity Bill, was created in June, 1942, "to secure the effective and coordinated development of coal and to pro-mote economy and efficiency in the supply, distribution, use and con-sumption of fuel and power."[3]

Reorganization of coal mining naturally came first, not only because it was generally in a technically lamentable and socially deteriorating condition, but also because it was the foundation upon which both the fuel and power system, and in turn, the entire industrial system of Britain were based. Given this, "Obviously the next stage is to take appropriate measures to reorganize the electricity industry" for the simple reason that "the supply of electricity and, in particular, its dis-tribution, is at present organized on a basis which must be regarded as completely out of date. In due course, the gas industry will come under review and an appropriate measure for re-organization introduced into Parliament."[4]

---

[1] W. Stanley Jevons, *The Coal Question* (1865), cited by the PEP Report, *The British Fuel and Power Industries* (London, 1947), p. 59 [hereafter referred to as *PEP Report*].
[2] D. L. Burn, *Economic History of Steel-Making* (Cambridge, 1939), p. 10.
[3] *Hansard*, Vol. 432, col. 1406.
[4] *Loc. cit.*

As with coal, "appropriate measures" were to begin with nationalization of electricity and gas supply. The two acts which did this constituted the second step in the unified development of British fuel and power along modern technological lines. Once this step was taken, Labour believed that the possibility of evolving a national plan for coördination of fuel and power as a foundation upon which might be erected an adequate postwar industrial system, fully able to take care of the economic needs of a Britain dedicated to expanding mass standards of living, might then be at hand.

But the successive submission to Parliament of the "appropriate measures," first for electricity, then for gas, was destined to arouse a progressively more stubborn resistance. On the surface, this reception seems somewhat paradoxical. Both electricity and gas fall more readily than coal into the category of natural monopolies which are, to employ the American judicial *patois,* "peculiarly vested with a public interest." They share this distinction with other types of public utilities—sewage and water supplies, streets and highways, transport and telecommunications, and so forth—and proposals for their nationalization would seem, consequently, fated to meet only with an opposition which could readily be disarmed by analogy and logic.

That this should have been particularly true in postwar Britain is borne out by three other facts. First, public ownership of public utilities was widely extended and generally accepted by Conservative and Liberal, as well as Labour, supporters. Second, in the field of electricity supply, a serious inroad on private ownership had been made in 1926 when the Conservative government established the Central Electricity Board with authority to develop on a national basis a unified power transmission system. And, finally, municipal ownership of electricity and gas undertakings was widespread throughout England, and the advance of municipalization had not, at least since the First World War, appeared as a political issue to divide the national parties. If, consequently, nationalization of electricity and gas meant carrying out a similar policy on a national basis, precedent—in the shaping of which all the political parties of the past had had a hand—would seem to lie entirely on the side of the proposed changes and to give no support to those who opposed them.

Yet the Opposition was not disarmed. On the contrary, the growing bitterness and resourcefulness with which it contested each successive step in the argument showed that vastly more was at stake than appeared on the surface.[5] This impression is further reinforced by the observation that each side began debate by appearing to concede the principal argument of its opponents. Labour conceded that both electricity and gas were, in sharp contrast with coal mining, relatively modern, virile, well-managed and progressive industries. And the Conservatives conceded both the need and desirability of unified development, and the desirability of public ownership and the general success of municipal enterprise in these fields.

Thus these two nationalization proposals are almost as important for what they do not show directly regarding the contest over future nationalization as they are for what they offer in terms of a rounding out of the picture of Labour's plan for fuel and power.

THE ELECTRICITY ACT

The act establishing the British Electricity Authority (BEA) became law on August 13, 1947,[6] and the vesting day was set as April 1, 1948. Under the act the BEA was to supersede the Central Electricity Board in control of the transmission of electric power, and to take over all the properties of private companies and local authorities engaged in power generation for public distribution, and power distribution for the consuming public. It was not to engage in distribution itself, this function being discharged under the act by area boards operating under BEA general direction, nor was it to have direct control over the North of Scotland Hydro-Electric Board.[7]

With respect to transmission, the act merely transferred the national grid system from the Central Electricity Board to the BEA, and this involved no principles of ownership or function. The CEB, as pointed out above, was established by a Conservative government in 1926,[8] to

---

[5] Standing Committee E on the Electricity Bill spent twenty-four days on its proceedings, and Standing Committee D, thirty-six days making its official report on the Gas Bill as first presented. The first explored in detail every possible argument, and the second began with these to elaborate every conceivable objection to the extension of nationalization.

[6] The full title reads: "An Act to provide for the establishment of a British Electricity Authority and Area Electricity Boards and for the exercise and performance by that Authority and those Boards and the North of Scotland Hydro-Electric Board of functions relating to the supply of electricity and certain other matters; for the transfer to the said Authority or any such Board as aforesaid of property, rights, obligations and liabilities of electricity undertakers and other bodies; to amend the law relating to the supply of electricity; to make certain consequential provision as to income tax; and for purposes connected with the matters aforesaid." 10 & 11 Geo. 6, Chap. 54. The act, including 6 schedules, is 124 pages long.

[7] This board was established by the Hydro-Electric Development (Scotland) Act in 1943 to have sole responsibility for generation, transmission, and distribution of electricity. It is responsible not to the central authority (BEA) but to the Secretary of State for Scotland. Nevertheless, its functions are to be closely coördinated with those of the BEA.

[8] The Electricity (Supply) Act of 1926 received Royal Assent on December 15, 1926, and became operative from that date.

develop a national scheme of high-tension transmission lines which would span the entire island, and which would purchase power in bulk from selected generating stations for wholesale delivery to distribution outlets. Under its administration Britain developed what is probably the finest national grid system in existence. The main outlines were completed by the middle thirties. By 1944 this system was made up of 3,614 miles of 132,000-volt and 1,528 miles of 66,000-volt transmission lines having a transformer capacity of 13,422,750 kva, and it purchased from 141 selected stations, having a generating capacity of 11,254,081 kw., some 39,445,940,000 kwh. of current for supply to the distribution network.

The record of the CEB was one of outstanding performance in terms of adequacy of supply and economy of operation both in peace and war. During the war, however, there had developed a serious power shortage, and defense regulations had given the CEB authority to provide and operate generating stations. This situation brought into the open a feeling that had long been growing that the separation of generation and transmission was highly artificial, and that certain difficulties, both technical and accounting, could not be overcome without making the wartime arrangement permanent. In a supplemental memorandum issued by the Incorporated Muncipal Electrical Association in February, 1944, some of the advantages of transferring generating stations to the CEB were said to be:[9]

a) To facilitate the efficient planning and siting of new, and development of existing, generating stations by eliminating the limitations inherent in the existing dual interests in those matters.

b) To enable a properly planned and long-term programme of development in station design to be carried out.

c) To effect substantial savings in engineering costs by the avoidance of the existing duplication of effort in designing new stations or extending existing ones.

d) By comparison of operating results and methods to raise the general standard of operating efficiency.

e) To extend the field for the utilization of very low-grade fuels by the construction of power stations specially designed for such fuels and situated in the areas where they are produced.

f) To improve the standard of technical ability among power-station engineers, designers, and operators by organizing adequate training; by interchange of staff between various power stations to increase experience; and by enabling appropriate personnel to obtain experience in foreign practice.

g) To facilitate the attainment of a National Standard Bulk Supply Tariff.

[9] As summarized, *PEP Report*, p. 310.

h) To facilitate the investigation into, and possible development of, district heating schemes for the utilization of low-grade heat not at present used in the generating cycle, which, in the national interest, might be used for the heating of domestic and commercial premises and for industrial process heating.

No serious exception was taken to these points in debate on the Electricity Bill. All that they mean is that further economies, possibly as great as those already realized by the CEB, could be effected by extending rationalization of generation in accord with already existing policies, and by unifying it with transmission. The latter, in its last annual report, had "estimated aggregate savings of £145,000,000 in capital expenditure as compared with the expenditure which would have been incurred had there been no grid" and tariffs had been reduced from an average of 1.65*d*. per kwh. to 1.08*d*. over an interval which has seen the price of coal increase by two and one-half times and other costs advance accordingly.[10] Since demand was increasing with amazing rapidity,[11] and since much of the existing plant was old[12] and small or inefficient,[13] a vast new construction program would have to be launched.[14] From past experience it seemed reasonable to expect that economies similar to those already effected might be realized in the future if the necessary machinery for carrying through the appropriate rationalization of generation could be provided.

This the bill proposed to do, and on this point there was no effective opposition. But the Government's proposal to include distribution among undertakings to be rationalized met with the bitterest and most determined opposition. And this opposition was undaunted by the fact that the Government rested its case, as it had already done in the debate on coal (with the Reid report), in effect, upon a report on electricity distribution which had been made by a committee set up by a Conservative government.

---

[10] *Financial Times*, March 24, 1948.

[11] On July 22, 1947, Isaacs said that "The demand for electricity has risen by 70 per cent since 1939 and is still rising." *Home Affairs Survey*, No. 15, July 29, 1947. "Generating capacity at CEB selected stations rose from 8.3 million kw. to 11.3 million kw. in 1945," *PEP Report*, p. 17.

[12] "By the winter of 1947 2 million kw. of existing generating plant would be more than twenty years old" commonly considered the average life of generating plant. PEP, *Idem*.

[13] Between 1926 and 1939 the CEB had reduced the number of selected stations from 491 to 136—to which must be added 35 nonselected stations. Of these "14 of the most economical 50 per cent of the total number of units generated for the Board during the first eight months of 1939...." *Facts About Electricity Supply*, Planning Broadsheet no. 204 (PEP, March 30, 1943).

[14] "4.6 Mil. Kw. of new generating capacity were scheduled to be brought into operation over the period 1946–49." *PEP Report*, p. 17. During the interval 1948 to 1952 inclusive, the original plan was to add 9,474,450 kw. of new plant. This has been subsequently cut down by 1,635,250 kw. of new plant, as stated in the white paper on capital investment in 1948.

The McGowan committee had reported in 1935, said Shinwell,

in favour of a drastic reduction in the number of electricity undertakings which, at that time numbered 635. [It had] quoted as a glaring example of the need for reorganization, the state of electricity supply in the London area. At the time there were 82 undertakings of various kinds in the London area and even now there are 75 of them. These undertakings were controlled by 243 separate Acts of Parliament, Provision and Special Orders, many of which are extensions or variations of the original Statutes.

The McGowan Committee pointed out that the existence of such a large number of undertakings in the London District, supplying at different tariffs and voltages[15] and offering unequal facilities for the hire of apparatus and schemes of assisted wiring, was clearly detrimental to the furtherance of a cheap supply of electricity throughout the district. This had given rise to justifiable complaints by consumers. If Hon. Members look at a map of the electricity undertakings in the London area they will see that it resembles something like a jigsaw puzzle. Some undertakings are pockets inside other undertakings; the areas of the undertakings bear no relation to the technical requirements; private companies and local authorities are hopelessly intermingled.[16]

The same picture would hold for other large distribution areas in Britain,[17] and it held for the country as a whole. Companies bought up properties haphazardly, and on no plan or basis except that they might prove profitable. For example:

The Southern Areas Electric Corporation bought companies in Essex, Sussex, Devon and Hereford. The Lincolnshire and Central Electric Supply Company not only operate in Lincolnshire, but also in Cheshire, Cumberland, Argyll and Caithness. British Electric Traction are interested in companies operating in the Lothians, Sussex, South Wales, Kent and Somerset. Callendars, the cable manufacturers, control three undertakings in Kent, Ayrshire and Oxfordshire, while another company—Messrs. Johnson and Phillips—are responsible for three undertakings in Argyll, Westmorland and Sussex. How [Mr. Shinwell went on to ask] can the electricity supply industry be reasonably organized, when its control and ownership is manipulated in this fashion? What do we know of the terms on which these plant manufacturers sold their goods to the undertakings which they controlled? Why did they buy these undertakings? Even if they

---

[15] "At present the country suffers from the inconveniences of total absence of standardization in voltages or appliances. In 1936 there were as many as 43 different declared voltages for low and medium pressure supplies, ranging from 100 to 480 volts. A citizen moving from one part of the country to another, or from one London district to another must often scrap the whole of his electrical equipment because of these divergences. There are wide divergences in charges for similar services and consumers in many rural areas are poorly cared for." British Information Services, *Economic Record*, no. 40, Jan. 1–20, 1947.

[16] *Hansard*, Vol. 432, cols. 1408–1409.

[17] "Within 14 miles of Manchester Town Hall there are no fewer than 30 separate undertakings ... in Lancashire, there are no fewer than 50 undertakings ... in this country there are 2,500 lighting authorities, and from Slough to Hammersmith there are 15 different changes of lighting within a space of 16 miles. In the north of England, two miles of road come under 22 lighting authorities." *Ibid.*, col. 1497.

improved them, what did the improvements cost these undertakings? What control had the Government over the relations between these outside interests and the subsidiaries?[18]

The trouble with power distribution was therefore not caused only by technical confusion, overlapping, and obsolesence, but also by confusing tariffs, profiteering, and the exercise of other monopoly powers. The practice of capitalizing reserves accumulated from high charges, and thus concealing from the public high profit rates, was cited.[19] Special privileges operating to the disadvantage of the general investing public, such as the sale of ordinary shares to existing shareholders at rates considerably under market valuations, were accorded insiders.[20] And the advance of private monopoly in the supply of such a vital service to the general public was intolerable on any grounds.[21]

The Government rested its case in general on the findings of the McGowan report, but it could not accept that committee's judgment that nationalization should be postponed. If the McGowan committee could find that "past experience has demonstrated beyond question that any attempt to carry through on a voluntary basis a scheme of reorganization on the general lines we have recommended would be bound to fail"[22] then "Why after 50 years? Why not now?"[23] Surely, if fundamental reorganization were required within the industry, nothing was to be said for further delay.

What the Government was proposing, in short, was to extend the benefits of the CEB in the field of transmission—manifest in themselves and conceded by everyone—to generation and distribution. The machinery was to consist of the British Electricity Authority, to be known as "the central authority," and fourteen area boards, plus the North of Scotland Board. The BEA was

to develop and maintain an efficient, co-ordinated and economical system of electricity supply for all parts of Great Britain except the North of Scotland District, and for that purpose—
    a) to generate or acquire supplies of electricity;
    b) to provide bulk supplies of electricity for the Area Boards hereinafter established for distribution by those Boards;

---

[18] *Ibid.*, col. 1421.
[19] *Ibid.*, col. 1418.
[20] *Ibid.*, col. 1419–1420.
[21] For data on growth of monopoly, and in particular of holding companies in the field of electricity supply, see the pamphlet, *Electricity* (Labour Party [1947]), pp. 9–11.
[22] Cited by Mrs. B. A. Castle, in *Hansard*, Vol. 432, col. 1628.
[23] Hugh Gaitskell, Parliamentary Secretary for the Ministry of Fuel and Power (subsequently Minister of Fuel and Power), in summing up for the Government, *ibid.*, col. 1692.

c) to co-ordinate the distribution of electricity by Area Boards and to exercise a general control over the policy of those Boards; and

d) to provide supplies of electricity for consumers for whom the British Electricity Authority are required by any provision of this Act or may for the time being be authorized by the Minister to provide such supplies.[24]

Excluding the North of Scotland District—which was to perform all three functions (generation, transmission and distribution)[25] the division of functions consisted of the BEA taking over generation and bulk supply, and of exercising general supervision over the area boards, while the latter managed the distribution of current. For the latter purpose, as map 2 shows, the country was to be divided into 14 districts or areas. The 16 boards, to be known collectively as Electricity Boards, were charged by the act to:

a) promote the use of all economical methods of generation, transmitting and distributing electricity;

b) secure, so far as practicable, the development, extension, to rural areas and cheapening of supplies of electricity;

c) avoid undue preference in the provision of such supplies;

d) promote the simplification and standardization of methods of charge for such supplies;

e) promote the standardization of systems of supply and electrical fittings; and shall also promote the welfare, health and safety of persons in the employment of the Boards.[26]

In addition to its general functions, the central authority is empowered to manufacture electrical plant and electrical fittings and all electricity boards may "sell, hire, or otherwise supply electrical fittings

---

[24] *Act*, pp. 1–2.

[25] The reason for this special treatment of North Scotland lies in the dual concern over "the regeneration of the Highlands," which had been losing population and industries for generations, and the peculiar problems associated with hydroelectric generation which required unified development of the whole interconnected Scottish watershed system. With the exception of Wales, North Scotland is the only present source of hydroelectric power. Since the establishment of the North of Scotland Board in 1943, "work has begun on four major hydro-electric schemes, estimated to cost upwards of £16,000,000. The installed capacity of the generating plant proposed is 374,000 Kilowatts with an estimated annual output of 706,000,000." Lord Morrison, in *Hansard* (Lords), Vol. 150, col. 176. New and projected developments may double or treble the capacity. See in particular the report of the Cooper committee, *Hydro-Electric Development in Scotland*, Cmd. 6406 (1943). The need for regenerating the Highlands was great, but it is doubtful how much electrification would contribute toward this end. "How can the Western Highlands be roused from their plight?" the Industrial Correspondent asks. "Many glens once fertile, closed to make room for sheep, are still largely desolate. The Hydro-Electric Board is fulfilling its plans; yesterday brought the welcome news that another project for Ross and Cromarty has been approved, but the costs of producing the electricity have steeply mounted and it is probably wrong to expect that many large industries—apart from electro-chemical and electro-metallurgical plants—will be drawn into the area." *Times*, Jan. 22, 1949.

[26] *Act*, Section 1 (6), p. 3.

NORTH OF SCOTLAND
DISTRICT

14
SOUTH
WEST
SCOTLAND

13
SOUTH
EAST
SCOTLAND

11
NORTH

EASTERN

12
NORTH

WESTERN

10
YORKSHIRE

9
MERSEYSIDE
& NORTH
WALES

6
EAST

MIDLANDS

5
EAST
ANGLIAN

7

8
SOUTH

WALES

MIDLANDS

LONDON

3

2 SOUTH
EASTERN

SOUTHERN

4
SOUTH

WESTERN

SOURCE: Ministry of Fuel and Power. Adapted by E. N. Bryant.

Map 2. Boundaries of area electricity boards.

and to install, repair, maintain or remove any electrical fittings."[27] The area boards are to be assisted in the discharge of their functions by consultative councils with the duties:

a) of considering any matter affecting the distribution of electricity in the area, including the variation of tariffs and the provision of new or improved services and facilities within the area, being a matter which is the subject of a representation made to them by consumers or other persons requiring supplies of electricity in that area, or which appears to them to be a matter to which consideration ought to be given apart from any such representation, and where action appears to them to be requisite as to any such matter, and of notifying their conclusions to the Area Board, and

b) of considering and reporting to the Area Board on any such matter which may be referred to them by that Board.[28]

In order that the BEA might discharge its functions there was to be transferred to it the whole of the transmission system of the CEB, all privately owned generating plants and distribution networks which were not wholly or mainly producing and supplying current for their own consumption, and all such properties owned by local authorities except where capacity was wholly or mainly used for local transport. This transfer involved some 170 generating stations, 563 undertakings of which 362 were local-authority undertakings, a staff of 98,000 persons, some £370,000,000 to be paid as compensation to existing shareholders, and plans for development and expansion requiring an expenditure of £700,000,000 in England and Wales and £100,000,000 in the North of Scotland.[29]

Aside from the usual complaints about further extension of "doctrinaire" nationalization *per se*, the Conservative attack on the bill while it was on its way through Parliament, and as the final act appeared, concentrated on three main charges. The first was that the intentions of the bill, entirely laudable in themselves, were in process of being fulfilled under existing conditions, and that if these conditions were maintained all the requirements of the Labour government would eventually be met. The act of 1926 was held to provide the required authority for any additional regrouping of existing properties which further rationalization might find desirable.[30] If changes were required the "Electric-

---

[27] *Ibid.*, p. 4. In addition the central authority may supply "electrical plant"; its right to manufacture does not include the right to export.

[28] *Ibid.*, Section 7 (4), p. 11.

[29] *Ibid.*, Part II, "Acquisition of Electricity Undertakings," section 13, pp. 16–17. Also, Shinwell in *Hansard*, Vol. 432, cols. 1416–1418.

[30] Niall McPherson, in *Hansard*, Vol. 432, col. 1458.

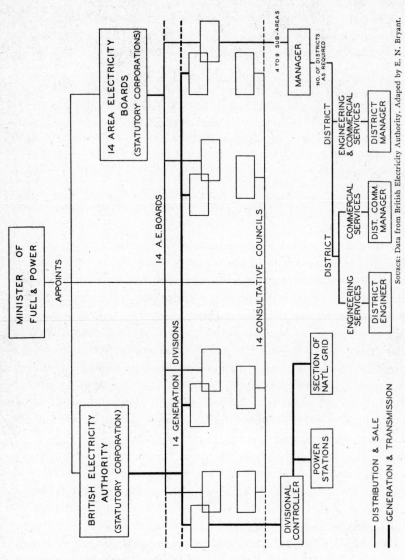

MINISTER OF FUEL & POWER

APPOINTS

BRITISH ELECTRICITY AUTHORITY (STATUTORY CORPORATION)

14 AREA ELECTRICITY BOARDS (STATUTORY CORPORATIONS)

14 GENERATION DIVISIONS

14 A.E. BOARDS

14 CONSULTATIVE COUNCILS

DIVISIONAL CONTROLLER

POWER STATIONS

SECTION OF NAT'L. GRID

MANAGER

4 TO 9 SUB-AREAS

DISTRICT

DISTRICT

ENGINEERING SERVICES

COMMERCIAL SERVICES

ENGINEERING & COMMERCIAL SERVICES

DISTRICT ENGINEER

DIST. COMM. MANAGER

DISTRICT MANAGER

NO. OF DISTRICTS AS REQUIRED

—— DISTRIBUTION & SALE

▬▬ GENERATION & TRANSMISSION

SOURCE: Data from British Electricity Authority. Adaped by E. N. Bryant.

Chart 2. Nationalized electricity in Britain: Basic organization.

ity Commissioners working on the lines of the McGowan report could give us a very good scheme."[31] It was obvious that the present was not, because of the fuel crisis (winter of 1947 and aftermath), the right time for "a major change and upset of this kind."[32] And furthermore, the major charges levied against the industry by the spokesmen for the Government simply were not true. Accepting the dictum laid down by Morrison as Lord President of the Council "that it is up to the nationalizer to prove the case for nationalization," Viscount Swinton found that "this is no case of inefficient or unprogressive industry." It has not failed the consumer. "Frequencies have been standardized. The voltage would have been standardized but for the war." The public has gotten a square deal. "Profits have been steadily ploughed back into the business."[33] And so also for other accusations levied against the industry.[34]

The second charge made by the Opposition appeared somewhat more damaging. The bill, they said, whatever the merits or demerits of the proposal to nationalize, was still a bad bill. To begin with, it vests all power to make policy decisions in the Minister of Fuel and Power. As shown in chart 2, the Minister appoints the chairmen and all other members of all the boards, and of the consultative councils. Board members, to be sure, must be appointed from among persons "appearing to the Minister to be qualified as having had experience of, and having shown capacity in, electricity supply, local government, industrial, commercial, agricultural or financial matters, applied science, administration, or the organization of workers," and of the twenty to

[31] Viscount Swinton, in *Hansard* (Lords), Vol. 150, col. 144. See especially the remarks of R. S. Hudson, in *Hansard*, Vol. 432, col. 1431.

[32] *Ibid.*, col. 145. Lord Barnby was worried for another and quite different reason. "It is only last week," he said, "when we were discussing this that I came straight from a luncheon at the American Chamber of Commerce where William Knox, President of Westinghouse International, had said 'You should pay less attention to nationalization and more attention to production.'" He (Lord Barnby) quoted a letter which he had "just received from a very prominent American industrialist, himself a Democrat, who is very well in touch with affairs at Washington and with the Administration" who said, "Many can see little difference between a British Labour Government that wants to nationalize everything in sight and a Red Government which has already shown just how it works. Americans generally do not like the way it works." Which led Lord Barnby to the conclusion that "I think this Bill is bad timing on nationalization." *Hansard* (Lords), Vol. 151, col. 871.

[33] *Hansard* (Lords), Vol. 150, cols. 141–142.

[34] Other arguments against nationalization—aside from those of a doctrinal character—were that the development of atomic energy might render the proposal completely obsolete (*Hansard*, Vol. 432, col. 1625); it would eliminate competition between gas and electricity which had benefited consumers (*Ibid.*, col. 1428); it would dislocate industry, and private companies were already promoting rural electrification (*Ibid.*, col. 1484); nobody but the T.U.C., "which votes for nationalization as a sort of duty" really wanted it anyway; and "there has been no great clamor for nationalization from the men engaged in industry ... The relationship between capital and labour in this industry has been very happy." Lord Balfour, in *Hansard* (Lords), Vol. 150, cols. 235–236.

thirty persons going to make up each of the fourteen consultative councils, from one-half to three-fifths must be appointed from a "panel of persons nominated from amongst members of local authorities in the area by such associations" and the rest must represent agriculture, commerce, industry, labor, and the general interests of consumers of electricity "and other persons or organizations interested in the development of electricity in the area."[35] The Minister must consult these interested groups, but he alone determines whether or not the appointee meets the qualifications.

The Minister, thus, is in the position of dictator over all the industry. For example, an advisory council, said Viscount Swinton—the most acidulous critic of the bill—is supposed somewhat to be "an independent authoritative tribunal. It is their right of appeal which really counts and yet here everything is left in the Minister's hands. The appeal from Caesar is to Caesar," and it is clearly necessary "that the appointment of these boards and executives should be in the central authority and not in the Minister."[36]

If this situation were not corrected, individual initiative and experimentation would be thwarted and the appointment of officers would tend to become political—not to mention the temptations of patronage. "Whether you agree or not with the suggestions that the McGowan Committee made in their Report," said Viscount Ridley, "the important thing clearly seems to be that we should have larger autonomous areas. Who owns the undertakings I do not really very much care, whether it is the public or private people, but what does seem important to me is that they should be run independently, efficiently, and with enterprise. And that is a state of affairs which I am quite convinced under this Bill can only be obtained by all strings pulling into the centre, a state of affairs which will be extremely difficult to achieve."[37]

The appointment of Lord Citrine as head of the CEB was cited as typical of what can, and is virtually certain to happen under the provisions of the bill. This was "clearly an instance of a political appointment."[38] Despite the requirement that the Minister must consult local authorities when making appointments to the consultative councils, the mere fact that he alone appoints them means that they will become

[35] *Act*, pp. 6, 10–11.
[36] *Hansard* (Lords), Vol. 150, cols. 146–147.
[37] *Ibid.*, cols. 184–185.
[38] *Ibid.*, cols. 191–192.

"stooges" of the Minister.[39] The same holds for all the boards. Altogether there are some 138 persons to be appointed to top positions on the boards "and somewhere between 280 and 420 members of consultative councils"[40] who are supposed to be watchdogs over the boards. Add these appointments to those which he makes to the Coal Board, and the Minister of Fuel and Power becomes a dispenser of patronage to the "boys" on an alarming scale.[41] Over all appointees and all staff members he possessed judicial as well as executive authority, and with respect to both persons and policies "he is authorized to adjudicate on matters which are normally decided by Parliament or the courts and there is no appeal from his decision."[42] Let these powers fall into the hands of "a super strong man . . . on the Government Front Bench,"[43] member of a "Gadarene Government"[44] such as this where "the wine of power seems to have gone to their heads," and the end may be that taking "all these powers into his own hands . . . he may use them with the same disastrous results which we have seen only too recently in Nazi Germany."[45]

Basic to every Opposition argument is the charge that the bill promotes undue centralization of authority in the hands of the Minister of Fuel and Power, and that this is especially bad when the decisions are to be made by a Minister responsible to a Labour government. Their case, that is to say, simmers down to an elaboration of the usual charges of bureaucratic centralism and state socialism which the Conservative party levels against all nationalization measures introduced by the Labour party. It is a case which was greatly weakened by the fact that the BEA was deliberately modeled after the pattern of the CEB, which it was to supersede, and which was, in turn, a creation of the Conservative party in its heyday of the middle twenties.

[39] *Hansard*, Vol. 432, col. 1427–1428.

[40] R. S. Hudson, *ibid.*, col. 1432.

[41] *Ibid.*, cols. 1432, 1438. In the House of Lords (*Hansard* [Lords], Vol. 150, col. 238), Hilaire Belloc's "Little Lord Lundy" was paraphrased by Lord Balfour to indicate where the "danger of patronage was."

> "We had intended you to be
> The next Vice-Chairman but three;
> The stocks were set, the boys were squared,
> The T.U.C. was all prepared;
> But as it is my language fails—
> Be off and govern Southern Wales."

[42] *Hansard*, Vol. 432, col. 1433.

[43] Lt.-Comdr. G. Williams, *ibid.*, col. 1495.

[44] Sir T. Moore, *ibid.*, col. 1503.

[45] Williams, *ibid.*, col. 1495. Sir T. Moore asked the indulgence of the House to summarize the whole outlook by misquoting a poem: "Into the Valley of Death, ride the carefree, ignorant and irresponsible Four Hundred," the "Four Hundred" being "the 400 well trained, well disciplined and well paid sycophants" making up the Labour M.P.'s, *ibid.*, col. 1501.

The impression of bitter and uncompromising struggle over un-essentials is not much relieved by an examination of the third line of criticism leveled by the Opposition against the bill. This had to do with the rates of compensation. The Government had proposed two rates of compensation; one for properties taken over from public authorities and the other for properties acquired from private companies. For the first, "The transfer of undertakings from the local authorities to the new organization set up by the Bill is a transfer from one form of public ownership to another. Local authorities have always displayed a sense of public duty and will not wish to make any profit from the transaction . . . The basis of compensation to the local authorities should be the transfer of their assets and liabilities to the New Boards."[46] For the private companies, the "holders of shares in the companies will be compensated on the basis of the average market value of the shares on certain dates; alternative dates are provided in the Bill and compensation is given on whichever is the more favourable to the shareholders."[47] For the latter this "compensation on the basis of market value" was regarded by Shinwell as "generous."

The Opposition regarded both as unfair because they penalized the undertakings which had been conservatively and efficiently managed, and which, instead of disbursing large dividends or, if public enterprises, applying earnings to rate reductions, had been plowing back funds into the business and both improving service and lowering rates.[48] Two principal objections were raised to the compensation rate for private companies. First, the basis should not be market values of pre-election dates when compensation was to be made in depreciated currency; this amounted to valuing "assets in 'Sound Andersons,' but paying for them in 'Inflated Daltons'!" This was no less than "legalized confiscation."[49] The only adequate basis was not market value as of some specific date or dates, but "net maintainable revenues" which would have included allowances for such items as good will and pay-

[46] Shinwell, *ibid.*, col. 1416.

[47] *Ibid.*, cols. 1419–1421. The alternative dates in the act are the average of quotations in the Stock Exchange Daily List (1) "on all six of the following dates, that is to say, the first, fourth, fifth, sixth, seventh and eighth days of November, nineteen hundred and forty-six" and (2) "the fifteenth day of February, the fifteenth day of March, the sixteenth day of April, the fifteenth day of May, the fifteenth day of June, and the sixteenth day of July, nineteen hundred and forty-five." *Act*, Clause 20, section 2, p. 32.

[48] For example, "Observe what you are doing, you are going here to penalize those who have been most conservative in their policy" and who have "followed the advice of the Chancellor of the Exchequer to plough back a large part of their profits into the business." *Hansard* (Lords), Vol. 150, col. 150, and *Hansard*, Vol. 432, cols. 1435–1436.

[49] *Ibid.*, col. 1436

ment for the power, as Shinwell put it, of very complexly organized undertakings of the holding company type[50] to manipulate prices against the public interest.

Nevertheless, most experts agree that stockholders got off rather well, and complaint about actual compensation has been surprisingly small. The same, however, is not true for public undertakings. Transfer of assets and liabilities could only mean that firms which had retired most of their indebtedness would be paid little, and those that had retired but little would be paid more. Critics here included Labour and Liberal M.P.'s as well as Conservative. Tunbridge Wells, they pointed out, would receive on this basis only £30,000, whereas the "capital outlay stands in the balance sheet at the moment, after writing down considerable sums each year out of profits, at £860,000."[51] The City of Glasgow, which had borrowed £11,670,000 for its electric undertaking and had repaid £9,000,000, would receive £2,870,000, while the City of Birmingham, which had borrowed £24,238,000 and paid back £8,600,000, would receive £13,570,000.[52] But more than this, once the properties were taken over, consumers in a district where electric rates could now be lowered, because indebtedness had been retired, would find themselves paying higher rates based upon costs for the new area which the bill would establish. Where profits had been used to lower tax rates, this source of income would now be cut off.[53]

Despite the belief, subsequently borne out by events, that this mode of compensating public utility undertakings was certain to cause a great deal of trouble in many specific cases, the Government won its point with an overwhelming vote. The other clauses in the act, though much criticized in certain details during committee hearings, were definitely of minor importance. With its passage Great Britain became the first major industrial country outside the Soviet Union to own and operate a completely unified power system which was coextensive with its national frontiers. In taking this step, the government acquired control of the second great division of the British fuel and power system. Gas was the third, and against its nationalization every argument, parliamentary device, and delaying tactic at the command of an aroused and resourceful Opposition was brought into play.

---

[50] *Ibid.*, cols. 1417–1418.
[51] *Ibid.*, col. 1494.
[52] *Ibid.*, cols. 1637–1638. Worse still, Glasgow is a "labour town" and Birmingham a "tory town." (I.e., a Tory administration had borrowed the money.)
[53] Two Socialist communities, Liverpool and Glasgow, it was pointed out, passed resolutions "to the effect that compensation should be on the basis of capital cost instead of the basis proposed in the Bill." *Ibid.*, col. 1509.

The Gas Act

"How," asked Gaitskell in opening debate on the Gas Bill, "can we really achieve co-ordination in the sphere of fuel and power as a whole—which is, after all, one of the purposes of my Ministry to carry out—unless we have public ownership in all three cases?" Clearly, "since the coal and electricity industries have already been nationalized, the gas industry must be also." Not, however, out of aesthetic considerations "based on the beauties of symmetry," but because the case for the nationalization of gas "rests upon three propositions: first, that the present structure of the industry is not conducive to maximum efficiency; second, that the present legislative framework is a major obstacle against achieving great efficiency; third, that from every angle the most suitable structure for an efficient gas industry can be achieved only by organization under public ownership."[54]

These three propositions were then examined in detail, the basic data, again, being drawn from an earlier and quite exhaustive report of a committee, known as the Heyworth committee, established by the conservative Coalition government in 1944, by whom it had been called upon "to review the structure and organization of the Gas Industry, to advise what changes have now become necessary in order to develop and cheapen gas supplies to all types of consumers, and to make recommendations."[55] Relevant to Gaitskell's first proposition, the Heyworth committee had found that, "The direction of required change is clearly marked, namely towards groupings into larger units. This is preponderantly the view of the Industry itself. It is in no sense a revolutionary idea; it is entirely consistent with past history, which shows a steadily accelerating trend towards integration." From grouping into larger units the committee believed would come "further reduction of production costs (a) through higher carbonizing efficiency; (b) through better labour utilization and reduction in maintenance costs; and (c) through improvement in load factor." Improvement in labor conditions, economies in capital charges, and improvements in both distribution and sales policies would also follow.[56]

That there had been a trend towards amalgamation within the industry was entirely correct. Between 1920 and 1938 the number of

---

[54] *Hansard*, Vol. 447, cols. 219–220.

[55] Ministry of Fuel and Power, *The Gas Industry: Report of the Committee of Inquiry*, Cmd. 6699 (1944). [Hereafter referred to as *Heyworth Report*.]

[56] *Ibid.*, paragraphs 230–231, pp. 39–40.

statutory undertakings had decreased from 798 to 703.[57] By 1946 this number had further decreased to 680. In addition there were some 366 nonstatutory companies, mostly small and serving isolated local communities. Most of the companies, statutory and nonstatutory alike, were relatively small. Thus, in 1945, out of 1,064 companies, 560 of the smallest concerns, or more than half, sold only 3 per cent of the total supply, while 28 of the largest undertakings sold 52.2 per cent of the total. Of the statutory group, there were, in 1946, 275 local authority undertakings which sold 36.4 per cent of the total gas made, and 405 private companies which sold 60.8 per cent.[58]

While the correlation is not rigorous, data published by the British Gas Council (see table 12) indicate quite clearly that size does have a definite relation to costs and prices. Larger size units were clearly desirable from this point of view alone. But more than mere size is involved. As map 3 shows, the supply areas of undertakings form a crazy-quilt pattern which bears little superficial resemblance to a rational scheme of development. Such joining together as the process of corporate amalgamation had brought about in the past was largely at the financial and top-policy control level, not at the physical and operating level. Properties of some 18 holding companies in 1938, for example, included 242 subsidiaries which were widely scattered over the country.[59] In the large London area alone, where the conditions were ideal for regional unification, there were still some 35 different supply undertakings in 1943.[60] Similar areas of high population and industrial concentration showed similar patterns.

Gaitskell made much of this state of affairs in developing the case for nationalization. He cited his own constituency of West Riding as a case in point. In this area there are

a large number of fairly big local authorities—the Corporation of Leeds, Halifax, Bradford and so on. There is also one of the more modern developments under private enterprise—the West Yorkshire Grid, created by the United

---

[57] *Ibid.*, par. 15 and table, p. 4. A statutory undertaking is either a corporation or limited liability company operating under Parliamentary statute, and possessing rights and obligations associated with eminent domain and rate control. The term as used in the Heyworth report includes both undertakings owned and operated by local authorities and by private companies. "Non-Statutory Gas Companies are normally limited liability Companies having no Statutory Powers and possessing no right to break open streets and bridges otherwise than by the consent of the Highway Authority" and selling less than 30,000,000 cubic feet of gas a year. British Gas Council, *The Gas Industry: Facts and Figures* (London, 1948).

[58] *The Gas Industry*, tables, pp. 6 and 7.

[59] Joan Mitchell, *The British Gas Industry Present and Future*, Research Series, No. 103 (Fabian Publications, 1945), p. 23.

[60] British Gas Federation, *Report on a Survey of the Gas Industry in Great Britain* (1943), pp. 27–29.

TABLE 12

NUMBER OF GAS WORKS AND PERCENTAGE OF TOTAL WORKS IN EACH CATEGORY OF CAPACITY, 1934–1938, PRODUCING GAS AT SPECIFIED RATES PER THERM[a] INTO HOLDER

Cost per therm[a] into holder	Capacity, in cubic feet per day											
	20,000,000 and over		10,000,000 up to 20,000,000		5,000,000 up to 10,000,000		1,000,000 up to 5,000,000		500,000 up to 1,000,000		Below 500,000	
	no.	pct.	no.	pct.	no.	pct.	no.	pct.	no.	pct.	no.	pct.
Below 3d.	8	72.7	10	55.5	12	30.8	37	23.9	9	8.1	6	1.6
3d.–4d.	3	27.3	8	44.5	20	51.3	61	39.4	36	32.4	23	6.3
4d.–5d.					5	12.8	39	25.2	39	35.1	52	14.3
5d.–6d.					2	5.1	15	9.6	21	19.0	71	19.5
6d.–7d.							2	1.3	5	4.5	62	17.0
7d.–8d.							1	0.6	1	0.9	56	15.3
Over 8d.											95	26.0
Totals	11	100	18	100	39	100	155	100	111	100	365	100

SOURCE: Adapted from British Gas Federation, *Report of a Survey of the Gas Industry in Great Britain* (1943), p. 11.
[a] 1 *therm* = 100,000 B.T.U. = 200 cu. ft. of gas of 500 B.T.U. per cu. ft.

Kingdom Gas Corporation. When that grid was set up and coke ovens constructed at Hemsworth to feed it, the local authorities opposed it as far as they possibly could; they would not allow the pipes which were to form the grid to pass through their areas, far less actually take gas from it. Yet to anybody who looks at the matter objectively, here is an overwhelming case for planning the area as a whole on the basis of the coke ovens which are there already. It would be possible to achieve this if we had a single authority for gas in that area. It is not possible to achieve it without that. As a matter of fact, two or three years ago my Ministry did their best to get together the various authorities in that district in order that we could plan some sort of grid. We had to abandon the attempt; it was altogether impossible to make them work together.[61]

An indefinite number of similar examples could be cited. It had proved impossible to get some thirty to forty small gas undertakings in South Wales to participate in a grid development which would have drawn heavily upon new large by-product coke ovens, being built in connection with steel reorganization and Coal Board plans, for cheap supplies of gas available in bulk. It would seem highly desirable to unify into a single grid network the areas of London and the seaside towns where the same capacity could serve the former whose peak load comes in winter, and the latter whose peak demand comes in the summer holiday season. What these cases establish is "that the evidence of the need for grid integration is overwhelming."

The Conservative reply consisted of arguing that the needed improvements could be effected without disturbing the current organization of the industry and of repeating, with some circumlocutions, the statements to that effect which had previously been advanced by the British Gas Council. Complying with a request from the Ministry of Fuel and Power on December 3, 1946, that the council send representatives to discuss with the ministry "major questions of broad policy" regarding the "planning for the future organization of the Industry under the Government's proposals for nationalization," the council, after having pointed out their opposition to the policy of nationalization, had nevertheless made a series of suggestions which they felt could be carried through by the government with the aid of the machinery at the council's disposal. Although, if nationalization were inevitable, the council was prepared to coöperate,[62] still they felt that

---

[61] *Hansard*, Vol. 447, col. 221.

[62] The British Gas Council "was given a mandate by its Member Undertakings at District Meetings held in July, 1946, in the terms of the following Resolutions:

A. That this meeting of the representatives of member Gas Undertakings is not in favour of the principle of Nationalization of the Gas Industry and is not prepared to collaborate to bring such Nationalization about.

B. That this meeting of the representatives of member Gas Undertakings is prepared—if

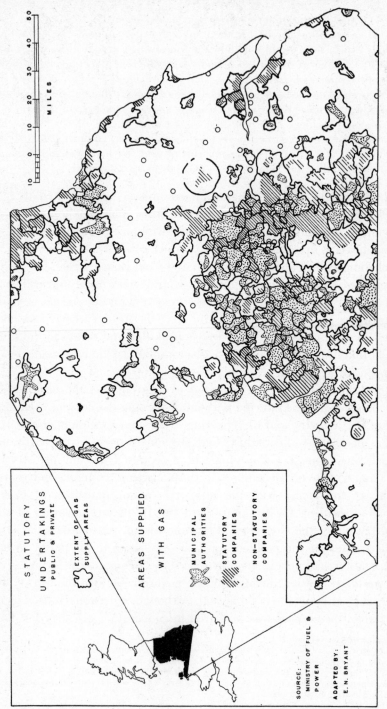

Map 3. Gas supply areas: Section of England and Wales showing prenationalization pattern.

"Recourse to Nationalization, or the expedient recommended by the Heyworth Committee, is not necessary or desirable to secure 'groupings into larger units.' The methods of geographical integration adopted in the past should be encouraged and facilitated, aided by an Integration Tribunal, to which could be referred any integrating proposals which could not be agreed, compliance with the findings of the Tribunal being obligatory. There are many large Undertakings, or groups of associated or contiguous Undertakings, which form a natural focus for the development of integration."[63]

Yet this position did not, at bottom, seem to be inconsistent with the Minister's main proposal, for the point at issue was largely that of the speed and comprehensiveness with which the integration should be carried through, and on this point the Gas Council was not prepared to argue, nor were its supporters in Parliament. Obviously, the speedier the better, and clearly the unit of organization was the gas supply area. It was also clear that these supply areas should be interlinked wherever possible by regional grids over the principal districts of heavy consumption, especially where pipeline networks were already juxtaposed and dovetailing of peak loads would make better use of capacity. If, as the Opposition—including the Gas Council—was prepared to concede, it was desirable that such reorganization be carried through at maximum speed, and if the steps that were currently being taken were too slow, too small scale, too inconclusive, and too suspect of manipulation to private advantage at the expense of the public (as the advance of the holding-company device indicated), then where was the case against nationalization? Particularly since the Heyworth committee— appointed by a Conservative government, and directed in the formulation of its recommendations primarily by businessmen—had found something of this sort necessary?[64]

There was little dispute over Gaitskell's second basic proposition "that the present legislative framework is restrictive." Most gas companies had originally grown up as local monopolies, subject to local legislation. A vast and complicated series of local laws, rules, and

---

Nationalization is to be effected—to co-operate with the Ministry of Fuel and Power in the detailed implementation of the Government's proposals, so as to ensure that the nationalized structure and organization of the Gas Industry are such as to maintain an efficient and economic gas service to the Public." *The Organization and Regional Boundaries of a Nationalized Gas Industry* (British Gas Council, 1947).

[63] *Heyworth Report*, p. 15.

[64] The Heyworth committee had recommended "compulsory purchase of all existing undertakings," grouping of properties into ten regions, and had advised that "the plan should be put into effect as a whole and not piecemeal." *Heyworth Report*, pp. 49–51.

regulations had grown up relating to both publicly and privately owned gas companies—there were "in force, up to 1937, no less than 3,278 Private Gas Acts and Special Orders"[65]—and they covered virtually all aspects of the conduct of business for both statutory and nonstatutory undertakings, and their price systems.[66] Crisscrossing at many different angles were similar national controls and regulatory measures. Significant national legislation, for example, had been passed relating to various important aspects of the gas business in 1920 (Gas Regulations Act), 1929 (Gas Undertakings Act), 1932 (Gas Undertakings Act), and 1934 (Gas Undertakings Act). A series of government inquiries, of which the more important in recent years had been the Gas Legislation Committee (Wrottesley) of 1931, and the Committee of Enquiry into the Gas Industry (Heyworth) of 1944, had meanwhile been making suggestions for reform of the industry, piecemeal and at large. The fact that the privileges and rights granted by the private acts were given by Parliament to local authorities, and that these could not be given except on condition of the exercise of certain controls by the national government, meant that the government was already mired down with a vast mass of regulatory detail which it urgently needed to shed.

Neither the industry nor the Opposition in Parliament took issue with this argument. On the contrary, some simplification of the legislative and regulatory controls had long been an objective of the industry, and constituted one of the principal *raisons d'être* for the establishment of the British Gas Council. Thus, it seems to have been conceded that to the need for technical rationalization must be added the need for sweeping away a complicated, overlapping, and thoroughly out-of-date cobweb of controls exercised from a multiplicity of legislative and administrative sources. But what of the third proposition that public ownership is the only way of achieving the desired results?

[65] According to *The Gas Industry: Facts and Figures*, 2,106 of these were Private Gas Acts, of which 1,080 related to local authorities and 1,026 to gas companies, and 1,172 were Special Orders, of which 377 related to local authorities and 795 to gas companies.

[66] Most important of the aspects of business organization and management subject to legislative control were: definition of area, amount of land which might be purchased, supply of gas to public premises, rules governing gas pressure and calorific value, accuracy of meter, gas prices, maximum dividends, methods of raising capital, use of investment funds, report of accounts and returns, and use of by-products. Regulations varied according to whether the company in question was classified as a maximum-price company, a standard-price (sliding-scale) company, or a basic-price company, each type of which came under different basic legislation.

Since public ownership had been recommended by the Heyworth committee,[67] and since the British Gas Council, though reluctant, was prepared to coöperate in reorganization of the industry under a nationalization act—the British Gas Council, in fact, expected to become the National Gas Board under the act, and to maintain its existing staff and most of its policies—was any other solution even sensible? Leaning on the Heyworth report, Gaitskell thought not. The Opposition would oppose it on the grounds, he said, that it would create controversy, that it could be introduced but slowly and over a number of years, and that it could not be "applied to the gas industry in the absence of similar treatment for its competitors." The arguments of the British Gas Council were essentially similar.

But, he went on to point out, the absence of nationalization would also cause controversy, and there was scarcely anything visualized in the Government proposals which would cause more "delay, difficulty and confusion" that the proposals of the British Gas Council itself. The Heyworth report answered the second argument, and the prior nationalization of coal and electricity supply answered the third. As for the fear that the gas industry under government ownership would lack "initiative, responsibility, enterprise and inducement" the Heyworth report recognizes that "all these things . . . are more likely to be achieved under public enterprise than under private enterprise."[68]

Three points stand out in the Opposition's defense of the *status quo.* The first, that the industry, from a technical point of view, was highly progressive and virile, would seem to be a very important issue, but it fell on barren ground since it was not seriously contested by the Government. The second, that the bill was a bad bill, came to rest primarily on general points which had already been presented in the debates on coal and power, and they seem to have been advanced without great enthusiasm, and more or less as a matter of routine; the only feature distinguishing debate on the Gas Bill was the almost complete absence of controversy over compensation. But the third point was a different matter. Here the issue was not unification of the industry, or

---

[67] Paragraph 245 reads: "Regional Boards should be set up by Act of Parliament covering the whole of England, Scotland and Wales. Each Board should acquire all the existing undertakings—municipal, joint board statutory company and non-statutory company—in its area, and should have the responsibility of initiating any new development which is found to be commercially desirable in areas within its regional boundary which are not at present included within the boundaries of any existing undertaking." *Heyworth Report,* p. 42.

[68] *Hansard,* Vol. 447, cols. 225–226.

the nature of the bill, but the further extension of nationalization. The time had come, the Opposition felt, not "to speak of many things," but of one thing: the necessity for calling a halt to nationalization before it was too late.

On the first point, Brendan Bracken for the Opposition rejected only the "pessimistic and necessarily superficial" tone of the Heyworth report, and the implication of the Government that the gas industry had become a "sleepy old monopoly . . . We shall try to show the House," he said, "that gas is one of the most vital of all British industries. It is not only a great distributor of fuel and power, but it is a great and ever-growing chemical industry, with an immense and fascinating future." The industry was not inefficient. On the contrary, "The British gas industry is recognized as the most efficient in Europe, and has plenty of admirers in the USA." It was a lively industry which had to fight for its life. The impact of competition from electricity on the industry had been devastating; it had been put in the position that Dr. Johnson had spoken of when he "said that if a man knows he is to be hanged, it concentrates his mind wonderfully." Competition from "electricity concentrated the mind of gas as well as its energies . . . To survive, gas had to encourage personal service, salesmanship and zeal in finding new markets for its products. Competition has always been keen between gas and electricity [and] the answer of gas to such competition was wholly admirable."[69]

Since these facts were not in dispute, only two points could be made in their elaboration. The first was that this virility was adequate to carry out the unification of the area supply system and the technical rationalization which was incidental to this unification. Since not even the British Gas Council was prepared to argue that this was so,[70] the contention amounted only to the expression of a fear that a nationalized gas industry, no longer needing to compete with a nationalized electricity industry, would fall into ruin. But this issue turns on the conduct of nationalized industries, not the situation in hand.

[69] *Ibid.*, cols. 242–243.

[70] The British Gas Council, that is to say, accepted the general recommendations of the Heyworth report which were concerned with the necessity of regrouping areas on a most comprehensive basis. That it was able in its 1947 report, *The Organization and Regional Boundaries of a Nationalized Gas Industry*, to make recommendations for such regrouping in a comparatively short time shows that it had long been thinking along these lines. Nevertheless, there was nothing in its various statements on nationalization to indicate that it had much confidence that such reorganization could be brought about solely by independent and voluntary action. Among other things, this result was clearly impossible so far as the publicly owned gas undertakings were concerned.

As for the second point, the Gas Bill,[71] and the subsequent Gas Act, "follows closely the lines of the Electricity Act" with the one important difference that, while under the latter act the British Electricity Authority governs the area boards, under the Gas Act, the area boards are the centers of authority. Since the leading point made by the Opposition against the Electricity Act as finally passed centered on this very difference, and since in the process of formulating its proposal the Government had, on this score, practically adopted intact the leading proposals of the Heyworth committee, it seemed difficult for Opposition spokesmen to criticize the bill very severely for having, in effect, yielded to their contentions.

To digress briefly, both the Heyworth committee and the British Gas Council had placed their emphasis upon regional organization. The first proposed to divide the country into ten regions, and the second into thirteen. The criteria of division into areas accepted by the former were adopted by the latter. The difference in number of regions is a result of a postwar survey by the Gas Council. With minor variations in detail, the Gas Act accepted the data of the survey. The division of the country into twelve area boards is shown by map 4. In keeping with its regional-decentralization emphasis the act begins by placing full responsibility for the conduct and management of gas supply in the hands of the area boards, who are to become the owners of the properties to be transferred. They are charged with the duty, "(a) to develop and maintain an efficient, co-ordinated and economical system of gas supply for their area; (b) to develop and maintain the efficient, co-ordinated and economical production of coke by them; (c) to develop and maintain efficient methods of recovering by-products obtained in the process of manufacturing gas."[72]

Under these general powers the area boards are authorized to manufacture and distribute gas, to buy from and sell in bulk to other area boards, to manufacture and sell any or all coke and chemical by-products of gas production, both to deal with the purchase, sale, instal-

---

[71] The bill was introduced in Parliament on January 22, 1948, and was passed by the House of Commons on February 12, 1948. It is known as the Gas Act of 1948, vesting date, May 1, 1949. Its full title reads, "An Act to provide for the establishment of Area Gas Boards and a Gas Council and for the exercise and performance by those Boards and that Council of functions relating to the supply of gas and coke and certain other matters; for the transfer to such Boards as aforesaid and to the said Council of property, rights, obligations and liabilities of gas undertakers and other persons; for co-ordinating the activities of Area Gas Boards and the National Coal Board relating to carbonization; to amend the law relating to the supply of gas; to make certain consequential provision as to income tax; and for purposes connected with the matters aforesaid." 11 & 12 Geo. 6.

[72] Gas Act, Section 1 (1).

SCOTLAND

11
NORTHERN

10
NORTH
WESTERN

9
NORTH
EASTERN

6
EAST
MIDLANDS

8
WALES

7
WEST
MIDLANDS

5
EASTERN

4
SOUTH
WESTERN

3
SOUTHERN

1
NORTH THAMES

2
SOUTH
EASTERN

SOURCE: Ministry of Fuel and Power. Adapted by E. N. Bryant.

Map 4. Boundaries of area gas boards.

lation and repair of all equipment and plant required in the discharge of their duties and—after consultation with the Gas Council—to engage in the manufacture of such equipment (except for export). Throughout the act attention is focused on the area boards, which are established and designed to be highly autonomous both in interpretation of the details of policy, and the management of gas supply undertakings.

Above the board, the Gas Council is set up to serve as an advisory body to the Minister of Fuel and Power, "on questions affecting the gas industry and matters relating thereto, and to promote and assist the efficient exercise and performance by Area Boards of their functions." In addition, "The Gas Council shall have power, *if so authorized by all the Area Boards or a group of Area Boards,* to perform services for, or act on behalf of, the Boards concerned in relation to matters of common interest to those Boards" and it "shall have power (*a*) to manufacture plant required by Area Boards, to sell or supply such plant to Area Boards, and to install, repair, maintain or remove such plant; (*b*) to manufacture gas fittings and coke fittings except for export, and to sell or supply such fitting."[73]

The Gas Council is also to serve as a negotiating body with trade unions, it is charged with the duty of developing and managing long-range research programs and personnel-training systems, and it has control over both long-term borrowing and current operations of the area boards when they get themselves into financial difficulties. With respect to this last contingent authority, "It is the function of the Gas Council to set up a guarantee fund to which the Area Boards will contribute. The purpose of the fund is, in effect, to give the Treasury the security which they naturally require if they are to guarantee the British Gas Stock through which the industry will raise the finance it requires. The Area Boards can draw on the guarantee fund if they are unable to meet the capital charges on their part of the British Gas Stock. If they do not come to the Council because they can pay their way, the Council leaves them alone, but if they come to the Council because they are in financial difficulties, and say 'Will you help us to pay our debts to the Treasury?' then the Council can issue directions, subject to the approval of the Minister, until they get out of the mess they may have got into."[74]

Thus the Gas Council is a central body which is to "be mainly ad-

---

[73] *Ibid.*, Section 2, pp. 3–4. (Italics mine.)
[74] *Hansard*, Vol. 447, col. 229.

visory and federal in character," while the area boards have "the main responsibility," Gaitskell went on to explain, "not because we think there has been over centralization in every case, but because in this case it is proper. There is no question of a national grid here; gas is a local service, and we think that to a great extent it should be decentralized."[75] To further reinforce this emphasis, each area board is to be kept under constant local surveillance through the establishment of a Gas Consultative Council, one-half to three-quarters of the members of which are to be "appointed from a panel of persons nominated from amongst members of local authorities" and the remainder from persons "to represent commerce, industry, labour and the general interests of consumers of gas and other persons or organizations interested in the development of gas in the area."[76] Finally, the preëminence of the area boards over the Gas Council is secured by the provision that all the members of the Gas Council, excepting only the chairman and the deputy chairman, are to "be the persons for the time being holding the office of chairman of an Area Board."[77] The Gas Council, in short, is under the majority direction of the area boards.

Since this structure was more or less precisely what the gas industry had suggested, and since it also seems to square entirely with the criticisms that the Opposition had made of the Electricity Bill, it would seem that opponents of nationalization would have considerable difficulty mustering an argument against the act on the grounds that it centralized authority. Nor, with one exception, did they expend much energy attempting to do so. The exception dealt with the fact that the Minister of Fuel and Power not only appointed all the members of the area boards, their consultative councils, and the chairman and vice-chairman of the Gas Council, but was also free to issue and interpret all policy directives to all these agencies—including those concerning their relationships with the Coal Board and the British Electricity Authority—within the framework of the act. Admittedly, this exception is an important one, since under it a degree of *de facto* centralization of authority and administrative control might be arrived at which would be fully as comprehensive as those formally granted under the other acts. Yet, surprisingly enough, very little was made of this argument.

On the contrary the whole basis of disagreement was shifted back to the ground accepted by the Government as valid for the application

---

[75] *Ibid.*, col. 228.
[76] *Gas Act*, Section 9, p. 9.
[77] *Ibid.*, Section 5, p. 5.

of nationalization measures *per se*. In the words of Brenden Bracken
for the Opposition, "Government supporters generally rest their case
for nationalizing an industry on three grounds—firstly, that Parliament
should control an industry like gas that affects most of the homes of the
country and many of the industries of Britain; secondly, the State
should step in where private enterprise has been manifestly inefficient; and thirdly, the State must take over an industry suffering from
chronic labour troubles. There is a fourth argument used by those who
strongly favour nationalization of gas, and it is the trilogy argument
put forward by the Secretary of State for War. According to that argument, gas is complementary to electricity and coal."[78]

The first was dismissed with the observation that there was already
a plethora of law regulating gas and, since this point seems neither to
meet the case made by the Government and conceded by the industry
nor to be altogether relevant anyway, it should be, for all practical
purposes, dropped. On the second point, with the exceptions noted
above (particularly with respect to the smaller companies), the Government, by conceding that the industry was progressive and efficient,
had refuted itself. The third point, strangely enough, came in for a
good deal of attention. The industry, said Bracken, not only does not
suffer from labor troubles, but it has evolved a system of copartnership
which gives labor a share interest in the well-being of the industry as
a whole. This copartnership is literally a panacea for Britain. "It can
answer the Government's prayer for an effective incentive to steady
production." Though copartnership "is not popular with many trade
union leaders—and employers" yet it "is one of the best ways of providing the good life that our people deserve. It can provide not only
social security . . . The idea that lies behind co-partnership is one of
the most constructive of our time" and "a proper system of co-partnership would solve most of the Government's present labour difficulties."[79]

Yet this point seems to have been advanced without serious intention
of following it up, nor was it, in fact, driven home. If, as Bracken conceded, organized labor was against it, there was little to be said for
pursuing the suggestion; which, however laudable, would be rejected
by the Government out of hand. The Opposition was left with the fourth

---

[78] *Hansard*, Vol. 447, cols. 241–242.

[79] *Ibid.*, col. 254. Violently rejected by Labour here, copartnership became the basic
formula for Labour's own proposals for private enterprise in general. See chapter xiii below
on the development councils.

argument—the unified development of coal, electricity, and gas—and their case against it came down to arguing on behalf of competition between alternative types of fuel and energy supply. Since even here the Government was prepared to agree—in fact to insist—that there must be full freedom of consumer choice, not too much could be made of this last redoubt. Not, at least, until some alternative answer could be provided to Gaitskell's question—"How can we really achieve co-ordination in the sphere of fuel and power as a whole—which it is, after all, one of the purposes of my Ministry to carry out—unless we have public ownership in all three cases?"[80]—which went beyond saying merely "let matters take their natural course." And no such suggestion was forthcoming.

The general argument against further nationalization under a Labour regime was, finally, all that the Opposition could offer here. The usual strictures were repeated. The board members would be "creatures of the Minister"; the boards would each be a "farcical body" composed of yes-men; the Minister of Fuel and Power was already overworked, and could not be helped out by "a Council of Puppets"; "team-spirit" would be lacking; the "consumer is afforded no real protection in the Bill, save by the setting up of a Consultative Council of Consumers—whatever that may mean"; the compensation was inadequate and amounted to confiscation; and so on and so on. From all such arguments the somewhat rhetorical conclusion was drawn that the gas industry should not be thus yoked and trussed up, but allowed "the measure of freedom it has enjoyed. During its long life it has been the good servant of most of Britain's homes. It renders inestimable service to industry. Its charges have always been regulated by Parliament. It is the pioneer of many new industries and it can start many more. It is eager and qualified to serve the many and complicated needs of the new industries by which prosperity can be restored to Britain."[81] It is, in short, the goose that lays the golden egg, and the Labour party has learned nothing from the experience of the dolt who in the fable on true prudence was foolish enough to cut the bird's head off.

When the question of compensation arose there was little more to be said than to repeat the arguments that had been used against the compensation clauses of the Electricity Act, since the provisions of the Gas Bill were identical in content with those of its predecessor. The

[80] *Ibid.*, col. 219.
[81] *Ibid.*, cols. 251–252.

capital value of the industry was estimated at some £167,000,000, and this estimate was based on market values, not on net maintainable revenue. Here, again, the dates selected were criticized. So also was the manner of taking over undertakings owned and operated by local authorities. As an example, the City of Paisley was cited, the capital of whose "undertaking is £600,000 with a reserve fund of £70,000 and outstanding loans of £136,000" and which, for this undertaking worth £600,000, would receive only £66,000 if the bill were passed.[82] Other examples could be given *ad infinitum.* The effect of the bill consequently would be to strike a body blow at the savings of private investors, at employees (through depriving them of the benefits of copartnership), and at municipalities.

The significant thing about comments such as these is that not even those who made them seemed to believe that they provided adequate arguments for estoppage of the bill. Even as they were argued, the specific points were dwarfed by the major issue—the extension of nationalization itself. That this was so seems to have been recognized by the leader of the Labour party in summing up for the Government just prior to division on the bill in the House of Commons. His statement is for this reason interesting, but is made doubly so by the additional reason that it seems to have led him to a conclusion which could hardly have been more mistaken.

"The interesting thing about these Debates on the socialization of industry," said Herbert Morrison, Lord President of the Council, "as the process of transformation from capitalist private industry to socialized industry goes on, is that each piece of socialization seems to go through the House more quietly than the one before. One would think that, the more that was done in this direction, the bigger the row would become. Take this Debate. Nothing could have been quieter and more sedate than this has been. It has been almost as quiet as the Debate on the Parliament Bill. My explanation for this very interesting and significant development is that, as the Debates go on, the Opposition are steadily being converted to the point of view that on the whole we are right and they are wrong."[83]

Yet nearly three months later—after Standing Committee D had chewed up and quarreled over virtually every fragment of the bill to the extent of 36 sittings and 2,192 columns of record, and the Lords

---

[82] See, in particular, the comments of Lt. Col. Elliot, *ibid.*, cols. 391–392.
[83] *Ibid.*, col. 470.

were promising to go the committee one better—the *Economist* characterized the then current debates on the Gas Bill as an endurance test. "Regarded," it went on to point out, "when it first appeared as among the less controversial of the Government's measures for nationalizing industry," the bill "has proved a dark horse. It has given the Government a remarkable amount of Parliamentary trouble, and caused Mr. Herbert Morrison" radically to change his tune from the quotation cited above, and to speak "at the Labour party conference of 'foolish, old-fashioned, nineteenth-century obstruction.' In short, Mr. Morrison thought the Tories were filibustering. He went on to utter the threat that if the Tory obstructionists wanted to go on with this kind of 'foolery,' which was contrary to the working of Parliamentary institutions, they were asking for more reforms of Parliamentary procedure."[84]

To be sure, the *Economist* found that the result of this elaborate pulling and hauling was the adoption of many amendments which at least the Opposition believed would mean that "the future control of the gas industry will, as a consequence, be more efficient and less political than it promised to be" and it felt constrained to side with the bill's opponents on the criticism that the compensation clauses, particularly those relating to payments for gas undertakings owned by local authorities, were unreasonably rigid. But an inspection of the record of the sittings of Committee D shows much less concern over streamlining a government bill, and much more of a determination to take a stand against the bill which would employ to the maximum every advantage of Parliamentary tactic and maneuver to delay, harass, and undermine. Thus it appears as a sort of dress rehearsal for the stand taken by the House of Lords. This impression is confirmed by the Opposition's concentration on the compensation clauses, and by the great concern shown over the apparent discrimination against public authorities shown by the bill. Why, Labour asked, should the Tories be weeping crocodile tears over the threat of the big bad wolf of national socialized undertaking to blow down the houses of socialized undertakings maintained by municipalities.

On this point Morrison seems to have sensed the intentions of the Opposition more accurately than he had on the earlier occasion. If he retained any doubt on this score, the reports of debates on the bill given in the Opposition press would have laid them completely at rest. Viscount Swinton served notice at the outset that the bill would be

---

[84] *The Economist*, May 22, 1948, p. 855.

FUEL AND POWER: ELECTRICITY AND GAS   165

fought tooth and nail. Lord Rennell, a Liberal member of the Opposition, found that "the Bill was one of a series that reminded him of the Wagnerian Ring of the Nibelungs. Amid roars of laughter" he proceeded: "First there was the Coal Act, which might be called Rhinegold, or Black Gold. Then there was Siegfried Shinwell striking sparks from the anvil as he made speeches to the gods. Now we have a well armed Brünhilde going up to the Socialist Valhalla in a flame of gas." Most of the comment was in a grimmer vein. Viscount Cecil of Chelwood found that despite the Government's repudiation of bureaucratic collectivism in favor of democratic socialism, it had here put forth a bill which was itself the very quintessence of bureaucratic collectivism. Viscount Buckmaster left nothing more to be added to the Tory case when, demanding that the gas industry should be set free of the fetters that the Government was fastening on it, he jeered, "the Moloch of nationalization demands yet another sacrifice. Steel is not ready for the sacrifice, so gas—equally innocent, equally unwilling—is offered up instead."[85]

THE COÖRDINATION OF FUEL AND POWER

That the ultimate object of these three nationalization measures—coal, electricity, and gas—was to smooth the way for a program having as its purpose the coördination of all aspects of the development of fuel and power, at all levels and for all users, the Government had never left in doubt. The three had been linked in *Let Us Face the Future* in a statement favoring "public ownership of the fuel and power industries."[86] Gaitskell had been explicit about it in opening debate on the Gas Bill, as had Shinwell in the previous debates on the Electricity and Coal bills. Behind these declarations lay many years of Labour party agitation. The "Mines for the Nation" campaign of 1919 had included gas and electricity among those industries subject to "the principles of public ownership,"[87] and subsequent annual conferences of[88] the Labour party repeated the demand at fairly regular intervals. At least this was the theory. Was it anything more?

Despite the emphasis on coördination among the three, barely hinted at in earlier years and becoming clear-cut only with the actual intro-

[85] *Daily Telegraph*, June 3, 1948.
[86] *Let Us Face the Future*, p. 6.
[87] *Report of the Twentieth Annual Conference of the Labour Party* (1920), p. 181.
[88] Aside from coal, the primary interest was in power. It was not until the thirty-seventh annual conference at Bournemouth in 1937 that gas supply industries came back explicitly into the picture. See the *Report* for that year, p. 277.

duction of the Coal Bill, it seems true both that it was the dawning realization of the larger implications of this position which strengthened at once the determination of Labour to carry through all three measures and the determination of the Opposition to fight them by every means at its disposal, and that, though the implications are now recognized, Labour has done little thus far to plan ahead for effectively carrying out the necessary scheme of coördination among the three industries. The idea is there, but little more. Nevertheless, this inter-industry coördination of the three nationalization programs obviously carries with it the most far-reaching implications for the entire British economy. More specifically, it seems scarcely conceivable that the three fuel and power acts can be carried to their logical conclusions—technologically and in economic terms—without forcing direct governmental interference in a steadily widening range of heavy large-scale and key industries, and thus an extension of planning far beyond the metes and bounds of the specific programs as they appear at the moment. As an incident thereto it follows that much of the supplementary governmental machinery for offering information, giving advice, and exercising some degree or other of administrative control—even though much of it may ostensibly have been established for specific and technically unrelated problems and more or less on an *ad hoc* basis—appears more and more as parts of a jig-saw puzzle which should possess the configurations of a significant pattern, and which the current of events and the logic of industrial organization must slowly force the Labour party to fit together and to accept on pain of loss of any gains from steps already taken.

And finally it would appear to follow as night follows day that, once the steps already taken are consolidated in a more or less effective organizational structure which has succeeded to an independent existence by severing the cord which connected it directly to the nurturing but different structure of the immediate past, the departures will be so drastic that there will exist no possibility ultimately of escaping the necessity to go forward and thereby to effect the wholesale transformation of society on a fully socialist basis, with its corollary either of the total abolition of capitalist society or the relegation of its fragmented and small-scale remnants to the minor interstices and the unprofitable fringes of the new society. That is, irrespective of their merits on other grounds, on the combined socialization and planning assumptions under which nationalization has been begun by the Labour government there will be no alternative to this choice but failure to effect any significant reorganization of the sort needed to restore Britain to a viable future and still keep a "Socialist" system—even of the sort advocated by the apostles of the Third Force.

It is virtually impossible to escape the conclusion that it was some such view of these emerging even if distant prospects, which was the actual subject of debate and around which the eddies of controversy swirled during the latter stages of the Gas Bill, and which, however clearly or imperfectly sensed on either side, constitutes also the heart of the further issue of the nationalization of the steel industry. Before turning to consider that critical case in chapter v, it may be worth while briefly to indicate some of the outlines of further change, anticipated by fuel and power nationalization, which may be derived directly from these very acts themselves and from their setting in other plans and programs of the Labour party which were known to all Parliamentary contestants. These may readily be summarized—though their details ramify endlessly—under three main headings: fuel and power raw materials, processing and delivery of fuels and power, and the use and substitution patterns of use of these by various types of intermediate and ultimate consumers. It is impossible to say how far Labour plans actually to go; it is only possible to be reasonably certain that the arguments, premises, and conclusions advanced in the promotion of the three fuel and power acts make reasonably clear that this must be the furrow for the turning of which Labour has set, not its hand, but a nationalized tractor, to the plow.

PROGRAMS FOR FUEL AND POWER RAW MATERIALS

As table 13 makes clear, Britain's fuel and power-generating resources are almost exclusively limited to coal. Only about one-third of one per cent of all domestic fuel—even after adding small amounts of exploitable minor fuels and energy such as cannel coal, anthracite duff, sewage gas, and wind and solar energy (atomic energy is still not technically feasible at commercial rates)—comes from sources other than coal, and only about ten per cent comes from abroad. More significantly still, although there are some possibilities of further extension of hydroelectric power development the amounts that may be added from such sources are small. The demand for oil imported from abroad is expanding so rapidly elsewhere—the American consumption, for example, expanded between 1946 and 1947 by an amount which was larger than the entire British consumption for the latter year[89] and the rising cost of transport overseas, combined with decline in the ratios of new reserves to total consumption in many of the more important fields, has already reached such levels that Britain must view with grave misgivings any further tendency to rely more heavily on petroleum fuels. This is particularly true since the rising cost of these imports is both significant and of a secular and long-run character, and so also is

TABLE 13

UNITED KINGDOM: PRIMARY SUPPLIES OF FUEL, 1945

Primary sources	Available supply		Estimated efficiency of utilization	Net useful therms supplied
	Quantity	Million therms[a] (estimated)		
			per cent	million therms
Coal (excluding colliery consumption) (million tons)......	166.6	53,000	18	9,600
Oil (from indigenous petroleum and shale) (million tons)......	0.1	42	25	10
Imported petroleum products[b] (million tons)...............	9.0	3,800	25	950
Hydroelectric power (billion kwh)........................	1.0	34	75	25

SOURCE: Adapted from *PEP Report*, table 100, p. 328.
[a] Average calorific value taken as coal = 320 therms per ton; petroleum products = 420 therms per ton (1 therm = 100,000 btu).
[b] Including motor spirit.

Britain's need for closing the import-export gap by holding down imports to the minimum.

Only coal can be obtained on advantageous terms from internal sources and more or less at will. Coal, in short, is almost literally the sole foundation of the fuel and energy requirements of Britain, and coal output alone can easily be increased to meet growing needs. Yet, as a wasting asset, it must be conserved to the maximum.

Thus the tendency exists to view coal and power as a unit not only at the raw-materials stage, but at every step in the extraction, refining, and use of coal. This view is seen in its clearest expression on the scientific end. Under the National Coal Board, a Scientific Department and Establishment Branch serves as a liaison body to connect the research

[89] World oil consumption was 256,000,000 tons in 1938, 364,000,000 tons in 1946, and 397,000,000 tons in 1947. The comparable figures for American consumption are 147,000,000, 234,000,000 and 254,000,000 respectively, and for British consumption 11,000,000, 13,000,000 and 16,000,000 respectively. *Financial Times*, April 30, 1948.

activities of the board with those of the Gas and Electricity boards and via various departments of the Department of Scientific and Industrial Research (DSIR) with virtually all research having to do with fuel problems. Most important of these organizations, perhaps, is the Fuel Research Station, organized in 1917 and consisting of the "Fuel Research Station at Greenwich and nine Coal Survey Laboratories in the various coalfields of Great Britain." Its objectives "are to investigate, in the broadest national interest, the nature, preparation, utilization and treatment of coal and other fuels and the products derived from them."[90] In the conduct of this work, "The Fuel Research organization maintains close contact with the research work of other organizations including the National Coal Board, the British Coal Utilization Research Association. A standing Consultative Conference on Fuel Research has been established to coordinate all work on fuel research. A Central Abstracting Bureau has been established at the Fuel Research Station for the preparation of Fuel Abstracts."[91]

Each of these fuel research agencies tends to have for its span of interest the entire range of problems of the whole industry to which it is attached, and to see its problems in terms of the industry considered as a unit. In this, of course, they merely reflect in the scientific field a manner of looking at scientific and technical problems which had given rise, in the field of production, organization, and management, to central coördinative councils, institutes, trade associations, etc., long before the government introduced its various nationalization measures. Thus when the problems of fuel and industry are viewed from either the scientific and technological end or from the organizational and management end, they have come, over the years and cumulatively, to appear to be (1) coextensive with the industry—coal, gas, coke, power— (2) coextensive with fuel and power as a whole, and (3) coextensive with all stages and levels of production from mining and water usage clear on through to the ultimate user. Concretize this view of the interconnected tissue of problems of fuel and power utilization into an implementing framework of administration and management, and we have before us the structural outline of the future system in this many-sided field.

In coal production alone the problem of technical efficiency, from the coal face on through to all processes of utilization, has come increas-

[90] Statement of the Fuel Research Station in *Industrial Research, 1947* (Todd Reference Books, 1947), pp. 121–123.
[91] *Ibid.*, p. 123.

ingly to appear to be inseparable from that of reorganization on an area basis, and this problem of planning on an area basis has, in turn, proven to be insoluble on the technical side except in connection with such considerations as those of size and location of colliery workings, unification of colliery operations with coking, gas, and other fuel utilizing industries, and the location of other lines of closely related industries, and on the human side except in terms of considerations which are at once coextensive with the problems of incentives on the job, occupational training and selection, job opportunities in other industries, housing and town planning, safety and health, standards of living and social security, and many others. More than that, the technical set of problems cannot be solved in isolation from the human set of problems and vice versa. And, finally, each set constitutes an organon of propositions each of which must be solved more or less simultaneously and continuously with the others.

The problem of coal-getting, that is to say, once undertaken on the basis visualized under the Coal Act, overlaps in a multitude of ways with allied activities which seem, on the same assumptions, incontinently to demand and to require coördinate handling on a similar basis by like-minded and functionally interdependent agencies. Coal mining means, under the new dispensation, extracting and making maximum use of coal and all other minerals found mixed with it in sizable quantities (such as nonferrous metals, iron, and—possibly in Yorkshire—potash), and thus extension of organizational tentacles into other fields. Wherever settling takes place from underground operations, and particularly in open-cast mining, where the soil stripped off the surface must be returned for agricultural purposes, the problems of coal mining are linked with those of land planning and agricultural usage. Because in each case the unit of calculation is now the area, the Coal Board must set itself to work these problems out with the Ministry of Town and Country Planning and the Ministry of Agriculture.

In hydroelectric development in Scotland and Wales, the pattern being evolved appears as an adaptation of the one pioneered by the TVA, where the use of water for power generation is linked in a multiple-purpose project to water use for all purposes, including recreation and municipal water supply (e.g., for the City of Glasgow in the Loch Lomond District), and all land use on the watersheds, including the nature of the crop, afforestation, methods of soil cropping and care, and use for park and recreational purposes. In the development of both water and coal resources, there has also been a strong tendency to effect control backward over the manufacturers and suppliers of machinery, equipment, and other materials needed in their development, and forward over the users of raw, semiprocessed, or processed materials and services, even if the materials and services supplied are sold to plants not officially under the control of the industry.

This is particularly true of coal, and was established as a government policy by the provision in the Coal Act which includes among the functions of the Coal Board that of "producing or manufacturing any goods or utilities which are of a kind required by the Board or for it in connection with the working and getting of coal or any other of their activities . . ."[92] This means, in effect, that the Coal Board possesses power to determine the market for coal machinery and equipment, and also the specifications for their construction and the prices at which they may be sold. In technical parlance, it is a monoposonist. But here the need and the power of the monoposonist reaches upward in the technical ladder of production as well as downward, and, furthermore, it is not a mere question of product or functional interdependence, in the market sense of the term. Added thereto, and in its ultimate implications vastly altering the whole set of relationships is the fact, to borrow a figure, that these interdependencies have grown, willy-nilly, a sort of connective tissue. Between and among them they possess something analagous to a common set of venous and arterial systems, and they are united by ligamina that bind directly action to action, and function to function.

FUEL PROCESSING AND POWER DEVELOPMENT

This ligaminous character of the interlinkages which require, on Labour's tacitly accepted planning assumptions, interprocess, interindustry, and interfunction coördination by employment of scientifically contemporaneous methods is more easily seen and more readily grasped at the second stage or level of fuel and power development. So numerous and complex are the networks of these interlinkages that it will be possible to illustrate here by mentioning only a few of the more important and better known.

Coal-gas-coke.—In 1946 the gas and coke industries used 40,900,000 tons of coal out of 176,700,000 tons of the coal produced in the country.

---

[92] *Coal Industry Nationalization Act,* section 1, p. 2. Similar provisions are found in the Electricity and Gas acts.

In 1945, when the total amount of coal available and used by the gas and coke industries was slightly less, but the ratio to total coal production (166,600,000 tons) was about the same, 2,300,000,000 net useful therms of gas were produced, of which 1,800,000,000 were produced by coke ovens and the balance by gas works. Of the 1,800,000,000 therms produced by coke ovens, all but 200,000,000 were consumed by works—mostly steel—to which the coke ovens were attached. The balance of 200,000,000 therms was sold to gas undertakings for sale through their distribution networks.[93] The implications of these trends are most far-reaching indeed.

The percentage of coal turned into gas and coke is rising steadily, and will continue, if plans currently afoot are continued, to rise perhaps even more rapidly in the future. The over-all importance of this trend from the point of view of fuel economy may readily be grasped when it is realized "that to provide all the heat services obtained before the War from Gas and Coke (which involved the carbonization of 19 millions tons of Coal) would have needed at least 50 million tons of Coal had it been used raw."[94] Thus, from the point of view of fuel conservation, everything is to be said for converting with the maximum speed from raw-coal firing to gas firing or electrical energy. This means expansion of local networks, regional grids, and, wherever possible, interregional grids. Every step taken in this direction means widening the area and increasing the rigor of control over the chemical quality of gas, pressures, and constancy of supply, and by so much as these steps are taken, they link all forms of gas supply directly to fuel in such a way as steadily to convert coal mining into a public utility function. Once, that is to say, industrial, commercial, and domestic users have converted their fuel plants to a gas basis they will demand, almost without realizing it, that a continuous flow of gas of constant qualities and proper pressures is available, and consequently that coal be mined continuously and distributed in an uninterrupted flow.

The percentage of gas produced and sold by coke ovens is rising slowly, but significantly. "In 1921, 14 Gas Undertakings purchased 1,325 million cubic feet of Coke Oven Gas. In 1942, 52 Gas Undertakings purchased 52,000 million cubic feet of Coke Oven Gas. The proportion of Gas bought from Coke Ovens by Gas Undertakings to the aggregate of Gas available for sale by the Gas Industry has increased from 8.5% in 1938 to 12% in 1945."[95] In certain districts this

---

[93] *The British Fuel and Power Industries*, pp. 326, 328.   [95] *Ibid.*, p. 19.
[94] *The Gas Industry: Facts and Figures*, pp. 18–19.

percentage is much higher, as table 14 indicates. The significance of this trend lies in the fact that the coking industry, and the industries—most notably steel—most dependent upon a continuous supply of coke and coke-oven gas, are in process of becoming sufficiently large-scale suppliers as to become indispensable in supplying gas for distribution to the public.

How important this may become is seen in table 14, for these are all cities possessing large-scale steel works (potteries in Stoke-on-Trent),

TABLE 14

Gas Purchased from Coke Ovens, and Total Gas
Consumption in Selected Areas, 1945

District	Cubic feet per annum	
	Coke oven gas purchased	Total gas supplied
	millions	millions
Sheffield.................	12,714	15,100
Newcastle-upon-Tyne.....	6,849	11,633
Stoke-on-Trent............	1,974	3,739
Derby...................	2,230	3,149
Rotherham...............	1,507	2,259
Middlesbrough............	1,851	1,854

Source: *The Gas Industry: Facts and Figures*, p. 19.

or able to draw upon near-by gas surplus from steel-operated coke ovens. In these areas, to some extent prototypal of further extension of gasification of coals, two rules hold; coke and gas requirements must be met by coke ovens juxtaposed immediately to, and organically bound up with, iron, and steel processing,[96] and when optimum-size coking installations are provided, the surpluses of gas flowing from these coke ovens (as well as deficits flowing to them) to the public utility gas network binds them into this utility supply, and hence gas, coke, and iron and steel works are bound together in the joint production of quantities of gas no one of which can be dispensed with in maintaining the necessary public supply. Add to this the tendency, when modernizing iron and steel production, to introduce simultaneously complete integration from raw materials to basic iron and steel shapes, continuous heat treatment from blast furnace to rolls or molds, and flow production which

[96] Of the 109,870,000,000 cubic feet of gas produced by the coking industry in 1945, 44,047,000,000 cubic feet were consumed by the steel industry, and 51,440,000,000 were taken by gas undertakings. *Loc. cit.*

makes no provision for storage between stages other than that necessitated by normal repairs and changeovers, and we have a metallurgical industry wherein coke making, and in an almost equally binding manner iron and steel processing, are taking on a public utility character. This is true since and because each separate step in processing under these methods constitutes a link in a chain of production which cannot be broken without destroying the power of all other links to function. On this showing, and quite aside from other considerations, the application of the logic underlying the program for fuel and power coördination, as advanced by spokesmen for the Ministry of Fuel and Power in the Labour regime, to these aspects of the central problem, would require that iron and steel be considered public utilities under the same central administration.

The same generalization will hold for the chemical by-products side of the picture. In 1947, when the gas industry carbonized 22,500,000 tons of coal to produce 12,500,000 tons of coke and 484,607,000,000 cubic feet of gas, it also produced 162,000,000 gallons of oil, 27,000,000 gallons of benzole (synthetic gasoline) and 87,000 tons of ammonia. By rough estimate, the gas supplied per pound of fuel expended was able to provide as much or more heat than if it had been used for fuel purposes alone, and "the market value of the Gas, Coke and by-products produced is approximately 3 times the cost of the Coal to the Undertakings."[97] Thus, while amply justifying itself in economic terms, the gas industry at the same time promotes conservation by making better use of the basic raw material and becomes a large producer of basic chemicals.

If this process of chemicalization of coal ultimately envelops the major part, if not the whole, of the coal supply—and so far as technical, conservation, and economic considerations are concerned, such, with minor exceptions, would appear to be the long-term result of current trends—are fuel and power industries to become gigantic chemical industries as well? Use of coal, for example, as a basis for benzol supply through application of liquefaction processes, and as a foundation for rubber and artificial fibers (e.g. nylons)—and these and similar trends based on coal are definitely to be counted on—will not only bring fuel and power into the field of chemicals, but could very well make them a preponderating force in the British heavy chemical industries. And here, with respect at least to further refinement of the more important

[97] *The Gas Industry: Facts and Figures*, p. 17.

bulk supplies of by-product chemicals, the same reasons for direct vertical linkage with the succeeding (chemicals) stage of production are to be found as appeared in the preceding (gas, coke) stages, and as are to be found for linking these sideways to the iron and steel industry. How far is Labour prepared to go down this path? Is it prepared to move for the nationalization of the chemical industry, and its integration with fuels and power by the methods used to connect the segments of coal, gas, and electricity to each other, or these as a group to iron and steel?

Suppose, for sake of argument, it were. Then at what point does the Labour government propose to break off? Consider the evidence of chart 3. This chart shows the possibilities that lie ahead of the gas industry through utilization of the by-products of the chemical treatment of coal which is part of the gasification process. Here it is, once again, not merely that chemical treatment of coal permits the further production of these by-products, but also that it is necessary to utilize the by-products in order to make the breakdown at each step economically feasible, that the argument for joint exploitation of the more important bulk by-products under unified direction is overwhelmingly strong on both technical and commercial grounds, and that there is no place in the chain, from the raw coal to the last of the most highly refined of the end by-products, where a clear-cut case can be made for separating any processing step from the processing step which preceeds it. Every link of the chain from coal to end-product, or, to change the figure, all the branches, twigs, and leaves of the chemical tree with a trunk of coal, are interdependent. Where technological considerations are less binding, then commercial, marketing, and other considerations—as the history of the great private combines of Imperial Chemicals, DuPont, and I. G. Farbenindustrie have shown—supervene to call for central management and administration of most (perhaps logically all) branches of this chemical complex. Does the effective coördination of fuel and power take Labour, in short, to the door of another room marked "Committee for Drafting a Bill to Nationalize the Chemical Industry?"

Coal-electric power.—The case for joining coal and electricity seems so completely valid as to silence opposition, and so, for all practical purposes, were the arguments for linking generation and distribution to transmission. Similar reasons hold for pooling in this same nationwide network power generated from all sources, and thus, power from hydroelectric as well as steam developments. The over-all effect of such a system should be—and is intended by the Labour government to be—a supply of electricity so reliable and so cheap that it will, when paired

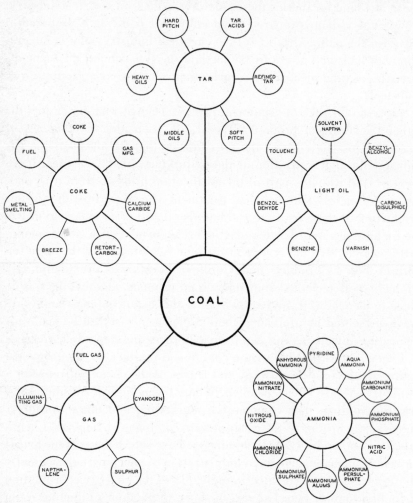

Chart 3. Principal by-products of the chemical breakdown of coal.

with gas similarly administered, gradually result in the conversion of virtually all heat and energy requirements in industry, shops and offices, and the home to this basis (electricity and gas, or electricity or gas). What are the implications?

Since most of this power comes from steam, and since the efficiency of steam generation is largely dependent upon large boiler and turbine units using high-temperature steam fed in at high pressures, there is growing interest in the development of combined heat and power steam-generating plants capable of supplying in bulk, for district heating purposes, either bleeder, or, as it is sometimes called, back-pressure steam from the generating process. Developments along this line have been highly successful in New York, Hamburg, Dresden, Moscow, Leningrad, and a number of other places. Elaborate plans have been developed for introducing such a system on a comprehensive basis in Paris. Such steam (or alternately, hot water) networks based on power generating stations have reached lengths of 44 miles in Leningrad and delivered 33,000,000 therms of heat a year, 12.4 miles in Dresden and delivered 4,760,000 therms a year, and 20 miles in Hamburg and delivered 12,500,000 therms a year. Plans for Moscow call for supply from this source of up to 85 per cent of its total heat requirements.

Several similar plans are under way in Britain. One engineer has summarized the great advantages of by-product district heating. He takes the average efficiency of individual heating in towns at 35 per cent owing to the predominance of coal fires, and he assumes the heat losses of distribution systems for large areas to be 20 per cent. On this basis the annual electric power generation for a heat supply of 305 million therms would be 3,660 million KWh. The heat in the steam required to generate this amount of electricity in a thermal electric station would be 135 million therms and the exhaust heat output of the turbines would be 366 million therms, making a total of 501 million therms. Thus, assuming a boiler efficiency of 85 per cent, the required heat could be supplied by an annual coal consumption of 590 million therms. The generation of 3,660 million KWh. in up-to-date condensing stations with a heat consumption in coal of 12,000 B.Th.U. per KWh. would require 439 million therms, and the provision of 305 million therms of heat by individual heating at 35 per cent efficiency would require 371 million therms in coal, giving a total of 1,310 million therms. This gives a balance in favour of district heating of 720 million therms.[98]

Such savings in fuel, particularly in a country like Britain which is starved for fuel and which must conserve the maximum from its dwindling resources, are not to be ignored. Furthermore, under favorable circumstances, it means both cheaper electricity and cheaper heat to the ultimate consumer.[99] But the capital costs of such combined operations are high, and "favorable circumstances" pose some very

[98] A. Margolis, "The Growth of District Heating in Russia and Germany," *Engineering*, Oct. 8, 1943, as summarized in *PEP Report*, p. 138.
[99] See the *Report of the Conference on Fuel and the Future* (Ministry of Fuel and Power, 1946).

interesting problems. Because heat loss through distribution networks is bound to be very high, the efficiency of steam or hot water distribution rises in proportion to the increase in the volume carried short distances. This means that generating plant should be located either in or very near dense population centers, or where office, commercial, and manufacturing demand for such heat is very high. Thus the establishment of a combined heat and power station has a very important bearing on both town planning and industrial location. Furthermore, once heat requirements within a consumption area are shifted from individual units to this common supply, demands for heat take on a public utility character which necessitates the production of electric current in parallel volume. The problem of dovetailing power and heat peaks then becomes paramount, and the best chance of doing so is to be found in interconnection of networks and maximum volume and variety of consumers.

If, on the other hand, new plants are constructed at or near coal measures, they become a major factor in forcing the pattern of new town development and the location of industry within the country. In either event, resort to these highly desirable methods of fuel utilization both favors and is conditioned by a corresponding reorganization of domestic and commercial heat requirements, and this, in turn, means redesign of housing to permit a shift from open coal heating to indirect or central heating, and the reorganization of industrial and housing developments wherever the source of heat is a central heat pool. Thus the agency in control of such an unfolding plan for better fuel utilization becomes a power in town planning, occupational diversification, industrial location, the manufacture and supply of heat-using equipment in the radius of influence, and so *ad infinitum*. The planning and coördination of the one sphere means, on the basis of the Labour party's assumptions, planning and coördination in the other. And the planning of each must also be coördinated with the planning of the other.

The mechanization of coal mining operations, which to a large extent governs the level of OMS in mining, greatly increases the amount of coal waste in the form of dust. If, however, electric plant is located at or near the pit and the volume of this waste is large enough, it can be changed from a liability to an asset in the form of valuable fuel for generating power. Where the volume of fuel of low calorific value is large enough, power generation may make an ideal fuel scavenger, and the economical use of this by-product of mining modernization may, accordingly, play an important role in the further extension of mine mechanization. But so to view the matter is also to plan on supplying the generating plant with this by-product on a continuing basis and under circumstances where the over-all supply of available heat and power will be combined with gas and coke (from expanded gasification of coal) on such a scale that the centralized coal-gas-power-heat-chemical by-products complex possesses a powerful gravitational pull on a wide variety of other industries, and via these, on population itself. At the heart of any such complex is the coal mine, which now becomes, among other things, the most important unit in a series of continuous, public-utility supply services. Coördination here means once again a widening of the arc of interservice and interfunction planning.

Fuel and power developments along the lines traced above have also an important bearing on both transportation and the whole apparatus for the distribution of coal. Wherever power generation and/or gas production plants are located near a colliery, coal shipments by rail or water will tend to disappear entirely. Alternatively, where similar generating and producing plants are located at major consumption centers some distance from the coal pits, coal shipments will tend increasingly to be made up of full train or barge loads moving directly from pits to the consuming plants. In either event, and in proportion as concentration of pit operations has resulted in few large-scale, mechanized collieries, and as the elimination of direct firing of coals in large numbers of small domestic and industrial units by tapping electric or gas grids results in concentration of the points to which coal shipments are made, the result is bound to be a great reduction in ton-miles of road and rail haulage of coal. It is conceivable that it might mean a halving of the ton-miles hauled, and even more than a halving of the man power required to handle the coal at all points from coal pit to consumer.

First should come a great dropping off of rail haulage. The importance of this fact for the railroads can readily be seen when it is recalled that more than half of the total freight ton-mileage handled by British railroads is coal. The loss of nearly half of this revenue, which would be siphoned off mostly from lines already suffering from thin traffic, might very well mean a shrinkage of revenues on these same lines which would cause wholesale abandonment of track, and, quite possibly, far-reaching reorganization in the rest of the main-line trackage and rolling stock. At any rate, it is clear that gas and power networks may become substitute transportation systems on a large scale.

This should be added to the effect upon transportation of the industrial and population relocation which unified development of gas and power systems promotes, as outlined above. The result is the need—on the Labour government's coördination assumptions—for a common and unified, or coördinated, plan for fuel and power development and transportation.

A second consequence would be the elimination of the whole complicated, inefficient, and man-power-absorbing system of coal distribution step-by-step with and at the same speed as the conversion of fuel and power to the new footing. The Coal Board cannot long avoid coordinating distribution of coal with its mining and fuel utilization schemes. If, as has been estimated, there are some 150,000 retail coal outlets, large and small, the displaced man power would be very large indeed. What follows is that the coördination of fuel and power does not permit drawing a line between mining and fuel and power development and wholesale and retail distribution. The coördination argument means taking hold of this as well.

Fuel and power consumption.—The economical use of fuel and power by the ultimate consuming unit is the last link in the chain of relationships which define the level of conservation and efficiency in the use of energy supplies. It was estimated, for example, that between the two world wars "the average thermal efficiency of Gas appliances was increased by about 20%. It is estimated that a 10% increase in the thermal efficiency of all Gas appliances (*a*) conserves about one million tons of Coal a year; (*b*) saves the consumer in the aggregate several million pounds sterling a year; and (*c*) assists the sale of Gas competitively to the same extent as a 10% reduction in price."[100] Yet, despite facts such as these—and they might be multiplied almost indefinitely—it seems clear that vast changes are in prospect, and that the coördination of fuel and power thesis applied to these problems involves still further extensions of the tentacles of control and regulation.

Although two-thirds of the gas sold in Britain is purchased by domestic users, and the "ratio of meters to population is 1 to 3.7, which means that nearly every household in the country has a gas supply, and that 41 millions of the total population of 48 millions are served by Gas in their Homes,"[101] still gas supplied only 8 per cent and electricity only 2 per cent of the fuel consumed by domestic consumers in 1945, while coal supplied 78 per cent. At the same time the estimated effi-

[100] *The Gas Industry: Facts and Figures*, p. 20.
[101] *Ibid.*, p. 8.

ciency with which gas was used was three times as high as that with which coal was used, and electricity was five times as high.[102] Why should coal be used so extensively? The answer is simply because practically all houses—and the separate rooms of most houses and flats—are equipped with open coal grates. Houses are built that way, people are accustomed to this type of heating, and the whole national system of domestic fuel supply is built up on this basis.

Furthermore, the same thing holds for nondomestic use. Despite the urgency of the fuel shortage, the great and growing interest in fuel conservation, and the need for increasing the efficiency of fuel usage at all levels, scarcely more than one-third of British coal was treated before use in 1945. More than half of all coal used was burned raw by industrial and domestic consumers.[103] Not only was it true that more than one-quarter of the coal was used by domestic consumers in this wasteful and uneconomical way, but this usage is the principal source of Britain's appalling smoke nuisance. From these countless thousands of little fires goes up into the air by weight "2.7 per cent as soot or semiliquid tarry globules, 0.3 per cent as ash, and 2.4 per cent as sulphur dioxide, a total of 5.4 per cent."[104] From domestic coal fires alone "the Heating and Ventilating (Reconstruction) Committee of the D.S.I.R. have estimated the cost of pollution . . . (excluding the cost of unburnt smoke) at over 5s per ton of coal used for domestic purposes."[105] This cost is partly expressible in terms of extra cleaning bills, damage to buildings and library collections, and part—mainly the effect upon health—is difficult if not impossible to calculate.[106] Yet though some progress has been made in recent years, "some 2½ million tons of smoke in the form of unburned portions of the coal substance are poured into the atmosphere" in Britain every year.[107]

[102] PEP Report, p. 337.

[103] In 1945 the railways consumed 15,000,000 tons of raw coal, collieries 12,000,000 tons, general industrial 43,000,000 tons, and domestic consumers 53,000,000 tons, and of coal treated before use 21,000,000 tons were carbonized at gasworks, 20,000,000 tons at coke ovens, 500,000 tons at low temperature, and electricity generation and hydrogenation took respectively 24,000,000 and 400,000 tons. Norman Smith, Gas Manufacture and Utilization (British Gas Council, 1945), pp. 22–23.

[104] Domestic Fuel Policy: Report by the Fuel and Power Advisory Council, Cmd. 6762 [Simon Report] (Ministry of Fuel and Power, 1946), p. 44.

[105] PEP Report, p. 342.

[106] For an interesting summary see Alexander Macgregor, "Smoke and the Public Health" in Proceedings of the Edinburgh Conference, 1947, of the National Smoke Abatement Society, pp. 94–98. See also the society's recent pamphlet, Guilty Chimneys.

[107] Proceedings of the Edinburgh Conference, p. 4. "These losses may be several times greater than the loss of visible smoke, so that there must be a total loss equivalent to about 10 million tons of coal a year," according to Sir George Elliston in a Presidential address before the Society. Times, Oct. 1, 1948.

What follows from facts such as these for the proponents of the coördination thesis? The implications are wide-ranging indeed, and they need only be mentioned for their bearing upon further control and regulation to be grasped. One approach leads to the conclusion that "the efficient use of fuel and smoke abatement are practically synonymous, but it is only through the strong and continued co-operation of all sections of the public that the campaign can be brought to a successful conclusion."[108] This means coördination of coal, coke, gas, electricity; all local authorities; town and country planning, and all housing and trading estates; housing and health; manufacture and use of all fuel and power appliances, domestic and industrial.

Another approach leads to the attempt to solve the problem of dovetailing of daily and seasonal peak loads of the several services, and of loads of those services which happen to be joint one to another (e.g., power and back-pressure steam, or gas and coke). This extraordinarily complicated problem is solved, if at all, primarily by widening the range and types of consumers, increasing the volume of consumption, and establishing discriminatory tariffs which build up off-peak usage (e.g., electrification of railroads) in such a way as to link the problems of individual consumption to those of the manner, mode, and prices at which each individual and class of consumer draws from the central energy pool.

They are, that is to say, problems of coördination and planning of alternative lines of consumer services of virtually all types and at all levels. Coördination to solve the problem of efficiency in the field of fuel and power, in short, brings the Ministry of Fuel and Power face to face with the need of making efficiency in related lines consistent with the freedom of consumers' choice. Not only freedom of choice, however, in the fuels to be used, but also in such things as the manner and times when they should be used, the prices they are to pay for alternatively useful services, the location of their homes and their jobs, the conditions affecting health and the modes of living themselves, the types and quality of the services that transport them to and from their jobs, and so *ad infinitum*. The Ministry of Fuel and Power must attack these problems directly, or it must attempt to work with other agencies in their joint solution if it is to accept the next step in coördination, upon the basis of which the first step has already been taken.

[108] *Domestic Fuel Policy*, p. 44.

CHAPTER V

Iron and Steel

Let no one suppose because we are here building for the future rather than for the present, and proceeding by evolutionary rather than revolutionary steps, that the proposals in this Bill are devoid of historic significance. This great reform removes from the private sector of our economy to the public the industry which is the citadel of British Capitalism. It transfers to Parliament and the community that power to dominate the economic life of this country which now resides with the steelmasters in Steel House.

It will enable our steel industry, which through its key position could do so much to lessen the severity of trade depressions, to become an effective national instrument for planning full employment. It will offer greater security to those who work in it. It will enable our home consumers to get the steel they require at low cost. It will enable the Colonies to get the steel called for by their development plans. It will enable us to cooperate the better with the peoples of Europe in the revival of the industrial prosperity of that continent and the strengthening of its democratic foundations. It is for these great ends that we are asking Parliament to make Britain's iron and steel monopoly the servant rather than the master of the British people.—George Strauss, Minister of Supply, November 15, 1948.

PRIVATE MONOPOLY in the iron and steel industry, said the 1945 Labour manifesto, *Let Us Face the Future,* "has maintained high prices and kept inefficient high-cost plants in existence. Only if public owner-ship replaces private monopoly can the industry become efficient."[1] The mere suggestion made Churchill boil with rage. "What," he demanded to know, "is the British industry which stands forth as a model, beating all previous records as a great producer? It is the steel trade, in which there has never been an industrial strike for 40 years, which is beating all records at this very moment in spite of the uncertainty by which it has been disturbed and hampered . . . The lifebuoy to which we were clinging in our distress is to be turned into another millstone to drag us down into the depths—and all for the sake of the Socialist programme alone. How unworthy of our country in its dire need!"[2]

POLITICAL OVERTONES OF THE IRON AND STEEL BILL

Thus were the issues joined. Both the Labour and the Conservative parties felt that the question of whether or not to nationalize the steel industry placed them literally at the crossroads. Labour felt it could not go back on its 1945 campaign promises without facing serious and pos-sibly large-scale defections in its own ranks which might, conceivably,

[1] *Let Us Face the Future,* p. 7.
[2] Broadcast, as reported in the *Times,* Feb. 15, 1948.

cost it the 1950 elections. Yet it could not go forward without risking
wholesale and well-organized opposition from powerful British business circles—opposition which it felt, rightly or wrongly, might result
in widespread business sabotage of its whole administration at a time
when it felt that it must appeal for this very business support as a condition to solving its postwar production crisis. Nor, yet again, could it
temporize indefinitely without risking a split in its own ranks which,
beginning at Cabinet level,[3] might well ramify throughout all layers of
the various groups whose combined support provided its mass following.

The Conservatives were also faced with a veritable Hobson's choice.
After steel what? Consider, said Captain Lyttelton, Conservative
spokesman and a director of the armaments firm of Vickers, the fact
that manufacture of the main products of the iron and steel industry
"ramifies into almost every crevice of British industry. It goes into the
chemical trade . . . into the production of sulphuric acid, sulphate of
ammonia and creosote. It goes into the electrical industry, in the manufacture of welding equipment; into structural steel, in the manufacture
of things like the Sydney Bridge; it goes into the railway equipment
industry, in the manufacture of axles, tyres and wheels for rolling
stock. It ramifies in every direction and finally, of course, it gets into
the miscellaneous industries where we find that the Government will be
engaged in making umbrella frames and florists' wire."[4] Later on in the
debate Anthony Eden, summing up the case for the Opposition, found
that the *Manchester Guardian* succinctly described the position of Labour when it said that "there is no point after this at which the advance
towards the extinction of private capital in British industry could be
halted."[5] The Tories found themselves defending a last major rampart
before the onrush of the socialist state which threatened their existence
as a political force of any importance whatsoever.

[3] It is quite generally believed in informed London circles, both friendly and hostile to
the Labour government, that of the top government personnel, Aneurin Bevan was the real
driving force behind the introduction of the Steel Bill, and that he was supported by Dalton,
Shinwell, Strachey, Griffiths, and Cripps. The opposition was headed by Ernest Bevin and
Herbert Morrison. The articles and editorials of the *Tribune*, commonly supposed to be a
"Bevan paper" would bear out the former conclusion, and Ernest Bevin's consistent playing
down of socialist heresies the second. One Labour M.P., George Edwards, had been dramatically expelled from the Party at the 1948 Scarborough conference for openly opposing
the nationalization of steel. Another group, the so-called Keep Left Group, though chastened
by party disciplinary action over the Nenni telegram affair, virtually demanded action on
steel as a condition to any further support at all. Also, delay was quite obviously creating
a good deal of unrest in certain trade union circles—not including, however, the steel union—
and hence a good deal of uneasiness in T.U.C. councils.

[4] *Hansard*, Vol. 458, col. 89.

[5] *Ibid.*, col. 480.

Both sides were agreed that this was a battle over a strategic height of major logistical importance. Thus nationalization of the iron and steel industry was inevitably bound up with the problem of the generalized extension of state ownership and operation of all large-scale and more or less monopolistically organized business in the country. For each participant every step in the debates, every thrust and counter-thrust, was made against the background of the 1950 elections, when by common agreement not only the question of steel, but most of Labour's past legislation and all its future plans would be fought without let or hindrance.

It is true that this political atmosphere is not conducive to an objective search for a scientifically defensible and economically valid solution of the problem of what to do with the steel industry in a socialist society; against its lights and shades it becomes virtually impossible for anyone, participant or outside observer alike, to separate truth from falsehood, and fact from dissimulation. Every issue has been obscured by a thick cloud of bias, tendentious verbiage, and innuendo. As debate unfolded much of this battledore and shuttlecock was genial and witty; some of it was bitter and steeped in vitriol.

One Opposition spokesman found the bill to nationalize the iron and steel industry a mere "semi-hybrid . . . certain to prove sterile." It was, again, a "Strauss's mouse, a mouse, however, which has enough meat on it to keep the rats on board a sinking ship."[6] Churchill snorted. "This is not a Bill," he said, "it is a plot . . . an operation in restraint of trade . . . a burglar's jemmy to crack the capitalist crib."[7] A colleague found the Labour leaders to be "gamblers with the best interests of the nation and unworthy of the high position of trust which they hold."[8] Labour had presented a "squint-eyed" bill, "lifting their hats to the Left wing in the party and, at the same time, trying to lift it to the Right wing, and have gone squint-eyed in the process."[9] Worst of all, it was Communism.

This latter theme became more dominant as the debates progressed. The argument followed the familiar pattern: ". . . the Government are power drunk. They want to have an all-powerful concentration at the centre; a little group of oligarchs—'we are the masters now'—flanked by the Patronage Secretary and supported by the obsequious majority

---

[6] Hugh Fraser, *ibid.*, col. 148.
[7] *Ibid.*, col. 228.
[8] *Ibid.*, col. 288.
[9] R. Jennings, *ibid.*, col. 294.

behind treading all together in unison the totalitarian road."[10] National-izing an industry of this sort is pure Marxism as laid out in the *Communist Manifesto*.[11] "As this Bill shows," said Churchill warming to his subject, "they are the handmaids of Communism, and prepare the way at every step for its further advance."[12] The analysis given by the incumbent Minister of Food, John Strachey, had once made an identical point, when he said, "It is impossible to establish Communism as the immediate successor to capitalism. Hence Communists work for the establishment of Socialism as a necessary stage on the road to Communism."[13]

Labour replied in a similar vein. Among its spokesmen was a small steel industrialist who found that "the case for the socialisation of the steel industry cannot be gainsaid. Steel and insurance are the remaining citadels of 20th century privilege and no society moving towards a Socialist economy, can afford a menace within its midst such as the Iron and Steel Federation. The anachronism of a few self-appointed men responsible to no one but the financial interests they represent, meeting in secret and arriving at decisions affecting profoundly the life of the nation, is a negation of democracy and constitutes what has been accurately described as one of the greatest sources of private political power in modern society. Further, the spectacle of 'steel barons' peddling their armaments around the world is an affront to the Christian conscience and can no longer be tolerated." The industry as a whole has been "Maginot minded" for 30 years; it is neither free, nor enterprising; it is run by "industrial adventurers, these twentieth century Drakes, Hawkins and Raleighs" such as Sir Andrew Duncan—industrial tycoon extraordinary and director of the Iron and Steel Federation—whose dictatorial powers are so formidable that it may be said that "whenever Sir Andrew Duncan sneezes the industry catches cold."[14]

Above all, no person in his right mind could applaud "these aboriginal war-cries of Mr. Churchill,"[15] and, as for promoting communism,

---

[10] Selwyn Lloyd, *ibid.*, col. 307.

[11] H. Strauss, referring to the "Socialist Party's own introduction to the *Communist Manifesto*, Centenary Edition," where "they claim a common inspiration with the *Communist Manifesto*." *Ibid.*, col. 130.

[12] *Ibid.*, col. 226. Had he not once said a good many years ago: "A strong dose either of Socialism or Communism will kill Britannia stone dead, and at the inquest the only question for the jury will be: Did she fall or was she pushed?" *Ibid.*

[13] Quoted by Captain Marples from John Strachey, *The Theory and Practice of Socialism* (London, 1936), *ibid.*, col. 431.

[14] S. N. Evans, in *Hansard*, Vol. 423, cols. 874–875, 877–878.

[15] Those who do so "run the risk of being told that the Conservative Party is an extinct volcano, of which the only sign of life is a faint wisp of smoke over the crater, emanating from the dying embers of Mr. Churchill's cigar." Lord Winster in *Hansard* (Lords), Vol 141, col. 735.

unless democracy can subdue "these citadels of power" by peaceful electoral means, then it faces "the ugly alternative . . . that any such change which is to occur must be brought about by other and more violent means and it is because we are preventing that that Socialist democracy is the true barrier against Communism."[16] On the contrary, "that Toryism, which has no understanding of the people and is a reaction against the people, is most likely to stimulate Communist revolution and Communist violence."[17]

As may be seen, both sides played to the galleries. But not as an idle gesture. They were in dead earnest. With all eyes constantly cocked warily for newspaper comments on what was about to be said, the facts, it is true, suffered the tribulations of the guests of Procrustes. But since the debate was political throughout, this could not be helped. With the elections of 1950 in the offing, the big question was how each might gain the maximum support from the politically unattached voters who go to make up the great intermediate middle-class layers. Thus the future of steel, far more clearly than any other program inaugurated under the Labour government, became at the very outset indissolubly linked with the issues surrounding the future of the Labour party and its whole socialist program.

This confusion over steel was worse confounded by the peculiar circumstances under which the debates over nationalization became entangled in partisan politics. A major constitutional issue was involved; that of the reform, or even total abolition, of the House of Lords.[18] This is because it has been technically possible for the Lords, under their powers to delay enactment of Commons' legislation, to prevent for two

---

[16] Sir Stafford Cripps, in *Hansard*, Vol. 458, col. 326.

[17] Herbert Morrison, *ibid.*, col. 494.

[18] In an editorial, published on June 23, 1948, the *Times* summarized the position of the Opposition when it said, "The Lords' rejection of the Parliament Bill makes it humanly certain that, failing an early general election, the Bill will be driven through by the vote of one House only, fought though it will be at every state. Behind this legally permissible procedure . . . lies a grave constitutional conflict . . . The Government is responsible to Parliament—not to the House of Common's majority which it must needs have." If the Lords were abolished and a single Chamber, the House of Commons, were to become the sole legislator, then legislation would speak for the elected majority, not for the people, and "The nationalisation of iron and steel is precisely such a measure as may invoke the duty of the Upper House to the people. There is a strong presumption that the mass of the people do not want it: Mr. Morrison himself . . . implies that in the broad national interest it would be a mistake. Yet it is promised, for reasons obviously partisan, by a three-year old Government which prefers to assault the Constitution rather than await the verdict of the people." To which Labour replied that the nationalization of steel having been in their campaign platform, *Let Us Face the Future*, clearly they had a mandate from the electorate which the Lords could not nullify without undermining constitutional procedure, and since the Lords were prepared to do so anyway, their power to estop legislation must be curbed. Actually the House of Lords had not rejected the bill; it only appeared that they might do so.

years the enactment into law of any legislation coming before them. The debates in the House of Lords over the Gas Bill showed a determination to put a stop to further nationalization at all costs, and so the Labour government was forewarned that its plans to nationalize steel, against which even more determined opposition was certain, were impossible of fulfillment unless the power of the House of Lords to delay legislation was curbed. Hence it came about that the question of what to do about the House of Lords began by the middle of 1948 to take precedence over all other issues.

In getting snarled up with this issue, the nationalization of steel became involved with deep-rooted British traditions, political, social, and cultural. Here the Labour party has run into the sort of dilemma which came very close to wrecking President Roosevelt's whole New Deal program in the United States when he undertook reform of a Supreme Court whose adverse decisions were blocking further advance along the chosen path. Each in its own country (Supreme Court and Lords) is the major obstacle, in a system of checks and balances, to the quick expression of popular sentiment. But far more than the Supreme Court, the House of Lords is part of a vast, deep-rooted, and sentiment-laden conservative system, a system which also embraces the Royal House, and which has by long use and wont come to be viewed by Conservatives, Liberals, and Labour—by patriots of virtually all parties and persuasions generally—as a symbol of British tradition, cultural achievement, stability, power, and Empire.

Thus nationalization of steel must needs wait upon this politically dangerous reform of the House of Lords. While the delay caused by this complication was being endured, it also happened that much of the case for the nationalization of steel, on the grounds chosen by the Labour government, was growing weaker; viz., that of the necessity of reorganizing the steel industry as a whole in order to secure greater industrial efficiency. As will be pointed out, while the condition of the steel industry still leaves very much to be desired, throughout the postwar period it has shown some remarkable progress in the enhancement of the volume of production, gaining higher output per employee, and lowering costs of output. So it happened that where the Labour government must make the most haste, it has been able to make the least.

The dilemma was politically serious, but it was also not altogether clear how it could be solved politically. At best, it appeared, Labour was loath to attack the problem at all because nationalization of steel was clearly anathema to American businessmen. Ordinarily this would not matter. But Sir Stafford Cripps has knowingly made himself responsible for the fixed belief that without Marshall Plan aid Britain could not solve the problem of the import-export gap, and that this solution holds the key to Britain's postwar revival—not to mention the success or failure of the Labour government's whole economic and social program. If, then, American aid is indispensable, and if this aid—proffered by an American Congress dominated by American business interests, and to be administered along business lines by an American businessman, Paul G. Hoffman—can be received only on American conditions, what is to be said about American disapproval of the nationalization of steel, advertised, as it was, as a major step on the road to the socialist society which American business abhors?

At a critical point in the steel discussions in Britain the news came that, when questioned about "his attitude towards British nationalisation policies," Hoffman had "said that if the British Government asked for E.C.A. [Economic Co-operation Administration] shipments to modernise the steel industry and then announced that the industry would be nationalised, the shipments would probably be denied."[19] Though this opinion was delivered, as it was later explained, quite obviously to quiet a Congress which was out of sympathy with the socialist program of the British Labour government, and though it did not specifically say that aid to Britain would not be given because of its nationalization measures,[20] nevertheless the damage had been done. The statement was received in London by Government spokesmen with stunned silence.

While, as subsequent events established, it was the official position of both the British and American governments that the Marshall Plan was to involve no interference in the internal affairs of recipient countries, yet the Italian elections showed clearly the American intention not to give aid where it suspected the political intentions of the dominant party. The Opposition was gleeful. Here was an unexpected break in the argument for them, and Churchill and his supporters made the

---

[19] *The Daily Telegraph*, May 14, 1948.

[20] "You don't get results in a transition period," he added. "On the other hand, a request for machinery for the coal industry, which was all ready nationalised, would probably be granted, since that would lead to increased production of coal immediately." *Ibid.* The issue, in other words, was not nationalization *per se*, but only the disturbing effects of transition which nationalization would involve, yet this was precisely what the Opposition benches were arguing in Parliament—not only about steel, but also about every other nationalization measure brought forward by the Labour government. It was also the position taken behind the scene by the American Embassy in London.

most of it. Britain, Churchill said, was "living on subsidies by loan or gift provided by taxes on the hard-working and heavily-burdened people of the United States . . . They gave us a loan which I welcomed, and helped forward to the best of my ability, a loan of £1,000 million. Now, under the Marshall Plan, which had its origin traceably in the movement for a united Europe, they are giving us £300 million a year now and for several years to come." This aid is all that has kept Britain from being subjected to widespread unemployment, as after the First World War.[21] On this aid "the Socialist Government and Socialist policy are living from month to month and from hand to mouth," and yet the policies of this same socialist government were akin to those of Henry Wallace who had just been repudiated in the recent American elections. The implication was obvious: Nationalization of steel might cause withdrawal of further American aid, and bring about a fatal collapse of Britain.

It is in the face of facts and events such as these, and against such a background of issues—past, present, and future—that the Labour government toyed for three years with its program for the nationalization of the iron and steel industry, and finally brought in a measure which represents a compromise that it evidently thought would extricate it from the most trying of all its numerous postwar dilemmas. As planned, the measure would take effect after the reform of the House of Lords, cutting down the time for which it can delay legislation from two years to one year, has passed into law, and would make possible the setting of the vesting day for the Steel Act on May 1, 1950. Later, but before the date of the 1950 general election had been set, the vesting day was changed to "January 1, 1951, or within eighteen months thereafter," the actual date to be determined by the Minister of Fuel and Power. This change insured that it would follow the election and made it possible for the issues involved to be thoroughly discussed in the course of the election campaign. Thus the problem of the nationalization of the steel industry is politically the most important and strategic of all the various nationalization proposals introduced during Labour's first five years of office.

[21] Top Labour leaders agree, Churchill went on to say: "Last April [in Manchester, the Lord President of the Council, Herbert Morrison, said], 'We would be facing big cuts in rations and a million or two people on the dole if our generous and far-sighted friends and allies in America had not come to the rescue.' [And the Minister of Health, Mr. Bevan] although I think he is the driving power behind this Bill—endorsed the statements of the Lord President of the Council, when he said at Scarborough [annual Labour conference, 1948] a month afterwards: 'Without Marshall Aid, unemployment in this country would at once rise by 1,500,000.'" *Hansard*, Vol. 458, cols. 216–217.

THE HISTORICAL ANTECEDENTS OF THE STEEL BILL

Not until the great depression of the thirties did Labour add the iron and steel industry to its lists of those industries which were ripe for socialization. In 1931 the Labour party included iron and steel, along with power and transport, among the "most important basic industries" which "should be reorganised as public utilities on the basis of National ownership and the participation of the Workers in the responsibilities of management and control."[22] In 1932 the "executive of the Iron and Steel Trades Confederation . . . presented to the then Trades Unions Council . . . a complete case for public ownership and control." Two years later, the T.U.C. "adopted the scheme . . . unanimously."[23]

Neither group reversed itself after taking this original position, though it was not until 1942 that the Labour party made the issue a major plank in its postwar program.[24] Even then steel never appeared in the forefront of discussion. What seems to have been primarily responsible for its inclusion in *Let Us Face the Future* was the belief that the scale of the technical reorganization required in order fully to modernize the industry could only be carried out with government assistance, and that to do so under the existing circumstances would serve only to consolidate a complete monopoly under the auspices of the powerful Iron and Steel Federation. The latter, in turn, would then be in such a strategic position astride the vast complex of closely related machine, manufacturing, construction and other allied metallurgical industries that it would be able at will to make or break the whole of Labour's postwar program. This holds with special force in the critical sector of export trade, where in 1948 some 32 per cent of the total tonnage of steel and steel products was shipped overseas, and was able to account for 43.2 per cent of all exports by value.[25]

THE RECORD OF PAST EFFORTS AT CONTROL

Before turning to the question of the degree of efficiency or inefficiency which characterized the British steel industry on the eve of the nationalization proposal, it will be worth while noting the character of the previous steps which had been taken to effect reorganization of the industry. Of these, three are of particular importance: the establish-

---

[22] *Report of the Thirty-First Annual Conference of the Labour Party* (Scarborough, 1931), p. 321.
[23] Jack Jones, in *Hansard*, Vol. 458, col. 237.
[24] Ronald Mackay, *ibid.*, col. 400.
[25] *Report of the ECA Mission to the United Kingdom*, Vol. I (1948), chart 22, p. 21, and tabular data, p. 31.

ment of the Import Duties Advisory Committee (IDAC) on March 1,
1932, the formation of the Iron and Steel Federation in April, 1934,
and the setting up of the Iron and Steel Board on October 2, 1946 as
the successor to the wartime Iron and Steel Control (inaugurated in
1939). It was what Labour felt to be the total failure of these organizations properly to effect the right type of steel reorganization which led
directly to the Iron and Steel Bill.

The IDAC was established by the National government shortly after
the demise of the second Labour government in 1931, and signalized
a sharp changeover in British trade policy to a wide-ranging system of
tariff protection. The new organization—sometimes referred to, after
the name of its chairman, as the May committee—found its *raison
d'être*, so far as the steel industry was concerned, in

the acute depression from which the industry suffered during the decade preceding 1932 [and which it believed] was largely due to causes beyond its control. The huge and urgent demands made upon it during the Great War caused
a large and hasty expansion of existing works or erection of new works in a
manner which was often haphazard—almost inevitably so in the circumstances
of the time—and in the last stages of the War always very costly, with the result
that when war demands ceased and the short-lived hectic post-war activity came
to an end the industry found itself with much redundant plant, some of which,
though representing the highest degree of technical efficiency, could not under
the post-boom conditions earn sufficient to cover the heavy capital charges incurred in construction. The difficulties caused by the slump in demand were
intensified by the severe competition from foreign works aided by the depreciation of currencies, or the reduction—and in some cases complete wiping out—of
capital charges by reason of that depreciation, or the restoration of works out of
Reparations . . . the combined effects of foreign and domestic competition during
the period when the general trade depression had reduced demand to a minimum
were a fall of prices and production to very low levels, with the consequence that
great losses were incurred, and the industry became heavily indebted to the
banks and was quite unable to carry out adequately the desirable reconditioning
and modernising of its plant or to take full advantage of new technical developments.[26]

As the National government saw it, two things were then necessary:
protection from foreign competition and protection from domestic competition. The first took the form of recommendations for the imposition
of ad valorem duties of one-third "on most grades of steel, for a short
period, their renewal being conditioned upon reorganization of the

---

[26] *Report of the Import Duties Advisory Committee on the Present Position and Future
Development of the Iron and Steel Industry*, Cmd. 5507 (1937), pp. 11–12. [Hereafter referred to as *IDAC Report*.]

industry."[27] Since this did prevent the continued large-scale importation of low-priced foreign steel, the duties were increased to 50 per cent in 1934, and steps were taken to promote "the formation of a comprehensive organisation capable of exercising a powerful influence on the conduct of the industry, and" to enable it "to negotiate with its foreign competitors on equal terms. This has only been achieved by giving the industry a quasi-monopolistic position in the home market."[28]

This new organization was the Iron and Steel Federation—which the May committee felt would "foster a spirit of co-operation" by employing to national advantage its "machinery set up to control development"—and enjoyed from the outset semigovernmental status. Since it was supposed to exercise influence (if not direct power) which was coextensive with virtually all phases and aspects of the British iron and steel industry, and since this was the alternative which both the industry and its Conservative supporters in Parliament were prepared to submit to the proposed nationalization, it is worth further examination. The formula was "self-government in industry," the powers were those of a cartel, and the sanctions were those supplied by the National government. As reorganized in 1945, the scope of the authority and the machinery of this version of self-government is shown in chart 4.

The main objects of the Federation, as outlined by staff members in personal interviews with the author in the summer of 1948, may be summarized as follows:

1) To render efficient service to the community.

2) To provide self-government for the iron and steel industry within the framework of government policy.

3) To develop all branches of the industry to the greatest possible extent, particularly those producing for export or supplying other industries producing for export.

4) To maintain full and regular employment.

5) To insure reasonable and steady returns to labor employed in the industry and to investors who put their savings into the industry.

6) To unite the industry for common purposes while allowing sufficient decentralization of management to give full play to enterprise and initiative so that the organization may be the servant, not the master, of the industry.

7) To set up an executive body which is properly representative of all sections of the industry, elected in such a fashion as to ensure that the best men get to the top.

8) To set up machinery to provide constant survey, investigation, and planning within the industry.

---

[27] D. L. Burn, *Economic History of Steel-Making* (Cambridge, 1939), p. 449.
[28] *IDAC Report*, p. 23.

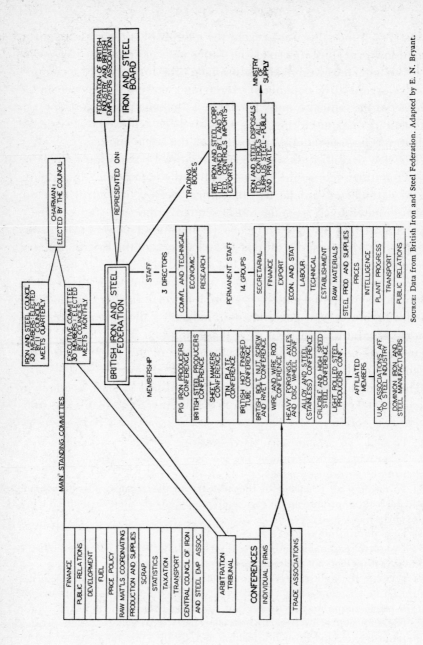

Source: Data from British Iron and Steel Federation. Adapted by E. N. Bryant.

Chart 4. Organization of the British Iron and Steel Federation before nationalization.

The executive committee is then supposed to conduct all the affairs of the Federation, including the management of the two trading bodies; coördinate the work and interests of the various conferences; conduct the various standing and *ad hoc* committees, represent the industry in all negotiations—domestic and foreign—affecting the interests of its membership, and serve as a negotiating body with labor unions and with all government departments having an interest in, or power over, one or more of the activities within the Federation's purview. Each of the conferences, in turn, is supposed to play a somewhat similar role in guiding all the corporations and trades associations which constitute its membership.

It requires little perspicacity, and but small knowledge of recent history, to recognize here a supercartel of the type which not even the Germans succeeded in effecting for any major industry until the rise of the Nazis in the early thirties. There is a close analogy, in fact, between this organization and that of the *Reichsgruppe industrie* as it was developed by the Nazis under the National Economic Chamber, except that the grouping of the metallurgical sections followed a somewhat different system of classification.[29] It represents a high level of development along the lines of what the *Economist* early in the war referred to as Britain's "feudalistic system of cartel Control" where there exists "an orderly organisation of industries, each ruled feudally from above by the business firms already established in it, linked in associations and confederations and, at the top, meeting on terms of sovereign equality such other Estates of the Realm as the Bank of England and the Government . . . This is of the order of ideas . . . that is admirable for obtaining security, 'orderly development' and remunerative profits for those already established in the industry—at the cost of an irreducible body of general unemployment. It is emphatically not a set of ideas that can be expected to yield the maximum of production or to give the country wealth in peace and strength in war."[30]

This view of the *Economist* seemed to Labour quite adequately to

---

[29] See, e.g., Robert A. Brady, *The Spirit and Structure of German Fascism* (New York, 1937), chart at end of book, and Franz Neumann, *Behemoth* (New York, 1942), Pt. II, chapters 2, 3, and 5, particularly the chart on p. 246.

[30] "The Economic Front," *Economist*, Dec. 9, 1939; "The Cartelisation of England," *Economist*, March 18, 1939; and "A Check on Production," *Economist*, June 15, 1940. *The New Statesman and Nation*, March 8, 1945, added a revealing comment: "We shall be confronted with a strongly entrenchd co-operative organization of industry on a restrictionist basis—not unlike the Italian fascist economy—impossible to unscramble. Unfortunately the influence of Trade Union leaders is exerted—unwittingly—in the same direction to the ultimate disadvantage of those whose interests they think they represent. But the record of the Duce's system surely does not invite imitation."

summarize the subsequent achievements of the Iron and Steel Federation. Prices were raised and stabilized to permit the survival of high cost producers; foreign competition was largely excluded and a cartel agreement was worked out with foreign competitors (following which tariffs on most products were first lowered to around 20 per cent ad valorem and then raised by a flexible formula to suit the industry's felt need for protection); two affiliated corporations were established, one for central buying and selling of virtually all iron and steel imports and heavy steel exports (The British Iron and Steel Corporation Ltd.), and one for the control (mostly price) over imports of ore and surplus government and private steel supplies (Iron and Steel Disposals Ltd.);[31] certain types of costs, most important those of ore, were equalized throughout the industry and financed out of a fund raised by the levying of tonnage charges paid into a central pool; and technical modernization, after making a few hesitant starts, was tapered off without beginning to cope with the underlying problem.[32]

Aided after the middle thirties by the beginning of the new armaments program, the results were gratifying to the industry. Home prices advanced for heavy plate from 160 shillings per long ton in 1933 to 213 in 1937, and for export from 155 to 220.[33] Other prices showed a similar behavior. "According to the Board of Trade figure, taking the 1930 price as the basis, at 100, there was a general rise in steel prices from 98.7 in 1934, to 139.1 in 1938. What is more startling are some of the prices which go to make up the index figure. Pig iron rose from £3 2s. 6d. per ton in January, 1934, to £5 9s. 0d. in 1938, ship plates from £8 16s. 3d. to £11 8s. 0d., and soft basic billets from £5 12s. 6d. to £7 17s. 6d. Thus there was a 30 to 40 per cent rise in British steel prices after the formation of the Federation."[34]

One result was that many important British steel-using industries had to pay higher prices than did their foreign competitors. According to one industrialist,

In January, 1939, whereas our American competitors were able to buy cold rolled steel sheets for motor car bodies at £14 a ton, Austin, Morris and the others were having to pay £21 5s. American cold drawn one per cent. nickel bars

[31] From data supplied by the Iron and Steel Foundation.

[32] "Now while the technical changes involved in the major expansions sanctioned in 1936 were impressive, the schemes scarcely reflected any advance towards a well devised ground-plan for the British industry; indeed two of them positively stood in the way of such an advance." Burn, *op. cit.*, p. 506.

[33] *Ibid.*, table XL, p. 455.

[34] John Wilmot, Minister of Supply, in *Hansard*, Vol. 423, cols. 846–847. These figures were not disputed by the Opposition.

could be bought at £21 5s. after being brought across the Atlantic, carriage, insurance and freight paid at Tilbury, whereas British manufacturers wanted £33 11s. United States cold drawn five per cent. case-hardened nickel bars were £28 8s. a ton at Tilbury, whereas the British manufacturers wanted £45 6s. More recently, in November, 1945, Stewart and Lloyds prices for oil equipment for Trinidad, was from 29 per cent. to 47 per cent. higher, free on board, than those of their Pittsburg counterparts. In the matter of barrel tanks, Oklahoma prices showed an advantage to the same buyers, the Trinidad Petroleum Development Co., of from 91 per cent. to 135 per cent. A large London industrial concern of my acquaintance has recently had a tentative inquiry for £1,250,000 worth of capital equipment for Russia. In the building up of this capital equipment they required steel castings. They went to Scotland for a price and were quoted £148 a ton. They thought this was rather more than a joke, and got in touch with American firms. I have here a cablegram received today, and the American price free on board is £62 a ton. It is the same specification and the same metal.[35]

The effect upon corporate profits of price, in a period which was shifting from a buyers' to a sellers' market, was as might be expected. According to Davies, although most of the leading steel concerns lost money, and United Steel earned less than one per cent before the establishment of the Iron and Steel Federation, "by 1937 all were earning more than 10 per cent on their capital, the lowest being Guest, Keen and Nettelfolds which earned 11 per cent and the highest Hadfields with 32 per cent. Exceptionally Standton Iron earned 8 per cent on its capital in 1932 but tripled it by 1938 when 24 per cent was earned. Similarly, while Whitehead Iron earned 12 per cent that year it multiplied its profits by nine times by 1937–8 when 74 per cent was earned on its capital."[36] It is "no wonder," said John Wilmot, that "the vital industries, the consumers and customers of iron and steel, such as the manufacturers of motor cars and engineering products generally, all greatly interested because they depended so greatly on iron and steel, protested these increases." He went on to quote Lord Nuffield, motor car magnate, from the *Times* of Aug. 21, 1937, who spoke of the success of the steel industry as "a perfect ramp, an absolute ramp . . . big cigars and nothing to do . . . It is asked why we cannot produce a cheaper motor car. The steel manufacturers in this country are doing their best to get all they can from the present position. They are overcharging us. Since they had the duty their price has gone up by 25 per cent."[37]

---

[35] S. N. Evans, *ibid.*, cols. 875–876. These figures also were not disputed by the Opposition. The last item was conceded specifically by R. S. Hudson for the Opposition, *ibid.*, col. 1109.
[36] Ernest Davies, *"National" Capitalism* (London, 1939), p. 73.
[37] *Hansard*, Vol. 423, col. 847.

Thus enhanced profits came mostly from higher prices gained through the exercise of cartel controls, and not from lower costs through reorganization of the sort which it was anticipated would follow upon the establishment of the IDAC in 1932, and its advocacy of the principle of self-government in industry embodied in the Iron and Steel Federation. The May committee, to be sure, had heavily underscored the need for reorganization in wholly unmistakable terms, and it had found some developments for the better before the outbreak of the war,[38] but as Burn and others have pointed out, there was, on the record to date, little evidence that the Federation took this task very seriously.

Perhaps, as some of its spokesmen appeared to believe, the Iron and Steel Federation lacked the necessary power to do so anyway. Whether this was so or not, it seems entirely clear that the official position taken by the Federation was that all such reorganization must be undertaken by individual members on a purely voluntary basis, and that to this end the best it could do was encourage further merger, amalgamation, and trustification behind the screen of protection, and provide certain additional services to the industry of more or less the usual trade association type—such as those supplied by the British Iron and Steel Research Association, founded in 1945[39] when the eminent threat of nationalization was already visible on the horizon although the plans had been drawn before the threat was clearly recognized. But, of course, if this were really true, then it was also true that the Federation was more interested in saddling the country with the vast liability of a gigantic monopoly organization, than of effecting a thoroughgoing technical reorganization of this vital sector of the national economy.

At any rate, this was the picture as the Labour government saw it when it came into office in 1945. Their first step, after announcing its intention to nationalize the industry, was to scrap the wartime Iron and Steel Control—set up at the outbreak of the war in 1939—under which the government had assumed central direction of industry policy, and set up in its place an interim Iron and Steel Board to prepare the way for the measures which were to follow.

[38] In its second Report the May committee had said, "Further investigation of the position led us to the conclusion (that had been reached in almost all previous enquiries into the industry) that the grant of protection would not suffice to place the industry in a position to play its proper part in the national economy unless it were accompanied by a considerable measure of reorganization." *Import Duties: Recommendations of the IDAC*, Cmd. 4181 (1932), p. 2. This position was reiterated in the 1937 Report, cited above, and some progress was reported. But the latter also indicated clearly that the task had scarcely been begun.

[39] For a description of this central research organization see The British Iron and Steel Association, *Metallurgia*, 36 (Sept., 1947), 253–256.

PRELIMINARY STEPS TO NATIONALIZATION

With respect to no other nationalization measure did the Government proceed with such caution. The most canonical Fabian tactics were employed at every step of the way—the Government literally feeling its way to a compromise solution. In the first announcement on the subject after the 1945 elections, Wilmot said merely that the Government intended "extending a large measure of public ownership to a large section of the iron and steel industry"[40] and proposed the establishment of a caretaker control board for the intervening period. A month later debate was opened on a motion definitely intended to feel out the strength of the Opposition and the sentiment in the country as a whole. It read, "That this House approves the decision of His Majesty's Government to bring forward proposals for transferring to the ownership of the nation appropriate sections of the iron and steel industry with a view to its efficient organisation in the public interest."[41]

Simultaneously with the submission of this motion, the government submitted to the country as a white paper a special report on the iron and steel industry which had been prepared by the Iron and Steel Federation (and the Joint Iron Council) at the request of the wartime Coalition government.[42] Since it was on the basis of the plans submitted in this report that the Labour government rested much of its case for the nationalization bill introduced later, it will be necessary to glance briefly at the proposals laid out in this report.

In its terms of reference to the iron and steel industry, the Coalition government "asked the industry to submit, within six months, a plan to be carried out in five years embodying the major improvements and new construction necessary to put the industry on an efficient operating basis. In formulating the plan, priority should be given to new plant at the finishing end of the industry which would increase exports; to schemes to reduce fuel costs and consumption; and to schemes to enable a greater proportion of output to be produced by large scale production methods. The industry were also asked to supply informa-

---

[40] This was on April 17. *British Economic Reports*, Aug. 5–19, 1946.

[41] *Hansard*, Vol. 423, col. 842.

[42] *Iron and Steel Industry, Reports by the British Iron and Steel Federation and the Joint Iron Council to the Minister of Supply*, Cmd. 6811 (1946). The Iron and Steel Federation's part of this report had been independently published in December, 1945. The Joint Iron Council consists of "two members of equal representative status," the Council of Iron-foundry Associations, founded in 1941, and the Council of Iron Producers, founded in 1945. These two are closely interlocked, and the latter represents about 75 per cent of the volume of national iron castings production. *Ibid.*, pp. 45, 104–107.

tion on the adjustments between firms which may be necessary to ensure the full loading of efficient plant . . ." and, "when submitting their plan, to make any proposals they think necessary for Government support during the period of modernisation." The plan "should, when agreed, constitute the basis of action for the Government and the industry."[43]

The Federation stated the "objects of the plan" which it later submitted to consist of three major tasks:

i) To make good the further modernisation and development which would have taken place during the last six years had there been no war. Under war conditions, the Government was unable to allow the industry to continue the process which it had begun several years before the war of systematic modernisation and development.

ii) To enlarge steelmaking facilities to bring them into close relationship with the higher demand for steel products that may be anticipated in the post-war years as compared with pre-war.

iii) To ensure the most effective use of plants by concentrating production, with due regard to the availability of raw material and the distance to markets, into efficient units of appropriate size.[44]

Thus it was laid down by the Federation as a basic proposition that its purpose before the war had been to secure "effective progressive modernisation" of the industry, and that this result would have been achieved by "the 1950's" but for the war.[45] The Federation estimated that home steel requirements by 1950–1955 would run around 13,000,000 tons, and export about 3,000,000 tons (ingot), and concluded that its "modernisation plan involves replacement and expansion in 7½ years equivalent to about 40 per cent. of the capacity of the industry at a cost of £168,000,000"[46]

This was then elaborated in terms of the leading steel producing districts of Great Britain; the requirements for iron ore, new and old scrap, raw materials, imports and domestic production, fuel needs, and other supply problems at different stages of iron and steel production; geographic location and relocation of the necessary plant (including plants to be scrapped) by sizes and types of plant (specialized, integrated, etc.), by processes and types of products, and by corporate enterprises; plant efficiencies, costs of production, capital requirements, and modes of financing; and the timing schedule on which all the anticipated changes were to be effected. On this last point, "the general plan in-

[43] *Ibid.*, p. 7.
[44] *Loc. cit.*
[45] *Loc. cit.*
[46] *Ibid.*, pp. 9 and 36.

volves the building of 4¾ million tons of blast furnaces and about 6 million tons of steel ingot capacity. The precise rate of building will depend on a number of factors, including the extent to which part of the rolling mill plant can be imported. The aim, however, is to start construction progressively on the whole of the plan within the five years from 1946 to 1950 and to complete it by the middle of 1953, i.e., within about 7½ years."[47]

There were certain conditions attached to the plan which must be complied with before the separate steps could be taken. The industry felt that although it had the wherewithal "to meet approximately half the cost of the programme out of its resources" and that the remainder could be had by the usual methods of financing,[48] still it would have to be assured of man power and materials priorities, and the whole program would have to be fitted in with the government's plans for the industrial growth of the development areas. Furthermore, since the "plan is based on the full loading of efficient plant," it must be protected from extreme fluctuations in demand; full employment policy required that the necessary "stability of demand . . . further be assisted by an import policy which arranged only for such imports as are necessary to balance efficient production in the U.K."; there should be a favorable taxation policy which would permit early writing off of capital and depreciation charges; and coal and high-grade imported ores should be managed with benefit of a firm policy which would guarantee the industry adequate supplies at low cost.

Relations with other industries which would be affected by the contemplated changes could be worked out with them. Thus, for example, the plan was based upon the assumption that cheap, but low-grade, domestic ores would supply 60 per cent of the total demand, and that the necessary increased capacities in ore mining and coke supply would be forthcoming.

The recommendations of the Joint Iron Council were, in effect and for all practical purposes, worked out along similar lines, although the scale of the recommended reorganization involved much less of a fundamental change in the structure of the iron industry than in the much larger and far more important steel industry.

It was against the background of these reports that Wilmot set up the caretaker Iron and Steel Board for the interim between the introduction of the motion to bring forward a nationalization bill for the iron

[47] *Ibid.*, p. 23.
[48] *Ibid.*, p. 36.

and steel industry, and the actual introduction of the anticipated bill. As Wilmot put it, "During this period, in order to see that the industry is carried on, that it secures, despite the current shortage, the necessary supplies of materials required both from home and abroad, and that the modernisation schemes proceed smoothly and rapidly, we intend . . . to set up a Control Board. This Board will take over those functions, together with responsibility for the regulation of production and distribution, and for advice on prices—functions so far performed by the Iron and Steel Control."[49]

Since this board was the successor to the wartime successor of the prewar IDAC., it came heavily to figure in the subsequent debates on the nationalization bill. In judging its purpose, "It is completely false to suggest," said Wilmot, "that this Control Board, upon which I shall invite to serve representatives both of managements and workers in the industry, will be asked to design the pattern of nationalisation. Nothing of the kind. That the Government have already determined. But in seeking technical guidance upon difficult practical problems of severance in particular cases, the Government will certainly avail themselves of the best technical advice of the individual members of the Board in their individual capacity. The functions of the Board are quite definite and for a limited period."[50]

On August 20 this was further amplified by a statement from the Ministry of Supply that "the Board should concentrate . . . on the supervision of the development and reconstruction of the industry and on the exercise of such continued direct control function as may be necessary in such matters as production, distribution and prices. It will not, however, be part of the functions of the Board or of the members of the Steel Industry to advise the Government in connection with plans for public ownership. The preparation of such plans, with a view to the submission of proposals to Parliament, will be treated by the Government as a separate matter. The Iron and Steel Federation has intimated that the industry will associate itself with membership of the Board on this basis and will press on with the modernisation programme with all possible speed."[51]

On September 5 the names of the members of the board were announced to the public. Its constitution[52] and the manner in which it ful-

---

[49] *Hansard*, Vol. 423, col. 854.

[50] *Ibid.*, col. 855.

[51] Ministry of Supply, *Press Release*, Aug. 20, 1946.

[52] "The members of the Iron and Steel Board were announced by the Minister of Supply on September 5. The Board consists of an independent chairman, two other independent

filled its functions drew high praise from the Opposition leadership in Parliament. It seemed to Churchill, in fact, that it provided the government with all the controls needed for so vital an industry and functioned so well that it entirely dispensed with the Government's case for nationalization. "In the Steel Board," he said, "which the Government's policy forces out of existence by their plans of nationalisation, we had an instrument at once powerful, flexible and comprehending, under which modern needs and emergencies in all their variations, many of them unforeseeable, could be dealt with as they arose."[53] This was high praise indeed. Nevertheless the Government, as George Strauss (successor to Wilmot as Minister of Supply) put it, "had never conceived the Iron and Steel Board as anything more than a stop-gap. It was clearly stated by my predecessor at the time of its establishment that the Board was set up to link the industry with the Government until nationalisation could be effected. The members of the Board have performed their difficult task admirably, but this setup is and always has been in the Government's opinion wholly unsuitable as a permanent method of control."[54] Accordingly, it was dissolved on the eve of the introduction of the Iron and Steel Bill.

Before turning to the bill, introduced for its second reading on November 15, 1948, it will be necessary to review briefly the general nature of the most important charge brought by the Government against the industry, viz., that of its failure effectively to reorganize itself in a manner and on a scale which the country's postwar needs required. The center of this claim was based on the industry's past record of technical backwardness. What were the facts?

TECHNICAL STAGNATION IN THE IRON AND STEEL INDUSTRY

The technical backwardness of the British iron and steel industry has long been a bitterly debated subject in British business and political

---

members, one of whom is still to be appointed, two members drawn from employers in the industry and two from the appropriate trade unions. They are: Sir Archibald Forbes, Chairman, who has experience both as a distinguished industrial executive and a Government official; Sir Alan Barlow, a Treasury official since 1942; Mr. A. Callaghan, general secretary of the National Union of Blast Furnacemen, ore miners, coke workers and kindred trades; Mr. Lincoln Evans, genral Secretary of the Iron and Steel Confederation and a member of the General Council of the Trades Union Congress; Mr. G. H. Lathan, chairman and managing director of an iron and steel company, president-elect of the British Iron and Steel Federation and Technical Adviser for the steel industry on the Government Finance Corporation for Industry; Mr. R. Mather, chairman and managing director of the Skinningrove Iron Company." British Information Services, *Economic Record*, no. 30, Aug. 26–Sept. 9, 1946, p. 4.

[53] *Hansard*, Vol. 458, col. 220.
[54] *Ibid.*, col. 56.

circles. In his incisive and indispensable history of the steelmaking industry in England, Burn tells of the caustic criticism leveled by Continental writers at the inferior exhibit put on by British iron producers at the Paris Exhibition of 1867. "According to the *Edinburgh Review* it was no longer a matter of conjecture that England had lost first place and was fast retrogressing," for the Exhibition "afforded evidence of our decline upon the largest possible scale."[55] Nor did she ever completely catch up with best practice abroad. Both German and American production from the eighties on tended to stay well in the lead, and although great advances were made in many branches of the British industry, by the outbreak of the First World War there were few lines in which its technology did not lag far behind.

After the war the condition became chronic, and during the decades of the twenties and thirties, the problem of what to do with the iron and steel industry crept ever more frequently into public discussion. In 1930 the Sankey committee[56] found "the smelting and coke-making branches of the industry wholly antiquated and inadequate; ore mining and steelmaking less so, but still in need of great expenditure."[57] Although "only a comparatively few (steel) plans were entirely out of date," the extent of the overhaul required called for new investment of £15,000,000 or more, regional amalgamations, and (Burn surmises) extensive locational changes.

After the establishment of the IDAC and the founding of the Iron and Steel Federation a modernization program was launched. By the outbreak of the war the total expenditure on this work was estimated to have run around £50,000,000. Yet it also seems clear that not only was the task scarcely begun, but that even the changes made were in many respects of such a nature as scarcely to improve the situation. What was needed, as Burn points out, was a fundamental change in the ground plan of the entire industry. Without this fundamental reorganization, piecemeal changes, however good in themselves, may very well represent merely a waste of capital resources. A brief review of the condition of the industry at the end of the Second World War will show why this is true.

---

[55] Burn, *op. cit.*, p. 3.

[56] The report of this committee, Burn says, "was confidential, but became available in Germany. Summaries in German newspapers were translated and published in England. The version used here was published in *Ironmonger*, Nov. 29, 1930, pp. 67–68. The accuracy of the record has never been questioned." *Ibid.*, p. 436, n. 4. The relevant data are reviewed in great detail in T. H. Burnham and G. O. Hoskins, *Iron And Steel in Britain, 1870–1930* (London, 1943).

[57] Burn, *loc. cit.*

Modern steel production is highly mechanized in all stages, from raw material to finished product, and the close technical linkage of the various steps in production favors a high degree of vertical integration of the primary stages of production. Chart 5 shows the leading technical interconnections of the industry, and illustrates the problems which technical modernization of the British iron and steel industry must face. Owen, one of the industry's most uncompromising critics, believes that in the various processes involved in the handling of raw materials "in no single one does Britain fulfil the most elementary requirements. In the proper preparation of raw materials, the blending of coke, blending, drying and sintering of ore, and the preparation of richer ore mixtures, in the use of waste gases to reheat the blast, Britain is hopelessly in arrears as these economies mostly come with increased size and integration. The same applies to the use of mechanisation for loading and charging and the elimination of laborious manual labor."[58]

High cost of raw materials is also due to lack of mechanization in coal mining,[59] the failure to construct more modern large-scale and by-product coke ovens,[60] and location of plant in high-cost ore areas. Concerning location, Burn comments that "there is a surprisingly wide range of raw material costs, and a very large part of the British output is made from the more costly materials. In 1937 the raw material costs for pig-iron in Northhamptonshire were from 40s. to 45s. a ton; in Lincolnshire from 50s. to 55s.; elsewhere—in the more famous centres—from 60s. to 70s. Seventy per cent of the iron was made in the high-cost areas, nine per cent in the low cost. It was estimated in 1944 that post-war raw material costs in the cheap area would be approximately 70s. to 75s. per ton of iron; in coastal areas, using imported ore,

[58] Henry Owen, *Steel—The Facts* (London, 1946), pp. 33–34. Since the data given and the argument advanced in this book has been the subject of some rather heated controversy, a request was made by the author for a detailed check on the accuracy of both fact and opinion from the point of view of the Iron and Steel Federation. The research staff of the Federation gladly complied. Unless otherwise indicated, all data and argument contained in this book and cited below have thus been cleared as accurate by the Iron and Steel Federation. The memorandum from the Federation, from which I am (by request) not free to quote directly, was dated August, 1946. At the time of my request in April, 1948, the federation had nothing new to add to that memorandum. Hence it will be assumed that the Federation will agree that the facts cited are substantially correct unless they are refuted in the memorandum in question.

[59] "Pithead prices in this country are £2 a ton as compared with 12s. 6d. in America. At two tons of coal to a ton of steel, the pithead price of coal here is £4 per ton of steel against 25s. in America." Sir A. R. Duncan, in *Hansard*, Vol. 423, col. 1029. Thus the coal cost in Britain is more than three times as high, even though the wages paid in British coal mining are less than half the American average.

[60] In 1937 "the central units talked of in 1931 had not been built and many of the new batteries were too small to realise all possible economies." Burn, *op. cit.*, p. 485.

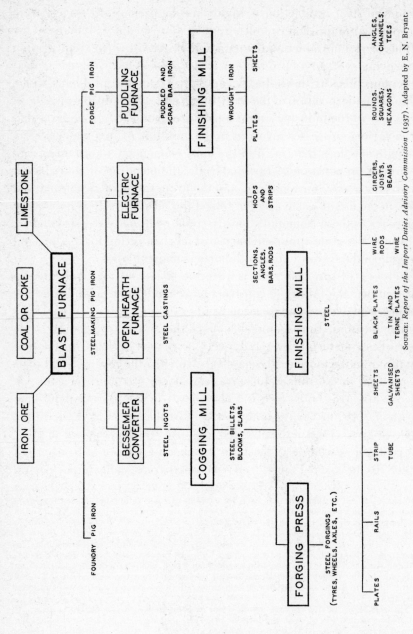

Chart 5. Interconnections of the iron and steel industry.

Source: *Report of the Import Duties Advisory Commission* (1937). Adapted by E. N. Bryant.

100*s*. to 105*s*. . . . The low-cost area is also the area where the only remaining large deposit of iron ore in Great Britain occurs."[61]

About blast furnaces, Owen says, "The average stack sizes for the leading countries in 1927 was (in tons): U.S.A., 506; Germany, 307; Belgium, 184; France, 172; Britain, 118. The average production of furnaces in blast in 1937 was Britain, 68,000 tons; Belgium, 81,600 tons; Luxemburg, 90,300 tons; Germany, 127,700 tons; U.S.A., 254,400 tons . . . In 1934 the average production of [British] furnaces in blast was 62,178 tons; in 1938, 68,600 tons; in January, 1946, they were working at the rate of 74,620 tons a year. In the three years, 1936–1937, only 76 of the 246 furnaces were scrapped, only 48 built. Between 1939 and 1945 (both inclusive) only four furnaces were built and 11 scrapped."[62]

Since efficiency is largely a function of size, these data require no comment. The same condition exists with respect to open-hearth furnaces. "In 1938 there were still one-quarter (113 out of 446) open-hearth furnaces of under 50 tons capacity, half between 50 and 80 tons (226 out of 446) and only 51 of over 100 tons."[63] One result is high fuel consumption per ton of steel produced, which the United States in 1927 had "down to 28 cwts. whereas in 1944 Sir William Larke still talked in terms of two tons of coal per ton being needed . . ."[64] Though the Iron and Steel Federation's plan anticipated reducing the quantity of coking coal per ton of pig iron produced from an average of 33 cwt. to 27 cwt., this figure for pig iron is only slightly under the American figure for finished steel twenty-three years earlier. Another interesting comparison is given in the fact that in Germany "one thousand tons of pig iron in 1913 required the consumption of 1,115 tons of coke; by 1924 this had fallen to 1,079, and by 1929 to 1,015."[65]

Bad location of plant in relation to raw materials, markets, and interrelated processes, coupled with high railroad rates and underdevelopment of internal waterways, canals, and coastwise water-transport

[61] D. L. Burn, "Recent Trends in the History of the Steel Industry," *Econ. Hist. Review*, XVII (1947) : 96.

[62] Owen, *op. cit.*, p. 33. Thus the condition was one of long standing. Alfred Edwards, who subsequently opposed the nationalization bill and was expelled from the Labour party for his pains, referred to the "days on the Tees" when "we saw pig iron coming from India into that district. Half our blast furnaces were out—why? Because 50 per cent. of them were nothing more than junk and have been absolutely obsolete for more than 20 years." *Hansard*, Vol. 423, cols. 1060–1061.

[63] Cited from statistics of the Iron and Steel Federation for 1938, Owens, *op. cit.*, p. 37.

[64] Cited, *ibid.*, from Burnham and Hoskins, *op. cit.*, p. 187, and *The Financial News*, Oct. 6, 1944.

[65] Robert A. Brady, *The Rationalization Movement in German Industry* (Berkeley, 1933), p. 111.

facilities, means very high transport costs. Owen finds that although Britain has a natural transport advantage, "in the U.S.A., the average haul of raw materials for the iron and steel industry is 750 miles, France 200 miles, Belgium 160 miles, Germany 150 miles, and Britain only 45 miles"—the average transport cost per ton-mile in Britain was nearly double the American figure.[66] Total freight charges ran to about 20 per cent of the cost of the finished steel. A special problem is provided by overseas shipment of iron ore, which "to bring freights down effectively . . . requires the use of ships of 10,000 tons and upwards, and the use of specialized unloading equipment which will give the ships a quick 'turn around.' Only a few of the coastal steel-making areas can accommodate the big ships, and few have adequate unloading gear. And it is equally important that if imports are to come in in big ships and the costly specialized unloading gear is to be fully employed importing must be concentrated at far fewer points than at present. Unloading equipment which can turn around a 10,000-ton ship in a day can discharge some 2,500,000 tons of ore in a year. The British import of ore runs at about 8,000,000 tons. But ores are imported still at upwards of twelve ports—most not adapted to the big ships—and the number seems by present plans more likely to rise than to fall."[67]

The catalog of retardation within the iron and steel industry seems to expand indefinitely. In the construction industry, which uses close to one-third of the entire domestic demand for steel products, little attention has been paid to adjusting specifications for tensile strength to load-carrying requirements, with the result that much more steel is used than is necessary. By altering these specifications "about 14 to 16 per cent. in weight of steel can be saved in building construction and as much as 23 to 25 per cent. in water-tube boilers, to take only two examples."[68] Improved steel specifications for other steel products would yield economies of 15 to 25 per cent from the general substitution of higher tensile strength steel, and at lower production cost because of the capacity of the mills to run longer without changing rolls. By adjusting the specifications to the use for which the steel is ordered, the substitution of light-gauge sheet steel for hot-rolled sections would

[66] Owen, *op. cit.*, pp. 40–41. For heavy finished iron and steel the American figure was 45*d.* per ton mile, the British 94*d.* For blooms and billets, the comparable figures were 43*d.* and 78*d.* respectively. This discrepancy, however, may be largely or wholly a result of the higher ton-mile costs associated with short hauls, although such a fact taken by itself would not indicate that British rates were unnecessarily high.

[67] D. L. Burn, "Recent Trends in the History of the Steel Industry," pp. 96–97.

[68] *Engineering*, March 4, 1949, p. 206.

save 30 to 50 per cent of the weight required.[69] Mill economies here are tied up with the entire structure of British industrial use of metallurgical products, and the need for thoroughgoing overhaul of metal specifications if advantage is to be taken of modern continuous processing methods is obvious.

In general the industry has grown like Topsy. The picture of the typical British steel mill, said a writer in the *Times,* is frequently that of "sprawl! The net result is a heavy proportion of obsolete equipment, or equipment requiring major overhaul and reconstruction . . . There are too many works which 'sprawl'—there is no other word for it— works which are a tangled riddle of gaps, corners, adjacent shops alternately empty and overcrowded, illogical separation, unbalanced and tortuous routes and methods in the handling of materials. The works where these things exist are works which are old and have too much past history incorporated in their layout. Some of them are reaching a stage where major reconstruction, involving heavy expenditure is becoming imperative, with the alternative of scrapping and building on a new site."[70]

The lack of integration exists at the plant level, between and among plants, within areas, and on a national basis. Virtually all authorities are agreed that there still exists a "relative absence of the integrated plant, combining coking ovens, blast furnaces and steelworks alone."[71] Economies involved run the gamut of operations. Speaking of the Scottish steel industry, a steel industrialist (Stewart, of Stewart and Lloyds) in an address before the Town and Country Planning Association said that "Scottish steel works, with one exception (Clydebridge), are not integrated . . . they have no coke ovens and no blast furnaces and have to manufacture gas specially for smelting cold pig iron and scrap, whereas in an integrated work the flow of materials from one operation to the next with the minimum of handling and the maximum conservation of heat, and the use of the blast furnace and coke oven gas, combine to reduce the cost of production to a level unattainable in unintegrated works . . ."[72]

But however serious lack of integration was at the given plant, it was still more serious when related to the geographic dispersion of industry.

[69] *Loc. cit.*
[70] *Times,* Feb. 2, 1945. Cited also by G. House, in *Hansard,* Vol. 423, cols. 1091–1092. See also W. Monslow, in *Hansard,* Vol. 458, col. 145. This *Times* editorial was written before Professor D. L. Burn joined the staff.
[71] Owen, *op. cit.,* p. 36.
[72] Cited by Mrs. Jean Mann, in *Hansard,* Vol. 458, col. 433.

An unusually large percentage of both pig iron and billet steel traveled from mill to mill, incurring additional transport and reheating costs.[73] Capacity of mills in one area would not be adjusted to those of supply mills located in other areas. Bottlenecks were common at every stage from raw material to finished product.[74] In short, the whole locational structure of the industry was bad and needed readjustment. Until something was done about this general pattern, individual changes, however desirable in themselves, were likely to cancel one another.[75] "That is why," Burn comments, "in central planning, if it is undertaken, the choice of location must be the primary consideration." In the past, "In general, a local market grew up around new steel works when the market did not initially exist (as a consumer of wrought iron); for example, steel shipbuilding in Scotland and on the north-east coast. It was useful to be near steelmaking to avoid heavy cost of carriage."[76] Expansion of steelmaking capacity was thus likely to take place in those lines which these new user industries required. The reciprocal influence of each upon the other tended to reinforce the tendency of the steel works not to seek new location, and of the user industries to demand greater rather than less diversification and differentiation of product. Furthermore, such effects of this interaction might very well be strengthened rather than weakened after local sources of either coal or iron ore had been exhausted.

If, in turn, growth did lead to some degree or other of plant specialization and product standardization the better to supply larger markets, there then arose competition for distant markets where other steel works were resident, and thus a tendency—heavily reinforced by the importance of overhead costs in this capital-intensive industry—to cut-

---

[73] "About one-third of the pig iron produced in 1938 (2,043,200 tons out of 6,761,000 tons produced) was not worked up into steel or other products at the furnace works but were sent elsewhere. Cumberland, the North-East Coast and Lincoln produce a surplus of pig iron which they send to make up the deficiency in Scotland, South Wales, the Black Country, Lancashire and Sheffield ... In 1935, 2,864,000 tons of pig iron was travelling about the country, costing £966,378 in transport freight, and adding 6s. 8½d. a ton to the cost of the foundries or steelworks as a result." Owen, op. cit., pp. 36–37.

[74] Ibid., p. 42.

[75] For example, the Colville Steel Co., the largest steel producer in Scotland, caters largely to the shipbuilding, ship machinery, and auxiliary steel consuming industries of the Clyde, a considerable percentage of its iron ore and scrap come from overseas, and much of its final product is shipped overseas. Yet, despite the much lower cost of water transportation—possibly averaging not much more than one-third of rail—and the high cost of transshipment, water-to-rail, and rail-to-water, in making detailed changes with a view to plant modernization in the Glasgow area Colvilles has given up every one of its important tidewater plants, and new mills or mill additions are constructed on the assumption that at least 50 per cent of iron and steel will be cast into pig and shipped elsewhere for reworking. Similar cases were cited by Hugh Dalton, in Hansard, Vol. 423, col. 1113.

[76] Burn, "Recent Trends in the History of the Steel Industry," p. 97.

throat competition. This situation creates an ideal environment for resort to cartel tactics, and the general effect of cartel policies is to freeze plants at their existing technical levels, and to bind them to their existing locations. Hence, when improvements take place in individual mills, they tend to occur as patchwork within the existing plant layout, and at old high-cost locations. Should these high-cost areas also be classed as depressed areas, political considerations may result in pressure being put on the industry by both the government and trade unions not to move to low-cost areas. On the contrary, as the decision to revive steelmaking in the southern Welsh district of Ebbw Vale illustrates, they may compel modern plant developments to take place in the areas least fitted, so far as costs are concerned, for the change.[77]

Thus it happens that piecemeal technological modernization may march hand in hand with technical stagnation and obsolescent plant, so that prices stay high and productive efficiency low. Lewis Ord, an experienced British industrialist, quotes the estimates cited by Dr. Rostas, that if the postwar output per man-hour in the British iron and steel industry be given as 100, that the American figure would be 495, or nearly five-fold.[78] This may be excessive; it compares with Burn's estimate that, using "a slightly misleading criterion, in the years just before the war productivities per man year in the American, German and British steel industries were in the ratio of 5 : 4 : 3." Although, furthermore, it depends somewhat upon the type of product, the year, and the method of quoting respective prices whether American or British prices are rated lower, "what is really more significant . . . is that the American industry could sell at prices slightly above or slightly below the British and yet pay wages almost twice as high."[79] Since the war the discrepancies have apparently remained substantially the same, although some British prices have actually fallen to the American level.

Without going into further detail, all the leading facts point to the serious need for a wide-ranging and fundamental reorganization of Britain's postwar iron and steel industry on a national basis. Factors "implicit in the physical environment," and "common to many British

[77] "The political strength of the old high-cost locations has been increased; and, in spite of the energetic provision of new industrial facilities under the Development Area policy, efforts to avoid the migration of steelmaking from old sites and old areas which are now unsuitable are, if anything, more effective now than before the war. Trade Union opinion has proved to be very strongly attached to the existing distribution of production—'balanced development' is called for, which means 'equal shares' for all areas." *Ibid.*, p. 101.

[78] Lewis C. Ord, "Anglo-American Comparisons, an Industrialist's Advice," *Soundings*, Dec., 1948, pp. 50–56.

[79] Burn, "Recent Trends in the History of the Steel Industry," p. 95.

industries" may play roles of some importance,[80] but the principal causes of the technical backwardness of the British iron and steel industry are of the type indicated above. Hence it comes about that the problem of steel modernization is coextensive with the problems of the number and size of newly integrated plants, degree of standardization of product and plant specialization, level of transport costs (and transport efficiency as a whole), the nature of raw materials supply, resort to by-product utilization, the structure of the demand and geographic distribution of the leading user industries, and, above all, plant locations. These problems, in turn, are tied up with industry policies of a cartel character; governmental policies associated with economic stabilization and the export drive; town and country planning and the whole range of population and industry relocation problems associated with them; trade union policies regarding equal sharing of development by areas, and special attention to the development areas; and so on *ad infinitum.*

Although much concern was shown, especially in the early stages of discussion of the government's anticipated plans for the steel industry, over the question of inadequate total plant capacity, this tended to drop out in face of the industry's willingness to scale their plans upward. At the time of the second reading of the bill, the industry had decided to plan an increase to 18,000,000 tons annual output.[81] Although some labor spokesmen talked in terms of 22,000,000 or 23,000,000 tons, and G. D. H. Cole—"that charming writer of fiction," as Captain Lyttelton commented acidly—"has got the figure up to 26 million tons," this issue was soon dropped.[82]

Interestingly enough, the Opposition did not in the main seek to deny the facts regarding the general condition of the industry. While there were some vigorous defenses of the industry against some of the more extreme charges of inefficiency and high prices, and although an occasional member could speak with a trembling voice on behalf of "these great cathedrals of industry,"[83] for the most part the Opposition merely

---

[80] Such as low-quality ore or long haulage for high-quality ores on the physical side, and low levels of scientific personnel and "the structure of the capital market" on the institutional side. *Loc. cit.*

[81] Lyttelton, in *Hansard,* Vol. 458, col. 82.

[82] Cole estimates domestic need by 1953 at 20,000,000 tons on the assumption of an increase over prewar of 150 per cent by volume of exports of products such as ships, vehicles, and other types of ferrous-metal-goods-using industries, and 6,000,000 tons for primary export purposes. G. D. H. Cole, *Why Nationalise Steel?*, New Statesman Pamphlet (1948), p. 19.

[83] Including at times, Labour M.P.'s. One, E. L. Mallalieu, said, "I can assure this House ... that inside these great cathedrals of industry there is absolutely nothing medieval. There one hears the clang of metal and the roar of fire and the hiss of steel as it issues skywards.

insisted that the past was the past, and that the evidence cited against the industry and the Iron and Steel Federation reflected a condition which was itself the product of the distortions introduced by the two world wars, the great depression of the thirties, and the consequent long period of capital shortage which prevented carrying through the program of plant modernization which had begun with the reorganization investment of £50,000,000 between 1936 and the outbreak of the war. Furthermore, that although the industry might be in part to blame for present conditions, Governments of the past shared definite responsibility for what Labour was now condemning.

The Government's case rested on the need for the reorganization, and its general unwillingness to allow so vital a change in the national economy to be carried through at the discretion, and on the terms, of such a monopolistically organized and cartel-minded body as the Iron and Steel Federation. Not alone, however, because of the role which the federation would play, but because there was a need for a ground plan for the industry which would fit into other plans for industrial development and social change whose implications reached far beyond the confines of any single industry. What were these plans for the steel industry? And, far more important, how did the proposed nationalization of iron and steel serve to promote plans for reorganization of this vital industry?

THE IRON AND STEEL BILL

A first question—far from academic because it concerned the whole problem of British industrial organization—arose over the meaning of the iron and steel industry as an industrial category. Even if it should be conceded that the necessary reorganization could only be effected by first bringing the industry under national ownership and direction, still, what were its metes and bounds? Where does the industry begin, and where does it end? This turned out to be one of the most difficult problems facing the Government, which ended by abandoning an attempt to unravel in favor of cutting the Gordian knot.

At night it is not just the red light above an altar which sends men's thoughts heavenwards...," *Hansard*, Vol. 458, col. 115. Lt.-Col. Hunt, Chairman of the Hallamshire Steel and File Co. is one of the very few who sees absolutely nothing the matter with the British steel industry at all. He finds it "solvent and united, with a quality of output unequalled anywhere and a rate of production of the highest on record... There was no branch of the steel industry which was out of date, and the entire industry represented a system which was sympathetic, flexible, go-ahead, responsible, and 100 per cent. efficient." As reported by the *Times*, Oct. 6, 1948, from a speech in Sheffield at Cutlers' Hall. This evaluation, of course, does not square at all with that given by the Iron and Steel Federation in submitting its program for postwar modernization.

In the earlier motion "to bring forward proposals for transferring to the ownership of the nation," the problem seemed virtually insoluble.

The iron and steel industry [Wilmot said] lies at the base of the whole of our industrial life. Its workers, over 300,000 strong, supply the raw material for by far the greater part of our magnificent engineering and shipbuilding industries. Its production is one of the keystones of our military defence, and the basis of our main export trades. The livelihood of millions of our workers depends on the provision of iron and steel of the right quantities, and at the right prices. In fact, it is scarcely possible to think of any human activity which does not depend, either directly or indirectly, on iron and steel. Farmers could not feed us without the ploughs and the tractors and the complicated agricultural implements which have now become the tools of their trade. Travel depends even more on the product of this great industry, from which it draws the raw material for its great ships and locomotives. Cotton spindles, printing machines, motor cars, and an ever increasing variety of household goods, all spring from iron and steel. New uses are constantly being found for the products of this industry. We now make, not only baths and sinks from steel, but are even planning to make complete houses from it. Iron and Steel is as much the lifeblood of the nation as is coal.[84]

Suppose, however, that modernization had led, or should lead, to increased vertical integration of the industry—whether backward from the finishing industries, as with the Ford Motor Company, or forward from raw materials to one or more of these multitudinous fabricating and finishing industries, would not matter. Does one then include them also in the category of the "iron and steel industry?" There are five "broad divisions of the industry," Wilmot went on to say. "The first is the mining and quarrying of ore. Second is the production of pig iron by smelting the ore in blast furnaces. Third is the production, from pig iron and from scrap, of steel ingots which, in the next and fourth stage are manipulated into various shapes, such as plates, sheets, strips, rods, tubes, and a thousand others. Fifth is the production of iron castings from pig iron or scrap and the production and the manipulation of wrought iron. That is the main set-up."[85]

All these sections would be taken over, which would have been all very well; but the technical interlinkages do not stop there. "Beyond this, there are various other finishing operations, some of which are so closely integrated with the actual iron and steel-making as to be virtually one process. We intend in such cases to include the whole plant. In other cases, the finishing processes are more easily separated, and

---

[84] *Hansard*, Vol. 423, col. 845.
[85] *Ibid.*, col. 853.

are often carried on in separate or independent works. There, we intend to review the field, section by section and firm by firm, in consultation with the industry, before deciding on the exact boundary in each particular case."[86] But what about these boundaries? Were there any principles which might assist the Government in making its decisions?

There were four major questions to be answered. First, where forward integration had gone all the way through to include the finished (fabricated and processed) material sold to the ultimate consumer and this integration could be justified on its own technical and economic (cost) merits, would nationalization include the finishing industries too? The second (and partially overlapping the first), was raised where the industry was directly interlaced with the engineering and construction industries; bridge making, shipbuilding, industrial and office building construction, etc. Integration, Sir Andrew Duncan, director of the Iron and Steel Federation, pointed out, between the two industries is close, and has sometimes been promoted by one industry and sometimes by the other. "The organisation of the [engineering] industry recognises that its firms overlap into so many of these engineering activities and it provides machinery by which the main problems in the steel-making processes—can be looked at and settled co-operatively for large and small firms alike." So closely related are the two that they cannot be put asunder, and yet "if these proposals go through, the Government would own the largest bridge building unit in the country, and 30 per cent. of the constructional engineering plant of the country." It would be engaged also in "all kinds of industrial enterprises such as making printing machines, locomotives, floating docks, barges, bridges, buildings and great public structures such as the new House of Commons"—activities which in some cases engaged "as many as 80 per cent. to 90 per cent. of the employees of some firms . . . outside the scheduled industries."[87]

A third problem was that of the inclusion of armaments firms. Referring to the Blackpool conference of the Labour party in 1935, K. Zilliacus pointed out that the Minister of Foreign Affairs (Ernest Bevin) had said that "our party has always stood for the abolition of the private trade in and manufacture of arms. We stand for it today.

---

[86] *Loc. cit.*
[87] *Hansard,* Vol. 458, cols. 384–385. He estimated that "under these proposals (given in the Bill) it is also true to say that the State will secure a foothold in 101 other industries and will own firms whose interest in iron and steel is a very small portion of their activities." *Loc. cit.*

We are pledged to the hilt and our pledges will be carried through." Between the two wars a ballot on "Peace Through Collective Security" had led to the casting of 10,500,000 votes for the nationalization of the arms industry, and Lord Halifax, in a memorable speech on March 27, 1945, had upheld the belief that the private manufacture and sale of arms was a leading cause of war, and was hence intolerable.[88] Because, said a colleague, "The iron and steel industry is a basic industry for armaments," it follows that "on that aspect alone, the industry ought to come under public control."[89] A spokesman for the Liberal party supported the view.[90] Furthermore, the government, by maintaining its war-constructed ordinance plants as peacetime producers of finished engineering and consumer goods products, was already up to its neck in both fields.[91]

Finally, there were the foreign affiliates of the various British concerns whose business the government would be taking over under the bill. These were scattered all over the world—in the Dominions, the Crown colonies, and in many foreign countries. Were they to be taken over too?

These were among the leading issues absorbing Labour attention, and to some degree or other dividing its ranks[92] during the interim between the introduction of the motion and the final introduction of the

[88] *Hansard*, Vol. 423, cols. 1080–1081.

[89] G. House, *ibid.*, cols. 1093–1094.

[90] Emrys Roberts, *ibid.*, col. 1094.

[91] Not to mention, of course, the government naval yards and other military construction and supply industries. For the Birmingham industrial exhibit in 1948 a catalog of products produced and services performed for sale by the government's ordinance plants was printed. The Royal Ordnance factories were described as "one of the finest productive organisations of the country," producing 25 classes of products (this is an incomplete listing) : I. *Heavy or Medium Engineering:* forgings (all types) ; castings (non-ferrous) ; fabrication by electric welding up to 15–20 tons; machinery—light, medium, and heavy; fitting and erecting "of any units or components" already machined; wood work, from logging mills to finishing shops; boxes, packing cases, wagon bodies; simple factory or office furniture. II. *Light Engineering:* assemblies, sub-assemblies, or components for a wide range of machinery; engines, winches, gears, etc.; "repetition work for Automatics and High Speed Capstans"; repair and overhaul of light vehicles; small metal pressings; ceramics, refractory, and porcelain work for heating units; steel cabinet work; non-ferrous strip rolling. III. *Miscellaneous:* preservation, identification, and packing of stoves; clothing manufacturing and reconditioning; paper and cardboard, cartons; precast cement components; electroplating; chemical indicators; vitrous enameling; pellet pressing and tabloiding; pulping, grinding, etc. of plastic substances; bulk laundry work and boot repair. IV. *Chemicals:* oleum, ammonium nitrate, formaldehyde, calcium chloride; hydrochloric acid; sulphuric acid; nitric acid; hexamine. Ministry of Supply, *Royal Ordinance Factories* (n.p., n.d.).

[92] Leading, among other things, to the resignation of John Wilmot, Minister of Supply, who would not go along with the decision to include all the holdings of the individual firms whose names were listed under the bill introduced later, and to the expulsion from the Labour party of George Edwards for openly opposing the introduction of the bill—although he had warmly supported the original motion. Wilmot was engaged as a private citizen in the iron and steel trades. He seems not to have been well liked in top Government circles.

enabling bill. The solution provided by the bill,[93] was to take over all the properties held by a list of 107 companies.[94] To assist in arriving at this list, the government set up the classification of iron and steel concerns[95] shown in table 15.

On the basis of this list, any firm producing more than the amounts indicated will be taken over, and all firms not acquired, but producing more than the minimum listed in the third column, must be licensed. Licenses are to be issued to this intermediate group "on such terms and

TABLE 15

IRON AND STEEL ACTIVITIES

Activity	Minimum output qualifying for acquisition	Minimum output requiring license
	tons	tons
The working and getting of iron ore..............	50,000	5,000
The smelting of iron ore in a blast furnace with or without other metalliferous materials...........	20,000	5,000
The production in the form of steel (including alloy steel)..	20,000	5,000
The changing of the cross-sectional shape of steel by hot rolling in a rolling mill..................	20,000	5,000

conditions as the Minister thinks fit" including the length of time for which the license may be held, "limiting the extent to which any of the said activities is to be carried on, controlling the maximum price of the products of those activities," and the imposing of restrictions under which the goods may be sold.[96] Firms under the minimum figure may proceed as before.

[93] Introduced to second reading in November, 1948. The full title read, "A Bill to provide for the establishment of an Iron and Steel Corporation of Great Britain and for defining their functions, and for the transfer to that Corporation of the securities of certain companies engaged in the working, getting and smelting of iron ore, the production of steel, and the shaping of steel by rolling, and of certain property and rights held by a Minister of the Crown or Government department; for the licensing of persons engaged in any such activities; for co-ordinating the activities of the Corporation, the National Coal Board and the Area Gas Boards relating to carbonisation; and for purposes connected with the matters aforesaid." 12 Geo. 6.

[94] Listed by name, Bill, Third Schedule, pp. 58–60.

[95] Bill, Second Schedule, p. 57.

[96] Bill, Sect. 27 (2). "Those between 5,000 and the datum figure may either double their 1946–47 production, or achieve the datum figure, whichever may be the less. They can go, moreover, beyond this with the permission of the Minister after he has consulted the Corporation." G. R. Strauss, in Hansard, Vol. 458, col. 65. One exception was made on the datum figure, namely the Ford Motor Company. The exception was made, said Strauss, not as had been suggested, "because of representations received from any American interests—we have received none—but because we thought that this company, which produces pig iron primarily for the purpose of the manufacture of its cars and tractors, two highly specialised products, should properly be excluded." Ibid., col. 64. Since one of the objects of the bill

As for the firms taken over, G. R. Strauss could "see no reason why publicly-owned companies should not be able to pursue the same industrial activities as the companies were able to pursue when they were

TABLE 16

BASIC PROCESSES

Product and status under the bill	Production (thousands of tons)	Percentage of total production
Iron ore		
To be acquired..............................	10,812	97.5
To be licensed..............................	273	2.5
Not affected................................	......	....
Pig iron		
To be acquired..............................	7,595	97.6
To be licensed..............................	175	2.2
Not affected..............................	14	0.2
Carbon steel ingots		
To be acquired..............................	11,763	99.6
To be licensed..............................	35	0.3
Not affected..............................	12	0.1
Alloy steel ingots		
To be acquired..............................	511	93.7
To be licensed..............................	24	4.3
Not affected..............................	11	2.0
Rerolling		
To be acquired..............................	5,268	93.1
To be licensed..............................	296	5.2
Not affected..............................	97	1.7
Sheet		
To be acquired..............................	1,177	94.1
To be licensed..............................	57	4.6
Not affected..............................	16	1.3
Plate		
To be acquired..............................	1,609	97.3
To be licensed..............................	43	2.6
Not affected................................	2	0.1
Tinplate		
To be acquired..............................	584	88.0
To be licensed..............................	75	11.3
Not affected..............................	5	0.7

privately owned. The marginal activities of the companies have not been undertaken by accident. They have been developed by the present owners of the industry as a part of the efficient exploitation of the processes of steel-making, and there is no reason why the Corporation

was reorganization of the industry to secure greater efficiency, and since vertical integration of the type secured by Ford is wholly in keeping with this trend, the exception makes no sense at all, nor was any other explanation than the one given by Strauss ever forthcoming.

should not embark on its task with the same technical and administrative advantages as its predecessors."[97]

Based upon 1947 figures, table 16 shows the proportions of basic processes in the three classifications established by the bill and table 17 the proportions of certain other types of production taken over with the 150 "daughter concerns" owned by the 107 companies thus acquired.[98]

TABLE 17

DAUGHTER CONCERNS

Product and status under the bill	Production (thousands of tons)	Percentage of total production
Heavy forgings		
To be acquired	61	45.5
Not affected	73	54.5
Drop forgings		
To be acquired	35	15.8
Not affected	186	84.2
Steel castings		
To be acquired	48	23.0
Not affected	160	77.0
Tyres, wheels, axles		
To be acquired	202	94.3
Not affected	12	5.7
Wrought iron and steel, tubes, pipes and fittings		
To be acquired	492	67.2
Not affected	240	32.8
Hard and mild steel wire		
To be acquired	343	60.0
Not affected	229	40.0
Cold rolled strip		
To be acquired	182	72.4
Not affected	69	27.6
Bright steel bars		
To be acquired	104	40.7
Not affected	152	59.3

As for the outside activities, some "idea of the extent to which the publicly-owned companies will be engaged in outside activities can be gained from the figures of employment. The companies concerned employ a total of about 300,000; 200,000 of these are directly employed in what I call Second Schedule activities; about another 30,000 to 35,000 are employed at the finishing end of the business in tubes, wires, and iron founding. Of the balance of 65,000 to 70,000, 12,000 are engaged in the manufacture of bolts, nuts and screws, some 35,000 are

[97] *Ibid.*, col. 61.
[98] Both tables adapted from *Home Affairs Survey*, Nov. 2, 1948, pp. 27–28.

engaged in general and constructional engineering, 7,000 to 8,000 in other metal working industries, including non-ferrous metals, and some 5,000 to 10,000 are engaged in miscellaneous employments such as chemicals, etc. The biggest block is constructional and general engineering. A labour force of 35,000 is admittedly impressive, but it represents less than 4 per cent. of the total number employed in engineering and the other 96 per cent. will still be employed under private ownership."[99]

There were anomalies galore, and the Opposition was quick to point them out. For example, not only the Ford Motor Company but Vickers, the great armament combine, was also excluded from the listed "Companies Which Fulfill Condition for Vesting of Their Securities" even though this same list included two wholly owned Vickers' subsidiaries, English Steel Corporation and Darlington Forge. Both of these latter companies produced a wide range of finished products; English Steel turned over to Vickers some 300,000 of its annual output of 420,000 tons of ingot steel which the latter turned "into finished products including finished machinery."[100] More serious still, since the bill authorized the government, in taking over any company, to conduct any line of business permitted under the firm's articles of incorporation, there was virtually no limit to the lines of business into which the government might not enter at will.[101] This might not mean anything

[99] G. R. Strauss, in *Hansard*, Vol. 458, col. 61.
[100] Lyttleton, *ibid.*, cols. 89–90.
[101] For example, a partial list of these activities which might be conducted by the English Steel Corporation, as read in committee, included the following: "the trades or businesses of iron masters and founders, steel makers, steel converters, colliery proprietors, coke manufacturers, machinists, makers of armour plate and bullet proof plates, miners, smelters, tin plate makers, manufacturers of agricultural implements and other machinery, tool-makers, brass founders, metal-workers, boiler-makers, mill-wrights, machinists, iron and steel converters, smiths, wood-workers, builders, painters, metallurgists, electrical engineers, water supply engineers, gas-makers, farmers, printers, carriers, and merchants, and to manufacture, repair, let on hire, and deal in machinery, implements, rolling-stock, and hardware of all kinds and to carry on any other business (manufacturing or otherwise) which may seem to the Company capable of being conveniently carried on in connection with the above or otherwise calculated directly or indirectly, to enhance the value of any of the company's property and rights for the time being.

"To purchase, acquire, rent, build, construct, equip, execute, carry out, improve, work, develop, administer, maintain, manage or control in any part of the world works and conveniences of all kinds, including therein roads, ways, railways, tramways, carrying or transport undertakings, by land, water, or air, stations, aerodromes, docks, harbours, piers, wharves, canals, reservoirs, water rights, water works, water-courses, bridges, flumes, irrigations, embankments, hydraulic works, drainage, iron, steel, ordnance, engineering and improvement works, gas-works, electrical works, telegraphs, telephones, cables, timber rights, saw-mills, paper and pulp mills, crushing mills, smelting works, quarries, collieries, coke-ovens, foundries, furnaces, factories, warehouses, hotels, viaducts, acqueducts, markets, exchanges, mints, ships, lighters, postal services, newspapers, and other publications, breweries, stores, shops, churches, chapels, public and private buildings, residences, places of amusement, recreation or instruction, or any other works." Selwyn Lloyd, in Standing Committee C, *Official Report; Iron and Steel Bill*, Eighth Sitting, Jan. 19, 1949, cols. 385–386.

more under government administration than it had under private—most of the authorized powers never having been used anyway—but it made a strong talking point for the Opposition who feared that nationalization of iron and steel opened up endless possibilities for permeation and spread of government competition throughout wide ranges of the manufacturing industries.

THE GOVERNMENT'S PLAN

The Government's proposal was to transfer the entire stock ownership of the 107 iron and steel companies to a new government corporation to be known as The Iron and Steel Corporation of Great Britain, consisting of "a Chairman and not less than four nor more than ten other members . . . appointed by the Minister from amongst persons appearing to him to be persons who have had wide experience of, and shown capacity in, the production of iron and steel, industrial, commercial or financial matters, administration or the organisation of workers."[102] With a view to avoiding dislocation, and out of "anxiety to preserve the most valuable fruits of this industry's past activities and successes," it was proposed "to keep intact the identity of the individual concerns. Their personnel and internal organisations, and such *esprit de corps* as they may have achieved, will be unaffected. Indeed, on the morning after vesting day the only difference for them will be that the ownership of the securities has changed hands. The companies will continue to win ore, produce iron and steel and sell their products as before."[103]

If, then, nothing more than mere transfer of ownership was contemplated, did the Government have any plan for reorganization of the industry at all? The Opposition thought not.[104] The industrial correspondent of *The Times,* who favored far-reaching and drastic overhauling, anticipated the contents of the bill with a statement which was destined to be widely quoted. Reviewing the announced plans against the background of postwar regulation of the steel industry, he wrote,

The Government, in fact, have contributed nothing to steel policy and learned nothing. They have not worked out what precise functions of supervision a Ministry or a Steel Board might exercise or what standards of judgment should be applied to determine the economic worth of particular projects in the in-

---

[102] *Bill,* Sect. 1 (1) and (2).

[103] G. R. Strauss, in *Hansard,* Vol. 458, col. 63.

[104] E.g., ". . . there is no plan of any kind whatever showing how this industry is going to be run when it is taken over under this Bill—no plan at all." Lyttelton, *ibid.,* col. 79. ". . . neither in the Bill nor in the speech of the Minister in moving the Second Reading . . . has there been given the slightest indication of a policy or plan for the industry." H. Strauss, *ibid.,* col. 125.

dustry. They have neither calculated what the consequences might be of abandoning the industry's present price practices nor tried to measure the long-term cost of supporting steel production at high cost sites. They have done nothing to entitle them to judge the industry, let alone to take it over, and by their fixed attention to the dogma of nationalization they have left unheeded and unsolved the real problems of the industry's future.

In what way and by how much will costs be reduced by nationalization? How much more will costs be reduced with nationalization than without? Will production—and productivity—rise or fall? Will the workers become more or less exigent? What principles will be applied to prices and investment? How will nationalization make it more possible to apply the right principles in the right way than under private ownership and management? The Government have not answered these questions because they do not know the answers. It is a decisive objection to the policy which they propose that it is a major diversion from the many urgent questions revealed by a study of the history of the steel industry in the past generation.[105]

The *Economist* had similar doubts.[106] The *Manchester Guardian* found that so far as the problem of monopoly was concerned, "What the Government has failed to show is that the transfer of ownership will contribute anything at all to the solution."[107] Worse still, the Opposition argued, the bill sets up "nothing more nor less than a holding company" which combines "the *mort main* of a holding company . . . [with] an incompetent, abstruse company which can make no decision,"[108] since the unit of policy implementation is to be the board of directors of each corporation taken over. The new corporation, in short, would appear to be a nonentity so long as it continues with its intention to keep alive "each and all of the steel companies and the boards, the fees, the articles of association and the subsidiaries,"[109] and to do so is meaningless if the corporation is to exercise any coördinative authority at all. As for coördination: "Inevitably, instead of having 107 completely autonomous units each carrying their own responsibility, authority and risk taking, we shall have concentrated in the proposed Corporation at the top, all authority and risk taking . . . Directors and managers may still be called directors and managers, but they will and must in fact

[105] "Post-War Investment and Price Policy: Second of Two Articles on Steel and the State," *Times*, Oct. 26, 1948. That this article was written by an outstanding authority on the history and current organization of the steel industry, who, furthermore, had served as a sympathetic consultant to the Government on the need and the implications of reorganization of the iron and steel industry prior to the introduction of the bill, and who was, accordingly, thoroughly familiar with the background of the Government's proposals, necessarily lends a great deal of weight to this judgment.

[106] Editorial and article, "The Steel Bill Examined," Nov. 6, 1948.

[107] Cited by R. W. G. Mackay, in *Hansard*, Vol. 458, col. 389.

[108] Hugh Fraser, *ibid.*, col. 149.

[109] Lyttleton, *ibid.*, col. 87.

become executive officers. Their work is bound to change in character and shrink in significance."[110]

The Government refused to be drawn into debate on this point. Strauss ventured the opinion that there would "have to be some coordinating machinery between the nationalised and the non-nationalised sections of the industry," and that within the nationalized sectors the government as shareholder in the corporation would play a more active role than shareholders of most private business were wont to assume. It should play an active part, "not by interference with the day to day management of each works, but in planning the overall efficiency of the industry and seeing that those plans are carried out. That means that where directors are weak, or management is below standard, the Corporation will cut out the deadwood, and, in consultation with the boards concerned, strengthen their organisations by the appointment of new men, many of whom, I hope, will be drawn from ranks not normally considered for posts of higher responsibility."[111]

Certainly it is clear that the Government submitted no plan for the reorganization of the industry at all. Whether they had in the background a plan which might apply to even the 107 companies to be taken over, nobody could say. Nothing exists in the literature of the Labour party, nor in any discussions in Government circles since the introduction of the bill, which seems capable of throwing any further light on the subject. Aside from plans for the machinery of administration, and certain broad development programs, the presumption seems strong that no clear-cut reorganization plan exists,[112] though it is always possible, of course, that one may be in the preliminary stages.

The corporation, as the sole owner of the 107 companies taken over, is to have "power to carry on those activities or any other activities which the companies, together with their wholly owned subsidiaries are authorized by their memoranda of association or charter to carry on, but may not extend the companies' powers without the consent of the Minister." With such consent it may acquire or set up new companies,

---

[110] Sir Andrew Duncan, *ibid.*, col. 386.

[111] *Ibid.*, col. 63.

[112] Alfred Edwards, the man expelled from the Labour party for his opposition to the party's proposals to nationalize the steel industry, and himself a "director of several companies, including Teesside blast furnaces" was quite sure that "the Government has no plan for steel. I am on the subcommittee for iron and steel and we have never been consulted once ... I criticised the Government for putting control of nationalised industries into the hands of capitalists and Civil Servants—a policy which gives us the worst of both worlds is suicide to the industries, and treachery to the country ... as Mr. Shinwell said, there was confusion of thought on nationalisation and insufficient preparation." *Daily Telegraph*, May 10, 1948.

undertake newly authorized activities and discontinue or restrict any line of activity.[113] It must see that the activities of the companies taken over are managed so that steel products "are available in such quantities, at such prices, and or such types, qualities and sizes as the Corporation consider best in the public interest."[114] To this end it may carry out the appropriate "capital development and reorganization," and provide "for training, education and research."[115] It must make an annual report to the Minister which the Minister must lay before both houses of Parliament,[116] and it must conduct the affairs of the companies under its direction in compliance with the substance of the enabling law and the directives of the Minister who is authorized to interpret it. The corporation is not to be exempt from taxation,[117] must balance its books as though it were an ordinary private corporation,[118] and in planning and carrying out "any programme of capital development or reorganisation of activities relating to carbonisation, the Corporation shall consult with the National Coal Board, with the Gas Council and with any Area Gas Board in whose areas those activities are or are to be carried on; and in planning and carrying out any such programme in respect of their activities relating to carbonisation the National Coal Board shall consult with the Corporation."[119]

There is a provision, usual in the Labour government's nationalization proposals, for the appointment of committees to represent interests of consumers.[120] An Iron and Steel Arbitration Tribunal, appointed by the Lord Chancellor, is to be set up to adjudicate disputes arising under the act and regulations made by the Minister under authorities granted by the act.[121]

As for the development program, nothing has ever been said beyond revision of the Iron and Steel Federation's estimate of £168,000,000 required for its own program by 1953. One estimate given during the debates was that when due allowance was made for price increases, the total capital expansion currently planned and under way will run to "at least £300 million."[122] Even this figure, however, represents no substantial change from the Iron and Steel Federation's own estimate,

---

[113] *Bill*, Explanatory and Financial Memorandum, and clause 2; clause 4 (4).
[114] *Ibid.*, clause 3.
[115] *Ibid.*, clause 4 (2) and (3).
[116] *Ibid.*, clause 4 (6).
[117] *Ibid.*, clause 9.
[118] *Ibid.*, clause 29. It may also sue and be sued (clause 10), and support or oppose bills in Parliament (clause 8).
[119] *Ibid.*, clause 45.
[120] *Ibid.*, clause 6.
[121] *Ibid.*, clauses 41–43.
[122] R. W. G. Mackay, in *Hansard*, Vol. 458, cols. 394–395.

and it is possible that it is, if anything, somewhat under the currently anticipated expenditures as revised since the original plan was first sketched. Thus it gives no clue to what the government may anticipate—if it anticipates anything definite at all—by way of further change once it takes over the 107 concerns.

FURTHER ISSUES RAISED BY THE DEBATES

But for the House rule which limits debate on the second reading of a major bill to three days, and the decision of the Government to limit the committee hearings to 35 sittings, there is no doubt that the discussions would have dragged on interminably. Even as limited, the official record is voluminous,[123] and the outpourings on the subject of virtually all shades of opinion in the daily and weekly newspapers and periodicals was in keeping therewith. The Opposition's position was that this bill differed essentially from all other nationalization proposals. "In this Bill," said Ivor Thomas, "we are entering an entirely new field. It is a highly competitive and highly complex industry, with great international ramifications. No comparison with other industries can properly be made."[124] While the Government might, and did, dispute the range of difference, it did concede that the issues centered in the proposed nationalization of iron and steel were of a far more vital character than had been the issues in any of the other bills, and that with this proposal it might very well be effecting a crossing of the Rubicon from which there could be no turning back. It is a critical point, said Dalton, in "the Socialist advance." The Government, in nationalizing coal and proposing to nationalize the iron and steel industry, was "now entering upon the key regions of the heavy industries."[125]

---

[123] As Ian Mikardo put the matter somewhat whimsically, on the assumption that speakers deliver "at an average rate of 160 words a minute" or "9,600 words an hour" a single sitting of two and a half hours would record 24,000 words. Making allowances of 20 per cent "for interruptions, for formal business, for discussions on procedure and for some of the irrelevances of hon. Gentlemen opposite" in thirty-five sittings the committee would compile 672,000 words, or "roughly equal to the combined size of Genesis, Exodus, Leviticus, Numbers, Deuteronomy, Joshua, Judges and the two Books of Samuel." An Opposition critic commented acidly that even this impressive verbal achievement "only represents one word per 50 tons of steel produced annually and therefore, it is quite inadequate." F. J. Erroll, in Standing Committee C, *Official Report*, Seventh Sitting, Dec. 16, 1948, cols. 313–314.

[124] Thomas, *ibid.*, col. 315. His comparison is interesting: "There is a fundamental difference between this Bill and previous nationalisation Measures. In the case of coal, there were special reasons, in the relations of employers and employed, why some change was necessary. In the case of gas and electricity, the principle of public ownership, had already been conceded over a very wide field. In the case of the railways there were special reasons why that part of our transport system might be brought into public ownership."

[125] "Here we are at the moment of the passing of a great industry from private to public hands. In the progress of the Socialist advance, we have now got past the first lines of banking and public utilities and transport; the advance is now entering upon the key regions of the heavy industries, first, coal and now iron and steel." *Hansard*, Vol. 423, col. 1015.

In this mood, each side literally "threw the book" at its opponents. All the arguments pro and con to be found in the debates on the other nationalization measures were repeated in this one, but the overtones were bitter, there was little by way of compromise on principle, and every resource was deployed to win any point, however small, both in Parliament and in the general reporting to the public. There was no avoiding the conclusion that in this case the "advance of Socialism" had passed beyond the point where the Tories could possibly express any sentiment for, or cite any precedent of their own making which might favor, any aspect of this nationalization measure. Only in reference to iron and steel does the Conservative *Industrial Charter* take, without reservation of any sort, a categorical position against nationalization *per se*.[126] And only here did the Labour government find its entire future to be at stake in any failure to steer successfully through the exceedingly dangerous waters between the Scylla of the dissatisfaction of its own mass following and the Charybdis of a successful appeal by the Opposition for British middle-class votes, which might be cast for the Conservatives should American support be withdrawn.

Furthermore, at very nearly every important point in the debates each side was continuously on the point of giving up entirely its most important single strategic position. On the Labour side, its strictures on the past record of the iron and steel industry for technical backwardness lost very nearly all of their persuasive power in face of the concession that the industry was rapidly making up for certain of its past failings. More than that, at the very time in which past shortcomings were being detailed at great length, official spokesmen for the Labour government—most notably Herbert Morrison and Sir Stafford Cripps—[127] were heaping eulogies upon the iron and steel industry for the manner in which its increases in productivity were contributing to postwar recovery. The Government still further weakened its case for nationalization as a precondition to technical modernization, by presenting virtually no argument at all on the current shortcomings of the steel industry, even though—as the above references on the relation-

---

[126] *The Industrial Charter* (Conservative and Unionist Central Office, 1947), p. 26. A partial exception is their condemnation of nationalization of certain parts of road haulage, but this is not expressed in the same unmeasured and uncompromising terms applied to the iron and steel industry.

[127] The Opposition made general use of their statements. For example, H. Strauss pointed out that "in press interviews after press interviews, and official document after official document issued by the Chancellor of the Exchequer, he holds up this industry as a shining example and offers very serious criticism of the nationalised coal industry." *Hansard*, Vol. 458, col. 124.

ships between this general problem and vertical integration and location show—the fundamental problems of reorganization of the industry as a whole had scarcely been touched. And, as if to clinch the case against itself, it not only offered no alternative scheme for the future but not even an intimation of the way in which it would proceed to coordinate and improve the industry once it possessed the power to act directly. Thus its whole case was left hanging in mid-air.

On its side, the Conservative group left the charge of monopoly within the industry either unanswered, or answered with such weak and tepid arguments that they lacked force enough to get more than passing reference by even the most favorably disposed of its press supporters. Peter Roberts, for example, found five types of competition still existing in the industry. Competition with other businesses for exports; competition between firms as evidenced by the expansion in output of some of them; competition in efficiency; competition in quality of products; and competition in labor and skill. Thus, he concluded, "Private industry under supervision, under the present set-up, is definitely competitive."[128]

Yet for all practical purposes, this argument did not and could not answer the Government arguments at all. The heart of the Government's case was that the industry was riddled with cartel and cartel-like policies relating to price control, production restriction, quota allocations, and central direction over broad investment policies, and that, among other things, these practices had "built into" the industry a vast assortment of insufferable inefficiencies whose excision required surgical treatment, and that it was nonsense to expect the industry to perform these severe operations on itself. Nor was it much of an aid to the Conservative case to point out that the high and expanding degree of the Iron and Steel Federation's control over these details of conduct of business had been carried through before and during the war with the advice, consent, and aid of the government. These were Conservative, or (for the duration of the war) Conservative-dominated governments, and they had highly approved of the formula of self-government in business. "What," asked Morrison, "is this State supervised, cartelised, monopolistic capitalism if it is not the very Nazi economic system? It is also similar to the so-called and miscalled system of 'public' corporations of Mussolini, about which he theorised in Italy but did not do much . . . the Tories are sitting at the feet of Dr. Schacht."[129] A similar

[128] *Ibid.*, col. 463.
[129] *Ibid.*, col. 488.

thesis runs through the analysis of the past history of these industry-government relations in the iron and steel industry made by one of the Government's strongest and most energetic supporters, Ernest Davies, who holds that the net result in the past has been that predecessor Governments aided the creation of a protected monopoly for the steel industry which generally exploited the consumer and aided nobody else.[130]

Yet if the industry's defense on this point seemed weak, so also was the Government's attack. This is true because at precisely the time it was attacking the principle of self-government in business as applied to the steel industry, it was also energetically promoting and eulogizing a similar formula in textiles and various other industries under the device of the development councils.[131] Though neither the Opposition nor the Government paid much attention to this it would seem that it was not the principle of self-government which was at stake, but only its application to "a producers' combine, primarily concerned with the producer's interest" of "the size, importance and structure of the steel industry . . ." It is this, said Sir Stafford Cripps, which "demands the change from private to public monopoly control."[132]

There is no need for further elaboration of the pros and cons of the argument on this point. Very little evidence was cited by either side, and in the end the argument boiled down to a statement by the Opposition that the Government already possessed adequate safeguards under its Iron and Steel Board, while the Government contended that these were not relevant to the problem of vesting positive decisions in the hands of an agency whose primary concern must be the public welfare and not private specialized interests. In effect, all other issues were subordinated to the problems of industrial reorganization and monopoly, and these were centered in steel as the citadel of British capitalism.

This fact is outlined even more sharply in the minor issues. Of these, four are of special interest. The first had to do with labor relations and working conditions in the industry. An attempt was made by the Opposition to prove that within the industry labor leaders feared nationalization;[133] that labor relations were, and long had been, excellent in the iron and steel trades—a point which was conceded by the Government

---

[130] Davies, *op. cit.*, chapter iii, "Steel's Protected Monopoly."
[131] For a description of the development councils, see chapter xiii following.
[132] *Hansard*, Vol. 458, col. 319.
[133] *Hansard*, Vol. 458, col. 84; for the labor reply on this point see *ibid.*, cols. 115–121; 237–238, and 278.

spokesman, G. R. Strauss;[134] and that wage rates were high in the industry as a whole.[135] Contrariwise, they argued, there were good reasons for believing that labor will work less hard in the industry if the Government takes it over;[136] that nationalization will not create full employment;[137] and that the net effect of the proposed change will be to "create a race of sycophants, of men hanging on their immediate bosses' smile"—[138] not to mention the total disregard of the rules and principles of good management which occurs when political power is fused with special interests, such as those promoted by trade-union leaders in which political reliability is bound to be a factor which will lame the capacity of management to make quick and effective decisions.[139]

Needless to say, the Labour reply on all these points was in the mood of emphatic rebuttal. Writing in the *Tribune*, for example, Mikardo found that so far as labor conditions were concerned, "the Report, published in 1947, of the Joint Advisory Committee on Conditions in Iron Foundries is probably the most slashing indictment of a privately-owned industry since Elijah chastised the prophets of Baal."[140] On this score, virtually everything was wrong with the industry that the imagination might conjure. As for labor efficiency under nationalization, the worker will not let its own government down,[141] and the participation of the worker through the device of the works councils will not only interest men in efficiency,[142] but will also reverse the tendency toward the "servile state" implicit in the past relation of employer to labor.[143] The issue, in short, was not economic but political.

On a second point, that the industry had been largely supported in the past by government subsidies of something like £22,000,000 a year,[144] that was not the whole of the story. This cost to the government

[134] "Fortunately the relationship between workers and managements in this industry has on the whole been good," but there were some exceptions. *Ibid.*, col. 74.

[135] E.g., *ibid.*, col. 425.

[136] *Ibid.*, col. 140. This was a very frequently repeated argument—with production under nationalization in the coal industry cited as evidence.

[137] *Ibid.*, col. 469.

[138] *Ibid.*, col. 417. The workman, said Col. Hutchison, will be in the position described by Shakespeare, "Oh, how wretched is that poor man who hangs on princes' favours"—the princes being now the government bureaucrats.

[139] Capt. Marples, *ibid.*, cols. 425–427.

[140] "Black Record—Story of the Steelmasters," *Tribune*, Aug. 6, 1948, pp. 7–8. Iron foundries, incidentally, are not included in the bill.

[141] E.g., *Hansard*, Vol. 458, cols. 277 ff., 287, 154, and 241.

[142] *Ibid.*, col. 248.

[143] *Ibid.*, col. 290.

[144] This was itemized as follows (reference is apparently to the year 1947): "Payments to the industry in respect of imports of steel, £8,600,000; pig iron, £345,000; scrap, £4,800,000; contribution towards freight of imported iron ore, £7,300,000; subsidy in respect of production of home ores, £700,000. Total £21,745,000." S. N. Evans, *ibid.*, col. 103.

was supplemented by "higher prices to be charged in the home market . . . at the cost of consumers generally," and at the social price of a technically retarded industry in the hour of the country's direst need.[145] But at the same time, this argument lost much of its force by the incorporation into the bill of a clause making possible the indefinite continuation of substantially the same type of subsidy after the Government had nationalized the industry.[146]

On the third point, that the introduction of the bill would disturb and upset the industry, and consequently lame production at a vital point in postwar economic recovery—the point at which the Opposition expected to find themselves heavily supported by American concern over implementation of the Marshall Plan—the facts were otherwise. At no time before, during, or since the introduction of the bill did the industry appear to falter in its steady recovery from war conditions.[147] On the contrary, the Government argued, it was the very prospect of nationalization which spurred the workers in the industry to show the increases in production which the Opposition was now citing as proof of the capacity of the industry to improve under private auspices.[148]

The fourth point seemed to the Opposition much more important. It was the problem of compensation. Bitter as the debate on the relevant clauses were on this point, the issue, however, was comparatively simple. The Government simply proposed that there could not be any "fairer criterion than the old well-established one, the price their prop-

---

[145] Sir Stafford Cripps, *ibid.*, col. 315.

[146] Clause 5 reads: "Where the Corporation have acquired, with the general or special approval of the Minister, any imported materials for the purpose of the carrying on by them or any other person of any of the activities specified in the first column of the Second Schedule to this Act, or any imported iron or steel in any form, and the total cost of such imported materials or iron or steel, including any expenses incurred in or in connection with the transport thereof and any import duty payable thereon, exceeds the price at which any such imported materials or iron or steel are sold in Great Britain by the Corporation, the Minister may, with the approval of the Treasury, pay to the Corporation out of moneys provided by Parliament an amount not exceeding the difference between the cost and the price aforesaid." This clause is italicized in the bill.

[147] See, e.g., the article "Steel Economy Campaign," *Engineering,* March 4, 1949, p. 206.

[148] "One would assume from hon. Members of the Opposition that the increase in the last 12 months of nearly a million tons of steel was created by some magician resident in the Steel House or in the Tory clubs of Great Britain. It is the result of the great sacrifice and effort made by these men who are now working under this Socialist Government, their own Government, and working under the firm, solid pledge of nationalisation." Jack Jones, in *Hansard,* Vol. 458, cols. 241–242. On the other hand, there can be no doubt but that the Steel House executives felt that the most crushing answer to the demand for nationalization was to show that the industry could and would improve efficiency as a patriotic duty, and entirely irrespective of the Government's intention to take them over. Specifically it seemed to them to be the most appropriate answer to the charge that the monopoly characteristics and cartel-like policies of the industry militated against increase in productive efficiency. Nevertheless, striking as some of the increases in productivity have been, they still do not begin to cope with the potentialities inherent in the type of fundamental change in the ground-plan of the industry mentioned by Burn, *op. cit.*

erty is fetching in a free market," and since "the Stock Exchange is a free market where the securities are constantly changing hands between willing buyers and willing sellers . . . There can, therefore, be no more equitable way of ascertaining the value of the steel securities concerned than the Stock Exchange quotations arrived at in this way."[149]

This, said the Opposition, is wrong in principle. Summarizing the debate, *The Economist* found that the whole issue rested upon the Government's contention that this method of valuation was fair because stock-exchange prices ". . . are the result of dealings in a free market between willing buyers and willing sellers. The flaw in this argument is that the commodity which can be bought in that market is not the commodity the Government wants to buy; it is only a tiny fraction of it. The price at any moment is determined merely by the marginal demand and the marginal supply at that moment. Buyers 'for control' habitually negotiate outside the Stock Exchange; and, when the initiative comes from them, almost invariably have to pay substantially more than the market price. At that price an overwhelming proportion of holders are neither willing nor reluctant sellers; they are not sellers at all. And to deem them to be willing sellers at the price acceptable to the few who do sell at a particular moment is bound to be unfair."[150]

Furthermore, the Opposition argued, the Government in so valuing the securities to be acquired had both broken a pledge and been guilty of an act of bad faith. The pledge was the assurance given at the time of the introduction of the motion to bring forward a bill to nationalize the iron and steel industry that "whatever the final method and basis adopted . . . proper allowance will be made in assessing compensation for the results of any expenditure incurred from now onward, on approved schemes of development or rehabilitation."[151]

Now "the peach . . . is going to be valued as a lemon," for in the intervening two and a half years there had been heavy capital investments involving advance of funds on the security of this pledge. Worse still, the government made a special appeal "to the leading firms not to increase but to 'plough in' their dividends and the co-operation which they have received in consequence," has definitely affected the market.[152] The industry had coöperated, dividends had been kept down, new

[149] G. R. Strauss, in *Hansard*, Vol. 458, cols. 69–70.
[150] *The Economist*, Nov. 20, 1948, p. 845. See also, *Hansard*, Vol. 458, cols. 158, 267 ff., 282, 466.
[151] Cited by Capt. Peake, in *Hansard*, Vol. 458, cols. 158–159 from statements made by Government spokesmen in *Hansard*, Vol. 423, cols. 838, 853, 854, 1004.
[152] Churchill, in *Hansard*, Vol. 458, col. 230.

investments had been made, the government had licensed schemes under which capital expenditures up to £100,000,000 were currently being financed, and all this only to be betrayed. "Never," Captain Peake said, "has a fly walked, or flown, so innocently into the spider's web."[153] Since stock market prices had been depressed by these actions,[154] the Government had in effect rigged the prices it now proposed to pay.

The Government reply was that the facts did not bear out the Opposition argument. Impending nationalization and "voluntary limitation of dividends did not in fact depress the price of industrial shares as a whole" as may be shown by the fact that "at the end of October, 1947, steel shares were 142.6; others were 149.8 [1938 prices = 100]. At the end of February steel was 151.8; others were 149.6. Steel has passed the rest . . . At the end of May, 1948, steel was 166.9 and all industrials were 161.7. At the end of October, steel was 173 and others were 161.7."[155] Furthermore, what these prices represented was earning power and future prospects based upon such things as past knowledge, past investment, past good will, but also on government protection from foreign competition, direct subsidies to the industry, government-regulated prices for steel products, past high profits rates due to government-stimulated war and postwar demands, etc.

The Government's plan, accordingly, was to take stock market quotations for these securities as of the average of the mean quoted in the *Stock Exchange Official Daily List* for the period from October 1 to October 25, 1948, or the middle of the month for the first six months of 1945—whichever was the higher—and exchange for these such amounts of British Iron and Steel Stock newly to be issued by the government as will, "in the opinion of the Treasury" be "at the general date of transfer of a value equal to the value of the securities" taken over and appraised in such a fashion.[156] The value of the quoted securities, "eliminating the duplications of capital where one company owns that of another company" will total "£243 million in respect of £134,500,000 of paid-up capital. On the average, £101.6 will be paid for every £100 of loan stock; £1 10s. on the average for every £1 Preference share, and £2 6s. 8d. on the average of every £1 of Ordinary stock."[157]

---

[153] *Ibid.*, cols. 160–161.
[154] That this had happened was the judgment of the *Stock Exchange Gazette*, Nov. 6, 1948, supported by the *Financial Times*, cited by H. Strauss, in *Hansard*, Vol. 458, col. 132.
[155] Sir Stafford Cripps, *ibid.*, cols. 313–314.
[156] *Bill*, clause 14.
[157] Sir Stafford Cripps, *Hansard*, Vol. 458, col. 311.

Since "everything belonging to or affecting the business of the company as at October, 1948, is fully taken into account in the price of the shares," and for ordinary shares the October "prices were, on the average, the highest that have been realised over the last ten years the shareholders are getting a very favourable deal."[158] In addition, under clause 16 of the bill, there was to be an official stockholders' representation of any company taken over, whose duty it would be to protect stockholders in working out the details of compensation. All in all, some Government supporters felt that the deal was overgenerous to say the least.[159] Whatever the relative merits of the argument, the compensation provisions certainly did not seem to justify the heated charges of the Opposition that they amounted to confiscation and robbery, and they were on balance at least as generous as those allowed in the other nationalization cases.

There were two further issues which appeared in the debates, but which were not followed through. Both are of extraordinary significance for the possible success of any proposed reorganization, and failure to consider either is likely to nullify any expectation of improvement the Government may entertain—however optimistic—from the new direction which they hope to give to the industry. The first is the problem of foreign competition, and the second is the relation between iron and steel development and relocation and all those general plans—ranging from those coming under the administration of town and country planning to those involved in regional and industrial development in general—for population relocation and industrial planning.

The first point entered the debates only as commentary on plans for expansion of total iron and steel capacity. Foreign steel capacity, it was pointed out, has been greatly expanded during the war,[160] and all the planned new capacity may not actually be needed. But far more important is the fact that much of this new capacity is in low-wage countries, where the costs of production are apt to be indefinitely below

---

[158] *Ibid.*, cols. 317, 311.

[159] See the data submitted by Jenkins, *ibid.*, cols. 131, 133–137.

[160] "Have the Government calculated on the increased capacity of foreign countries? Is it realised that the Canadian output has already been trebled? Is it realised that the European countries, with the exception of Germany, are approaching their pre-war figure, that Luxembourg, Poland, South Africa, and Sweden have passed it? Is it realised that the United States of America, with its enormous production figures, is in the course of doubling them? What is going to happen when all these come into operation and play on the international market? If we double the inter-war demand, as it was experienced, we find a total demand of 16 to 17 million tons, which will be taken care of by the existing plan. But is a permanent doubled demand likely?" Col. Hutchison, *ibid.*, col. 414.

British levels for this reason alone. In certain countries, most notably Germany and Japan, American plans call for raising permitted output to new levels, and in these areas, accordingly, low wage costs will be coupled to new and more or less modern plant. Hence they will enjoy a double advantage over the British. Where this is not so, as in the United States, higher wage costs are largely offset—if not already more than offset—by correspondingly higher productivity, and are coupled to a volume of output so preponderatingly great as to lend enormous pressure for the resort to discriminatory and dumping practices the instant the industry is faced with any marked degree of underutilization.

These factors lay extraordinarily great emphasis upon the need for a far more drastic overhaul of the British iron and steel industries than has been brought to light by any plans submitted to date. But almost equally important is the second neglected aspect: the connection between any such reorganization and other schemes for population and industrial relocation and development. On this subject, only one feature has come in for any significant discussion at all, and that is the plan for expanding iron and steel plants in the development areas (previously known as distressed areas). However desirable this may be on its own merits, it contributes comparatively little to the central problems involved in the badly needed reorganization of the iron and steel industry. Surveying the whole postwar British picture, it is probably entirely accurate to say that for the more important heavy-industrial, and a wide cross-section of the light-industrial (machinery, metal products) centers of Britain, there can be no solution to the problem of industrial location and development until the plans are laid for steel; that population relocation—and with that the whole range of problems associated with town and country planning, housing, etc.—depend upon the plans for industrial location and development; and that even the general social security program—social insurance, health, full employment, etc.—cannot reach far beyond the emergency level in its efforts to ameliorate the lot of the laboring population as a whole until the plans for population relocation have been resolved on both the regional and national levels.

Thus the reorganization plans behind the nationalization of the iron and steel industry must necessarily play a pivotal role in the whole of the Labour government's postwar recovery and reconstruction program. Yet so far as one can tell, except for the actual transfer to public ownership, no plans exist as yet which are at all capable of dealing in a realistic fashion with this problem of "what to do with steel" in all its complexity, or with the realities which define the urgency for rapid, wide-ranging, and drastic action.

Nor, as will appear in following chapters, are there any broadly co-ordinative physical plans relating to the vast complex of problems in the other spheres of the national economy with which the fortunes of the iron and steel industry are so intimately linked, and where similar solutions on a similar scale must soon be sought as a condition to national viability.

CHAPTER VI

National Transport

Whenever Parliament deals with any great basic service which represents an overhead charge on the whole of industry, Parliament establishes a monopoly. The fact that it is broken up into hundreds of thousands of monopolies does not alter the fact that the whole of the legislation of this country has proceeded in the direction of establishing the principle of monopoly in the field of transport, but we have always denied the nation the advantages of co-ordination, unification and integration among all the forms of its transport services ... as services move in this direction, they must be publicly owned and publicly run, with the whole of their affairs subjected to Parliamentary and public examination.—Alfred Barnes, Minister of Transport, December 16, 1946.

THE LABOUR CASE for nationalization of internal transport was based on five main points. First, public transport media of virtually all types—excepting only small-hire and personal-service facilities, such as supplied by taxicabs and small local haulage—are natural monopolies possessing power to manipulate the interests of all persons, groups, and parties within society, and such power cannot be allowed any longer to remain in private hands. Second, coördination between and among the several media of a type and on a scale necessary to achieve effective unification at lowest capital and operating costs for the various types of traffic movements can only be realized when basic management decisions are vested in a single authority. Third, excepting only certain specialized types of local traffic, the very nature of the complex regional traffic patterns of an industrialized economy requires that the unit of top policy determination be at least coextensive with national—not local and regional—frontiers.

To these three arguments, which apply more or less equally to any national industrial system,[1] two others which applied specifically to Great Britain were added. The first of these was that the scale of the existing duplication and overlapping of traffic media in Britain, plus

---

[1] They apply, of course, equally—and perhaps even more forcibly—on an international basis where, depending upon the type of traffic medium, the appropriate geographic frame of reference is rarely coterminus with national frontiers. Thus, with internal waterways it is clearly the watershed or interwatershed (watersheds interconnected with canals) area, with railways and highway facilities it is the continental (sea-bound) land mass, with maritime shipping the world's sea lanes, and with airways the unit is global. The Inland Transport Committee of ECA had under continuous review throughout 1948 the problem of unified European traffic networks for rail, road, and waterways media which consider Britain as an integral segment of the Continental system. See the summary, *Times*, Nov. 4, 1948. Proposed as a "symbol of Western Union," there has been a revival of interest in London in a channel tunnel linking Britain directly with Continental traffic arteries. *Times*, Sept. 15, 1948.

the extent of their technical backwardness and consequently the proportions of the necessary investment required to effect the needed reorganization, required financial resources which only the government was able to command, and necessitated a type of unified financial planning for transport which only a national public institution could carry through. This was all the more important since, finally, the nature, quality, and cost of transport was bound to be a determining factor in all of the Labour party's plans for industrial and population relocation, and the whole range of problems involved in the vast programs both of the nationalized industries and of town and country planning.

All such arguments were lent additional support, Labour spokesmen for nationalization contended, by the simple fact that the issue of public ownership and operation of transport was not, and virtually never had been, in dispute as such. Gladstone had been "speaking as a Tory" when as early as July 8, 1844, "he moved the Second Reading of a Bill for Government purchase of the railways."[2] Sixty-four years later the great Liberal, David Lloyd George, upon leaving the office of President of the Board of Trade in 1908, reported that under his direction the board had drawn up "a complete Bill for the nationalisation of the railways, and that there was in his documents with the Bill a letter from every one . . . of the 113 managers of those companies saying that it was the only thing to do."[3] Even Churchill, now leader of the Conservatives, had, when classed as a Liberal at the end of the First World War, "given his blessing to nationalisation" in no uncertain terms.[4]

Nor had the more general arguments for public ownership of the railways changed essentially since the earliest days. Virtually from the beginning, Labour spokesmen for nationalization pointed out, the railways had employed their monopoly position to prey on the public.

[2] Douglas Jay, in *Hansard*, Vol. 431, col. 1842. Upon the basis of some six reports of a committee of inquiry set up under his auspices as president of the Board of Trade, "Gladstone produced his Bill and secured the Act of 1844" proposing "state purchase on the following basis. At the end of fifteen years the Government should have the option of purchasing any new line 'whatever the amount of profits'; the Government terms would be twenty-five years' purchase of the annual divisible profit calculated on the average of the last three preceding years" provided it was not "in excess of 10 per cent." George Ridley, *The Railways, Retrospect and Prospect* (Labour Party, 1942), p. 7. In a memorandum to Lord Palmerston (then Prime Minister) in 1864 Gladstone reopened the subject by forwarding the recommendation of "a man named Galt" for state purchase of the railroads. *Times*, Dec. 22, 1948.
[3] C. Davies, in *Hansard*, Vol. 431, col. 1658.
[4] In a manifesto called *The Next Five Years*, Sir Arthur Salter, author of the 1932 Salter report on transport reorganization, independent member of Parliament and frequent braintruster of conservative policy, had written about "the last group of industries" which "is composed of those suitable for complete socialisation. We suggest it should include such industries as transport, electricity supply, some forms of insurance. Transport is an obvious example." Quoted by Douglas Jay, in *Hansard*, Vol. 437, col. 89.

In 1844, when there were only 2,000 miles of railway line in Britain, Gladstone had found that the railways had gone "among the individual traders very much like a triton among the minows, and the effect had been, in many cases, highly inconvenient to them. They had shown that their arrangements for communication, not merely upon the lines of railway, but off them, were affected and deliberately controlled by the companies" and there was every reason for believing that "as the country became covered with a closer network of railroads, then difficulties and hardships would be increased . . ."[5]

Gladstone had prophesied correctly. Over the intervening years the exercise of these monopoly powers had led to the expected results: disorganization, technical backwardness, high costs and high rates, and low quality of service. Sir Eric Geddes, echoing the sentiments of Churchill and Lloyd George, had said in 1919 that private enterprise in railroads "makes for colossal wastes" and his indictment, made by a nonsocialist more than a quarter of a century ago, leaves little for a socialist to add to the story of the railroads at the end of the Second World War. "The transportation agencies," Sir Eric Geddes had said then, "will be comparatively barren and sterile in economy and development until this unified control is brought in . . . This will come as a shock to some who believe in individualist effort . . . The railway interest is a community interest. Agriculture has got to be developed. The State must come in and make economies possible . . . If you cannot get efficiency by means of private management, then nationalise . . . We must not commit the folly of our predecessors and allow the development of every system on its own principles, and of every system according to the whims and notions of those who introduce it . . . Transportation is the greatest power that we have for bringing prosperity to the community . . . We must eliminate wasteful haulage; we must standardise . . . One of the first acts which the Government will take will be to acquire on fair terms the private wagons of the country."[6]

Subsequent history had confirmed Geddes' judgment. So bad, indeed, had the internal transportation situation become in the later thirties that not even the railroads were able any longer to present a united stand against nationalization. For example, a leading railroad executive had come out openly for nationalization in 1937. Writing in the *News Chronicle* on December 29, 1937, William Whitelaw, chairman of the London and North Eastern Railway, one of the "big four" railroads of

[5] *Hansard*, Vol. LXXXVI, William IV, 7th and 8th Victoria (1844), col. 489.
[6] Quoted by W. Monslow, in *Hansard*, Vol. 431, cols. 1682-1683.

Great Britain, had "advocated nationalisation of the railways" with the suggestion that "after purchasing the railways, the Government should set up a body to control both road and rail transport. This public body might be run something like the London Passenger Transport Board or the Port of London Authority." Of course, "one of the principal obstacles to overcome is the deep-rooted political prejudice against the word 'nationalisation.' But this is not a political problem. There is no doubt in my mind that State ownership would result in rationalisation and improvement which would reduce the costs of both passenger and industrial transport."[7]

There was, furthermore, a great deal of anticipatory legislation which demonstrated, incidentally, a step-by-step realization that the proposals incorporated in the bill under discussion must sooner or later determine government policy. "Under the Regulations of the Forces Act, 1871, the Government took control of the railways at the outbreak of the war in 1914. The Defense of the Realm Act and Regulations of 1914, and similar previous Acts, have enunciated the principle that in times of public necessity, the Crown was always entitled to take over private undertakings."[8] In a similar fashion the government had assumed management control in the Second World War, first over the railroads and subsequently over virtually all types of transport.

A series of major legislative acts had helped to ease the way for the action now contemplated. The Railway Act of 1921 "has simplified the problem of nationalisation" by amalgamating "125 companies, with all their managers, and 700 directors" into "only four companies, with their general managers, and 102 directors."[9] A first step in the same direction was taken for passenger transport by road with the passage in 1930 of the Road Traffic Act which divided the country into thirteen traffic areas, each of which was placed under the administration of three traffic commissioners whose duty it was to see that unnecessary services were eliminated, and that fares, routes, and time tables were established on an orderly and unified basis. Similar controls were extended to goods traffic by road under the Road and Rail Traffic Act of 1933, an act which was memorable also in that it represents the first step taken in the direction of unification of road and rail media.

Of even greater importance was the passage in 1934 of an act setting up the London Passenger Transport Board to take over the ownership

---

[7] Cited by Douglas Jay, *ibid.*, col. 1842.
[8] Monslow, *ibid.*, col. 1683.
[9] *Loc. cit.* This statement is not strictly accurate.

and management of "over 14 local authority undertakings and some 70 private undertakings,"[10] with a view to fusing them into a single, unified passenger-transport system covering—with the exception of main-line road and rail transport into the city—the entire metropolitan area of greater London. The manifest and universally recognized advantages of this unification had served as a sort of large-scale "pilot plant" operation to establish the feasibility of similar unification of the entire internal traffic network of England's compact industrial system. Even the Conservatives had come to recognize the desirability of this last step when they had gone along, under the Coalition government, with post-war proposals which called for virtually the equivalent of what was being submitted by the Labour party in the Transport Bill of 1946.

Finally, for those inclined occasionally to look abroad for inspiration and guidance, there was the status of railways in the British Commonwealth. "In Canada," Barnes pointed out, "55 per cent of the railway mileage is already State-owned. In Australia and New Zealand, 95 per cent is publicly-owned. In the Union of South Africa, 81 per cent is State-owned." In the world as a whole 45 per cent of "rail transport is already publicly-owned or State-owned."[11] And if such a conservative paper as the *Financial Times*, so dearly beloved by the Opposition, can find that "the complete co-ordination of transport by means of a scheme of unification is now the only way to get the best possible service at the lowest economic cost,"[12] how, then, could even the Government's most bitter critics fail to realize the inevitable need for the bill which had just been laid before the House of Commons?

At any rate, the Government argued, here again it had a mandate from the public. It had won the 1945 elections on the basis of the program laid down in *Let Us Face the Future*, where the proposal to nationalize the whole system of internal transport had been made absolutely explicit.[13] The proposal was the result of over fifty years of agitation, beginning with the declaration by William Matkin, president of the T.U.C., in 1890, that the railroads were mismanaged, "their servants overworked and poorly paid" and "often extortionate goods

---

[10] "... the Act establishing it was passed by a Conservative Government in 1934, although it was prepared by the Labour Government which preceded the Administration." A. J. Barnes, in *Hansard*, Vol. 431, cols. 1624–1625.

[11] *Ibid.*, col. 1622.

[12] Cited by Morrison as of "either the 2nd. or 3rd. Sept.," *ibid.*, col. 2074.

[13] "*Public ownership of inland transport.*—Co-ordination of transport services by rail, road, air and canal cannot be achieved without unification. And unification without public ownership means a steady struggle with sectional interests or the enthronement of a private monopoly, which would be a menace to the rest of industry." *Let Us Face the Future* (London, 1945), p. 7.

rates have a baneful influence on the trade of the country."[14] Again in 1897, and in wholly unambiguous language, the T.U.C. passed by unanimous vote a resolution to the effect "that the time has now arrived when the railways of the country should be taken over by the Government in pursuance of the Act of 1844" and it instructed its Parliamentary committee "to press this matter upon the attention of the Government."[15] The general tenor of this demand was reiterated in subsequent T.U.C. congresses down through the years.

But the demand for nationalization of transport on the part of Labour's organized supporters did not begin and end with railroads. The T.U.C. added municipalization of tramways in 1892 and docks in 1896. In 1905 it demanded nationalization of canals for the first time. In 1918 it fought against return of the railroads by the government to their private owners, and in 1920 it favored the "co-ordination of transport system" as a whole. The Labour party itself first proposed nationalization of railroads in 1908. In the following year it added waterways. In 1917 it took the position that the railways should not be returned to their owners at the end of the war, and in 1937 it included nationalization of all internal and coastwise transport among its "four vital measures of reconstruction" with a statement that "competition in Transport, especially between private undertakings, is wasteful, inefficient and dangerous. A National Transport Board will therefore be set up to coordinate Transport by Road, Rail, Air, and Coastwise Shipping, and to own and operate the Railways and such other Transport Services as are suitable for transfer to Public Ownership . . ."[16]

The Opposition might laugh—as they did—but in face of the fact, said Barnes, that "the Labour Party, the Trades Union Congress, the Co-operative Congress . . . who have been speaking for the organised workers and consumers of this country for many years . . . have stated quite clearly in published documents, and in many other ways, their firm conviction that these transport services should come under national ownership,"[17] and since the issues had been stated clearly in the recent electoral contest, it follows that "both the principle of nationalisation, and our clear intention, have been submitted to the electorate, and have received their endorsement." The case for nationalization was thus complete.

[14] *Report of the Twenty-third Annual Trades Union Congress* (Liverpool, 1890), p. 28.
[15] *Report of the Thirtieth Annual Trades Union Congress* (Birmingham, 1897), p. 70.
[16] *Report of the Thirty-seventh Annual Conference of the Labour Party* (Bournemouth, 1937), p. 277.
[17] *Hansard*, Vol. 431, col. 1618–1619.

THE PROBLEM OF COMPENSATION

It was against such a background of opinion, legislative experimentation, and historical evolution that the Labour government's bill for a once-for-all solution of the national transport problem was introduced and pushed through the two houses of Parliament. Yet debate which should, on such a showing, be short and simple, was lengthy and a "hard-hitting one on both sides," and, as Morrison added somewhat ruefully, "I have never known, on any Bill introduced by this Government, or indeed by any other Government for quite a long time, such a vigorous campaign conducted as we have seen on this Bill."[18]

The debates were remarkable for another and quite unexpected reason. Throughout all phases of the debates and committee discussions the Government avoided all phraseology designed to "sell socialism," and so—in its desire to prove that it had been at all points anticipated by nationalization and control measures which had been introduced or proposed by previous nonsocialist governments—it assumed an almost apologetic tone in defense of the bill before it. Nor did the Opposition, aside from occasional spirited thrusts, attempt to raise the much maligned ghost. For its part it concentrated attention largely on compensation provisions in the bill, and on extension of nationalization into the general field of road transport. More astonishing still, both sides ignored almost entirely the central issue at stake, that of the technical reorganization of transport as a whole. Aside, that is to say, from frequent emphasis upon what Morrison somewhat whimsically referred to as "the magic word 'coordination,' "[19] the Government had virtually nothing to say about how efficiency, coördination, unification and integration, technical modernization, and so on were to be effected. Virtually all the basic arguments for planning were absent from its presentation.

So also for the Opposition. Not only did they concentrate most of their attention on compensation and the inclusion of road transport, but much of their attack on these features seemed to be quibbling over minor points, when, indeed, not to be downright frivolous. The really

---

[18] *Ibid.*, col. 2071. An unusually large, well-organized, and amply financed campaign had been conducted throughout the entire country by a Transport User's committee, which appears to have been improvised for the occasion, and which, among other activities, endeavored to pressure Parliament with a flood of telegrams and letters—many drafted by use of formulae suggested to them—from all different types of transport users protesting the proposed nationalization. Specimens of the telegrams are given by Morrison.

[19] *Ibid.*, col. 2078.

important problem of the overhaul of the British transport system had so completely dropped out of the picture at one point that Sir Arthur Salter, himself an opponent of the bill, was moved to remark: "I do not propose to follow the Hon. Member for Enfield [Ernest Davies] on the subject to which he devoted most of his time, namely, compensation. This is not because I have nothing to criticise in what he said, nor because I think that the subject is not important. But I have taken the view, both upstairs and down here, that on the whole, rather too big a proportion of our time has been spent on questions of compensation. I do not say that too much time has been spent on this subject, but, rather, that too little time has been spent on other parts of the problem. After all, what really matters to the country is whether or not, from the point of view of the user of transport a more efficient transport system is provided by the Bill."[20]

Thus it came about that, with minor exceptions,[21] the Opposition accepted the statements on the condition of British transport media, physical and otherwise, made by the Government in its criticism of the past reign of private enterprise in this vital field. Two objections, however, were entered more or less for the sake of the record. As a sort of parenthetical comment it was pointed out that contrary to the situation obtaining in most other industries where nationalization measures had been proposed, "there has never been an inquiry into the technical merits of the various proposals for the industry as a whole," and it is essential that such "a public and impartial inquiry . . . should take place, and that these proposals should be exposed to public and impartial hearing." Such an inquiry would "be completely dangerous to the half-baked proposals in this Bill," and "legislation should be postponed until it had taken place."[22]

The Government had anticipated this criticism with the statement that "there have been some five major Acts of Parliament dealing in some respect or another with this problem, and there have been about

---

[20] *Hansard*, Vol. 437, col. 70. In committee stage Jay summarized the growing irritation of the Government at Opposition tactics when he commented that "I would also affirm that a number of speeches were made in the Committee, by the Opposition, before the Guillotine was introduced, which were calculated to spend time rather than to improve the Bill. If that is a definition of obstruction, I say there was obstruction." *Ibid.*, cols. 93–94. On the record this complaint seems justified, but it is also true that the Government never seriously attempted to bring the debate around to the central issue as stated by Salter.

[21] A partial exception is to be found in the comments by J. A. Sparks concerning increases in railroad efficiency, but Sparks was speaking for, not against, Labour in making the very points which one normally would have expected the Opposition to have made the most of, yet which it scarcely bothered to note. *Hansard*, Vol. 431, col. 2051.

[22] Major Sir David Maxwell Fyfe, *ibid.*, col. 1640.

20 important inquiries, many of them of a character which the opposition interests are now demanding."[23] Furthermore, Barnes went on to add, "we are living in a period in which action is very desirable, and inquiries can be very dangerous in their consequences."[24]

Strangely enough, the Opposition made very little out of this curious remark. They did point out that although "inquiries can be dangerous," they may be rendered no less necessary because of that when such a momentous step is to be taken. This was especially so since the Government, at the very moment it was arguing the tremendous importance of securing a general trade recovery in Britain, was also taking "the wildly irresponsible course" of having "the attention of every operator engaged in transport deflected from his ordinary work of serving industry into looking at what will be, and must be, his position under these nationalisation proposals."[25] But this point was not followed up.

Nor, for all practical purposes, was the second quondam reservation. The run-down condition of the railroads, the Opposition insisted, was itself largely a product of the strain placed on them during the war when normal replacement and repair were reduced to those required on an emergency basis only. Since the government ran the railroads during this period, and was therefore itself at least partly responsible for the conditions in which it now found transport, the least it could do was to give the railroads a chance to rehabilitate themselves. This seemed especially desirable in view of the fact that the Minister of Transport "knows as everyone knows that the railway companies had their plans ready for renewals, replacements and new works, and to take his own example, he knows it was planned and that everything was prepared to rebuild Euston Station."[26] Other examples might be cited *ad infinitum.*[27]

---

[23] Barnes, *ibid.,* col. 1618, and Morrison, col. 2076. As Strauss, Parliamentary Secretary of the Ministry of Transport, pointed out, just before the general elections of 1945 the Liberal party had issued, under the chairmanship of Sir Seebohm Rowntree, a pamphlet entitled *The Future of British Transport* which concluded with the statement that "we ... recommend that the control and ownership of railways and the long distance road haulage and passenger transport industry should be transferred to a public utility corporation." *Ibid.,* col. 1992.

[24] Barnes, *loc. cit.*

[25] Fyfe, in *Hansard,* Vol. 431, col. 1640.

[26] *Ibid.,* col. 1638.

[27] E.g., planned at the time the government took over the railroads were the following schemes: "(i) Manchester-Sheffield electrification, estimated to cost £6,200,000. 'This scheme will increase the capacity of this important cross-Pennine route, 60 per cent of which traffic is coal. It will allow for quicker turn-around of locomotives and wagons and save 180,000 tons of coal per annum, while releasing 180 locomotives.' (ii) Woodhead Tunnel, estimated to cost £2,500,000. This tunnel is located on the above-mentioned route, and age and structural defects make its replacement necessary. (iii) East and west extensions of Central Line (London Passenger Transport Board), and Sheffield electrification (L.N.E.R.)." *Home Affairs Survey,* Dec. 9, 1947.

Yet, as indicated, neither of these two Opposition points was heavily underscored in the debates, and they seem to have been mentioned only to be dropped. Clearly a thorough reorganization of the internal transport system of Britain was necessary before the required changes and repairs could be made, and the Opposition appears to have been at a loss for alternatives to the Government plan which could even begin to grapple with the problem.

But compensation and the question of the inclusion of road transport involved issues of an entirely different order of magnitude in Opposition eyes. Both, the Opposition felt, involved a fundamental issue of principle. But this principle soon proved a double-edged sword. With respect to compensation the heresy consisted of accepting the conventional competitive supply-and-demand valuation of transport securities as they might be determined on the free market of the stock exchange. But in the arguments on nationalization of road transport the heresy consisted of eliminating precisely those aspects of cut-throat competition which the more ardent upholders of the competitive, free-enterprise system had long been seeking to wipe out by private agreement. It is small wonder that under these circumstances principle soon came to resemble a chameleon facing the well-nigh irresolvable problem of crossing a Scotch plaid.

The heart of the debate soon became compensation, and since this issue has come subsequently to play such an important role in the various cases made for and against the Labour government, it will be necessary to discuss the argument at some length.[28] Centering attack on the compensation provisions applying to the railroads, the Opposition found them to be no less than "a compromise between the law of the jungle, and the artificial restrictions of the Zoo," and this to the tune of "a confiscation figure of something like £17 million." The hardships to be endured by security holders, including "poorer people and widows" were grievous and evil.[29]

The basis of compensation to railroad security holders chosen by the Government was to be that of market values as quoted on the stock exchange on certain selected dates. The Minister of Transport explained "briefly what influenced the Government to come down on this side of the market price for railway passenger traffic, passenger transport, and canal shares," in the following terms: "In the first place, it covers adequately the securities that are involved. Sixty-nine of the quoted

[28] For a discussion of the issues in road-rail coördination, see pp. 264–272 below.
[29] Major Cooper-Key, in *Hansard*, Vol. 431, cols. 1867–1868.

securities of Part I of the Fourth Schedule[30] represents 98 per cent. of the nominal value of all the securities involved. Therefore, this method which we have adopted, which is quick and easy in its assessment, covers, to all intents, the whole of the securities that are affected. The dates from 1st to 8th November, 1946, represent very favourable quotation dates. The alternative of the middle monthly quotations for the six months prior to the Election, February to July, 1945,[31] gives an advantage in certain cases. Therefore," he felt, "we have adopted a simple, easy, and fair method that gets equitable compensation and avoids considerable difficulties" which "recognizes, on the one hand, the rights of dispossessed owners to reasonable compensation and, on the other hand, the right of the State to benefit from the use of its own credit."[32]

This meant, in the end, payment of £1,000,000,000 for all rail and canal securities in the form of 3 per cent transport stock, "repayable optionally in 1978 and finally in 1988."[33] Since, the Government argued, the basis of this appraisal was stock market valuation, and since, as the *Financial Times* had stated in commenting on the bill, "The market is the place where all differences of that sort are valued in arriving at daily quotations," it follows that "the investor is doing no worse, in terms of capital values, than if he had chosen to sell his stock in the market around current prices."[34] And the stock exchange, Hugh Dalton reminded his listeners, is the Holy of Holies, not for the Government, but for the Opposition who were denouncing the Government as though it were resorting to economic heresy.

The leading newspapers, accordingly, approved of the basis selected.[35] The Government had "gone to the independent arbitration of the Stock Exchange quotations" and Dalton, who did not want "to put very dangerous ideas into the heads of some . . . hon. Friends," pointed out that the stock exchange regarded itself as "a scientific recording instrument"[36] based upon the principle that the "higgling of the market

[30] The third schedule of the *Act*, pp. 145–146, names the "Bodies Whose Undertakings are Transferred to Commission," and the fourth schedule, pp. 147–151, itemizes the "Securities to be Replaced by British Transport Stock."

[31] See *Transport Act*, Section 17, pp. 24–26 in particular.

[32] *Hansard*, Vol. 431, col. 1627.

[33] *The Economist*, Jan. 3, 1948, p. 25.

[34] Cited from the *Financial Times* by Dalton, in *Hansard*, Vol. 431, col. 1803.

[35] Comment on the bill was cited from the three leading Opposition newspapers, *The Daily Telegraph*, *The Times*, and the *Financial Times*.

[36] He quoted from a stock exchange memorandum which said: "The Stock Exchange may be likened to a scientific recording instrument which registers, not indeed its own actions and opinions, but those of private and institutional investors all over the country, and indeed, all over the world." *Hansard*, Vol. 431, col. 1805.

gives a value which is just good enough for both buyer and seller." At this equating point, "the two sides to the bargain . . . close and complete the bargain, one to buy and the other to sell." To illustrate he went on to recall how "on one occasion an employer offered a barrel of beer to his workers; they drank it, and he asked them how they liked it. They replied, 'Well, governor, it was just right.' He asked them, 'What do you mean, just right?' He was told, 'Well, if it had been a bit better, you would not have given it to us, and if it had been a bit worse, we could not have drunk it.' " And that, said Dalton, "briefly, is the philosophy of the Stock Exchange. It is to that philosophy that we have appealed in this Bill. Those prices are just right; they are just right in terms of certain quotations taken on certain days" and those quotation dates provide "as the basis of compensation a market value which gives a higher price than any comparable period which could have been chosen for a long time past."[37]

It is, perhaps, needless to point out that the question of fairness of compensation could not here—or elsewhere for that matter—be settled except on a more or less arbitrary basis, since there are no objective criteria for valuation which are, or indeed can be, wholly free of interest bias. For the Government it was pointed out that many of its constituents saw no reason why any compensation should be given at all.[38] But if, ignoring its own heretics, full and fair compensation was truly to be given, it could not be offered on the basis of payment for run-down physical assets which were highly over-capitalized—largely as a result of high payments to landowners, lawyers, and others as the systems were built up.[39] Furthermore, the railroads had been immensely profitable, for "since the coming into operation of the Railways Act, 1921, no less than £880 million has been paid in the form of interest and returns upon the shares, that is, virtually the whole of the capital has been repaid in the period since 1921."[40]

More to the point, the Opposition wanted the Government to pay in terms of net maintainable revenue or for actual capital expenditure. The first could not be calculated except on assumptions which "would have to be made in regard to the policy which would be adopted other than nationalisation"[41] if one were looking to the future, or to the

---

[37] *Ibid.*, cols. 1806, 1817.
[38] Referred to by Douglas Jay, *ibid.*, col. 1843.
[39] "The capitalisation figure per route mile in this country is £56,000 as against £31,000 in France, £24,000 in Germany and £14,000 in the United States of America." A. J. Champion, *ibid.*, col. 1833.
[40] *Loc. cit.*
[41] Dalton, *ibid.*, col. 1820.

peculiar circumstances under which revenue had been maintained in the past. Looking ahead, revenue must be calculated as a function of rate policy, capital investment, and operating expenses involved in modernization, and, above all, the nature of competition with other transport media. And looking backward, one saw that wartime profits had been maintained by the railroads through not keeping up repairs and replacements and eating up their real capital. At the same time dividends were received largely from rentals paid to the railroads by the government to the tune of £38,000,000 a year.

If one were to go back further, railroad earnings during the thirties were a very uncertain quantity. "Take the Southern Railway," said G. R. Mitchison, "one of the more prosperous ones. In 1935 it was getting nothing; in 1936 it was getting ½ per cent; in 1937 1½ per cent., and in 1938 nothing . . ."[42] Share prices reflected these fluctuations in earnings, and in face of these records the Government was offering steady returns at fairly high levels. For example, said Jay, for "Great Western ordinary the compensation price is 59¹⁄₁₆. In January, 1939—and I took the first working day of each year so as to be perfectly fair—the price was not 59 but 28; in January, 1935, it was 51; if the highest level it touched in 1932 is taken, because it was a depression year, the price was only 48¾. Thus the compensation price is a far higher price than that of 1939, 1935, or 1932. Take the L.M.S. ordinary. The compensation price is 29½. In January, 1939, that stock stood at 13½; In January, 1935, at 21; and the highest point it touched in 1932 was 20⅝."[43]

If one were to take the second alternative proposal, payment for actual capital outlay, the amount involved would run, on the basis of the "estimate of the 'Economist' on 23rd November . . . just under £1,200 million,"[44] or some £300,000,000 above the stock market valuation as of the dates given. If, on the other hand, the net revenue claimed by the railroads' spokesmen as maintainable were £40,000,000 per annum, then the government would have to pay £1,600,000,000 or 76 per cent more than the stock market figure. In contrast with either of these two positions was the fact that the stock market rated the value of shares in terms of past records, current performances, and future prospects in the absence of proposed nationalization. The very fact that it was low showed that the prospects of the railroads were very poor in-

[42] *Ibid.*, col. 1702.
[43] *Ibid.*, col. 1848.
[44] Dalton, *ibid.*, col. 1819.

deed. If, said Dalton, the window were opened to competition, "and if it is very free competition—well, maintainability descends rapidly towards zero."

Alternatively, Dalton undertook

to console anybody who thinks that the railway stockholders are being ill-treated, by putting the compensation terms in another form . . . Let us take the total compensation contemplated for the railways under this Bill—£908 million. If the net maintainable revenue were put at £40 million—although I think that it is too high and could not be maintained anyway—that would represent 22.7 years' purchase. That would mean that the risk on all the railway's capital on this basis would be measured by an interest rate of about 4½ per cent., including all the speculative junior stocks, and if we were to break that up it means that—on the basis of 22.7 years' purchase—on the senior half of the capital we should put the yield at 3 per cent. which is not much above the Government gilt-edged level, and a risk of 6 per cent. on the junior half. Having regard to the very doubtful net revenue prospects in the future I think this is very generous. Let me quote the other figure. If we take the average net railway revenue of 1935–37 it will be found that the compensation we propose represents about 25 years' purchase, so really it cannot be said that they are being skinned alive, as the right hon. Gentleman so picturesquely put it. Many an eel would be happy if that were its fate.[45]

The Opposition reply was to point out that different stock market dates gave different quotations, and different shares on given dates showed different results. Little was made of this point, however, though clearly it might have been pursued to considerable advantage. Aside from arguing for the alternative basis of valuation—net maintainable revenue and real capital investment[46]—the Opposition centered its attention on three arguments. First, that it was improper for Parliament to set the value, for this was to solve an economic problem by political means. Second, that the whole matter should be referred to an impartial tribunal. And third, that serious injustices would be perpetrated on certain classes of security holders—principally upon owners of debentures as against shareholders, and upon trust funds which were largely dependent upon such debenture holdings as against private individuals.

Of these three, only the last received much detailed attention.[47] Dalton conceded knowledge "that some 29 per cent. of the total stocks, at

[45] *Hansard,* Vol. 431, cols. 1820, 1821–1822.

[46] Occasionally, though only by parenthetical reference, a third alternative was hinted at, that of replacement value, which would total something like £2,000,000,000. See remarks by R. Assheton, *ibid.,* col. 1891.

[47] See, in particular, comments by Assheton, *ibid.,* cols. 1887–1890. The Church of England, he said, would lose £200,000 income per year. Income of "hundreds of country rectories and vicarages" would be reduced, superannuation and other insurance accounts would be diminished. Col. 1890.

present value, are trustee stocks held in England and Wales"[48] but he insisted also that trustees were among the railroad security holders who would gain by greater security of return on government shares, and that the injustices to some were counterbalanced or more than counterbalanced by better returns to others. But even more significant, security holders were very lucky to get off so well under the circumstances, for the government was virtually in the position of paying them a good price for run-down properties with a future which, in the absence of nationalization, was dark indeed. Nothing less than a fundamental reorganization of the entire internal transport system of Britain was called for, and failing that—which only the government was prepared for, and had the necessary resources to carry through—where would they be? Furthermore, the government could not undertake this task too heavily burdened with a compensation debt, much of which was, on any showing, the price of the folly and mismanagement of the railways in the past.[49]

At this point the Government rested its case so far as compensation for railway securities was concerned. Relatively little opposition arose over the proposal to make the payment in British Transport Stock and not in British government stock, although choice of the former carried with it the principle of making "interest payments . . . a first charge on revenues."[50] Nor was much made of the fact that the principle of compensation employed in nationalization of the railroads differed from that applied in other transfers to public ownership.[51] In general both

---

[48] *Ibid.*, col. 1811.

[49] Nevertheless, the government did contrive a method of redeeming indebtedness out of current income which confers on the Transport Commission a back-breaking load. Clause 93 states that "the Commission shall charge to revenue in every year all charges which are proper to be made to revenue, including, in particular, proper allocations to general reserve, proper provision for depreciation or renewal of assets and *proper provision for redemption of capital* . . ." (Italics mine). Professor Walker rightly comments, "If this clause means what it says, and there is no reason why it should not, the Commission will have to find, out of the difference between their receipts and costs, the additional net revenue—it may be as much as £20,000,000 per annum—required to pay off £1,000,000,000 British Transport Stock before A.D. 2000 . . . Loaded with this obligation, it may take a generation or more before traders and public begin to enjoy the economies of co-ordination so confidently predicted by the supporters of the Act." Gilbert Walker, "The Transport Act of 1947," *The Economic Journal*, LVIII (March, 1948) : 17.

[50] See the comment by Jay, in *Hansard*, Vol. 431, col. 1850, which seems to indicate a difference of opinion in Government circles on this point. See, also, the comment by Walker, footnote 49 above.

[51] W. S. Morrison was an exception. He objected that the Government "makes the rules" to suit itself: "The Bank of England has been paid for in one way; Cable and Wireless in another; the coalmines in yet another, and this Bill adds to the confusion by containing four different compensatory devices to be applied according to whether railways, road transport undertakings, the undertakings of local authorities or privately owned railway wagons are being taken. The absence of any coherent principle is . . . an alarming prospect . . ." *Hansard*, Vol. 431, col. 1788.

sides seemed to accept the rule that expediency should govern, provided the device employed could be justified strictly on its merits in each separate application. This seems to be the reason that relatively little objection was raised to the payment for rolling stock of road hauliers and privately owned railway wagons at the rate they would bring on the resale market, and without inclusion of any goodwill allowance.[52]

A somewhat more valid point was raised in criticism of the compensation features contained in clause 27 of the act, relating to ports and harbors, which provided "not a lump sum represented by British Transport Stock, but an annual consideration in lieu thereof equal to the present commitments under the sinking fund contribution, plus interest on outstanding loans until such time as the sinking funds are sufficient to redeem the securities issued in respect of the stock of the dock undertaking," which would mean, for example, that the Port of Bristol Authority, for assets which are worth £11,050,000, would receive roughly £5,175,000.[53] By this action the government would acquire "assets costing £5,875,000" without compensation to the City of Bristol. A similar result could be shown for the assets taken over from the Port of London Authority and the Mersey Dock and Harbour Board.

Yet the point, once having been made, was not followed up. For the purpose in hand, the central fact brought out by the debate on compensation was that all groups realized that nothing less than a thorough reorganization of internal transport was called for. All other issues, including compensation, were subsidiary in the sense that nationalization, or, at least, the anticipated changes which lay behind the intent to nationalize, was virtually inescapable anyway.

THE BRITISH TRANSPORT COMMISSION

The Transport Bill was passed and received the royal assent on August 6, 1947, and is known as the Transport Act of 1947.[54] The scope and scale of this "largest and most extensive socialisation measure," as

---

[52] See, e.g., further remarks by W. S. Morrison, *ibid.*, cols. 1790–1792, and Lt.-Col. Dower, cols. 2043–2044.

[53] W. A. Wilkins, *ibid.*, col. 1676.

[54] The full title reads: "An Act to provide for the establishment of a British Transport Commission concerned with transport and certain other related matters, to specify their powers and duties, to provide for the transfer to them of undertakings, parts of undertakings, property, rights, obligations and liabilities, to amend the law relating to transport, inland waterways, harbours and port facilities, to make certain consequential provision as to income tax, to make provision as to pensions and gratuities in the case of certain persons who become officers of the Minister of Transport, and for purposes connected with the matters aforesaid." (10 & 11 Geo. 6, Chap. 49.) The act consists of 128 sections and 15 schedules, and totals 170 pp.

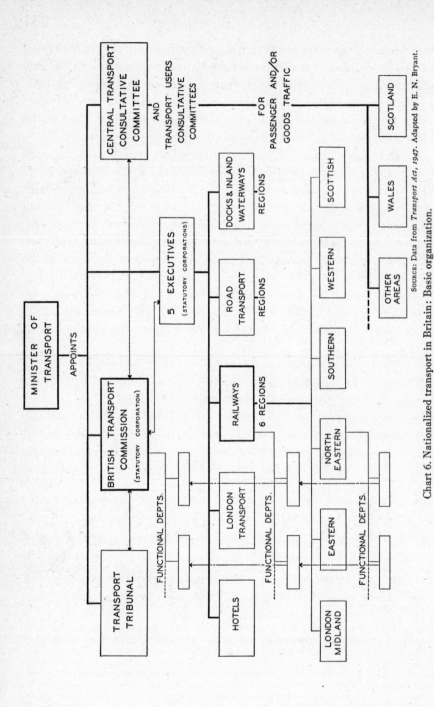

Chart 6. Nationalized transport in Britain: Basic organization.

SOURCE: Data from *Transport Act, 1947*. Adapted by E. N. Bryant.

Barnes referred to the act, was truly staggering. On the vesting day, January 1, 1948, the properties taken over from railroads alone consisted of 52,000 miles of track, 13,500 stations, 20,000 locomotives, 45,000 passenger carriages, 1,235,000 freight wagons, 100 steamships, 70 hotels, 50,000 houses, 9,000 horses, 25,000 horse-drawn vehicles, and 11,000 motor vehicles. In addition the government took over wharves and docks at 76 places containing 95 miles of quay, and it acquired ownership of some 1,640 miles of navigable canals and internal waterways. In acquiring the London Passenger Transport Board, it took over the largest and most complicated underground network in the world and some 7,000 busses and coaches, 900 trams, and 1,750 trolley-busses. It will, finally, eventually acquire from long-distance road haulers and bus companies some 34,000 motor vehicles (including the 11,000 owned by the railways) and a large number of bus and lorry terminal facilities and miscellaneous properties.

The railroads on vesting day employed roughly 680,000 persons. Ultimately it was believed that the Transport Commission would have direction over from 1,000,000 to 1,250,000 workers. The capital investment involved in taking over the railroads, canals, and the London Passenger Transport Board was estimated at roughly £1,065,000,000. The scale of operations was equally Gargantuan. "In 1946 the railways moved two hundred and sixty-two million tons of freight, and carried one thousand two hundred million passengers," and the London Passenger Transport system handled "over four thousand million passengers, and "our canals moved over ten million tons of freight."[55]

The broad outlines of the machinery set up under the Transport Act are shown in chart 6. At the top, appointed by and directly responsible to the Minister of Transport, is the British Transport Commission, consisting of a chairman and from four to eight members. To it are transferred directly all the properties nationalized under the act, and in it are vested all the powers deemed necessary to manage, extend, or curtail these properties in the future on a going-concern basis. Actually, it is to exercise its management functions by setting up boards which act as agents for the commission, to be known as "executives," the members of which are also to be appointed by the Minister of Transport, and are to be jointly responsible to him and to the Transport Commission. The act provides for five such executives, namely, "the Railway Executive,

[55] From an "extract from a broadcast talk by the Rt. Hon. Alfred Barnes," Minister of Transport, on January 1, 1948, as given by, Central Office of Information, Reference Division, *Nationalisation in Britain, II, 4: Transport*, No. R. 1563, p. 12. [Mimeographed.]

SOURCE: Associated British and Irish Railways. Adapted by E. N. Bryant.

Map 5. British railways.

the Docks and Inland Waterways Executive, the Road Transport Executive and the London Transport Executive and, as from the appointed day, an Executive known as the Hotels Executive."[56]

As indicated, each executive is to become the general management body for one of the properties taken over under the act, and are to be made up of a limited number of especially qualified persons—presumably not less than four nor more than eight, though, as indicated by the Railway Executive, the number may be higher on occasion—serving on a full time basis. The Railway Executive, for example, "would be the employer of staff and the authority for contracts and would deal direct with the public. The executive would be composed mainly of functional officers, six members out of nine being responsible for certain departments of railway work. These are: public relations, stores and estate; staff and labour negotiations and welfare; passenger, freight and commercial development; operating and marine; civil engineering and signalling; mechanical and electrical engineering."[57]

Each such executive may, subject to approval by the commission, regionalize its work as it sees fit. The Railway Executive, as shown on map 4, is divided into six regions: (1) London Midland Region, (2) Western Region, (3) Southern Region, (4) Eastern Region, (5) North Eastern Region, and (6) Scottish Region. Each of these regions more or less closely corresponds to the area served by one of the former big-four railroads, or some principal division of one or more of these lines. Similar patterns may be used for internal waterways and for road passenger and freight transport.

Paralleling the Transport Commission and its several regional divisions—which are not, it appears, necessarily identical with the regional divisions of its several executives—are to be Transport Consultative committees. The one which is to be advisory to the Transport Commission is to be known as the Central Transport Consultative Committee, and the regional ones are to be known as Transport Users Consultative committees. Of the latter, there may be either separate committees for freight and passenger traffic, or a single committee for both lines of service. No size for these committees is specified in the act, but they are to consist of representatives of "agriculture, commerce, industry, shipping, labour and local authorities," certain other "persons nominated by the Commission," and "not more than two additional members" to be added by the Minister "if he thinks fit."[58]

---

[56] *Transport Act*, Section 5, Clause 2, p. 11.
[57] *Home Affairs Survey*, Dec. 2, 1947, p. 39.
[58] *Transport Act*, Section 6 (4), pp. 13–14.

Finally, there is to be established a Transport Tribunal, which "is the Railway Rates Tribunal renamed. It will take over the powers of the Railway Rates Tribunal, the remaining jurisdiction of the Railway and Canal Commission, and the remaining jurisdiction of the High Court on transport matters,"[59] and this amounts to possession of "full jurisdiction to hear and determine all matters whether of law or of fact" concerning ownership, transfer, claims for damages, etc., as they relate to transport—rights which are similar to those relating to other matters possessed by the regular high courts of England and Scotland.[60]

There was singularly little Opposition criticism of this machinery beyond the routine application of certain standard adjectival derogations. The bill "gives an unexampled opportunity for political patronage and jobbery." It would mean "increased cost to the consumer." There would result a "loss of enterprise and initiative" throughout the transport field. The transport workers would insist upon a closed shop.[61] The bill had the air of hasty improvisation, and was proposed without benefit of adequate inquiry into the important facts. Nor was the time ripe. Change would now upset revival of industry, and this change would make "the Minister of Transport a dictator."[62] The Minister was challenged "to give an illustration of any country where there is a complete monopoly of all transport, except Germany and Russia."

The Minister seems to have quite fairly summarized debate on the administrative features of the bill when he replied that despite "some substantial improvements to the Bill . . . the main structure has been preserved unimpaired" and the "commission remains as the supreme policy body." He had not, he went on to say, "discerned any condemnation of the proposal of the Commission as a policy body, or of the Executives as management instruments as such, or of the parallel machinery of the Consultative Committees for the purposes of voicing the needs of trade and industry, and the traveling public. It is quite true that the numbers of the Commission have been subjected to criticism, and the Minister's power of appointing Executives has been challenged and discussed at some length. But the main plan of the Commission" and its supplementary machinery were substantially unaltered.[63]

[59] Barnes, in *Hansard*, Vol. 431, col. 1633.
[60] See *Transport Act*, Part V, "The Transport Tribunal and Transport Charges and Facilities," and Tenth Schedule, "Provisions as to the Transport Tribunal," pp. 162–163.
[61] Fyfe, in *Hansard*, Vol. 431, col. 1647.
[62] Sir Cuthbert Headlam, *ibid.*, cols. 1669–1670.
[63] *Hansard*, Vol. 437, col. 46.

Yet it is difficult to avoid the conclusion that the Government may have done itself a distinct disservice in sidestepping criticism along these lines. Considering that the purpose of the Transport Act of 1947 was to coördinate and unify internal transport throughout the British Isles, the machinery established seems to contain some very obvious weaknesses. Since all members of the Transport Commission, the various executives, and the consultative committees receive their appointments from the Minister of Transport, and hold their tenure subject to his pleasure, it seems clear that the Minister of Transport, not the Transport Commission, is the real executive authority, and under these circumstances the device of the independent autonomous public corporation can have but little real meaning since it is, in effect, a mere operating division of the Ministry of Transport. This interpretation is reinforced by the fact that neither the Transport Commission's own executives, nor the consultative committees attached to them, hold tenure from it, but from the Minister, and by the numerous clauses in the act which lend the Minister general authority—without at any point defining the limits of such authority—to give instructions and to make decisions relating to the conduct of the commission's duties. In reality the Minister, not the commission, is the executive authority for both transport as a whole, and for the several executives in charge of the various traffic media.

By so much as this may not be true, the hierarchy of command consists at each level—beginning with the Transport Commission and its various executives, and down through the regional organization as a whole—of a board or committee, not an executive officer. So far as authority may be needed to coördinate across the board at any given level, there is lacking in any one person the power to make a decision. This is because the commission and all its executives are organized along functional lines, so that, "the chain of command leads direct from the department in the region to the members of the Executive responsible for the particular function concerned."[64] This holds for each level of authority in relation to each level above it, which means, among other things, that virtually any local issue involving coördination at the lowest level with other functional authorities at that level may be passed up all the way to the top before it is remanded for settlement

[64] Gilbert Walker, "The Transport Act of 1947." Professor Walker adds the comment that this is a "highly centralized departmental type of administration usual among the small compact railways of the nineteenth century" but probably poorly adapted for the large-scale operations visualized under the 1947 act.

below. It is hard to see how a more awkward and cumbersome device for securing rapid and responsible decision making than this might have been devised.

But the worst is yet to come. Despite all emphasis on the need of handling the problems of traffic movement as though each type of media and service were but a single aspect of a unified traffic system, the management of each was divided among the several transport executives. Each such executive is then to coördinate the functions allocated to it on a national basis, and for this is to select its own regional division. This has meant in practice that the functional breakdown within the separate executives varies from executive to executive, and that the regional breakdown is left to the discretion of each executive, with the result that, so far, in no two branches of transport do regional divisions coincide. Thus the railways have six regional divisions. The canals and internal waterways with which they are to be integrated have five. The Road Executive has decided to divide Britain into "ten or twelve divisions, and the Road Transport Executive will suggest to the Commission a series of large areas for passenger transport."[65] Should it then develop that the British Transport Commission, in furtherance of plans for further promoting transport coördination—and numerous references would seem to justify the inference that these are being prepared—should establish its own regional offices, confusion would seem to reign supreme.

Finally, as if to complicate things to the uttermost, the tendency seems to be to place all real executive authority in London, and thus to centralize the regional problems of traffic coördination to the maximum. Four out of six of the regional offices of the Railway Executive, for example, are located in London. A fifth is located in York, and the sixth in Glasgow.[66] Even if the other executives do not follow this lead, the fact that one executive centralizes in London and the others do not may prove a major complicating factor.

If these sources of possible administrative weaknesses are taken, not separately, but in combination, the effect would seem to justify the Opposition complaint that the intentions of the Government were to construct a vast centralized transport bureaucracy without paying any particular attention to the way in which large scale and complicated functions should be organized in order to remain manageable.[67] Vir-

---

[65] *Home Affairs Survey*, March 3, 1948.
[66] *Home Affairs Survey*, Dec. 2, 1947.
[67] See, e.g., the remarks of Quintin Hogg, in *Hansard*, Vol. 437, col. 88.

tually all the administrative weaknesses in this bill were already beginning to show in the organization of the National Coal Board by the time the transport "appointed day" had rolled around, yet the bill's sponsors seemed to have learned little from previous mistakes.[68]

It is difficult to say just what the devising of this cumbersome administrative machinery indicates. If merely ignorance of administrative theory and practice, then the mistakes made are not very serious, since they can readily be corrected. But if they indicate failure to understand the nature of the problem of genuine traffic coördination then they are serious mistakes indeed. How serious may readily be shown by a quick survey of the transport problems to be solved.

RAILROADS AND INTERNAL WATERWAYS

All parties agreed that the railroads were in a badly run-down condition at the end of the war. The Southern Railroad was a partial exception, but the lamentable state of the London and North Eastern more than made up for that. The generalization covers rolling stock, stations, track, service, and the relationship between the railroads and other traffic media. A few data will show the scale of reconstruction required.

At the beginning of the winter of 1946–47 no less than 3,700 locomotives "out of a total book stock of 20,242, were out of service for repairs."[69] The locomotives on the London and North Eastern were "on the average, . . . over 32 years old."[70] They were also almost completely unstandardized as to type, and over wide ranges of construction and repair locomotive parts were not interchangeable. In place of some 35 to 40 types required by analysis of work to be performed, there were over 400 at the time the Transport Commission took over.[71] Nor were types adequately specialized as to type of traffic. Relatively little had been done on such problems as scientific analysis of locomotive haulage, capacity, efficiency of operation, fuel economy with various loads and at various speeds, the relative economies under various traffic densities of steam, diesel, and electric traction, and equipment and facilities for repair at the roundhouses.

---

[68] Partial recognition of their situation is reflected in the establishment, December 16, 1948, of the British Transport Joint Consultative Council, made up of representatives of the five executives, and the five leading transport trade unions, "to provide regular opportunities for exchanging information and views on inland transport problems and the activities of the British Transport Commission and their executives." *Times*, Dec. 17, 1948.

[69] *Labour Party Year Book, 1947–8*, p. 195.

[70] *Hansard*, Vol. 431, col. 1621.

[71] In a general announcement concerning plans for standardizing rolling stock early in 1949 it was suggested that the number of types of locomotives might be reduced to twelve. *Times*, Jan. 4, 1949.

Much the same picture held for passenger carriages and freight wagons (the usual English expression for open freight cars; closed boxcars are called "goods wagons"). Of the latter "over 20 per cent," said Barnes, "are obsolete and should be scrapped and 50 per cent are over 35 years old."[72] In November, 1947, more than a month before taking over under the act, it was estimated that "nearly 200,000 wagons were under or awaiting repair" out of a total of about 1,250,000, and that there "were over 54,000 fewer wagons in operation than a year ago, and over 80,000 fewer than in 1945.[73] Worse still, very few of these wagons were of 40 tons capacity, and the vast majority of them were under 25 tons capacity. None of them were equipped with automatic couplings. Very nearly half (570,000) had been privately owned, and details of construction varied endlessly from merchant to merchant and from line to line. Few of them were, except for the chassis, of steel construction. The picture for passenger carriages was somewhat better, though still bad in comparison with best practice abroad. All-steel carriages, for example, were rare, and automatic couplings were found on only a limited range of specialized equipment.

As for roadbed, "maintenance work on the permanent way was in arrears to the extent of 10,000,000 sleepers and some 328,000 tons of new steel rails,"[74] and much road ballast was in bad shape. Some tunnels and bridges were too small for the larger equipment, and the light weight bull-head type rail—though standard throughout the British railways system—is wholly obsolete.[75] Terminal facilities were in a similar condition. "Terminal goods sidings for the reception of . . . trains in the Midland coal field," for example, "were built in the 19th century. They were built to contain and deal with trains consisting of 25 eight-ton wagons. That is the capacity of a good many of the terminal goods sidings. At the present time it is quite a normal load to have 90 wagons of from 12 to 15 tons to be dealt with."[76] Furthermore, turn-around was slow. It was found during the war that, mainly through improved turn-around, the railroads were capable of handling 50 per

---

[72] *Ibid.*, col. 1629.

[73] *Home Affairs Survey*, Nov. 25, 1947.

[74] *Labour Yearbook.*

[75] The new heavy flat-bottom rail—long since standard on American and most Continental lines—is "59 per cent stronger vertically, and 136 per cent stronger laterally" than the super-seded bull-head type, "will require about 16,900 fewer components" including fastenings, etc. per mile, is easier to maintain, keeps better alignment, makes for quieter and smoother riding, etc. *Home Affairs Survey*, Feb. 8, 1949. The official reason for the continuation of the obsolete bull-head type was Britain's lack of hardwoods for cross-ties, yet most American railroads where the heaviest equipment is to be found—e.g., practically all of the western lines—have always used softwoods.

[76] J. Harrison, in *Hansard*, Vol. 431, col. 1857.

cent more than they did before the war,[77] and that cutting down the time when wagons would be detailed under load to 48 hours would increase the capacity of the railroads to move "750,000 additional tons of traffic every month."[78] Despite the wartime achievements there were great possibilities of further improvement.

A multiplicity of small stations, closely interspersed along the lines, handling small loads, and requiring frequent stops for both freight and passenger service meant also slow speeds and small trainloads. A horse-and-buggy mentality still governs railway operations, said Davies. "The railway companies today still operate on the basis of a large number of small local stations which are so located that the goods are collected within a distance in which a horse and cart would still be able to operate"[79] with the "net result . . . that the average speed of the goods train in 1938 was just over nine miles an hour, which was an incredibly low speed. The official figure, published by the Ministry of Transport, regarding the net ton haul per engine hour, if we include shunting, amounts to 461, whereas if we exclude shunting it amounts to 968."[80]

Nor was the situation much better in passenger transport. Testifying before the Royal Commission on Transport in 1931, Lord Monkswell "pointed out that as long ago as 1848 the Great Western Railway ran a train from Paddington to Didcot, a distance of 53 miles, in 47½ minutes, or, in other words, at the rate of 67 miles per hour, while the fastest booked train on any British railway today runs at 62 miles an hour, and the average of the best runs is not more than 55 miles an hour."[81] Local services were even worse, and reminded one of the Victorian era. Over the country as a whole, consequently, for passenger service "the average train miles per hour is only 15."[82] Automatic train control was wholly lacking.[83] There has been little change for the better since 1931.

Nor was the general service of a very high quality. Mr. Dalton spoke of "those dingy railway stations, those miserable, unprepossessing res-

[77] *Production and Engineering Bulletin*, 3 (March, 1944) : 143.
[78] *Ibid.*, 3 (July, 1944) : 313.
[79] "Since January, 1948, ten branch lines and twenty-five stations and halts have been closed altogether or closed to passengers." *Times*, Feb. 21, 1949. These were mostly very short or narrow-gauge lines. These excisions are very small indeed in view of the probability that real overhaul would show from one-fourth to one-third of linage, on an integrated road-met traffic basis, to be wholly obsolete.
[80] *Hansard*, Vol. 431, col. 1649.
[81] Cited by Champion, *ibid.*, col. 1831.
[82] Davies, *ibid.*, col. 1650.
[83] *Ibid.*, col. 1831.

taurants, all this apparatus for sleeping and eating, makes one ashamed as an Englishman when one is travelling abroad and sees how well the thing is done in Continental Europe, Western Europe, in Sweden and France . . . Still more do we feel that if we go to America and Canada. One feels very much ashamed in Canada of this branch of private enterprise in the old country. That is one reason why the tourist traffic is not so easily attracted here. The railways are in very poor physical shape."[84] This impression will be pretty well verified by any casual traveler moving around Britain in the postwar period. Where the service is not inferior and the products of low quality, the prices are very high.[85]

As for the canals, they "have really been allowed to fall into disuse." Of the some 2,200 miles of canals "the railways own something like 35 per cent" and they are declining in importance chiefly for this reason. Once they carried some 40,000,000 tons of goods a year. "In 1938 . . . that figure had dropped to about 13 million tons."[86] Though some "40,000 people lived on the system,"[87] it was a precarious existence eked out with benefit of equipment and facilities even more out of date than those of the railways. Most of this waterways network is largely if not wholly out of date. "There has been practically no coordination and consolidation" of British internal waterways facilities, Fenelon writes. The "various local systems . . . were planned piecemeal in the constructional period, almost without relation to each other. There is no uniformity of depth, width, general conditions, or in dimensions of locks, tunnels or overbridges. . . . Canals built to suit one kind of boat are generally unsuitable for other types, and thus only the smallest barge can navigate for any distance. On the Continent and in the New World 600 ton barges are usual, whereas in Britain the maximum is often below 100 tons and may fall as low as 40 tons."[88]

Coördination between the two media of rail and internal waterways occurred at very few places, and at most terminal points of the two systems did not exist at all. The situation with respect to docks and

[84] *Ibid.*, col. 1809.
[85] There are some notable exceptions. The station newsstands and bookstalls are excellent, and the porter and baggage room service is—although badly run down at the heel and overmanned—still fast, convenient, and cheap.
[86] Davies, in *Hansard*, Vol. 431, cols. 1659–1660.
[87] *Home Affairs Survey*, Jan. 1, 1948.
[88] K. G. Fenelon, *Transport Coordination* (London, 1929), pp. 37–38. Freight rates on the canals vary endlessly. "The network has . . . hitherto been managed in small uncoordinated fragments; the method appropriate to the period of turnpike roads." Robert F. Aickman, Chairman, Inland Waterways Association, in a letter to the *Times*, Sept. 30, 1948.

harbors was not much better. Many of the docks and harbors were in bad shape, had inadequate warehouse, loading, and handling equipment, channels and berthing space were frequently unsatisfactory for larger boats and specialized types of cargo, and very little had been done about specializing various ports for handling different types of shipments. But even more important, very little had been done to unify shipping needs with ports and harbors and with other internal transport media.[89]

The detailed management of inland transport facilities was further complicated by a veritable jungle growth of charges and rates. Speaking of railroad rates alone, the Royal Commission on Transport reported that "the railway companies have informed us that under the principles now guiding the fixing of railway rates, goods are classified on a system based principally on their value or ability to pay, but conditioned, to an extent which varies considerably with different goods, by their convenience of carriage. The present classification and system of rates and charges based thereon may be said to be a combination of value, packing and weight."[90] The London Chamber of Commerce found "that in practice it is hard to discover any guiding principle in the classification itself," but irrespective of "whatever the principles may have been upon which the standard rates were fixed, they have been nullified to a great extent by the system of exceptional rates, of which millions are in force at present."[91] The Minister of Transport "had been informed that there are some 40 to 50 million different rates in existence" and, hence, "one of the most beneficial results of this Bill will be, if we can simplify the jungle of rate charges, that now prevails in our railway and transport industry."[92]

Furthermore, the general level of these rates was high. Colin Clark has estimated that in 1935 the average charge of moving freight in England was five times as high as in the United States and 70 per cent higher than in France.[93] The significance of such transport inefficiency can be appreciated when it is realized that in 1925 freight charges account for some 30 per cent of the market price for pig iron, and a correspondent in the *Times* stated in the early forties that of a "selling

---

[89] See, e.g., remarks of Major Ungoed-Thomas, in *Hansard*, Vol. 431, cols. 1877–1881, and G. R. Straus, cols. 1987–1988. Interesting in this connection, also, is the *Report of the Working Party on Turn-Around of Shipping in the United Kingdom Ports* (Ministry of Transport, 1948).

[90] Cited by the Ministry of Transport, in *Hansard*, Vol. 431, col. 1634.

[91] Cited, *loc. cit.*

[92] *Ibid.*, cols. 1633–1634.

[93] Colin Clark, *Conditions of Economic Progress* (London, 1946), p. 32.

price of 46/11¼ per ton for coal, 12/3¼, or more than 25 per cent represents transport costs between the pit and the merchant's depot alone."[94] These cases do not appear to be exceptional.

UNIFICATION OF ROAD AND RAIL FACILITIES

An even greater weakness in the postwar British internal transport system is to be found in the failure adequately to unify road and rail traffic facilities. There are two possible bases for unification. First is differentiation of traffic between the two, with each medium specializing in the types of traffic for which it is especially qualified to provide a superior or lower cost service. Second is the possibility of managing the flow of traffic from point of origin to destination so that two or more of the traffic media—trucks, buses, railroads, canals, and waterways—would coöperate to handle those separate parts of the movement for which each had a marked advantage. These two possibilities are closely related, and since it will rarely happen that the one excludes the other, planning for virtually every traffic medium must take into account the simultaneous performance of both functions.

This may be illustrated from the classical statement of the Labour case for nationalization of transport written by Herbert Morrison. In *Socialisation and Transport,*[95] where he builds his argument around the plan which he had originally formulated in 1931 and subsequently seen carried through by the succeeding Nationalist government in the London Passenger Transport Board, he spoke of "transport needs for which the railway is not the best medium" and cited the examples of "light traffic, branch routes connecting sparsely populated areas, or rural areas with the great towns: door to door deliveries for moderate distances, and so on." A like generalization holds, in turn, for railways, canals, coastwise shipping, and road haulage. Thus, a "unified, comprehensive transport system would concern itself primarily, not with capturing traffic for this or that form of transport, but with determining the most economical method of meeting this or that public requirement."

The enormous practical importance of this view becomes immediately apparent when it is realized that if, as has been estimated, buses and road hauliers in Britain were to take over entirely all "light traffic, branch routes connecting sparsely populated areas, or rural areas with the great towns" in which—all factors bearing on costs and services

---

[94] Cited in *Railways for the Nation* (London, Labour Research Dept., 1945), pp. 14–15.
[95] (London, 1933), pp. 88–89.

included—they enjoyed a distinct advantage, it is probable that the route linage of the British railway network could be shrunk by one-third.[96] Over most of these thin traffic routes the railways are definitely unable to meet both overhead and operating costs, and on some routes it is impossible to meet even one of these costs. But bus and truck facilities can, with an appropriate system of schedules and rates, provide better and cheaper service and at the same time operate on a going-concern basis. An inevitable precondition is the development of a national rate structure for all these various services.[97]

The implications for the railroads are obvious. By abandoning these lines they would reduce both overhead and operating costs per volume of traffic hauled not only through ridding themselves of these unprofitable operations, but also by being able to abandon many stations, loading yards, warehouse and special handling facilities at the junction points of these lines with the routes of denser traffic upon which they would now be able to concentrate. At the same time rolling stock, trackage, and terminal facilities would be given much higher capacity, load, and diversity factors as a result of concentration upon heavy carload, trainload, long-distance, through, and fast traffic. From the resultant economies in rail transport it should be possible to finance the complete overhaul required on British main line railroads which all experts agree are long overdue—including the extensive electrification proposals of the Weir committee.[98] And all this could be accomplished while providing not only superior road service at lower costs for the areas abandoned, but also a superior rail service through providing a uniform pick-up and delivery service as a result of the practice of interchange of traffic at all the common road-rail terminals.[99]

[96] Estimate of a leading official of the Ministry of Transport and an outstanding authority of the economics of railway transport, made personally to the author in 1948.

[97] Thus Sir Cyril Hurcomb, chairman of the British Transport Commission, admitted that "fares and charges . . . are the crux of the problem of fostering and integrating the transport services." *Times*, Oct. 28, 1948. This is badly misplaced emphasis—the real problem is technical overhauling—but it underscores a present difficulty.

[98] "When I was Minister of Transport I appointed a Committee under the chairmanship of Lord Weir on the electrification of railways . . . The Weir report on railway electrification recommended electrification, and held that it would give a profitable return of 7 per cent." Herbert Morrison, in *Hansard*, Vol. 431, col. 2079. This figure, though a rough estimate, is doubtless too low for a thoroughly reorganized railroad system, since the advantage of electrification rises in proportion to the density of traffic, the length of the haul, and the weight of the load—all changes which road-rail unification are designed to underwrite to the maximum.

[99] This raises the question of the nature of plans for road construction. There are two general lines of emphasis. One is the construction of trunk roads, as a national network of major highways, and the other is the construction of special-purpose roads. There are seven classes of the latter, the most important being that for heavy "solid-tyred vehicles and vehicles whose statutory speed is less than 20 m.p.h." *Home Affairs Survey*, Nov. 9, 1948.

As indicated, the possible economies from reorganizing internal transport along these lines were very great. The contrasting historical facts were reasonably clear, and, with minor exceptions, beyond dispute. Beginning slowly during the twenties, but with growing rapidity during the thirties, bus and road-haulier systems had been siphoning off increasing percentages of profitable railroad traffic. A single illustration will show how drastic this threat to the railroads appeared to be. British railway freight traffic in "general merchandise Classes 7 to 21," which include "practically the whole range of manufactured goods ... although mounting (until 1938 at least, the latest date for which prewar statistics are available) to one-sixth of the total railway tonnage—yielded almost half of the gross revenue from freight; and during the twenty years before the war (1939), at a time when the estimated potential (railway) traffic was rising by one-third, the actual tonnage of general merchandise originating fell by one-quarter."[100] Contrariwise, the railroads lost practically none of their tonnage of classes 1–6, consisting primarily of coal, minerals, heavy merchandise, and in general, heavy, bulky, and low-value traffic.

The result was a fall of average revenue per ton-mile. But this was not all. Aside from high-value freight in general, the really lucrative traffic for both rail and road lies in dense traffic areas, or between major traffic centers. Road hauliers concentrated on this traffic, since it meant full loads both ways. For the railroads the results were a decline in volume of traffic where operating conditions (high capacity and factor ratios) were favorable, without any corresponding reduction in either overhead or operating costs being possible, and an increase in the proportion of revenue drawn from short-haul thin traffic and feeder lines which were likely under normal circumstances to be operated at a loss anyway. To some degree or other, the same appears to have been true of passenger transport. The irony of this situation was heightened by

---

There are two interesting comments to be made on this last classification. First, "solid-tyres" are and have been obsolete for a quarter of a century, and second, efficient traffic of the type visualized should travel upwards, not of 20 miles per hour, but 30 to 60 miles per hour. One would be hard put to find a better example of the degree of cultural lag in British thinking about problems of industrial technology. Yet a later effort to "raise the speed of heavy lorries from 20 m.p.h. to 30 m.p.h.," and at the same time to "transfer some traffic to the railroads," met with strenuous opposition from representatives of lorry drivers. *Times*, Feb. 28, 1949. Here again is an example of "the little less" which is strangling so much of postwar British recovery effort—where, as a high British government official expressed the matter dourly, "every interest, taken by itself, has just *a little more* to gain from *not* making the change than from making it," and, hence, resists change whenever it affects its future.

[100] Gilbert Walker, "Road and Rail: A Transatlantic Comparison," *Journal of Political Economy*, LIV (Dec., 1946) : 517. See also his exhaustive book on the subject: *Road and Rail* (London, 1942).

the fact noted above, that for a given volume, the shorter the distance, the smaller the load, and the thinner the traffic the greater is the relative advantage, cost-wise, per ton-mile of road over rail.

In introducing the Transport Act, much was made of the fact that both passenger and freight hauliers were becoming large-scale and nation-wide combinations. Table 18 gives a summary of passenger traffic by road on the eve of the war and shows a very rapid rate of concentration. By 1938 there were three dominating groups. Describing

TABLE 18

OWNERSHIP OF BUSES AND COACHES IN GREAT BRITAIN

Vehicles in possession	1932–33		1937–38	
	Number of operators	Total vehicles owned	Number of operators	Total vehicles owned
1–4...................	5,269	9,369	3,786	7,130
1–14..................	6,111	15,347	4,539	12,643
15 and over...........	323	30,893	259	36,731
Total...............	6,434	46,240	4,798	49,374

SOURCE: Cited by Walker, in *Jour. Pol. Econ.*, LIV:517, from *Annual Report of the Traffic Commissioners* (1939).

"how the road transport system came into a private monopoly jointly with the railways," Douglas Jay went on to say that "by the Railways Road Transport Act, 1928, the railways were given power to run road vehicles. They made very little use of that power, but what they did was to buy up controlling shares in practically all the private bus companies in the country. At the same time, two great private holding companies, Thomas Tilling and British Electric Traction, joined in that process and bought controlling shares in the same companies. By about 1938 we had a system whereby, as far as I have been able to discover, private companies owning over 90 per cent. of all the private buses in the country were as to more than 50 per cent. owned ultimately by Thomas Tilling, B.E.T. and Scottish Motor Traction in Scotland, and as to over 40 per cent. by the railways. That combine owned nearly 100 private bus companies, and employed something between 60,000 and 100,000 men."[101]

The combination tendency was somewhat less marked in the motor freight business. "In 1936, the only year for which figures are available, 80,000 of the 134,000 trucks licensed for hire were in possession

[101] *Hansard*, Vol. 431, cols. 1844–1845.

of operators owning four vehicles or less. Fleets of four to twenty-four accounted for another 36,000 vehicles, raising the accumulated proportion to 80 per cent. Only 6,000 (7.4 per cent.) were included in fleets of a hundred vehicles and over, and these included the substantial numbers of pick-up and delivery vans owned by the four main-line railways and the few railway affiliates. In addition, 350,000 trucks were owned by persons and companies doing their own carrying (including retail delivery services), making a grand total of half a million or so trucks in all."[102] Such data would seem to indicate that road haulage was truly the small man's paradise, and the gestation ground for individual initiative.

Yet this is only part of the story. In 1933 the Road and Rail Act required all road hauliers to obtain a license to operate from the chairmen of the area traffic commissions who, for this function, were made the licensing authorities. Three classes of licenses were issued: "A," public carriers when the vehicles were used solely for hire; "B," mixed carriers, when operators used their vehicles partly for hire and partly for their own trade or business; and "C," private carriers, when operators used their vehicles solely for their own trade and business.[103] A Tory government proposal, though opposed by some of the road hauliers, the act seems to have favored consolidation of operations sufficiently well to make possible the presentation of a unified front by the industry in conducting the "Square Deal" negotiations with the railroads in 1938. Under this arrangement the railroads and road hauliers agreed to the elimination of rate cutting and other competitive practices with a view, apparently, to effecting a working arrangement for sharing traffic between the two.

This "standstill" agreement, the Labour government argued, had the effect of enabling two more or less monopolistically organized groups to avoid even the type of competition which might have forced the continued rationalization of each, but without making adequate provision for unifying traffic between the two media. Hence, it was doubly damned, and in the normal course of events one could look forward to the time when a vast private combine would manage internal British transport problems as it saw fit without necessarily devoting much attention to the public interest in improved and cheaper transportation. A proposal for just such a combine was actually advanced in 1939. It was rejected in favor of the wartime Road Haulage Or-

[102] Gilbert Walker, *Road and Rail,* p. 505.
[103] *Nationalisation in Britain, II, 4:Transport,* p. 8.

ganisation under which the government was enabled to pool road facilities on a national basis under its war emergency powers. In 1946, however, the recently organized (1945) peak association of the hauliers, the Road Haulage Association, and the Railway General Managers' Conference got together on a program for national coördination, which they presented in their *Memorandum to the Minister of Transport: Coordination of Road and Rail Freight Transport.*[104]

This memorandum seems at first glance to meet all the Government demands for improving road-rail transport. Paragraph 20 even went so far as to declare that while "cooperation between road and rail services ... is the immediate problem," it is recognized, however, "that the solution of the road/rail problem is only one step towards the coordination of all forms of inland transport services." The real difficulty, however, was that effective power over road operations would be placed in the hands of area organizations which would be "formed under the auspices of the road haulage industry managed and operated under the direction of the hauliers concerned ..."[105] and would result, consequently, in centralizing national management of road traffic in the Road Haulage Association. Even though lip service was paid to the need for unifying and modernizing road-rail transport, this would amount to the arrogation by a private organization of what are necessarily governmental functions, and at the same time would tend to eliminate those very same small operators whose champions the Road Haulage Association was so loudly claiming itself to be.[106]

The effect of the haulier proposal would not only be to confer what is properly public authority upon an all-inclusive private and monopoly-minded body, but it would also leave the matter of technical rationalization of both railroad and road haulage entirely to the pleasure of the industry. The record of neither industry in the past was good, and that of railroads was distinctly bad. Furthermore, the current

---

[104] (Main Line Railways and the Road Haulage Association, 1946.) See also, Robert Allan, *The Royal Road* (London, 1946), chapter iii.

[105] *Memorandum to the Minister of Transport*, paragraph 5 (ii) and (iv).

[106] The proposal, said C. Davies, amounts to a mere formalization of a postwar procedure whereby the "Road Haulage Association set up regional sub-committees before which all applicants for 'A' and 'B' licences were invited to attend and they, being for the most part members of the Association and subjects to certain relations with it, had to appear. When they did, the result of their application for a licence was prejudged. The small man coming before such a sub-committee seeking his 'A' licence and hearing that the Road Haulage Association intend to oppose his application before the licensing authorities, decides not to proceed with that application." Knowing that he would meet with opposition from association attorneys before the licensing authority, the little man would give up, only to go away with a handout of "anti-nationalisation literature" where he could "read that under nationalisation the small man would be squeezed out." *Hansard*, Vol. 431, cols. 1651–1652.

state of affairs was clearly intolerable. Consequently, in bringing forth the Transport Bill the Government proposed that "this monopoly should be extended and eventually covered by the State . . . Any road haulier whose business is predominantly engaged in the transport of goods over 40 miles is brought within the compulsory terms of the Bill." At the time the bill was introduced, Barnes said, ". . . there are 'A' licensed vehicles to the number of 86,000, and there are roughly 19,000 holders. 'B' licensed vehicles number 53,000 odd, and there are 27,000 holders. Of the 'C' licensed vehicles, there are 306,000, and 149,000 holders." Of these, "some 2,000 to 2,500 undertakings will be brought within the compulsory terms of the Bill, and the number of motor vehicles involved will be approximately 20,000."[107]

If the vehicles taken over from the railroads upon their acquisition by the government be added, then the total to be acquired under the act would run between 30,000 and 35,000. Hence, outside acquisition under the bill, "there will remain some 100,000 'A' and 'B' vehicles, and about 300,000 'C' vehicles used by traders for the carriage of their own goods."[108] Nationalization of road haulage, that is to say, was to include less than one-tenth of the vehicles engaged in the industry.

Certain classes of goods transport were exempted entirely. Such were "bulk liquids in tanks, meat and livestock, furniture removals and similar specialised traffic,"[109] including all haulage by farmers operating their own vehicles. All road hauliers "are free to operate with a 25 miles radius" and all "C" licenses up to 40 miles, but all operating over 25 miles must receive permission to do so. The purpose of giving this special concession to the "C" licenses was belief that this "40-mile limit will enable all retail trade, and the vast bulk of manufactured and merchanted commodities to be undertaken by 'C' licenced traffic without any disturbance." But for this traffic, beyond "the 40 miles' limit, there must be no uncertainty as to what we aim to achieve," and hence the "C" licensee "will have to prove his case to the licensing authority, and will have to prove that it is a legitimate traffic for his own business."[110]

As for the "A" and "B" licenses, the Government would acquire them if either the total weight or the "total receipts of the undertaking from ordinary long distance carriage for hire" exceeded half the total

---

[107] *Ibid.*, col. 1630.
[108] Lord Pakenham, in *Hansard* (Lords), Vol. 147, col. 879.
[109] Barnes, in *Hansard*, Vol. 431, col. 1630.
[110] *Ibid.*, col. 1631.

weight or receipts of the enterprise in question for the base year 1946.[111] Thus the purpose of the act is clearly the elimination of road-rail competition for long-haul traffic on the tacit assumption, apparently, that this will automatically bring about the desired coördination within each and between the two media. Otherwise there is no mention whatsoever of differentiation by traffic media between thin and dense traffic areas, nor is even a side glance thrown at methods for achieving unification between short- and long-haul road traffic. A government monopoly of what must, when "C" traffic is added, be considerably less than half of long-haul freight movements, is effected, and that is all.[112]

Even less, apparently, was intended with respect to road-passenger services, where the "procedure to be adopted is for the policy Commissioners to promote area schemes, after consultation with the local authorities in their areas." Ultimately the intention is that "they shall be brought completely into an integrated national transport service,"[113] but "integration" here apparently means the same as it does with road haulage. This nationalizing of road transport, that is to say, comes out to a definition of coördination in terms of monopoly ownership of long-distance haul or local-area schemes, and not in terms of the two possibilities discussed at the beginning of this section. That this conclusion fits the facts is indicated by the observation made above that after the passage of the act the separate road-haulier and road-passenger systems under the appropriate road-transport executive were so organized as to integrate parallel services on a national basis, but not to unify services among the several media on either a regional or a national basis. Furthermore, it seems clear that the organization of the several executives internally along functional lines will tend still further to underscore the emphasis upon handling the separate problems of each medium on a self-contained basis, and thus to defeat—or, at least, to render very difficult carrying out—the original and stated intentions of the act—which explicitly declares it to be "the general duty of the Commission ... to provide ... an efficient, adequate, economical and properly integrated system of public inland transport and port facilities within Great Britain for passengers and goods ..."[114]

---

[111] *Transport Act*, Section 41 (1), (*a*) and (*b*), p. 55. Certain special exemptions relating to the base year follow in the balance of Section 41 and in Section 42.

[112] Since the act there appears to have occurred a considerable expansion of "C" facilities, and a corresponding withdrawal of high-grade traffic from public media.—Speech by Sir Cyril Hurcomb to the Mansion House Association on Transport, March 25, 1949. *Times*, March 26, 1949.

[113] *Ibid.*, cols. 1631–1632.

[114] *Transport Act*, clause 3 (1), p. 8.

Should it happen, finally, that the several executives turn out to be more or less independent rate-making authorities, in the sense that the commission delegates to them its control over "charges schemes" so long as each complies with the injunction that costs must be covered out of revenues,[115] and so far as the facilities within its jurisdiction are concerned, then the tendency to substitute "duopolist" competition for "an integrated inland transport as a whole" would be, as Walker suggests,[116] strong indeed. There are at least two powerful influences operating in this direction. The first is the tendency to think in terms of the 1946 proposal of the main-line railways and the Road Haulage Association, which favored formulation of "a National Rates structure based on road factors" to parallel "a Railway Rates structure" similarly conceived and "capable of correlation with the road rates structure."[117] In these terms, correlation is bound to mean division of traffic between the two media in terms of costs as they would be determined within each medium considered as a self-contained traffic system.

Such an interpretation might seem questionable were it not that the act specifically recognizes "the traders 'freedom of choice' between the several services offered,"[118] except as the commission may seek to influence decisions by appropriate manipulation of rates within and between the two media. The commission is limited, that is to say, in its efforts to secure coördination between road and rail, to adjustment of rates to induce customer choice to comply with its plans. Since it could only accomplish this by an organization of traffic which is inconsistent with the system of separate executives for the several media—equipped, as they are, with their varying patterns of regional and functional division of management—the effect of this freedom of choice is to concentrate attention upon independently determined charges schemes, and thus to "perpetuate the present distribution of traffic between road and rail, itself one of the grounds of complaint against the present uncoordinated system . . ."[119]

COÖRDINATION OF COASTWISE AND OVERSEAS TRANSPORT

At its annual conference in 1937 the Labour party passed a resolution declaring that "competition in Transport, especially between private undertakings is wasteful, inefficient and dangerous." Accordingly, it

---

[115] *Transport Act*, clause 77 (1), p. 100.
[116] Walker, "The Transport Act of 1947," p. 22.
[117] *Ibid.*, p. 4.
[118] *Ibid.*, p. 21.
[119] *Ibid.*, p. 22.

urged that "a National Transport Board . . . be set up to coordinate Transport by Road, Rail, Air, and Coastwise Shipping, and to own and operate the Railways and such other Transport Services as are suitable for transfer to Public Ownership . . ."[120] in a similar vein the T.U.C. in its *Interim Report on Post-War Reconstruction*,[121] gave a priority rating among the industries to be nationalized, because of their "vital importance to the life and well-being of the community," to two groups. The first was "Fuel and Power (including coal, gas and electricity)," and the second was "Transport (including railways, canals, road transport, coastwise shipping, and internal airways)." Similar sentiments are found scattered throughout the literature of these two interlocking labor bodies.

Nevertheless, when the bill to nationalize transport was introduced, coastwise waterways were not included in the list of industries ripe for nationalization. So far as this part of transport was concerned, the bill limits itself to making provision for the establishment by the Minister of Transport of "a Coastal Shipping Advisory Committee" on all matters jointly affecting "the interests of the Commission and those of persons engaged in coastal shipping."[122] Even in the debates on the bill the suggestion nowhere appears that coastwise waterways be included. Yet if the purpose of the act be truly to achieve unification and technical rationalization over all parts of the more closely related segments of the interconnected transport web, this seems a strange omission.

Strange for a number of reasons. For one thing, coastal shipping over large areas of England—particularly on the long north-south-axis haul—appears to be as serious a competitor for rail traffic in major classes of low-value, bulky, heavy, and through haulage as do the road hauliers for high-value and light-weight freight. Furthermore, situations appear in coastwise shipping leading to cut-throat competition and allied practices of the very types which were so much deplored when they cropped up elsewhere in the internal transport system. Rate structures cover coastwise shipping where it reaches in many places deep into the interior—e.g., the Tyne, Severn, Clyde, and Thames—in direct competition with, and as an indispensable part of, the canal-internal waterways facilities and shipping fleets now belonging to the government. It is difficult to tell where the functions and provinces of

---

[120] *Report of the Thirty-Seventh Annual Conference*, p. 277.
[121] Trades Union Congress, *Supplement to the General Council's Report*. Section I, "Trade Unions and the Post-War Period" (1944), p. 9.
[122] *Transport Act*, Section 71 (1), p. 96.

the one begin and of the other end. In England, perhaps more significantly than any other place in the world, coastwise shipping is truly part of the seamless web of internal transport.

There are two other compelling arguments which would seem logically to have brought coastwise shipping under the plans of the Transport Act. First, so far as the appropriate data on the condition of coastwise shipping exist, they would suggest that these facilities in Britain are as technically backward and inefficient as virtually any other section of the internal (domestic) transport system. Tugs, barges, steamers, docks, harbors, warehouses, and virtually all aspects of coastwise shipping are generally in a serious state of arrears and burdened with old-fashioned, out-of-date, run-down, and inefficient equipment. The seriousness of this condition is even more heavily underscored by the fact that the major coastwise shipping terminals also serve internal waterways and canals, railroads, and road hauliers. That these terminals are badly in need of repair is recognized by including them among the facilities to be nationalized. But at best, this is only half the story.

The other half is that where land and water haulage meet, efficiency rests as much or more on the nature, timing, and methods of routing and handling the flow of harbor traffic as it does on the port facilities for handling transference from land to water and from water to land. How clearly this is the case can be seen by glancing through the *Report of the Working Party on the Turn-Round of Shipping in the United Kingdom Ports*, cited above. The routing of traffic through various ports, the shortage of railway wagons in general and of specific types for handling specialized cargoes such as iron ore, wheat, coal, and most foodstuffs, the problem of repair and maintenance of shipping facilities, the complicated problem of decasualizing labor at the various ports by maintaining an adequate supply of the various types of skilled labor to handle cargoes, and at the same time, such a flow of the right types and quantities of cargo as to keep the labor fully occupied—these are typical of the problems which require simultaneous and coördinated planning and management.[123]

---

[123] See, in particular, the "Working Party Team Reports," in the above-mentioned *Report*, pp. 19–36, dealing with the number of activities and ministries involved in the solution of detailed problems of goods handling at the more important ports such as Bristol, Glasgow, Hull, Manchester, and London. Mechanization is meeting strenuous trade-union resistance. A good example is the strike induced by the attempt to introduce "an unloading, transporting, and stacking machine" at Butler Wharf (London), capable of reducing dock labor by one-third. Wherever introduced, there have been strenuous union protests. *Times*, Nov. 4, 1948. At Butler Wharf the strike was settled by postponing introduction of the machine! *Times*, Nov. 10, 1948.

So to put the matter, however, necessarily raises a similar question with respect to overseas shipping. To be sure, the object of the Transport Act was to make possible unified planning of a coördinated and integrated internal transport system. Nevertheless, the Transport Act has not been supplemented by any other act, nor even by a proposal, designed eventually to nationalize overseas shipping. Yet it is impossible to avoid the question of what is peculiar about the structure, operating conditions, present status, national importance, etc. of overseas shipping which takes it outside the criteria applied to other transport media when the act of nationalizing them was being carried through. Virtually all that was said about coastwise shipping applies in some sense or other to overseas shipping—although efficiency levels are much higher in the latter—and there must be added to these the fact, more vital to England than to any other major industrial power in the world, that overseas shipping is literally her lifeline. The flow of goods and passengers to and from England—regular, of very large volume, properly timed and distributed between and among the various ports—is absolutely essential to national livelihood, and the shipping arteries that converge on England are related to internal shipping of all types as the tentacles of the octopus are related to the body to which they are attached.

The exclusion of overseas shipping from the category of transport agencies to be nationalized—from the facilities, that is to say, which must be "unified, coordinated, and integrated" because of their common bearing on all interests going to make up the national welfare—is especially difficult to account for in view of nationalization of overseas airways. "In 1946 the Labour government passed the Civil Aviation Act, under which it set up three government corporations enjoying among them a monopoly of all British scheduled air services. The British Overseas Airways Corporation (B.O.A.C.) was to operate the North Atlantic, Empire and Far Eastern routes, the British South American Airways Corporation (B.S.A.A.C.) was to operate the South American routes, and the British European Airways Corporation (B.E.A.C.) will be responsible for internal services within the United Kingdom and for those between the United Kingdom and the Continent."[124]

Apart from its possible relation to the question of nationalization of overseas shipping, the Civil Aviation Act is remarkable for several

---

[124] Central Office of Information, Reference Division, *British Civil Aviation*, No. R. 1367 (1947), p. 1. [Mimeographed.]

features which have an interesting bearing on the Labour government's concept of transport unification under socialism. To begin with, the actual nationalization of airways was initially carried through not by the present Labour government, but by the prewar Conservative government under authority of the British Overseas Airways Act of 1939. Following enactment of the bill into law in August, 1939, the B.O.A.C. was established in November, 1940, as a wholly owned government corporation with a monopoly of scheduled overseas air traffic.

What led the Conservatives to this apparently novel (for Conservatives) solution of the problem of British airways development? Why nationalize a young, swiftly expanding, technically dynamic, and admittedly highly competitive industry? Particularly, why should a Conservative government, dominated by businessmen, seek this type of solution? These are important questions, both for the general issue of what and when to nationalize, and for the specific puzzle of why the Labour government sought to build on the Conservative foundation— with such relatively slight change in policies—when it came their turn to meet the problem of airways development and management. ·

Four factors converged to favor the solution of nationalization, and this solution was reached in three major steps. Of these four factors, the most important was at first that of government subsidy of airlines. It was heavy government subsidies to the infant industry which led the Conservatives to take the first step on the road to nationalization, pursuant to the publication of the report of the Civil Air Transport Subsidies Committee (Hambling committee),[125] by establishing in 1924 Imperial Airways, to be the "only State-subsidised company to represent British interests abroad."[126] Though the terms of reference were somewhat broader, it was a similar concern over subsidies which led the Conservative government to implement the report of the Cadman committee[127] by setting up the B.O.A.C. in 1938. The same concern underlay the Labour government's white paper on Civil Aviation,[128]

---

[125] *Report on Government Financial Assistance to Civil Air Transport Companies*, Cmd. 1811 (1923).

[126] *British Civil Aviation*, p. 6.

[127] *Report of the Committee of Inquiry Into Civil Aviation*, Cmd. 5685 (1938). The committee recommended (p. vii) that the total of government subsidies to airlines be raised from a previous annual maximum of £1,000,000 to £3,000,000. "We emphasize that British Civil Aviation cannot compete with subsidised foreign aviation unless it is completely subsidised" (p. 13).

[128] *British Air Services*, Cmd. 6712 (1945). "H.M.G. [His Majesty's Government] recognise, however, that if air transport is to fulfill its function of providing services in the Public interest, some measure of State aid may be necessary to support essential but unremunerative services" (p. 5).

which stated the case for the enabling act of 1946. The common theme which ran through all these reports and discussions was that civil aviation could not be made viable—particularly in competition with subsidized foreign companies abroad—without large and continuing government aid, and that the government could not indefinitely continue to give this aid without insisting that the industry organize itself in such a way that it would economize in its operations to the maximum, and by so doing at the same time develop along lines which would guarantee its eventual capacity to stand on its own feet financially.[129]

It is entirely natural that concern over this problem should have led, cumulatively, to a consideration of the second factor, that of the inherently monopolistic character of air traffic. Here it quickly became evident that an essential condition to successful air transport was, first, adequate and comprehensive meteorological, sondage, and supplementary radio-navigation aids, and that these must necessarily be provided as a common service to all aircraft on the basis of the most comprehensive geographic coverage possible. This was not only a government function, but also one which could only be carried out on an international footing, and hence it called for the establishment of a wide range of intergovernmental aids to navigation.[130] For analogous reasons it soon became evident that such factors as the intimate connection between the vast complex of necessary air-navigation aids and airfield and airport operations, the heavy initial investment and high maintenance costs of the appropriate large-scale and properly planned airfields, and the possibility of planning the capacity of such airfields so that each major traffic center might be able to handle the traffic of all comers—that all such factors favored nationally owned systems of airfields, constructed, operated, and managed in keeping with codes and standards established by international agreement.

It became increasingly evident that the nature of the traffic problems associated with large-scale and long-distance air transport favored a unified network of air routes, air schedules, and supplementary airfreight and passenger facilities operating over and using such a system

---

[129] In an address before the Royal Aeronautical Society, Peter G. Manfield, "Director General of long-term planning and projects at the Ministry of Civil Aviation" estimated that "air transport could become self-supporting within seven years, and in ten to twelve years it should have achieved a sound commercial status without direct subsidy on any route." *Times*, Oct. 1, 1948. In 1948, "volume of operation" had increased by 39 per cent; operating costs had decreased by 21 per cent; staffs had been reduced by 3,000, and the deficit per ton-mile had been reduced 39 per cent (total deficit, April–September: 1947, £4,690,000; 1948, £3,991,000). *Home Affairs Survey*, Jan. 4, 1949 and Feb. 22, 1949.

[130] For a survey of the organizations charged with these functions, see Sir Oswald Mance, *International Air Transport* (Chatham House, n.d.), pp. 14–16.

of airfields. Airways, in short, seemed to fit snugly into the category of natural monopolies. Virtually all the economic and technical factors alike favored this view. The logical result, consequently, would seem to be the establishment of an international air-transport monopoly, and this conclusion has actually been drawn by British and other airways experts abroad.[131]

Failing the necessary conditions for achieving this ultimate solution, however, everything is to be said for unifying each national airways system so that it may become truly competitive with other similarly nationally unified air systems. The third factor favoring nationalization, consequently, is the somewhat paradoxical need for national monopoly in order to meet international competition. Thus Imperial Airways was given a monopoly of British overseas air transport in 1924, B.O.A.C. in 1940, and the three government corporations set up by the Labour government in 1946.

In each, the failure of the previous piecemeal subsidy and regulation program to effect complete unification has led to revamping. Thus in 1935 British Airways, Ltd. was established to take over from Imperial Airways the whole of the British-European traffic, and the Air Transport Licensing Authority was set up for the purpose of effecting some degree of coördination among the numerous companies operating domestic routes. In the 1939 reorganization, B.O.A.C. took over some of the former, and some eighteen companies flying internal routes were consolidated into National Air Communications and given a virtual monopoly of domestic airways. The 1946 act of the Labour government finally reverted to the general pattern of the 1939 arrangement by dividing the field between three major monopoly groupings.

Before this last step was taken, however, the fourth factor, differentiation between the traffic to be handled by airways and that to be handled by steamship lines, began to play a part, and here the case for specializing traffic between the two, and for planning rates, terminals, traffic interconnections, and, in general, for managing both on a unified basis, is quite similar to that relating to railroad and road traffic. Just as trucking is most efficient for short-haul, feeder, and special classes of intermediate-distance traffic, leaving to the railroads the long-haul, bulky, heavy, fast, and through traffic, so overseas airways should

---

[131] See, e.g., the proposal of Lord Brabazon, "Thirtieth Wilbur Wright Memorial Lecture," *Journal of the Royal Aeronautical Society*, Oct., 1942, p. 256, and the summary of the Spanish, French and Swiss proposals as summarized by Mance, *op. cit.*, pp. 77–79. See also "Labour's Support for World Airways" cited in *Hansard*, Vol. 418, col. 361.

handle the extra-fast, extra-long-haul, very high value, lightweight traffic and leave to shipping short-haul overseas movements in virtually all types of traffic, and intermediate and long haul in bulky and heavy traffic. It might seem that the ordinary operations of competition would lead to such differentiation, but clearly, in the Labour view at least, this had not happened in the past, and hence circumstances compelled them to seek a solution in this sphere through complete unification of all public-carrier, long-distance internal transport and of most short-haul, rail, water, and local, public-utility passenger transport. Why not, then, apply the same principles to overseas transport?

The Conservatives had themselves been moving along the path of intermedia traffic coördination for airways before the Labour victory at the polls in 1945. Although leaving shipping and railroads in private hands, they were proposing, nevertheless, an arrangement which they believed would unify traffic between these two networks and one governmentally owned public air-transportation system and two semiprivate airways. This was the essence of the so-called Swinton Plan, under which "in the Commonwealth, including the Atlantic route, the shipping companies with their established organisation and local connections, were to be associated with the B.O.A.C., although not as a predominant partner. On the European and internal routes the partners were to be the railway companies, the short sea shipping lines, the travel agencies and the B.O.A.C., the B.O.A.C. to be in a minority position. On the South American route the British shipping lines, in coöperation with the B.O.A.C., but making the larger contribution of capital and management, were prepared to operate a new company . . ."[132] The two latter companies were to operate wholly without subsidy, and "new entrants were to be permitted on new routes."

In rejecting this proposal of the Conservatives on the grounds that it was the flimsiest sort of political compromise,[133] the Labour government in nationalizing all airways accepted the thesis that airways were

---

[132] Harold Macmillan in debate on the Civil Aviation Bill of 1946, *Hansard*, Vol. 418, col. 335.

[133] Lord Swinton, said Herbert Morrison, summing up for the Government, must have argued somewhat as follows: ". . . he said, 'What can I do to get some scheme through this Cabinet of conflicting points of view?' He said, 'I will have three corporations,' and he had three. He had one with substantially, if not predominantly, a railway interest. He said to himself, 'That will square the railway interests.' He had another with a very strong shipping flavor about it, and he said, 'That will square the shipping people, the Conservative believers in private enterprise.' It was real political genius. It satisfied both the railway Conservatives and the shipping Conservatives. Finally, he produced a public-ownership corporation, the B.O.A.C., and he said, 'That is for the Socialists.' . . . That was the Swinton plan, one for the railways, one for shipping and one for the Socialists." *Ibid.*, col. 425.

a natural monopoly and thus necessarily a public function,[134] and at the same time rejected the concept—accepted by it as basic in coal, electricity, gas, internal transport, telecommunications, etc.—that the desired coördination required a single, central, unified body in charge of both administration and management, and completely by-passed the question of unifying air transport with either rail or shipping.

The first is completely consistent with the Labour position on nationalization, but the second and third are in direct contradiction to it. For the second, the Government's case was made to rest on grounds which were borrowed straight out of the mouth of the Opposition. "If the Government were to set up one corporation to run all British air service," said Ivor Thomas, Parliamentary Secretary to the Ministry of Civil Aviation, "there would be a danger that one man at the top might impose his ideas throughout the whole organisation. Moreover, if there were one exclusive corporation, a man with a strong personality, whose ideas differed from that corporation, might find himself, despite great abilities, excluded from the field of civil aviation."[135] Not only does this contradict directly the position taken in the other nationalized industries—involving an argument which Labour had pooh-poohed whenever it arose—but also the principal justification offered for separate companies was that overseas air traffic was "a highly competitive international business."[136]

On its own showing, and in terms of virtually the whole of the past history of British transport, this would have seemed to favor setting up not three companies, but one, since, as the argument runs, unified management alone could provide the necessary economies in operation, pooling of experience, and so on which were required to make British competition with foreign companies really effective. Furthermore, this very same necessity to meet foreign competition would seem to underscore the case, not for abandoning, but for carrying through along rational lines, the differentiation and specialization of traffic between airways and shipping. In principle, there is virtually nothing in the relationship between shipping and airways to distinguish this problem from that arising from the conditions in internal transport, for which unified control was sought by the Labour government in Parliament.

---

[134] This is not strictly accurate. All nonscheduled air traffic, both internal and external, might stay outside the public fold, though in practice such private air lines have been subjected to increasingly stringent governmental control.

[135] *Hansard*, Vol. 418, col. 317.

[136] See, e.g., George Lach, "Comparison with other Public Concerns: A Reply to *'Britain's Air Lines: A Critical Scrutiny,'* by Oliver Stewart," *The Listener* [weekly publication of the BBC], Feb. 12, 1948, p. 248.

If, as appears to be true, the only Labour answer to this criticism is to reply that the policies and operations of the three airways companies are coördinated through the offices of the Ministry of Civil Aviation, then, of course, the latter becomes the real administrator, and the three air corporations cease to be independent, autonomous, public bodies. Instead, legal fictions to the contrary, they can only be regarded as management subdivisions of the Ministry. In this event, the arguments employed for setting up three corporations instead of one fall to the ground. The new competition would be competition within the family, and not between independent policy-making bodies. There would then be little to distinguish the latter type of competition from that which every large and well-conducted organization attempts to stimulate between and among the various divisions, functions, and members of its staff. This competition would be little aided by the device of three corporations; conversely, it would be wholly consistent with one.

No machinery whatsoever has been devised by the Labour government for coördination between airways and shipping abroad, nor between airways and railways either at home or abroad. Nor, finally, are there as yet any plans in view for coördination of overseas transport, whether by air or water, with the domestic transport system. Yet the arguments advanced for the latter (coördination of internal transport) are virtually certain to raise these problems in the not very distant future.

FURTHER IMPLICATIONS OF UNIFICATION

There are several other important fields of economic activity in which consistent application of the formulae underlying the arguments advanced in favor of the Transport Act will call for continued extension of transport planning, and hence, most probably, of further extension of nationalization. Foremost are the engineering industries immediately associated with the construction activities of the nationalized transport media and the supply of equipment required by them. Here—as in the coal, electricity, and gas industries—the British Transport Commission is given the power, subject to certain specific limitations, "to construct, manufacture, purchase, maintain and repair anything required for the purpose of any of the activities of the Commission."[137]

Save for the proviso that the commission may not "engage in the building of ships, except lighters, barges or like vessels of a gross tonnage not exceeding one hundred and seventy-five tons,"[138] there exists

[137] *Transport Act*, clause 2 (2) (*a*), p. 3.
[138] *Ibid.*, clause 2 (2) (*i*), p. 4.

only the general prohibition of manufacture of equipment beyond the specific needs of the transport arm or service in question as determined by the preëxisting companies whose properties have been taken over under the nationalization act.[139] Thus the commission may construct rail roadbed, bridges, harbors and docks, hotels and housing (for railroad staff), locomotives and other rail rolling stock, and virtually all types of road equipment, with the limitations noted above. If, as appears evident, the technical modernization of transport facilities in Britain is to require the production of supplies and equipment running into hundreds of millions of pounds, then the Transport Commission is bound to become heavily interested in wide segments of the more important engineering industries. At any rate, it seems impossible to read the relevant clauses in the bill—particularly those relating to the authority granted to the Ministry of Transport to interpret—without coming to the conclusion that the latitude permitted the Transport Commission would allow it to become eventually, if it so chose, almost the sole supplier of the entire engineering requirements of all phases of the transport network taken over. This would make of the Transport Commission the leading engineering firm in Britain.

So far as may be made out from the act, the relevant Parliamentary debates, and other official criticism and commentary, there seems to exist no plan to solve the problem of the bearing this degree of nationalization of engineering and manufacture may have upon heavy industries in general. By the same token, there does not seem to be much more of a plan with respect to the bearing upon all future transport programs of the conversion of the fuel and energy system to an electricity and gas basis. Here it seems clear that every successive step taken in this direction must result in the transfer in whole or in part of shipments by water, rail, and road, to "shipments" by power line and gas main, and that the articulation of the latter, accordingly, must have a very significant bearing upon the scale, types, and location of transport facilities.

The mere fact that all such media have now been nationalized provides absolutely no guarantee that relations of interdependence, complementarity, or even of duplication and overlapping, will be planned and worked out on an appropriately scientific basis. What is

---

[139] E.g., clause 2 (4) (a) prohibits the "manufacture in any one fiscal year" by the commission, "otherwise than for purposes of experiment or research, chassis for road vehicles substantially in excess of the total of the number manufactured in a year" normal in the operations of the companies taken over. The same rule holds for other types of supplies and equipment.

preëminently needed at this point is a comprehensive physical plan, laid out on a national basis, in which transport is looked upon as a vital component to be coördinated into over-all plans for population and industrial location.[140]

To supply this nationwide physical plan was the function of the Town and Country Planning Act of 1947. Here at last was the agency which appeared to have been designed to pull together all the scattered threads of policy relating to nationalized and nonnationalized industries, and to weave them into a consistent and meaningful pattern. If such were the intentions behind town and country planning, then certainly transport must be servant to its plans, and what one previously failed to understand in the programs for British transport outside this frame of reference would soon begin to take on meaning when examined within it. Such appears to be the official Labour view, and, hence, further discussion of transport reorganization in Britain must necessarily become subordinate to the issues underlying that physical plan.

---

[140] A prominent government official commented on this point as follows: "There is a long way to go before any comprehensive 'plan' is made. In my own view, we are just as likely to go in for less as for more planning in the future. The task is very complicated and political pressure is strong against adopting radical solutions. In practice it is sometimes easier to use the forces of the market, so that no individual Minister can be blamed for changes." This seems to be a fair appraisal of the dominating position in Labour government circles, but, of course, it is also a position which is apt to result in little by way of the large-scale, comprehensive technical overhauling and intermedia coördination which constitute the heart of the British transport problem.

CHAPTER VII

Telecommunications

Yesterday it was coal; today it is Cables. The Socialist advance, therefore, continues. But I believe that this stage is not controversial. I understand the Opposition do not intend to divide against the Bill ... This is not only a means of Socialist advance; it is also a practical measure of United Imperial Policy.—Hugh Dalton, May 21, 1946.

ON THE SURFACE at least, nationalization of cable and wireless would seem to be the least important of all the measures introduced for expanding the area of public ownership since the Labour party's advent to office in 1945. There was no mention of it in *Let Us Face the Future*. It was never underscored in the Labour party's annual conferences or at successive T.U.C. congresses. When the bill was introduced it met with no determined opposition. Debate was short and desultory. The Government's case for the change was couched in the most conventional terms, and it was justified by reference to advantages and interests of which one would normally have expected to hear from the lips of die-hard Tories. The bill received unanimous approval.

Once passed, the act all but disappeared from public discussion. Its presence among the accomplishments of the Labour government is rarely noted by friends or enemies. It is never listed by His Majesty's Loyal Opposition among the sempiternal transgressions which a chastened future must disavow in a more penitential mood. Neither the Labour party nor the T.U.C. took the trouble to explain or justify the act to its membership in any special pamphlet or popular "discussion series." In the two widely circulated surveys of Labour's early record— one strongly pro-Government, and the other not unsympathetic—the best it received was a single footnote reference.[1]

Seemingly thus issueless, it contrasts with most of the other nationalization acts, mild as some of them are. In adding overseas cable and wireless networks to an already governmentally owned and operated overseas telephonic system and a complete and comprehensive internal telecommunications system, the bill dealt with a situation which contrasts sharply with that covered by the Transport Act, where the previ-

[1] John Parker, *Labour Marches On* (London, 1947), does not mention cable and wireless at all. A survey, J. E. D. Hall, *Labour's First Year* (London, 1947), gives it a single footnote reference on p. 206 in a chronology of Labour bills.

ous importance of the public and private sectors was almost exactly reversed. Nor, as with the Transport and Coal bills, was nationalization here occasioned by gross inefficiency and a felt need for thoroughgoing reorganization. It differed from the Gas and Electricity acts, in that there appeared to be no issue of further extension of nationalization in order to make possible unified operation of functionally and regionally interdependent networks. No principle of broad socialist policy, such as that which surrounds the proposed nationalization of iron and steel, was at stake. No problem of long-term planning, such as that underlying the Town and Country Planning Act, the Agricultural Act, or the various working-party and development schemes of the Board of Trade, appeared as the *raison d'être*. Though the Cable and Wireless Act appeared, like the Bank of England Act, as a mere formal shift in ownership in an already public-minded service, there was nothing here to compare with the role which the financial acts were to plan in the long-term planning of the economy. Nor, finally, were there any humanitarian angles as in the Social Insurance, Health, and Empire Development acts.

Yet, so to consider the matter suggests in itself the possibility that the act may possess a special significance of its own. Possibly it might indicate, better and more simply than any other nationalization measure, the metes and bounds of the area of agreement between the Labour party and its Conservative opponents. If this were so, then it would merit a little more attention than one might otherwise be inclined to give it. For, once having defined the areas of agreement in principle, the differences in both theory and practice might then come more clearly into view.

To see what there may be in this supposition—as well as better to understand the act itself—it will be necessary to go briefly into a few background facts.

The Telecommunications System of the Post Office

In England, as in most European countries, the telecommunications services of telephone and telegraph have long been conjoint functions of the publicly owned and operated post-office system. The three services, in fact, have virtually grown up together, as complementary communications networks under unified management, from the time at which it became clear that each was to become a web whose boundaries would be coextensive with the national frontier. The British Post Office, in this sense, dates from the introduction of the penny post by Sir Rowland Hill in 1840. The private telegraph systems were transferred to the Post Office in 1870, and the telephone lines in 1892. Since then each has appeared merely as a division of a common national communications system, and a balanced relationship between them has always been maintained. They are kept continuously coördinated with one another at all levels from the central headquarters in London down through the various regional and local divisions and offices. Local post offices, numerous and conveniently located, are also local telephone and telegraph offices where one not only conducts postal business, but also sends telegrams and makes telephone calls.

So far as technology and costs are concerned, this is an ideal arrangement for the two wire services. Their engineering problems are the same, their equipment involves identical, or largely similar, supply, maintenance, and repair facilities, and in recent years technical developments enable them to use simultaneously the same sets of wires. It has proved easy in practice to make the dispatch and delivery of telegraphic messages a service which can use the ordinary post office facilities, and thus avoid the additional expense which maintenance of separate offices would involve. Messages may be sent and delivered over the telephone, and copies can be mailed with the next postal delivery.

The principles involved in this pooling have been extended to the supplying of other similar services. Thus, although parcel post is not quite so highly developed in England as in the United States, it has nevertheless become a very significant merchandising distribution system in Britain. In 1946–47 the Post Office delivered 250,000,000 parcels. The post offices and stations, the mail cars and trucks, and the deliverymen who handled ordinary mail and mailed telegrams also handled the parcels, and such cost studies as the British Post Office has made indicate that it could continue to expand this service indefinitely at decreasing costs per package handled. Potentially, that is to say, the parcel-post system might well become a national unified delivery service for packages which could make of it a major—perhaps the only—transportation and distribution facility for this class of traffic.

Similarly, the British Post Office has operated since 1861 a national postal savings bank for small investors. It has grown enormously. "The number of savings bank transactions in the year 1946/47 was 117 million. On December 31, 1946 there were approximately 24 million active deposit accounts in the Post Office Savings Banks, with the sum of £1,982 million to their credit. In 1945 the average amount due to each deposit in active accounts was £83 18s. 3d."[2] Not only does this make of the Post Office the largest savings institution in Britain, but under a Labour regime which is committed to raising the income of the working classes—who use its services most extensively—and lowering the income of the upper brackets—who use it the least—the relative importance of this banking system in the huge new savings and investment program is being vastly enhanced. Here also, the question naturally arises as to whether or not this machinery might be extended, like the other functions discharged by the Post Office, to handle all, or nearly all, British savings, with advantages and economies similar to those realized in the other services.

Thus far the extension of the postal savings function has been accompanied by a reduction in the cost of handling small accounts which seems to be directly analogous to the economies arising from unified operation of the mail, wire, and parcel-post services. Efficient, well-ordered and managed, convenient, and easy to understand and use, it is handled in the same offices and through the same facilities which provide communication and delivery services. Furthermore, the staff and facilities handling this type of traffic can handle other public service activities with similar results. The money post handles a vast traffic in payments and cash-on-delivery transactions both at home and abroad. The Post Office handles payments of old-age, widows-and-orphans, army, navy, unemployment, and health insurance. In its offices are to be found the application forms, blanks, and facilities for taking out and making payments of local taxation licenses, PAYE (Pay As You Earn) adjustments, motor vehicles licenses, and licenses for wireless and television receiving sets.

With the addition and expansion of each new function, new personnel has been taken on, new facilities have been created, and new problems of management and administration have arisen. In 1946 there were approximately 350,000 persons on the Post Office payroll. Only the vast British coöperative movement compares with it as a service institution in number of employees,[3] the scale and complexity of opera-

---

[2] *Home Affairs Survey*, Jan. 6, 1948, p. 12.

[3] In 1948 the British coöperative movement employed "some 330,000 workers, of whom 60,000 are employed by the wholesale societies, and most of the remainder by the retail distributive societies." K. Bennet, "Labour Relations in the Co-operative Movement," in N. Barou, ed., *The Co-operative Movement in Labour Britain* (London, Fabian Society, 1948), p. 74.

tions, and the well-nigh universal availability of its national service network. But with the continued spread of the post-office system, the pooling of plant, facilities, and personnel, the general effect of reduction of both overhead and operating costs per volume of traffic handled, the quality of the service, the extraordinary convenience to the public—these and other advantages continue to be found possible and realizable.

Not, however, as a matter of course. There are certain rules to be observed, certain principles to be followed, and certain dangers to be avoided. These involve problems which are largely, if not wholly, of the type commonly referred to as bureaucratic; because of them the British government has found it necessary in the past to subject the operations of the Post Office to searching inquiry. The most recent investigation, and the one which has been primarily responsible for the present organization of the Post Office, led to the Bridgeman report.[4] This is a very important document not only for the Post Office, but for all large-scale public and private establishments. Because of limitations of space it must suffice to point out a few of its more important recommendations having a direct bearing upon the policies of the Labour government when it resorted to the nationalization of cable and wireless in 1946. There were three closely related conclusions of special interest.

1. *The general and over-all problem was not that of ownership, nor of size or complexity of the operations, but of good organization versus bad organization.* No question was raised as to whether any activities or functions were properly to be managed by a public authority, or should be grouped under a single administration. All this was taken for granted. Hence most of the committee's recommendations concerned the application of various well-accepted administrative rules for grouping interdependent functions and activities, for relating centralized policy coördination with decentralized authority and responsibility, for developing types and methods of selecting, training, and arousing the interest and coöperation of personnel, and for other ways and means of heightening efficiency of production and smoothness of operations. Put the other way around, all the efficiencies, sense of staff participation, means of securing continuous technical modernity, and the like could be achieved in such a public, large-scale, complex, multifunction, national network of services if organization was scientific, resources were adequate, and personnel policies proper.

---

[4] *Report of the Committee of Enquiry on the Post Office*, Cmd. 4149 (1932).

2. *As a corollary, the communications network should be even more closely interrelated in the future.* Thus it followed that the committee, while recommending segregation and regrouping of various activities by function, rejected the suggestion that the communications networks of mails, telephone, and telegraph, be transferred "either in whole or in part, to an independent authority of the Public Utility Company or Statutory Corporation type"[5] and the alternative suggestion that the latter two "Electrical Communications" together, "or the Telephone Service by itself" be similarly set off as an independent unit.[6] As for the first, the committee stated that had they been concerned with the problem "of inaugurating for the first time in this country a new system of communications . . . there might be advantages in having the Telephone and Telegraph Services conducted by an independent Administration divorced from direct Government control"[7] yet the interdependencies that had grown up over the years showed numerous advantages from joint operation by a central authority, and even if this were not so, the common use of buildings, joint use of counter staff, and other aspects arising from the past fusion presented an overwhelming case against separation.

In telephone and telegraph, "plant is largely identical and interchangeable. Telegraph and telephone wires are run on the same poles and in the same cables, and by the practice of superimposing, the same wires are used simultaneously for both telegraphic and telephonic transmission. These factors involve a common maintenance and construction staff."[8] The two systems had grown together and the fusion between them should be maintained.

3. *The outward expansion of the wire services to include all overseas communication, particularly wireless facilities, was taken as a logical, obvious, and entirely desirable extension of the preëxisting domestic telecommunications networks.* This is brought out very clearly in an early part of the report, dealing with overseas facilities owned and operated by the Post Office, where the committee comments: "Ten years ago telephone communication with places abroad was inefficient and was confined to Paris and Brussels and a few towns in their vicinity. Today, telephone communication by wire is maintained with the whole of Europe except Turkey and Greece and extends as far as Ceuta, in

[5] *Ibid.*, paragraphs 48–49, p. 18.
[6] *Ibid.*, paragraph 53, p. 20.
[7] *Ibid.*, paragraph 50, p. 19.
[8] *Ibid.*, paragraph 52, p. 19.

Morocco. The development of 'radio-links' in telephony has added the whole of the North American continent as well as Australia, New Zealand, South Africa and Egypt to the intercommunicating systems reached directly from the British Post Office system, and further developments are impending. It is now possible to communicate by telephone from Great Britain with more than 93 percent of the telephone subscribers of the world."[9]

The Bridgeman report was written in 1932. Subsequent developments in the telecommunications field have been entirely in line with the committee's generalization. The case for fusing overseas and domestic telecommunication networks of all types, wire and wireless alike, into a single operating mechanism has been made stronger by virtually every new technical development in telecommunications. Yet the greater part of the facilities for telegraph communication with Commonwealth countries was in the hands of a privately owned and operated monopoly.[10] It was as a partial corrective to this inconsistency that the bill to nationalize the cable and wireless facilities was introduced by the Labour government.

THE PRIVATE OVERSEAS NETWORK

The first major step toward the development of a unified external telecommunications system came with the Imperial Wireless and Cable Conference of 1928[11] which brought together representatives of both public and private interests of Britain and the Commonwealth. The occasion was the "position created by the competition between the beam wireless telegraph services," owned and operated by the United Kingdom Post Office, and "the submarine cable telegraph services" under which the cheap rates of the former were threatening the financial prosperity of the latter. The result was the establishment of two private companies. The first was known as Cable and Wireless Holding Co. Ltd., "a merger company owning practically all the shares of the old

[9] *Ibid.*, paragraph 31, p. 14.

[10] This somewhat understates the case, since it refers only to British owned properties. According to Post Office authorities, "Cable and Wireless Limited never handled anything like one half of the telegraph communications between the United Kingdom and other countries nor did it ever handle exactly any United Kingdom telephone traffic at all. As regards the telegraph traffic, the bulk of the services to the Continent of Europe were operated by the Post Office, with competition to some of the countries from the Company. The telegraph services with Denmark and Sweden were operated by the Great Northern Telegraph Company of Denmark, which also had services with the Far East. In the Western direction something like 80 per cent of telegrams exchanged with the United States were operated by two American companies (Western Union and Commercial Cable Co.) who also carried traffic to many other parts of the world."

[11] *Report*, Cmd. 3163 (1928).

cable companies and the Marconi's Wireless Telegraph Company Ltd." The second was an operating company known as Cable and Wireless Ltd. "with a capital of 30 million shares of £1 each holding all the communication assets of the above-mentioned wireless and cable companies, certain cables previously owned by the Governments of the Commonwealth, and a lease of the beam wireless stations in the United Kingdom then owned by the United Kingdom Post Office."[12]

Under this arrangement privately owned overseas cable and wireless facilities were merged, and to this merger were added the government's own "beam wireless telegraph service." Since the Post Office continued to operate not only all external telephone services, both cable and wireless, but also the British-owned telegraph cables to Europe, the operationally desirable complete technical unification was still not possible. As a condition to giving approval to this new arrangement the British and Commonwealth governments retained three controls: 1. Two directors of the operating company, including the chairman, had to be approved by the British government. 2. The operating company was "required to consult, in regard to questions of policy as distinct from ordinary business and management, the Imperial Communications Advisory Committee (now the Commonwealth Communications Council), a body comprising representatives of the United Kingdom, the Dominions, India and the Colonies. The Committee were given certain regulatory powers as to proposed increases in telegraph rates." 3. Fifty per cent of net revenue in excess of £1,865,000 had to be used for "reduction of rates or such other purposes as the Advisory Committee might approve."[13] In addition the Post Office was to receive an annual rent payment of £250,000 for the lease of its beam wireless facilities.

The amalgamation, to repeat, was not complete. The "distant ends" of the beam system continued to be operated in Canada, Australia, South Africa, and India by companies associated with Marconi's Wireless Telegraph Company Ltd., and were not included in the reorganization. Down to the time of the nationalization of cable and wireless these arrangements remained unaltered. Certain of the dominion governments participated in the ownership and operation of both cable and wireless.[14] And "certain telegraph services with Europe and the external

---

[12] *Cable and Wireless Ltd.; Proposed Transfer to Public Ownership*, Cmd. 6805 (1946), p. 2.

[13] *Ibid.*

[14] In Canada, Australia, and New Zealand, Cable and Wireless Ltd. operated the overseas cable services independently of wireless; in South Africa and India they were operated together. Wireless services in the first three were operated respectively by the Canadian

telephone (both cable and wireless) services of the United Kingdom were . . . reserved to the United Kingdom Post Office." Foreign-owned services, although competing, were still not affected. It appears, furthermore, that the reorganization was much more of a financial than an operating merger of the various properties involved. The new company, for example, regarded its holdings in dominion-operated companies with which it was affiliated "as investments and [did] not attempt thereby to control the policy of the companies."

The world-wide business contraction of the thirties brought the new company so close to financial insolvency that a new set of arrangements was proposed by the government in 1938.[15] The annual rent charge of £250,000 was cancelled, the governmentally owned beam service was transferred intact to Cable and Wireless, and in consideration thereof the Post Office received 2,600,000 Cable and Wireless shares with a par value of £1 each (total capital: £30,000,000), and the "standard revenue" was reduced from £1,865,000 to £1,200,000 per annum. The various Commonwealth governments reaffirmed their desire to work in close coöperation with the new company. But much more important, under the agreement the basic rate was to be reduced to 1s. 3d. per word, and 10d. per code word.

The results of this second reorganization were astonishing. First, partly as a result of somewhat more complete fusion of the two alternative types of service, cable and wireless, and partly as a result of the cutting of cables during the ensuing war and the necessity for further expanding radio facilities in anticipation of further impairment of cable facilities, the wireless service was vastly extended. As volume increased, it was found that wireless messages could be sent at a fraction of the cable cost. Second, the fusion gave Great Britain the only unified world telecommunications network, and thus a certain degree of monopoly of the huge volume of both Commonwealth and international traffic which grew so rapidly as a result of the necessity of keeping the expanding military frontiers in continuously close contact with each

---

Marconi Company (50 per cent of whose shares were held by Cable and Wireless), the Amalgamated Wireless (Australia) Ltd. (18 per cent of whose shares were owned by Cable and Wireless and 51 per cent by the Commonwealth government), and the New Zealand government (with no participation by Cable and Wireless). In South Africa the joint services were operated by the Cable and Wireless of South Africa Ltd. (80 per cent owned by Cable and Wireless), and in India by the Indian Radio and Cable Communications Company Ltd. (75 per cent of whose shares were owned by Cable and Wireless). *Ibid.*

[15] Details are set forth in *Cable and Wireless Limited:* statement of proposed changes in the arrangements between His Majesty's Government and Cable and Wireless Limited, and of a reduction in Empire cable and wireless rates. Cmd. 5716 (April, 1938).

other. And third, the low rate of 1s. 3d. was an Empire-preference rate which virtually eliminated all competition within the Empire, and began to divert much traffic from competing facilities. In 1944, according to *Fortune*,[16] "A U.S. seaman in Capetown cabling four words to New York finds himself paying $4.50 while his Canadian buddy sends the identical message to Montreal for $1.20. In 1939 an 'empire' press rate of a British penny (1.7 cents), which British newspaper publishers had been seeking, was put into effect. These and earlier rate reductions not only increased the purely British traffic but diverted business from U.S. carriers."

By the end of the war, according to *Fortune*, British cable and wireless was "handling with impaired facilities and reduced staffs five times the traffic of 1938," and it had begun and was swiftly carrying through the development of a world-girdling network of radio transmission facilities which was necessarily, and at the outset, being geared to handle a large volume of traffic. The postwar outlook of Cable and Wireless Ltd., consequently, would have been very rosy but for the American reaction, which soon led to two principal American countermeasures. First, a series of proposals for amalgamation of American holdings which might possibly give the American companies an eventual double advantage over the British—being less weighted down with expensive cable properties (the possible combination of American-owned cables being much smaller than the British cable system), and being largely based on wireless facilities constructed in various theaters of war operations at government expense and subject to indefinitely large government subsidies in the future as a by-product of the postwar American concern over its dominating role in world "security." The second countermeasure, dimly forecast by various events early in the war but becoming increasingly plain as the Allies marched to victory, consisted of an increasingly insistent demand for free access to Empire territories on an equal footing with British interests and was centered on the growing American adherence to the doctrine of world free trade, a doctrine which was virtually certain sooner or later to strike a body blow at the British system of Empire preference.

There were other factors contributing to the need for once again considering the possibility of further reorganization of British overseas telecommunications. The Post Office was not satisfied with the existing arrangements, nor did the dominions think they were "adequate for

---

[16] "U.S. and World Communications," *Fortune*, XXIX (May, 1944) : 281.

a Commonwealth telecommunications system." Consequently a study of the various alternative steps to be taken in order to reorganize the whole system was made and the Bermuda conference was held. Published reports of the study stimulated further American interest along the lines indicated above, and the conference rendered even more imperative vigorous and far-reaching reorganization of the British network. Complicated in detail, the over-all picture from this point on is comparatively simple; the net result was nationalization in 1946.

Two Empire conferences on communication were held, one in 1944 and one in 1945. At the earlier conference the Commonwealth Communications Council had to solve two central problems. Explicitly, it must find a way of satisfying the demand of the dominions for a larger share in the administration of the Commonwealth telecommunications system. Implicitly, but more important, as the Bermuda conference was to show, it must seek ways and means of securing the utmost technical, organizational, and operational rationalization of which the system was capable. In consideration of the first, it "recommended the establishment of a series of public utility corporations in the United Kingdom, in each of the Dominions and in India, each corporation being owned by the local Government, but linked by an exchange of shareholding between the United Kingdom corporation on the one hand and the Dominion and Indian corporations on the other; the Commonwealth Communications Council acting as a clearing house for information as the essential co-ordinating authority on behalf of all the Governments."[17]

This recommendation appears to have been satisfactory but for one thing: it was not believed, particularly by the British delegates, that the "degree of central co-ordination essential to secure the consolidation and strengthening of the wireless and cable system which was felt to be imperative" would be effected by the proposal. Internal rationalization, in other words, had become the issue. To discover how this could be effected, Lord Reith was sent to tour the Commonwealth countries on a mission "to explain the difficulties felt by the United Kingdom Government and to explore alternatives." Pursuant thereto, a second Commonwealth Telecommunications Conference was held, in London in July, 1945, on the eve of the general elections which elevated the Labour party to power. Attended by "the Governments of the United Kingdom, Canada, Australia, New Zealand, South Africa, India

[17] Cmd. 6805, pp. 4–5.

and Southern Rhodesia" it made recommendations which the Labour government a year and a half later was to incorporate virtually intact into its own nationalization measure.

Before considering how best to consolidate the findings of this second Empire conference through appropriate legislation, the new Government saw fit to act upon the last of the conference's five proposals— which was to undertake negotiations with foreign telecommunications interests—and on the initiative of the United States, joined in calling the conference which convened in Bermuda in November and December, 1945. The result of this conference, attended by British, Commonwealth, and United States representatives, amounted to an astonishing tactical victory for the Americans, for it opened what may prove to be an unbridgeable gap in the British telecommunications system of Empire preference. The Government's own summary requires no elaboration:[18]

The Bermuda Agreement provides for substantial reductions in telegraph rates between certain countries of the Commonwealth and the United States, and contemplates the eventual introduction of a world ceiling telegraph rate of 1s 6d. per word, subject to the agreement of foreign administrations. The Agreement includes a statement of the principles to be adopted in determining whether a direct wireless telegraph circuit should be established between two countries, the intention being that this statement should be presented for consideration at the next International Telegraph Conference. Broadly the proposal is that such circuits should be opened when justified by traffic or service needs, and the adoption of the principles suggested would enable the problems referred to in paragraph 6 above [direct wireless telegraph circuits between the U.S. and various Dominions, India, and British Colonies] to be very largely met. The countries represented at the Bermuda Conference recognised the important strategic role which cables play in a coordinated telecommunications system, and agreed that to secure the optimum development of telecommunication services, research and development work in both cable and radio communications is essential.

It was against the background of events leading up to the Bermuda conference, and for the direct purpose of implementing the resulting agreement, that the Labour government introduced its bill to nationalize cable and wireless.[19]

---

[18] *Ibid.*, p. 8. Subsequently—since the summer of 1947—the American policy has shifted from rate decrease to rate increase, with the result that Imperial preference has been considerably strengthened.

[19] "The present Bill is a necessary step towards the implementation by the United Kingdom of the Bermuda Agreement. The United Kingdom Government regards the Agreement as a settlement likely to be of immediate benefit to the peoples of the Commonwealth and of the United States, and as a valuable contribution towards the settlement of world telecommunication problems. This view is fully shared by the Governments of the Dominions and India." *Ibid.*

NATIONALIZATION OF CABLE AND WIRELESS

The Cable and Wireless Act,[20] under which the government took over the share holdings of the previous owners of Cable and Wireless Ltd.,[21] received the Royal assent on November 6, 1946 and came into effect on the first of January, 1947. The short, but vital, discussions on the second reading of the bill make strange reading. The Government, for example, advocated the change on behalf of Imperial preference, which the Bermuda agreement had all but wiped out so far as the United States was concerned,[22] and which socialists were not supposed to favor anyway,[23] while the Opposition (led by Oliver Lyttelton) supported the measure because it consolidated cables permanently into an Imperial communications network—the purpose which had originally led to the establishment of Cable and Wireless Ltd. in 1929—which would meet with the expressed approval of the various Commonwealth governments.

Five reasons were advanced for the nationalization measure. Four were submitted by Dalton for the Government, and one was offered by the concurring Opposition. All were centered on the results of the Bermuda agreement. The Government submitted (1) that nationalization would further unify cable and wireless networks, (2) that it would consolidate the network of Empire communications, (3) that it would hold together the remnants of Imperial preference, and (4) that it would eliminate an otherwise impending rate war with the United States. The Opposition's point was that nationalization involved an Anglo-American pooling which made possible the survival of the British Empire!

[20] The full title reads: "An Act to bring the share capital of Cable and Wireless Limited into public ownership, to provide for the cost of making certain payments to that company in connection with reductions in its charges and for purposes connected with the matters aforesaid." 9 & 10 Geo. 6, Chap. 82.

[21] Listed in the First Schedule to the act with holdings, as of April 18, 1945, as follows: The Eastern Telegraph Co., Ltd., 10,750,660 shares; The Eastern Extension, Australasia and China Telegraph Co., Ltd., 6,709,853 shares; The Western Telegraph Co., Ltd., 5,301,646 shares; Marconi's Wireless Telegraph Co., Ltd., 2,529,413 shares; The Eastern and South African Telegraph Co., Ltd., 1,291,854 shares; The African Direct Telegraph Co., Ltd., 301,763 shares; The West Coast of America Telegraph Co., Ltd., 205,379 shares; The West African Telegraph Co., Ltd., 188,243 shares; and The Europe and Azores Telegraph Co., Ltd., 121,189 shares.

[22] "The Bermuda ceiling is to be 1s. 6d. a word compared with the present Commonwealth ceiling of 1s. 3d." Dalton, speaking for the Government, *Hansard*, Vol. 423, col. 210. But this differential represented a major American triumph, since it was infinitesimal compared with the one preceding (see *Fortune, op. cit.*), and it was subject to a future revision in which the more important cards were held in the American hands. See below.

[23] See chapter xii following.

The first two points may be taken together. It is very difficult to be sure what they mean. As was shown clearly at the 1945 Commonwealth Telecommunications Conference, following the Reith mission, some way had to be found for effecting a closer working arrangement between the publicly and privately owned sectors. When the beam service of the Post Office had been merged with Cable and Wireless in 1938, it excluded wireless telephony, and certain European telegraphic services, which were left in the hands of the Post Office, and radio broadcasting, which was left in the hands of the British Broadcasting Corporation (BBC). The merger, in other words, was a fusion of telegraphic services only (except for those European services still operated by the Post Office). The nationalization act went no further; it seemed neither to alter the technical *status quo,* nor to anticipate doing so in the future.

This seems all the more curious since concurrent technical developments had begun to favor closer fusion between the transmission facilities of these three media—telegraphic, telephonic, and radio transmission. There had been four particularly important lines of development: 1. The engineering advance which made it possible to dispense entirely with separate telegraphic lines on land (by sending telegraphic and telephonic messages simultaneously over the same wires by use of different frequencies) opened the same possibilities for overseas cables. 2. When cables were a common transmission system for telephone and telegraph overseas, the case for linking them directly to domestic wire networks in a single operating communications web was doubly strong. 3. Developments in radio transmission, particularly in the use of high frequencies, FM, and television had begun to revolutionize the relationships between wire and wireless facilities. Short-wave transmission from powerful stations made possible the building up of long-distance air communications through appropriately spaced relay stations which could be entirely alternate (independently or as stand-by) to wire and cable, or which could be spliced in to become relay parts of a combined wire and wireless network (and vice versa). 4. At the same time FM and television, being limited by the very high frequencies employed to horizon-to-horizon broadcasting, could have their range of communication enlarged only by means either of closely juxtaposed relay stations, or by "piping" through the regular wire and coaxial cable networks. Once again, use of different frequencies made this possible without interfering with the normal use of the wires and cables for the usual telephonic and telegraphic purposes. This was an especially important development for Britain, since for overseas broadcasting—something which the world-wide ideological conflicts following the Second World War rendered of unusual importance to the British, particularly if they were to hold the Empire together—the only means available for transmitting abroad by FM and television lay in "piping" through the cable network.

If the primary purpose of the nationalization had been technical rationalization of all overseas telecommunications it would have seemed impossible for the act completely to by-pass (as it did) all reference to developments along these lines. On the contrary, by establishing a separate and independent corporation to manage the properties taken over (similar to those operating the other nationalized industries) the Government appears to have decided that cable and wireless networks overseas should, if anything, be even more sharply separated from both domestic and overseas nontelegraphic wireless services. Though subsequent action placed the new board of directors—having the same rights and duties in respect to the properties of the company as had the old one under private enterprise—under the general supervision of the Postmaster-General, yet it was clearly the intention to segregate the operations, management, and general policy of cable and wireless in an organization which would operate independently and as an autonomous unit.

Hence, it seems clear that the reason for this decision rested not on grounds of the need for technical rationalization, with which it is inconsistent, but the better to satisfy the Dominion governments where the degree of government participation in both ownership and management was not only large, but was also definitely on the increase. Furthermore, the Labour government was committed to giving virtual independence to three of its more important colonies, India, Ceylon, and Burma, where, as already seemed evident, the move to nationalize cable and wireless holdings was bound to prove irresistible. Some formula had to be found, consequently, for reconciling the growing lack of harmony between the parent British company and its various Empire affiliates. The obvious answer was to reverse the previous development towards privatization, and to nationalize cable and wireless. This view is consistent with the findings of the Reith mission, and the recommendations of the 1945 Commonwealth Telecommunications Conference.[24]

[24] See, e.g., the summary, Central Office of Information, Reference Division, *Nationalisation in Britain*, *I*, no. R. 1391, pp. 10–11. Lord Reith had once been a member of the Board of Directors of Cable and Wireless.

The third reason for nationalizing cable and wireless, namely, that it strengthened the system of Imperial preference, was plainly not in accord with the facts. The only argument that could be advanced on its behalf was that the "Bermuda rates still maintain the margin of Imperial Preference"[25] but it was a very thin margin compared to previous ones, and even this residue was seriously threatened. The proof that was adduced by Dalton to show that the maintenance of Imperial preference was the object of the bill rested on a curious argument. Couched in highly tendentious language, the impression was given that Imperial preference was conceived by wedding the mutual desires of the Commonwealth and Labour governments in a program which was being forced through in the teeth of bitter opposition from the Tory benches.[26] It was contended, furthermore, that, with the express approval of the Opposition, Cable and Wireless Ltd. "had in mind—and they admit that they had in mind—changes which would involve the eventual abolition of Imperial Preference altogether." Dalton hoped, therefore, that "the Opposition . . . will rally for once to the support of Imperial Preference."[27]

The truth seems to be that the Commonwealth countries wanted the recommendations of the 1945 telecommunications conference carried out the better to give them a hand in the management of overseas communications networks in their own territories, and to strengthen the hand of the local governments against the stranglehold of a private monopoly. They favored the tendency of the Bermuda agreement to lower rates on the growing volume of traffic with the United States, and the impetus it should give to further rationalization of the general network with the possible result of still lower rates within the Empire. The company, on the other hand, appears clearly to have viewed the negotiations at Bermuda as a hard-bargaining affair in which the British had a very great short-run advantage[28]—a more extensive and closely unified network, and more experience in its operation—and, consequently, were in a position to negotiate a *modus vivendi* with the Americans which would, in effect, constitute a "gentleman's agreement" that might

---

[25] *Hansard*, Vol. 423, col. 210.
[26] "I say that all the Dominion Governments, including Canada, South Africa, Australia, New Zealand, Southern Rhodesia and the Government of India have accepted these recommendations. They are all lined up together, and those whom this bond of Empire has united let no Conservatives seek to tear asunder. We are very alive to this threat to Empire Preference from the other side of the House." *Ibid.*, cols. 204–205.
[27] *Ibid.*, col. 210.
[28] "No wonder the Chairman of the Federal Communications Commission said that it was one Conference when the concessions were all one way, as the U.S. had virtually nothing to offer or trade with." Derek Walker, *ibid.*, col. 239.

reserve the bulk of past preserves for future undisturbed British enjoyment. The result would then have been another world cartel arrangement for effective division of territory. The price thereof was a common rate which was higher than the British were used to inside their own territories, and lower than the Americans had previously found profitable outside.

None of this sounds as though the Opposition was opposed to Imperial preference—which it was not and never had been. Rather, the reverse seems to be true. Nevertheless, it is also true—and in this the Opposition appears, not without some reluctance, generally to have concurred—that nationalization of cable and wireless was at once the essential condition to meeting demands of the Commonwealth countries, and necessary in order to carry out the Bermuda agreement. The major stimulus on the latter point, however, came from the fear of a rate war with the United States.

That this fourth reason for nationalizing cable and wireless was far more important than the three previously outlined, was brought out very clearly in Dalton's statement. Had it not been for the Bermuda agreement, he said, "American companies would have conducted a rate war, which they have already started. There has already been a very considerable rate war, and, in face of that, Cable and Wireless would have been compelled either to reduce their rates in step with the American companies, or else they would have lost a large amount of business to the American Companies."[29] Contrariwise, the Bermuda agreement established rates which could be defended on their own merits.

The implications of this statement are in closer keeping with the facts than the argument about Imperial preference, as the *Fortune* analysis of the year before made quite clear.[30] Here, the combination or merger of the American companies in a directly competitive worldwide telecommunications network, which would be heavily concentrated on the cheaper wireless transmission facilities,[31] and—especially important—which would have at its command seemingly limitless resources which Britain could not possibly match was something that

[29] *Ibid.*, col. 209.
[30] "U.S. and World Communications," *Fortune*, XXIX (May, 1944) : 281.
[31] "What we were seeking to do at the Bermuda Conference was to seek an Anglo-American Agreement, as in so many other fields, which would give us a practical working compromise between the American preference for wireless working and our own insistence on a balanced Wireless and Cable system." Dalton, *Hansard*, Vol. 423, col. 211. David Eccles believed that the Bermuda agreement involved "disgraceful concessions...as one of the conditions of the American loan." *Ibid.*, col. 231.

appeared capable of beating the British to their knees. On the long pull, that is to say, and under the circumstances under which future competition between the rival networks would have to be conducted, the advantage lay with the Americans. The question was, consequently, how good a bargain could be made with the Americans before the advantage had shifted overwhelmingly to their side, and what the conditions necessary to carrying it out were. The Bermuda agreement was the answer to the first, and the nationalization to the second. Hence it seems highly probable that following Bermuda, cable and wireless would have been nationalized by whatever Government was in power. Despite all the political fanfare, in other words, the dominating issue was one on which British parties were in united agreement.

The solution was dictated not only by considerations such as those sketched above. There was another aspect which did not enter directly into the discussions, but which dominated the unverbalized background. An overwhelming majority of the American companies, already discussing merger, were private companies. In the mood which prevailed in postwar America, the vast system of wartime military wireless which had been developed on a world-wide basis was virtually certain sooner or later to be turned over to the American overseas telecommunications companies, either by sale or lease, at very low rates. Generally speaking, also, the American government has favored cartel arrangements overseas wherever its nationals did not enjoy equal advantages under free trade. In the struggle to effect, and subsequently to revise, any such cartel arrangements, American companies would be practically certain to move uninhibited by any of the ordinary scruples which might limit similar moves at home. Antitrust legislation has no meaning for American policies abroad, and its political and economic interests abroad required a readily available telecommunication web with the widest possible geographic coverage.

The one thing to do, if Britain was to hold its own, consequently, was to lift the whole future of British telecommunications from the economic plane to a political one. This was most easily effected by nationalization of the British monopoly. By this sudden maneuver the British Hercules might be able to keep a part of his swiftly dwindling margin of advantage over the American Antaeus whose power now seemed to be expanding geometrically. Furthermore, once the American advance was halted, a new rationale might be evolved, to transmute the past reality of bitter rivalry into (at least) the outer semblance of a happy copartnership. Though this last and more lofty reason for effecting public ownership of cable and wireless was most heavily emphasized by the Conservatives, Labour concurred. David Eccles saw clearly "the fact that this Bill brings us right up against a major change in the relations between the British Empire and the Commonwealth and the United States." The issue, said this spokesman for the Conservative party, was the survival of "Christian Democracy."[32]

The ideas submitted on this point are interesting not only because they were advanced primarily by Conservative members of the House, but also because they were destined eventually to be accepted by the Labour party and increasingly to dominate its plans for future Empire development. Eccles' elaboration was soon to be heard in slightly altered versions from numerous Labour leaders. "The survival of the Commonwealth and British Empire," he continued, "depends upon the faith of the Anglo-American peoples in the ideals of democracy. No man is right to put obstacles in the way of the propaganda of that faith . . . we ought to sit down with the Americans and work out an area of free speech and expanding prosperity so wide and so powerful that the United Nations could rest upon that special relationship while the building up of the world society is going forward . . . In my judgment there is no survival for the British Commonwealth and Empire except upon the basis that we and the Americans never go any more into Conference thinking 'well, the time may come when we shall have to fight each other.' It is a case of pooling everything now, or losing out by ourselves. This is my answer to the argument about the loss of foreign exchange."[33]

Throughout the world there was "a race in ideas." The alternative to "Christian Democracy" was the "horrible propositions which threaten to engulf civilisation once for all. No one who cares for the British way of life could overestimate the value of cheap and swift communications in spreading our news, our thoughts, and our ideals. I do not think any price would be too high to pay for unity of moral outlook among all peoples."[34]

This sentiment was already running as a leitmotiv through the Labour government's representations in the United Nations conferences, in its discussions concerning British participation in Marshall Plan aid and the unification of Western Europe, in early British trade union par-

[32] *Ibid.*, col. 226.
[33] *Ibid.*, cols. 231–232.
[34] *Ibid.*, col. 226.

ticipation in the World Federation of Trade Unions and subsequent withdrawal from it, and it was destined soon to be found running through other discussions of Empire Development.[35] In its fully developed expression, and embellished with moving sentiments, it presented the picture of Britain and the United States marching, henceforth, arm-in-arm along the main highways and through all the byways of the world. Despite occasional differences they would stand shoulder to shoulder, and speak with a common voice. The voice would everywhere instruct and dramatize the Anglo-Saxon way of life. To the miserable, the downtrodden, and the near-heretical it would show the manifold benefactions, material and spiritual, which might flow from freely imitating this palpable product of two thousand years of progress in Western civilization. The words spoken to the downtrodden might emanate from Whitehall and White House, but they would pour in dulcet tones from the countless termini of the vast and swiftly proliferating web of world-wide telecommunications.

All this represents, so to speak, the public-relations aspect of the nationalization act. But it was not very well handled; a good basic script, an adequate cast, but a rather listless performance. Possibly this is because the act, like the 1945 conference and the Bermuda agreement, had in it too much of a sense of bowing to necessity; a necessity in which the overtones of hard bargaining were too loud to permit the softer notes of sentiment and idealism to be heard. Both in the discussion of the various aspects of the issues and debates, and in what was written about them there seemed to be almost as little enthusiasm as there was general want of significant difference of opinion.

So far as the bill was concerned, what was there to debate about anyway? The Opposition could complain that the "administrative machinery provided in the bill was 'inept,' " and that "the phraseology is, as usual, comfortably vague, and is couched in that flatulent official English which is designed, it would appear, to conceal rather than disclose the meaning." A governmentally owned corporation might not, merely because of change in ownership, run things "efficiently" any more than any other of the government's boards.[36] There was no quarrel with the financial provisions, and financial provisions made up almost the whole of the bill presented.[37] Properly administered—though how

[35] See chapter xiv following.
[36] Oliver Lyttleton, in *Hansard*, Vol. 423, cols. 218–219.
[37] The amount of the compensation was to be settled between the company and the Treasury directly, and in default of agreement by a tribunal of three members made up of

Labour could properly administer anything was a mystery to the Tories—the terms of the transfer complied with the most conservative canons of good financial taste.

THE COMMONWEALTH TELECOMMUNICATIONS BOARD

The act cleared the way for the government to take over by merely appointing a new board of directors to the already existing corporation. Since appointments are made by the Postmaster-General, and directors are thus responsible to him on larger matters of policy, we have here a slight variation on the device of the "independent, autonomous government corporation." Over the bulk of its operations, the links of Cable and Wireless with the Post Office appear, for example, to be almost as loose as those of the BBC. In fact, a subsequent piece of legislation, however desirable it may be on other accounts, tends to remove overseas telecommunications still further from Post Office administration. Under the proposed Commonwealth Telegraphs Bill, read for the second time in the House of Commons on March 22, 1949, the estates and interests of Cable and Wireless Ltd. [with minor exceptions] in land in Great Britain (including the wireless stations,"[38] and some 5,000 out of 13,000 employees, will be transferred to the Post Office,[39] leaving the remaining overseas properties under the conjoint direction of the established company and a newly organized Commonwealth Telecommunications Board which is to be broadly representative of the "partner" Commonwealth governments.

Under this arrangement it would appear that the future of Cable and Wireless would, as anticipated, be expected to work out somewhat as follows: (1) The past division of overseas telecommunications properties between those owned and operated directly by the Post Office and those operated by Cable and Wireless, would be maintained. (2) Just as the British government has acquired the private holdings of Cable

---

a chairman nominated by the Lord Chancellor and who must be "a Lord of Appeal in Ordinary or Judge of the Supreme Court," an accountant "to be nominated by the President of the Institute of Chartered Accountants of England and Wales" and a person to be nominated by the Governor of the Bank of England who is "experienced in matters of finance or business." *Act*, Section 2 (1). The basis selected is "net maintainable revenue," which had already been rejected in other cases (most notably in transport). The whole of the act—which is very short—is concerned entirely with these financial arrangements and the problem of transfer. When the final reward was made, the private owners (the Treasury owned 2,600,000 out of 30,000,000 shares) organized into the Cable and Wireless (Holding) Group received £32,195,000 of the £35,250,000 for appraised value of the properties taken over. *Times*, Feb. 2, 1949.

[38] *Commonwealth Telegraphs Bill*, 12 & 13 Geo. 6, "Explanatory and Financial Memorandum."

[39] *Hansard*, Vol. 463, col. 231.

and Wireless, so also might each of the dominions acquire such privately owned telecommunications services as are administered by its own nationals, or otherwise fuse them into a pattern which would permit of some degree of unified operation. (3) The several partner governments would then be represented on the Commonwealth Telecommunications Board.[40] (4) The board would serve in an advisory and promotional capacity to each of the partner governments, for relay—by whatever arrangements exist for relating the appropriate governmental departments with the given operating companies—to each of their own separately established operating companies,[41] and (5) the British coördinating authority will be the "External Telecommunications Board on which the company will be fully represented."[42]

Thus the field of telecommunications is, in effect, divided among several organizations. The Post Office possesses all domestic telephone and telegraph networks, all overseas telephone facilities, and certain overseas telegraph (European continent) services. Cable and Wireless possesses all non-European overseas telegraph networks belonging to the British government. The various dominions possess, or unify by some formula, all such properties—segregated or not segregated into domestic and overseas—as may belong to them or to their own nationals. BBC possesses all domestic and overseas radio-broadcasting facilities not included under the direct administration of either the Post Office or Cable and Wireless. Coördination of the British government's overseas facilities is to be handled by the External Telecommunications Board when the problem is purely British, but by the Commonwealth Telecommunications Board wherever it affects the interests of the dominions.[43] Agreements between any of the partner governments and other foreign telecommunications interests—including compacts with such organizations as the International Telecommunications Conference[44]—may be handled directly by the Post Office, or by its External Telecommunications Board, or by the Commonwealth Telecommunications Board (on the initiative of any partner government).

[40] *Bill*, First Schedule, Pt. I, "Constitution."
[41] *Ibid.*, "Functions," pp. 12–13.
[42] Wilfrid Paling (Postmaster-General), in *Hansard*, Vol. 463, col. 233.
[43] Section 9 of the bill makes special arrangements for "Extension of system of Pooling Telegraph Revenue," but this does not include power to make such arrangements with the partner governments.
[44] The International Telecommunications Conference, in turn, is a coördinating body for a considerable range of specialized international telecommunications bodies whose work, in the aggregate, covers the entire field of international telecommunications. A good description of these organizations is given in Sir Osborne Mance, *International Telecommunications* (London, Royal Institute of International Affairs, 1943).

In all this there is a rough resemblance to the situation which gave rise to the three corporations set up to handle overseas airways. But the principle of division in this case is in part functional and in part territorial. Except in the preparation and actual broadcasting of programs by the BBC, neither of these criteria of separation square very well with the facts of technology, the conditions necessary for efficient operation, or the requirements for adequate policy unification and coördination. On the contrary, it appears to have been the intent of the law to remove Cable and Wireless—like BBC—as far as possible from the direct control of the Post Office. But although an excellent case could be made for such independence for the BBC on the grounds that it should be removed from direct political guidance by the party or Government in power, this does not apply to Cable and Wireless at all.

The nationalization of cable and wireless, consequently, appears to have been the result of a purely Empire decision. Domestic politics played a minor role; international politics, relating in particular to internal Empire unity and partly to the Empire *vis-a-vis* the United States, played the compelling part. The change was effected by a paper transfer, in the consideration of which, management, technical, engineering, and long-range planning factors—except as amended in small part by the Commonwealth Telegraphs Bill—came in for scarcely any thought or discussion at all. This is all the more strange when it is recalled that, confused as the corporate picture of telecommunications in the United States may be, there can be no doubt but that whatever fusion in American telecommunication service may result from the Bermuda agreement will bring American overseas networks into an effective working arrangement with both the American Telephone and Telegraph Company and Western Union. The financial resources which such a working combination would possess could not possibly be matched by either Cable and Wireless itself, or by any combination of resources at the disposal of the British Post Office.

CHAPTER VIII

Social Security: Social Insurance

This Bill is founded on the Beveridge Report . . . It seeks to provide security for all. It seeks to provide equal benefits in exchange for equal payments . . . The Bill brings before us a really comprehensive scheme which seeks to provide for the citizen some security from his birth right to the time of his death and, indeed, even a death benefit after death.—Prime Minister Attlee, February 7, 1948.

The main feature of the Plan for Social Security is a scheme of social insurance against interruption and destruction of earning power and for special expenditure arising at birth, marriage or death. The scheme embodies six fundamental principles: flat rate of subsistence benefit; flat rate of contribution; unification of administrative responsibility; adequacy of benefit; comprehensiveness; and classification.—*Beveridge Report.*

OF ALL LABOUR government measures the one most generally acceptable at home and the one most widely and most favorably known abroad—particularly in the United States—is unquestionably Social Security. This is partly because of the very wide attention given to the Beveridge reports on which it is based.[1] Several circumstances contributed to this result. Universally acclaimed at home, a cheap American edition of the second *Report* retailing for only a dollar, was sold on the bookstands of the United States from one end of the country to the other. Here and elsewhere throughout the world, the reports were taken, in effect, as both a more or less official statement of the Coalition government in England (in which all parties were joined) and as a sort of informal manifesto concerning the type of postwar world which the allied Anglo-American governments were resolved to bring into being.

[1] Actually there were two reports, of which only the first and far more influential was official. The first was the report of the Interdepartmental Committee on Social Insurance and Allied Services, of which Sir William Beveridge was chairman. This committee was appointed by Arthur Greenwood, Minister without Portfolio, on June 10, 1941, and its report— *Social Insurance and Allied Services* (London, HMSO, 1942)—was submitted on November 20, 1942. (Hereafter referred to as *Bev. Rep. I.*) The second report, *Full Employment in a Free Society*, though a sequel to the first report, was not the result of the work of an official governmental committee, and hence appears under the personal authorship of Sir William Beveridge alone. It was privately published in November, 1944. (Hereafter referred to as *Bev. Rep. II.*) The first report was, by agreement with the government, signed by Beveridge alone, "so that the departmental representatives would not be associated in any way with the views and recommendations on questions of policy which it might contain." (*Bev. Rep. I,* p. 11.) Although the second report appears also under the personal authorship of Beveridge, it too was written on the basis of data largely supplied by government departments, and while in continuous consultation with much the same cross-section of official personnel who participated directly in the first report. (See *ibid.,* pp. 13–14.) The two reports taken together are regarded by Beveridge as a unit, the concentration of the first being on the whole range of "social services," and that of the second on "full employment" without which the first cannot be long sustained.

It might, in a sense, be taken as the first programmatic expression of the general ideas which were expressed in the Atlantic Charter and the declarations concerning the Four Freedoms.

This effect was heightened by the dramatic circumstances under which each of the two reports were first circulated. Two months after the appointment of the Beveridge committee, the Atlantic Charter had been announced to the world in a magnificently staged spectacle (August 14, 1941). Six months later came the almost equally spectacular joint Declaration by the United Nations (January 2, 1942). For Britain these events were identified with the turning point of the war. The first Beveridge report was issued in final form shortly after the United States had entered the war; it came, in other words, as part of an expression of the basic and fundamental ideas for which the titanic world-wide struggle was being waged, and it's recommendations were patently considered to outline the social reforms which would follow an Allied victory.

The second report came in November, 1944, as the victory was being clinched in a war which had arisen out of the very conditions of long-drawn-out world depression with which the report was coming to grips. It would be hard to imagine a more favorable setting. The recommendations of the second report were generally held to provide the key to the success of the highly publicized first report. It was issued at the very time when world-wide attention was being directed towards the postwar period, and in which the most anxious concern was being expressed over preventing another and possibly even more disastrous holocaust in the future. It directed attention to the causes underlying the current conflict, and it offered a cure for preventing another. But even more important, it offered a therapy which was bound to be highly satisfactory in the inner policy-making circles of the Western world, for it held to the view that full employment could be achieved without destroying any significant feature of the prevailing capitalist economic order.

There are some differences between the general positions of Keynes and Beveridge, but for these purposes (at least) they are of minor importance.[2] The general Keynesian position held two strategic advantages of immense importance. On the one hand, it held out the comforting prospect of an efficient cure for what had up to the present time proven a crippling and cumulatively more disastrous weakness of capitalist

---

[2] For a brief summary of the areas of agreement and disagreement between the two see *Bev. Rep. II*, pp. 90–101.

society, namely, recurrent and world-wide depressions. It promised to do this by strengthening that very system and not, like other suggested remedies, by still further weakening it with an eye toward its ultimate destruction. And on the other, it showed a way out of the Western dilemma at a time when emphasis in the world-wide ideological struggle was beginning to shift from a war against Fascism toward what would soon be known as the "cold war" against Communism. Capitalism could eat its cake and have it too in the very face of the mass unrest which had threatened to drive it out of power in the whole of the Western world. All doubt on this score seemed at rest when it was recalled that the formula for full employment also carried with it, and seemed indissolubly linked to, the formula for social security and "freedom from want." It was this very same "want," in the form of mass impoverishment, disease, insecurity in almost every conceivable human risk, hunger, and hopelessness, which dogged the steps of most of the world's population virtually everywhere from birth to death.

Thus, the two reports could not only be put out by a Coalition government, but because of this timing factor could enjoy the support—in principle if in not all phases and aspects of practice—of Conservative, Liberal, and Labour alike. Most were for them; few dared be against them. Furthermore, whichever party should enjoy the opportunity of carrying the appropriate enabling laws into effect was certain of mass support both at home and abroad. As it gradually became clear that Britain's future, for the postwar transition period at least, rested upon American support, the general adoption of the Keynesian formulae for peacetime maintenance of full employment in the United States[3] was certain to assure British legislators of widespread official American endorsement. Against social security not even the most rabid Conservative opponents of Labour could arouse much support at home, and the permanent residue of Keynesian-oriented New Deal American sentiment cut off opposition abroad at the only point where it mattered very much.

Finally, there was another peculiarly strategic aspect to Labour introduction of such measures. The social security acts were the very

---

[3] Section 2 of The Employment Act of 1946, setting up the Council of Economic Advisers to the President, was written as "An Act to declare a national policy on employment, production, and purchasing power, and for other purposes." Section 2 is directly inspired by Keynesian doctrine. One of the council's three first codirectors, Leon Keyserling, was a convert to the "consumption" emphasis of Keynesian doctrine, as may be seen by his contribution published in *The Winning Plans in the Pabst Postwar Employment Awards* (Pabst Brewing Co., 1944).

quintessence of the type of legislation which epitomized both the long struggle of organized labor for recognition and its most recognizable legitimate claim for redress of grievances. They attempted to correct notoriously malefic conditions, in the fight against which, labor, throughout its long career of struggle, had received the maximum degree of support in liberal, humanitarian, and most religious circles. "Social Security Legislation," a Labour party brochure explains, "commenced in this country with the first Poor Law of Elizabeth."[4] Since those early days the long slow struggle—memorialized in thousands of reports of factory inspectors, poor-law authorities, countless special studies and investigations, and pamphlets and books beyond number—has consisted of one hard-won victory after another, and has enlisted as it has gone along increasing support outside labor ranks.

For the British workers, it is the one "line of socialist advance" which, despite numerous short-run setbacks, has nevertheless given them the most striking proof of the power of organized mass pressure to get results in the face of the most recalcitrant opposition, and the clearest evidence of the essential justice of their cause. Furthermore, it is the one which reaches all members of the laborer's family—the women, the children, the sick, disabled and infirm, and the aged. And to all it carries the lesson of the peculiar merit of the British gradualist approach. Sidney Webb's words are worth quoting. The "fourth line of the socialist advance," he wrote in 1916, is "the constant elaboration of the collective provision, for those unable to provide for themselves, of whatever may be regarded for the time being as the national minimum that the modern State undertakes to secure to every citizen. We need only mention the ever increasing collective expenditure on the infants and the children of school age, on the sick and infirm, on the blind, the deaf, and the crippled, on the mentally defective of all kinds, on the prematurely invalided and the aged, on the widowed mothers of young children; and now even on the able-bodied man or woman unable, amid the complications and fluctuations of modern industry, to find wage-earning employment."[5]

---

[4] Alban Gordon, *A Guide to the National Insurance Act, 1946,* with an introduction by James Griffiths, Minister of National Insurance, Labour Discussion Series, No. 8 (Labour Publications Dept., 1946), p. 5.

[5] Sidney Webb, *Towards Social Democracy? A Study of Social Evolution During the Past Three-Quarters of a Century* (Fabian Society, 1916), p. 39. The other three lines of social reform were (1) "progressive extension of collective ownership and administration"; (2) "progressive assertion of the paramount control of the community over such land and industrial capital as is still left in individual ownership"; and (3) state use of "its power of taxation in such a way as partially to redress the inequalities of income that private ownership of the means of production involved." *Ibid.,* pp. 38–39.

The Conservatives would not have been able to attack this "fourth line of socialist advance" as it appeared in the social security legislation of the Labour government even had the events of the war not forced their hand. Past tactics and events had long since immobilized their capacity for effective opposition even where the will was still strong. For one thing, in giving ground to increasingly resolute and threatening demands for remedial factory legislation, trade union recognition, manhood suffrage, and similar reforms inaugurated throughout the nineteenth century, they were also necessarily giving ground to poor-law reform, workmen's compensation for industrial accidents, and the steadily widening range of social reform in general. All these aspects of reform—political, social, economic, and even cultural—were so closely and indissolubly tied together that advance along one line carried with it, or at least opened the way for, closely related reform in other lines. Furthermore, the total inadequacy of private charity to deal with even the more insistent problems of emergency relief had been driven home to the upper classes in unmistakable terms. The very scale of the need required state action if it was to be tackled at all. Thus it came about that the long and extraordinarily successful reform campaign which absorbed the active years of Lord Shaftesbury's life, though meeting at times with bitter opposition in Tory ranks, was almost perfectly adjusted to the *Realpolitik* of the general social situation.

Not, of course, that Lord Shaftesbury was in any sense a cynic. The contrary was most certainly true. But the formula which underlay his general thinking and program for action was one which could, and ultimately did come to, appeal to the advocates of practical politics in Tory ranks. Shaftesbury was a passionate Christian and his reform inspiration came largely from the Evangelical movement.[6] In a formally theocratic state—which England still is—where most of the leaders of church and society had always been drawn from the same closed circles, this was, on its own merits, a very effective line of attack. But suppose, also, that Christian salvation could lead to a type of social reform which would, in Bismarck's famous expression, "bribe" the working classes, and deflate their class-conscious hostility by making minimum concessions in the sphere of social insurance? While there is no evidence that Shaftesbury was influenced by any such considerations, some of the Evangelicals themselves—most notably, John Wes-

[6] See, e.g., J. Wesley Bready, *Lord Shaftesbury* (New York, 1922), particularly chapter xxii.

ley—were.[7] But much more important, the point had been brilliantly grasped by Disraeli long before Bismarck appeared on the scene.

In 1844 Disraeli wrote his novel *Coningsby; or, The New Generation*, and followed it one year later with his even more famous *Sybil; or, The Two Nations*. In the first a man of genius from the upper classes preaches and promotes a heroic doctrine of redemption for the nation, and in the second the nation of the rich is to succor the nation of the poor. After describing the miserable lot of the poor in the most moving terms, he issued his call on behalf of "a free Monarchy and a privileged and prosperous people" to the youth of the nation to take up the cure of this otherwise ruinous social malady. "We live," the novelist wrote, "in an age when to be young and to be indifferent can be no longer synonymous. We must prepare for the coming hour. The claims of the future are represented by suffering millions; and the Youth of a Nation are the Trustees of Posterity."[8] Nearly thirty years later, in his famous speech at the Crystal Palace, Disraeli laid out the program of the Conservative party in terms of three great objectives: "(a) to maintain our Institutions, (b) to uphold the Empire, and (c) to elevate the condition of the People."[9] There followed a series of legislative acts of which the more important were Public Health Act (1875), Sale of Foods and Drugs Act (1875), Employer's and Workmen's Act (1875), Conspiracy Act (1875), Artisan's Dwellings Act (1875), Friendly Societies Act (1875), the Merchant Shipping Act (1876), and the Education Act (1876). These acts are held by Conservative propagandists in Britain today to have supplied, respectively, "the real foundation of public health administration today"; the fulfillment of Disraeli's cry for "pure air, pure water, the inspection of unhealthy habitations, the prevention of the adulteration of foods"; guarantee of the right to strike as "the greatest boon ever given to the sons of toil" (Odgers of the T.U.C.); the first step in the elimination of "the rookeries which disgraced our urban civilisation, and made decent life almost impossible for those who lived in them"; prompted friendly societies by insuring "the adoption of sound rules, effective audit, and rates of payment sufficient to maintain solvency"; provide "for the safety and protection of seamen"; and "made education compulsory throughout England and remedied many defects in the existing education system."[10]

[7] See, e.g., J. L. and Barbara Hammond, *Lord Shaftesbury* (London, 1923).

[8] *Sybil; or, The Two Nations* (London, 1845).

[9] *Conservative Social and Industrial Reforms 1800–1945* (Conservative Political Centre, 1947), p. 17.

[10] *Ibid.*, pp. 17–20.

A. Macdonald, "who termed himself a Liberal and Labour M.P.," was held to have declared in a speech during 1879 that "Conservatives have done more for the working classes in five years than the Liberals have in fifty."[11] This theme in Conservative propaganda has recently been revived, and in the brochure referred to it is made to appear that virtually all the significant social legislation of the past century and a half of British history has been put across by Conservative governments, and the implication is strong that this has been done in the face of what they felt to be the muddled thinking of the Liberals and the even more muddled thinking of Labour.[12] The fact that most of this legislation was, virtually without important exception, fought bitterly by Conservative governments when it was first proposed, and that, when this was not so, Conservative-sponsored social legislation made only those concessions which the Conservative leaders felt they must make to retain control of the government, does not eliminate the fact that their own propaganda has long committed them to taking additional minimal steps along Sidney Webb's "fourth line of the Socialist advance.

There was a final reason why the Conservatives could not effectively oppose the new social security legislation when faced with the appropriate bills for Parliamentary action, and because of which Labour leaders could count on Conservative support as though all parties conceded as a matter of course the essential desirability of the new welfare proposals. It was the heavy emphasis on Christian duty that has been, since Shaftesbury and Chadwick, a part of British social legislation. Mockery and sentimentality were mixed in Disraeli's endorsement of earlier legislation; cynicism and piety in Bismarck's more widely heralded German social insurance legislation of the middle 1880's. But the Church of England was compelled by the close identification between the Evangelical movement and the new reform program to take an active and growing interest in assuming the leadership. From the days of Shaftesbury on the reform movement within the Anglican Church became increasingly strong.[13]

---

[11] *Loc. cit.*

[12] "... the Conservatives fought and won the battle against *laissez-faire* [the Liberal gospel], under which the worker was regarded as a commodity to be bought or sold in the open market. Today the Conservative Party fights to protect the British people against the growing menace of socialism under which all the means of production, distribution, and exchange will be owned by an all-powerful state and the status of the individual worker will be reduced to that of a cog in a great machine." Under Conservative governments of the past "the State has increasingly concerned itself with the improvement of the social conditions of the people and the protection of the individual from exploitation." *Ibid.*, p. 56.

[13] "The religious humanitarians like Shaftesbury were able to cooperate with the scientific humanitarians like Chadwick. They were efficient and they got things done. But neither of

There was a special reason why this reformist movement within the churches, Evangelical and Anglican alike, should have been so effective in convincing much of Labour's rank and file of the sincerity of Tory support for state aid to social welfare: it was thoroughly in harmony with the Christian piety of the outstanding Labour leaders. As is well known, the founder of the Labour Party, Keir Hardie, took his socialism very largely from the Sermon on the Mount.[14] At the annual T.U.C. congresses and the Labour party conferences the sense and atmosphere of Christian piety are sometimes so strong that an American would have to seek familiar parallels in some of the mass movements emanating from the Los Angeles area during the days of the depression.[15] Of the great Labour party personalities of recent years, perhaps the two most widely admired and respected in labor ranks were Arthur Henderson and George Lansbury. The first "found in Wesleyan Christianity a strong fountain of inspiration which lasted him all his days." Of the causes leading to Henderson's socialism "the predisposing factor was Methodism."[16] Much the same was true of Lansbury, who saw the salvation of Britain to be possible in the future only if all—rich and poor, Lord and commoner, Conservative and Labourite, capitalist and socialist—would "enlist" as he once put it, "in one great army under Christ's banner, accepting His teaching literally and in all its fulness, determined in every deed to fight against the devil and all his works,

them had much respect for public opinion and for the votes of the majority. Both in their own way were equally authoritarian, though the authoritarianism of Chadwick looked forward towards a centralised bureaucracy, while that of Shaftesbury looked back towards the paternal authority of a Christian State. If one must find a label for Shaftesbury's political views, I would describe him as a theocratic Conservative: nor does he stand alone in this respect; the Victorian reaction against economic liberalism was to a great extent inspired by the same principles. Coleridge and Southey, Carlyle and Ruskin, F. D. Maurice and Cardinal Manning, even Gladstone in his earlier period, were all in their various ways theocratic Conservatives, and these men contributed perhaps more than any other to the formation of the characteristic type of Victorian humanitarianism." Christopher Dawson, in *The Listener*, April 22, 1948, p. 656.

[14] See the very interesting sketch of Keir Hardie's life in Margaret Cole, *Makers of the Labour Movement* (London, 1948).

[15] It is interesting to note that most of these Christian inspired mass movements in the United States begin either in the Los Angeles area or soon gravitate west, and that the overwhelming bulk of the adulants are of British origin, usually one or more generations removed. The so-called Bible Belt is predominantly English, Scotch, and Welsh; typically Methodist, Baptist, Christian Church, and splinter sects which have broken away from these groups; their characteristic doctrinal outlook is made up of a blend of primitive Christian egalitarianism (centering on the Sermon on the Mount), and social Utopianism; they are typically "anti money-power" (Wall Street), clannish, strong on domestic and family virtues, revivalist, opposed to strong drink, etc. They are also the source of most of the early movements for social welfare programs. Examples are the Townsend Plan; Ham and Eggs; Mankind United; the Utopian Society. See, e.g., Marcus Bach, *They Have Found a Faith* (New York, 1946), and Carey McWilliams, *Los Angeles County* (Boston, 1946).

[16] Cole, *op. cit.*, p. 249.

and by God's good grace to establish the Kingdom of Heaven on earth."[17] A similar outlook, possibly somewhat more astringent in its more characteristic expressions, underlies the thinking of a number of the leading figures in the contemporary Labour government.[18]

In light of considerations such as these it should occasion no surprise that the social insurance bills should have been presented virtually as coalition measures, and that the call for all good Britishers and true to rally round the common cause met with practically no dissent at all. In introducing the National Insurance Bill, James Griffiths reminded the House of Commons that "to a large extent this is a Bill consolidating existing Measures" most of which have "already been before Parliament, fully debated, and which have stood the practical test of many years of administrative application."[19] Furthermore, said Arthur Greenwood, in summing up debate for the Government, "Every party at the last General Election was pledged to the broad principles of the plan." Hence there was no reason why "hon. Members opposite" should not "help it on the Statute Book."[20]

Nor, in fact, were the Opposition disinclined. R. A. Butler for the Conservatives said of it, that "We regard this plan as part of the mosaic or the pattern of the new society . . . This Bill forms part of a series of Bills . . . which . . . foresaw the pattern of the new society long before this Parliament was ever thought of . . . The whole philosophy lying behind these Measures, in which, I must make it quite plain, we have played our part and shall play our part, is that the good things of life shall be more widely shared; we look forward to a society of which the more unfortunate members are free from the direst dread of penury and want."[21] A colleague who wished that the word "National" might displace "Social" in the title of the bill, resented disparaging remarks

---

[17] George Lansbury, *Your Part in Poverty* (London, 1917).

[18] Seventy-seven Labour representatives from the two Houses of Parliament belonged to the Parliamentary Socialist Christian Group at the time of the 1948 (Scarborough) conference of the Labour party. Among these are the following members of the Cabinet: A. V. Alexander, Minister of Defense; Sir Stafford Cripps, Chancellor of the Exchequer; J. Chuter Ede, Secretary of State for the Home Department; Viscount Jowitt, Lord Chancellor; and G. Tomlinson, Minister of Education. There are also two ministers not of Cabinet rank, Arthur Henderson, Secretary of State for Air, and Lord Pakenham, Chancellor of the Duchy of Lancaster. See, *In This Faith We Live*, a pamphlet issued by the Parliamentary Socialist Christian Group, with a foreword by Sir Stafford Cripps, where he says, "Christianity is the one force great enough to provide the dynamic power which can stabilize and strengthen progressive democracy."

[19] *Hansard*, Vol. 418, col. 1744.

[20] *Hansard*, Vol. 419, cols. 102, 105.

[21] *Hansard*, Vol. 418, cols. 1767–1768. Butler is also the leader of the Conservative group which is responsible for such publications of the Conservative Political Centre as the pamphlet, *Conservative Social and Industrial Reforms 1800–1945*, referred to above. See also David Clarke, *The Conservative Faith in a Modern Age*, with a foreword by Butler.

from the Government benches, and he wanted to "say, therefore, speaking on behalf of my Party, that we welcome this Measure wholeheartedly."[22] There was no division of the House at the end of the long debates on the second reading of the bill, and but three dissenters rose to dispute the chorus of "Ayes" which moved the bill along.

In a similar diapason of goodwill and harmony the social security acts passed into law. The question naturally arises: despite the historical facts mentioned above why should such interparty harmony prevail? If this social security legislation was really such a characteristic expression of the Labour party's general social program, how could the Conservatives support it so freely, and at the same time remain pledged to fight the program of which social security was such an important part on the grounds that the new socialism was certain to become the ruin of British society as a whole?

The Web of Social Security Acts

It is important to note at the outset that all the social security legislation submitted by the Labour government during its first term of office is based upon the first Beveridge report (official). There is no legislation directly connected with the second report (unofficial)—except, of course, in the sense that all legislation having as its general purpose to increase production, find markets, improve Britain's foreign trade position, and the like may be regarded as tending to promote "stability at levels of full employment." There is, however, no direct attack, no general enabling legislation, no consciously avowed program, no expressed plan for implementing the recommendations of the unofficial second report. There is only the broad sentiment (e.g., *Let Us Face the Future*) that the general objective is to achieve this result. This is true despite the fact that the case for coördination of miscellaneous legislation is at least as great—and far more vital—in this area as in the area covered by the first report.

What the separate measures which have an indirect bearing upon full employment (summarized in the foregoing chapters dealing with nationalization and in the following chapters dealing with other aspects of the Labour recovery and development programs) demonstrate is that the more important social security legislation must still lie in the future. It is the more important both on its own merits—since all parties concede that the major problem of social security is the elimi-

[22] Osbert Peake, in *Hansard*, Vol. 419, col. 84.

nation of unemployment—and because it is also generally recognized that the objectives of the legislation based on the first Beveridge report cannot be achieved effectively or be long sustained unless the prior problem of unemployment has been solved.

This position has been heavily underscored by Lord Beveridge himself, and it has been accepted by Labour spokesmen without important reservations. Beveridge spoke of "five giants" which block "the road of reconstruction." These are, he said, "Want, Disease, Ignorance, Squalor and Idleness." Each must be attacked in its turn, but the elimination of "idleness" induced by involuntary unemployment is a basic assumption for the destruction of the other "giants."[23] Arthur Greenwood was even more emphatic. "In a transition period," he said, "and probably afterwards, sickness and accident may befall workers, and so, therefore, we need a social security service to prevent want during days of adversity and to avoid human deterioration. *But the first line of attack must be a full employment policy,* for without the production of wealth there will be large scale unemployment and its consequences, and without it we cannot sustain a proper standard of life for our people—*not even for those at work, and certainly not for those who are in difficulty and in awkward circumstances.*"[24]

It is also interesting to note that, although social security in this more restricted sense—as the provision of a minimum of all the basic needs and necessities of the entire population—draws a rough line between insurable and noninsurable contingencies, yet health, though falling in the former category, is not covered by the same legislation nor included under the same administration. This seems rather odd in view of Beveridge's insistence upon "a unified system covering all risks" in which he included the entire range of medical services,[25] and the frequent insistence of supporting organizations, as it was put by one powerful Labour party group, that "all the social services should be co-ordinated under one Minister who might be called 'Minister of Health and the Social Services.'"[26]

[23] *Bev. Rep. I,* pp. 6–7; see also "Assumption C. Maintenance of Employment," pp. 163–165.

[24] *Hansard,* Vol. 419, col. 99. Italics mine.

[25] As outlined, e.g., in his speech before the Conference on Social Insurance, convened by the International Labour Organisation of the League of Nations Union, at the London School of Economics, November 23, 1925 and reproduced as evidence by the Scottish Miners Federation Approved Society, in *Memoranda from Organisations;* Appendix G to the report by Sir William Beveridge, Cmd. 6405 (London, 1942), Paper 21, "Social Insurance and Allied Services," pp. 124–126.

[26] *Ibid.,* Paper 4, "Memorandum of Evidence by the Parliamentary Committee of the Co-operative Congress," pp. 17–20.

This division does not, furthermore, square with the contents of the National Insurance Bill as given by Griffiths at the time of its introduction. Past legislation had, he said, been handled in a typical British fashion. Successive Parliaments, he went on to say, had "passed a series of measures and so the system has grown up in a haphazard piece-meal, way much like a patchwork quilt. How patchy the quilt is, can be gleaned from the fact that the mere enumeration of the Acts of Parliament which are superseded by this Bill, takes three pages of print in the Schedules, and the Acts which we amend take another nine pages. For a long time past it has been apparent that what was needed was a co-ordinated plan for weaving all these together in a unified, comprehensive scheme covering the whole Nation." Hence, it was the purpose of the bill to consolidate "into one scheme, the existing schemes of insurance against sickness, unemployment, and old age."[27] Nevertheless, health and medical aid were taken care of in separate legislation. (Because of this, and certain other problems of administration which were associated with that measure, it will be dealt with separately in the following chapter.)

Health aside, social insurance legislation is laid out in four principal acts. The first and most important was the National Insurance Act of 1946, whose primary purpose was the consolidation of all existing legislation covering the more common types of social insurance.[28] The second was a supplementary law known as National Insurance (Industrial Injuries) Act, passed almost simultaneously with the National Insurance Act to take the place of the earlier workmen's compensation laws, and to handle the entire range of injuries arising out of employment.[29] The third act, known as the National Assistance Act of 1948, was strictly speaking not an insurance act at all. Its purpose was to terminate the existing poor-law and to substitute a system of supplementary aids to take care of special cases of individual need

[27] *Hansard*, Vol. 418, cols. 1743, 1745.

[28] As indicated in the full title of the act, which reads: "An Act to establish an extended system of national insurance providing pecuniary payments by way of unemployment benefit, sickness benefit, maternity benefit, retirement pension, widows' benefit, guardian's allowance and death grant, to repeal or amend the existing enactments relating to unemployment insurance, national health insurance, widows', orphans' and old age contributory pensions and non-contributory old age pensions, to provide for the making of payments towards the cost of a national health service, and for purposes connected with the matters aforesaid." 9 & 10 Geo. 6, Chap. 67.

[29] The full title reads: "An Act to substitute for the Workmen's Compensation Acts, 1925 to 1945, a system of insurance against personal injury caused by accident arising out of and in the course of a person's employment and against prescribed diseases and injuries due to the nature of a person's employment, and for purposes connected therewith." 9 & 10 Geo. 6, Chap. 62.

which might not be covered in full by the regular insurance measures.[30] The fourth act is the Family Allowances Act, which specified a system of supplementary allowances for all families of two or more children under school age and for especially needy families.

These four, together with the National Health Service Act, constitute the separate pieces "of a grandly conceived mosaic," all of which "fit together" and none of which "should be judged singly or apart from the whole."[31] There are six principal objects of the legislation. The first and more general object is to unify, round out, supplement, and tidy up all past social legislation in Britain into a coherent pattern which will take care of all the insurable, semi-insurable, and technically noninsurable personal risks which the ordinary person could not normally foresee, or foreseeing, still of necessity lack the resources adequately to make provision for. All such risks and cases of need are regarded by the Labour government's social security experts as a proper care of the state, and the new legislation lays upon the state the responsibility for seeing that machinery is devised for handling them. Technically, only insurable risks should be classified as insurance; the rest is state aid.

A second purpose is to bring the entire structure of contributions and benefit payments under a single ministry, with the former handled by a single stamp payment made at regular intervals, and the latter managed either by direct payments from the Ministry of National Insurance, or via the appropriate ministry administering the supplementary aids—the Ministry of Health for medical services, or the Ministry of Education for the various school and family supplementary aids—for which the benefits are to be paid.[32]

A third and corollary object was to eliminate duplication and overlapping of administrative machinery throughout the country for administering, separately and more or less in isolation from each other, various special aspects of insurance and relief. There was much ad-

---

[30] The full title reads: "An Act to terminate the existing poor law and to provide in lieu thereof for the assistance of persons in need by the National Assistance Board and by local authorities; to make provision for the welfare of disabled, sick, and other persons and for regulating homes for disabled and aged persons and charities for disabled persons; to amend the law relating to non-contributory old age pensions; to make provision as to the burial or cremation of deceased persons; and for purposes connected with the matters aforesaid." 11 & 12 Geo. 6, Chap. 29.

[31] Gordon, *op. cit.*, p. 7.

[32] "Until recently, to take one or two examples, sickness benefit was a matter for the Ministry of Health, unemployment insurance for the Ministry of Labour, and workmen's compensation for the Home Office. I think it is much more sensible that these closely linked schemes should be under the control of a single Minister," etc. But by this Griffiths means "benefit payments." The same, however, holds for contributions. *Hansard*, Vol. 418, cols. 1737–1738.

ministrative tidying up to be done. A fourth object—outstanding in the National Assistance Act—was to remove the social stigma long attached to the receipt of poor-law relief by removing cash assistance from the local authority administration associated with Poor Law to a central government administration, and by substituting a personal for a family means test. A fifth object was to fix the maximum rate of contribution which all could pay and a rate of benefit related to need irrespective of the amount of the contribution.

Before turning to the actual provisions of the related acts to see how these objectives were carried out, there is a sixth objective which needs to be examined somewhat more at length for the simple reason that it raised again, though in a rather peculiar way, the whole issue of nationalization. This matter came up in connection with the taking over by the central administration of the work of the approved societies, most of which were very closely associated through common ownership and administration with the business of industrial assurance (mostly small policies for the provision of death and burial benefits). As subsequent events were to bring out, the abolition of the approved societies served to open the way for the proposal to nationalize all industrial assurance,[33] and may prove to be the thin, opening wedge to eventual nationalization of all insurance. The 1949 Labour party manifesto, *Labour Believes in Britain,* urges not only the nationalization of industrial assurance, but goes on to point out that "splitting off industrial assurance from the remaining business of the companies would lead to confusion and inefficiency. Labour therefore proposes that all the industrial assurance companies, the biggest being the Prudential and the Pearl, and the larger collecting societies, should be taken over as they stand."[34] But is this really a good stopping place either?

The Approved Societies and Industrial Assurance

Approved societies were set up under authority of the National Health Insurance Act of 1911 as autonomous financial units for the purpose of administering funds drawn from the state on the basis of the number of members. They are of several types, but they

can be grouped under five main heads according to the kind of office or society with which they are associated, namely Friendly Societies, Friendly Societies

---

[33] "Only one major recommendation of the Beveridge Report has not yet been carried out: the proposal to convert industrial assurance into a public service ... The nation's social security plan will be completed when industrial assurance itself becomes a great social service." *Labour Believes in Britain* (London, 1949), pp. 19–20.

[34] *Loc. cit.*

without branches, Industrial Life Offices, Trade Unions and Employers' Provident Funds.[35] Friendly Societies, whether with or without branches, are engaged in the main in voluntary insurance against sickness on a mutual basis. But many or most of them, in addition to sickness benefits, give benefits for death or maternity, and recently they have undertaken a growing amount of endowment and deposit insurance. The Industrial Life Offices are engaged primarily in insurance for burial expenses and other expenses connected with death, but like the Friendly Societies have developed in the direction of general life insurance and endowment insurance . . . The primary function of Trade Unions is in dealing, on behalf of their members, with employers in regard to terms and conditions of work. But a large number of them also provide insurance benefits of various kinds for unemployment, sickness, old age and other contingencies; most, but not all, of the Trade Unions with which Approved Societies are associated have a friendly side. Employers' Provident Funds are societies consisting of persons entitled to rights under superannuation or other provident funds established for the benefit of persons employed by one or more particular employers."[36]

Approved societies might exist for several purposes, and with varying rates of benefit payments depending upon the membership. "For example, an Approved Society associated with the banking industry had a lighter sickness risk than one associated with mining. Many societies concentrated on attracting the lighter risks. Approved Societies were allowed to expand any surpluses which they accumulated on certain benefits which were additional to the standard rate. Some increased the rate of sickness benefit, others provided grants in aid for dental, ophthalmic, convalescent treatment and so on. Thus the situation arose that a scheme intended to provide a flat rate of benefit for a standard contribution, the less needy received more than those whose more frequent illness and lower income made them the more needy of the benefits of the scheme."[37]

There were several weaknesses in this scheme. Benefits were unequal, and not adjusted to the structure of need. The distribution of societies throughout the country was fortuitous and haphazard. According to Beveridge the total number of units which were valued separately, and whose benefits might differ from those of other societies,

[35] The two basic enabling acts under which these various societies, administering state funds under the approved societies scheme, were set up were "the Collecting Societies and Industrial Assurance Act of 1896, which first made separate provision respectively for Collecting Friendly Societies, and for Industrial Assurance Companies," and the Assurance Companies Act of 1909. Wilson and Levy, *Industrial Assurance* (London, 1937), pp. 74–81.

[36] *Bev. Rep. I*, pp. 23–24.

[37] From the "personal opinions of one of [the] experts" of the Ministry of National Insurance, and made available to the author through the kindness of the Ministry of National Insurance under date of May 13, 1949. (Hereafter referred to as "Expert's Opinion.") Needless to say this "opinion" is completely unofficial and personal.

was about 6,600 despite the fact that sustained efforts had been made at concentration. "Even where a society starts with a definite local association its members may move, so that any Approved Society may carry on business in any part of the country. In any moderate sized town the insured persons are likely to be scattered among some hundreds of societies and branches, each of which has to make arrangements for administration of cash benefits to members entitled to them."[38] Also, and in some respects even more important, their linkage with the types of organizations listed above made it possible to promote the private business of the administering body "by the access to house and to persons afforded by the operation of the State scheme. It is only by this means that the Industrial Life Offices were able to push industrial assurance on to State contributors. The door to door agents of industrial assurance firms were, of course, generally the same agents through which State health insurance was administered but the business was financially separate and the Approved Societies were governed by statute, regulation and rules entirely distinct from any private insurance."[39]

Under the new act (1947) the government merely decided that the approved societies were no longer administratively appropriate or adequate to handle a now greatly expanded state-subsidized insurance scheme. But this decision was also heavily influenced by past association with industrial assurance. Before the war the scale of this latter business had been immense. "In 1939 there were 103,000,000 policies of industrial assurance in force, more than two-and-a-quarter policies for every man, woman, and child in Britain. The sums assured amount to £1,668,000,000, and the Assurance funds to £455,000,000. The amount paid in claims on death was £24,000,000 and the amount paid in claims on maturity was nearly £11,500,000. The premiums received were over £74,000,000 and the expenses of management were nearly £24,000,000, exclusive of dividends to shareholders amounting to over £1,750,000 after payment of £1,600,000 as income tax. In addition to premiums, the companies and societies received in 1939 nearly £20,000,000 as interest on investment."[40] About four-fifths of this business was done by 14 private companies; roughly one-fifth by the 146 collecting (friendly) societies.[41] The former, consequently, are much

---

[38] *Bev. Rep. I*, pp. 50–51.
[39] "Expert's Opinion."
[40] *Bev. Rep. I*, p. 250.
[41] The friendly societies are frequently referred to as "collecting societies" because their premiums, being payable at intervals under two months, are usually collected by house-to-

larger than the latter—a situation which is enhanced by the fact that the private companies are usually also affiliates of very large life insurance companies doing an ordinary commercial life insurance business. Furthermore, the private companies are highly concentrated. One company, the Prudential Assurance Co., Ltd., received a third of all the premiums paid to private companies, and the other companies were closely allied in an Industrial Life Offices Association which enabled them to operate as a more or less unified group with respect to policy terms, premium and benefit rates, etc.

Distinguished by law from ordinary life insurance, industrial assurance[42] was literally "poor man's insurance" which was both costly in proportion to the poverty of the premium payers, and profitable in proportion to the poor man's inability to meet even these limited obligations. Speaking of the premium income of £74,000,000 in 1939, Beveridge comments that it is literally "built up of pennies, six-pences and shillings, collected for the most part week by week from a large proportion of all the households of Britain."[43] In 1934 the Cohen committee found that the average whole-life policy (payment on the death of the life assured) called for a premium payment per week of $2\frac{3}{4}d.$ on an insured amount of £14 8s. 0d.[44] In 1940 analysis of the same type of policies for 19 of the largest offices showed that the "average premium . . . was about 3d. a week and the average sum assured, including bonus, was just under £15."[45] More than 80 per cent of all such policies were limited to payment of burial expenses.

To negotiate the taking out of such policies, collect the weekly or fortnightly premiums (door-to-door), and generally to manage the business of such a large number of small policies by such a large num-

house canvassers either on a weekly or fortnightly basis. Their policies cannot exceed £300, they pay no shareholder's profits and they are exempt from the income tax. Many of the friendly societies, however, do not collect on this basis and, hence, are not "collecting societies." This is most likely to be so where the friendly society makes provision for sickness or other benefits in addition to those for burial purposes.

[42] There are three distinguishing characteristics. In contrast with ordinary life insurance, industrial insurance (1) generally requires no medical examination of the insured person, (2) the consent of the person to be insured is not required (most policies being taken out by one or more members of the family on other members), and (3) the policies "carry no right to a share of profits disclosed on valuation, that is to say the with-profit policies which form so large a part of ordinary life assurance"—although some of the private companies do voluntarily make some such provision, and the profits of the friendly societies belong to the members. *Bev. Rep. I*, p. 250.

[43] *Loc. cit.*

[44] *Report of the Committee on Industrial Assurance and Assurance on the Lives of Children under Ten Years of Age*, Cmd. 4376 (1934), p. 5. (Hereafter referred to as *Cohen Report.*)

[45] *Bev. Rep. I*, p. 250. The remainder, made up of endowment policies, averaged 8d. weekly premiums on £23 (face value) of insurance policy.

ber of companies and societies was expensive and wasteful. The Cohen committee found in 1932 some 51,573 whole-time agents, 15,961 "spare and part-time" agents—293 deputy agents, and 2,675 special canvassers—a total of 71,502 persons—engaged in the business.[46] At the time of the outbreak of the war Beveridge estimated the total number of full-time agents employed by the private companies to be about 65,000.[47] The estimated average total cost to the policyholder in 1937 was "37.2 per cent, or nearly 7/6 in the £ or 4½d. in the shilling of the premiums received."[48] While some reductions had been effected in these costs over the years, they still remained unconscionably large, and the necessary condition to their reduction historically had been growth and consolidation of companies, and dominance in the volume of business by the private companies.[49]

Such figures, however, underestimate the cost to the policyholder for a number of reasons. A series of investigating committees, most important of which was the Cohen committee, had found that this business was plagued by virtually every known type of abuse of which it seemed capable. Outstanding, however, was the grievous burden of lapsed policies. Since most of these reflected payments which had already been made and which the economic resources of the policyholder would not permit him to keep up (or, at any rate, which he did not keep up) they constituted in general a heavy tax on the very lowest income groups for which no benefit was received at all. Of 10,708,864 policies issued during the year 1929, 4,854,473 were forfeited by failure to pay subsequent premiums, and while, as the Cohen committee pointed out, "most of the lapses occur within a few months after the policies are effected . . . before any large amount of premiums has been paid upon them" nevertheless "in the aggregate the loss to the payers of the premiums must . . . be considerable."[50] The Beveridge figures are even higher.[51] If the total nonrecovery on payments made on lapsed policies

---

[46] *Cohen Report*, Appendix B, pp. 110–111.
[47] *Bev. Rep. I*, p. 250.
[48] *Ibid.*, p. 257.
[49] Between 1887 and 1937–1940, expenses including commissions had decreased as a percentage of premiums from 44.0 to 29.0 for private companies, and from 44.2 to 40.0 for the friendly societies. Expenses plus dividends, however, raised the former figure for the private companies in 1937–1940 to 32.9 per cent. *Ibid.*, table XXVII, p. 259.
[50] *Cohen Report*, Appendix A, pp. 108–109, and text, p. 34.
[51] "It may be estimated . . . that in the last years before the present war, about 10 million policies on an average were issued each year, and about 6¾ million policies were ended prematurely each year. Of these ¾ of a million were policies not taken up; about 3¼ million represented outright forfeitures after the policy had been taken up, and premiums paid upon it; and about 2¾ million were converted into free policies for reduced sums or surrendered for cash." *Bev. Rep. I*, p. 264, and table xxx, p. 265.

were added to the costs mentioned above, it is probable that on the total outlay of all persons seeking industrial assurance the return in the form of benefits never averaged more than 50 per cent, and it may actually have been considerably less.

While there is considerable evidence of improvement along these lines in more recent years, yet it seems probable also that the strictures of Sidney Webb on the system of industrial assurance made at the time of the First World War, were still generally valid on the eve of the new legislation. Since they are so widely known in Labour circles, and are so frequently referred to, his conclusions are worth quoting in full:[52]

A more serious question is the urgent necessity for putting a stop to the evils connected with the whole system of Industrial Insurance. At present the great mass of the wage-earners (usually the wage-earners' wives) are persuaded, by the army of plausible agents, to pay 18 million pounds a year for insurance, almost entirely for 'Burial Money.' This heavy tax—twice as much as the wage-earners pay to the State for all the benefits of the National Health Scheme; more than is levied in Germany on all the parties concerned for a universal provision for sickness, accident, maternity, invalidity, old age and widowhood—is very largely consumed in costs. In round numbers, eight millions goes in expenses, three-quarters of a million in dividends to shareholders, and eight millions in claims; whilst the balance goes to increase the Insurance Fund, which provides for meeting future claims. The poor people are willing enough to insure, but they misunderstand the contracts into which they are persuaded to enter. Four-fifths of all the policies lapse in less than five years, without becoming claims. Though 10 or 11 millions of new policies are taken out each year, the number in force rises only by less than one million annually, and, though practically every person in the wage-earning class is insured at some point in life, at least 30 per cent of the deaths among that class are uninsured at death. Nor is there any possibility of preventing this huge cost, these incessant lapses, and this high proportion of deaths without 'Burial Money'—still less any prospect of securing any proper provision for widows and orphans—so long as the matter is left to anarchical private enterprise and the tender mercies of the Industrial Insurance Companies and Societies. In the face of incessant competition they simply cannot dispense with their extravagantly costly method of personal canvassing and collection. The only possible remedy for the evils of Industrial Insurance is to bring in the power and the organisation of the State. This can hardly be done for Industrial Insurance alone.

As Webb's summary suggests, industrial assurance, though costly to the policyholder, appears also to have been quite profitable—in some cases inordinately so—to the companies. One of the most extreme cases cited by the Cohen committee eighteen years later was, ironically

[52] Sidney Webb, *How to Pay for the War* (London, 1916), p. 193.

enough, that of the Salvation Army Assurance Society, Ltd. It was found to have drawn, in return for "sums amounting to £24,000 . . . paid into the life assurance funds of the Society from Salvation Army resources" during the years 1895–1897, some £83,853 in the year 1930 alone. Along with "£10,000 taken to the Staff Pension Fund 12 per cent of the industrial premium income of the year was withdrawn from the policyholders." Another company, the Blackburn Philanthropic, which had been transformed from a mutual into a proprietary company, issued in 1912 some £800,000 in shares to 373,262 members who paid nothing for them. In 1930 it was found that "9 directors and the secretary now hold between them 86,713 shares and that 59 persons (all of whom hold at least 100 shares each) being superintendents, inspectors and agents or persons living at the same addresses as directors and other officials own, in total 58,659 shares. Of the balance, no fewer than 446,723 shares are owned by 639 persons, each of whom possess more than 100 shares." Although this transfer may have involved some payments among shareholders, still no money had ever been paid into the company by any shareholders. Yet "the company now pays a dividend of 3⅓ per cent., free of tax, on the authorized capital" (£1,000,000), which represents "6 per cent. of the premiums paid by industrial policyowners."

Again, one of the larger offices, the London and Manchester Assurance Co. Ltd., transferred in 1930 "the equivalent of 8.3 per cent of the Industrial Assurance premiums" out of profits "to proprietors and staff accounts." Since "expenses and commissions absorbed 42.7 per cent the total applied to purposes other than benefits to policy owners represented no less than 51 per cent of the premiums."[53]

From subsequent data submitted to both the Cohen and Beveridge committees it would appear that these individual examples are not far out of line with the picture of profits in this field of insurance in general. Furthermore, it also appears that this line of insurance, sold almost entirely to the poor, is, despite its relatively high cost to the policyowner, still more profitable than ordinary life insurance which is sold typically to middle and upper income groups. Sample data on eight companies showed that while the "sum of expenses and dividends" averaged 33.7 per cent in 1937 for the industrial branches and only 16.0 per cent for the ordinary branches, yet the average dividends to

[53] *Cohen Report*, pp. 24–26.

shareholders was 4.2 per cent for industrial and 2.6 for the ordinary. Furthermore, and probably for the same reason, the volume of the premiums paid in the industrial branches of ten companies (for which data were obtained), plus those paid by "all societies," was nearly double that of the ordinary branches. Premiums in the first totaled £64,176,300 and in the second £31,012,900.[54] The industrial assurance business, in other words, was more than twice as large as ordinary life and almost twice as profitable.

The high cost, which brought such high profit to the stockholders out of this traffic in dire need, to the impecunious policyowner was paralleled by the total inadequacy of the benefits provided to meet the burdens and risks for which industrial assurance was issued. All authorities are agreed on this.[55] Nor was this inadequacy made up by the various services supplied by state insurance programs which had preceded the passage of the 1946 National Insurance Act. Hence, for the vast proportion of the insurable industrial population the two did not materially supplement each other.

It was for reasons such as these that the Labour government decided not to "work through the Approved Societies," but instead to take them over almost intact. But in so moving, Labour forswore for the time being nationalization of industrial assurance, even though it had long been included among the leading demands of its supporters. In the early days when the friendly societies were first being organized there had been some occasional resistance to this idea,[56] but the inadequacies of the system, plus the prevalence of obvious abuses in certain branches of the trade, soon united labor ranks in favor of nationalization. In 1911, for example, the T.U.C. wanted "the Government to secure appointment of a Royal Commission or of a Parliamentary Committee to inquire into the whole field of industrial life assurance with a view to its nationalisation."[57] A year later the demand was renewed, with the hope being expressed that the Postmaster-General might "give consid-

[54] *Bev. Rep. I*, Table XXIX, p. 262.
[55] Some criteria are laid down in *Bev. Rep. I*, p. 31, which indicate the extent of the inadequacy of these organizations.
[56] Thus the T.U.C. in 1886 passed a resolution opposing any "projected legislation on national insurance . . . calculated to destroy and sap our trade and friendly societies" which proposals for nationalization might promote. *Report of Nineteenth Annual Trades Union Congress*, p. 48. The Webbs at one time shared this fear that the state might "enter into competition with the friendly societies and the insurance companies." See Beatrice Webb, *Our Partnership* (London, 1948), p. 417. This fear, however, was completely removed later, and the Webbs became ardent supporters of the nationalization of life insurance as a whole.
[57] *Report of the Forty-fourth Annual Trades Union Congress* (1911), p. 163.

eration to the question with a view to the establishment of a satisfactory system of State Life Insurance."[58] The demand was frequently repeated thereafter.

A like emphasis runs through the Labour party conferences. The 1912 conference, for example, echoed the 1911 demands of the T.U.C.[59] The 1916 conference passed a resolution favoring the "acquisition by the State of the railways, mines, shipping, banking, and insurance."[60] In 1933 it suggested a variation on the theme by proposing "taking over of Industrial Assurance by a Public Utility Corporation with a statutory monopoly."[61] Other Labour pronouncements have consistently run in a similar vein. "Any system of complete co-ordination of such services," a *Memorandum of Evidence by the Trades Union Congress*[62] to the Beveridge committee said in summing up its case, "involves either the abolition of Approved Societies, in their present form, or handing over to such Societies services now under National or Municipal control. The whole aim and purpose of social service is completely inconsistent with the furtherance of commercial interests and there should be no room for that in the new scheme."

After reviewing the mass of evidence and the various recommendations submitted to it by various interested organizations, the Beveridge committee concurred. "The approved society system in its present form" it concluded, "has served its purpose and had its day. Without belittling in any way the services rendered by all kinds of societies in the launching of health insurance, it is possible to decide that the time has come to make health insurance national. The reasons leading to this conclusion may be summed up under two heads: first, that the approved society system is inconsistent with the policy of a national minimum; second, that the approved society system has disadvantages for insured persons and involved unnecessary administrative costs, while the compensating advantages which it may provide for such persons can be obtained in other ways."[63]

The solution by the Labour government of the problem of the approved societies was as follows: First, they decided "that it would be impracticable to use the Societies as organised bodies in the administration of the comprehensive scheme of social provision now contem-

[58] *Report of the Forty-fifth Annual Trades Union Congress* (1912), pp. 255, 290.
[59] *Report of the Twelfth Annual Conference of the Labour Party* (1912), p. 108.
[60] *Report of the Fifteenth Annual Conference of the Labour Party* (1916), p. 135.
[61] *Report of the Thirty-third Annual Conference of the Labour Party* (1933), p. 13.
[62] Cmd. 6405, pp. 13–17.
[63] These are summarized in detail, *Bev. Rep. I*, pp. 28–32.

plated,"[64] and hence that the Government would favor a comprehensive and fully coördinated scheme, no part of which could well "be delegated to anybody" because "we have to do the job ourselves, for we cover the whole of the nation."[65] Second, so far as the structure of benefits covered in the two basic national insurance acts are concerned, "all approved societies as such will be wound up."[66] The whole, that is to say, of the types of preëxisting insurance covered by the new acts was to be absorbed by the new administration. But, by the same token, in the third place, all insurance, industrial or otherwise, not covered by the acts, is still to remain in the hands of the companies to which the approved societies had been attached.

This last point was in partial keeping with the pledge given by the Labour party on the subject of national insurance and approved societies on the eve of the elections in which, in response to direct questioning from their own membership they said, "The Labour Party is of the view that in our future social insurance scheme, the system of approved societies shall be abolished with the exception of bona fide friendly societies and trade unions, which have a long and honourable record of work in both public and voluntary health insurance, and should be free to come in if they so wish."[67] Under the act this position was altered two ways. In the first place, the friendly societies were not "brought in," but allowed to exist alongside of the national service so long as they provided supplementary and additional benefits only. As such they could not only continue to exist, but their facilities might be expanded indefinitely under authority of the sections of previous acts not repealed by the current legislation. In the second place, although the commercial companies were still allowed to exist under this provision, for all practical purposes it was clearly anticipated that the effect would be their virtual dissolution in this general field. This was brought out in the debates when G. S. Lindgren, the Parliamentary Secretary to

---

[64] James Griffiths, in *Hansard*, Vol. 416, col. 564, and repeated in the debates on the second reading of the National Insurance Bill, *Hansard*, Vol. 418, col. 1763.

[65] *Loc. cit.*

[66] Gordon, *op. cit.*, p. 30. Section 66 (1, b) of the act states that "all assets of any approved society which are attributable to business under the enactments previously repealed; [and] (c) all assets of the body charged with the administration of any special scheme under section seventy-three of the Unemployment Insurance Act, 1935, which is in force immediately before the appointed day, except in so far as these assets are not attributable to any other scheme; shall in so far as they are determined in accordance with directions of the Treasury to be of a revenue nature become assets of the National Insurance Fund, and in so far as they are determined as aforesaid to be of a capital nature become assets of the National Insurance (Reserve) Fund."

[67] Cited, *Hansard*, Vol. 418, col. 1794.

the Ministry of National Insurance, stated that "friendly societies are not interfered with under this Bill. It is approved societies, and the difference between approved and friendly societies is very considerable . . . Friendly societies are not mentioned in the Bill and they are not concerned."[68]

Once the line had been drawn between the area of insurance which the government was to take over and the area which was to be left to the societies and the companies with which the approved societies had been connected, it followed that the Government definitely rejected any idea of immediately extending nationalization any further into the general field of insurance—life or otherwise. This was true despite the fact that insurance in general had frequently been on the T.U.C. and Labour lists of businesses to be nationalized, and despite some rather strong insistence during the debates that it now be included. The case was put most strongly by one of the Government's supporters, who pointed out that "the Government and the State have always been interested in insurance in which there was no profit." After having reviewed a number of illustrative cases, Steele went on to add, "Then again, we have this new insurance Measure which is to be an insurance against poverty and ill-health and which makes provision for old age. Why not enter the business of fire, accidents, theft, and all those other things in which some benefit and profit can be made . . . If we as a Government undertake all these measures in which there is no profit, why not take into account all the other kinds of insurance and make sure that any profit that is got from insurance will be returned to the people as a whole . . . Let us make this Bill a little more comprehensive, and let us have provisions for the Minister to go into the whole field of insurance . . . I ask the Minister to let us have a really comprehensive scheme and go into the whole question of insurance."[69]

It appears quite clear that the rejection of this plea—and past T.U.C. and Labour party resolutions of which it was a consistent expression—provides the secret to the almost unanimous support which the national insurance bills received from all parties. Without tarrying much longer on these details, it is worth while pointing out that this action did nothing to clear up the matter of the nature of the Labour government's long-run intentions regarding the field of insurance in general. There

---

[68] *Ibid.*, col. 1812. This is not, of course, quite correct. The intent of the bill was clearly to siphon off from all societies, friendly and approved alike, the business covered specifically in the bill, and now made the exclusive preserve of the Ministry of National Insurance. The bill did, however, give special preference to the friendly societies.

[69] *Ibid.*, cols. 1836–1838.

are not only past commitments to be taken into account; current interest among its followers in further extension of state control over the field of insurance is also very widespread. Even were this at present wholly in the minor key, however, there are four reasons advanced by its partisans why Labour is apt not to drop its interest in further extension. Separately no one may be decisive, but together they may well be irresistible.

First is the fact, brought out with a great wealth of detail in the Beveridge report, that private insurance has been an exceedingly profitable business.[70] Since, as will be pointed out below, none of the benefits planned under the national insurance acts are entirely on a self-sustaining basis, and the necessary Treasury subsidies are, accordingly, large, and since virtually the whole of the supplementary social security legislation, i.e., national assistance and health, is entirely removed from any actuarial foundations whatsoever, the whole general social insurance mosaic is necessarily a losing business. It would be surprising indeed if there were no demand that these losses, inescapable however well the schemes are managed by the government, be offset in part by being pooled with the very considerable gains accruing from the profitable sectors of the business. This is particularly so, since it appears from the evidence that if this were done, insurance as a whole— of which social insurance then would be the principal losing sector— might just about, or perhaps slightly more than, pay for itself.

A second, and almost equally convincing reason is the fact that the social insurance program is clearly a minimum program, and there is very much to be said for making it possible for additional benefits, calling for additional contributions, to be arranged by the insured at will. This was recognized in part in the act, when it specifically exempted from the purposes of the act those classes of business carrying benefits above the minimum, which were not to be affected by the law. But the act goes further. It recognizes the possibility that it may be desirable for those insured under the act to extend their benefits by making additional contributions without going outside the new administration. Section 27 (1) provides that "any body of persons claiming to represent, or to be entitled to be treated as representing, insured persons of any class and their employers may submit to the Minister a scheme for supplementing the rights conferred on those insured persons

---

[70] *Bev. Rep. I*, Appendix E, "Administrative Costs of Various Forms of Insurance," pp. 277–286. Considerable data are included on profit rates.

by this Act, whether by providing for additional payments in cases for which benefit is provided by this Act, or by providing for payments in other cases, or otherwise."[71]

Thus it might very well be that the machinery set up under the act for minimum purposes could be indefinitely supplemented to take care of one or all of the additional insurance requirements of the persons covered in the act—which is theoretically everybody—and with corresponding extension in the coverage of the act to include more and more types of life and liability insurance.[72] Such a possibility suggests a third reason why Labour may be interested in extending the scope of the acts beyond the minimum level, viz., the belief that reductions may be effected in the costs of managing these other types of insurance which are strictly comparable to those which might be effected by taking over industrial assurance, and which may possibly be even larger. Here again the Labour position was outlined by Sidney Webb in 1916.[73]

We have here, in fact, one of the most glaring examples of waste due to competition. The hundred and thirty companies and societies compete strenuously with each other for new insurers. They maintain extensive offices and staffs; they expend vast amounts in advertising and other expenses; with the exception of four companies, they pay out large sums in commissions on new business; they keep in the field something like a hundred thousand agents (perhaps three-quarters of them "full time"), all in order, really, to induce people to pay their premiums to this office rather than to that![74] It is true that the effect of this competitive advertising and solicitation is also to make a large number of people insure who would not otherwise do so at the time and perhaps not at all; but much of this "forced business" is of very doubtful social value—in fact, seven out of every ten of the new policies thus obtained (principally those for the smallest amounts) are actually allowed to lapse! And though competition among the offices reduces their net profits to a point at which the life business is often said to be scarcely remunerative, it is not at all so effective in keeping down the price charged to the insurer. So intricate are the calculations and so varied are the conditions of the policies that the ordinary person is unable intelligently to compare one offer with another. Several hundred different life policies lie

---

[71] Further provisions detail at considerable length just how this may be carried out in actual practice.

[72] Experts in the Ministry of National Insurance take exception to this interpretation on the grounds that the intention of the framers of the act was to make possible continuation under the new scheme of supplementary insurance schemes, but that the government is not to contribute (by subsidy or otherwise) to such schemes, nor to encourage their further growth. This is doubtless correct, but it does not require modification of the statement above.

[73] *How to Pay for the War.*

[74] In submitting their case against future listing of industrial assurance as "ripe for nationalization" before the Labour party executives the leading companies argued that even though there were "fourteen companies and 136 collecting societies ... already 98 per cent of the premium income is concentrated in fifteen offices," and hence rationalization through concentration under nationalization was not called for. *Times*, February 22, 1949.

open to the choice of any would-be insurer in the United Kingdom, and are actually being sold every day at varying prices for their incomprehensibly varying advantages. To a skilled actuary the best of these offers seems to differ from the least advantageous to the extent of at least 30 per cent for "without profit" policies, and by as much as 50 percent in the extreme range of policies "with profits." The continuance of business at such varying premiums proves that competition does not secure to the customer the cutting down of prices to the lowest possible figure.

The total cost of "Management," that is, of (i) getting in the 50 million pounds of premiums, (ii) of issuing some 10 to 12 millions of new policies annually, (iii) of making the necessary investments, and (iv) of paying fewer than one million claims, amounts to 12 million pounds a year. This—in comparison with the cost of the work done by the Inland Revenue or the Post Office—is an enormous sum. Calculated on the aggregate of the total receipts, on the total annual investments, and on the total payments for claims, amounting altogether to about 100 millions, it comes to something like 12 percent on the cash transactions. It is much more than all the working expenses of our vastly greater banking system, with its 10,000 branches in the United Kingdom. Out of every pound paid in the Life Assurance premiums, no less than four shillings and ninepence disappears in expenses. There ought here to be an opportunity for a substantial national saving.

Webb believed the collection costs for ordinary life policies to be higher even than for industrial assurance. Whether this was so or not, "the very heavy cost . . . imposed on the 'ordinary' insurer" was due "(a) partly to the large amounts paid (in most cases) to solicitors, bank officials, and other agents, as commission, both on new business among different staffs, to the extensive multiplication of office premises, and to the embarking on expensive advertising in all sorts of ways; (c) partly to the fees taken by a quite unnecessary profusion of Directors—over 1500 in number—amounting, it is estimated, to something like a quarter of a million sterling annually, and to the salaries paid to the officers of the needlessly numerous separate staffs—all of these items being greatly swollen by the competition among so many companies and societies; and (d) partly to the handsome dividends in the comparatively few shareholder's concerns, which are taken by the little knots of proprietors to whom they belong."

There is a fourth reason for extending nationalization of insurance which is supported by Labour. It lies in the fact that the insurance companies are major financial institutions, second only in importance to the commercial banks. They are, thus, giant repositories of savings,[75] and

---

[75] "One of the best ways to save is through insurance. The nation's Social Security plan will be completed when industrial insurance itself becomes a great social service." *Labour Believes in Britain*, pp. 19–20.

are collectively a major force in the gathering, guidance, and flow of
investment funds. With the growing reliance of Labour upon Keynesian
types of employment equilibrium devices, this becomes a balancing
factor of major importance. Furthermore, insurance differs from banking in that it is inherently concerned primarily with safe, low, conservative yield combined with the maximum security. Risk, venturesomeness,
and speculation are reduced to a minimum, or should be reduced to a
minimum. Thus, on the basis of the conventional arguments about
bureaucratic administration, insurance constitutes the very type of business to which the methods of the civil service are the most perfectly
adapted. The government is also in a position to give the maximum degree of security, and the universal pooling which it might effect naturally spreads the risks on the widest possible basis. Thus the advantages
of an efficient bureaucracy combine with financial considerations of
vital importance to the over-all recovery and development program to
make the case for nationalization of all life insurance seemingly overwhelming.

How important each of these arguments may actually be in discussions among Labour party stalwarts behind the scenes, it is difficult to
say. Certainly personal investigation by the writer uncovered none who
were willing to take sharp issue with Sidney Webb's general conclusion
of 1916 "that the Government should take over compulsorily, by
Act of Parliament, the whole business of Life Assurance, and conduct
it, as a public service, by a state Insurance Department."[76] One or
another of the four reasons will discreetly be advanced sooner or later
in any conversation where the question is brought up. But in general it
will be discussed only with reluctance.[77] The social insurance acts are,
as a group, probably to be regarded as only the first step in a "one-
step-at-a-time" program for further incursions into the field of insurance.[78] For this reason, in addition to its own specific merits, the
present "minimum program" is worth examining a bit more closely.

[76] *How to Pay for the War.*

[77] See, e.g., the statement by Griffiths, in *Standing Committee Debates on the National Insurance Bill,* p. 262.

[78] This is sharply disputed by Ministry of National Insurance spokesmen. But *Labour
Believes in Britain* specifically lists all industrial assurance on the nationalization agenda
for the future and part of nonindustrial assurance (in that the state is to take over all of the
insurance business of the larger industrial-assurance concerns), and Labour party experts,
commenting on the manuscript of this book, specifically say, "The Labour Party in its recent
declaration of policy, *Labour Believes in Britain,* reaffirms its belief in the nationalization of
the insurance industry." (Forwarded to the author by courtesy of the Ministry of National
Insurance, May 17, 1949.)

THE SCOPE AND CONTENT OF THE MINIMUM PROGRAM

It is not necessary for present purposes to go very far into the actual detail of the contributions, benefits, and machinery set up for administering the Social Insurance Act. There is already a vast explanatory literature on the subject, including a number of excellent and very compact summaries issued by the Ministry of National Insurance, and, furthermore, much of this literature is known and available to the

TABLE 19

CONTRIBUTIONS FOR MEN AND WOMEN UNDER THE NATIONAL
INSURANCE ACT OF 1946

Category	Weekly rate			
	Men		Women	
	s.	*d.*	*s.*	*d.*
Self-employed (18 and over)..........	6	2	5	1
Self-employed (under 18).............	3	7	3	1
Employee (18 and over)..............	4	11	3	10
+ Employer......................	4	2	3	3
Employee (under 18)................	2	10½	2	4
+ Employer......................	2	5½	1	11
Nonemployed (18 and over)..........	4	8	3	8
Nonemployed (under 18).............	2	9	2	3

SOURCE: Houghton, *The Family Circle*, pp. 16–17.

interested American public. The central facts, however, may briefly be summarized, and certain points of emphasis noted for their bearing on the general Labour government program.

In tables 19, 20, and 21 are shown the more important data on the system of benefits and contributions contained in the National Insurance Act, and in table 22 the equivalent data on the National Insurance (Industrial Injuries) Act, compared with those for the old Workmen's Compensation Act and the Coalition government's proposals.

With respect to no other legislation for which it is responsible does the Labour party speak with such unmeasured pride as when it considers this body of acts as a whole. Speaking over the BBC network on July 4, 1948, the day before the appointed day on which the new acts were to go into force, Prime Minister Attlee hailed the event as "a new and proud chapter . . . in Britain's social history." "Since 1945," he went on to say, "a series of Acts have been put on the Statute Book which strike at the very roots of poverty and for the first time in our

TABLE 20

GRANTS AND WEEKLY BENEFITS FOR SELF-INSURED WOMEN, SINGLE AND
MARRIED, UNDER NEW AND OLD SCHEMES

Benefit	New scheme	Old scheme	Married woman's benefit from husband's insurance	
			New scheme	Old scheme
	s.	*s.*	*s.*	*s.*
Unemployment	26	22	None[b]	None
Sickness (first 6 months)	26	15	None[b]	None
Sickness (after 6 months)	26	9	None[b]	None
Maternity (13 weeks)	36	None	20[c]	None
Widowhood (first 13 weeks)				
No children	36	10	36	10
Widow and child	43½	15	43½	15
Widowhood (after 13 weeks)				
No children	None[a]	10	None[a]	10
Widow and child	33½	15	33½	15
After age fifty	26	10	26	10
Orphans	12	7½	....	....
Old age	26	10	16	10
Maternity (grant)	£4	£4	£4	£2
Death (grant to heirs)	£20	None	£20	None

SOURCE: Houghton, *The Family Circle*, pp. 20-21.
[a] Ten *s.* if married to insured man before July 5, 1948; 26*s.* if incapable of self-support by reason of infirmity.
[b] See table 21.
[c] Four weeks.

TABLE 21

GRANTS AND WEEKLY BENEFITS FOR MEN UNDER NEW AND OLD SCHEMES

Benefit	New scheme	Old scheme
	s.	*s.*
Unemployment		
Man without dependents	26	24
Man with wife and child	49½	45
Sickness (first 6 mos.)		
Man without dependents	26	18
Man with wife and child	49½	18
Sickness (after 6 mos.)		
Man without dependents	26	10½
Man with wife and child	49	10½
Old age		
Single man	26	10
Man with wife under sixty	42	10
Death (grant to heirs)	£20	None

SOURCE: Houghton, *The Family Circle*, pp. 14-15.

history provide for a minimum standard of living below which no one may fall ... Today the inspired dreams of our pioneers of social justice have been translated into the most advanced social legislation to be found in any part of the world ..."[79] Calling for "the willing co-

TABLE 22

COMPARISON BETWEEN WORKMEN'S COMPENSATION, COALITION GOVERNMENT'S PROPOSED INDUSTRIAL INJURIES SCHEME, AND LABOUR GOVERNMENT'S INDUSTRIAL INJURIES ACT, 1946

	Single man or woman	Single man or woman with adult dependent	Married man	Married man with child
	s.	*s.*	*s.*	*s.*
WORKMEN'S COMPENSATION ACT				
First 13 weeks (maximum).............	35	35	40	45
After 13 weeks (maximum)............	40	40	50	55
COALITION GOVERNMENT'S PROPOSALS				
Injury benefit (first 26 weeks).........	40	56	56	63½
Disablement benefit				
Basic maximum.....................	40	40	40	40
Maximum rates with unemployability supplement........................	60	76	76	83½
INDUSTRIAL INJURIES ACT, 1946				
Injury benefit (first 26 weeks)[a]........	45	61	61	68½
Disablement benefit[b]				
Basic maximum rate[c]...............	45	45	45	45
Maximum rates with unemployability supplement........................	65	81	81	88½

SOURCE: Houghton, *The Family Circle,* pp. 20–21.

[a] Sickness benefit (including allowances for one adult and one child) under the National Insurance Act is, subject to certain conditions, payable to an industrial pensioner during periods of incapacity, if an unemployability supplement is not in payment.

[b] If an accident is fatal the scheme provides pension allowance or gratuities for certain prescribed dependents as compared with a lump sum (maximum £400 or £700 if there are children) under the Workmen's Compensation Act.

[c] A constant-attendance allowance of up to 40s. a week may be paid to a person with maximum pension (Coalition government's proposal was 20s.).

operation of every one of us" James Griffiths spoke of the new scheme as "more than an Act of Parliament; it is an act of faith in the British people" that they can carry through a system which "will provide for everybody without exception: men, women and children, young and old, rich and poor, married and single, employer and employed, those working on their own account and those not working at all."[80]

[79] Douglas Houghton, *The Family Circle: The Story of Britain's New Age of Social Security,* with a Foreword by C. R. Attlee (Labour Party, 1948).

[80] *Family Guide to the National Insurance Scheme,* prepared by the Central Office of Information for the Ministry of National Insurance, with a Foreword by The Rt. Hon. James Griffiths, M.P., Minister of National Insurance (London, 1948).

There may be some pardonable exaggeration in all this. Allowing 26s. ($5.20) a week for a man without dependents and 49s. 6d. ($9.90) a week for a man with wife and child for unemployment seems decidedly grim. So do many other of the payments. But that it is an enormous advance over the past in virtually every important respect is wholly beyond question. The Labour government, all its critics and detractors to the contrary, has a justifiable right to look upon this legislation as a great and significant step in the direction of the social security objectives for which it feels that it has fought so long and against such bitter and unrelenting odds. Furthermore, despite the air of finality with which so much of the official commentary greeted the rounding out of the program, there is no reason for believing that the last word has been said or the last proposal advanced for improving the status of the underprivileged ranks of the British public. Clearly further advances are intended; the acts themselves are so worded that far-reaching changes may be made in the future within the framework of the authority already granted. And there is no special reason for believing that even further legislation may not be contemplated.

Against this background of opinion, and without any intention of detracting in the least from the credit due the Labour government for what has already been accomplished, it will be worth while examining certain features of the program which indicate the nature of the compromises already made, and the possible changes which must be considered in the future. Some of these involve decisions already made which are, at first glance, quite puzzling and very difficult to square with past declarations of long-run policy.

A first point to be noted is that although all the explanatory literature pertaining to the social security acts generally refers to the grandly conceived mosaic as insurance, taken as a group they are set up in such a way as to disassociate contributions from any clear-cut actuarial relationship to benefits. (This is shown in table 23.) Thus the total cost to the Exchequer rises from 32 per cent of the estimated income in the first year of operation of the schemes (this figure is a rate, not a sum, since the schemes were to begin on July 5, 1948), to 40 per cent in 1958, 51 per cent in 1968 and 57 per cent in 1978—the point at which the schemes will, by rough estimate, be fully rounded out on a permanent basis. If the sums estimated for "Assistance" are not included (they are not considered insurance in the program), the percentages are somewhat smaller, but they rise somewhat more rapidly, being 26, 35, 47, and 55 per cent for the four years respectively. When the schemes are fully developed, in other words, benefits will exceed total contributions plus interest income by over 14 per cent.

It should be pointed out, incidentally, that the schemes do not, of course, begin from scratch. At the time the acts were passed (1946) there was more than £713,000,000 available in the form of transfers

TABLE 23

FINANCE OF SOCIAL SECURITY SCHEMES, INCLUDING STATE ASSISTANCE
(In millions of pounds)

	1948	1958	1968	1978
Estimated expenditure				
Benefits.................................	454	548	681	752
Assistance...............................	57	53	45	36
Total.................................	511	601	726	788
Estimated income				
Interest on reserve funds.................	21	21	21	21
Insured person's contributions............	177	191	191	178
Employers' contributions.................	138	145	146	136
Exchequer direct contributions..........	82	84	84	79
State annual subsidy....................	36	107	239	338
State assistance........................	57	53	45	36
Total.................................	511	601	726	788
Total cost to Exchequer...................	175	244	368	453

SOURCE: Gordon, *A Guide to the National Insurance Act, 1946*, p. 35. These data have since been altered in certain minor particulars.

from the previous Health Insurance Fund (£250,000,000 in December, 1944), Unemployment Fund (£375,000,000 in December, 1945) and Pensions Fund (£88,000,000 in March, 1945). This sum, it was believed, would be augmented by the day of commencement of the schemes (July 5, 1948) to between £750,000,000 and £800,000,000, and a sum of this size would be kept as a permanent (revolving) reserve fund upon which a minimum return of approximately £21,000,000 annually might be earned. In addition there is to be transferred to the National Insurance Fund "the sum of one hundred million pounds" out of assets taken over from the partial liquidation of the approved societies.[81]

[81] *National Insurance Act*, Section 11 (1). There are certain discrepancies in these data. All estimates of benefit totals neglect to indicate the difference between total contributions

Direct subsidy, furthermore, is not limited to regular and fixed supplementation of the schemes for which contributions are paid, technically the insurance schemes, or to meeting the costs of supplementary schemes such as those provided under the National Assistance Act—for which there are no contributions at all. Since in all of the schemes for which there is assumed to be some actuarial basis for contributions (formerly including health, not now in the classification) some time must elapse before the amounts paid in will warrant the payment of full benefits, the acts vest in the Minister authority to supply all or part of the additional funds required during the transitional period. Also, the amounts of contribution may be varied upward or downward for any or all types of insurance whenever in the opinion of the Minister the change will help to maintain "a stable level of employment,"[82] or he may wholly exempt certain classes of insured persons from making any payments at all for limited periods of time and in special circumstances which seem to him to call for relief.[83] Finally, since an even greater latitude is permitted for extending the outgoing payments under those parts of the grand mosaic which are technically of a noninsurance character, the National Assistance and the Family Allowance acts, the amounts to be supplied by the state may be still further increased by mere administrative action—subject, in the more important cases, to Parliamentary approval.

For reasons such as these, the total amount which the government may be called upon to supply in the form of subsidy over the entire mosaic is quite indeterminate. Only one part, the direct weekly (Exchequer) supplement to contributions, is linked quantitatively to the insurance feature;[84] the balance is supplied by "annual lump sum payments . . . calculated to equal the amount by which the weekly contributions and supplements and the interest on the Reserve Fund falls short of the total required to provide the cost of benefits and administra-

---

and in-payments and total benefits and assistance which is involved in the administration of the act. It has been estimated that the total payroll would run around 35,000 full-time persons, and, of course, office expenses (equipment, buildings, supplies, etc.) will be fairly large. Also, the addition of the funds transferred from the approved societies to the National Insurance Fund would raise the total to £900,000,000, and thus also the estimated income from interest on the fund.

[82] *Ibid.*, Section 3 (1).

[83] *Ibid.*, Section 5 (1) lists three principal reasons: "Periods (i) of unemployment or of incapacity for work; (ii) of full time education or of full time unpaid apprenticeship; (iii) when they are not in receipt (or are deemed in accordance with the regulations not to be in receipt) of an income exceeding one hundred and four pounds a year." For the latter, suspension of payments means loss of rights to benefits.

[84] *Ibid.*, Section 2 (3) (a) and (b), and Part V of the First Schedule.

tion."[85] Furthermore, since for at least one major type of payment, un-employment, there is no known means of estimating future costs at all, the state grants may quite conceivably be suddenly increased or de-creased by very considerable amounts. Such payments, to be sure, would come only in part from insurance contributions; the balance must come out of any special funds made available by special Parlia-mentary grants. But this is only to say that the line between actuarially grounded insurance supplemented by state contributions which may vary (at least for insurance), and these other contributions from the state for constituent parts of the technically noninsurance forms of wel-fare assistance—which may vary even more—is at best hard to maintain, and that, whether maintained or not, the total burden of the state may vary indefinitely for the mosaic as a whole.

More important is the question whether this should be called an insurance system at all. Noninsurance social service facilities are out-right state obligations but not necessarily lacking actuarial founda-tion, as illustrated by the National Health Service Act. Insurance legislation is based on actuarial data which calls for a schedule of in-going payments (contributions) and for another schedule of outgoing payments (benefits). The first are divided between employers and em-ployees and the government, and are set at fixed rates including the amounts to be added by the Exchequer. But if the mosaic is really a mosaic, and hence to some extent interdependent throughout its parts, then the total benefits, which are paid out of contributions made by the insured supplemented by state funds (insurance or noninsurance), be-come increasingly larger and the state subsidy rises very rapidly indeed. Assuming that the estimates given in table 23 more or less cor-rectly forecast the future, total contributions (employers, employees) begin in 1948 at £315,000,000 and increase to £336,000,000 in 1958, £337,000,000 in 1968, and drops to £314,000,000 in 1978. The two types of government subsidy referred to above (excluding both interest on reserve fund and state assistance) for these same years are £118,000,000, £191,000,000, £323,000,000, and £417,000,000 re-spectively. The latter constitute 27 per cent of the total of these two figures for 1948, 36 per cent for 1958, 49 per cent for 1968, and 57 per cent for 1978.

But even this is not quite the whole of the story. The employer's con-tributions constitute a legitimate business cost, and may be so reported

---

[85] Gordon, *op. cit.*, p. 34. The lump sums are specified in Section 2 of the act.

for tax purposes. It is generally believed that much, if not all of this
will be recovered either in the price of the products or services sold, or
in tax deductions—or by some combination of both. If the first, then
the employer's share would resemble a sales tax, and being regressive
in its incidence would mostly be paid by the lower income groups. If
the latter, it will be paid out of taxes, and the government subsidy will
amount to the following percentages for each of the decennial periods:
59 in 1948, 63 in 1958, 70 in 1968, and 74 in 1978. If circumstances
permit the employer to resort to either or both devices, he will pay less
than the amount which he appears to be paying—less in direct proportion to his capacity to shift. Any circumstance which permits him to
shift any part of his contribution decreases, in effect, the proportion of
all contributions, and correspondingly increases the subsidy.

Hence, if the government subsidy is to be 57 per cent or more (up to
74 per cent) of the total of in-payments, and the contributions 43 per
cent or less (down to 26 per cent) when the system is fully developed,
it is true, of course, that the insurance feature steadily declines in importance. More than that, the same facts mean that the case for insisting
on contributions has already shrunk in importance so far that one might
well wonder why any are required at all. Why, in other words, was it
not decided to pay the whole amount out of taxable income, and avoid
thereby the complications and additional expense involved in the elaborate bookkeeping, additional staff and other facilities, required in
maintaining a system of contributions? This is a particularly interesting
point, since so to finance the whole scheme would not make it any more
or less free, but merely so alter the incidence of the burden as to square
it fully with that of the tax system as a whole. Since most taxes in England are already steeply progressive,[86] the choice of the Government was
between a source of income which was wholly progressive in its income
incidence, or one which was but partly so.

The first course of action is the one which a Labour government
might be expected to follow, and there are still other reasons why this
would seem its logical course. It has generally been argued by Labour

[86] a) Both income and inheritance taxes are steeply progressive; (b) the ratio of state
income from these taxes to tax revenue from all sources is very high; (c) the incidence of
real estate taxes, both in the city and the country, is highly progressive (in terms of capacity
to pay) largely because these holdings are so highly concentrated; (d) the same holds for
all taxes on unearned income, the rate here being almost double for earned income; and
(e) subsidies of one sort or another advanced out of state revenues to keep retail prices of
controlled products low, coupled to direct control of prices and rentals, tend to prevent the
shifting downward of tax burdens assumed by many different classes of higher income
receivers.

spokesmen that social security is not, as the Conservatives contend, the enemy of mass habits of saving, but the absolutely indispensable condition to it.[87] If this is true the advantage to the objectives being pursued by the Labour government from shifting the payments now made by employees directly onto the tax system would be considerable. It would, by increasing taxes, decrease the savings of persons in the upper income brackets (the greater part of whose savings are invested in private business and industry not under government control) and in so doing promote the Government's plans for effecting a painless, but still considerable redistribution of income. Total national savings would not be affected, however, since at lower income levels the money previously paid out as contributions to the social security schemes would, the assumption is, now be saved in the form of deposits in savings accounts. Finally, the overwhelming majority of these savings accounts would be Postal Savings—in England the poor man's savings system par excellence—the investment and financial resources of which are wholly at the disposal of administrative authorities who have been appointed by the government.

Needless to say, the critical assumption in this argument is that the savings made possible to the lower income brackets through elimination of contributions would be deposited in the Postal Savings banks. Should this be true, the amount of savings under the administrative control of government agencies—so far as they might be affected by the mode of financing the social security schemes—would be double what they are now. This would, of course, give the government control over a greater percentage of the national income.

Despite lip service to the doctrine contained in the assumption, however, the Government seems not to have accepted its own contention very seriously. Not only has it failed to make use of the social security program to effect a partial redistribution of income and gain greater control of the national wealth but it has established rates for each class of persons paying the contributions which are not a percentage of earned income, as they might logically be and as some wished to see

---

[87] "I have heard so often the suggestion made ... that if anything is done in this way by means of State provision, you will stop people saving. I can remember that suggestion being made at the time of the introduction of the old age pension of 5s. a week at 70. Of course, it did not happen, but, as a matter of fact, one's own experience proves that if you have something, at all events, to build on, it is easier to add to it, than if you are in the precarious position that you cannot get the first little bit ... Our experience in this country has shown that State provision does not kill private savings any more than—one of the most remarkable things—heavy taxation prevented giving to the community." Attlee, in *Hansard*, Vol. 418, cols. 1901–1902.

them,[88] but a flat rate. The system of rates, in other words, is regressive within the framework of the contributions scheme—so regressive, in fact, that it is doubtful whether any amount of frugality would make possible savings in the lowest income brackets after these payments are made.[89] Thus the Government chose a basis for collections which, on its own argument, discourages savings the most at precisely the point where it desired to encourage them the most.

Furthermore, in choosing the mode of levying contributions it laid a heavier burden on the earned income of the employee and a lighter burden on the unearned income of the employer—the former share hovering around 56 per cent of the total contributions to be paid from 1948 to 1978, even on the assumption that the employer actually pays the levy out of net income, and does not succeed in shifting some or all of the burden onto other shoulders. Finally, by rejecting levy on the basis of capacity to pay—the system which dominates the whole of the British tax system—the Government also made impossible any shift of the burden from the earned income category toward the unearned income category.

Another reason for supposing that the Government did not take its own argument very seriously lies in its general acceptance of the Keynesian analysis of the conditions conducive to the maintenance of full employment. According to Keynes, with any given aggregate national income savings vary directly, and expenditure for consumers goods ("propensity to consume") inversely (i.e., as a ratio) with the level of income. Hence, so long as the Government is attempting to keep down expenditures on behalf of capital formation with a view to industrial modernization, and maximizing exports and minimizing imports, anything that holds down standards of living might seem desirable. But this means that the Government has sacrificed the direct

[88] "Under the system as now laid down in the Bill, I think it is rather unfair to ask a man who is earning perhaps £3 to £4 a week to pay 4s. 7d. out of his wages by way of contributions. I think it is rather excessive. It is true, of course, that if there are any workers—I have yet to meet them—earning £10, £12, £14 and £16 a week, these deductions may be quite reasonable. I suggest to the Minister that a far better system would be to introduce contributions on the basis of a percentage of the total income which might be earned. By this means those who are earning most . . . would in fact pay the most. This system of percentage deduction from total incomes could, in fact, also be adopted so far as company incomes are concerned. My suggestion therefore is to make a four or five per cent deduction from the total income of all people. This could be deducted by the Chancellor from the Income Tax returns. It would obviate a lot of detailed work for the Ministry of National Insurance, and would do away with the suggested system of one stamp, and a national insurance card." Arthur Lewis, in *Hansard*, Vol. 418, col. 1806.

[89] For some, it was estimated, "the contribution . . . comes to almost one-fifth of the income" of those in the lower brackets who must make contributions. R. A. Butler, *ibid.*, col. 1762.

social objective of redistribution of income to the objective of full employment through high and stable production. Which is another way of saying that these two appear to it more as alternatives and less as complementary measures. In view of the low morale prevailing in many sectors of the British economy, social security will then have had the effect of lifting the worker up only once again to cast him down.[90]

Without pursuing this aspect of the subject further, it may parenthetically be noted that the structure of the system of collections chosen is necessarily complicated by this admixture of insurance, semi-insurance, and supplementary aids. For insured persons alone there are three classes and rates of contributions, outright public "gift" (i.e., health services), and three different structures of benefits. The three classes of insured persons are:

Class 1 (Employed Persons). Those who work for an employer under a contract of service or are paid apprentices. Most people who work for wages or salary are in this class. They are also insured under the Industrial Injuries Scheme.

Class 2 (Self-Employed Persons). Those in business on their own account and others who are working for gain but do not work under the control of an employer.

Class 3 (Non-Employed Persons). All insured persons who are not in Class 1 or 2.[91]

The rates not only differ among these three classes, but within each class they are also different for men, women, boys and girls. Furthermore, "there are special rates of contribution for men and women serving in His Majesty's Forces and for foreign-going seamen."[92] There are different rates of contribution for different classes of persons for different types of benefits. This is true, despite the fact pointed out above, that for all except a part of the limited range of formally classified insurance, the scale of contributions throughout the whole "grandly conceived mosaic" is so small, relative to the total cost, as to create an unbridgeable hiatus between the two.

---

[90] "For a generation I have lived with the consequences of insecurity, but to those who profess to fear that security will weaken the moral fibre and destroy self-respect, let me say this. It is not security that destroys, it is insecurity. It is the fear of tomorrow that paralyses the will; it is the frustration of human hopes that corrodes the soul. Security in adversity will, I believe, release our people from the haunting fears of yesterday, and will make tomorrow not a day of dread but a day of welcome. I believe that security will release their gifts and energies for the services of the nation." James Griffiths, *ibid.*, col. 1758.

[91] *Non-Employed Persons*, National Insurance Leaflet 42 (London, 1948). There are estimated to be roughly 19,250,000 persons in the first class, 2,750,000 persons in the second class, and 10,000,000 persons in the third class.

[92] *Employed Persons*, National Insurance Leaflet 40 (London, 1948).

Thus, so far as contributions are concerned, the government's chosen method of financing, in addition to being inequitable (in the sense of capacity to pay) in the strictly insurance sector of social security, and only vaguely related by types of risks to any clear-cut actuarial foundation, is also difficult, cumbersome, and possibly quite costly to administer. The substitution of a single stamp payment for all the previous separate payments was, of course, a very great step forward. But it is difficult to see why the board was not swept entirely clear. The only argument[93] which Labour people advanced on behalf of the general idea lying behind the choice made was, to paraphrase, that "it is not a good idea for the worker to get the idea that he is getting something for nothing." Yet the latter was precisely the argument used in connection with the health program. All the literature refers to the health program as one which gives "free medical attention and service for everybody." This, of course, is true only in the sense that in-payments are wholly and frankly disassociated—though quite clearly it would have been relatively easy to devise an actuarial basis for the appropriate system of beneficiary contributions. Is it not possible that if the same amount of time and effort devoted to explaining the present complicated scheme had been given to explaining how and why social insurance and supplementary welfare services were not and could not under any circumstances be free—how one contributed in taxes to what one received in benefits—it would have greatly simplified giving the general public an adequate and proper understanding of the philosophy underlying the whole program? And with this the government would have saved itself, employers, and the public alike a great deal of time, trouble, and unnecessary expense.

A somewhat similar, though possibly less serious, question is raised in connection with over-all administration. Despite all the elaborate argument on behalf of unification of social security under a single centralized national administration, benefits are actually administered by various ministries. Collections and certain classes of benefits[94] are administered by the Ministry of National Insurance. All health and

---

[93] The reason has also been advanced that "the history of the Poor Law and the vast development of Thrift organizations which have been features of the working class movement particularly in the last century, [in particular] the hatred of charity and the desire to secure benefits 'by right' are more powerful than a theoretical illogicality, which arises from the large State subvention." "Expert's Opinion." But this same "charity" in the past included health services and these are now "free," and since when has it been, indeed, a Labour belief that state aid of such a type was "charity?"

[94] Principally as defined in the National Insurance and National Insurance (Industrial Injuries) acts, excepting sickness.

medical expenditures are administered by the Ministry of Health. The Ministry of Labour participates in the administration of industrial injuries disbursements. Other ministries are involved in some cases; for example, benefits paid out to servicemen are administered in part by the ministries concerned with the armed forces, and school lunches— closely allied to the juvenile health program—are under the aegis of the Ministry of Education. Although important steps were taken toward centralization, the minimum national social welfare program of the government, in other words, appears to fall short of the degree of central administration which was sought in the new legislation.

Furthermore, alongside the regular government agencies there exists a vast medley of private and voluntary associations whose stated functions are in many respects closely related to those being performed by the government, when not actually in large part duplicative of them. To illustrate:

Foremost amongst societies providing general social service are the National Council of Social Service and the Family Welfare Association. The National Council of Social Service was established to create a closer link between the machinery of Government and the voluntary activities of the ordinary citizen; to co-ordinate the activities of local councils of social service; and to bring together national organisations concerned with special aspects of social welfare in such groups as, for example, the National Old People's Welfare Committee, and the Standing Conference of National Voluntary Organisations. The Family Welfare Association works on personal lines to help any individual or family in need or difficulty. It has a number of District Committees in London and family case work agencies affiliated to it in the provinces.[95] There are many other similar private charitable organizations.

All of these so-called voluntary associations are dealing with problems, situations, and needs which are overwhelmingly below the "Plimsoll line" of minimum need as defined in the numerous statements of intention put out by the Labour government. If, then, it was the purpose of "the grandly conceived mosaic" to provide a comprehensive and complete system of planned security below this line, why were these various voluntary associations, most of which are ostensibly and publicly based on the much hated (according to Labour spokesmen) private charity, allowed to continue? While there is no reason to doubt the word of Government spokesmen, who disavow any desire to eliminate them entirely, there can be no question but that, unless their func-

[95] Central Office of Information, Reference Division, *Social Services in Britain*, No. R. 1333 (1947).

tions are to be shifted to problems which are not (because they cannot be), handled by the Government machinery, their continued existence raises doubt as to the adequacy of the program.)

It seems likely that their functions will be left unimpaired during the transition period required to get the fully rounded government program completely under way. Once that program is functioning properly it is possible that the Government will find itself, in effect, slowly "nationalizing" them, either by assuming certain of their social security functions directly or by gradually forcing most of them out of business through further extension of the minimum program.[96]

There are many other problems associated with the launching of the new social insurance program, but these are mostly of an administrative character. Very few policy issues of importance are involved. The over-all administrative structure planned for the Ministry of National Insurance is of such nature that, within the limitations noted above, it is one of the better organized of the new programs set up under Labour government auspices. It began operations on July 5, 1948 with an already highly experienced staff made up in part of persons transferred from the former social security agencies which had been absorbed into the Ministry of National Insurance, and in part of persons recruited from the approved societies whose functions had been taken over under the National Insurance Act. The estimated staff requirement of 30,000 persons seems comparatively small for a national network of regional and local offices which is designed to administer such a wide range of functions in direct contact with the whole of the insured population. The wide range of discretion left to the Minister of National Insurance covers virtually all phases and aspects of the related authorities under his administration, and permits him by the issuance of interpretative regulations to introduce a great deal of flexibility and general capacity to adjust in order to meet almost any conceivable contingency.

SUMMARY

The social insurance acts are based directly on the first Beveridge report, and constitute the major proportion of the remedial program contemplated under the Beveridge program. The rest of its minimum

[96] Such an intention is generally, and in most cases emphatically denied by Government spokesmen, which may very well mean that the voluntary associations will enjoy further existence. But their functions are supplementary to the minimum program, and bound to be eroded by any further extension of that program, e.g., as may be illustrated by the passage of the Married Women (Maintenance) Bill. *Ibid.* See also the *Home Affairs Survey Supplement on Social Services in Britain*, R. 1737.

program is made up of the welfare aids which are directly supplementary to the social insurance acts, and the health program. The success of the minimum program of the first Beveridge report itself depends upon the solution of the problem of full employment with which the second Beveridge report deals. On this latter program there is very little by way of direct legislation, although there is a good deal of detailed planning which has a bearing upon the problem.

The social insurance acts involve a limited amount of nationalization so far as the approved societies are concerned. So much of the business of the societies and companies to which the approved societies were attached as remains above the minimum program anticipated by the government may still be kept by them, although the acts definitely permit extension of the Ministry of National Insurance into this sphere as occasion may seem to justify. The line, consequently, is not at all clear-cut. Nevertheless, in general the acts reserved to the government direct administration of the whole of the government welfare measures below the minimum line. One of the reasons for doing this was to eliminate the abuses of industrial assurance which had become such a blot upon the administration of the approved societies, especially those conducted under the auspices of the commercial companies. With these abuses eliminated, the Government rested, and did not move to absorb the general run of life insurance, nor even industrial assurance above the "minimum" line. That this decision was dictated solely by considerations of expediency is clear from the intimation in Labour's 1949 manifesto, *Labour Believes in Britain*, that sooner or later it will yield to the long-standing popular demand for the nationalization of large portions of the general field of life insurance.

Strictly speaking, only a very limited cross-section of the new social security program can be said to provide insurance in the ordinary sense of the term at all, since for the general program "contributions" are removed too far from any direct quantitative relation to benefits to have any actuarial significance at all. Within the limited range of insurance, use of the system of flat-rate payments pays lip service to insurance principles. But it is also regressive in its incidence, a principle which the Government rejects in its tax program, and which is inconsistent with its long-run plans for using fiscal (and other) means for redistributing wealth.

At the same time, by choosing to finance a limited portion of the program from contributions instead of by an additional tax levy, it appears to be linking contributions to benefits when in fact the hiatus between these is so great as to render such linkage meaningless. Furthermore, by the amount of the contributions the program itself is regressive in its incidence, and regressive in a way which shifts the burden onto earned income and away from unearned income, as well as from the higher brackets to the lower. Since it is also true that the major part of the funds for the social welfare program comes from the government, most of the money necessarily comes from sources where the principle of the progressive levy is basic. Hence, one might infer that the method of financing is a mere compromise with a tradition which the Government may not feel itself indefinitely bound to respect, and that sooner or later steps will be taken to shift the financing, in whole or in part, to some other footing.[97]

In summary, then, it would be logical to suppose (1) that social insurance will be supplemented in time by a full employment policy, the program for which has not yet been laid out, but which should be aided by whatever income-stabilizing effect social security payments may promote, (2) that the entire range of life insurance will sooner or later be taken over, or "nationalized," and (3) that much or all of the financing of the minimum program will eventually be shifted to taxes. That is to say, these three steps would be the ones which the past pronouncements of the Labour party, the general logic of the position they have taken on the relevant points, and the logic of the steps already taken would combine to urge them to take. In light of these circumstances, the existing national insurance and the supplementary welfare aid acts might be regarded as a typical example of the Fabian gradualist approach.

---

[97] By the end of the nineteenth century, "the idea that for certain basic contingencies of adversity all members of a trade, profession or association should pool their risks had firm grounds in experience, and it was these agencies which had so developed which were quick to form Approved Societies to put into operation the State health insurance scheme *in addition* to their private side. From the conception of a flat contribution rate for a standard benefit within a group developed the consciousness of the wider communal responsibility of all members of the State for the basic needs of the less fortunate. The tradition of independence remained, however. The benefits must be by right and not by need. They must be paid for by contributions and not from taxation. The experience of Unemployment Assistance and the operation of the Poor Law in the 30's, have only reinforced this conception. The State, of course, provides large sums from direct taxation and there is a limit to the contribution which anyone can afford to pay. But this distinction between benefit by right and assistance by need is still very deeply felt." "Expert's Opinion." There must be a great deal in this argument, for it is repeated too frequently to be ignored. Yet I found great skepticism in many Labour circles over this interpretation of the workingman's attitude towards state social security aids, and, of course, none of it applies to the health program— which is ostensibly "free" and comes wholly from the state!

Whether or not this is true remains to be seen. The health program would appear in general to justify the above interpretation; on the surface the Conservative acceptance of the compromises effected by the Labour government does not. But at the same time, Opposition nervousness over the insurance acts—perceptible in detail throughout the various debates—has come out more clearly and unambiguously in the health program. Here sweet reasonableness seemed more clearly to be giving way to the suspicion that underlying the whole program was a heresy which was no part of the original Beveridge plan.

CHAPTER IX

Social Security: Health

One of the first merits of this Bill is that it provides a universal health service without any insurance qualifications of any sort. It is available to the whole population, and not only is it available to the whole population freely, but it is intended, through the health service to generalise the best health advice and treatment. It is intended that there shall be no limitation on the kind of assistance given—the general practitioners' service, the specialist, the hospitals, eye treatment, spectacles, dental treatment, hearing facilities, all these are to be made available free.—Aneurin Bevan, Minister of Health, April 30, 1946.

"HEALTH, LIKE PEACE, is indivisible," a Labour party pamphlet explains, "and a health service which includes only some branches of medical care and excludes others would constantly defeat its own ends."[1] The National Health Service Act places "an obligation ... upon the Minister to provide, in the health sense, to 'each according to his needs.' This is a cardinal Socialist principle ..."[2] and need in this sense is at once coextensive with the entire range of illnesses and disabilities which may afflict any person at any time, with the medical needs of all the population without regard to occupation, station, or capacity to pay, and with all aspects of the interrelated fields of therapy, prevention, and environmental conditions of work and living which predispose toward illness or health.

An adequate and comprehensive national health service must, all Labour party spokesmen are agreed, be coextensive with this structure of need. Just what is involved? Suppose, first, that nothing is done. Suppose the conditions which prevailed on the eve of the Second World War were once again to be regarded as normal. The normal would mean a level of ill-health which, causing the country "a direct loss of over £300,000,000 annually," a productivity loss of "over 30,000,000 working weeks"[3] a year, indicated an inadequate, badly distributed

---

[1] Hilde Fitzgerald, *A Guide to the National Health Service Act*, with an introduction by the Rt. Hon. Aneurin Bevan. M.P., Minister of Health (Labour Party, 1947). [Hereafter referred to as *L.P. Guide.*]

[2] Capt. William Griffiths, in *Hansard*, Vol. 422, col. 370.

[3] *PEP Report on the British Health Service* (1937). "This figure takes no count of most illnesses lasting less than four days, or of those for which benefit is not claimed, or of the sickness of the millions who are outside the provisions of National Health Insurance because they work on their own or earn more than £5 a week. It may well represent under half the total loss." S. Mervyn Herbert, *Britain's Health*, a Pelican Special based on the PEP Report, with a Foreword by Lord Horder (London, 1939).

(with respect both to geographic distribution of population and capacity to pay), and essentially emergency "sickness service," and an untold and incalculable loss of security and happiness which weighed most heavily on those least able to bear the load. This load was heavy indeed, and the belief persisted that much, perhaps eventually most, of the loss might be prevented in the future if appropriate steps were taken.

To keep the separate steps in line with progress toward the ultimate goal is possible, however, only if a very wide view is taken of the problem. "It is . . . well," said the Parliamentary Secretary to the Ministry of Health in discussing the problems of building a health service, "if we remind ourselves that health is a positive thing, and that our essential health services are pre-eminently those which deal with environmental factors like nutrition, food policy, priority classes for milk, school meals, living conditions, housing and public services, working conditions, leisure-time activities and social and economic security."[4] But this is to say that planning for medical care is possible only within the framework of national planning of the physical environment of the entire population of Britain—at work, at home, and during leisure hours. It is to say that the problem of the nation's health is one which can be solved only by a long-run double shift in emphasis: first, from therapy to prevention, and second, from mere medical preventive measures to the reconstruction of the entirety of the environing circumstances and conditions which are necessary to sustain the medical achievements.

In the over-all Labour program, the National Health Service Act was sandwiched between two general sets of legislation. On the one hand, it was regarded as a component of that portion of the general social security program which stopped short of (but was related to) the general problem of maintaining full employment, and which was centered in the social insurance acts. The Health Act was considered a part of the minimum level program intended not only to secure the lower income levels against both normal and abnormal risks of the types which cannot be readily provided for by the average person, but also to put a floor under the general standard of living. On the other hand, the health program was looked upon as a constituent part of the plans for reconstruction and rehabilitation of individual and social life in gen-

---

[4] J. John Edwards, "Building a Health Service," *Public Administration* (Summer, 1948), p. 1.

eral—a program which included slum clearance, housing, town and country planning, and many other allied and supplementary measures for establishing a new and higher level, literally a new way of life, for the population as a whole.[5]

But at the same time, the Health Act possessed a particularly distinctive characteristic. The object of this act was regarded as an absolute good of such an essential nature that the standards of service to the least and poorest should be as high as to the greatest and most affluent. Here there was to be absolute (or, at any rate, very nearly absolute) equality. No aspect or special line of service was to be limited by capacity to pay, nor linked in detail with any system of personal payments whatsoever. Lazarus as well as Dives was to get the best which the best of medical science could offer. In this sense the National Health Service Act was unquestionably the most radical of the nationalization measures introduced by the Labour government.

Such, at least, was the theory. As is not unnatural, practice departed somewhat from theory, but because the theory was based on this idea of absolute good, and the act provided a practical implementing agent for the first steps toward the achievement of the double shift in emphasis referred to above, it possesses a somewhat special interest for students of the Labour program. The question quite logically arises: If health is an absolute good, then why not education, recreation, housing, and the standard of living in general? Why should equality stop at any specified minimum, giving each a right only to some of the good things of life; the right to enjoy a minimum education, a minimum social security, a minimum standard of living—and but a minimum of these minimums? Why should not each have equal access to the entire social heritage within a society whose function it is to see that all handicaps, economic and social, are henceforth removed, wholly and without let or hindrance?

These questions take on a rather special interest because the Labour party's health program was formulated and the act introduced under the administration of Aneurin Bevan, who is not only the farthest to the left of the leaders of the Labour government, but who also enjoys unquestionably the widest and most rapidly growing personal popularity among the rank and file of both the Labour party and the T.U.C. He is, furthermore, an astute politician, and appears slowly to have

[5] As one government expert expressed it, "The Health Service is a government expenditure in just the way road maintenance is and every resident is eligible without any test." Communication to the author, May 18, 1949.

evolved within the loosely organized sponsoring bodies behind the Labour party something approaching the American concept of a political machine. The scale of his immense personal influence is indicated by the steel nationalization bill which he appears to have put over almost singlehanded. He is frequently referred to as Labour's "next Prime Minister"; and it was quite widely believed that whether Prime Minister or not, Aneurin Bevan would exercise vastly enhanced powers in the councils of the Labour party after the 1950 elections—win, lose, or draw. Bevan's general position seems clearly in line with an affirmative answer to the questions indicated above. In Lancashire shortly after the Labour victory of 1945, he told the cotton textile workers, "Homes, health, education and social security—these are your birthright."[6] In subsequent speeches "birthright" appears to possess in Bevan's mind the meaning given it in the National Health Act. Yet here he appears to be as much the heir of Shaftesbury, Chadwick, and Lloyd George as of the Webbs and Labour socialism.

The Labour Case for a National Health Service

A survey of past labor agitation for health legislation leaves no doubt but that Bevan accurately interprets the popular understanding of the content of man's natural birthright so far as health, at least, is concerned. References to well-thought-out health problems in the T.U.C. literature are few and far between, but their tenor is unmistakable whenever the subject comes up. A speaker in 1874 noted that "the health of the people had been so far neglected and demoralised in many instances as to threaten the extinction of the perpetuation of a healthy race."[7] It was their "right . . . to take hold of such matters" and see that this situation was completely altered. The race was at stake. This theme has been hammered home at virtually every Labour party conference since the party came into existence at the turn of the century. In 1905 the Labour party held that "the time has come for the provision of meals for school children at public expense."[8] In 1907 they held that "it is the duty of the State to provide the machinery necessary to cope with rapid development of . . . pulmonary and tubercular consumption" and the conference was to instruct "the Labour Party to draft and introduce into the House of Commons as early as

[6] Cited, *Time*, March 21, 1949, p. 29.
[7] *Report of the Sixth Annual Trades Union Congress* (1874), p. 3.
[8] *Special Conference on Unemployment and Provision of Meals for School Children at the Public Expense* (1905), p. 70.

possible a Bill for the establishment of National Sanitoria throughout the United Kingdom."[9] Four years later they demanded "Nationalisation of our Hospitals and Dispensaries, and also . . . the provision in all congested areas of maternity wards in order that the best medical aid may be at the service of all classes of the community without the delays, uncertainty and disorganisation inseparable from the present charitable system."[10] In 1911 they wanted feeding of school children supplemented by school clinics for complete medical service to school children which would be "free of cost to the parents."[11]

Another resolution in that same year went the whole distance, demanding "a State Medical Service" which "was a real medical service—hospital treatment and treatment for diseases that required operation and a service that would be applied to everybody."[12] In 1918 this demand was spelled out in definite and unmistakable terms. It is worth quoting, since it shows that the program which Bevan inaugurated on the vesting day, July 5, 1948, was almost a verbatim copy of the one laid out by a Labour conference thirty years earlier. The resolution, moved by Dr. Marion Phillips of the Women's Labour League,[13] and carried by unanimous vote, read:

That this conference declares that the organisation and development of a unified Health Service for the whole community are questions of urgent importance, and that steps should be taken without delay to establish a Ministry of Health based upon Public Health Services, and entirely disassociated from any Poor Law taints.

It further declares,

a) That to such a Ministry of Health should be transferred all the Health Services now coming under the Local Government Board, Board of Education, Home Office, Privy Council, National Health Insurance Commissions and Poor Law Acts.

b) That a Department for the care of Infancy, Maternity and Old age, largely staffed by women, should be established, and increased powers be given to Central and Local Authorities for work of this kind.

c) That all duties relating to Housing should be transferred to the new Ministry, and that in this Department also the services of women should be fully utilised.

d) That there should be no representation of special interests, such as those of Insurance Societies in the formation of such a Ministry.

---

[9] *Report of the Seventh Annual Conference of the Labour Party* (1907), p. 62.
[10] *Report of the Ninth Annual Conference of the Labour Party* (1909), p. 88.
[11] *Report of the Eleventh Annual Conference of the Labour Party* (1911), p. 86. This resolution was introduced by Miss Margaret Bondfield of the Women's Labour League, who was subsequently one of the most powerful figures in the shaping of Labour party policies.
[12] *Ibid.*, p. 106.
[13] *Report of the Seventeenth Annual Conference of the Labour Party* (1918), p. 124.

e) That the Public Health Committees of the Local Authorities, with such further provision as is necessary in view of their increased duties on the lines of the composition of the Educational Committees, should be the centres of local administration.

f) That the Public Health Acts should be extended so as to include within their scope all those duties now so inadequately provided under the Poor Law, and all further services that are necessary to secure and maintain the health of the community.

The Labour party, with a few minor exceptions, never departed from this position. In 1942 it officially endorsed the recommendations for health service as embodied in the first of the two Beveridge reports, and in 1943 it elaborated this case in great detail in a pamphlet which received wide national circulation.[14] Its argument had three main points. First, the standard of health in England was very low; second, ill-health was more general and more serious in the lower income brackets; and finally, the existing health services were wholly inadequate to deal with the problem.

It would carry discussion too far afield to review the evidence for each contention. The huge and exhaustive survey by PEP in 1937 makes any attempt at short summary look ridiculous. But certain facts may be noted for their bearing upon the decisions which Labour saw fit to make when it proceeded to draw up legislation intended to improve the situation.

Although great progress in raising the British standard of health had been made in the past, it lay chiefly in the eradication of epidemics. This is brought out very clearly in table 24. "From this table it can be seen that the great epidemic diseases have, in the main, been conquered. For example, during 1848–72 there were, in all, 695,000 deaths from cholera, smallpox, and typhus—or roughly, 28,000 a year among a total population of under 20 millions. On the other hand, there were only 1,914 deaths (mainly from typhoid and paratyphoid fevers) from these dread diseases during the decade 1931–40, or 191 deaths per year among a total population twice as large. This enormous decline has been brought about by the vast improvements achieved during less than one hundred years in the field of sanitation, hygiene, water supplies and housing."[15]

The central problem, in other words, was no longer that of preventing the sudden spread of epidemic diseases, but of dealing with diseases

[14] *National Service for Health* (Labour Party, 1943).
[15] Lord Horder, *Health and Social Welfare* (London, 1948), p. 84.

and ailments which were endemic in the life of the nation. Diseases whose action might be slower, though no less deadly, and whose causes were either obscure (e.g., cancer) or whose eradication was resisted by powerful interests which might be adversely affected economically by preventive action (e.g., tuberculosis communicated from infected cattle). For the most part, however, this change in the nature of the

TABLE 24

DEATHS IN GREAT BRITAIN FROM ALL CAUSES, 1837 AND 1937

Causes in 1937 and, in brackets, corresponding groups for 1837	Deaths, July–Dec., 1837	Deaths, July–Dec., 1937, in population of same size
All causes...............................	148,701	84,010
Smallpox................................	5,811	Nil
Measles, scarlet fever [measles, scarlatina]....	7,252	255
Whooping cough...........................	3,044	209
Typhus, typhoid and paratyphoid [typhus]...	9,074	47
Erysipelas...............................	482	80
Respiratory and disseminated tuberculosis [consumption, decline]....................	27,754	4,188
Pneumonia, pleurisy, congestion of lungs [pneumonia, pleurisy, hydrothorax]........	7,055	4,542
Maternal mortality [childbed]..............	1,265	339
Violent deaths...........................	4,845	4,206
All other causes..........................	82,146	70,144

SOURCE: Registrar-General, *Annual Review for 1937*, as reproduced in Lord Horder, ed., *Health and Social Welfare* (London, 1948), p. 84.

principal disease hazards did not seriously alter one significant fact; the incidence of ill-health was still heaviest among the lower income classes—those who were most greatly in need of adequate medical care were least able to provide for it.

In earlier periods, as the elaborate data of the Poor Law Commissioners and the reform legislation promoted by England's great "pioneer of modern sanitary science," Edwin Chadwick,[16] makes clear, the death rate of the lower income classes from the spread of epidemics was many times as high as that of the upper classes for the simple reason that the poor lived in the physical surroundings which gave rise to the epidemics, and which helped spread them with maximum speed once they arrived. In later periods, although the death rate had dropped

[16] For a fascinating review of the lifework of this remarkable character see R. W. Richardson, *The Health of Nations: A Review of the Works of Edwin Chadwick* (London, 1887), 2 vols.

for the population as a whole and the average life expectancy had risen markedly,[17] the incidence of ill-health remained pretty much as it had been before.

The reasons for this are legion, and all are associated with poverty. Malnutrition, for example, is almost always attributable to poverty, and diseases caused by malnutrition, accordingly, are found almost entirely among the poor. According to Sir John Orr, "At the beginning of the present century, in some industrial towns, more than half of the children in the poorer districts suffered from rickets to such an extent that those who recovered were left with permanent deformities of the skeleton."[18] There had been some progress, but in 1936 he found that 50 per cent of the population were still not receiving adequate amounts of certain foodstuffs which are necessary to maintain health.[19] Rickets were still prevalent in 1927, as was shown by the report of a committee set up in that year by the Board of Education which "concluded that out of a random sample of 1,638 children in L.C.C. (London County Council) schools, 87.5 per cent showed some sign of rickets, and 66.1 per cent two or more signs. The measurements of 100 women attending Stockton-on-Tees ante-natal clinics showed that 41 per cent had abnormal pelvises due to rickets in childhood. A statistical analysis of the records of 41 children attending child welfare centres at Stockton-on-Tees yielded interesting material. The children who provided this material were those who had attended the centres for one year or more and whose health records were comparatively full. It was discovered that 43 per cent of them had rickety stigmata, 24 per cent decaying teeth, and 31.2 per cent were suffering from anaemia. A definite correlation between the conditions mentioned above and bad feeding was noticed."[20]

Tuberculosis, which remains high on the list of causes of death, "is generally agreed to be a poverty disease . . . The mortality from pulmonary tuberculosis," for example, "was found to be about three times greater among Class V, the unskilled workers, than among Class I, the upper and middle classes" in a survey by the Registrar-General in 1921–1923.[21] It is associated with low dietary standards—particularly

---

[17] In 1841 only 17 per cent of the population of England and Wales (15,914,000) were 40 years of age and over; in 1945, 45 per cent of the civilian population of these two countries (39,206,000) were 40 years of age and over. Horder, *op. cit.*, p. 407.

[18] Sir John Orr, *Nutrition in War* (Fabian Society, n.d.).

[19] Sir John Orr, *Health, Food and Income* (London, 1937).

[20] *PEP Report on the British Health Service*, pp. 322–323.

[21] *Ibid.*, p. 285.

the shortage of fats—bad working conditions, and overcrowding. One study of a group of women between 15 and 25 years old, for example, showed that tuberculosis was sharply on the increase in overcrowded areas in the period from 1911 to 1932, and markedly on the decrease where the "average density of persons per room" fell beyond a certain point.[22]

Further illustrations might be given indefinitely; more recent data show substantially the same picture up to the outbreak of the Second World War. In general, "The lower the family income falls, the lower . . . is the standard of health. The infant mortality rate has been reduced to some extent in all classes of society, but the richest class has benefited nearly twice as much as the great bulk of the nation from the new knowledge that has made this reduction possible . . . In 1936 the infant mortality rate per 1,000 live births in Glasgow was 109 (which exceeds the rate in Tokio or Buenos Aires). In Gateshead it was 92; London, 66; Surrey, 42! . . . Tuberculosis is twice as prevalent amongst the poor as amongst the well-to-do, and the average stature of the well-to-do is three or four inches greater than among the poor."[23] Again, "while sixty-two out of 1,000 people die from consumption among those who have comfortable stipends, the figure is 126 per 1,000 among those belonging to the poorer classes of the community . . . The rate of mortality from measles is seven times greater among the poorer members of the community than it is among those who are in a different position."[24]

Even where medical facilities of some sort or other were available, the poor were either too poor to be able to pay when fees were charged, or too ignorant of their own actual health conditions to know when to go to medical officers or clinics when the services were free. In 1910 the Webbs, in a remarkably compact survey of the existing state of medical care for the poor, found that "nearly one-third of all the two million persons who sought Poor Law relief last year did so suffering from sickness, and the greater part of them on account of disease or in-

---

[22] Over this time interval it had increased by 70 per cent where there were over 1.15 persons per room in the county boroughs, by 13 per cent in the county borough and 21 per cent in the administrative counties where there were between 1.00 and 1.15 persons per room, and by 15 per cent in the administrative counties where there were between 0.85 and 1.00 persons per room. When the number of persons per room dropped to between 0.55 and 0.70, however, the death rate had dropped by 24 per cent for county boroughs and by 26 per cent for administrative counties. *Ibid.*

[23] *National Service for Health*, p. 5. Overcrowding, slum conditions, and mass poverty in general are roughly proportioned to the incidence of infant mortality shown in the above-mentioned figures.

[24] The Lord Archbishop of York, in *Hansard* (Lords), Vol. 143, col. 31.

firmity, *which largely because it had not been treated when it should have been,* had gone so far that the patient was unable to work."[25] In 1939 a "survey of the conditions of 1,250 married working women, based on information collected by the Women's Health Inquiry Committee," showed that most women did not consult a doctor until their condition had become so serious that it could no longer be ignored, and that even then less than half of them sought medical advice which resulted in professional treatment of the seven most serious ailments.

This investigation is especially interesting, since it was based on a sample where "every possible safeguard was taken that the cases, necessarily few in number, from each district, social or economic class, should not in any way be selected from those women who were known to be in bad health."[26] Of those reporting illness, in reply to direct questions, there were 1,837 cases falling into "the seven specially analysed ailments." Of the 558 cases of anemia, 38 per cent were professionally treated; the other cases and percentages were as follows: headaches, 291 and 30 per cent; constipation and/or haemorrhoids, 273 and 36 per cent; gynaecological trouble, 191 and 59 per cent; bad teeth, 165 and 43 per cent; rheumatism, 258 and 56 per cent, and bad legs, 101 and 60 per cent. Of all cases reporting these seven ailments, 44 per cent "asked advice and followed it"; 9 per cent "asked advice and did not follow it"; 16 per cent "took only 'home' or chemist's remedies"; and 31 per cent "took no advice or remedy" at all.

There were five classes of income (as determined by "housekeeping money"[27]) covered in these cases, ranging from a low of 4 shillings or under per head per week, to over 10 shillings. Taking these two ex-

---

[25] Sidney and Beatrice Webb, *The State and the Doctor* (London, 1910), p. 246. Italics in the original.

[26] Margery Spring Rice, *Working-Class Wives, Their Health and Conditions* (London, 1939), p. 22.

[27] The five classes were: 4s. per head per week and under; 4s. 1–6d.; 6s. 1–8d.; 8s. 1–10d. and 10s. 0d. The class limits appear to read from the lower class to the first higher. "Housekeeping money" is a well-nigh universal institution in Britain, particularly in lower income ranks—although it is widespread even in the upper income brackets—and requires a word of explanation. It is typically a conventionalized sum which is more or less standard by occupation and income levels, which is given to the wife by the husband on a weekly basis, and on which she is supposed to "make do." Out of this sum she is to meet all ordinary running expenses of the family. Extras, such as large expenditures for durable goods and vacation money, come out of the husband's surplus. The amount of this surplus is typically not known by the wife, since she ordinarily does not know either the husband's current income, nor the amount of any accumulated savings. Surplus over housekeeping money in the possession of the husband goes for cigarettes, drinks, gambling (horses, dogs, or football pools as a rule), and savings. Thus housekeeping money does not necessarily indicate the family's capacity to spend, nor even the income rank of the breadwinner. According to F. Zweig, *Labour, Life and Poverty* (London, 1948), p. 14, housekeeping money is more often a fixed sum than a percentage of earnings, and "very often comes down to 50 per cent."

tremes for all seven ailments, in the lowest income group there were 415 cases, of which 121, or 30 per cent, asked advice and followed it, and 161, or 40 per cent, took no advice or remedy at all. For the upper income group there were 161 cases, of which 93, or 58 per cent, asked advice and followed it, and 28, or 18 per cent, took no advice or remedy at all. While the number of cases is small, and hence the percentages given must be used cautiously, nevertheless, it is believed that they report the general situation as a whole with relatively small margins of error. If this is true, they show a close inverse correlation between income and frequency of both complaints and the taking of effective remedial action. So far as the sample may be taken as representative—and it is in keeping with a vast mass of similar or analagous data—it appears that not only is disease more widespread as one goes down the income scale, but also that it is either endured as an inevitable consequence of poverty, or not even recognized as illness at all. Furthermore, when discovered by medical examination, it is usually advanced to the stage where only remedial medical care is possible and preventative measures can have little effect, and it is frequently not followed up in such a way as to make even remedial medical care effective. There exists throughout society, if these data are correct, a vast submerged, undiscovered, and untreated incubus of illness, which lies so heavily on those in the lower income brackets that among them extended periods of good health are virtually unknown.

The principal feature of this altered problem of ill-health is that condition associated in contemporary dietetics with "hidden hunger," or lack of proteins, vitamins, calcium, and other essential ingredients of a properly balanced diet. There is now an extraordinarily wide range of diseases and ailments associated with bad dietary standards, old age, sedentary habits of living, and various specialized occupations; often persons put up with these for long periods, and on many occasions all their lives, without doing anything about them, and not infrequently without realizing even that they are ill until the sickness has reached an acute stage. These diseases attack people in all classes and conditions of life, although they are usually more severe as one goes down the income scale.

To cite a single example, at the Peckham Health Centre in London it was found in the course of an eighteen months' medical examination of "1,530 individuals (men, women and children) of the family members of the centre" that "in only 9 of these has nothing wrong been found, and 83% have something the matter and are doing nothing about it. Of this group, the doctors say that 'the majority are unaware that they are less than perfectly healthy . . . The most exuberant sense of well-being may be associated with most serious disorder. Hence the recognition of well-being as a cloak covering every sort of disorder is of primary importance.' "[28]

Of the group "doing nothing about it" most considered themselves in a state of well-being. Fifty-nine per cent of all cases suffering from disorders, in fact, reported this reaction, while only 32 per cent suffering from disorders reported what the Peckham Centre medical staff called a sense of "dis-ease," or conscious realization that everything was not all right.[29] A subsequent examination of 3,911 persons of both sexes, members of 1,206 families, revealed 1,673 out of 1,946 males, or 86 per cent, suffering with "disorder," and 1,880 out of 1,965 females, or 96 per cent, suffering from "disorders." All men after the age of fifty-six, and all but four women after the age of thirty-nine, had "disorders" of one sort or another. This condition of the men, it should be noted, existed even though 90 per cent of those of employable ages were employed and practically all of these had insurance doctors to whom they could report, and many had factory welfare supervisors. Furthermore, within the family, the health of the breadearner was a primary concern and hence more attention was paid to it.

The diseases from which these people were suffering ran virtually the entire gamut from mild disorders to advanced stages of cancer, tuberculosis, heart disease, etc., and for women included almost every malady with which the sex may be afflicted. It must be remembered that these data indicate the state of health of the people of Britain after a hundred years of health legislation which has succeeded in, among other things, virtually eliminating epidemics.

From such data, Labour drew the conclusion that the national health services were inadequate, too expensive for the vast mass of the population, unorganized and uncoördinated, and able to cope with the problem, even in the regions possessing the better medical facilities, primarily on a remedial or emergency level. For all practical purposes preventive medicine for the impecunious did not exist, and environing factors conducive to good health were still, in many areas, almost wholly lacking.

[28] Cited, *ibid.*, p. 30. The percentage given as 83 should be 81. See the following paragraph.
[29] Drs. Innes H. Pearse and Luc H. Crocker, *The Peckham Experiment: A Study of the Living Structure of Society* (London, 1943), p. 13.

This was, to repeat, the condition of Britain after a century of health legislation meant to deal with the problem on a national basis. "The first central body to be created in an attempt to supervise and standardise public medical services throughout the country was the General Board of Health set up by the Public Health Act of 1848."[30] The principal efforts of this board were concentrated on control of epidemics, and the creation of sanitary sewage, water supply, and other facilities which were a precondition thereto. The next big step was taken in 1875 with the passage of the Public Health Act, creating local government boards which were, under the supervision of the national authority, charged with the duty of extending sanitary control over widening phases of the problem of health protection. This act, described as

by far the most important measure during that period . . . forms the basis of much of the structure of present-day legislation covering such matters as:

Water supply; general sanitary provisions, including sewerage; supervision of markets and slaughterhouses; highways and streets and buildings; labourers' dwellings; common lodging houses; public nuisances; investigation of offensive trades; provision against infection in suspected houses, etc., including destruction of infective bedding, etc., and removal of infected persons to hospitals, including those coming in ships; provision of hospitals; appointment of officers—Medical Officer of Health, Surveyor, Inspector of Nuisances, Clerk and Treasurer; appointment and proceedings of Committees; rating and borrowing powers; protection of officers from personal liability; alteration of areas and union of districts; constitution of Port Sanitary Authority, etc.[31]

To implement this program "the structure of local government was reorganized so as to place the direct administration of public health and welfare services, with the exception of the Poor Law Service, in the hands of a single set of popularly elected bodies, the councils of counties, boroughs, urban and rural districts, known generically as 'local authorities.' "[32] Thus the organization of British local government as it exists today is largely a by-product of this second great step in the direction of public health control—a fact which is worth keeping in mind when we turn to the National Health Service Act which places so large a burden of administration under the new program upon these very same local authorities.

The next big step came with the passage in 1911 of the National Health Insurance Act, which for the first time "provided free medical

[30] Central Office of Information, Reference Division, *Medical Services in Britain*, No. R. 1237 (London, 1946), p. 2.
[31] *Health and Social Welfare*, p. 89.
[32] *Loc. cit.*

treatment and sick pay for the general body of workers by the method of compulsory insurance financed by contributions from workers, employers and the national Exchequer. The scheme was administered centrally by a new Department, the National Health Insurance Commission; but much of the detailed work fell on 'Approved Societies,' mostly the old Benefit Societies, or 'clubs,' and on local Insurance Committees. The Local health authorities found no direct place in the new scheme."[33]

In 1919 the Ministry of Health was set up to take over "the Local Government Board, the National Health Insurance Commission and functions of the Home Office in relation to mental diseases"; its duties were enlarged so as to give the ministry control over working-class housing, and especially "to take all such steps as may be desirable to secure the effective carrying out and co-ordination of measures conducive to the health of the people."[34] Along the way, and both before and after the establishment of the new Ministry of Health, there had been a considerable mass of supplementary and consolidating legislation which steadily widened the area of public regulation, control, and direct service affecting the health of the population. Thus a Cleansing of Persons Act of 1897 permitted local authorities to provide facilities "for cleansing and disinfection of people infected with vermin"; a Public Health (Regulation as to Food) Act of 1907 tightened up and extended the control of local authorities over various aspects of sanitation respecting food; a Public Health (Tuberculosis) Act of 1921 made provision for establishing special facilities for detection and treatment of tuberculosis; a Public Health Act of 1925 "still further increased the powers of Local Authorities in connection with public sanitation and hygiene" and required them to assist in the care of blindness and eye disease; the Public Health Act of 1936 consolidated the powers of local authorities and gave them additional powers over "environmental and individual health services, particularly those in regard to maternity and child welfare." Other legislation supplemented these authorities still further. Thus mental disorders were dealt with in The Lunacy Act of 1890, the Mental Treatment Act of 1930, and the Mental Deficiency acts of 1913 and 1938; and many other acts were passed relating to maternity and child welfare, factory conditions and industrial health, provision for special diseases (e.g., Cancer Act of

[33] *Ibid.*, p. 90.
[34] Cited, *ibid.*

1939), control and regulation of hospital services, town planning, housing, and social welfare in general.[35]

So far as medical care—as distinguished from general preventive measures—is concerned, the most important piece of previous legislation was the 1911 National Health Insurance Act (NHI). This had been the product of a series of political compromises. The Conservative position,[36] as expressed in the majority opinion of the famous report of the Poor Law Commission of 1909, which provided the basis for the 1911 act, was that publicly provided medical care should be confined to the destitute, and should be dispensed by local poor-law authorities and by charitable (voluntary) hospitals and dispensaries. Everyone else should pay in full for medical care, supplied on a free-enterprise basis by the profession. It should be a primary purpose of those administering aid to the needy to stimulate them to self-help, and to encourage them to resort to voluntary prepayment schemes organized by friendly societies, charitable bodies, and by the doctors themselves.

The minority opinion of the 1909 commission, written by the Webbs, argued that the majority position would only result in constant pressure to develop poor-law and sanitary (public health) local authorities on a piecemeal basis, with resulting confusion and overlapping. There should be only one type of local authority, a public health authority set up on a county and county-borough basis. Since "deterrence," as proposed by the Conservatives, is irrelevant to medical care, the local authority should include environmental and protective hygiene in its services. Although it was not necessary for the care to be comprehensive, it should be available to all who needed it, rich and poor alike, with the requirement that the poor who were unable to pay the full cost would pay according to their means and receive supplementary aid at need from the local assistance authority. Although the act was administered according to the principles embodied in the Conservative report, the opinions of the Webbs had great influence on future legislation.

The health legislation sponsored by the Liberal party under the leadership of Lloyd George, which culminated in the establishment of the Ministry of Health in 1919, rejected all means tests, and sought to build up a system of prepayment, leaving the muddle over poor-law and

[35] An excellent summary of this legislation is given in very compact and readable form in *Medical Services in Britain*, pp. 1–43.

[36] I am indebted to Francois Lafitte for most of what follows on the historical background of the National Health Act. This information was given in a letter to the author, written in June, 1949.

public health service undisturbed and, in effect, superimposed a third and quite unconnected system for partial medical care for manual workers only. The Liberals expected later to provide care for wives and children, and make provision for hospital care and other features, but this was never done. The net result of these improvisations was that a sort of piecemeal development and expansion took place outside the stereotyped national health insurance scheme established by the act of 1911 in which new duties were given, as occasion seemed to demand, to various local authorities and voluntary hospitals.

After the First World War, Chamberlain attempted to meet the Webb's demand for rationalizing local government medical service by transferring administration of the poor law to counties and county boroughs' public assistance committees, and by transferring the hospitals of the same local authorities to their own public health committees. Services of borough and district authorities were not transferred to counties and county boroughs. Meanwhile the regionalization of the hospitals, about half of which were in the hands of local government authorities, won increasing support within medical circles. It was advised by a council of eminent doctors appointed by the Minister of Health in 1920, and it was made the condition to the receipt of government aid offered voluntary hospitals following an official inquiry in 1921. After 1930 growing competition from municipal hospitals led the voluntary hospitals to attempt their own regional organization. The Nuffield Provincial Hospitals Trust attempted in the later thirties further to promote regionalization by making regional surveys of hospital needs and facilities, and by grants of money.

Along the same lines, the British Medical Association began itself to foster prepaid medical service.

A Royal Commission on NHI in 1926 had dwelt on the multiplicity of *ad hoc* medical schemes, found in the development of municipal and voluntary services an insuperable obstacle to extending NHI, and had argued that "ultimately" all medical care services would have to be provided by a unified public organisation based on local authorities, which would involve a total divorce of medical care from social insurance. This commission included men such as Sir John Anderson who were the reverse of Socialists. The BMA by then was keen on NHI, which fitted in well with private practice and left doctors pretty free of lay control. They feared local-government employment, they campaigned for full payment of specialists for hospital work (voluntary hospital work was voluntary and unpaid for most doctors), and therefore demanded inclusion of all forms of medical care for nearly everybody in NHI. Their scheme of reform of 1930 and revised scheme of 1938 and the great publicity they made for them—at a time when Governments did little or nothing—did nearly as much as Labor or Liberal propaganda to work up popular support for a comprehensive and "free" service. Yet the BMA was never at any time under perceptible Socialist influence and its leaders were nearly all political conservatives. Extension of NHI *a la* BMA would have entitled at least 90 per cent of the whole population to free medical care of all kinds. Having gone so far the BMA would not justify its later insistence on shutting out the remaining 10 per cent. A scheme like NHI, with all its administrative complexities, was understandable when designed for a minority of the population; to use it to exclude a small minority was not feasible, and all political parties saw that quickly enough. Finally the Medical Planning Commission, set up by *all* important doctors' organizations (BMA, Royal Colleges, etc.) in 1940, produced a blueprint for a service in *1942* anticipating most all that has since been done.[37]

It is interesting to note that both legislation and detailed changes in the direction of a fully comprehensive prepaid "free" service met successively with less and less organized opposition. Liberals, Conservatives, and Labour representatives all participated, and there was no important point at which the Labour party was seriously out of line or in disagreement with the views of other spokesmen. It played in most discussions a minor part, and for a long period one of its more important proposals—to turn the voluntary hospitals over to the government—would have been unacceptable even to its own membership, since this alone would scarcely have broken the hold of poor-law traditions on the municipal hospitals. These traditions were abhorrent to the doctors, and constituted the gravamen of the demand for change in the administration of social services in general which underlay, for example, so much of the writing of the Webbs.

Thus, in 1944 the Coalition government issued a white paper in which changes which would simplify and strengthen the whole general administration of public health in the postwar period, and greatly to expand its scope and improve its quality, were proposed. In the direct formulation of these suggestions the Labour party had had little hand, they were difficult if not impossible for all except the "diehards" of either Liberal or Conservative parties to oppose, and, in effect, even the leading organizations of the British medical profession were pledged to support them. Health centers were to be established throughout the country "at which general practitioners might attend," specialist and consultant services were to be rapidly extended, and "the

[37] *Ibid.*

coordination of all the existing services in the joint interest of efficiency and economy" was to be carried through.[38] It was while these proposals were being generally discussed throughout the country that the general elections of 1945 took place, and the new Labour government introduced and carried through its National Health Service Act.

Before turning to that act it is worthwhile repeating that the net result of the previous extensions of public health and medical services had gone so far, and had already come to envelop such a wide cross-section of the related phases and aspects of the problem, that the Conservatives found themselves in a position which robbed them of any effective opposition to Labour's proposal. Indeed, the official spokesman for the Opposition in the House of Commons, Richard Law, saw fit to preface his criticisms of the bill with what would appear as a most extraordinary concession had his party not already been committed to the bill's contents.

> I am anxious, [he said] to make clear our position on these Benches in regard to the principle of a national, comprehensive, 100 per cent health service. Of course we accept that principle today, as we accepted it in 1944, when the Coalition White Paper was published. I assure the Minister that on this side of the House we are just as anxious as he is, or any of his hon. or right hon. Friends by his side or behind him are, to give the people of this country the fullest possible benefits which can come from the acceptance of the principle of a comprehensive service. I hope the Minister will understand that. We accept the principle, and we accept the consequences that flow from it. We understand, for example, that once we are committed, as we are gladly committed to the principle of a 100 per cent. service, we require an enormous expansion and development in the health services as a whole. We understand, once we accept the principle, that we are committed to a far greater degree of coordination, or planning as it is usually called, than we have ever known before.[39]

After this concession, the Opposition was left with almost no basis for criticism of the bill. The whole of their case was summarized in the statement that the bill which the Conservatives would have offered "would have differed from this Bill only in" that it "would not have attempted to control, own and direct the hospital service of this country or to interfere with that age old relationship which exists, always has existed, and in our view ought to continue to exist, between a doctor and his patient."[40] The weakness of this position is that the overwhelming majority of those who had just elected the Labour government had

---

[38] *Medical Services in Britain*, p. 43.
[39] *Hansard*, Vol. 422, cols. 66–67.
[40] *Ibid.*

never been in a hospital and had had few if any relationships with a doctor at all, and upon the rare occasions when they had, had received only emergency medical service, provided largely or wholly at public expense, and only in the direst extremities of both health and purse.

But this did not dawn upon the Opposition until it was entirely too late to make any effective criticism at all. On the contrary, they proceeded to implement this objection by one of the most misbegotten "Amendments on Order Paper," placed to supplant the second reading of the bill, which imagination could contrive for such a memorable occasion. This amendment read:

This House, while wishing to establish a comprehensive health service, declines to give a Second Reading to a Bill which prejudices the patient's right to an independent family doctor; which retards the development of the hospital services by destroying local ownership, and gravely menaces all charitable foundations by diverting to purposes other than those intended by the donors of trust funds of the voluntary hospitals; and which weakens the responsibility of local authorities without planning the health services as a whole.[41]

Offered by H. U. Willink, former Minister of Health in the wartime Coalition government which had been responsible for the white paper of 1944, on behalf of Winston Churchill, wartime Prime Minister and now leader of the Opposition, the widest possible publicity was given this tactical misadventure. Furthermore, the Opposition in choosing Richard Law for its official spokesman picked the son of the man who had "led the Opposition to the 1911 Bill"—the very bill which Labour revered because it had pioneered the way for all subsequent public health legislation. Labour spokesmen, ably seconded by Liberal support,[42] easily succeeded in turning rout into farce with the result that the Opposition degenerated to the point of submitting no more than a rather diffident running diatribe on more or less inconsequential issues, liberally spiced with comments on Victorian morality.

[41] *Ibid.*, col. 222.

[42] "It seems rather unfortunate that the right hon. Gentleman [Law] ... should have had to open for his party yesterday because I am sure he will recollect the part played by his revered father who led the Opposition to the 1911 Bill. Exactly as this Amendment is today, so it was then. They could not say 'Yes' and they did not dare to say 'No,' so they invented a sort of new middle Conservative way of trying to get the best of both worlds. Obviously the intention was to wreck the then Bill while paying lip service to the necessity of creating a new medical service available to the poor of this country." Clement Davies (Liberal party leader), *ibid.*, col. 249. Nor did the Opposition learn much from this initial blunder, as may be shown by their complete rout, after having launched a determined attack upon the subsequent and rather startling increases in the cost of the program at the end of the first few months experience. See, e.g., "Mr. Burn's Defence of Health Service Costs," *Times*, March 18, 1949.

Thus it came about that on this theoretically most radical piece of Labour legislation, there was, in effect, no real opposition at all. The main principle of 100 per cent service having been conceded, the Opposition had no plan to submit as an alternative, and so the Parliamentary Secretary found himself in a quandary when called upon to reply. "Rarely, if ever," he said, "in a first day's Debate on a Measure of this magnitude can the Opposition in this House have stated so weak a case as that which was stated yesterday from the benches opposite."[43] Summing up at the end of the Commons debate for the Government, Arthur Greenwood spoke in a similar vein. "We have listened to an exhibition of logic-chopping which has not added much to the argument, and I am bound to say, at the outset of my speech, how sorry I feel for the Opposition. They have been in office so long that they are now in a semi-comatose condition . . . I have never known an Opposition so feeble on so great an issue as the Opposition has been in this Debate."[44]

THE NATIONAL HEALTH SERVICE ACT, 1946

The National Health Service Act[45] was passed on November 6, 1946, and came into effect on the same vesting day, July 5, 1948, which witnessed the introduction into practice of the social insurance laws. This "comprehensive service" is "designed to secure improvement in the physical and mental health of the people of England and Wales, and the prevention, diagnosis and treatment of illness"[46] of all sorts for the whole of the population of Britain.

Administratively the services fall into three main divisions: hospitals which are to be owned directly by the Ministry of Health, but whose administration falls under the control of a system of regional hospital boards; medical services provided by the local health authorities; and general direction of the work of medical practitioners, and their auxiliary drug and other supply services, which are to be under the direction of local executive councils. All are directly or indirectly responsible to the Ministry of Health. Before turning to a more detailed discussion of these three principal divisions, there are a few points which need to be noted.

---

[43] *Ibid.*, col. 206.
[44] *Ibid.*, cols. 397–398.
[45] The full title reads: "An Act to provide for the establishment of a comprehensive health service for England and Wales, and for purposes connected therewith." 9 & 10 Geo. 6, Chap. 81. Separate enactments applied substantially the same provisions to Scotland and Northern Ireland.
[46] *Act*, Sect. 1 (1).

1. *Nationalization is limited.* Only the hospitals are nationalized. The physical properties already owned by local authorities and other groups, such as private clinics, are to remain in possession of their former owners. So also will the new health centers to be constructed or converted from existing facilities, by the local authorities. Supply services, such as chemist shops, and manufacturers and distributors of surgical instruments, drugs, artificial limbs, glass and optical equipment, etc. remain within the province of private enterprise. Doctors are not "nationalized," though most of them are now to be nationally paid. They may or may not enter the service, and if they enter they do so for the most part on something less than a full-time basis.

2. *"Comprehensiveness" is limited.* Since, "broadly speaking, the service aims to give anything held to be *medically necessary*," the emphasis of the bill is on the curative, not on the preventive side.[47] Preventive medicine is possible, and is even stressed, but authority to combat most of the environing conditions (except housing), such as overcrowding and bad nutrition, which are detrimental to health, is not given to the Ministry of Health, but to other authorities. The same is largely true of industrial medicine. Within the field of medicine proper, the program is again heavily oriented in terms of minimum requirements. Patients requiring special services at hospitals or from practitioners, and special equipment not provided in the program, are permitted to have them without recourse to the health service program. With ambulances, as with most other services, local health authorities are free to provide the service directly or to make arrangements with efficient voluntary organizations (private voluntary societies), or to combine both methods. No provisions of the act cover the private practice of doctors who do not enter the service at all (estimated in 1949 to be about 5 per cent of the total),[48] or the extra services requested by patients willing to pay for them. In many cases these may involve very large sums of personal expenditure.

3. *It is not a free service.* Though an entirely obvious point, it is essential, to avoid misunderstandings, to realize that this is so except in the sense that receipt of service is wholly disassociated (except where extra services are requested) from the direct payment of any amount

---

[47] Francois Lafitte, in a personal letter to the author, June, 1949. "In the Bill unfortunately the phrase 'comprehensive health service' is used. It is a comprehensive health service from the curative point of view, but the right hon. Gentleman is also the head of the Ministry which will be responsible for the local authorities carrying out the preventative side, which is so important." Clement Davies, in *Hansard*, Vol. 422, col. 254.

[48] Francois Lafitte, *op. cit.*

by the recipient at any time. The Labour party has taken the trouble to make it clear that *"the Service will be free at the time of treatment;* no matter what medical treatment is needed, it will be available, and there will be no fees to pay (apart from certain small charges for repairs of spectacles and dentures and for home helps). But the service will be paid for by all of us through our National Insurance Contributions, taxes, and rates."[49] Of these three, the first, on the original estimates, was to consist for England and Wales only of "a sum of approximately £32,000,000 to be transferred annually to the Exchequer from the National Insurance Fund."[50] Local rates were to pay for part of the service, originally estimated to amount to roughly £6,000,000 for the first year of operation. The entire balance is to be paid out of tax income by the Exchequer. This sum was originally estimated as over £100,000,000 for the first year.

4. *The medical profession maintains effective control over all professional aspects of the program.* Although the Minister appoints all officers, certain persons will hold their positions *ex officio* (because of holding offices in organizations over which the Minister has no control) and he must consult with professional bodies before making appointments, and must distribute the appointments among the various divisions of the medical profession and other interests affected. To illustrate: The Central Health Services Council established under the act is constituted as follows.[51]

The number of members of the Central Council shall be forty-one of whom six shall be the persons for the time being holding the offices of the President of the Royal College of Physicians of London, the President of the Royal College of Surgeons of England, the President of the Royal College of Obstetricians and Gynaecologists, the Chairman of the Council of the British Medical Association, the President of the General Medical Council and the Chairman of the Council of the Society of Medical Officers of Health, respectively; and of the remaining thirty-five members, who shall be appointed by the Minister,–

a) fifteen shall be medical practitioners of whom two shall be selected for their knowledge of mental illness and mental defectiveness;

b) five shall be persons, not being medical practitioners, with experience in hospital management;

c) five shall be persons, not being medical practitioners, with experience in local government;

d) three shall be dental practitioners;

[49] Stephen Taylor, *National Health Service,* Labour Discussion Series no. 6 (Labour Party, 1946).

[50] *L. P. Guide,* p. 32.

[51] *Act,* First Schedule, p. 65.

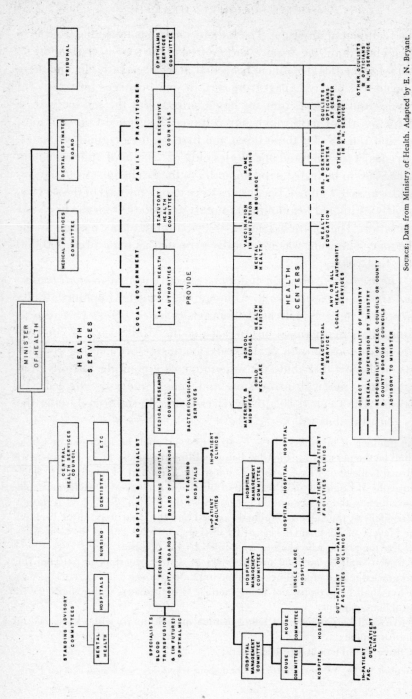

Chart 7. Organization of British National Health Service.

Source: Data from Ministry of Health. Adapted by E. N. Bryant.

e) two shall be persons with experience in mental health services;

f) two shall be registered nurses;

g) one shall be a certified midwife; and

h) two shall be registered pharmacists;

and before appointing any of the persons specified in subparagraphs *a* to *h* respectively, the Minister shall consult with such organisations as he may recognise as representative of those persons.

The Minister must consult the council, and this council must advise the Minister on any matters relating to any aspect of the conduct of the service which either of them think requires change or policy decision.[52] The same holds for the standing advisory committees, as given at the top of chart 7, for mental health, hospitals, nursing, and dentistry. These latter may be set up at will, but must be constituted "partly of members of the Central Council" and partly of other persons, whose appointment by the Minister must, however, also follow the lines of consultation and representation indicated for the council itself.[53] While the Minister may "by order vary the constitution of that Council,"[54] he must first consult with the council. The central council must "make an annual report to the Minister on their proceedings and on the proceedings of any standing advisory committee" set up under the act, but the Minister must also lay this report before Parliament.[55]

With these preliminary observations, the rest of the program can be more readily understood in connection with the separate administrative divisions.

THE HOSPITALS

The "nationalisation of hospitals," the Labour party *Guide* comments, "is the most far-reaching change for which the Act provides."[56] A hospital survey had found that "there is no hospital system now,"[57] and that hospital services in England were, over the country as a whole, inadequate for the needs of the new health service by virtually every criterion. On the second reading of the bill, Bevan had declared that the British "hospital facilities are available where they are least needed. In the older industrial districts of Great Britain hospital facilities are

---

[52] *Ibid.*, and Sect. 2 (1).

[53] *Ibid.*, Sect. 2 (3).

[54] *Ibid.*, Sect. 2 (2).

[55] *Ibid.*, Sect. 2 (5). He may, however, after consulting with the council, refrain from laying all or any part of the report before Parliament if he is convinced that so to act would "be contrary to the public interest." *ibid.*

[56] *L. P. Guide*, p. 8.

[57] *The Hospital Surveys: The Domesday Book of the Hospital Services* (Oxford, Nuffield Provincial Hospitals Trust, 1946).

inadequate. Many of the hospitals are too small—very much too small. About 70 per cent have less than 100 beds, and over 30 per cent have less than 30. No one can possibly pretend that hospitals so small can provide general hospital treatment."[58]

There were two general types of hospitals: voluntary hospitals, originally supported out of fees and private endowments, and public— mostly municipal—hospitals, supported mostly by public funds. Most of the voluntary hospitals, however, were coming to rely heavily upon public sources of funds. In one hospital, "in 1905, forty years ago, our income was made up entirely of voluntary gifts, that is subscriptions, donations and legacies, but last year—45 per cent. of our income came from public authorities, from patients and from central funds for serv- ices rendered . . . to-day our voluntary hospitals are only partially voluntary."[59] Even then they were frequently compelled to resort to the most extreme, and at times highly ludicrous,[60] measures for making up the ever-recurring deficits. As with the municipal and other public hos- pitals, the size of the new and modern hospital, and the scale of the neccessary expenditure—involving an outlay of £2,000,000 pounds or more—is "entirely outside the scope of voluntary effort."[61]

Much the same held for public hospitals. Most of them (over 2,000 in England and Wales) were hampered by inadequate facilities and obsolete equipment, had too few beds, and were understaffed with doctors—particularly specialists—and nurses, so that the country re- quired a huge extension of hospital buildings, and drastic modern- izing of their whole layout, equipment, and staffs. But that was not all.

[58] *Hansard*, Vol. 422, col. 44. "The experiences of the past decade have revolutionized our ideas regarding hospital planning. It is now considered that the ideal unit is an institution containing from 800 to 1,200 beds." Lord Inman, in *Hansard* (Lords), Vol. 143, col. 52.

[59] Lord Inman, *ibid.*, col. 50. "Voluntary hospitals during the past twenty years have been greatly dependent on local authorities for contributions for services rendered; hospital beds, maternity and child welfare clinics, tuberculosis dispensaries, and V. D. Centres." Sir Arthur S. MacNalty, *The Reform of the Public Health Services* (Oxford, Nuffield College, 1943). MacNalty was formerly chief medical officer of the Ministry of Health.

[60] "Some of your Lordships may have seen, just before the war, a large hoarding [bill- board] outside one of our best known hospitals on which it was stated: 'We require 10,000 people to sell soap for us.' That institution was so desperately hard up that the committee had purchased a quantity of soap to sell again at a profit. Another well-known hospital en- gaged a staff of 200 canvassers to go from door to door selling stationery. All sorts of weird appeals were organized to intrigue the public into giving. There were banquets of humour, midnight matinées, flag days, and Bridge tournaments. Indeed, the hospital administrator, like the Athenian of old, spent his time in doing little else but seeking to hear of some new thing." Lord Inman, *ibid.*, cols. 50–51. He had gone, he said, over to the United States to "beg funds" some years ago. On Sunday he attended "service at the well-known Fifth Avenue Presbyterian Church," and his heart sank when he heard the first hymn announced. It was, "Guide me, oh thou great Jehovah, Pilgrim through this barren land." It was time, he felt, to be done with "stunt appeals to maintain our work."

[61] *Ibid.*, col. 52.

The geographic distribution of hospitals bore little relation to the structure of need. In three counties of North Wales—Merioneth, Caernarvon, and Anglesey—having a population of 200,000, there were less than 500 hospital beds. "The result is that patients are waiting for from six to nine months for admission to hospital. People who should be treated as in-patients are being treated as out-patients. In the whole of Merionethshire there is not a single fever hospital, and people have died on the way to a fever hospital which was a considerable distance away."[62] In a mining district (Leigh) in Lancashire having a population of 85,000, where there was only "one hospital catering for the whole constituency, the Leigh Infirmary, a small hospital completely inadequate to the needs of the district . . . At this hospital catering for 85,000 people a waiting room for the out-patients . . . will not hold more than 40 people. The people waiting for treatment go into the corridors, overspill outside, and wait there whatever the weather."[63]

But even in the areas where hospitals were most plentiful and the service more adequate, the shortages of beds, facilities, and staff were frequently acute. A medical report, made in 1945, dealing with the Greater London Area, which has a population of 14,000,000, showed "that there is in the area a deficiency of beds for acute medical and acute surgical cases; a deficiency of beds for tuberculosis; a deficiency of beds for maternity; very bad provision indeed for the clinic sick, and only a very small amount of provision for the clinic sick from voluntary sources . . . The distribution of hospitals over this area is very haphazard . . . We have . . . in one part of London, Middlesex and Surrey, good municipal services and good voluntary services, but in two other counties very little is done. In fact, there is a terrible patchwork all over this very large area."[64] Whether facilities are adequate or not, coöperation between and among them is a haphazard affair, and frequently impossible. Dr. Guest believed that "the question of combining voluntary and municipal hospitals is so complicated when considered from the standpoint of the country as a whole that, unless it is done on a national scale, I am convinced it cannot be done at all."[65]

Such, at any rate, was the case as seen by Government spokesmen. Bevan also felt that "it is repugnant to a civilised community for hospitals to have to rely upon private charity,"[66] and service at the public

---

[62] Emrys Roberts, in *Hansard*, Vol. 422, col. 135.
[63] H. Boardman, *ibid.*, col. 284.
[64] Dr. L. H. Guest, *ibid.*, cols. 293–296.
[65] *Loc. cit.*
[66] *Ibid.*, col. 47.

hospitals was tainted with their past association with the poor laws. To accept service from them carried a stigma to many people and this should be swept wholly away. But why nationalization? There was not much dispute over the facts of shortage of beds, inadequate facilities and equipment, staff deficiencies, etc., but there was serious question on this move. Not, however, strange as it may seem, on the issue of public ownership. In this case, the issue was not of public versus private ownership, but of national ownership and direction versus local ownership and direction.

The proposal of the Government was "to create an entirely new hospital service, to take over the voluntary hospitals, and to take over the local government hospitals and to organise them as a single hospital service . . . to provide the people of Great Britain, no matter where they may be, with the same level of service." This would mean rounding out hospital services into "effective hospital units," each of which would be associated with a medical school. Then, "if you grouped the hospitals in about 16 to 20 regions around the medical schools, you would . . . have within those regions the wide range of disease and disability which would provide the basis for your specialised hospital service. Furthermore, by grouping hospitals around the medical schools, we should be providing what is very badly wanted, and that is a means by which the general practitioners are kept in more intimate association with new medical thought and training."[67]

Contrariwise, handing over the voluntary hospitals to the local authorities, or requiring them to construct hospitals of a size and type to meet local needs and to provide the staff and facilities which modern medical science requires, would create obvious and irreducible handicaps. "Many of the local authorities in Great Britain have never been able to exercise their hospital powers. They are too poor. They are too small. Furthermore, the local authorities of Great Britain inherited their hospitals from the Poor Law, and some of them are monstrous buildings, a cross between a workhouse and a barracks . . . or a prison. The local authorities are helpless in these matters. They have not been able to afford much money." While some local authorities "are first class" it is also true that "the local authority area is no more an effective gathering ground for the patients of the hospitals than the voluntary hospitals themselves." To try to make the local authorities responsible for the hospital program, hence, would mean "that once

---

[67] *Ibid.*, cols. 49–50.

more we shall be faced with all kinds of anomalies, just in those areas where hospital facilities are most needed, and in those very conditions where the mass of the poor people will be unable to find the finance to supply the hospitals . . . because the local authorities are too small, because their financial capacities are unevenly distributed" they "could not be effective hospital administration units."[68]

Yet aside from an occasional reference to the bill, as one member of the House of Lords put it, as "just another step on the slippery road leading to nationalization,"[69] not even this last position of the Minister was seriously disputed. In fact, so far as the proposals relating to the hospital service were concerned, the only serious disagreement came over two matters. The first was settled, in part at least, on the Opposition's terms. The second involves a fundamental point of administration.

The first disagreement was over the proposal to take over the private endowments of the voluntary hospitals and put them into the general fund. Numerous objections were raised, and in face of these the Government decided to permit "the teaching hospitals" to retain "all their liquid endowments," while some "£32 million belonging to the voluntary hospitals as a whole" was to be left in their possession.[70] This it was argued, would not only leave intact the important donations which had been made in the past for specialized services, but would also encourage future donations of a like sort.

The second point had to do with the separation of provisions of the act relating to the hospital service, managed on a national basis, from those relating to the general practitioners, the health centers, and other facilities which were to be managed on a local basis. Here the Government proposed an arrangement which seems effectively to have destroyed all determined opposition. Under the law the country has been divided into fourteen regions, each of which "has a natural university medical centre as a focal point." Four of these center in London, "each having part of the metropolis with gathering grounds extending far beyond the metropolitan boundaries."[71] Each area has a regional hospital board appointed by the Minister, consisting of a chairman and an undefined number of persons appointed after consultation "(a) with the university with which the provision of hospital and specialist services

[68] *Loc. cit.*
[69] Lord Lyle, in *Hansard* (Lords), Vol. 143, col. 82.
[70] Bevan, in *Hansard*, Vol. 422, col. 62.
[71] L. John Edwards, *op. cit.*

in the area of the Board is to be associated; (*b*) . . . with such organisations as the Minister may recognise as representative of the medical
profession in the said area or the medical profession generally; (*c*) . . .
with the local health authorities in the said area; and (*d*) . . . with such
other organisations as appear to the Minister to be concerned."[72] Before
filling vacancies the Minister must consult the board. "At least two of
the members of the Board shall be persons with experience in mental
health services."

Each regional hospital board has under its administration a series
of general-purpose hospitals, so equipped that they can offer all the
regular and specialist services which make it possible for a truly
modern hospital to handle all types of cases. The hospital management
committee is to be made up of a chairman and other persons appointed
by the board after consultation "(*a*) . . . with any local health authority
whose area comprises the area or any part of the area served by the
hospital or group; (*b*) . . . with any Executive Council whose area comprises the area or any part of the area served by the hospital or group;
(*c*) . . . with the senior medical and dental staff employed at the hospital or the hospitals of the group . . . and (*d*) . . . with such other
organisations as appear to the Board to be concerned."[73]

In addition, attached to each medical university, of which there is to
be at least one in each region, there are teaching hospitals, each governed by a board of governors having the same status as a regional
hospital board. Each board has a chairman appointed by the Minister,
and other members similarly appointed, with "not more than one-fifth"
each drawn respectively from persons "nominated by the university
with which the hospital is associated . . . nominated by the Regional
Hospital Board, [and] nominated by the medical and dental teaching
staff of the hospital." The balance is to be made up of "persons appointed after consultation with . . . local health authorities and other
organisations."[74]

All the assets and liabilities of the hospitals taken over are transferred to the Ministry of Health. All management is in the hands of the
regional boards and management committees, each of which is to be
a "body corporate with perpetual succession," etc. Two features of this
arrangement are of special interest. First, actual administration is in
the hands of committees. There is no provision made for establishing,

[72] *Act*, Third Schedule, p. 67.
[73] *Ibid.*, p. 68.
[74] *Ibid.*

either before or after the vesting day, any more compactly centralized management responsibility. Furthermore, the committees are all large. The average regional board appointed under the act has twenty-six members, the average board of the teaching hospitals ranged "between sixteen and twenty-nine, the average number being twenty-eight," and the hospital management committees of the regular hospitals varied "between ten and thirty."[75] Whether this "two-tier" system of management of vast and complicated services by large and cumbersome committees—"the drowsy syrup of the democratic state"[76]—can be made to work successfully or for long seems highly doubtful. On this point the Labour government seems in danger of overlooking a first principle of proper and efficient management: the undivided centralization of authority in the hands of a single individual at each and every level of executive responsibility. It is one thing to place policy control in the hands of committees, so long as they are treated as purely administrative bodies,[77] but to place management executive responsibility directly in such hands has everywhere else proved to be a mistake which is almost always fatal.

The second feature is that, as with the Central Health Services Council, the preponderating control within the committees is in the hands of the medical profession itself.[78] This seems to have drawn the teeth of the opposition within the profession to the hospital program as a whole. But what quickly became apparent in the debates is that it was not public ownership of hospitals—not, even, in fact, their nationalization—which most disturbed the medical profession. It was the belief that it was the purpose of the act to "nationalize" the doctors and dentists by converting them into full-time salaried employees of the state.

[75] "Progress in the National Health Service. The Hospital Service: A Report on Recent Developments," *The Hospital*, Nov., 1948, pp. 487–501.

[76] "Nowadays the spare time of a specialist is taken up by attendance on committees which are the drowsy syrup of the democratic State. When recently a Professor of Medicine retired from a London school he was found to be on thirty-two committees. That is perfectly fatal to the product of life." Lord Moran, in *Hansard* (Lords), Vol. 143, col. 40.

[77] "This *might* be the relation between the H.M.C. and the (single individual) hospital manager (we have professional hospital managers)—much depends on the H.M.C.'s willingness to trust him. It is the relation between R.H.B. and *its* chief officers." Francois Lafitte, *op. cit.*

[78] According to the previously cited report printed in *The Hospital*, the membership of the regional boards appointed after vesting day showed 26 per cent from local authorities, 21 per cent from the voluntary hospital field, 20 per cent from the medical profession, and 15 per cent from the universities. Part of the first group and all of the last three groups are drawn from the medical profession.

EXECUTIVE COUNCILS AND THE MEDICAL PRACTITIONERS

With respect to the medical profession, there were certain preliminary facts to be faced. One was the maldistribution of doctors. For example, "In the South Division of Bristol, which has one of the biggest single housing estates in the country and has a population of 34,000, there is not one resident medical man. Efforts to induce people to go have so far failed. In the town of Taunton, which is not far away and has a population of approximately 40,000, there are 56 registered medical practitioners."[79] Again, "In South Shields before the war there were 4,100 persons per doctor; in Bath 1,590; in Dartford nearly 3,000 and in Bromley 1,620; in Swindon 3,100; in Hastings under 1,200. That distribution," said the Minister of Health, "of general practitioners throughout the country is most hurtful to the health of our people," and needs seriously to be altered.[80]

The regional distribution of specialists is even worse—as the data on hospitals and clinics referred to above help heavily to underscore. But perhaps even more important, there is a great shortage of both general practitioners and specialists. It was pointed out that the Teviot committee believed that the standard of treatment anticipated in the National Health Service Act would require a three-fold increase in dentists within twenty years.[81] There was also a shortage of all types of auxiliary workers and of facilities for training them, and incentives were lacking to hold those who chose to enter the field. An outstanding example is the shortage of nurses. An investigation of the Nursing Recruitment Service in 1948 shows that of 2,937 nurses completing their training between June, 1946, and February, 1948, in some sixty-eight hospitals in the London area, "15.5 per cent. gave up nursing altogether; 3.4 per cent. went abroad; 0.9 per cent. entered the Services; 8.1 per cent. entered non-hospital nursing employment; 36.6 per cent. went on to midwifery training, and 3.5 per cent. took up other training courses; leaving 32 per cent. who remained in hospital employment." Similar nationwide results would mean that not more than half the number of nurses previously estimated to be entering the service would actually

---

[79] Arthur Greenwood, in *Hansard*, Vol. 422, col. 401.

[80] *Ibid.*, col. 53. I am obligated to Dr. Mark Daniels of the Tuberculosis Research Unit of the Medical Research Council for the observation that these data indicate more a shortage against an ideal or medically adequate scheme than a relative shortage. He refers to data showing that "there are more doctors per 100,000 population in England than in any other country except the U.S.A."

[81] Mrs. Corbet, *ibid.*, col. 268. See also *Final Report of the Inter-Departmental Committee on Dentistry* [*Teviot Report*], Cmd. 6727 (1947), pp. 45–48.

be doing so.[82] Almost everything was the matter with the nursing profession: inadequate training, low pay, bad living conditions, lack of status, poor future prospects. So serious has the shortage of nurses become that it appears to be partly paralyzing essential hospital services. In the summer of 1948 one estimate found 30,000 hospital beds in London alone to be unoccupied for this reason.

Facts such as these, however, were not really in dispute. The big question was whether or not it was the intention of the Government to make full-salaried civil servants of the doctors. Contending that this was so, the British Medical Association (B.M.A.) conducted large-scale and quite effective opposition to the bill, going so far at one time as to threaten the Government with wholesale sabotage of the new service by the doctors unless they could be satisfied on this point.[83] The general position of the Labour party on this point was not clear, and comments made during the debates in Parliament did not go very far toward further clarification. The Socialist Medical Association, closely allied to the Labour party, stated, while the debates were still under way, "We still insist that the best service, the perfect doctor-patient relationship, and the highest form of team work will be possible only when the service becomes one employing whole-time salaried officers."[84] Bevan himself had not helped to quiet the fears of the Opposition when he stated in his opening remarks that it was his belief "that the medical profession" was not yet "ripe . . . for a full salaried service."[85] Furthermore, the Labour party had previously made a definite commitment on the point. In its pamphlet, *National Service for Health,* published in 1943, it said that "in the Labour Party's opinion it is necessary that the medical profession should be organised as a national, full-time, salaried, pensionable service."[86] Many Labour M.P.'s were still prepared to fight for this principle. It was pointed out that most doctors in the teaching hospitals and on the staffs of the medical colleges were on a full-time salaried basis, not to mention those working for the various branches of the armed services, most doctors on industrial payrolls,

---

[82] *The Hospital,* Sept., 1948, pp. 385–386.

[83] A national plebiscite circulated by the B.M.A. carried the question: "I agree to abide by the decision of the majority and undertake not to enter the service if the answers . . . reveal a majority against undertaking service." 24,066 answered this question in the affirmative; 4,494 in the negative. *Home Affairs Survey,* Feb. 24, 1948. Nevertheless, 21,341 doctors and 4,500 (approximately) of the dentists had signed up by vesting day (July 5, 1948). *Daily Telegraph,* July 12, 1948.

[84] Quoted by Law, in *Hansard,* Vol. 422, col. 78.

[85] *Ibid.,* col. 55. This statement was repeated the following day in the Government rebuttal by the Parliamentary Secretary to the Minister of Health, *ibid.,* col. 214.

[86] *Op. cit.* Also cited by Mr. Reid, in *Hansard,* Vol. 422, col. 392.

and many other doctors working for public bodies, both local and national, and that these included services which were admittedly of the highest technical order of excellence, and areas where the most substantial contributions were being made to the advancement of medical science.

Thus it was feared that the compromise proposed by the Government was only another example of the gradualist tactics of Labour. This fear was lent additional support by the Government's proposal to put an end to the sale of practices, which had long been one of the more serious financial obstacles to entering the profession and one of the most lucrative sources of gain at the end of a profitable career.[87] With this was linked the problem of redistributing doctors. Under the law as proposed, "A doctor newly coming along would apply to the local Executive Council for permission to practise in a particular area. His application would then be referred to the Medical Practices Committee. The Medical Practices Committee, which is mainly a professional body, would have before it the question of whether there were sufficient general practitioners in that area. If there were enough, the committee would refuse to permit the appointment. No one can really argue that this is direction, because no profession should be allowed to enter the public service in a place where it is not needed. By that method of negative control over a number of years, we hope to bring about over the country a positive redistribution of the general practitioner service."[88]

This "proper distribution," said Bevan, "kills by itself the sale and purchase of practices . . . an evil in itself . . . tantamount to *the sale and purchase of patients*" because it is a transfer in which they have no voice, and thus one which, in passing the patient from the old doctor to the new, robs them of the free choice among doctors which the medical profession has been so insistent should be maintained at all costs. Although Bevan had "never admitted the legal claim" of doctors for compensation for the loss of this privilege, nevertheless, he also conceded that very great hardships would be inflicted upon doctors now practicing if there were no compensation.[89] Accordingly he accepted the

[87] "It was," Lafitte, *op. cit.*, points out, "the doctor's substitute for a pension," but as such was uncertain in amount—being high for some, and inadequate for others—and laid a burden on the incoming doctor which was frequently prohibitively high for young doctors not in possession of independent means.

[88] Bevan, *ibid.*, col. 54. It was hoped, however, that special financial inducements for going to the less preferred areas would eliminate almost entirely the need for compulsion. Supply and demand for medical practitioners would become similar to that regulating the distribution of school teachers.

[89] "Many of these doctors look forward to the value of their practices for their retirement. Many of them have had to borrow money to buy practices, and, therefore, it would, I think,

B.M.A.'s own figures, and a global sum of £66,000,000, based on actuarial estimates, was set up, out of which compensation for loss of the right to sell existing practices could be paid. Claims must be entered by the individual doctor, adjudicated in "consultation with the medical profession," and paid upon retirement or death. The sum arrived at will in the meantime be paid interest at the rate of 2¾ per cent per annum.

Upon passage of the National Health Service Act it became illegal for any doctor "entered on any list of medical practitioners undertaking to provide general medical services . . . to sell the goodwill or any part of the goodwill of the medical practice of that practitioner."[90] If, however, the doctor in question does not choose to have his name placed on the list, or, if once placed on it, he withdraws it in order to practice privately outside the area of the executive council on whose list his name was registered, then he may freely sell his practice as before.[91] Since doctors are not required by law so to enter their names, since once having entered they may withdraw at will, and since private practice for regular fees may be charged even by doctors who do enter the service whenever the patient is willing to pay fees for services which are in excess of those provided for under the act, the ministry felt that these compensation provisions were most liberal.

Those who entered the service were then subject to certain measures of direction. If they were already in the state-supported medical service, they might from the start practice where they already were. Those joining the service after vesting day could go anywhere they liked, save to those areas which were closed to additional doctors because they were deemed to be already adequately staffed. All doctors were subject to the rules and regulations laid down by the duly constituted authorities as provided under the act. Yet while the system of payments was subject to national regulation, general administration was set up on the principle of self-government by the medical profession.

According to provisional estimates, certain doctors engaged in general medical practice would receive a fixed annual salary of £300; each would receive capitation fees averaging 15s. 2d. for every patient

---

be inhuman and certainly most unjust, if no compensation were paid for the value of the practices destroyed." *Ibid.* (The global sum might be decreased if less than a minimum number of doctors [17,900] signed up for the service; a contingency which did not arise.) The sale of dental practices was still permissible under the act, though this does not appear to be of much importance in the dental profession.

[90] *Act*, Sect. 35 (1).
[91] *Ibid.*

on his list.[92] Some might be guaranteed certain additional income consisting mainly of special annual "inducement payments . . . to encourage doctors to practise in areas which are sparsely populated or otherwise unattractive; supervision fees for the training of assistants; payments in respect of the provision of drugs and appliances."[93] To finance these payments, a central fund was to be established, calculated at a rate "equal to a capitation fee of 18s. a head of 95 per cent of the population," producing an estimated total of £40,826,250. On the assumption that the minimum number of doctors would sign up for the service (17,900—by the middle of 1949 about 19,900 were in), this sum would then be divided as follows: £1,000,000 for mileage payments, £5,370,000 for fixed annual payments (£300 each), and capitation fees estimated roughly at 15s. 2d. per patient.

The ordinary medical practitioner's gross income was then estimated to run as follows (exclusive of receipts from private practice and obstetric service, but inclusive of the £300 fixed sum): "1,000 public patients, £1,058; 2,000 patients, £1,816; 3,000 patients, £2,574 and 4,000 patients, £3,332." Extra income, to be paid out of a "fund exceeding £400,000 a year will be available for discretionary payments when there is a call to practise in difficult and unpopular areas."[94] These rates have subsequently been revised so that gross income minus expenses—estimated to run 40 per cent of gross for a doctor having 2,000 patients, and to decline to 33⅓ per cent of gross for a doctor having 4,000 patients—would leave a net income rising as follows: 2,000 patients, £1,090; 2,500 patients, £1,317; 3,000 patients, £1,606; 3,500 patients, £1,920; and 4,000 patients, £2,222.[95]

Somewhat different schedules have been worked out for dentists and various classes of specialists. Dentists were initially paid so well that a special investigation in early 1949, based on "an analysis of the earnings of 5,078 dentists from October 1948, to March 1949" showed "that 1,066 were earning at the rate of over £6,000 gross a year, and of these 333 were exceeding £8,400 gross."[96] After reducing compensation "to about 20 per cent. of the gross fees" it was estimated that they

---

[92] Made up of payments for regular patients on his lists, treatment of persons temporarily resident in his area and not on his list, treatment of emergency cases, services of a second doctor to administer an anaesthetic, and (in certain areas) "in respect of mileage." *Remuneration of General Practitioners*, Ministry of Health Regulation (April, 1948).

[93] *Ibid.*

[94] *Home Affairs Survey*, Dec. 30, 1947, p. 30.

[95] *Home Affairs Survey*, Aug. 24, 1948, p. 21.

[96] "In order to obtain a gross income of £4,800 the dentist has to spend at least 55 per cent. of the fees he earns on materials, wages, etc." Letter by C. H. Housden to the *Times*, Feb. 26, 1949.

would "produce for the fully employed, experienced, single-handed dentists a net annual income of £1,778."[97]

Medical specialists came off even better. Following the report of the Spens committee,[98] the Ministry made what was almost universally acclaimed as an extremely generous offer. While "specialists under thirty-five before the war earned an average £1,202," under the offer "they are virtually guaranteed net incomes from all sources of about £2,000 a year at the age of thirty-two, rising to £3,000 a year at forty; and a third of all specialists are promised considerably more." These last may expect income from "distinction awards" made by "a committee of eminent medical men, which will add £500 to the annual salary of one specialist in five, £1,500 to the salary of one in ten, and £2,500 to that of four in every hundred." Furthermore, "in addition to secure salaries and a system of pensions which adds 8 per cent. to their real value, the new service offers specialists paid holidays, payment of their most important expenses, continuance of salary during periods of ill-health, and paid leave for study and other activities necessary to professional efficiency."[99] So favorable, in fact, have been the conditions offered to specialists that recruitment of general practitioners may be seriously endangered.

Administration of national health service relating to medical practitioners comes under the Medical Practices Committee and the Tribunal at the national level, and under executive councils at the local level. These are to be manned almost wholly from the medical profession, and are referred to as medical self-governing bodies. Under the law, "the Medical Practices Committee shall consist of a chairman, who shall be a medical practitioner, and eight other members of whom six shall be medical practitioners. Of the said six medical practitioners, at least five shall be persons actively engaged in medical practice."[100] This body has complete control over all applications of doctors to work with the national service, and their allocation to a given area. The Tribunal "deals with complaints about doctors, dentists, pharmacists, oculists and opticians," and is composed of a "practising barrister or solicitor of not less than ten years' standing appointed by the Lord Chancellor," and two other members, one of whom is a representative of the execu-

---

[97] Announcement of the Minister of Health, Aneurin Bevan, as reported in the *Times*, May 20, 1949.

[98] *Report of the Committee on Remuneration of Consultants and Specialists* [Spens Committee], Cmd. 7420 (London, 1948).

[99] "Medical Salaries," editorial, *Times*, March 17, 1949.

[100] *Act*, Sixth Schedule, p. 72.

tive councils, and one of whom is drawn from a panel representative of the various branches of the medical profession.[101]

This principle of self-government[102] is extended to the local executive councils, for which there is to be one for each of the local health areas. These councils, which are also to be bodies "corporate with perpetual succession and a common seal and with power to hold land without licence in mortmain," are to be made up of "a Chairman appointed by the minister and twenty four other members." Of the latter, eight are to be appointed by the local health authority for the area of the executive council, four by the Minister, seven by the local health committee, three by the local dental committee, and two by the local pharmaceutical committee.[103] It is the duty of these self-governing councils in each local area "to make . . . arrangements with medical practitioners for the provision by them as from the appointed day, whether at a health centre or otherwise, of personal medical services for all persons in the area who wish to take advantage of the arrangements, and the services" provided under the act.[104] They have, in other words, general administrative authority over local medical, dental, and allied practitioners in the local area.

Francois Lafitte, an eminent British health authority, has summarized the activities of these executive councils as follows:

The executive council is fundamentally a *joint committee* of the local health authority and the local doctors, dentists, etc., to which are added a few "independent" local citizens chosen by the Minister, and usually comprising people prominent in welfare organisations. They do *not* have complete authority over the local professional men. They do not employ them and cannot order them about. The contracts of the professional men (conditions of service, duties, code of conduct, etc.) are uniform in all areas and determined centrally. Executive councils have very limited powers to add special conditions to those contracts (e.g. requiring an elderly doctor not to have more than, say, 1500 patients, or allowing him a basic salary if he can prove financial need) ; their main duty is to make sure the doctor carries out his contract, to sit on disputes between doctor and patient, to arrange schemes of mutual aid and proper distribution of

[101] *Ibid.*, Seventh Schedule, pp. 72–73.

[102] Referring to the Medical Practices Committee, the Parliamentary Secretary comments, "That is called direction. What then, in the name of conscience, would be the definition of professional self-government? Where, may I ask, is there any other service paid out of local funds or out of national funds where anything approaching that amount of self-government exists?" *Hansard,* Vol. 422, col. 212.

[103] *Act*, Fifth Schedule, pp. 71–72. These local committees are to be representative of the respective professions in the local area, and of lay interests—mostly drawn from the local health authority. *Act*, Sect. 32 (1).

[104] *Ibid.*, Sect. 33. A British Medical Guide has been organized by the B.M.A. to protect interests of doctors in negotiations with the government over their matters, and to serve as a "collective bargaining" agency on terms and conditions. *Times*, March 31, 1949.

doctors, to decide whether more or fewer doctors are needed, to advertise vacancies and select candidates (subject to final decision by the central Medical Practices Committee), and to draw up plans for health centres (which cannot however be imposed by them, since statutorily local authorities are responsible for the plans).

Professional self-government is much more developed in the local medical, dental, ophthalmic etc. committees—the representative bodies of the local professional men—which work with the executive councils. These are recognised by statute and are given important duties. On many issues executive councils cannot act without consulting them (though not bound to accept their views) ; and disputes not involving patients—e.g. one doctor's complaint about another's behavior, or that of a Ministry inspector against a doctor or a chemist—must in the first instance go before the professional committee, with appeals to the Tribunal or the Minister.

All these procedures are adapted, with very little change (except that functions have been extended) from the National Health Insurance scheme, where they have been tested for a generation. The principal novelty lies in the close link of the executive council with the local health authority—in NHI insurance agencies predominated, and the professional element was smaller. Executive councils are not practitioners' councils.[105]

What did the doctors and the Opposition have to say to all this? Lord Moran seems to have summarized criticism quite adequately when he commented that it had been throughout the debates "tethered to the earth" and had "never become airborne"; on the contrary, it had "been totally lacking in idealism."[106] It had revolved entirely around practical issues, and when the government was prepared both to make wide concessions on self-government and to forego full-salaried service for the general practitioners, the Opposition disappeared from sight. The Council of the British Medical Association decided on May 5, just two months before the vesting day, "that in spite of the insufficiency of the safe guards to the profession's freedoms and the misgivings of a substantial section of the profession," nevertheless "to advise the profession to co-operate in the new service on the understanding that the Minister will continue negotiations on outstanding matters, including terms and conditions of service for consultants and specialists, general practitioners, public health officers and others."[107] On the eve of vesting day, Dr. Guy Dain, chairman of the council, felt very optimistic indeed. "The fight is over," he said, "the public, after July 5, will get the very best service that doctors can give. We shall make the public

[105] Francois Lafitte, op. cit.
[106] Hansard (Lords), Vol. 143, col. 44.
[107] Home Affairs Survey, May 11, 1948, p. 32.

medical service of this country the finest that is humanly possible. The negotiations with the Minister of Health and his department have resulted in the protection of the freedom of the public and the medical profession in most of the things which doctors have thought to be most important."[108]

THE LOCAL HEALTH AUTHORITIES AND THE HEALTH CENTERS

The "third instrument to which the health services are to be articulated is the health centres," the provision of which is "imposed as a duty on the local authorities."[109] Two important points were raised: Was this—Bevan had anticipated the criticism—to create an unworkable "trichotomy in the services," and were the local health authorities good units to which to delegate such a wide range of functions as the act devolved upon them?

The act, it will be noted, imposed upon the local authorities two sets of health services. They must "provide, equip, and maintain to the satisfaction of the Minister premises, which shall be called 'health centres' " where facilities will be available for general medical, dental, pharmaceutical, and specialist services performed by the respective professions, and they must manage a wide series of special health and welfare services. As chart 7 shows, the latter include a maternity and midwifery service (inclusive of ante- and postnatal clinics), child and school welfare and medical service, home-health and nursing service, local mental-health service, facilities for vaccination and immunization, and an ambulance service. In addition the local authorities are responsible for health education, and they may establish services for prevention of illness, care and aftercare, and domestic help for sick persons. For some of these services, particularly those which are voluntary, it may make additional charges.

Some of the centers will be large, some small, and services and facilities need not be identical in each. At "large centres . . . there will be dental clinics, maternity and child welfare services, and general practitioners' consultative facilities, and there will also be smaller surgeries where practitioners can see their patients."[110] What then is to be the relation between these centers and the regional hospital system? Or,

---

[108] *Home Affairs Survey*, June 22, 1948, p. 25. This included the further undertaking, on the suggestion of the Royal College of Physicians, that Bevan "make it statutorily clear that a whole-time service will not be brought in by regulation but would require further legislation to make it possible." *Home Affairs Survey*, April 4, 1948, p. 25.

[109] Bevan, in *Hansard*, Vol. 422, col. 58.

[110] *Ibid.*, the London County Council has decided, e.g., to set up 162 health centers under authority of the act. *Home Affairs Survey*, Feb. 22, 1949, p. 35.

again, between them and the executive councils similarly organized on a local basis? One critic asked "whether it is desirable to divide the health service into three watertight compartments by vertical lines: the hospital and consulting services in one division, the general practitioner services in another, and the local authority services in a third."[111] Maternity service, for example, will come partly under the regional hospitals, and hence under regional administration; partly under the local health authorities; and partly under the direction of persons responsible to the executive committees. "For maternity purposes the whole service should be continued by a single body. If the double control is to continue, as it appears from the Bill, it will lead to a disruption of what is beginning to be a logical conclusion, and I feel that some means must be found to co-ordinate and not separate the maternity services."[112]

Thus there appears to be some considerable possibility of duplication and overlapping of territories and functions, and of multiple jurisdictions within the given territories. But there is a much more serious point in the very nature of the local health authority itself. Under the law the local health authority shall be "for each county . . . the council of the country and for each county borough . . . the council of the county borough."[113] Each such local authority will establish a health committee, responsible to it alone, a majority of whose members must be drawn from its own ranks. Hence there may occur a complete lack of coördination between local authorities, which cannot be controlled by the ministry, except by power of the purse.[114]

But there is an additional difficulty. Speaking of the hospital services alone, the *British Medical Journal* observed that "One of the obstacles in the way of a rational hospital service that gives full scope for local responsibility and enthusiasm is the existing chaos of local authority government. Reform of the hospital service has had to precede reform of local government."[115] Although this is undoubtedly a handicap for

---

[111] Richard Law, *ibid.*, col. 68.

[112] Dr. Clitherow, *ibid.*, col. 95.

[113] *Act*, Sect. 19 (1). Joint boards may be established for two or more counties or boroughs or divisions of same. *Ibid.*, Fourth Schedule, pp. 69–70.

[114] On this administrative problem Francois Lafitte, *op. cit.*, comments that " 'trichotomy' after all is a great improvement on the preceding 'kilotomy.' We had well over 1,000 independent hospital authorities before; now we have less than 20. We had over 500 different local authorities actually providing various non-hospital services; now we have only 150, and never more than one in the same place. Moreover, much of what local authorities did before was optional; the new authorities all have a *duty* to provide services. Trichotomy creates problems of coordination; it has even split up a few services formerly unified (e.g., the Croydon maternity service) but those problems are far more manageable than those of 'kilotomy.' " See also appendix 5.

[115] May 11, 1946, p. 726.

the new hospital service, the establishment of the regional organization has largely by-passed the problem in this branch of the medical program. But for the practitioners' executive councils, and for the health centers, the program rests squarely on the foundation of the existing local authorities with the result that their future expansion must take place within the framework of this political structure. Yet, as will be pointed out later in connection with town and country planning, this same system of local authorities has been found wanting on many another score, and nothing is so certain as the probability that thoroughgoing reform of the county and borough system is one of the major tasks which lie ahead. Every new function assigned to these same authorities is bound further to complicate that reorganization if and when it takes place. Here again is a case where gradualism may have unwittingly multiplied the intricate involutions of the Gordian knot which the Government on its chosen approach must needs unravel, not cut through.

The provisions for the executive councils and the health centers did, however, give the *coup de grace* to those who feared that the National Health Act would unduly centralize authority, destroy local initiative, and take management out of the hands of the profession. The trichotomous arrangement may make administration difficult at many points of contact,[116] but it is difficult to find in the organization an effective justification of the fear of bureaucratization and regimentation.[117]

[116] Francois Lafitte, *op. cit.*, adds the following comment: "Generally I think the whole structure of the service could be made clearer if it were pointed out that they are divided into two groups: second line and first line. Second line services are regionally organised and wholly State-financed. First line services are locally organised in 145–150 county and county borough areas. The essential difference in content is that first line services centre essentially around the patient as a person with a family and home known personally to the doctor, welfare worker, etc.: they deal with him initially and try to serve him in his home or near to it. Second-line services are essentially specialist, involving complicated apparatus, buildings, etc., though they operate outposts (e.g. tuberculosis clinics) and sometimes come to the patient at home (visiting specialists). First-line services themselves are divided into two classes under separate, but connected, management: those directly controlled by local authorities, the cost of which is half rates and half taxes; and those controlled by joint professional-local authority committees (the mixed executive councils), comprising services that never were part of local government, but have been taken over and extended from NHI and are wholly State-financed. The two branches of the first line service have a common interest in the development of "health centres" in the management of which they will be jointly involved. These health centres will ultimately become the common focus of *all* the first-line services, merging the doctor's private office with the clinics, midwifes' offices etc. of the local authority. They will be the counterpart of the hospital as the focus and base for team work in the second line service; on the development of focal institutions for the first-line service depends the future pattern of British medicine. Without it general practitioners, dentists, home nurses, health visitors, midwives will continue to work in isolation, even jealousy. If health centre practice is developed, it will certainly lead in the end to unified management of *all* first line services, probably by a system of reformed local authorities with added professional elements of some kind."

[117] This includes the fear also of government "sanctions." Those who worry about these, the *Lancet* (a British medical journal) warns, "will do well to remember that any Act which

AUXILIARY AND SUPPLEMENTARY SERVICES

A Ministry of Health announcement addressed to the general public states, "Your doctor will give you a prescription for any medicines and drugs you need. You can get these free from any chemist who takes part in the Scheme. In some country areas the doctor himself may dispense medicines. The same is true of all necessary appliances. Some of them will be obtainable through hospitals; some your doctor can prescribe for you. There will be no charge, unless careless breakage causes earlier replacement than usual . . . All necessary fillings and dentures will be supplied without fee . . . If you need glasses, these will be provided without charge . . . you will get . . . if necessary, a new hearing aid invented by a special committee of the Medical Research Council . . . They will be supplied free, when ready, together with a reasonable allowance of maintenance batteries."[118]

Thus all drugs, equipment, and special mechanical aids required for therapeutic purposes will be supplied along with the medical service. Only special services, or "specially expensive types" of equipment—spectacles, dentures, etc.—which are not medically necessary (if necessary they are "free") will involve extra charges. Home services for virtually all phases and aspects of the health program may be supplied at need, though special attention is paid to nursing mothers, children under five, and illnesses which it seems more advisable to handle in the home than in the clinics or the hospitals.

As mentioned earlier, there are several health services which have not been brought under the control of the Ministry of Health through the new act. For example, the Ministry of Fuel and Power is responsible for the health services in mining, the "Ministry of Pensions for the care of those injured in war (only to a limited extent, e.g., limb-fitting), the Ministry of Transport for the safety and health of seamen and other workers . . ."[119] The Ministry of Education is responsible for the school feeding program, the school medical service, and for special

---

sets out to assume a service to the people must contain some sanction for governmental use if unforeseen circumstances should threaten a breakdown of the Service. Such a sanction was written into the National Health Insurance Act [1911]: It gave the Minister power to suspend N. H. I. regulation in a particular area, and initiate there any form of service (not excluding a whole-time salaried service) that he thought appropriate. Yet during the last thirty years this power has only once been used, and the profession has hardly been aware of its existence." There is no reason for supposing that instrumentation of this bill will involve "unjust use" of similar powers. Nov. 16, 1946, p. 720.

[118] *The New National Health Service* ("throwaway," undated).
[119] *Health and Social Welfare*, p. 95.

schools for mentally defective, maladjusted, and physically handicapped children. The Ministry of Labour, with the exceptions of mining and transport, is responsible for industrial health, industrial accident, industrial disease, and industrial rehabilitation services. Nearly all of the other ministries exercise jurisdiction over some special medical services.

In all of these cases it is anticipated that close liaison will be maintained between these other ministries and the Ministry of Health. The same holds for all the social services, governmental and private. The former range from social insurance to town and country planning, and the latter from voluntary youth organizations to the Marriage Guidance Council. Directly related to the medical program is the work of such voluntary associations as the National Council of Associated Children's Homes, the National Council for Maternity and Child Welfare, the Central Council for the Care of Cripples, and the National Council for Mental Health.[120] In addition, there are many special educational and research agencies whose work has a direct bearing upon the problems and activities of the Ministry of Health. Especially significant is the Medical Research Council, established in 1920 and directly subject to the general direction of the Privy Council. Operating with a fund of about £380,000 (1947) subscribed by the government, and supplemented from numerous private endowments—such as those from the Nuffield and Rockefeller foundations—its work is carried on partly in central laboratories located in London (National Institute for Medical Research, Hampstead and Mill Hill), and partly in hospitals, clinics, universities, and other medical and biological research institutions scattered over the country.[121]

Just how all these various agencies—voluntary and public; national and local; therapeutic, preventative, environmental, and research—will be knit in with, and related to the work of the national health service it is too early to say. It seems probable that experience will reveal a great deal of duplication and overlapping at points, and if so it will take considerable time and experiment to smooth them out. Thus far these activities, closely related to the new health service though they are, do not seem greatly to have been remodeled or seriously reshaped. Which

---

[120] An excellent and very compact summary of the work and organizational liaisons of those associations is given in Central Office of Information, Reference Division, *Social Services in Britain*, No. R. 1333 (1947).

[121] A quite complete catalog of the various societies, research foundations, institutes, and other bodies interested in medical and health research will be found in *Health and Social Welfare*.

would not matter much, if there is something by way of a plan for effecting interdepartmental, interfunctional, and interagency coördination. Whether there is such a plan, nobody can say—either on the evidence available to the general public, or available directly upon inquiry from the Ministry of Health itself.

THE HOUSING PROGRAM OF THE MINISTRY OF HEALTH

Two of the more important environmental services vitally affecting the national health service fall directly under the jurisdiction of the Ministry of Health: housing and water. The latter includes "the central administration of water supply, sewerage and prevention of river pollution."[122] Here again the Ministry of Health works almost wholly through local authorities—county, borough, and municipal. Projects developed by these bodies are submitted to the Ministry of Health, which is responsible for coördinating the local planning schemes. If they are approved, then they may be financed in whole or in part from loans advanced through the instrumentality of the Ministry of Health. Increasingly, the exercise of this function has brought the ministry up against the fact that the local authority is a poor basis for such planning. For example, "So far as river pollution is concerned, the view is now held that there can be no substantial improvement until control is vested in a comprehensive authority which will be responsible for the whole of a catchment area or groups of catchment areas" organized on a drainage basin basis.[123] Many other interests are involved: agriculture, town and country planning, hydroelectric power generation (Scotland and Wales), industrial relocation and development, etc. A national water plan, in short, is called for which would lift this whole problem largely, if not wholly, out of the jurisdiction of local authorities. Presumably it is the function of the Central Water Advisory Committee—broadly representative of "all water interests"—to perfect such a plan some time in the near future. None exists as yet.

Much the same relationship between local authorities and the Ministry of Health exists for housing. Although housing control is under its jurisdiction, it operates primarily as a counseling, promoting, checking, and coördinating agency for the local authorities. The latter have had power to build ever since 1890; between that time and 1939 local

---

[122] Ministry of Health, *The Work of the Ministry of Health.* [Booklet for new staff members.] (London, n.d.), p. 42. See also the *Housing (Financial and Miscellaneous Provisions) Act,* 1946, 9 & 10, Geo. 6, Chap. 48, and *The New Housing Bill* (HMSO, 1949), summarized in *Home Affairs Survey,* March 8, 1949

[123] *Ibid.,* p. 43.

authorities built roughly a quarter of all the houses constructed throughout England (approximately 4,000,000 houses). After the Second World War the housing shortage became so acute that the Ministry of Health entered much more actively into control of the whole field. It was estimated that at the end of the war the British housing shortage was, by minimum housing standards, approximately 2,000,000 houses. This was partly the product of total cessation of housing construction during the war (previously running around 350,000 houses per annum), and partly the result of war damage. It has been estimated that "out of about 13 million houses in the United Kingdom at the outbreak of war in 1939, nearly 4½ million, about one in three, were damaged or destroyed by enemy action. 210,000 houses were totally destroyed, and 250,000 were so badly damaged as to be uninhabitable, besides 4 million that received slight damage."[124]

The scale of this problem of housing shortage made necessary energetic nationwide action. But there were difficulties. Most important was the shortage of building materials, particularly timber, nearly all of which had to be imported from abroad in a period of acute shortage of foreign exchange. Other housing materials were also in relatively short supply—bricks (until 1948), cement, lime, plaster, plumbing and heating installations, etc. Furthermore, rentals and construction costs were high, and in most cases wholly out of the reach of those who needed new accommodations the most. The government moved into this situation with a program which called for building 750,000 houses by the end of 1948.

The initiative typically comes from the local authorities or from private contractors who must, in order to obtain the necessary building materials, first obtain the approval of the local authorities, who may then refer the matter for approval to their own local planning board or committees. Before materials can be allocated the plans must be submitted to the Ministry of Health. They must include the number and types of houses, and their location, estimated costs, materials specifications, and labor requirements. When the plans have been processed by the Housing Division of the Ministry of Health, the local authority is then able to issue the appropriate licenses, or contract with private building firms to do the necessary work, with the assurance that the required manpower and materials will be forthcoming. Approval likewise carries with it the right to obtain loans from the government, sub-

---

[124] *Home Affairs Survey*, April 13, 1948, p. 29.

sidy for construction costs if the housing is temporary—£220,000,000 having been allocated for this purpose by Parliament—and subsidies in lieu of higher rentals consequent upon higher construction costs. By the end of the year 1948, some 582,881 houses (425,720 permanent and 157,161 temporary) had been completed, and some 187,942 houses were under construction. Of the 425,720 permanent houses constructed, 306,470 had been erected by local authorities.[125]

Thus, although the goal set in the housing program has not yet been reached, the record of construction nevertheless constitutes a major achievement. Beside supervising construction, the ministry has made serious efforts to lower costs. Finding that in the distribution of building materials "monopoly, quasi-monopoly and restrictive practices have reigned almost unchallenged for many years" the Simon committee has recommended that the government take up, under the authority of the Monopoly (Inquiry and Control) Act,[126] an investigation of monopoly practices in this field, and that power be granted to:

a) Require the registration of all agreements relating to trade practices;

b) Declare individual agreements between manufacturers and merchants to be in restraint of trade and illegal;

c) Prohibit either a manufacturer or a merchant from exercising discrimination between customers in accepting orders; and

d) Control prices and margins.[127]

Because of high building costs, the acute housing shortage, and the belief that restrictive practices lead to high profits, there has been a recrudescence of a rank-and-file demand, frequently raised in Labour circles in the past, for nationalization of the housing industry. Thus far the Government has completely ignored this demand. A similar attitude has been taken to the closely allied demand for nationalization of land as a condition to carrying through a comprehensive low-cost housing program, and for holding down rentals.[128] In place of these proposals it has extended wartime rent controls, proposed antitrust investigations, and encouraged private employers to proceed with a variety of incentive systems to encourage higher labor productivity.[129]

---

[125] Private enterprise had constructed 80,209, housing associations 2,807, and government departments 3,228. Of the war-destroyed houses rebuilt, local authorities had rebuilt 8,187 and private enterprise 24,819. *Home Affairs Survey*, Feb. 8, 1949.

[126] For a discussion of this act see chapter xiii following.

[127] *Daily Telegraph*, April 28, 1948.

[128] See, e.g., the "National Executive Resolution on Housing and Town Planning," in the *Report of the Forty-third Annual Conference of the Labour Party* (London, 1944), p. 118.

[129] Paralleling the restrictive practices involved in the cartel-like contracts of the employer, or those of the trade unions, restriction on efficiency in the building trades in England is

Despite the achievments to date, it is hard to avoid the conclusion that postwar housing is still a rather chaotic affair. The initiative really comes from the local authorities, as indicated above, and these are—as will be pointed out in detail in the following chapter—bad physical planning units. The appropriate unit of reference should be, rather, the metropolitan area, the geographic region, or the "conurbation." It is impossible to separate housing construction from town and country planning, and these in turn from either population relocation or industrial location and development. So long as closely interrelated functions are divided among a number of largely independent and autonomous departments nationally, initiative and responsibility are split between local, regional, and national authorities, and all these bodies must operate largely without benefit of any visible plan to hold together—unify and coördinate—the interdependent web of activities on either a local or national basis, the result is likely to fall far short of both need and the possibilities of satisfying it for a long time to come.

The Social Welfare State and the Costs

The National Health Service Act has been held, by friends and foes alike, to epitomize the "social welfare" or "social service" society of the future which the Labour party is now in the process of rounding out. What will it cost? If the health data are any criterion, it will cost far more than anybody had anticipated. For England and Wales the original estimated cost of the health service was £152,000,000 a year. "Of this, £87 millions will be the cost of the hospital and specialist services; £45 millions the general practitioner, dental, pharmaceutical and eye services; and £8 millions the annual amount for compensation and superannuation for the doctors."[130] These figures proved far too low on virtually every item.

At the time the act went into effect, the total cost for the first nine months of the service was estimated at £150,000,000. Before the nine months were up (March 5, 1949) this figure had been upped to £208,-000,000, and was running at the rate of approximately £330,000,000

apparently a well-nigh universal phenomenon. A product of a variety of factors—past seasonal and chronic unemployment, fractioning of union jurisdictions among small craft unions which also means fractioning of work operations, etc.—the level of productivity is astonishingly low. The building industry absorbs over a half million men. Proper incentive systems, it is felt, might cut the labor requirements by from one-third to one-half. One example is cited where inauguration of a bonus system upped output 45 per cent according to the employers, and 70 per cent according to the union. *Economist*, June 19, 1948.

[130] Stephen Taylor, *op. cit.*, p. 16.

a year.[131] Some of the costs were transitional, and hence temporary.[132] But most of them were of an enduring character, and the prospect was that the second year would find the service running around £285,000,000 a year and that it would most probably increase further in the years to come. Hospital costs were up from a figure of £115,000,000 for the first nine months to £136,000,000; the dental service from £8,150,000 to £21,800,000; the practitioners' drug bill from £12,700,000 to £17,715,000, and "local authority services were costing two-and-a-half times as much as was expected." The most important reason for the increase seems to have been the "hidden demand," particularly for the care of eyes and teeth, the condition of which among Britons was much worse than had been estimated.[133]

If this is true, the enhanced costs of the service can hardly be attributed to anything more than a lack of foresight. What they indicate is that by and large the health service was needed more than even its most sympathetic proponents imagined and that costs may be expected to increase continually. On the basis of the record to date, there must be an enormous backlog of illness and impaired health which will require treatment before the service can catch up with emergency treatment and concentrate on sickness prevention on a big scale. And there are other reasons why costs are bound to increase. The average life span is increasing, and the amount of health care necessary will become greater as the percentage of older persons goes up. An increase in general practitioner's fees is due, and the increased demand for medical service means a corresponding expansion of investment in hospitals, clinics, research facilities, and all types of skills and staffs. Finally, it is almost inconceivable that the minimum standard itself will not be raised. With a few notable exceptions, regular hospital service in England, for example, cannot begin to compare with the average obtainable in the United States. On this score the general level of British service must be at least twenty-five years behind American practice. The general quality of dental work is equally behind the times. Although other services—such as those operating out of the health centers—cannot be

---

[131] The data are to some extent noncomparable because the latter estimates include Scotland.

[132] E.g., in the original estimates no allowance was made for the debts of the voluntary hospitals to be taken over. They were later estimated at £15,400,000, while £2,010,000 had to be added to the previous figure of £2,435,000 allowed for the debts of the municipal hospitals taken over. *Times*, Feb. 17, 1949.

[133] A supplementary estimate calling for Parliamentary approval of an additional £52,000,000 for various national health foundations spoke of "enormous misery already alleviated." *Home Affairs Survey*, Feb. 22, 1949.

duplicated in the United States, rates of pay and the general quality of care given in many areas are low by better British standards.

But when all this has been taken care of, there remains a second line of "poverty." Titmuss, in his *Birth, Poverty, and Wealth* found "that the excess of infant mortality among the poor over that of the wealthy was relatively higher in 1921–23 than in 1911, and relatively higher again in 1930–32 than in 1921–23. The causes of these higher class differentials in mortality are environmental diseases, bad housing, nutritional deficiencies, defective clothing, ignorance, inadequate medical care as shown in the differentials of higher infant mortality rising with the age of the infant."[134] Thus, despite notable gains, particularly between 1911 and 1939, the laboring class continued to fight what seemed always, speaking relatively, to be a losing battle; a battle which showed that even therapy is affected by adverse environmental factors, and that these cannot be separated from low standards of living. Poverty, Zweig has found, beggars all phases and aspects of living, including a general corruption of concepts of pleasure and preoccupations of leisure hours.

The influence, moreover, is not unidirectional only. Poverty impoverishes cultural standards, and degraded cultural standards tend to rob life of the very meaning and hope which are required to make possible improved incomes. Putting several confidential estimates together, it would seem possible that adequate incentives alone might increase the average per capita output of the British worker by a minimum of 25 to 35 per cent without any other change in investment, organization, or planning.[135] Low morale means a search for a quick relief from squalor, meanness, dullness, monotony, and boredom. In England this has led, among other things, to a vast increase in gambling. The total turnover in gambling during the postwar years has been estimated to be double that of the prewar period,[136] running in the neighborhood of £1,000,000,000 annually and involving the full-time employment of something like 230,000 people.[137] These data check fairly closely with

[134] Cited by Zweig, *Labour, Life and Poverty*, p. 117.

[135] Lafitte, *op. cit.*, believes this estimate is "overdrawn." Yet I must let it stand, for it is based on (a) very high and specialized (management engineering, etc.) British expert opinion; (b) observation on morale experiments in Britain, Germany, and the United States (e.g., the Hawthorne experiments) ; and (c) a background of some 15 years of specialized study of this badly neglected—especially in Britain—aspect of industrial civilization.

[136] Lafitte, *op. cit.*, comments that this is "a symptom not fundamentally of *poverty* but of new found money to spare and no idea how to spend it sensibly." But what does this mean if not impoverishment of values flowing from past impoverishment of life—which the "new found money" cannot materially relieve in face of the current austerity program?

[137] Cited in Churches' Committee on Gambling, *This Gambling* (London, n.d.). Of this total £450,000,000 was the turnover on horse racing, £400,000,000 to £450,000,000 on dog

the investigations in the London area made by Zweig, where he found that of the limited cross-section interviewed, one out of five workers bet regularly on football pools, and one out of three on dog races.[138]

Other pleasures which express to some extent a sense of mass frustration, lack of hope, and lack of interest tell a similar story. Smoking has increased the annual bill for tobacco since before the war by about 100 per cent; the total national expenditure on tobacco in 1944 was 10 per cent of the national income, or £506,000,000—double the annual health bill under the new act. The ratio of expenditure for "smokes"— expenditure tending to be fixed at relatively high levels regardless of income—rises rapidly as one goes down the income scale. The same is true of drinks. Regular drinkers who also smoke, Zweig estimates, spend approximately 50 per cent of their income in this way.[139] Where these expenditures run as high as this, "housekeeping money," which sets the standards of comfort for the entire family, is held down to levels which higher wages will not affect. It seems obvious that something must be done about "secondary poverty" as a condition to the elimination of "primary poverty," and the latter is the most important key to the health and welfare of the entire population.

It is against the background of facts such as these that the intent, purport, and possibilities of the national health program must be examined and evaluated. But they serve, at the same time, also to require painting the picture of the problem of social welfare in the "social service state" on a much larger canvas. If the impasto is the direct attack upon health and the allied social security and social welfare problems, the underpainting which gives tone and color to the whole is the complete physical reconstruction of the life of the people of England. The most important agency in this field is the Ministry of Town and Country Planning, to which it will now be necessary to turn.

---

racing, and £70,000,000 on football pools. "Gaming machines" (mostly American imported pinball and slot machines) accounted for £10,000,000.

[138] Zweig, op. cit., pp. 31, 40. "The average dividend is between £5 and £15 per 1s., which means that on an average about 100 to 300 lose while one wins." Ibid., p. 42.

[139] Ibid., p. 28. Lafitte, op. cit., comments: "Zweig is basically right, but his work is impressionistic and not amendable to statistical generalization. The passages cited overdo the gloom. The betting-smoking-drinking boom (now past its peak) is (among other things) a sympton of inflation, of greatly increased spending money in the pockets of aimless people unaccustomed to such prosperity." But Zweig's results are generally accepted by experts (such as Lafitte) as probably representative; the passages are cited for their bearing on the issue of "secondary proverty;" the data on the peak having been passed is statistically incomplete, and would appear to have occurred, if at all, by rigorous curtailment of certain imports (particularly cheaper tobaccos) and high prices (see the growing trade union complaints throughout 1948 and 1949 on the rising cost of living) ; and the end of Lafitte's last sentence does not require comment or elaboration—it states the whole case precisely!

CHAPTER X

Town and Country Planning

Labour believes in land nationalisation and will work towards it, but as a first step the State and local authorities must have wider and speedier powers to acquire land for public purposes wherever the public interest so requires.—*Let Us Face the Future.*

This Bill has been described as the most important for a century. I would not go as far as that, but I do say that it is the most comprehensive measure which has ever been placed before this House . . . The objects of town and country planning . . . primarily . . . are to secure a proper balance between the competing demands for land, so that all the land in the country is used in the best interests of the whole people.—Lewis Silkin, Minister of Town and Country Planning.

IN BRITAIN 50,000,000 people and the fourth largest industrial system in the world are crowded into an area somewhat smaller than the state of Oregon. In England alone—an area almost exactly the size of the state of New York—the population density is now well over 800 to the square mile, making it the highest in the world.[1] To feed, house, and employ such a huge and still-growing population in this tiny area, particularly in face of the politically irresistible demand for rising standards of mass consumption, requires ever more intensive use of soil resources, and ever more careful balancing of all the various competing demands of land. Thus, as the supply of land grows tighter in the "tight little isle," each piece of land which is not irrevocably committed to a specific use has become a battlefield in a continuous war among myriad forces, each seeking the land for its own use. So it happens that land planning is a "natural" for Britain, and it should occasion no surprise that no government or party has or ever has had a monopoly on the idea.

Against the background of the general shortage of land, the demand of each of the major alternative uses has, for one special reason or another, been growing more insistent, and each seems able to enlist much popular support. To illustrate, with respect to food and raw materials such events as the shrinkage of the Empire, the loss of over-

[1] The area of the United Kingdom—including England (50,328 sq. mi.), Scotland, Wales, Northern Ireland, the Channel Islands and the Isle of Man—is 94,279 sq. miles. Oregon has 96,981 sq. mi., and New York 49,576 sq. miles. In April, 1948, the estimated population of the United Kingdom passed 50,000,000 mark; the 1948 presidential election estimates gave Oregon a population of somewhat over 1,500,000, and New York around 14,500,000. The density of the population in England was computed on the basis employed in the *Report of the Royal Commission on the Distribution of the Industrial Population* [*Barlow Report*], Cmd. 6153. (1940), p. 13.

seas markets, the decline in overseas investment, the high and rising cost of overseas food imports, and the adverse trade balance conspire to favor cutting down the import of foodstuffs to the minimum, and by the same token to promote an expansion of the domestic agricultural acreage to the maximum. Like factors—intensified by the existence of a world-wide shortage of paper, pulp, timber, and other wood products, and the rising demand of the housing, furniture, publishing, plastics,

TABLE 25

ACRES OF AGRICULTURAL LAND USED FOR OTHER PURPOSES, 1927–28 TO 1938–39

| Year | Buildings and general constructional development | Sports grounds | Miscellaneous | | | Total |
			Aerodromes of Air Ministry	War office	Other or unexplained	
Annual average, 1927–28 to 1933–34........	42,000	10,000	600	200	700	53,500
1934–35..........	57,000	11,000	3,000	200	2,600	73,800
1935–36..........	55,000	13,000	10,000	1,500	......	79,500
1936–37..........	56,000	11,000	10,900	2,000	100	80,000
1937–38..........	56,000	14,000	12,200	4,700	700	87,600
1938–39..........	54,000	10,000	24,500	8,800	2,100	99,400
Total for 12 years..	572,000	129,000	64,800	18,600	10,400	794,800
Average per year..	47,650	10,750	5,400	1,550	850	66,200

SOURCE: *Country and Town: A Summary of the Scott and Uthwatt Reports* (London, Penguin, 1943), p. 35.

and similar wood-using industries—favor expansion to the maximum of domestic forest resources, and hence of acreage that can and may compete with grazing, agricultural, and other land uses. Similarly the demand for more coal at lower cost promotes resort to opencast (strip) mining at the price of temporary removal of land from agricultural use, and the demand for the restoration of land for the latter use compels opencast mining to restore land to agricultural usage with a corresponding increase in the costs of the coal.

Competing against these rising demands of the foodstuffs and raw materials industries for more of the fixed supply of rural land are all the demands for more space arising from the growth of urban communities. Table 25 shows for the last twelve prewar years the amount of agricultural land which has been lost in these various ways in England and Wales.

How serious a problem these encroachments on the countryside present may be grasped when it is realized that the total of nearly 800,000 acres shown by the table as lost to agriculture is more than 2 per cent of the land area of England and Wales available for all purposes (37,133,000 acres), and that these data mostly relate to the years of the depression when the amount of land taken up for the first two classifications was unusually low. Any attempt to make up for the depression and war-years neglect of such problems as slum clearance and those associated with relocation of population and industry—especially when coupled with the attempt to comply with the new standards of metropolitan, town, and country planning—can only mean an even greater urban demand for these limited acres for a good many years to come.

There are two further aspects to this urban encroachment on rural lands which combine to lend the problem of land planning in Britain a peculiar note of urgency. The first is that because of the location of the major and rapidly growing population centers[2] a large percentage of the land absorbed by the urban demand for space is likely to be good agricultural land. Before the war it was found that "approximately two-fifths of the total population dwell in the seven million-mark conurbations"[3] of London, Birmingham, Merseyside, Glasgow, Tyneside, West Yorks and Manchester, and that seven of the more densely populated areas, constituting only 27 per cent of the total area of Great Britain, "contained about 79 per cent of the insured population."[4] None

[2] It has been the contention of Town and Country Planning spokesmen (cf., e.g., letters to the *Times*, Feb. 2, April 11, and May 26, 1949, by F. J. Osborn, Chairman of Executive, Town and Country Planning Association) that the purpose of the new controls was largely to see that any needless diversion from agriculture of good farm land be eliminated, and it has been pointed out that even in good farm land areas it is frequently possible to locate large tracts on low quality hill, upland, and moor for building and similar purposes. But the tendency to take good farm land for these purposes is there nevertheless. A delegation from the Central Landowners' Association to the Ministry of Agriculture stated that "according to one estimate, 2,500,000 acres might pass out of agricultural use within the next 30 years if land were to be taken at the rate prevailing between the wars. This would be equivalent to 10 percent of the total grass and arable acreage of England and Wales." *Times*, Feb. 8, 1949. Again, Essex farmers complained that the contemplated construction of new reservoirs and "the creation of the new towns of Harlow and Basildon" would absorb 20,000 acres of good farm land. *Times*, Jan. 13, 1949.

[3] *Barlow Report*, p. 12. The term, "conurbation" apparently "owes its origin to Professor Patrick Geddes, who wrote many well-known works on Town Planning during the first quarter of the present century. He uses it, but without any precise definition, to indicate what he calls 'city-regions,' or 'town aggregates' such as Greater London, but his use of the term is a wide one; he would, for instance, include Liverpool and Manchester and the Lancashire millions generally in a single conurbation which he christens 'Lancaston.' " *Barlow Report*, p. 6.

[4] *Ibid.*, p. 24. The seven areas are given as (1) London and the Home Counties, (2) Lancashire, (3) West Riding, Notts, and Derby (4) Staffs, Warwick, Worcs, Leics, and Northhants, (5) Northumberland and Durham, (6) Mid-Scotland, and (7) Glamorgan and Monmouth.

of the conurbations, and only one of the specified areas (Glamorgan and Monmouth) are to be found outside areas of good agricultural land, and two of the major conurbations (Merseyside and London) are located in the heart of the best and most intensively cultivated land in Britain.[5]

Since "good quality land" in England and Wales is limited to some 16,500,000 acres, the swiftly expanding demands of the conurbations and specified areas create an urban demand for land where Britain can afford it the least. And a second factor multiplies this demand. This is the Socialist outlook on life, which, however loosely held or fuzzily visualized, pledges those who hold it to make a Herculean effort to raise mass standards of living to levels formerly enjoyed only by the middle and upper classes. Any plan for raising standards of living in Britain must call for an eventual complete rehousing of most of the labor and lower-income population, and this rehousing must be carried out with due provision made for adequate park, playground, garden, green and open spaces, and attractively planned shopping centers, social and recreational centers, etc. Such plans are necessarily based on the assumption of a heavy and expanding use of land adjoining the immediate area of the major existing population centers. If American experience offers any lead at all—and the English are as much addicted to crowds as are Americans—the complementary program of lengthened vacations with pay, particularly if accompanied by cheap and convenient transportation, is likely eventually to require additional and vast extension of recreational and vacation facilities at the seashore, in national parks, and for other distantly removed publicly managed amenities. To plan these things for the millions instead of the few thousands is to cause the Labour demand for land to expand geometrically. Socialism, that is to say, adds a peculiar note of space urgency.

The problem of war damage tends, at the same time, to demand effective action along these lines at an early date. Very nearly every major metropolitan center suffered some degree of war damage, and in a few places—such as London, Birmingham, Coventry, Sheffield, and Manchester—the damage was very heavy. Large sections of these great metropolitan centers must be rebuilt. Frequently, as in London and Birmingham, reconstruction affects large and densely populated work-

---

[5] See, e.g., the land classification map of the Ministry of Town and Country Planning (in collaboration with the Ministry of Agriculture) based upon "a special investigation of the Land Utilisation Survey of Britain." The outline plan for the development of West Midlands (Birmingham area) calls for extensive expansion of rural farm lands.

ing-class and slum areas. War damage has made it easier to carry through slum clearance on a comprehensive basis, but virtually all such replanning almost of necessity compels reconsideration of the related problems of population location, industrial dispersion, transport, and so on for the metropolitan area as a whole, and the relation, in turn, of the latter both to the region in which it is situated and to the nation as a whole. Thus the German bombers which sought to destroy Britain served to dramatize the need for replanning her entire national system of land use, and to galvanize her leaders into making positive and constructive effort on a scale which would have seemed impossible in the more limited perspectives of prewar days. War damage, in short, adds to space urgency an acutely sensitized note of time urgency.

There is a final, but ultimately still more important, reason why land planning in Britain should have moved into the very center of postwar problems. It lies in the dawning consciousness that for nearly every step taken to mobilize national effort to achieve full employment on an enduring basis there must be taken a similar step toward the creation of a physical plan which will tie the loose ends together and implement general directives. Without some type or other of physical planning on a national basis, there is no possibility of successful economic planning in pursuit of any objective—full employment, the closing of the import-export gap, rising standards of living, or anything else. However urgent the other reasons for land planning in postwar Britain may be, this close interconnection between economic planning and physical planning would itself have forced Labour—or any other Government—sooner or later to come forward with something like the Town and Country Planning Act of 1947.

The Background of Town and Country Planning

The act is quite obviously a transitional measure. On any other assumption it falls far short of either the plans which one might have expected the Labour party to introduce, or which would have been consistent with the general tenor of expert opinion as it existed in Britain on the eve of the cessation of hostilities. Under the act land planning is administratively almost wholly disassociated both from industrial development and from agricultural development. (There even exists a persistent tendency to argue that so to relate these plans involves no less than totalitarian redirection, which is both unnecessary and undesirable.) It is to consist primarily of machinery for relating the plans of metropolitan centers, towns, and local governments, and other piece-meal programs undertaken under various authorities, to regional and national plans. Without containing in itself anything even remotely approaching a national physical plan, it clearly encourages thinking along such lines, and thus offers another example of the peculiar evolutionary approach to major social problems which is so dearly beloved by the Fabian-minded Labour leaders—not to say of most Englishmen in general.

This gradualist approach of Labour is illustrated in the history of its interest in town and country planning. It is reflected in the changing agitation for such planning by Labour itself; in the anticipatory legislation which Labour supported even when it did not initiate it; and in the recommendations of the more important special commissions on which Labour had representatives, and which were established to deal with the separate problems which the Town and Country Planning Act later attempted to bring under a single roof.

Labour's interest in land reform before the Second World War had little or nothing to do with land planning; it was largely manifested in the demand for land nationalization as a measure to skim off the unearned increment of the landlord class. Thus "for a generation or more the problem of land values and 'unearned increment' has been the subject of acute political controversy. The old Liberal battle song was 'God gave the land to the people,' " and where Lloyd George left off in his famous drive for land taxation for the purpose of siphoning off unearned increment, Labour took up the championship of the long overdue reform.[6] Due acknowledgments have gratefully been tendered by Labour leaders to the influence of Henry George and the single-tax agitation in the shaping of their ideas on the problem of land values.[7] During Labour's second brief tenure of office in the early thirties it introduced a typical single-tax piece of legislation in the Finance Act of 1931, which "set up . . . machinery for taxing land values." Since "several years' preliminary valuation work was necessary before [the] tax could become effective . . . long before collecting tax the Tory Government . . . repealed it."[8]

---

[6] *Town and Country Planning*, Labour Discussion Series, no. 12 (London, n.d.), p. 1.

[7] "The existence of these problems has long been recognised and various proposals put forward for their solution. Writing in the latter half of the 19th Century, Henry George brought the problem into the political arena with his proposal for a single tax on land values." Lewis Silkin, Minister of Town and Country Planning, opening debate on the second reading of the Town and Country Planning Bill in the House of Commons, January 29, 1947. *Hansard*, Vol. 432, col. 952.

[8] *Loc. cit.*

The first strong case for land nationalization was made by the T.U.C. in 1882. Since no true "title ever existed" in land, it held "that the land ought to be nationalised and that the increment in the value of land should be applied to the national purpose of reducing taxation." It is idle, they said, to talk about land law reform, since "no reform will be complete short of nationalisation of the land."[9] A similar proposal was defeated the following year, and again in 1886. But in 1887 the position was reaffirmed, and from that time on land nationalization and the total liquidation of landlordism became fixed T.U.C. policy.

The Labour party took up the theme at its first annual conference in 1901, varying the argument by "recognising that the inevitable tendency of privately-owned capital is towards combinations in monopolies known as Trusts," and stating its position by declaring "that the final object of all democratic effort must be to transfer all such private monopolies to public control as steps toward the creation of an Industrial Commonwealth founded upon the common ownership of land and capital and the substitution of cooperative production for use in place of the present method of competitive production for profit."[10] There was no departure from this position until after the disastrous failure of the second Labour government in 1931. By the latter thirties, however, the combination of continued world depression, rising interest in the success of the Soviet five-year plans, and the prospects of another possible world war combined to shift the grounds of action. Reconstruction was the order of the day, and the key to reconstruction was planning. And "national planning requires," they resolved, "that the use of land shall be controlled in the public interest. Without such control it is impossible to use the limited area of this country to the best advantage whether for agriculture, industry, or other purposes." Hence, "the land should belong to the people" as a condition to the necessary planning.[11]

This shift in Labour opinion from nationalization of land to effect income redistribution, to public ownership as a condition to land planning on a national basis, is also reflected in the long history of Parliamentary legislation having to do with one or another aspect of the problem. Some of this legislation, relating to such problems as health,

[9] *Report of the Fifteenth Annual Trades Union Congress* (Manchester, 1882), pp. 35–36.
[10] *Report of the First Annual Conference of the Labour Representation Committee* (Manchester, 1901), p. 20. The most elaborate and carefully reasoned statement of this version of British Labour's land nationalization ideas is to be found in appendix xii, *Report of the Twenty-Sixth Annual Conference of the Labour Party* (Margate, 1926), p. 336 *et. seq.*
[11] *Report of the Thirty-Seventh Annual Conference of the Labour Party* (Bournemouth, 1937), p. 277.

education, relief, the poor laws, slum clearance, and sanitation reach far back into the nineteenth century. But probably the first attempt to deal with the problem of land planning on a national basis was contained in the Housing and Town-Planning Act of 1909. Thereafter, there was a spate of remedial legislation—very important as background detail (especially the act of 1932) for the 1947 act, but too voluminous for summary here—which reflected the belief that each of the several problems affecting the use of land could be handled separately as they arose.[12] This period came to a close with the Second World War and the establishment of a series of special investigating committees for the purpose of reconsidering the national problem of postwar land planning, and of suggesting appropriate legislation for carrying their recommendations into effect.

The first and most important of these, the Barlow committee, was actually constituted in 1937. Before it could complete its report the outbreak of the war had served to reorient its investigations and findings in terms of the longer and larger perspectives of the postwar years. It was charged "to inquire into the causes which have influenced the present geographical distribution of the industrial population of Great Britain and the probable direction of any change in that distribution in the future; to consider what social, economic or strategical disadvantages arise from the concentration of industries or of the industrial population in large towns or in particular areas of the country; and to report what remedial measure if any should be taken in the national interest."[13] It found that the need for remedial action in terms of all three of the leading criteria which it had examined at length, "social, economic and strategical," was urgent, but capable of solution only if viewed in terms of a problem in planning which was coextensive with all the various facets of community life and industrial occupa-

[12] So far as town planning alone is concerned (for agriculture and industry see chapter xi and chapter xiii respectively) the more important measures were: The Housing and Town Planning etc. Act of 1919, making it obligatory for every borough or urban district of 20,000 population or over "to prepare and submit to the Local Government Board within three years a Town Planning Scheme in respect of all lands within the Borough or Urban District in respect of which a Town Planning Scheme may be made under the 1909 Act"; the Housing etc. Act of 1923 which extended this period to six years, and gave certain planning authority to the Ministry of Health; the Town Planning Act, 1925, which, with its Scotch counterpart, was the first act "to deal with planning as a separate question, consolidated the former planning enactments without introducing any remarkable new features"; and the Town and Country Planning Act, 1932, which repealed all former town planning legislation, and codified the law by clarifying the powers of local authorities, and granting general national supervisory powers to the Minister of Health. Central Office of Information, Reference Division, *Town and Country Planning in Britain*, no. R. 1483 (London, 1947), pp. 7–12.

[13] *Barlow Report*, p. vii.

tions; only when carried out on a national basis as a series of coördinative functions which would permit local initiative under central guidance; and only if for this purpose there was established by statute "a National Authority," taking "the form of a Board" and known as the "National Industrial Board," for "the purpose of making research into, advising upon, and regulating the location of industry."[14]

Appearances to the contrary, the National Industrial Board was not to serve as a positive planning body. It was to become an information-gathering, advice-giving, and suggestion-making agency to which were given some tentative and permissive powers of general regulation so far as London and the Home Counties (Beds, Bucks, Essex, Herts, Kent, Middlesex, and Surrey) were concerned. It was to collect and coördinate information relating to the location of industry and its bearing upon natural resources, to put out publicity and make annual reports, to give "advice to Government, local authorities and industrialists as to problems of industrial location" and to make on this subject a special report to the Board of Trade which would assist the latter to use its influence in carrying out the general directives of the report. With respect to London and the Home Counties, the board was to have power to pass upon private and public authority developments within these areas, but not power to take the initiative in shaping up positive plans for the areas in whole or in part.

The great merit of the Barlow report was that it showed beyond peradventure of a doubt that land planning in Britain must be carried out on a national footing, and under some degree of top ministerial direction. On the strength of its recommendations two additional committees were appointed to deal with special problems not fully covered in this first general analysis. The first of these, the Scott committee,[15] was set up in October, 1941 "to consider the conditions which should govern building and other constructional development in country areas consistently with the maintenance of agriculture, and in particular the factors affecting the location of industry, having regard to economic operation, part-time and seasonal employment, the well-being of rural communities and the preservation of rural amenities." In general the effect of its report was to bear out the findings of the Barlow committee, laying special emphasis upon the problem of the relationship between the location of industry in rural areas and the preservation of agricul-

---

[14] *Ibid.*, pp. 204–205.

[15] The full title of the committee's final report reads: *Report of the Committee of Land Utilisation in Rural Areas*, Cmd. 6378 (London, 1942).

ture, scenic attractions, and rural amenities. Like its predecessor, the Scott report favored the establishment of a national land planning body, in this case to be known as the Central Planning Commission, under the personal direction of a Minister of National Planning who would be responsible to a standing committee of all the ministers whose departments would be directly concerned in the activities of the commission.

The second of these two follow-up surveys was that of the Expert Committee on Compensation and Betterment, commonly referred to as the Uthwatt committee, which was appointed January, 1941, and made its final report in September, 1942. Congruent with its terms of reference,[16] the committee found a general failure over "the twenty years to adapt planning policy and methods to the needs of the situation" and hence "that the only way out of the confusion produced by the existing practice of compensation and betterment was to bring all land affected by planning resolutions into a single ownership where shifts of land value brought about by such planning could take place without the disturbances that inevitably took place where land was held in multiple ownership."[17] To this end the committee recommended "the immediate vesting in the State of the rights of development in all land lying out-side built-up areas (subject to certain exceptions) on payment of fair compensation, such vesting to be secured by the imposition of a prohibition against development otherwise than with the consent of the State accompanied by the grant of compulsory powers of acquiring the land itself when wanted for public purposes or approved private development."[18]

Administration of all lands and properties thus acquired or controlled was to be placed in the hands of a central planning authority on the double assumption that "national planning is intended to be a reality and a permanent feature of the administration of the internal affairs of this country,"[19] and "that 'planning' has a meaning not at-

---

[16] "To make an objective analysis of the subject of the payment of compensation and recovery of betterment in respect of public control of the use of land; to advise, as a matter of urgency, what steps should be taken now or before the end of the war to prevent the work of reconstruction thereafter being prejudiced. In this connection the Committee are asked to consider (a) possible means of stabilising the value of land required for development or redevelopment, and (b) any extension or modification of powers to enable such land to be acquired by the public on an equitable basis; to examine the merits and demerits of the methods considered; and to advise what alterations of the existing law would be necessary to enable them to be adopted." *Report of the Expert Committee on Compensation and Betterment*, Cmd. 6386 (London, 1942), p. ii [*Uthwatt Report.*]

[17] *Town and Country Planning in Britain*, p. 14.

[18] *Uthwatt Report*, p. 157.

[19] *Ibid.*, p. 11.

tached to it in any legislation nor, until recently, in the minds of the public" such that "National Development is added to planning." This latter expression means simply that "it is essential that there should exist means by which the requirements of agriculture, transport, public services and defence, as well as housing, industrial location, town siting and other matters can be given proper weight and considered as a whole." The necessary "coordination at the centre as respects the various Government Departments interested in particular aspects of planning" can be effected by setting up a "Minister for National Development" who would be freed of departmental cares the better to seek the appropriate technical counsel and to formulate the requisite schemes. The "broad principles of policy would . . . be settled by the Cabinet after consideration by a Committee of Ministers presided over by the Minister for National Development" while "the actual execution of the schemes and formulation of detailed plans would fall to the Government Department concerned."[20]

Omitting further details—it will be necessary to return to some of them later—the three reports agreed on a number of points. The need for action was urgent. The time for half measures was long since past. Planning was the order of the day. The new complication of war damage served only to underscore the case. The state would have to acquire control over all land development. To plan for the multiplicity of needs involved in each separate case and with respect to the entire range of interests affected, and in order to make the very best use of each area and region, required national action on such a scale that it could be effected only at the Cabinet level, where the power existed to coördinate the activities of all ministries concerned with physical planning.

There followed a second flood of town and country planning legislation. The Ministry of Town and Country Planning Act of February, 1943, established a new ministry and transferred to it the central land planning powers of the Ministry of Works and Buildings with a view to "ensuring consistency and continuity in the framing and execution of a national policy with respect to the use of land." The Town and Country Planning (Interim Development) Act of July, 1943, was designed to forestall land speculation which would render postwar plans difficult to carry through, and the white paper, *Control of Land Use* (Cmd. 6537, June, 1944), sought to define the aims of future planning policy. The Town and Country Planning Act of November, 1944, sought

[20] *Ibid.*, pp. 156–157.

to put land planning on a constructive instead of restrictive basis, largely through measures designed to strengthen the hands of local planning authorities, and to expedite their acquisition of land needed for local planning purposes. All such plans were placed under the general permissive authority of the new Ministry of Town and Country Planning.

To such measures as these were added a series of supplementary legislative acts designed to deal with related aspects of physical planning.[21] In combination with the other town and country planning acts, white papers, and findings of special investigation committees, these measures demonstrated clearly the need for some means of clarifying, unifying, and simplifying overlapping national and local authorities and jurisdictions as they related to physical planning, and for bringing the whole of the previous legislation and further proposals in this field, made by other Governments and parties, into more direct conformity with the social outlook of the new Labour government. This involved astonishingly few changes of a uniquely "Socialist" character. Such as they were, it was these changes which the Town and Country Planning Act of 1947 was, in part, designed to effect.

THE TOWN AND COUNTRY PLANNING ACT OF 1947

The act does not nationalize the land.[22] In a rather limited sense it does nationalize development value by "restricting the owners' interest in his land to the enjoyment of its existing use . . . and transferring to the State the exclusive right to derive financial benefit from the development of land or from changes in its use."[23] Thus the Labour government accepted as a basis of its "most comprehensive measure" the Uthwatt report, apparently saying to itself as it did so, in the words employed

[21] Two of these, the requisitioned Land and War Works Act of June, 1945, and the Acquisition of Land (Authorisation Procedure) Act of April, 1946, were interim measures having to do with transition from war to peace. The other two are the Distribution of Industries Act of June, 1945, and the Trunk Roads Act of March, 1946. The former will be dealt with more fully in chapter xiii.

[22] The full title reads: "An Act to make fresh provision for planning the development and use of land, for the grant of permission to develop land and for other powers of control over the use of land; to confer on public authorities additional powers in respect of the acquisition and development of land for planning and other purposes, and to amend the law relating to compensation in respect of the compulsory acquisition of land; to provide for payments out of central funds in respect of depreciation occasioned by planning restrictions; to secure the recovery for the benefit of the community of development charges in respect of certain new development; to provide for the payment of grants out of central funds in respect of expenses of local authorities in connection with the matters aforesaid; and for purposes connected with the matters aforesaid." 10 & 11 Geo. 1, Chap. 51 (August 6, 1947).

[23] *Economist*, June 19, 1948, p. 1005.

by a critic from the Liberal benches, "We will not take the inevitable decision; what we will do is suggest that there is a thing called the development value."[24] And that value—however it may be determined—may well prove so difficult to appraise that it will effectively nullify much, if not eventually all, of the main purpose of the act.

Why did the Labour party seek this way out? "Nationalisation is the final and best solution," said Silkin, speaking of the predecessor Acquisition of Land Act of April, 1946,[25] and clearly the principal reason for the "failure of town planning hitherto can be attributed to . . . the obligation on local planning authorities to pay compensation to an owner of land who in the public interest, is refused permission to develop."[26] In his review of previous legislation designed to promote town and country planning the Minister found compensation the perpetual *bête noire*. Elaborate and time-consuming efforts were required to establish "increment value" as was necessary under the laws of 1909 and 1931. The provisions regarding compensation in the 1932 act were such as to stultify the efforts of local governments to go ahead with significant betterment programs.[27] Silkin's predecessor in the Ministry of Town and Country Planning, W. S. Morrison, had found that "compensation and betterment" played a central role in the whole problem, and such also was the burden of the Uthwatt report and the Coalition white paper on the control of land use.[28] Surely compensation was the stumbling block and to Labour's spokesmen land nationalization was both the best method of hurdling it and the most acceptable to the Labour party's followers.

Nevertheless, in place of the needed final solution, the drafters of Town and Country Planning Act of 1947 sought to provide a means of handling this problem which they believed would facilitate physical planning without being, at the same time, inconsistent with the longer objective. The act, accordingly, is dominated by transitional devices centered around the related problems of compensation and development which its proponents saw throughout as merely two sides of a common coin. While there is no clean-cut division, broadly speaking, only thirty-six out of one hundred and twenty sections in the act are concerned even in part with problems of administration and actual

[24] Clement Davies, in *Hansard*, Vol. 432, col. 1004.
[25] *Hansard*, Vol. 418, col. 1203.
[26] *Hansard*, Vol. 432, col. 950.
[27] *Ibid.*, col. 952.
[28] *Ibid.*, cols. 953–954.

development plans; the rest are almost wholly preoccupied with the financial aspects of land acquisition and development. Furthermore, the implementation of the former rests almost wholly on the latter.

This may be shown directly from the act itself. Under the act, as chart 8 shows, the Minister of Town and Country Planning possesses formal power to coördinate all physical planning within Britain. He is, to be sure, subject to some Parliamentary controls in the discharge of his duties,[29] and wherever the activities of his ministry involve other ministries joint approval is required.[30] Within these limitations, the Minister is the sole fount of authority for all land planning covered by the intentions of the act. Three types of agencies derive their duties and responsibilities from this source.

The first of these is the Central Land Board, which will administer compensation and betterment. All directives come from the Minister, and it is solely responsible to him for decisions relating to all individual cases. District land valuers are to be used as agents wherever it is more convenient to delegate this authority.

The twelve regional controllers are an administrative innovation of the Minister, and are not provided for in the act. To them may be delegated such authority as the Minister may see fit, but they are purely creatures of his hand. Except as he may designate, the local planning authorities are in no sense responsible to them, and may, in fact, completely by-pass these agencies at will. There is, furthermore, no necessary connection between them and the Central Land Board.

The real planning bodies are to be the local authorities, who, for the purposes of the act, are to be the councils of the counties and county boroughs.[31] If a larger unit is desired, either by the local councils themselves or by the Minister, joint planning boards, made up of two or more local councils, may be established. It is anticipated that for cer-

---

[29] *E.g.*, a copy of every annual report of the ministry's Central Land Board must be laid before Parliament (sect. 1:8), and its expenses must be met out of moneys voted by Parliament (sect. 3:5) ; orders relating to lands taken over from the National Trust (a private venture incorporated by Parliament in 1907 for the preservation of historic monuments, and scenic attractions) are subject to Parliament procedure (sect. 5:5) ; ministerial "development orders" must be "laid before Parliament immediately after it is made" (sect. 13:5) ; Treasury devised schemes for payments out of the central fund for land compensation purposes must be approved by Parliament (sect. 58:6), etc.

[30] This is not strictly accurate. For example, under the Trunk Roads Act of 1946, the roads designated by the Minister of Transport as trunk roads must be accepted by the Minister of Town and Country Planning (sect. 8:1) ; housing is almost entirely under the Ministry of Health; the Ministry of Works may, independently of the Minister of Town and Country Planning, acquire building sites (sect. 41:2) ; and it is the Treasury, not the Ministry of Town and Country Planning, which makes the schemes for paying out funds for properties depreciated under the act (sect. 58).

[31] For the changed status of local government since the war, see appendix 5.

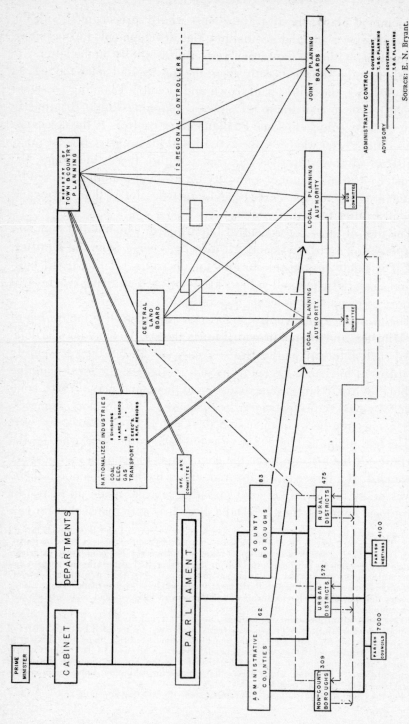

Chart 8. Basic organization of Town and Country Planning.

Source: E. N. Bryant.

tain areas, especially for the great conurbations referred to above, experience will quickly demonstrate the need for these larger local planning agencies.

The power of the Minister with respect to these three subordinate types of agencies is extraordinary. For the first two, he appoints and removes all officers, determines salaries, tenure, and the conduct of office. He gives instructions on the performance of their duties, and receives and amends reports made by them to him, and on his instructions. His powers with respect to the local planning authorities are extensive. He may, for example, amend their plans (sect. 6:3), make a local plan on his own initiative (sect. 7:1) give instructions to local planning authorities (sect. 11, 14, 15, and 16), receive and pass upon appeals made over the head of local authorities or independent tribunals (sect. 16, 18, and 19), revoke or modify any local order (sect. 26), compile local lists of buildings or monuments which are to be preserved (sect. 30:1), and compel local authorities to delegate functions to subsidiary local groups (sect. 34:1).

But his most important duty with respect to the local authorities is to see that they submit local development plans within a space of three years after the appointed day (the day when the act goes into effect). Each of these plans, which are to be reviewed in detail every five years, is based on a quite elaborate survey. The surveys are to cover physical factors such as water supply, soil fertility, and minerals; social factors such as housing, population, industries (whether expanding or contracting), open spaces, public buildings, etc.; and development plans or operations of other types of agencies including transport authorities, local industries, statutory undertakings, and government departments.[32]

The permitted coverage of these local plans is extraordinary. According to the act, any such local plan

shall include such maps and such descriptive matter as may be necessary to illustrate the proposals aforesaid with such degree of particularity as may be appropriate to different parts of the area; and any such plan may in particular—

  a) define the sites of proposed roads, public and other buildings and works, airfields, parks, pleasure grounds, nature reserves and other open spaces, or allocate areas of land for use for agricultural, residential, industrial or other purposes of any class specified in the plan;

  b) designate, as land subject to compulsory acquisition by any Minister, local authority or statutory undertakers any land allocated by the plan for the purposes of any of their functions (including any land which that Minister or

---

[32] See the outline given in the House of Commons by Silkin, in *Hansard*, Vol. 432, col. 962.

authority or those undertakers are or could be authorised to acquire compulsorily under any enactment other than this Act) ;

c) designate as land subject to compulsory acquisition by the appropriate local authority—

    i) any land comprised in an area defined by the plan as an area of comprehensive development (including any land therein which is allocated by the plan for any such purpose as is mentioned in paragraph (*b*) of this subsection), or any land contiguous or adjacent to any such area;

    ii) any other land which, in the opinion of the local planning authority, ought to be subject to compulsory acquisition for the purpose of securing its use in the manner proposed by the plan.

Furthermore, the act goes on to add, "a development plan may define as an area of comprehensive development any area which in the opinion of the local planning authority should be developed or redeveloped as a whole" for such purposes as "dealing satisfactorily with extensive war damage . . . conditions of bad lay-out or obsolete development, or for the purpose of providing for the relocation of population or industry or the replacement of open space in the course of the development or redevelopment of any other area, or for any other purpose specified in the plan."[33] At all stages of survey and discussion the services and facilities of the Ministry of Town and Country Planning and its various regional offices will be at the disposal of the local planning authorities.

When the provisional plan has been prepared, it is to be exhibited for public inspection and criticism. This will consist of making available to the public, maps, films, lectures, and special exhibits consisting of dioramas and other especially prepared visual, statistical, and supplementary material. "The people whose surroundings are being planned," said Silkin, "must be given every chance to take an active part in the planning process, particularly when the stage of detail is reached."[34]

Once the plan is completed, only major changes in projected development need be approved by the Ministry of Town and Country Planning. Although permission to construct industrial buildings of 5,000 square feet of floor space or over (there are some exceptions to this rule) must have a certificate of approval from the Board of Trade that selection of the site has been made in accord with national policy, and at various points further approval must be sought from other national and statutory undertakings, all such matters are henceforth to be cleared through

---

[33] *Act,* Sect. 5 (2) and (3), pp. 4–5.
[34] *Hansard,* Vol. 432, col. 963.

the office of the Ministry of Town and Country Planning which will then serve as a coördinative agency. The act establishes a special control over all outdoor advertising, which its proponents hope to see severely curtailed.[35]

Aside from serving as a general codification of all law relating to town and country planning, the most important departures of the new act were (1) to make compulsory the immediate drafting of ten-year plans by all the local authorities in England, (2) to clarify and facilitate the designation of land for purposes of development, (3) to lay greater stress on enlarging the planning unit to make it coextensive, wherever possible—as in the great conurbations—with the primary area of population and occupational interdependence, (4) to make it possible for all landowners definitely to know where they stand in relation to such development plans, (5) to settle the price of all land affected by these plans, and (6) to siphon off all future value increment of the land from all such developments into the coffers of the Treasury. With respect to virtually all aspects of both past legislation and the new codification, the interpretative powers of the Minister are very broad; he appears to have been given authority for complete and definitive planning on the most comprehensive scale.

And this would be true, were it not for the financial provisions of the act relating to compensation and development. The act leaves each landowner, unless his land is to be compulsorily acquired for public purposes, with the proceeds from its "existing use." But if the land was purchased before the act went into effect for an amount above that which would have been derived from its sale for existing use, because of its anticipated development value in some new use, or if the owner suffers a loss from any other difference between the two values, he may lodge a claim for compensation against the government, to which, under the act, will accrue all future value increments on such land. Thus land worth £50 for agricultural use but purchased for £200 for real-estate development, would—if the land were wanted for development use by the local authorities, and other factors remain the same—entitle the owner to recover £150 under the compensation clauses of the act.

[35] Section 31 of the act requires consent of the local planning authority for all display, and the "dimensions, appearance and position of advertisements which may be displayed," the site, and the length of time of the display must be approved. Dispute in connection with the exercise of this authority may be settled by an independent tribunal appointed by the Minister. This means severe regulation (of size, appearance, location, etc.) but not severe curtailment, except perhaps in beauty spots and ancient city districts of historic interest. Section 32 provides, *inter alia*, severe penalties for violations.

The national sum of all such individual claims for the loss of development values would then constitute the total which the government would have to pay in order to settle accounts with the past. But how large should this sum be? The Barlow committee believed that an intelligent guess based on 1937 figures would show the total of the allowable claims to be "somewhere in the region of £400,000,000."[36] The Uthwatt committee held that "a better conception of the amount involved may be obtained by taking the past rate of development of undeveloped land—using the phrase as meaning undeveloped land outside town areas—at 45,000 acres per annum and the average value of development rights as regards that land at £200 per acre. The resultant figure is £9,000,000. A valuer's method of arriving at a capital sum would be to multiply that sum by a figure representing an appropriate number of years' purchase."[37] The Government accepted the Uthwatt formula and came out with a "global figure" of £300,000,000.

The method of arriving at this figure was to multiply £9,000,000 by "15 to 16 years' purchase" and then to round out the "capital sum representing the true development value . . . to something of the order of £150 million. To this should be added a further capital sum representing the development and redevelopment value of land in built up areas" which Silkin estimated "would run to about the same figure." Adding these two figures the Minister got £300,000,000, which is exactly the amount of the global sum.[38] The global sum, once being set at this figure, cannot be altered without Parliamentary amendment to the act. Hence, if the total of the claims allowed by the district valuers comes out, for example, to a figure double the global sum, all claims will be scaled down by 50 per cent.

---

[36] *Barlow Report*, p. 119.
[37] *Uthwatt Report*, p. 41.
[38] Silkin, in *Hansard*, Vol. 432, col. 980. An advertisement placed by the Central Land Board in the *Times*, Feb. 11, 1949, read as follows: "The Town and Country Planning Act, 1947, transferred the development value in land and buildings from the individual to the State. (Development value is the difference between the actual worth of the property as it exists and as it is in fact being used, and its potential worth for development or for some other more lucrative use, e.g., agricultural—building; house—office.) This affects you in two ways. 1. If you owned or leased land or buildings on 1st July, 1948, you may have a claim on the £300 million fund provided for those who have lost the development value of their land. The Central Land Board's pamphlet S.1.A. explains how you may have a claim. The final date for claiming is now 30th June, 1949. (The Board will contribute towards professional fees incurred by claimants until 31st October, 1949, so long as the claim is submitted, and the professional adviser retained, by 30th June.) 2. If you propose to build, or to enlarge or to change the use of any buildings you own or lease, you will probably have to pay a development charge, equivalent to the increase in value of your property due to planning permission for the building, enlargement or change of use. The Board's pamphlet D.1.A. explains your position. Both S.1.A. and D.1.A. are obtainable from the Board's offices or the office of your local authority (in the L.C.C. area from the County Hall)."

So far as future development value (from the appointed day, July 1, 1948, when the act went into operation) is concerned, the developer pays 100 per cent of the difference between value[39] for the existing use and the value for the development use. This may be paid in a lump sum at the time of the development (and until it has been paid development cannot start), or in a series of regular payments over a period of time as determined by the Central Land Board.

Quite obviously compensation for lost development value and development value which is to accrue to the public in the future are closely linked. The formula applied to one—if for none other than political reasons and in order to comply with the accepted criteria of fairness in treatment of different persons in the same circumstances—will have to be applied to the other. Consequently, the amount of the compensation is a matter of vital importance.

Land interests, as might be expected, soon became quite vociferous in their denunciation of the figure. For some strange reason, not much was made of this point when the bill was in passage through the House of Commons. Throughout the debates Opposition attendance was low, and even debate on the vital issue of compensation failed to elicit from the Opposition benches much more than the usual adjectival derisions with which they were wont to greet all Labour proposals.[40] It might seem, at first blush, as though this might be explained on the grounds that the Labour government's program here was based directly on the formulae for determining land value found in the recommendations of the Conservative Uthwatt committee. In order to arrive at its low figure for "undeveloped land outside town areas" of £9,000,000—which was then to be multiplied by "an appropriate number of years' purchase"—the committee had definitely rejected floating value, which would have been decidedly more favorable to landed interests.[41] The same issue was involved in urban land and the same formulae were used to determine its value, which accounted for Silkin's second £150,000,000.

[39] Value, in terms of money, of the benefit to the existing land and buildings of the permission for the new development.

[40] On the second day of debate on the second reading of the bill in Commons Capt. Chetwynd pointed out that at no time on that day had Opposition attendance exceeded 15, and "at one point their numbers sank to 3." A Conservative member rose to protest that there were 29 members in attendance (142 Conservative members voted against the bill). *Hansard*, Vol. 432, col. 1168.

[41] By "floating value" they meant the potential value which the land in question might be speculatively held to have when used for any possible future use for which it might conceivably be employed. *Uthwatt Report*, pp. 14–15.

Not even the fact that Silkin was clearly guessing[42] when the figure was set appears to have disturbed the Opposition. Nevertheless, if the key to adequate land planning in Britain is truly to be found in the nationalization of development value at, or anywhere near, the 100 per cent figure, it is difficult to see how the new act can be made to operate, since the Central Land Board appears, in effect, already to have accepted the principle of payment at one third of this rate or less. That is to say, the law specifies 100 per cent, or the whole difference between the existing use value and future (developed) use value, but neither value has meaning until determined authoritatively for each specific piece of land. As the Central Land Board has proceeded, this value actually came out at roughly one third of what it was earlier anticipated, upon the basis of previous methods of calculation, the proper sums would be. The result has been that both the Conservative critics to the right and the Labour proponents of full land nationalization to the left have each been greatly strengthened in their opposition to this half-way measure.

Although it is very difficult—particularly for an outsider—to separate fact from fiction and rumor from historical reality in this badly complicated picture, the reasons why this dilemma arises from the act seem to be about as follows: (1) If the global sum for all lost development value should be, as some estimates would have it, not £300,000,000, but somewhere in the neighborhood of £1,300,000,000, then the general effect will be to scale all claims down to something like 25 per cent of their market value. (2) Since the global sum is fixed, no special concessions, e.g., to builders in underdeveloped and crowded areas, can be made to any group without scaling down the rate of payment of all other claims. (3) Whatever the payment finally allowed, it will not, it is estimated, be paid for more than five years after the claim has been entered. One result, consequently, is that (4) claimants who have entered into mortgage contracts—particularly common

<hr>

[42] At one time or another such points as the following have been made in this connection: (1) Both the Barlow and Uthwatt committees, upon the basis of whose findings the Government rested its case, were themselves clearly and admittedly guessing. (2) There was no particularly valid argument given for accepting the 15- or 16-year multiplier. (3) All estimates must depend upon assumptions underlying analysis of trends in land values, and these Silkin admitted were of dubious value when not, indeed, wholly inadmissable. (4) For non-urban lands the figure was rounded out and clearly could have been too high or too low by several millions, and the evaluating of urban land values at the precise figure of rural land values was a pure *tour de force* of the imagination. (5) Land value is difficult if not impossible, under the most favorable circumstances, to separate from other (e.g., constructional) values. (6) No national land value inventory had been made upon the basis of which any more precise guess could be risked.

among small holders—are subject to suit by mortgagees for balance due them in the absence of any payment at all during the interval of settlement and beyond the amount of compensation received, since the state, in effect, takes over development values free of mortgage (the private contractual relations of the individual being no concern to the government) but without relieving the mortgagor at any point of such prior obligations.

Furthermore, (5) wherever existing value is purely nominal because the land to be developed is vacant and currently unused—and such appears to be the status of much (possibly most) of the land needed for immediately foreseeable development purposes in Britain—the rate of payment upon compulsory acquisition is bound to be very low, with the necessary result that development charges are bound to be high. Under these circumstances, (6) the owner may choose either to develop the land himself, or sell it at some figure above existing use value—to which he may even be able to add the sum of his anticipated compensation claim—with losses realized or anticipated to be recovered out of future earnings from the developed property.

He will not, of course, escape the development charge if he develops the land himself, and neither will his purchaser if he sells. But among the consequences of this second alternative is that (7) sales above existing value may become an accepted practice with the direct result of forcing large-scale compulsory acquisitions of land at existing values by the Central Land Board and ahead of development needs, and the indirect result of psychological nullification of the act.[43] But a further result is that (8) if the burden is not to be passed on to the consumer in the form of higher purchase or rental prices—something which "the Building Materials and Housing Act, 1945, and . . . the limitations of the selling and letting prices of properties erected under license, should prevent"—then "what will inevitably happen is that developers who are limited to a selling or letting price which covers only the 'existing use' value and the Development Charge, but who are faced with a cost in their books of a development which includes the cost of the land bought on the old basis and the Development Charge, will have to cover their commitments somehow. One way to do it is to scamp the building, and so reduce the cost, and quality, of construction—the other way is not to

---

[43] "The Board is anxious not to use compulsion or to take action on a large scale. Some time ago, Mr. Bevan urged local authorities on no account to pay more than "existing use" value for land which they acquired. But if these measures do not have the necessary psychological effect on the market, what then?" *Economist*, Sept. 25, 1948.

build at all.'"[44] Both of these results are wholly opposed to the underlying purposes of the Town and Country Planning Act.

The following examples were given by a British valuation expert, himself thoroughly familiar with and generally sympathetic to the objectives of the Town and Country Act, as typical of the situations which arise from the attempt to apply the financial provisions of the act as they stand on the statute books.[45] Without attempting to pass on their validity, they are given here for whatever they may be worth:

a) In 1946 an ex-service man was demobilized and returned to his home in Bournemouth. He had been a small jobbing builder before the war. He purchased three plots of land for £130 each, obtaining an advance of £270 from his bank on the security of the three plots and their total purchase price of £390. The local authority has now acquired these three plots for 30s. (The "existing use" value of these unbuilt-on plots was purely nominal and only value they can have is value arising out of permission to build. Given permission to build they are again worth £130 each. The development charge is therefore £129 10s. 0d. for each plot.)

b) A schoolmaster's wife in Guildford purchased a building plot adjoining her house for £250 in 1946. It has now been compulsorily acquired by the county council for £1 in order that a police station may be erected on the site.

c) Trustees of a large hospital purchased a site for the probable extension of their hospital for £250,000 in 1946. The hospital has been nationalized but not the site for the extension. The trustees refused an offer of £300,000 for the site at the end of 1946; the land has now been valued, in the light of the act, at £110,000.

d) An estate developer purchased land before the war in Hertfordshire and laid it out as a building estate. The actual cost standing in his books is £25,000; the estate is being compulsorily acquired by the County Council for £1,400 and the estate owner would be bankrupt had he no other assets. (In protest he has employed a firm of demolition engineers to blow up the sewers and roads he laid in the estate.)

If these examples are in any significant sense representative, wholly aside from the question of any personal injustice[46] which may be done, they represent not compensation for development value foregone, but, since market prices govern development valuation, partial nationalization without compensation for existing land values—a principle in nationalization which the Labour government had repeatedly fore-

[44] Letter to the editor, *Economist*, Oct. 2, 1948.

[45] Given personally to the author in the summer of 1948: the expert, for obvious reasons, prefers to remain anonymous.

[46] In all these cases, it is necessary to keep in mind the fact that the owner has a legitimate claim to compensation for the loss incurred by the action taken. These claims are, of course, subject to the limitations noted above.

sworn until the white paper on the 1947 act was issued. But there is an obverse side to this coin. If compensation is to be made at low rates, what about nationalization of development rights in the future? While theoretically this is to be 100 per cent, actually the Central Land Board has, in effect, accepted the basis of war-damage compensation and is proceeding actually to take only about a third of this anticipated increment.

An example will illustrate what appears to be the actual procedure now employed by the ministry's valuation staff. Suppose that a piece of vacant land is to be acquired for development purposes. Because the land was vacant (unused) its value is purely nominal, and may be set at £1. On this land a building containing 40 flats of 10,000 cubic feet each is constructed at a cost of 2s. 6d. per cubic foot, or a total of £50,000. The flats may be rented for £300 a year each, bringing in a total for the building of £12,000 gross. Subtracting from this one-third, or £4,000, for "voids" (vacant flats), maintenance, repair, and general upkeep, will leave a net annual income of £8,000.

Accepting, as current practice in Britain does, the conventional figure employed in mortgage investment before the war of 16 years as a multiplier to arrive at the capital value of this net income would give a gross development value for the finished building of £128,000 (£8,000 × 16). Subtracting the £50,000 construction cost leaves a remainder of £78,000. This, however, is not the "true development charge." The government makes three additional allowances. First, £3,000 must be deducted from the previous net rental income (£8,000) as annual interest charges on construction costs (£50,000 × .06). This leaves £5,000. Determined by the same formula as before (£5,000 × 16) the capital value is now £80,000. From this must be subtracted the £50,000 construction cost.

From the remainder, £30,000, must be subtracted "existing value" before construction, or £1. The net remainder of £29,999 may then be said to constitute, for the purposes of the act, the "true development charge" when taken at the rate of 100 per cent. But if this amount is taken, it seems clear, the landowner will not build, for he gets nothing in return for his efforts and risk of capital. So some allowance must be made on this account. It was estimated by experts with experience in the work of the Ministry of Town and Country Planning (summer of 1948) that the development charge made by the Central Land Board in this case would probably be about £8,000. What of the other

£22,000? This would be left with the developer on the principle that the development charge will, in fact, have to be what a developer, or one of several competing developers, will pay for the opportunity to carry out the developments and build the flats. A market in development charges, hence, seems inevitable.

The scaling down of development charges from the rate anticipated under instructions issued pursuant to passage of the act to the amount developers are prepared to pay for the opportunity of developing means that the act is being nullified in what its spokesmen believed to be its most important provision, and the one around which are grouped all the more important authorities and initiatives which provided the *raison d'être* for the act. Hence, what has been substituted for "nationalisation of land," is not "nationalisation of development value" but a sort of specialized capital levy on land proprietors, old and new. And so long as free enterprise governs the development field, that would seem to be about all the framers of the act can do about it.

More than that, the complicated and involved clauses in the bill which relate to compensation and development appear to make administration most extraordinarily difficult. Speaking of this when the bill made its first appearance, one of the Government's strongest supporters commented that "it is unfortunate that, despite its 108 clauses and nine schedules, so much has had to be left to be filled in by subsequent orders and regulations—so much, not merely on questions of detail, but involving principles of high importance. The Bill will inevitably be shot at because of this, as a further example of the dangerous practice of 'legislation by order'; but this feature of the measure simply could not have been avoided unless the Government had been prepared to cut the knot by proposing to nationalise the land outright." One was left, the article went on to say, "to ruminate sadly on the reasons why this solution has been set aside," only to conclude that once again the British penchant for "muddling through" and improvisation had been substituted for thought-out plans and clear-cut principles.[47]

Turning from the financial clauses in the bill, one meets with a second major weakness of the act: whatever concerted planning is to be carried

<hr>

[47] *New Statesman and Nation*, Jan. 18, 1947, p. 44. Three reasons were believed to account for the Labour government's decision to seek this compromise solution: (1) land nationalization was not included in the Labour party's election program; (2) the detailed work necessary to provide the proper basis had not been done, because civil servants had spent all their time wrangling over details for a measure based on a compromise formula such as had been suggested by the *Uthwatt Report*; and (3) the bill was long overdue, and something had quickly to be improvised as a foundation upon which to proceed with some sort of physical planning.

out depends, initially at least, solely upon the local authorities. Numerous and in many respects very cogent reasons were given for this choice. It was held to be important to decentralize such a huge and complicated program as the planning and replanning of virtually the whole of the physical life of Britain. It was necessary to avoid rigidity and regimentation in dealing with widely varying conditions, social outlooks, and local interests, habits, and customs. Everything was to be said for encouraging initiative from the bottom, for obtaining the maximum amount of popular participation, and for arousing a local sense of pride in achievement. A plan, in short, to fit the people must come from the people, and remain at all stages acutely sensitive to their needs and aspirations.

Furthermore, as pointed out above, the act seemingly reserved to the Minister of Town and Country Planning ample resources for stimulating sluggish county and borough councils into action, and gave him power to go over their heads in the event gentler and more persuasive methods failed. But under all circumstances he must operate through them. Hence, the degree and quality of the national physical planning that might be brought about must arise mainly as a result of a hoped-for congruence among these local plans and confluence of them. Although they may be modified by the general guidance and tutelary coercions of the Minister, the initiative lies in local hands.

The strengths and weaknesses of this general procedure are obvious and familiar. Their bearing upon the postwar planning of the British Labour party can best be seen in two general types of schemes: those relating to the great conurbations, such as London and Birmingham, and to the new-towns program.

PLANNING THE CONURBATIONS: LONDON

There are seven great conurbations in Britain: London, Birmingham, Merseyside, Glasgow, Tyneside, West Yorks, and Manchester. Elaborate and adequate investigations as a basis for planning coextensive with the "conurbation" have been made for only the first two. An actual plan has been drafted only for the first.[48] But these two investigations and the London plan have received an extraordinary amount of publicity—both in England and abroad—and they are so clearly intended to be

[48] Patrick Abercrombie, *Greater London Plan 1944*, A Report Prepared on Behalf of the Standing Conference on London Regional Planning by Professor Abercrombie at the Request of the Minister of Town and Country Planning (H.M.S.O., 1945). The Birmingham survey was entitled, *Conurbation*, A Planning Survey of Birmingham and the Black Country by the West Midland Group (London, Architectural Press, 1948).

more or less prototypal of the pattern of general physical planning to be applied to all British conurbations that they illustrate all the points at issue.

The County of London plan is concerned primarily with a compact inner urban core of solidly built-up city known as the County of London, covering (in 1938) 116.95 square miles and having a population of over 4,000,000, which lies at the center of a metropolitan traffic area of 2,418 square miles and a population (1936) of over 10,000,000.[49] The Birmingham conurbation covered in the West Midland Group survey was an area laid out as "an irregular quadrilateral of 270 square miles, with Tettenhall, Stourbridge, Solihull, and Sutton Coldfield standing at its four corners. It contains the country's largest continuous built up area outside London, occupied by 2,150,000 people— 1,150,000 in Birmingham and Smethwick, 400,000 in the central Black Country zone, and 600,000 in the outer districts."[50]

In these two major surveys the case for the unified physical planning of the "conurbation" area has been dealt with at great length. The summary of the Birmingham survey given by the *Times* shows clearly the nature and complexity of the problems involved within such major urban areas themselves, and the bearing of planning within these areas on the concept of national physical planning as it is visualized in the Town and Country Planning Act of 1947.

The conurbation as a whole needs neither to seek new towns elsewhere for an "overspill" population nor to attract new trades in order to diversify the occupations of its citizens. Its essential problems are internal; maldistribution of people and resources and obsolesence of much of their physical equipment for work and home life. Some of its Black Country communities are too dependent on heavy metal trades for economic health and afford insufficient employment for women; but their needs can be met within the conurbation by a gradual shifting of suitable industries from farther west.

Apart from this the conurbation badly needs tidying up. The survey tells the usual story of an unplanned jumble of housing and industrial buildings, cramping factory expansion no less than social life, and of congestion and maldistributed open space. Its remedies are the accepted procedure of modern planners everywhere: to convert the sprawling urban mass into a set of well-defined communities forming an "archipelago of urban settlements, with each settlement isolated from its neighbors and set in green, open land, from which all develop-

---

[49] *London Statistics*, Vol. XLI, published by the London County Council. The Greater London plan, which includes the County of London plan, covers an area of 2,599 square miles and a postwar population roughly approximating that of the metropolitan traffic area of 1936.

[50] *Times*, May 20, 1948. The report, *Conurbation*, is probably the best and most exhaustive investigation of this sort produced in England or any other country since the war.

ment other than for agriculture or amenity is rigidly excluded"; to introduce wedges and dispersed patches of green into all the larger towns; and to segregate residential neighbourhoods from industrial and commercial zones in an orderly way.

One twentieth of the whole surface of the conurbation—an eleventh of its unused land—is a dreary desert of abandoned mine workings, tips, slag heaps, marl pits, disused canals, and derelict factory sites. In the Black Country 5,540 acres, a third of its total open land, is derelict. Some of it is now being reclaimed: the group holds that far more can be restored to use, and presents some illustrations of what might be done in particular places, especially by judicious and extensive tree-planting.

Renovation is inseparable from tidying up; extensive renovation of physical equipment is necessary. Factory buildings occupying 5,100 acres were surveyed, and 7 to 10 per cent of the total (in terms of floor space) was found to be so bad as to merit the description of slum factories requiring immediate replacement; another 25 to 33 per cent needs replacement within 30 years, though much of it could be reconditioned meanwhile. About one-fifth of all factory workers are employed in works which should be scrapped or reconditioned; and the group holds that the authorities should be able to describe minimum standards for all factory buildings, as they already can for cotton cloth works.

Residential slum clearance is even more necessary. Of 588,000 dwellings in the conurbation, 103,400 (17.6 per cent) are so old, crowded, and poorly equipped that they should be condemned as insanitary and pulled down as quickly as possible. In some areas, such as Darlaston and Cosely, a third of the houses are in this class, in several others more than a quarter. Another 95,300 old dwellings are similar in design and crowding, but lack the gross sanitary defects of the worst class; they should be replaced as soon as the latter have been dealt with.

These two classes of obsolete houses account for one-third of the conurbation's accommodation; in some places, like Dudley and Walsall, for over two-fifths. The conurbation's immediate minimum needs in mid-1945 are estimated at 128,000 new dwellings—sufficient to replace the worst slum houses and those destroyed by air raids, as well as to accommodate the increase of population since 1939. Since mid-1945 about 12,000 permanent and 6,300 temporary dwellings have been completed.[51]

This picture, with minor variations in detail only can be taken as typical of all the major conurbations.[52] In all there is an "amorphous

[51] *Loc. cit.*

[52] The major differences among them are the following: (1) The conurbations to the south and east—notably London and Birmingham—have been growing in population and relative industrial importance, while those to the north and west have been stagnating since before the First World War. Between 1934 and 1939, for example, Birmingham's population increased at the rate of 27,000 persons a year, while that of Greater London increased between the two wars by close to 1,500,000. (2) Industry in these conurbations is heavily concentrated in the lighter industries; in the north and west (with the partial exception of the Manchester and Liverpool areas, which although heavy-industry centers also concentrate heavily on

sprawl"—both within the central metropolitan area and the surrounding comglomerates of satellite towns and villages—of housing, industries, and social and cultural amenities, and each miscellany of urban bits and pieces is badly intraconnected by an inadequate helter-skelter of transport and communications facilities. In each, vast slum areas of overcrowded and derelict dwellings are splotched, like the malodorous encroachments of some wasting disease, over the central body of the urban mass, and each is effecting a creeping and disorderly outward invasion of a rotting countryside. In the center of each there is crowding and lack of parks and open space; on the periphery, disorder and the ruin of agricultural land. In none are location of dwellings and industries related to each other, and the linking arteries—themselves improvised in the past on a step-by-step basis—are perpetually clogged by ribbon developments which tend to nullify each major traffic improvement as rapidly as it is made.

This is a familiar story in all the great megalopolitan centers of the world, and a consideration of the ever more pressing problems presented by these huge formless agglomerations is everywhere making a case for orderly planning, against which few any longer argue, and which is written in letters so clear and bold that all who run may read. But it is also true that unless there is a master plan for an entire region, detailed planning within the region, however excellent it may be in various particulars, may worsen rather than improve the general situation. This is brought out by the Abercrombie report on the Greater London plan, which states that between the wars "the relationship between housing and industry was almost entirely ignored. Huge schemes of decentralized dwellings were carried out by local authorities, and vast housing estates were created by private enterprise, while unrelated trading estates, or 'parks of industry' on the one hand, and isolated factories on the other hand, largely abandoning the traditional industrial sitings, wallowed in the sea of suburban housing. The lack of focal points for the new community life became tragically evident. The two opposite tendencies only produced a jumble; industry, finding housing established, followed in the hope of recruiting local labour, while elsewhere industry arrived first and houses were then dumped around the factories."[53]

---

cotton textiles) on the heavy and basic industries. (3) London is to some extent a special case because of its preponderating size—in 1939 it contained about 15 per cent of the entire population of England and Wales.

[53] *Greater London Plan*, p. 2.

But this is only the beginning. There "is the paradox of houses for City workers built near factories, whereas the homes of those who work in the factories were still in the built-up area." Again, "modern transport attracts people to live away from their work where houses cost less, and thus suburban spread is encouraged; but only too often the housing spread, arriving first, creates a demand for further transport; and in each case the wheel turns a full and vicious circle," and the London Passenger Transport Board's system, magnificent when viewed from a purely transit point of view, nevertheless "creates new suburbs and then finds itself unable to cope with the traffic" resulting therefrom. And so *ad infinitum.* The general conclusion is that "the Regional Plan is not the sum of the wishes and proposals of these individual authorities, however much they may be conceived on planned lines."[54]

All this has been amply and fully demonstrated in the *Greater London Plan,* and a like realization underlies the magnificent survey of the Birmingham conurbation. In proposing, as the Town and Country Planning Act of 1947 does, to set up joint planning authorities to work out plans for all the conurbations similar to those detailed at such great length in the *Greater London Plan,* it has unquestionably taken the right step. But by the same token, it seems all the more difficult to understand why there exists no equivalent national physical plan, nor apparently any intention to formulate one. The paradox is greater because there is practically no aspect of the acknowledged need for relating local to regional plans within the conurbation which is not duplicated on the national scale in the relationships among the several conurbations themselves, and between them and the rest of the nation. Possibly even more important, it is quite clear that, as is demonstrated in the *Greater London Plan,* no conurbation plan can be worked out outside of the framework of a corresponding national physical plan.

For example, the *Greater London Plan* distinguishes three aspects of its over-all problem: "To locate population and industry more logically, to improve transport radically, and to determine a proper use of the land."[55] These require simultaneous solution, and to this end it makes five major assumptions: (1) Following the recommendations of the Barlow report, no new industry should be admitted to the London

---

[54] *Ibid.,* pp. 2, 3, 5. In Greater London an area of "2,599 square miles is divided up into 143 local authorities. In the area there is also a vast number of statutory authorities whose functions one way and another impinge upon planning, such as the Port of London Authority, the Thames Conservancy, Drainage and Hospital Boards, Gas and Electricity Supply, Railway and Canal Companies, etc. Of the 143 local authorities, nearly every one has a planning scheme prepared, or in course of preparation, independently of its neighbours." *Ibid.,* p. 1.

[55] *Loc. cit.*

area. "This involves consideration of the industrial future of London and its surroundings." (2) A corollary which is "inseparable from consideration of London's industrial future is the question of decentralisation of persons and industry from the congested centre" and a general "rearrangement of population within the Region." (3) A further corollary is that the "total population of the area will not increase, but on the contrary, will be somewhat reduced." (4) A supplementary assumption is that "the Port of London will continue to be one of the world's great ports," and (5) a final assumption is that the necessary "powers for planning will be available."[56]

It requires no great understanding to realize that the second and third of these assumptions depend almost wholly upon the first, and that the first, third, and fourth are capable of solution only on a national basis. Of these the first is clearly the more important, and this is recognized throughout the plan. In its "Planning Assumptions Affecting Industry" the plan places in the forefront the major assumption that "there will operate after the war a national policy governing industrial location, based on the Barlow Commission's findings, though modified sufficiently to make it applicable to the whole country, as an instrument of positive planning value, rather than a negative one."[57] There must be, in other words, a national physical plan governing industrial location, as a condition to making possible the solution of the problem of industrial location within the London region. Furthermore, as related "assumptions" make clear, this national plan for industry must be linked to a national program for maintaining full employment in order to prevent the "further drift of population from the depressed areas and other areas of low pre-war prosperity to South-East England, and in particular to Greater London," and to prevent "a further drift of population to our bigger towns" from agricultural and rural areas throughout the United Kingdom. Additional assumptions are derived largely, if not wholly, from these four, and these four, once again, depend directly on the first.[58]

---

[56] *Ibid.*, p. 5.

[57] *Ibid.*, p. 38.

[58] Even those assumptions which are less directly linked to problems of industrial location and development necessarily require national—not local or regional—action first. There are two of these: one is "that strategic considerations related to national defence will not be dominant factors in the post-war planning of the Region, either as regards types of industry, the size of industrial concentrations, their relationships to industrial populations, or the use and development of London as a great port," and the other, "that there will be the fullest possible measure of co-operation between the various Government and Service Departments for the purposes of operating the National Industrial Planning Policy in the Greater London Area." *Loc. cit.*

All the leading assumptions in conurbation planning, that is to say, which relate to industrial location and development, population distribution and growth, and to the transport media which serve the various areas, are based on considerations which are national in scope, not regional. But that is not all. Since the very scale of the reorganization—particularly in the face of postwar limitations on investment funds—requires the carrying out of conurbation plans one step at a time, it is highly important that the steps taken in each of the several schemes are at least roughly coördinated. To take an obvious example, any major geographic shifts in industries, and *ipso facto* of population, between rural and urban areas in or around the conurbations immediately set in motion a whole series of cumulative movements which might greatly enhance the drawing power of the conurbation in question at the very time that it was desired to prevent its further growth, and in so doing at the same time nullify in whole or in part plans for the depressed areas in particular and for decentralization in general. The same generalization would hold for the several steps taken in the replanning of the various conurbations themselves. If it is planned that London's population is not to grow, increase in population must take place elsewhere. If its industries are not to be expanded, other places must take on the new plants. Thus as London plans with respect to these matters it forces reconsideration of plans elsewhere, and plans elsewhere force reconsideration of its own.

What will be true at the inauguration of each plan will hold throughout all the various stages of its execution. Many factors conspire to force this coördinate development. The very scale of the operations will create keen competition for investment funds, and for the necessary materials and supplies. The draft each major scheme will make on limited resources will vary at different stages of development. More important, every single step will imply—where, in fact, it does not imperiously demand—replanning of important segments of the various national webs of transportation, communication, electric power generation and distribution facilities, gas and (in many cases) heat distribution networks, and so *ad infinitum*. All these are of necessity planned, in their major outlines at least, on a national and interregional footing.

Thus this problem which each conurbation planning authority faces—to proceed by stages to the fulfillment of its planning schemes—requires the fitting of the separate programs of development into the framework of a national development plan. But the existence or the general desirability of a central national plan for the purpose of relating regionally or functionally interdependent plans does not necessarily mean that such a plan should have priority in time, nor should it imply the construction of a rigid pattern into which the several regions and activities must fit their plans on pain of having them cut down or arbitrarily reshaped and altered to fit. On the contrary. No national plan of this sort, any more than any regional or local plan, can have much meaning unless it is based first on exhaustive and detailed surveys covering every locality and every local problem which requires solution at some point or other on a regional or national scale. These surveys must cover all local problems as seen from the local point of view, and all that may be handled on a local or regional basis without reference to the national scene ought quite obviously to be so handled. So far as the Ministry of Town and Country Planning is proceeding along this line, it is on the right track, and it is of necessity following a procedure which is designed to siphon off at each level the range of problems which require the relational effort between and among planning bodies at the next higher level, and thus avoiding much of the bureaucratization that results from congestion at the top.[59]

The point is merely this, that so to proceed also means that the desired coördination of activities and plans at each higher level depends upon the formulation of a plan at that level as soon and as rapidly as the interdependencies are clearly established. Where the relevant decisions are clearly national, they must be made on a national basis, and, as the London and other conurbation surveys have already shown, a large percentage of the decisions made within the region must wait until the national plan exists. Nor is this a matter of a plan, once conceived, serving henceforth as an inflexible pattern to which all subsequent situations, must be adapted. Trial and error, *ad hoc* decisions, con-

---

[59] I am indebted to Francois Lafitte of the *Times* for the following comment, with which I am in general agreement. "Given some sort of national strategy (broad industrial distribution, roads, railways, coalfields, airfields, ports, national parks, nature reserves, farm reserves, etc.) and an intelligible regional strategy, the whole of the rest of planning is far better done as locally as possible. Our local government is in a jumble (though Cole's views on reform are not the only ones), but nothing would make planning stink more quickly than to take it out of the hands of local authorities of some kind. When you get down to places it is communities that are being planned or replanned, people that are being disturbed; the more the planned are drawn into the process of planning the less they are likely to resist good plans because they do not understand them, and this is best done by having your (alert, imaginative) planning officers in town and county halls, and even be delegating much of the routine of planning regulation (as distinct from plan-making) to the sub-county authorities (districts, boroughs, etc.) It's an even bet that planning is going to stink anyway in 10 years' time, unless its present arbitrariness (inevitable in the early years of a new venture) can be rapidly lived down; to remove it altogether from local government would make this certain."

flicting interests, and a host of problems of one sort or another make it necessary to regard every plan, however large or small, as a changing, living, adjustable thing. The proper analogies are of an organic, not of a mechanical or architectural character. Nevertheless, there is another and possibly more compelling reason for believing that the decision of the Town and Country Planning Act of 1947 to go so far in the delegation of real planning authority to the local authorities—particularly in the absence of even tentative well-developed regional and national plans—may betray a fatal weakness. This inheres in the confused and jumbled nature of British local government itself, the relationships between these governments and the various ministerial departments and public utility authorities—including the whole of the nationalized industries and services—and the steps taken to solve the problem of interrelating the development programs of the latter.

The issues at stake in this general area of public administration are extraordinarily complex and intricate, and their independent analysis at this point would carry the discussion very far afield. Furthermore, it is an area where one must needs step warily, particularly an outsider lacking intimate knowledge of the inner workings of British regional and local institutions. Nevertheless, the bearing of certain aspects of this complex governmental machinery upon the problems of town and country planning is relatively simple, and, for the most part, quite obvious. Not only that, but it is also true that the problems they present are for the most part in no wise new, and have frequently been pointed out by British critics of high standing.

In planning for Greater London it was found that the area covered included some 143 local authorities, and that the effective carrying out of the conurbation scheme for the larger area would be possible only if planning of these individual authorities was subordinated to the over-all plan. This situation is duplicated nationally. There are in England and Wales alone 62 administrative counties and 83 county boroughs which, under the 1947 act, are to become planning authorities. In some cases, to be sure, they may be combined into joint planning boards. Supplementary thereto are 309 noncounty boroughs, 572 municipal districts, and 475 rural districts, all of which may exercise some degree of planning power. Finally, at the very bottom of the pyramid there are some 7,000 parish councils and 4,100 parish meetings whose functions may often very considerably affect the carrying out of planning schemes. The possible complications are numerous.

At the outset, the relationship between the administrative counties and these other local government bodies is in part that of a superior agency to its subordinates and in part that of a more or less independent and parallel authority with similar functions. Yet the former and the county boroughs are to be the local planning authorities as though this complicated arrangement of local government functions did not exist and the law makes no special provisions for effecting a consistent realignment between the regular and the special planning functions of these local bodies. Even when joint boards are set up, they may not follow any of the usual local government lines since the Minister of Town and Country Planning "may by order constitute those areas or parts as a united district for the purposes of this Act."[60]

Again, neither the administrative counties or the county boroughs are laid out in such a way that they can be divided up among the 12 regional controllers, established under authority of the act, and still be consistent with the patterns of regional interdependence shaped by the needs and plans of either the seven specified areas or the seven million-mark conurbations mentioned above. At least this cannot be done without cutting across county and borough lines. To illustrate:

One of the essential features of the five greatest English conurbations— Greater London, Greater Birmingham, Greater Manchester, Merseyside, and Tyneside—is that they all cut right across county boundaries, in such a way that no unification of them is possible without the inclusion of districts lying within more than one existing county. London laps over into Middlesex, Hertforshire, Essex, Kent and Surrey—even if no account is taken of the still wider dimensions of Sir Patrick Abercrombie's Greater London planning area. Greater Birmingham extends from Warwickshire into Staffordshire and Worcestershire. Greater Manchester spreads southwards from Lancashire into Cheshire and into a corner of Derbyshire. Merseyside's north bank is in Lancashire, and its south bank is Cheshire. Tyneside is similarly situated, partly in Northumberland and partly in Durham. In all these cases a unified conurban authority, capable of making *and of carrying out* comprehensive conurban plans, would have to take away considerable parts of more tha none County from the planning and plan-executing jurisdiction of the County Councils, as well as to absorb a number of at present independent County Boroughs.[61]

The same holds for most of even the smaller conurbations such as Sheffield, Leeds-Bradford, Bristol, and Plymouth.[62] Wherever parts of

---

[60] Act, Sect. 4 (2).

[61] G. D. H. Cole, *Local and Regional Government* (London, 1947), p. 141.

[62] Excellent summaries of town plans for British cities of varying size have been issued by Ascot Gas Water Heaters Ltd., London. They are known as *Ascot Town Plan Summaries.*

counties and their various subdivisions are assimilated to larger joint councils, the remaining parts must exist as rump councils. But no line of division—following existing local government boundaries or cutting across them at will—can bring them simultaneously into conformity with both the regional divisions of the ministry and the major conurbations without endless complications in virtually every aspect of either the normal conduct of local government functions or those relating to their new planning fuctions.

Closely related to such considerations is the fact that although the physical plans which these local authorities are to devise and carry into effect depend upon close liaison with the special statutory bodies, the various ministries, and the newly nationalized industries, nevertheless the regional coverage of one rarely corresponds with that of the other. In no two of the newly nationalized industries, for example, do boundaries of the regional areas correspond with one another. In the transport industry there are five executives, each of which has a separate and individual pattern of regional divisions. Furthermore, virtually every ministry having anything to do with internal affairs has its own scheme of regional divisions, which are rarely alike for any major district in Britain. Yet all of them are in some sense or other affected by, and in turn affect, county council planning, plans relating to the great conurbations and the specified areas, and the actions of the regional offices of the Ministry of Town and Country Planning. Hence, although the latter, under the 1947 act, is to serve as a coördinative and unifying agency, it is hard to see how this function can be discharged without a national physical plan which will bear somewhat the same relation to all these local agencies as the Greater London plan does to both the 143 local authorities and the "vast number of statutory authorities whose functions one way and another impinge upon planning" within that area.

Even with—perhaps especially because of—the devolution of planning initiative to the local government authorities as provided under the act, the need for reform in the whole general structure of local government is imperative. Admittedly, the problem is not new. As early as 1905 the Fabian Society proposed a "new Heptarchy" under which Britain would be divided into seven major regions. In 1919 Fawcett proposed a division into thirty, and the Ministry of Health a year later drew up a plan which would have divided the country into fifteen provinces subdivided into fifty-nine regions.[63] Among more recent

[63] Cole, *op. cit.*, p. 17.

proposals, Cole[64] has suggested dividing the country into fourteen major divisions. In a similar vein "the Labour Party solution (adopted at the 1943 Annual Conference) was regionalism, a two tier system of regional and area authorities. In the same year a N.A.L.G.O.[65] Reconstruction Committee put forward the perhaps most clearly thought-out of all the statements defending one-tier local government. It recommended a network of all-purpose authorities covering the whole country, each to be not less than 100,000 in population and not more than 500,000."[66]

Pursuant to this interest, the Labour government in 1946 set up a Local Government Boundary Commission for the purpose of reviewing the whole problem of local government boundaries, and for bringing in suggestions and recommendations for change. At the time of writing two reports have been issued.[67] They are interesting in the present connection for three special reasons. First, because they bring out in great detail the enormous differences in size and importance among the English counties.[68] Second, because they show the complexity of the county councils, which the Town and Country Planning Act of 1947 establishes as the primary planning units, and how varied they are in their patterns from county to county. (See map 6.) But third, and most important, they indicate that in the selection of criteria for tracing new local-government boundary lines the type of considerations that govern physical planning have been ignored almost entirely. This may be seen from the fact that the powers of the Boundary Commission exclude "jurisdiction over functions; yet the Commissioners write that their experience amply confirms a statement made by the Minister of Health, Mr. Aneurin Bevan, on 16 December, 1947: 'Everyone who knows about local government feels that it is nonsense to talk about functions and boundaries separately. They have to be taken together.' "[69]

[64] *Ibid.*, pp. 140–164.

[65] N.A.L.G.O. = National Association of Local Government Officials.

[66] *Labour Party Bulletin: Local Government*, VI (May, 1948) : 67.

[67] *Reports of the Local Government Boundary Commission* for 1946 and 1947, printed for distribution in 1947 and 1948 respectively by H.M.S.O.

[68] "The English counties include seven with a population of over a million and three with under 100,000. At one end of the scale is the giant Middlesex with 1,958,000 people and at the other, pygmy Rutland with 17,517, a hundred times smaller and less than the average size urban district. There are five counties with a rateable value over £10 million and two with under £300,000. A penny rate produces £88,143 in Middlesex, £55,230 in Surrey, £466 in Rutland and £1,080 in Huntingdonshire. There are 6,939 miles of county road in Devon and 274 in Oxfordshire. In 1945–46 there were 232,404 children on school registers in Lancashire and 126,854 in Surrey, although Lancashire and Surrey have something like the same rateable value. There is no end to the different ways of making comparisons. In the West Riding, for instance, 1,445,440 people inhabit 1,610,829 acres. In Middlesex there are 1,958,000 people in 148,691 acres." *Labour Party Bulletin: Local Government*, VI (Feb. 1948) : 24.

[69] *Ibid.*, VI (May, 1948) : 67. See also appendix 5.

Thus the Government seems to have piled the Pelion of recommended lines of therapy which are to some degree or other—perhaps primarily—irrelevant to the governing purposes of the Town and Country

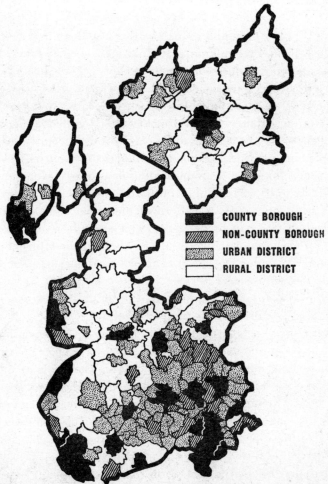

SOURCE: *Labour Party Bulletin*, February, 1948.

Map 6. Local-government boundaries. Lancashire and Leicestershire illustrate the degrees of complexity in the county pattern.

Planning Act on the Ossa of confused, overlapping, and generally obsolete forms of local government. In the absence of evidence to the contrary, there is no telling whether the proposed changes in local government would square any better than the existing system, bad as it may be, with the needs of conurbation planning, or with plans for unified regional development of the specified areas, or even with whatever national physical planning the Government has in mind—if, that is to say, it has the latter in mind at all. The very fact that it raised the question of local government reform in the way it did creates a serious question as to whether the Government sees the need for such a plan.

There are three special reasons why this last doubt may be raised in categorical form. First, planning at all levels, but particularly national physical planning, requires national decision as to the general disposition of land between its various agricultural and urban uses. Second, the same generalization holds for industrial location and development throughout the country. And third, the most significant single bit of comprehensive land planning to be carried out in detail (aside from that of the London, Birmingham, and Manchester conurbations) on the government's initiative, is found in the new-towns development, and this is likely to be successful in proportion as it is carried through in keeping with some general pattern of industrial and population decentralization (its avowed purpose), which, again, requires national, not local or even regional, decision. Yet, although the Minister of Town and Country Planning has power to amend local development schemes, and thus to exercise considerable influence in the actual shaping of detailed local plans, an examination of programs thus far formulated in these three sectors reveals comparatively little by way of schemes for drawing these related features of national development into some more or less coherent national plan, or even of any clear picture of the need for forming such schemes in the future. There is a great deal of legislation concerning each, and interdepartmental coöperation—Town and Country Planning, Board of Trade, Agriculture, Transport, Labour, etc.—may be able to achieve much of the desired coördination at will, yet little appears to have been accomplished which involves any serious departure from the *status quo* (before the Labour Government) on the national level. And that *status quo*, except for the existence of certain wartime controls, could be described as a "planned economy" only in a very narrow and limited sense of the term.

With respect to the agricultural program and plans for industrial location and development, it will be necessary to examine theory and practice at some length. The two following chapters will be devoted to this purpose. But for the new towns—whose program lies somewhere between both regional and national physical planning on the one hand, and agricultural and industrial planning on the other—the story is simpler and the issues more clear-cut and hence may be dealt with briefly before passing on to these other and more significant aspects of the larger national problems of town and country planning.

PLANNING THE NEW TOWNS

In 1945 the Government set up the New Towns Committee (Reith committee) with the following terms of reference: "To consider the general questions of the establishment, development, organisation and administration that will arise in the promotion of New Towns in further-ance of a policy of planned decentralisation from congested urban areas; and in accordance therewith to suggest guiding principles on which such Towns should be established and developed as self-contained and balanced communities for work and living." The com-mittee issued two interim reports, and a final report,[70] and most of its recommendations were incorporated in the New Towns Act of 1946.

Under the law, the new towns were to be established as independent government-sponsored corporations, solely responsible—until other-wise determined—to the Minister of Town and Country Planning, and vested with powers coextensive with all phases and aspects of construc-tion and management of the new towns from beginning to completion. They might be located at any place designated by the Minister, and be intended as entirely new towns in hitherto undeveloped territory, or as radical extensions and reorganizations of existing small towns. The corporations might be given "authority to hold, manage or dispose of any land or property in such a way as they think fit for the fulfillment of their purpose," take over, "if this is considered desirable in the inter-ests of amenity and public health . . . from Statutory Undertakers or Local Authorities the supply of gas, electricity, water, sewerage and other services in any area designated as the site for a new town,"[71] con-stitute itself as a "housing association within the meaning of the *Housing Act* 1936, and . . . provide any housing accommodations which Local Authorities are empowered to provide under the Act," and perform such other duties and exercise such additional functions as the Minister may find necessary in the carrying out of the tasks laid upon them.[72]

---

[70] The *First Interim Report*, Cmd. 6759, the *Second Interim Report*, Cmd. 6794, and the *Final Report*, Cmd. 6876, were all issued in 1946.

[71] Presumably the subsequent nationalization of gas and electricity generation and dis-tribution modified the New Towns Act with respect to these two services.

[72] An excellent summary of the two early reports of the Reith committee and of the New Towns Act is given in *Town and Country Planning in Britain*, pp. 23–25, and appendix F.

The new towns are to be of limited size, optimum population running between 30,000 and 50,000, and with related districts not to exceed 60,000 to 80,000. They are to have a "balanced social composition"; such a balance of industries, trades, and occupations as to make the town largely self-sufficient, and to keep it fully employed, and such a balance of activities, facilities, and amenities as may be required to provide each new town simultaneously with high standards of living and with a rich and adequate cultural life. As plans are being drawn, they include general layout of the location of factories, trading centers, residential quarters, recreational and cultural buildings and parks, and the provision of public utilities, transport, and other necessary services. They are to be located and constructed with a view to preserving both a balanced relationship between town and country and between the resulting new town and other nearby towns and major conurbations. A careful study of any one of them—Hemel Hempstead is a recent, but excellent example—would give an adequate picture of the general plan for the new towns.

Historically, the new-towns idea in Britain is the product of the confluence of many different streams of thought. Most important among them, however, are the romantic "garden city" idea—best exemplified in the famous towns of Welwyn and Letchworth—,[73] the concept of the "satellite town" or ring of "satellite towns" surrounding major metropolitan centers and the great conurbations, and concern over the reconstruction and viability of the distressed areas, where the local populations have been left high and dry as a result of the folding-up or migration of leading industries. (See chapter xiii following.) An additional stimulant has been the wartime experience with the beneficial effects on health and general outlook on life of the removal of population—particularly of women and children—from the major urban centers. There are many other causes contributory to the emphasis on the new towns, but it has only been recently that all have been subsumed in plans for population decentralization over the entire country.

That decentralization dominated the thinking behind the New Towns Act was made quite clear by Silkin at the time of its passage. Only by these means, he argued, was it possible to provide for the surplus populations of the larger towns. Initially some twenty new towns were planned for England and Wales—including extensions of existing

---

[73] The great pioneer was Sir Ebenezer Howard, the fiftieth anniversary of whose book, *Garden Cities of Tomorrow*, was celebrated at a dinner on October 6, 1948, with the Lord President of the Council, Herbert Morrison, as the principal speaker.

towns—capable of providing for 1,000,000 persons. And these were to be followed by many others. Eventually, it would appear, the new towns would absorb all those persons forced out of the big cities by the program of decentralization who did not drift into the smaller villages or into the open countryside.

But it is also evident that it might be—indeed is already becoming—impossible to tell where new-towns development began and replanning of old towns left off.[74] Clearly, on the Ministry's own showing, most of the major problems of planning in the great conurbations were mirrored in microcosm in many, if not most, of the existing medium-size and smaller cities of Britain. Thus it seems evident that conceptually, at least, new-towns planning for the lesser cities is to become more or less the equivalent of conurbation planning for the major cities, and that the patterns worked out here will eventually embrace virtually all those centers of population already existing outside the great conurbations as well as those which will be created by future decentralization.

Between conurbation planning and new-towns planning, in other words, the physical environment of virtually the whole of Britain's urban population would eventually be planned. If this is so, then practically all the generalizations made above in discussing the planning of the conurbations applies to the new towns as well. Indeed, the necessity of a national physical plan as a background and framework into which local planning should be fitted is even greater for the new towns, since most of them are likely to become satellites of the conurbations, and hence further to complicate the planning of the latter by a further widening of its area of reference. That is, this will be bound to complicate the planning of the conurbations unless new-towns planning is linked conjointly with conurbation planning into a national physical plan. .

Most of the early new towns, at least, are almost certain to be satellite towns. Of the first ten planned, six—Stevenage, Crawley–Three Bridges, Hemel Hempstead, Harlow, Hatfield, and Welwyn Garden City—"are sited within a sixty mile radius of London, and will be used primarily to relieve congestion in that city."[75] Two of the other four, Aycliffe and Easington (later to be called Peterlee) will be situated in Durham in the general neighborhood of the Tyneside conurbation.

---

[74] This was pointed out in detail by spokesmen for the Ministry of Town and Country Planning in a personal interview.

[75] *Home Affairs Survey*, June 29, 1948, p. 15.

Whenever new towns are planned as definite satellites to the conurbations, their fate and future prosperity will be unavoidably assimilated in the plans of the latter. The same would hold for all new towns built within the more densely populated industrial regions. But even where this is not true, new towns will appear as consumption centers of gas, electricity, and water, and as nodules on railroad and highway traffic arteries, which will require realignment and reconstruction of each separate public utility web and network, and a general relocation of industries and population within the whole country. "The sites for all ten of the new towns which have so far been designated," the official summary goes on to state, "have been chosen with very careful consideration of such matters as the size of the area, the accessibility of road and rail communications; the availability of water, gas and electricity, situation in the light of future industrial development, and the claims of agriculture."[76]

Here, "careful consideration" might mean that the Minister of Town and Country Planning had reference to some larger plan standing in the background, even though a given local plan was explicitly drawn only within either the local frame of reference, or within that of the conurbation (for a satellite town). This inference would seem to follow not only from such descriptions as that quoted above—and it is consistent with others emanating from the ministry—but also from the fact that the new town, when once developed, is both to aid and be a part of a national program of decentralization and to attain the status of an administrative county or municipal borough.

The New Towns Corporation is the landowner, land developer, and landlord in the area, but the local authority in the area is the old local authority (prefecture or rate-levying) aggrandized to embrace in its local government boundary the new town area. When development is finished, the corporation hands over its freeholds to the local authority at a valuation. Thus the new-towns program neither adds to nor subtracts from the previous problem of conflicting jurisdictions, and leaves the local authorities as the initiating bodies, with all the limitations for regional and national planning previously discussed.

Nevertheless, this would not matter should detailed investigation show that in actuality the Minister of Town and Country Planning, although not having a clearly formulated national physical plan of his own, is still consciously acting to move population in compliance with some reasonably clear-cut national plan for the development of in-

[76] *Loc. cit.*

dustry. Clearly plans for agriculture and industry (or in the absence of plans, what happens to them) will determine the location of most of the population of such a highly industrialized country as Great Britain. If there are plans for agriculture and industry, then the steps taken by the Ministry of Town and Country Planning will merely follow those taken in planning in these two fields. That is to say, the local authorities under his administration would simply be planning the appropriate facilities, living quarters, etc., required to make possible the fulfillment of these other plans.

In this event, the planning initiative of the local authorities would be limited to the mere devolution of a schedule of local adjustments required to comply with plans cast on a national basis and emanating from these two other sectors. This would be true even though the national (or regional) plans were constructed, as they should be, only after exhaustive surveys had shown the desirability of confining these plans to problems that exceeded the competence of the smaller body. While there might be some valid criticism of this procedure on the ground of its occasional cumbersomeness, the advantages of widespread and popular local participation in the shaping of the local plans would probably far outweigh the handicaps of less streamlined implementation.

But if national physical plans do not exist, then all the former criticisms apply. It would then appear that either in ignorance of the need for some national master plan, or in an excess of zeal for a highly specialized English version of democratic participation (or both), only a combination of good luck and heroic measures could prevent detailed local plans from adding confusion of exactly the same sort that the authors of the Greater London plan found to exist when they examined the results of previous piecemeal and uncoördinated planning by the multifarious and overlapping minor planning agencies operating within that area. Surely the necessity for the highly desirable popular participation can scarcely demand fouling up the picture in one any more than it does in the other.

In any event, the real determinants of centralization, of decentralization, and of population relocation are the plans and programs for agriculture and industry. Accordingly, before attempting to assess the full implications of the Town and Country Planning Act it will be necessary to look into what the Labour government intends to do in these two most vital areas of national life.

CHAPTER XI

Agriculture and Marketing

A General Enabling Act should be passed giving the State power to acquire all agricultural land and laying down the basis for compensation.—*Our Land, The Future of Britain's Agriculture.*

The right hon. Gentleman and the Government say that we must do something more and that it is not enough to let the economic principles of the world situation work themselves out. The Minister says we must guarantee prices and markets to ensure stability. With that, we on this side of the House agree. Because that is the underlying principle of the Bill, we do not propose to divide the House on Second Reading.—Captain H. F. C. Crookshank, Spokesman for the Conservative Opposition, January 27, 1947.

THE NEED FOR a national agricultural policy in Britain derives largely from concern over imported food supplies. Twice within the memory of living Britons this need has been brought home with startling and dramatic suddenness. In 1917, and again in 1943, submarine warfare brought the country face to face with impending starvation.[1] But in contrast with the period after the Treaty of Versailles, the end of the Second World War did not bring an end to the danger. This time there is no shortage of ships to bring the vital food from overseas, but there is a shortage of purchasing power to buy in the customary amounts. Because this is so, the new need is not for devices and maneuvers with which to circumvent a passing emergency, but for a long range program of agricultural planning to solve a major problem on an enduring basis.

REASONS FOR THE NEW PLANNING EMPHASIS

At the forefront of any discussion of a national plan for agriculture must be placed Britain's dependence upon food imports. From about half of total domestic food consumption in 1914 imports had increased to nearly two-thirds by the time of the outbreak of the Second World War.[2] In 1947, despite greatly enhanced domestic production, strict rationing of all imported food, and a persistent and well-organized

---

[1] For a good expression of the stimulus of war emergencies on British agriculture, see R. S. Hudson, "An Address [at the] 98th Annual Meeting of the Farmers' Club," *Journal of the Farmers' Club*, Dec., 1940, pp. 57–62. Hudson was at that time Minister of Agriculture.

[2] This is the commonly quoted estimate. E.g., "In peacetime . . . Our imports amounted to about two-thirds of our total supply, requiring about 20 million tons of shipping per annum." Sir John Orr, in *The Nation's Larder* (London, 1940), p. 59. But estimates do not agree. Some appear to be quoted in tonnage terms, some in value terms, some appear to include manufactured food products, others not. See, e.g., the data cited by Charles Smith, *Britain's Food Supplies in Peace and War* (London, 1940), p. 13.

system of export-import controls designed to lower food imports to the minimum, they still ran close to "three-quarters of the 1938 rate of import" and constituted very nearly half of the total of all imports.[3]

For certain items highly important from a dietary point of view, the degree of dependence upon foreign supplies was higher still. In 1937–38, the following percentages of the total of domestic supplies were imported: wheat as flour, 79 per cent; sugar, 73 per cent; butter, 91 per cent; cheese, 80 per cent; fruits and nuts, 74 per cent; bacon and ham, 68 per cent. Large percentages of even such foodstuffs as eggs (33 per cent), beef and mutton (52 per cent), and "other vegetables" (excluding, that is, potatoes, 36 per cent) were imported.[4] While some of these ratios have been considerably altered as a result of the wartime agricultural production drive and the rationing system, yet the general picture remains much the same. Thus, while there are increased supplies of grains (particularly wheat) and sugar from domestic production, the general livestock situation has seriously deteriorated, and the fats and oils shortage has assumed critical proportions.[5]

Meanwhile the secular long-run demand for food has been rising and is bound to continue to rise for a long time to come. A primary and possibly transitory factor is the increase in population. During the war and postwar years Britain's population increased, as a result of excess of births over deaths and of immigration over emigration, approximately 4,000,000. Whether or not future events will reverse this trend depends upon a number of circumstances, but none of them are apt to alter the picture seriously for some time to come. Far more important is the need for raising the nutritional standard of the population.

For large sections of the population these standards are, and have long been, deplorably low. Medical examination of 1,500,000 conscripted men in 1917–1918 showed the following results.

[3] Thus "food and feedingstuffs in 1947 totaled" (at current f.o.b. prices) £750,000,000 out of an import total of £1,574,000,000. The ratio for 1946 was approximately the same. Planned food imports for 1948 came to £390,000,000 out of £792,000,000 for the first half of the year. *Economic Survey for 1948*, Cmd. 7344, p. 11. These figures do not make allowance for reshipment abroad of foods processed from imports (comparatively small).

[4] Computed from data given by Charles Smith, *op. cit.*, p. 13. These percentages are based on tonnage figures. Value figures for the year 1935–36 are given in Lord Addison, *Policy for British Agriculture* (London, 1939), appendix v.

[5] Major declines from 1939 to 1946 were: sheep and lambs 17,985,659 to 12,816,501; pigs, 3,515,101 to 1,475,640; horses used for agricultural purposes, 714,004 to 436,784 and poultry (including ducks, geese and turkeys), 56,425,854 to 39,845,265. Sir George Stapledon, "The Agricultural Situation" in *Farming and Mechanised Agriculture, 1948* (London, 1948), p. 44. The domestic oils and fats shortage, for which the African Groundnuts Scheme was developed (see chapter xiv), was estimated to run in the neighborhood of 6,000,000 tons annually.

"Of every nine men of military age in Great Britain on the average three men were perfect, fit and healthy; two were on a definitely inferior plane of health and strength, whether from some disability or some failure of development; three were incapable of undergoing more than a very moderate degree of physical exertion, and could almost (in view of their age) be described with justice as physical wrecks; and the remaining man was a chronic invalid with a precarious hold on life."[6]

It is commonly believed that in the years between the two world wars British nutritional standards improved greatly. "Partly as a result of learning what foods are good for them," wrote one British food expert in 1940, "partly because the standard of living has been rising since the last War, the people of this country have increased their consumption of fruit by 88 per cent., of vegetables, other than potatoes, by 64 per cent. and the drinking of milk by about 50 per cent. since 1913."[7] Yet in 1936 Sir John Orr found that around "50 per cent of the population were not securing adequate amounts of certain types of foodstuffs. Subsequent inquiries while modifying have not substantially altered his conclusions. In the most recent survey of consumption,[8] it was computed that nearly half the population of Britain subsist on inadequate diets. Of these 16,000,000 probably do not spend enough to purchase the comparatively expensive protective foods necessary for proper nourishment, and the majority would find it very difficult to increase their food expenditures."[9]

Although wartime food controls in the Second World War are generally believed to have materially improved the standard of food consumption of the previously badly undernourished lower income brackets, there can be no doubt but that the standards are still seriously, not to say dangerously, low.[10] It is difficult to say just how much more

---

[6] Quoted in Smith, *op. cit.*, p. 2. It is pointed out that the above is possibly not a fair sample since it included men who were not already in the army after three years of war, and hence, must have included many more who were in general bad health than an earlier muster would show. Nevertheless, the results were properly termed "alarming."

[7] J. C. Drummond, "Food in Relation to Health in Great Britain During the Past Two Hundred Years," in *The Nation's Larder*, p. 14.

[8] Sir William Crawford and H. Broadley, *The People's Food* (London, 1938).

[9] S. Mervyn Herbert, *Britain's Health*. Based on the *PEP Report* (London, 1939), p. 175.

[10] For example, during the author's eight months' stay in England in 1948, his eleven-year-old daughter, in excellent physical condition at the time of departure from the United States and previously nourished by a balanced diet complying with best American dietary standards, developed anemia as a result of protein shortage. This happened despite the fact that her diet was carefully watched and was reinforced at times with food imports from America which were not available to most English children. Such an individual experience cannot, of course, provide a basis for generalization, but it did lead to making further inquiries over a wide range of British and American sources from which it was possible to draw two general conclusions: first, that British medical data did not adequately reflect the

food would be necessary to raise the average consumption to accepted minimum standards but there is no question but that increases would be large for many of the more important classes of food. A prewar estimate placed these increases at 12 per cent for meat, 16 per cent for butter, 20 per cent for vegetables (excluding potatoes), 25 per cent each for eggs and fish, and 50 per cent for fruit.[11] It is possible that postwar standards would increase these percentages still further.

Thus the demand for increased food combined with the high desirability, not to say downright necessity, of keeping food imports at rock-

TABLE 26

ACRES OF AGRICULTURAL LAND IN GREAT BRITAIN, 1891–1936

Year	Arable land	Permanent grass	Total
1891	16,484,664	16,433,850	32,918,514
1911	14,647,788	17,446,870	32,094,658
1921	14,967,303	15,906,372	30,873,675
1931	12,634,358	17,281,162	29,915,520
1936	12,095,761	17,359,730	29,455,491

SOURCE: Christopher Addison, *Policy for British Agriculture*, appendix ii, p. 287. (Slightly adapted.)

bottom has had the effect of arousing intense national interest in the status of domestic agriculture. But while there can be no question that concern over food supplies is primarily responsible for this changed attitude towards agriculture, it is also true that once attention was turned in that direction the depressed status of the industry gave cause for the gravest alarm. A long-run decline of British agriculture was found to have paced, step by step, the combined need for per capita increase in food consumption and rising dependence upon imports. Average decline in arable land, as given in table 26, reflects the changing long-run condition.

On the eve of the Second World War virtually everything was wrong with British agriculture. Farming methods were badly out of date, the land was deteriorating, and all classes of the farming population—owner occupier, tenant, agricultural laborer, and landlord alike—were becoming impoverished. For these conditions, which have been detailed at great length in a number of widely circulated books,[12] there

poor health of Britain's population; and second, that Britain's dietary standards were probably dangerously low.

[11] Smith, *op. cit.*, p. 12.

[12] See, e.g., Addison, *op. cit.* Also, the extensive bibliography in *Farming and Mechanised Agriculture, 1948*, pp. 319–323.

are a host of contributory causes. For present purposes they may briefly be summarized under three main headings.

1. *British import policy.*—While industry, trade, and finance, both at home and abroad, were steadily resorting to large scale and monopolistic forms of organization which had been successful in wringing from the government subsidies, subventions, tariffs, and other special forms of aid and protection, British agriculture remained largely unorganized and hence unprotected and unassisted. Domestic agricultural products competed on a virtually open, free market with imports from abroad, and both imports and home-grown products, once they had left the farmer's hands, were under the control of compactly organized food manufacturers and distributors with whom the unorganized and small-scale cultivator at home was wholly unable to bargain on an equal footing.

At the same time, the long-standing interest in keeping down the cost of foodstuffs in order to keep up the standard of living of the wage-earning class placed the most powerful kind of popular support solidly behind any change in this policy. Furthermore, Empire policy as it concerned both the dominions and a number of the leading crown colonies was wholly, and in a sense almost inescapably, opposed to any change in policies relating to domestic agriculture which would curtail the easy and free entry of products from these primary areas of British controlled raw-materials supply.[13]

2. *Special advantages of the foreign exporter.*—The most important of these was that large areas of land especially adapted for mass production of foodstuffs both before and after the advent of farm mechanization, were available in the countries from which Britain imported. In some of these areas, such as the West Indies, Africa, and India, cheap labor was abundant. Some, such as Canada, Australia, the United States, and Argentina, had precisely the kinds of extensive cultivation for which the newer types of agricultural machinery were the best adapted. And most of these areas possessed vast stretches of land which could be, and were, adapted to continuous cropping for long periods of time without the necessity of replenishing the soil. Soil-robbing, ultimately so catastrophic if practiced for long periods, was still a universal practice in most of the areas whose products competed on a large scale with those of British domestic agriculture at the time of the outbreak of the war in 1939.

[13] For more detailed discussion of this point, see chapter xiv.

There were additional advantages enjoyed by foreign competitors. Perhaps chief among these was the large-scale organization of virtually all stages of agriculture from breaking the soil to delivery of the finished product to the British market. Compared with English methods, most foreign agricultural production, distribution, processing, and financing was large-scale, closely organized, and monopolistically minded. Much of it enjoyed strong government support at home, a type of support which frequently—as during the twenties and thirties—promoted dumping of agricultural surpluses on international markets for almost anything they would bring in order to maintain domestic prices. As Britain had both the largest and the least-protected food market in the world, the effect of such practices abroad had a disastrous effect upon her domestic agriculture.

3. *British agriculture's lack of political friends.*—In broad outline, the Conservative party was itself closely tied in with, when not in truth to be regarded as the direct expression of, the type of landlordism which preferred fox hunts and deer forests to the extension of agricultural acreage,[14] or the reform of agricultural methods. The Liberal party had long been favorable to agricultural reform and improvement, but its free-trade stand—reaching back to the days of the repeal of the Corn Laws in the middle 1840's—had long inhibited the type of action on its part which could strike at the heart of the difficulty. When it finally saw the necessity of attacking the problem—which had so increased in magnitude that its proposals were already worthless—the party had disintegrated to a degree which made it impossible for it to gain support even for its mild program.[15]

As for the Labour party, it had never had much of an agricultural policy. It was much concerned with land nationalization and had championed the elimination of the "tied-cottage" system, but the vigorous attempt by the Minister of Agriculture during Labour's brief tenure in office in the early thirties, Lord Addison,[16] to work out a comprehensive scheme for revival of British agriculture, failed to arouse widespread support in Labour circles. "Throughout its history," a recent

---

[14] Some 7,000,000 acres of land in England and Scotland had been given over to game preserves in the middle thirties. By rough estimate the amount of cattle grazed on deer forest lands in Scotland had declined by two-thirds and the number of sheep by 60 per cent between 1920 and 1936. Addison, *op. cit.*, pp. 60–61.

[15] See, e.g., H. M. Trevelyn, *English Social History*, in particular, the famous 1926 *Manifesto* of the Liberal party, and *The Land and the Nation: Rural Report of the Liberal Land Committee, 1923–25* (London, 1925).

[16] *A Policy for British Agriculture.*

writer[17] comments, "the Labour Party has only taken an occasional, spasmodic interest in farmers and farming. Its panacea of land-nationalisation, now apparently in cold storage, was a tenurial rather than an agricultural reform;[18] it would have ended the landlord-and-tenant system, but would have had little direct effect on what farmers produce or how they produce it . . . The Party's leaders, like the Party itself, have always been more concerned over such sentimental issues as the tied cottage than with the agricultural essentials, like output per man-hour." Hence "it was natural that the Labour Party went into the 1945 Election without an agricultural policy of its own."

Thus agriculture as an industry has appeared in recent British history as a sort of political orphan. Nevertheless, the events of the war—aided in this emphasis not a little by the background of the depression of the thirties—urged immediate adoption by someone. The plight of agriculture was at long last generally recognized, and it surprised nobody that there was a sudden rush by all parties to sponsor plans and programs for its salvation. The presumptive heir to the honor had as grist for its thinking, in the evolution of a program of action, a widely varied series of expedients and improvisations which had been adopted, belatedly, hastily, and spasmodically in the past in order to meet random agricultural emergencies as they arose.

When Labour inherited the mantle of political authority in 1945 it became the residuary legatee of these miscellaneous improvisations; it might plan to continue with them, or to bring them to an end by proposing plans for a fundamental reorganization of agriculture. What it did was to attempt to pick a middle way between the two general courses of action. Hence it will be necessary to glance briefly at the historical background before proceeding to examine the implications of the path which was finally chosen.

THE MISCELLANY OF PREWAR IMPROVISATIONS

At the end of the Victorian era, Ernle points out, "The legislature was powerless to provide any substantial help"[19] to British agriculture, and this generalization might be extended to cover the interval up to the early years of the great depression of the thirties. Short of "substantial

---

[17] F. W. Bateson, "Wanted—An Agricultural Policy," *New Statesman and Nation*, May 8, 1948, p. 370.

[18] How true the statement is may be seen in what is probably the Labour party's most carefully worded statement on agriculture, as it appeared in appendix XII of the *Report of the Twenty-sixth Annual Conference of the Labour Party* (Margate, 1926), p. 336 *et. seq.*

[19] *English Farming*, p. 379.

help," however, it was possible for Parliament to provide a number of minor technical aids. Thus a series of Diseases of Animals acts, the first of which was introduced in 1894, attempted to control the spread of animal diseases, the most important of which was hoof-and-mouth disease. Similar Destructive Insects and Pests acts, reaching back to 1877, attempted similar controls over an allied field. Later, Housing acts provided governmental aids to rural housing for agricultural laborers; the Agricultural Credits Act of 1928 set up the Agricultural Mortgage Corporation to provide loans on agricultural mortgages; and similar acts were passed to assist one branch of agriculture or another to solve separate, pressing problems.[20]

"Substantial help" first came with the thirties when "the depression had demonstrated the need for the economic planning of agriculture"[21] on a more comprehensive footing. Three important pieces of legislation were introduced in quick succession. In 1931 came the first Agricultural Marketing Act. This was followed in 1932 by the Import Duties Act, and in 1933 by the second Agricultural Marketing Act.

The Import Duties Act provided for the first time a general protective tariff which covered certain lines of agricultural imports (though it exempted wheat, meat, live animals, and wool). It was reinforced by the Ottawa agreements of the same year, which increased certain preferential rates for Empire products.

The two Agricultural Marketing acts were far more important. As the case was later summarized by the Lucas committee:[22]

Amongst the many and complex factors which were responsible for the almost continuously depressed state of British agriculture in the period between the two World Wars, there was one which stood out for all to see. The marketing of British farm produce was in many cases markedly inferior to that of its foreign competitors. The channels of disposal were to a large extent, antiquated, circuitous and excessively costly. Moreover, whilst the British farmer was capable of producing the best products in the world, those products were not being adapted to consumer requirements or presented for sale in the manner best calculated to attract the customer. Prices realised compared unfavourably with those of imported products which, though often intrinsically inferior, arrived properly packed and graded and in a form scientifically designed to conform to consumer requirements. The ever-increasing flow of these graded products from

[20] An excellent summary of this legislation for the year 1923–1934 is given in George Walworth, *Feeding the Nation in Peace and War* (London, 1940), chapter vi, pp. 112–142.

[21] Isabella Williams, "Agricultural Legislation and Policy," in *Farming and Mechanised Agriculture*, 1948, p. 67.

[22] *Report of the Committee Appointed to Review the Working of the Agricultural Marketing Acts*, Economic Series, no. 48 (Ministry of Agriculture and Fisheries, 1947), p. 3. (Hereafter referred to as *Lucas Report*.)

overseas was a measure of the foreign farmers' competitive success in the British market. It was also a measure of the British farmer's failure to adapt his product and marketing arrangements to the requirements of his customers.

All this had previously been brought out at length in 1922 in the report of the Linlithgow committee, which believed that the development of a "marketing sense" among home producers was necessary to bring "production into relation with the requirements of the markets" by coöperative action which would include "standardising and improving the marketability of farm products," and "to increase the efficiency of the marketing and distributive machinery as a whole." Pursuant thereto, the Agricultural Produce (Grading and Marking) Act had been passed in 1928, under which the Minister of Agriculture was enabled "to prescribe standard grades, packages and methods of packing and to control the use, in association with the grades, of a common trade-mark—known as the 'National Mark'—to denote home produce of a defined standard of excellence."[23]

The results of this first effort at grading and standardization were, on the whole, disappointing, largely, it was argued, because the underlying difficulty with British agriculture was found in the fact that it "consisted of a mass of small-scale, highly individualistic producers, each of whom, whether from choice or through lack of machinery for organization, worked on his own. There were, and still are, some 446,000 farms in Great Britain, 346,000 of which comprise less than 100 acres each, 276,000 less than 50 acres. These small scattered producing units obviously lacked any coherent production or marketing plan. They had not even the advantage of a reliable and up-to-date system of market intelligence. Without organization they were powerless to emancipate themselves from the scramble of the market."[24]

The major difficulty, it appeared, lay in the lack of farmer organization, and the assumption was made that could this be provided at the marketing end it could not help but compel a general and cumulative reform of both production and distribution of agricultural produce. Hence, the two Agricultural Marketing acts were designed (1) to provide a legal basis for voluntary organizations of producers, (2) to extend to such recognized organizations the power "to protect themselves against a blackleg minority" by giving them the power to make decisions binding upon the whole of the agricultural industry in general, and (3) to supplement the authority of the officially recognized

[23] *Ibid.*, p. 4.   [24] *Loc. cit.*

private bodies of producers with such special aids and subsidies as circumstances might from time to time dictate. The result was the deliberate and state-supported extension into agriculture of a system of compulsory cartels which had come to dominate large and increasing areas of industry and trade in the British economy.

Thus, under the 1931 act,

home producers were enabled... to deploy an array of statutory powers far exceeding in range and effectiveness any that a purely voluntary organization, however comprehensive, could secure for itself. Producer Boards operating schemes under the Act could, in fact, take complete control of the whole home-produced supply of a commodity. They could make regulations governing the sale of the commodity at any stage between producer and consumer. They could limit the amount of the product that could be offered for sale, and they could use any method they liked for the sharing among members of the whole income derived from the sale of the product. In short, *they were given the powers of a statutory and inviolable monopoly* ... To these formidable powers the 1933 Act added the power to place a direct quantitative limit on sales by any producer and provided that any such limit might be based on the producer's past sales.[25]

Under authority of these acts the following marketing schemes were in operation before the outbreak of war:[26]

Hops Marketing Board (England)	established	9– 6–32
Pigs Marketing Board (Great Britain)	"	9– 9–33
Bacon Marketing Board (Great Britain)	"	9– 8–33
Pigs Marketing Board (Northern Ireland)	"	10– 1–33
Pigs Industry Council (Northern Ireland)	"	1– 1–35
Milk Marketing Board (England and Wales)	"	10– 6–33
Scottish Milk Marketing Board................	"	12– 1–33
Aberdeen and District Milk Marketing Board....	"	8– 1–34
North of Scotland Milk Marketing Board........	"	10– 1–34
Milk Industry Council (Northern Ireland)	"	8–16–34
Butter and Cream Marketing Board (Northern Ireland)	"	5– 5–36
Milk Marketing Association (Isle of Man)	"	4–25–35
Potato Marketing Board (Great Britain)	"	3– 9–34
Potato Marketing Committee (Northern Ireland) .	"	11–24–38
Potato Marketing Association (Isle of Man)	"	6–12–35
Egg Marketing Committee (Northern Ireland)	"	9–10–36
Fat Stock Marketing Association (Isle of Man) ...	"	10–25–35

[25] *Ibid.*, pp. 6, 8. Italics mine. Actually, there were two marketing acts in 1933. The second one made provision for the payment of compensation to producers for losses incurred under marketing schemes.

[26] Isabella Williams, *op. cit.*, p. 68. For more complete detail on interim legislation and farm and distributor organization see George Walworth, *op. cit.*, pp. 139–142.

In addition, in order "to give any necessary assistance to the producers of such commodities and in part to provide for marketing reforms" the "Government of the day" introduced special *ad hoc* legislation to permit the setting up of special commissions whose special function was to be the supervision of subsidy schemes and the exercise of certain additional regulatory and supervisory powers. Three such commissions were established: the Wheat Commission under authority of the Wheat Act of 1932, the Sugar Commission under authority of the Sugar (Reorganisation) Act of 1936, and the Livestock Commission under authority of the Livestock Industry Act of 1937. Similar commissions were proposed for milk and poultry, but neither had been established—the first because of opposition from "producers and distributors alike," and the second because of the outbreak of the war.

The Sugar Act also set up a British Sugar Corporation—an amalgamation of various British sugar refining companies—which had two main functions: "(*a*) to make contracts with sugar beet growers for the purchase of home-grown beet in accordance with terms and conditions decided upon in negotiation with the grower representatives and after consultation with the Sugar Commission; and (*b*) to process the beet with the highest possible degree of efficiency."[27] If the corporation was unable to come to a satisfactory agreement with growers, the Sugar Commission was authorized to determine the conditions and terms of contract. The commission could also determine the total maximum beet acreage to be grown, and the allocation of acreage to each grower, make inquiries relating to the sugar industry such as "beet freight rates and redistribution of factory capacity," and make recommendations for amalgation of existing refineries.

Although the special *ad hoc* commissions were looked upon as purely transitory devices for achieving some degree or other of "orderly marketing" until the industries over which they exercised control might be brought under the administration of regular marketing boards, the device of the semipublic corporation was quite obviously planned on a more permanent basis. Had it not been for the war it seems possible that most of the marketing boards might, in the normal course of events, have come gradually to assume powers and methods of procedure similar to those of the corporation set up under the Sugar Act of 1936. At any rate, incorporated in the various enabling acts and

[27] *Lucas Report*, p. 38.

special bits of legislation dealing with agriculture, and manifested in the several boards, commissions, and corporations set up as a result of them, are certain common ideas. These called immediately or eventually for a system of organization which possessed certain common characteristics:

1. There would exist for each major commodity, within each area or region of reference (county, England, United Kingdom, etc.), and for all levels of organization from the raw-materials (farmer) stage to the point of retail sale to the ultimate consumer, an organization which included all recognized suppliers or traders, and which would possess authority to act for the whole of the industry or trade in question. All suppliers producing for sale to others would be registered, licensed, or otherwise listed and brought directly under the authority of the central body.

2. Each such central body (association, board, commission, corporation) would be lent statutory authority which was coextensive with the industry or trade, and would possess a dual responsibility to its membership and to the Minister of Agriculture. Initiative in forming the central association would lie in the hands of the producer, and the central body would typically represent producer interests alone. The industry or trade, in other words, would be empowered to regulate its members on their own behalf, and to determine policy relating to other interests in the community subject to certain specified checks designed to provide general consumer protection. All consumer protection was purely advisory.

3. The central idea being "assured markets and guaranteed prices," the primary object was to establish an effective system of price controls. As the commissions and boards evolved they came to include some degree or other of most of the following:

   a. A cost-of-production price formula designed to be high enough to permit the last producer (with the highest costs) whose output was necessary to achieve the desired total output to survive, or—to employ the term used during and after the war—the "target" supply. The marginal supplier at this price would be the supply-line farmer or trader.

   b. Price, so determined, should include a "fair return" over cost to the least efficient producer. Should it, however, be set below this figure, the government would give a money subsidy to all suppliers to the equivalent of the difference between costs so determined and price as set.

   c. High grower costs might be lowered by supplementary subsidies such as provision of fertilizers, and the supply of scientific and other farming aids at government expense.

   d. The gap between costs and prices at the margin was to be set so that profit margins would not fall below a certain assured figure. Such margins would be set at all levels from producer to consumer.

   e. All suppliers must be registered or licensed by the commission or board as a condition to marketing output or receiving any benefits under the relevant controls.

4. Power to control prices meant power to control production, and, typically, power to determine whether or not new suppliers could join the industry. (For hops, the right to grow was limited to those producing hops at the time the act went into effect; thereafter the individual licensee had the right to transfer his license by sale.) Most of the boards, commissions, etc. attempted to restrict acreage, plant, number of producers or traders, etc.

5. Technical rationalization was intended to follow as a natural consequence of the effort to control price and restrict production. Ideas included improved species, better seeds, more mechanization, soil regeneration and better fertilizer technique, experimental processing plants (e.g., part v of the Livestock Industry Act of 1937 set up three experimental slaughterhouses), standards and grades, elimination of distribution costs, and many others.

Persons familiar with the American NRA codes (codes of fair-trade practice under the National Recovery Administration) and the AAA agreements (marketing agreements under the Agricultural Adjustment Administration) will recognize at a glance the general idea which underlay the British marketing therapy for agriculture; it is that of "self-government in business." The logical result would be wholesale cartelization of each agricultural industry and trade to which the common formulae were applied, and the end product would be the evolution of a British version of the "corporate state."

This was the Tory solution for the problem of British agriculture as it appeared on the eve of the Second World War. And it had the expected results. Producers "made little use of the Acts for the promotion of efficiency measures . . . In each case, price amelioration was the principal objective of these schemes."[28] With "their strictly limited powers of positive action" the consumers committees were not able to give "adequate protection to the consumer . . ."[29] There was "no reason for thinking that the efforts of producer marketing boards in the field of distribution resulted in the lowering of distribution costs."[30] The burdens on the taxpayer in the form of subsidy costs, and upon consumers in high prices and low quality or inferior service was allayed at few points, and made heavier and more onerous at others.

How the subsidy system worked out is shown by sugar, for which subsidies were first paid in 1924 under the 1925 Sugar Subsidy Act (retroactive for one year). Under stimulus of the subsidy acreage in-

---

[28] *Lucas Report*, p. 50.

[29] *Ibid.*, p. 52. "There is still no effective power given to the Consumers' Committees." George Walworth, of the Cooperative Union, Ltd., in a letter to the author, April 26, 1949. (Hereafter referred to as "Walworth Letter.")

[30] *Lucas Report*, p. 52.

creased nearly twenty fold—from 22,637 in 1925–26 to 404,000 in 1935–36, but of the £66,940,351 receipts "over 60 per cent (£40,292,077) was provided by State assistance." For the year 1936–37 "the State assistance was £2,576,000 in the form of subsidy and £2,675,000 revenue abatement, giving a total of £5,251,000."[31] Between 1934 and 1939 the Government paid local producers an average of a little over two and a half pounds subsidy per head for 7,703,970 cattle, or a total of £20,000,000. Basing his estimate on prewar data, Walworth found "that the subsidy necessary to bring all commodities to the British stabilised prices would be a subsidy of no less than £5.67 per acre of land (including rough grazings and uplands); in other words, the farmer's present claim is that he requires a subsidy of £5.67 per acre to make his business profitable."[32]

The Miscellany of Wartime Improvisations

Two major changes in the prewar pattern of agricultural control were introduced during the war years. A new ministry, known as the Ministry of Food, was set up to manage "procurement, marketing and distribution of foodstuffs," and the Ministry of Agriculture and Fisheries was given more power to stimulate home production. The results were temporary eclipse of the marketing boards and commissions and significant technical rationalization of the very sort which it had previously been hoped these same boards and commissions would foster. These results might seem at first glance to combine a double refutation of the prewar solution. Actually they served to convince their sponsors of the correctness of their former ideas.

Paradoxical as this may sound, it is easy to demonstrate. Avoiding details—which are very complex and concerning which there is still only a limited amount of verifiable data in published form—the establishment of the Ministry of Food resulted in the application of preëxisting marketing controls to all British food supplies, whether domestically grown or imported from abroad. "The Ministry of Food," the Lucas committee commented, "is a distributors' Ministry recruited largely from men drawn from the distributive trades. Inevitably it has become distributor minded," predisposed to the support and furthering of distributor interests as they had been evolved over the preceding

---

[31] Walworth, op. cit., pp. 444–445, 455. A good summary of British prewar experience with agricultural subsidies is given by J. A. Venn, "Agriculture and the State" in Agriculture in the Twentieth Century (London, 1939).

[32] Ibid., p. 130.

decade.[33] In assuming control over all "sales off the farm" the "Ministry of Food became responsible for subsequent stages of marketing, utilisation and distribution." These enlarged controls were a logical extension of the cartel idea underlying the familiar slogan of "assured markets and guaranteed prices" by way of which the Minister of Agriculture had originally sought merely to put a floor under producers' prices.[34]

The Ministry of Food, in other words, was controlled by the very people who had been responsible for the development of the marketing boards and commissions, and who were predisposed to find in the emergencies of war an occasion for applying to all aspects of food marketing and distribution the techniques and ideas which had served their interests so well—though on a piecemeal and experimental footing—in times of peace. The Food ministry became a central agency for coördinating all the various trade associations—producer, manufacturer, wholesaler, and retailer—engaged in the food trades by converting them into official or semiofficial representatives of the government. In this capacity they were charged with the duty of carrying into effect instructions given them by the government which were, almost in their entirety, consonant with the ideas and objectives of the superseded marketing boards and commissions themselves.

There were, however, two differences in emphasis. Regulations restricting supply gave way generally to formal policies for expanding supply, and food rationing was added to the former controls over processing, marketing, and distribution. In line with the agreed division of labor between the Food and Agriculture ministries, foodstuffs production was the primary concern of the latter (except where it related to plant and processing capacity). That part of the rationing program which dealt with general allocation of supplies was, on the other hand, wholly controlled by the Food ministry. Within these limitations the Food ministry came to represent a sort of central, or "peak," association of the organized business interests of the various branches of the British food industries.

Carried over into the postwar period by the Labour government— ostensibly as a transition measure but possibly to become a permanent fixture—the Ministry of Food in June, 1947, worked with and through the following organizations; 120 representing producers, 213 representing manufacturers, 217 representing wholesalers, 128 representing

[33] *Lucas Report,* p. 57.
[34] *Ibid.,* p. 45.

retailers, and 299 known as "general purpose organizations." With most of these it maintained "direct" liaison; with the balance liaison was "through a representative committee." In addition, the ministry established some 50 or more "companies under Ministry of Food control."[35]

For the management of this medley of associations and companies, the Ministry of Food is divided into 45 divisions. Under the Animal Feeding Stuffs Division, which is typical, there are 28 national associations, 50 local associations, and 13 "companies under Ministry of Food control." Of the national associations, 8 are producers associations, 12 are manufacturers associations, 6 are wholesalers associations, 6 retailers associations, 2 general-purpose associations, and 3 fall into the special category of consumers associations.[36] Roughly the same division holds for the local associations. Some of the national associations are themselves central, or "peak," associations, and this is true of 11 local associations which are "affiliated to the National Association of Corn and Agricultural Merchants," and 6 "affiliated to the National Federation of Corn Trade Associations."

This machinery applies to imported as well as to home-produced foods. Thus the Dried Fruit and Edible Nuts Division has under its jurisdiction one company under Ministry of Food control (National Association of Dried Fruit Port Services, Ltd.) and a series of "other" and "general-purpose" organizations. "Other" organizations include the British Food Mission (U.S.A.), the Dried Fruits No. 1 Supply Sub-Committee of the National Dried Fruits Dealers' (War-Emergency) Federation, three overseas "purchasers"—the Australian and South African governments and Andrew Weir and Co. (Iraq)—and the Edible Nuts Executive Panel. The executive committee of this last panel consists of the chairmen and vice-chairmen of associations representing the following trades: almonds, apricot kernels, Brazil-nut importers, cashew nuts, desiccated coconut, edible nuts in shell, hazel nuts, shelled walnuts, and South African groundnuts.

---

[35] From a mimeographed *Directory of Trade Associations and Similar Organisations in Contact with the Ministry of Food* (Revision), issued by the Information Branch, Public Relations Division, June, 1947, marked "Confidential" but freely available to any person inquiring of representatives of food industries. It is not complete nor is it accurate in all details.

[36] These are the National Farmers Union (membership includes 80 per cent of all British farmers selling to markets), National Farmers Union and Chamber of Agriculture of Scotland, and National Horse Association of Great Britain. Several national associations serve in more than one capacity. Thus, the Agricultural Co-operative Managers Association acts as a manufacturers association, a wholesalers association, and a retailers association.

According to representatives of various divisions of the ministry—who are virtually all also representatives (most actually remaining on the private payroll) of one or more of the various private trading companies and trade associations being governed by their particular division—the ministry operates almost exclusively through the existing national or local associations if these are well organized and possess the necessary machinery and personnel to serve as official agents of the government. When this is not so, or where it seems easier and simpler to set up an independent and central coördinating agency, the government then establishes "companies under Ministry of Food control." This category "is not limited to those in which the Ministry has shares but includes those in which there is Ministry representation or partial control."[37]

Typically, these companies are formed of, by, and for the benefit of, the industry, with the Ministry of Food maintaining only so much control as will insure that the company pursues the interest of the industry in compliance with the major policy-coördinating decisions of the ministry itself. The policy decisions are, in turn, made within the appropriate division of the ministry by industry representatives, who then transmit these decisions to those other industry representatives who make up the governing board of the "company under Ministry of Food control." The company may or may not be incorporated. If there is any share capital, it is generally put up by the industry involved, and any profits may be distributed by the company to stockholders as in any ordinary commercial enterprise.

These companies merit very careful examination for a number of reasons. First, they clearly represent the culmination of a process of growth in government-business partnership which is looked upon with high favor among business sponsors and managers, and may be regarded as one of the most perfect examples of the application of the formula of "self-government in business." Thus they are a different, but consistent, application of the formulae underlying the prewar marketing boards and commissions, and might be looked upon as a wartime and postwar adaptation of the ideas which led to the organization of the Sugar Corporation. Second, they appear as almost the complete opposite of the nationalization program of Labour in the sense that they make possible arrogation by private and vested-interest groups of formal governmental authority to implement policies which

---

[37] *Directory of Trade Associations*, "Introductory Note."

are primarily congenial to a specific industry or trade.[38] That these companies speak and act on behalf of the government is neither here nor there; their first loyalty is to the industry from which their membership is drawn, to which their officers sooner or later expect to return, and which in many if not in most cases, continues to pay its representatives in the Ministry of Food—who fix ministry food policy for the guidance of the companies—out of private corporate or trade-association funds. Furthermore, the general rule holds throughout that the commanding positions are held almost exclusively by representatives of the large—not the intermediate or small—companies.[39]

But there is a third and for present purposes much more important reason for stressing the importance of these "companies under Ministry of Food control." The "privatization" of public functions which they represent is almost the canonical opposite of nationalization, and consequently, they would appear to be wholly unacceptable to the Labour government. But not only have they been taken over and continued by that Government in the postwar period, but there are also some indications that Labour may make them more or less permanent fixtures and adapt the ideas underlying them to other economic activities. To cite a single example: very much the same general ideas appear to be shaping the program for the development councils—a program which is supposed to embrace the 80 per cent of British industry which is not to be the object of nationalization legislation.

Within the industry, Marcom Ltd. is considered to be one of the best and most highly developed of all the "companies under Ministry of Food control." It may, consequently, serve as a sort of guinea pig to illustrate the implications of the device.

Marcom Ltd. was set up, under the Companies Act of 1929, on July 4, 1940, as a government corporation having control over the whole of margarine and compound-cooking-fat processing, importing, and dis-

---

[38] In the 1950 election brochure, *Labour Believes in Britain,* there is evidence of some dissatisfaction with this arrangement. The party is now pressing for nationalization, for example, of the Wholesale Meat Supply Association, and the Sugar Corporation.

[39] For example, most of the policy-making staff in the Oils and Fats Division is drawn from Unilever, the giant combine which produces and controls approximately 83 per cent of all fats going into soaps, margarine, and similar compounds of edible oils and fats in Britain. This staff regularly draws paychecks from the Ministry of Food as government employees, makes them out to the Unilever Company, and then receives in return checks from Unilever as though they were regular employees of the company. Former Unilever employees on the staff of the Oils and Fats Division of the Ministry of Foods found this practice general, and "proof," as one high official of the ministry put it, "of what a wonderful company Unilever was to work for." The same story was freely given by representatives of the Meat and Livestock Division.

tribution. Behind it lay some earlier experimentation, the first step in which had been the imposition of industry control, on October 7, 1939, which eliminated proprietary brands in favor of one standard for each fat, fixed prices, and allocated raw materials on the basis of prewar output and in keeping with formulae laid down by the government. Numerous protests were made. Particularly effective were the complaints of the national press that the controls meant serious loss of advertising revenue. The result was decontrol and the reintroduction of brands on Noverber 11, 1939. There were certain restrictions, however. Total output was limited to prewar production; maximum prices were established for different grades; consumer prices and a code number identifying the producing factory had to be printed on the wrapper; and the percentage of cheaper margarine to be produced was fixed at the prewar rate.

In the following summer Marcom was set up to serve as the special coördinative agency on the basis of the formulae embodied in the decontrol order. Specifically, it was authorized to do the following things:

Manufacture, sell, and distribute margarine and domestic cooking-fat compounds in the United Kingdom, Northern Ireland, the Isle of Man, and the Channel Islands.

Act as agents for the Ministry of Food.

Rationalize and coördinate the resources of the industry.

Acquire and take over in whole or in part the business, property, liabilities, etc. of any person or firm in the industry and trades covered by the order.

Acquire and take over shares, stock, debentures, etc. in any other company carrying on a business directly or indirectly benefiting Marcom.

Purchase, lease, exchange, hire, or otherwise acquire any real or personal property, patents, trade marks, trade names, licenses, rights or privileges which the company may think necessary or convenient for the purpose of its business. Also to construct, maintain, or alter buildings required for any of its various activities.

Pay for any property rights acquired.

Borrow, raise, or secure payment of money by the giving of mortgages, etc.

Draw, make, accept, endorse, and discount bills and notes.

Grant allowances, gratuities, and bonuses.

Lend money.

Invest money.

Cause the company to be registered or recognized in any foreign place or country.

Divide proceeds among manufacturers.[40]

---

[40] This listing is given as it was detailed by a representative of the Ministry of Food with reference to the enabling measure setting up Marcom, and as checked with representatives both of Marcom and of companies coördinated by it and under its control.

These are formidable powers. They are, in brief, the type of powers ordinarily lent to private corporations in the normal conduct of business plus the right to represent its decisions as possessing the authority of the national government. Furthermore, these powers are lent by the act of incorporation to the leading executives of the affected trade associations; the directors of Marcom were initially the Joint Executive Committee of the Edible Oil Association of England and Scotland, representing all British margarine and compounds manufacturers. This committee had been set up at a meeting held in London on September 21, 1939, and attended by representatives of 60 out of 76 invited firms. The president of the association was in the chair; the previous president of the association was then in charge of the Oils and Fats Division of the Ministry of Food. Hence in setting up the Joint Executive Committee to negotiate with the ministry, the association was establishing machinery for negotiating with its own former president, a man (J. B. Van den Bergh) who, incidentally, was also a top executive of the giant Unilever combine.

Because Marcom was merely the new name for the Joint Executive Committee of the association, the effect was to transform the association into a privately operated government corporation. As such it needed little new capital.[41] Furthermore, the government was to pay all manufacturing, factory, general overhead, packing, selling, and distribution costs. Technically, also, all income was its property. Profits were then pooled: one pool for margarine, one for compounds. Originally Marcom was to distribute all profits received from the ministry, but after March 29, 1941, this function was taken over by Marcom's *alter ego*, the Joint Executive Committee. Profits were limited to the amount of profit during the twelve months preceding the outbreak of the war, for the production and distribution of one and one-third times the prewar tonnage.

Under these circumstances Marcom was granted exclusive control over all processing and distribution of all edible fats and oils. Competitors were either eliminated entirely or taken over by Marcom. Thus, for example, at the outbreak of the war it was anticipated that all imports of lard would cease. However, under Lend-Lease large quantities of lard were imported after June, 1941. The Lard Importers Association, largely dominated by American firms—Swift, Armour, Cudahy, Wilson—made strong representations to be allowed to handle the im-

---

[41] Initial capital was £100, divided into 100 shares of £1 each.

ports through their usual channels. Turned down by the Ministry of Food, they appealed to the American Embassy. The result was that they were allowed to participate as members of Marcom, whereby they turned over this business to Marcom, shared in the profits of the lard trade which they no longer handled,[42] and were granted three representatives on the board of directors of Marcom.

One result of these operations has been a reduction in the number of companies in operation. Lard imports led to the reduction of compound fat companies from 48 to 4. By April, 1943, the number of factories processing margarine had been reduced from 29 (at the outbreak of war) to 12. Meanwhile, all companies and/or plants retired continued to be paid their proportionate shares out of the profits pool as though they were still in operation. This has been referred to, wholly without benefit of satire, as "nationalization by compensation."

With slight variations in detail, such appears to be the general pattern for the other "companies under Ministry of Food control," and with similar variations, such also is the existing postwar pattern for all these companies under Labour direction. It remains to be seen whether or not this inverse nationalization, or "privatization," as it might be called, is to be incorporated in Labour's long-range program for the physical planning of agriculture. Before turning to this aspect of the question, it is necessary to glance briefly at the other general line of wartime improvisation—the enhancement of agricultural production.

The principal wartime powers of the Ministry of Agriculture were set out under the Emergency Powers (Defence) Act in the Defence (General) regulations of 1939. Most important of these were the following:[43]

Regulation 51. Acquisition of land (to increase food production).

Regulation 61. Preservation of land for purposes of agriculture.

Regulation 62. Control of cultivation and termination of agricultural tenancies (i.e., the issue of directions as to cultivation, use or management of land); the termination of tenancies if directions are contravened.

Regulation 63. Destruction of game and pests.

Regulation 66. Delegation of functions (see Cultivation of Lands Order below).

---

[42] Previously Marcom had received no profit on lard which it distributed. Now it was to receive 6s. 8d. per ton. Lard importers were to receive 20 per cent of Marcom profits unless the total tonnage of lard distributed fell short of 500,000 tons per annum, in which case they were to receive only 15 per cent. After the cessation of Lend-Lease, imports fell off rapidly, but lard importers continued to receive their agreed share.

[43] As outlined by Isabella Williams, op. cit., p. 71.

Regulation 67. The right to call for compulsory returns and to make use of them in any way required.

Under the Cultivation of Lands Order, 1939, the County War Agricultural Executive Committees (one for each of the 62 administrative counties of England and Wales) were established to exercise the Minister's powers under the Defence Regulations (Regulation 66 above). Thus a wide measure of decentralisation was achieved for carrying out the Ministry's policy to increase domestic food production.

An Executive Committee had in general from eight to twelve unpaid members, mainly farmers, each appointed by the Minister. Each Committee had a number of sub-committees dealing with various branches of the Committee's work such as cultivation, labour, machinery, land drainage, livestock, technical development, feeding-stuffs, insects and pests, horticulture, finance and general purposes, goods and services and war damage. Further decentralisation was effected by the appointment, within each county, of District Committees (there were in all 478 of these in England and Wales) whose chief responsibility was to keep direct contact with the farmers individually and to bring to the notice of the Executive Committees any case which called for action. To this decentralisation is largely attributable the success of the planning of the Ministry of Agriculture. In accordance with the needs of the country as a whole, plans for the acreage of all major crops were made and then broken down to a country basis and afterwards, again, by districts and parishes, to that of the individual farmers.[44]

Supplementary legislation, of which there were several important instances,[45] was designed further to increase the control of the Ministry of Agriculture and Fisheries over food production. There were three important innovations. First, the Minister could determine the total national acreage to be sown and cultivated, the amount of land to be used for different crops, and the allocation of crop acreages by districts and farmers. Second, he could set standards for good land usage, good cultivation, and good crop management, and in pursuit of this authority inspect to see that standards were complied with. And third, he could take over land which he believed was not being properly used and make such disposition of it as he saw fit for the duration of the war, in pursuit of his duty to see that the maximum output was obtained from domestic agricultural resources.

[44] A similar arrangement under the direction of the Department of Agriculture of the Secretary of State for Scotland was applied to Scottish agricultural production.

[45] E.g., The Agriculture (Miscellaneous War Provisions) Act of 1940 extended the system of prewar commodity subsidies and made special payments for plowing land; the Agricultural Wages Regulation Amendment Act of 1940 set up a national minimum wage; other acts made special provision to aid land drainage, establish a National Agricultural Advisory Service "for the improvement of agricultural education," and increase the resources of the Agricultural Mortgage Corporation from £13,000,000 to £31,000,000. Williams, op. cit., p. 71.

The over-all result of the application of these powers was that "by 1944 the acreage under crops in the United Kingdom had increased from 8,813,000 acres in 1939 to 14,548,000 acres, the acreage under wheat had increased by 82 per cent over pre-war, while the potato acreage was doubled. The output of the agricultural industry in terms of food value increased by 70 per cent. This expansion was achieved largely by a redirection of the whole farming economy so as to make possible the maximum production of direct human foods."[46]

This result, particularly against the background of the preceding trends in British agriculture, represents a revolutionary change of no mean order. It involved two major shifts in production, and raised two fundamental issues of long-term policy. The first shift was in land acreage. Between 1939 and 1944 some 7,000,000 acres of "permanent grass" had been plowed up. In the latter year a little under 10,000,000 acres remained in this category. If, as some experts believe, 4,000,000 acres in "permanent grass are all that is justified and necessary in England and Wales,"[47] area under tillage might be further increased by 6,000,000 acres. This would mean, in effect, a virtual doubling of British tillable acreage. Should it prove possible to raise output of the added acreage to something like prewar standards of production without undue cost—which some British soil experts believe feasible[48]—this would mean doubling of home production of cultivated crops.

The second shift in production was an increase in cultivated crops which brought with it a corresponding deterioration in the livestock position. As indicated above,[49] this had become very serious by the end of the war. Because "the greatest number of people can be fed from a given area of land when they are content to live wholly or mainly on a vegetarian diet, cereals, pulses, vegetables and fruits" and "when foodstuffs of animal origin are required, much more land is needed to feed people, because of the loss of food values in the conversion of vegetable

[46] Statement of the Minister of Agriculture and Fisheries, Tom Williams, in *Farming and Mechanised Agriculture, 1948*, p. 147.

[47] A. P. McDougall, "Our Flocks and Herds—Their Future," *Journal of the Farmers' Club*, part 4, 1946.

[48] For a general analysis of the possibilities of increasing British soil fertility, based largely on experience in New Zealand, see G. A. Holmes, *Revolution in Agriculture* (London, 1946). Interesting also is *The Land and the Nation: Rural Report of the Liberal Land Committee, 1923–25* (London, 1925), particularly chap. iii, pp. 31–38.

[49] Footnote 5, p. 447. Before the war roughly three-fourths "of the value of British agricultural output was in the form of livestock products and only one-sixth in farm crops." By 1945–46 these proportions had shifted to roughly one-half and one-fourth respectively. *The Agricultural Charter: A Statement of Conservative Agricultural Policy* (London, 1948), p. 8. George Walworth, "Walworth Letter," questions the reliability of the value figures.

foodstuffs into milk, meat and eggs by the animals concerned,"[50] this policy had its independent justification in times of war. But it also meant—with the single exception of milk[51]—a serious decline in home-produced protein foods and animal fats. British food standards have long been deficient in both; the war change and increased reliance upon domestic production meant a worsening of this dietary misbalance.

Because some of the increase in crop production resulted from the change-over from permanent grass, which was used for the grazing of sheep and beef cattle, to tillage, it seems impossible for Britain to plow up more of her grasslands without worsening her dietary standards (so far as home production is concerned) unless there occurs also a general overhaul of British agricultural methods in both crop production and animal husbandry. This, however, is tantamount to saying that the first or wartime "revolution in British agriculture" requires, so long at least as the objective of self-sufficiency in food is to be pursued, a second revolution in agricultural technique and land management.

Not, of course, that something has not already been done along this line. During the war the number of tractors used in British agriculture tripled, the amount of fertilizer used was doubled, and many other changes increased agricultural productivity. Nevertheless, as a sample postwar survey brought out in considerable detail,[52] there was still a great deal the matter with British agriculture. Much land was badly laid out; many farm units were too small; farm buildings were frequently inadequate or badly in need of repair; soils were inadequately classified and cultivation in many places was poorly adapted to soil types; many farms were poorly managed; there was a general lack in some areas of good roads, electricity, water supply, etc.; and both farm labor and farm tenantry relations were frequently such as to have an unfavorable effect upon productive efficiency.

[50] A. W. Ashby in *Post-War Britain*, p. 65. He cites the following statistics:

PERSONS MAINTAINED PER 100 ACRES

Crop	Edible Products	Persons
Wheat	Bread, beef, pork	208
Oats	Meal	172
Potatoes	Vegetables, pork	418
Mangolds	Beef	28
Mangolds	Milk	117
Swedes and turnips	Beef and mutton	20
'Seeds' hay	Beef and mutton	13
Meadow hay	Beef and mutton	12
Finest pastures	Fat beef and mutton	40

[51] Between 1939 and 1946 the total of cattle and calves had increased from 6,770,145 to 7,266,526, with a corresponding increase in veal supply, and a somewhat larger proportionate increase in milk output because of better feeding practices. Stapledon, *op. cit.*

[52] *National Farm Survey of England and Wales, A Summary Report* (Ministry of Agriculture and Fisheries, 1946).

Considerations such as these inevitably raised the two fundamental problems of long-term policy referred to above. First, what degree of self-sufficiency was actually possible and desirable, and if desirable, at what cost? Second, what type of national agricultural program was necessary in order to achieve the desired production and still be consistent with other aspects of land planning—such, for example, as those envisaged in the Town and Country Planning Act of 1947?

On the first, opinions vary widely. Some believe that Britain can be entirely self-sufficient. For one writer,[53] this is "dependent upon all our land being harnessed and farmed scientifically, upon security of tenure and upon the raising of the level of the farm worker to that of the town worker." According to a more widely quoted estimate by Colonel Pollitt,[54] for Britain "to produce the whole of her food-stuffs," which he believes entirely possible, "means bringing all ploughable land under an arable rotation, stocking it with more than double the head of livestock we have now, nearly doubling the number of men on the land, providing roads, water, electricity, drainage, buildings, implements, fertilizers, etc." To effect such a complete overhauling would require new fixed capital of £707,000,000—nearly a doubling of fixed capital per acre[55]—and new working capital of £483,500,000.[56] Pollitt believes this can be accomplished at a cost less than that required to supply Britain when two-thirds of her food had to be imported from overseas,[57] and will supply food of such variety and quality as will materially improve the dietary standards of the British public.[58]

Such estimates, however, are regarded by most British experts as "theoretical and not practical"; they are far less optimistic. But all are

[53] Arthur Smith, *Agriculture's Challenge to the Nation* (London, 1941), as reviewed in the *Journal of the Farmers' Club*, Dec., 1941, p. 97.

[54] George P. Pollitt, *Britain Can Feed Herself* (London, 1942), p. 3. For an interesting early statement of this position see Sir Charles Fielding, *Foods* (London, 1923). Particularly interesting is table XXI, p. 251. Fielding was formerly Director of Food Production.

[55] At prewar values for both figures, new capital would come out to £20 7s. per acre. The 1938 "assumed value" per acre was £25; the total fixed capital of a completely modernized British agricultural system would be £45 7s. per acre. *Ibid.*, p. 30.

[56] Of which £253,500,000 would be tied up in livestock, and £230,000,000 in "implements and machinery" giving a total of new capital of £13, 19s. per acre on 34,700,000 acres. (All figures are in prewar values.) *Ibid.*, p. 31.

[57] Using 1938 figures, home produced foods were value at £220,430,000, and imported foods at £437,427,940, giving a total of £657,857,940. The estimated cost of production of the food equivalents from domestic production under the conditions assumed would be £643,000,000. *Ibid.*, pp. 32–33.

[58] For this comparison he takes the proposed dietary of the *First Report of the Advisory Committee on Nutrition* made to the Minister of Health. This would raise the British diet from a per capita daily consumption (1934) of protein from 0.189 lbs. to 0.236, fats from 0.262 to 0.264, and carbohydrates from 0.909 to 1.003. *Ibid.*, p. 9. These latter figures are probably too low to maintain an adequate nutritional diet.

agreed that a vast increase in home production is possible. The so-called Cripps Four-Year Plan,[59] over the interval 1949–1953, entails an expenditure of £450,000,000 with which it is hoped to increase domestic production by 50 per cent—a figure which would amount to nearly double the prewar total, and which would reduce British food imports to roughly one-third of total requirements. But the fundamental question is how this is to be done.

The Conservative program, with sights set very much lower, calls for "long-term expansion of British agriculture based upon guaranteed prices and an assured market, a reform of distribution and marketing, a Workers' Charter providing status, incentive and security, effective priority for necessary capital development and measures for improving efficiency."[60] It calls, as detailed examination of its proposals will show, for a widening and extension of the series of prewar improvisations in production and marketing which have been outlined earlier in this chapter.

In the past, wherever they have faced the problem of agriculture at all, Labour spokesmen have insisted on going much further. Two things, they have held, are essential above all others. The first is national ownership of the land, and the second is land planning. The case for the first has been made largely on the ground that it was necessary in order to achieve the second.

In making this case, Labour has had the support of many eminent specialists. Thus Lord Addison, Minister of Agriculture in the Labour cabinet of 1930–31 finds that "the recognition of this fact is no longer a Party matter . . . it is now accepted by men in all political parties as the only way of doing the job." He cites, as an example, the opinion of A. G. Street, outstanding authority on British agriculture, who said: "More and more I find myself being forced to consider this problem (land nationalization) and more and more I am becoming convinced of two things in connection with it. *Firstly* that the nationalisation of the land of Britain is not so very far away; and *secondly* that it is the only thing which can provide a workable solution to the land problem of this country in all its aspects."[61] In a similar vein Sir A. Daniel Hall, dean

[59] *European Co-operation.* Memoranda submitted to the Organisation for European Economic Co-operation relating to Economic Affairs in the period 1949–1953, Cmd. 7572, p. 17.
[60] *The Agricultural Charter*, p. 40. This plan calls for postwar production which would be 150 per cent of prewar.
[61] *A Policy for British Agriculture*, p. 67. Italics in original. "Lord Addison still occasionally argues on land nationalisation, but I think, realizes that it is unlikely to be achieved in the near future. The stronger case is for the reorganisation of farms, but even Addison had to admit that the cost would be prohibitive." "Walworth Letter."

of British agricultural experts and formerly Chief Scientific Advisor, Ministry of Agriculture, gave it as his opinion after a long life devoted to the reform of British agriculture that "as the first necessary step in this reconstruction of the countryside the State will have to take over the ownership of the agricultural land, for only by doing so can the State make it fully available for its proper purpose—urban as well as agricultural. Again only the State as owner can protect this limited area of ours from the waste and misuse that comes from pursuing one end without regard to other vital interests that are involved."[62]

Such statements might be taken as providing the central text and point of departure, repeated *ad infinitum,* for the Labour party's program of agricultural reform.[63] But here, as in other nationalization plans, Labour spokesmen have always taken the strong position that nationalization is only a first step designed to clear the way for thoroughgoing technical and social reform, and it has become increasingly true that this view has come to be couched in terms of national planning of agriculture. As early as 1935 a Labour pamphlet spoke of "Labour's Great National Plan" which called for making "agriculture a public service under self-respecting conditions, paying its way, providing a fair living for those engaged in it, yielding a full return not only of agricultural produce but of health and happiness for our people."[64] Again, as Tom Williams put it, "It is not a question of freeing the farmer from the tyranny of the landlord, so much as providing the farmer with an effective landlord; unifying ownership, providing efficient management and organization, intensifying drainage improvements, and ensuring that such assistance as the State may provide for the industry will be used for the benefit of the farmer and the community, instead of filtering through to individuals who have nothing but a financial interest in the land."[65]

What specifically must such a national plan for agriculture do? Voluntary coöperation won't work on the production end; it has been

---

[62] Sir A. Daniel Hall, "Agricultural Planning and Policy," in *Industry and Rural Life.* Being a summarized report of the Cambridge Conference of the Town and Country Planning Association, Spring, 1942, edited by H. Bryant Newbold (London, 1942), p. 21.

[63] For typical examples see Sir Stafford Cripps, *The Economic Planning of Agriculture* (Labour Party, 1934) ; Lord Addison (Minister of Agriculture in the Labour Government of 1930–31), *Labour's Policy for our Countryside* (Labour Party, 1937) ; and Tom Williams (Minister of Agriculture in the 1945 Labour Cabinet), *Labour's Way to Use the Land,* one of a series of booklets entitled *Labour Shows the Way,* and edited by Clement R. Attlee, Prime Minister in the 1945 Cabinet.

[64] *Labour and the Land* (Labour Party, 1935).

[65] Williams, *op. cit.,* p. 87.

tried and it failed.[66] State aids in the form of "subsidies and bribes" not only do not improve things, but they consolidate vested interests and freeze maniford inefficiencies into all steps and phases of agriculture from the farm to the consumer's table.[67] Surely nothing short of a unified national policy, implemented by a national plan whose coverage and range of control were coextensive with those of all valid interests engaged in production and use of foodstuffs, would suffice. This, Labour's spokesmen have long been insistent, only socialism can accomplish. None of the plans or programs of either the other parties—Conservative and Liberal alike—even remotely touches the heart of the problem.

In detail, one might infer from perusal of the miscellaneous Labour literature on the subject that Labour seemed united on the idea that an adequate national plan for agriculture must provide for all of the following:

Land ownership should be vested in the hands of the state, and taken away from the idle gentry. "The bulk of the farmers of Britain do not own the land they farm . . . Approximately two-thirds of the land available for agriculture is owned by the aristocracy . . . the landed gentry [is] . . . a legacy from feudal times."[68] On the other hand "about 40 per cent of all farm-workers live in tied cottages," poorly equipped, from which they may be evicted at will by the landowner.[69] Lock, stock, and barrel, the remainder of the inefficient and unjust feudal system of land tenure must go.

Social Conditions in agriculture must be completely revamped. Living conditions, wages, health, village and country life in general, the provision of amenities, etc., are all parts of this problem. One is virtually compelled to infer from Labour literature that it is their position that the social side of the problem of land planning is coextensive with all aspects of the lives of the rural population.[70]

Crops and the techniques of farming should be completely modernized. Crop acreage should be decided on a national basis, and then broken down regionally and locally. Farm methods—all the way from soil improvement, planting, etc. through to harvesting, storing, and shipping—must be mechanized as far as possible, and brought up to best approved practices. Products, methods of cultivation, costs, prices, financing, etc. are different facets of a single problem of efficient cultivation. It might, that is to say, be inferred that Labour has in mind

---

[66] Cripps, *op. cit.*

[67] Williams, *op. cit.*, pp. 30–34.

[68] D. J. Diston and Michael Williams, *What About the Land* (Independent Labour Party, n.d.). Far more important now is the judgment that without thoroughgoing technical farm reorganization owner-occupants are likely to be no better off—they might, on balance, even be worse off—if tenancy were abolished entirely.

[69] *Rural Realities* (Labour Research Department, 1946), p. 3.

[70] See, in particular, the reasons given for "the drift from the land" in the *Scott Report*, pp. 16–21.

a national plan which must be coextensive with all land cultivation, and all techniques and problems of agricultural production.[71]

Farming, processing, and distribution of agricultural products must be discussed in a general context of ideas which imply that each is a different phase of the problem of agricultural production; they cannot be separately and independently dealt with. One might be led to the further inference that in the Labour view there must be a national farm plan, which would be coextensive with all phases of the preparation and supply of the agricultural product[72] up to the point where it is sold to the ultimate consumer.

Domestic agriculture, food imports, and agriculture in the Empire—not to mention non-Empire countries previously selling in large quantities to Britain—are interrelated in an intricate pattern. Certain products—consumer goods such as coffee, tea, spices, citrus fruit, tobacco, and industrial raw materials such as cotton, wool, sisal, and wood pulp—must be imported from abroad even if a program of "self-sufficiency" from domestic production is fully carried through. If not, the dependence upon other external supplies—notably in feeding stuffs, oils and fats, and grains—increases this emphasis. So far as one may judge from scattered Labour statements, in short, whatever may be proposed by way of a national agricultural plan would also envisage coördination of the domestic program with either or both Empire food planning and world food planning.

Agriculture, other land uses as visualized in town and country planning, and plans for ruralization of various industries are so closely related to each other that it is difficult, if not impossible, to tell where one begins and the other leaves off. Virtually all Labour pronouncements on the various aspects of the subject would lead one to conclude that in its view agricultural planning is a component of some type of national physical planning which visualizes the linkage in some manner or other of multiple-phase land planning with its general planning programs at all levels and stages of development—town, population, and industrial location and development.

It was against the background of a miscellany of ideas from which inferences such as these might be drawn by the unwary that the Labour government evolved its "plan for agriculture." It will be interesting to see how far it has gone in the process of carrying out the program which would seem to be implied by its previous statements of policy, and to examine the implications of the first steps taken for further legislative enactment.

[71] It is precisely at this particular point that inference departs most widely from observable reality.

[72] There are few exceptions in the Labour literature which would seem to invalidate this inference. To illustrate, a very great deal is made of the frequently cited example, that in 1938, when the sum total of domestically produced and imported foodstuffs was valued at £650,000,000, the cost to the consuming public totaled £1,500,000,000—giving a cost of distribution £250,000,000 larger than the entire cost of production. See, e.g., G. A. Holmes, *op. cit.*, pp. 118–125. It is difficult to say what such data means, but all are agreed that the costs of distribution are too high. Countless examples could be offered from the daily papers on this point, and also on the lack of coördination between production and distribution plans and policies.

Labour's Postelection Agricultural Program

On August 6, 1947, there was enacted into law a bill described, in an earnest peroration by the Minister of Agriculture, "as an agricultural charter and a farmer's Bible."[73] It bore the short and ambiguous title, "An Act to make further provision for agriculture."[74] This bill, Tom Williams said, "will place agriculture in its rightful place . . . as a senior partner in our economic system."[75] It would effectively codify and unify the prewar miscellany of bills, orders, and regulations having to do with agriculture, under which "millions of acres of cultivable land . . . lay derelict" and agriculture was regarded as "the poorest of poor relations."

Producing, as it did before the war, nearly £300,000,000 worth of produce, and "at this moment, well-nigh up to £600 million per annum," land is one of Britain's important natural resources, which must be used to the maximum to help close her import-export gap and still make it possible for her to feed her population well. Furthermore, the problems of agriculture could not be treated in isolation. They are closely interlocked with industry and other forms of planning. And, strange as this must have seemed at first to Opposition ears, Williams could "not claim sole authorship of this Bill. It is a product of the combined wisdom of all the different sections of the industry, and of the advertised views of the three major political parties in this House." Expert bodies, such as the Royal Agricultural Society of England, had found that farmers needed guaranteed prices, and in return for this "must accept an obligation to maintain a reasonable standard of good husbandry . . . and submit to necessary measures of direction and guidance, subject to . . . appeal to an impartial tribunal." The leader of the Tory Opposition, Winston Churchill, had made a "declaration of policy to electors in 1945 in which he said, 'Our policy will be one of stable markets and prices. In return for this all occupiers and owners of agricultural land must maintain a reasonable standard of good husbandry and estate management.' " The manifesto of the Liberal party had been even more forthright.[76]

Hence all had concurred in the leading provisions of the act, and "the provisions are fairly simply summed up in two words . . . 'sta-

---

[73] Tom Williams (Minister of Agriculture and Fisheries), in *Hansard*, Vol. 432, col. 625.
[74] 10 & 11 Geo. 6, Chap. 48. It is a lengthy document of 111 sections, 13 schedules, and 118 pages.
[75] Williams, in *Hansard*, Vol. 432, col. 625.
[76] *Ibid.*, cols. 625–626.

bility and efficiency' ", and "every considerable proposal in the Bill can be grouped under one or other [sic] headings." Part I of the act takes care of "stability" by the device of "assured markets and guaranteed prices." Part II takes care of "efficiency" by setting up methods of assuring "good estate management and good husbandry." And the balance of the act deals with tenurial rights (part III with agricultural holdings, and part IV with smallholdings), and problems of administration and ministerial guidance (part V is administrative and general). Since the Tory Opposition agreed that the core of British agricultural ills was to "guarantee prices and markets to ensure stability," and "because that is the underlying principle of the Bill" they did not propose to "divide the House on Second Reading," with the result that the bill passed into law without ever having been put to a vote.[77]

This seems a strange denouement for Labour's past utterances indeed. Gone completely is all talk of nationalization—beyond, that is to say, the faint hint that the subject might be reintroduced at some time in the distant future.[78] While markets are to be "assured" and prices "guaranteed," the act contains not even a side or parenthetical reference to the marketing acts, the wartime Ministry of Food distribution controls, or the whole complicated and involved subject of distribution costs. In debate the Minister of Agriculture would go no further than to state that clause 4, entitled "Power to Supplement Arrangements," was widely enough drawn to allow the application of any or all of the prewar machinery of the marketing boards and commissions.[79] But no provision was made, or, for that matter, even hinted at, for correlating the powers of the Ministry of Agriculture and Fisheries with those of the Ministry of Food.

Nor, again, is there a trace of a decision having been arrived at as to whether the Government should come down at top-policy levels on the side of maximizing the export drive or of deciding to promote agri-

---

[77] Said W. J. Brown, "This has, I think, been the most remarkable debate on Agriculture to which I have had the privilege of listening during my time in this House. For all of us are combined to bless the Minister of Agriculture, and this is practically without precedent. . . . We approve the principles of his Bill; we praise the Minister for having introduced it, and, in short, I have never seen such a happy family in my life in this House on the subject of Agriculture." *Hansard*, Vol. 432, col. 689. This was typical of the chorus of praise which greeted the Minister's proposals.

[78] "For better or for worse, nationalisation of the land was not part of our mandate for the present term of office." *Ibid.*, col. 638.

[79] This, however, applies only to the commodities listed in the first schedule of the act—fat cattle, fat sheep, fat pigs, cow's milk (liquid), eggs (hen and duck in shell), wheat, barley, oats, rye, potatoes, and sugar beet. Control over all other crops is to be implemented solely by "efficiency tests" as provided in part II. *Ibid.*, col. 630.

cultural self-sufficiency. There is not even a reference to Empire problems, though the Government repeatedly was pressed to answer whether or not they "accept the position that the home producer comes first and the Empire producer second."[80]

Equally puzzling is the omission of any reference to the problem of ruralization of population and industries, and of the whole medley of related problems concerning social relations—beyond some efforts to define more closely tenant and small-holder rights and duties—and conditions in the countryside. The Minister was willing to state that the Land Utilisation Division and the Forestry Commission of the Ministry of Agriculture and Fisheries would coöperate with the Ministry of Town and Country Planning. Beyond that he would not go. Hence there is nothing in the act which reflects any concern over the recommendations of the Scott report in this connection, and consequently no machinery was devised for correlating agricultural development with population relocation and industrial development under auspices of the ministries of Town and Country Planning, Fuel and Power, Supply, Transport, and the Board of Trade or with the plans of the ministries of Health and Social Insurance.

Finally, the act contains no provisions for any national physical plan for agriculture, nor any statements of policy which might serve as guideposts in the formulation of any such plan. This last omission is all the more surprising when it is recalled that on no point had the Labour party been so critical of the other parties, and that it had frequently and emphatically upheld those portions of the Scott report which came out most clearly for comprehensive postwar national planning of British agriculture. In fact, the Labour party seemed in the passage of this act to have been guilty of the very type of extemporizing and improvising against which the Scott report had warned most strongly.

Since, however, the Agricultural Act of 1947 was confessedly framed against the background of the Scott report, it may be worth digressing for a short space to see just what the Scott committee proposed should be done. Under the heading of "A Five-Year Plan for Britain" this Conservative-party-dominated committee had spoken on

[80] Captain Crookshank for the Opposition, *ibid.*, col. 884. Earlier, he had insisted that "the crux of the whole question" was whether "the home producer must come first and the empire farmer next?" (Col. 651.) Pressed for an answer, the Solicitor-General, speaking for the Minister, replied: "I have already said that the Government have kept themselves free to implement the policy embodied in this Bill, and that is a sufficient answer to the question." (Col. 884.)

behalf of long-range and comprehensive agricultural planning in words whose meaning was clear and unmistakable:

Throughout this Report we have stressed the importance of realizing that planning is a continuous and evolutionary process of national development. We have emphasized especially the need for long-term policies, for example in agriculture, to secure the necessary conditions of stability for satisfactory development. In the realm of forestry, planning involves looking ahead for at least a century; in constructional development possibly for even longer periods. In thus calling attention to the long-term character of planning there is danger that matters of real urgency, demanding immediate attention, may be deferred for future consideration. This is a very real danger: it is apparent at the present time when there is a not unnatural tendency to say that the immediate problem is the winning of the war and that all questions of planning and reconstruction can be considered when peace comes. Nothing could be more fallacious: for not only is the vision of the future the stimulus for the present, but plans must be made in advance and be ready when the time for their execution comes. As a nation we may have a genius for extemporisation, but our great failures, both in war and peace, have been due to a failure to think ahead and to make plans in advance.[81]

Concerned in all this "only with the parts of such a comprehensive plan as affect the countryside in contradistinction to the town," the Scott committee had recommended "that a plan be drawn up, consistent with the general policy for continuous national planning, of work to be completed within five years and that the execution of the work be undertaken accordingly." During the first year there was to be set up a "system of land classification for planning purposes"; the "standard procedure for co-operation between the appropriate town-planning officers and officers representing agricultural and rural interests" should be laid down; "panels of architects and planners" were to be set up; a "comprehensive investigation of electricity, gas, and water supplies" was to be completed; "the demarcation of National Parks" was to be completed and a "National Parks Authority" set up. Over the next five years the following were to be completed:

i) town and country planning schemes to cover the whole country so that there will be thereby a full indication of the areas where industrial zones are or are to be established and satellite towns or new settlements to be located;

ii) a definite number of houses for rural workers, the number to be decided by taking stock of the position at the time;

iii) a full survey of all villages and hamlets to determine the existing facilities for village social centres (including playing fields) and the drawing up of

[81] *Scott Report*, p. 89.

a plan for the provision where suitable of centres of the village college type and the opening in all counties of a long-term building program;

iv) programmes for electricity, water and gas, to be based on the survey to be made in the first year;

v) the National Park scheme with hostels, etc. in working order;

vi) the determination and signposting of all footpaths and bridle paths;

vii) rules, if any, for the control of access to the countryside, the use of commons and of highways and other rights of way;

viii) the elimination of unsightly advertisements, petrol stations, etc.;

ix) the registration of title.[82]

Lest there be any doubt about the nature of its planning ideas, the committee detailed at great length its specific "Recommendations and Suggestions." These included a system of "local planning" which "must be compulsory and not permissive" and which would blanket the entire country. All such "local planning schemes should be agreed by the Ministry of Agriculture before approval by the Central Planning Authority," and "every interest which in any respect transcends merely local interests, should be regarded as a national interest." At all points where the national interest dominated, there was to be a national plan, and in all places where agricultural planning involved close liaison with other government departments, divisions, etc. the necessary co-ordination was to be arrived at under the direction of the Central Planning Authority.[83]

The Scott committee was appointed by a Coalition government which was largely, if not wholly, dominated by the Tories. Hence, it seems paradoxical indeed that its report should be eulogized by Labour, and shrouded in silence by the Conservatives.[84] But it seems even more paradoxical that the central and dominating idea in that report—the "Five-Year Plan for Britain"—should have been both the primary attraction for Labour prior to the elections, and the aspect most completely ignored in its subsequent agricultural legislation. Finally, the sense of paradox is once again heightened by Labour's complacency in the face of the general support it won from its former enemies by accepting the Conservative formula of "guaranteed prices and assured markets" in shaping its own masterpiece of legislation in this field.

Was, consequently, Hugh Fraser of the Opposition correct in congratulating the Minister on the Agricultural Bill "for a number of

[82] *Ibid.*, pp. 90–91.

[83] See *ibid.*, part V, "Summary of Recommendations and Suggestions," pp. 91–99.

[84] The Conservative *Agricultural Charter* does not even make parenthetical reference to the Scott report. Careful survey of similar Conservative utterances shows that they are, with rare exceptions, equally reserved.

reasons, chief of which is that the normal procedure of Socialist legislation has been reversed?" The bill pleased him. To be sure, "the carrot is somewhat diaphanous," he said, but "the stick is hickory all the way up, with knobs on in the schedules."[85] A little later a colleague, Heathcot Amory, wished "to contribute a modest note or two to the symphony of welcome" with which the Opposition greeted the bill, since, as he went on to add, "the Labour Minister is now engaged in carrying out policies which had been formulated by his Conservative predecessor in office, the powerful mogul in formulating Tory policies in general, Mr. R. A. Butler."[86]

There seem three possible answers to Fraser's jibe. The first is that Labour has dealt in the past in terms of pleasing, but still (for it) mostly glittering, generalities to cover up the fact that it has no agricultural program at all. For the nonce, the answer given by a critic in the New Statesman and Nation, may serve as an adequate statement of this interpretation. "My criticism," he wrote, "of Mr. Tom Williams, the present Minister, is that he has not known, except in a vague sort of way, where he was going. Partly through circumstances beyond his control, he has lived from hand to mouth, achieving only a patchwork of improvisations."[87] This is the view accepted by virtually all of the critics of the Government as found, for example, in its own so-called "Keep Left Group."

A second interpretation is that the Labour party has actually gone over to the Conservative position. This would mean that it had really given up land nationalization as a long-run objective, that it intended to by-pass the principal recommendations of the Scott report relating to "national planning" for agriculture except so far as might be implied in the Town and Country Planning Act, and that it might be satisfied merely to extend a series of government aids to agriculture—scientific, technical, subsidies, etc.—which would assist individual farmers to be more successful as business entrepreneurs, and to adopt, with appropriate postwar adjustments, the general ideas underlying the prewar marketing boards, commissions, and corporations.

This second interpretation is, politically at least, a far more serious charge. To justify it a number of allegations can be, and have been, made. For one thing, the very nature of the Agricultural Bill of 1947 seems to bear it out. The whole Conservative prewar program for agri-

[85] *Hansard*, Vol. 432, col. 670.
[86] *Ibid.*, col. 697.
[87] F. W. Bateson, in *New Statesman and Nation*, May 8, 1948, p. 370.

culture might be summed up, as indeed it frequently has been, in terms of "guaranteed prices and assured markets," and this serves as a leitmotiv for Williams' "agricultural charter and farmer's Bible." Again, the Ministry of Food, born of wartime emergencies from the womb of Conservatism *in extremis,* has been kept by Labour. Not only kept, but its internal constitution as a "distributor's agency" remains unaltered and its power, in the pulling and hauling that has been going on continuously behind the scenes, increased at the expense of both the Ministry of Agriculture and Fisheries and the Ministry of Health. Control over food sanitation and inspection, formerly in the hands of the Ministry of Health, has been taken over by the Ministry of Food. A similar transfer, this time with Parliamentary approval, resulted in the removal of control over food standards from the Ministry of Health, where industry representatives could not control them directly, to the Food ministry, where they become the creature of big and powerful processor and distributor combines.

As for the Ministry of Agriculture, it is equally obvious, as has been insisted in the past by all parties from right to left, that processing and distribution are the preëminently strategic sectors of the agricultural control and development program. It makes relatively little difference what is accomplished at the production end, whether on behalf of the farmer, the tenant, or the consuming public, so long as the detailed management of processing and distribution is inefficient, and irresponsible (to the public). Consequently, it is difficult to avoid the conclusion that the Coalition government by the very act of setting up the Ministry of Food, and the Labour government by the very practice of continuing and extending its power and influence, have pushed the Ministry of Agriculture and Fisheries into a secondary and subsidiary position. The Ministry of Food, furthermore, is to be continued by Labour as a permanent department, the Minister to have Cabinet ranking. As matters stand, in the words of a Liberal critic of the Government, there are historically few more curious spectacles than that of the leftish theoretician for the Labour party, John Strachey, presiding, with benefit of a versatile repertory of brilliant socialist phraseology and supported by his personal office staff alone, in disembodied grandeur over a vast and complicated machinery for implementing policies which are in no part of his making, and which have been formulated in their main outlines by giant combinations of business which are opposed to the socialist tenets of the Labour government from center to circumference.

But there is a third possible interpretation of Labour's extemporizing and improvisation. It might be that the Labour party has not yet revealed its hand; that it is feeling its way slowly into the heart of this tangled and dangerous problem before deciding how to maneuver, what tactic to employ, what are to be the logistics of its long-term plan for subduing this antisocialist redoubt of its most bitter and uncompromising enemies—the snobbish and aristocratic masters of Britain's tradition-steeped fox hunts and deer parks. Labour has long and characteristically viewed the Tory part in such social terms; so to proceed against them would be thoroughly consonant with approved Fabian tactics. "One thing at a time," said one of the members of the Labour Cabinet when asked why only one part of the Labour program had been acted upon and another closely related aspect—ultimately far more important and strategic—had been completely by-passed. "Nationalisation of the land," Tom Williams said, "was not part of our mandate for the present term of office." "Then of the next?" one feels compelled to ask. Or, at any rate, "Sooner or later?"

This is not merely an academic question, for, upon the basis of past evidence at least, this is the decisive question upon the answer to which depends the whole character of future programs—or even the existence of such programs—for national physical planning for agriculture. There are only three things to go upon in attempting to find an answer. First is the possible further import of the Agricultural Act of 1947. Second is the possible acceptance of the Lucas committee's recommendations. And third is the possible existence of closely related plans in other sectors of the national economy which, when united with those evident in the field of agricultural production, might appear to trace a coherent pattern of evolving policy.

The first two of these possibilities may be dealt with here. The third refers back to the preceding chapter on town and country planning, and ahead to the two following chapters. For the first, consider briefly the leading provisions of the act. The first part, dealing with "Guaranteed Prices and Assured Markets" has as its stated purpose "enabling producers to plan ahead" as far as possible. To this end the Minister is to conduct "annual and special reviews of conditions" in agricultural industries, and, upon the basis of his findings, to devise formulae for, and to fix, minimum prices so that producers may know as far ahead as their requirements determine just what their prices and costs are to be. There is to be an annual review for "wheat, barley, oats, rye, potatoes or sugar beets" and other specified crops, and biennial reviews on alternate years for "milk, cattle, sheep, pigs and eggs."[88]

Thus knowing what his minimum prices are to be—and assured that if he cannot sell at those prices the government will make up the difference[89]—the government asks the farmer to be a good "estate manager and husbandman." For "the purpose of securing that owners of agricultural land fulfill their responsibilities to manage the land in accordance with the rules of good estate management, and that occupiers of agricultural land fulfill their responsibilities to farm the land in accordance with the rules of good husbandry,"[90] the act sets up "rules of good estate management and good husbandry." The first set of rules requires the owner to supply the proper type and amounts of fixed equipment, and to provide any other appropriate conditions which may be deemed necessary in order to make possible "good husbandry" on the part of the tenant. The second set requires the occupier or tenant to maintain "a reasonable standard of efficient production, as respects both the kind of produce and the quality and quantity thereof, while keeping the unit in a condition to enable such a standard to be maintained in the future."[91] The appropriate criteria are specified in detail.[92]

The Minister has the right to issue instructions regarding any or all of these criteria, inspect to see that instructions are complied with, take over the land and manage it himself or have it managed on his behalf if instructions are disobeyed, and do anything additional which is clearly within the broad intentions of the act. Relations between owners and tenants having anything whatsover to do with any of the foregoing criteria of efficient management and husbandry, or with other mutual rights and obligations under the law, are similarly codified and brought under the administration of the Minister of Agriculture.[93] Special provisions are made governing compensation for improvements made by tenants, for land whose value has decreased as a result of changes effected under the act, for land from which the owner or manager has been

[88] *Act*, Sect. 5 (1) and (2).
[89] *Act*, Sect. 4 (1) (b) (i) and (iii).
[90] *Act*, Part II, Sect. 9.
[91] *Act*, Sect. 11 (1).
[92] Permanent pasture and arable land are to be properly managed and cropped, fertility is to be maintained, adequate stocks of the right types of livestock are to be kept, fields are to be kept clean of weeds and pests, and animals of disease, good standards of breeding are to be followed, and the necessary maintenance and repairs of equipment, fields, and buildings are to be made. *Act*, (2) (a–f). Further detail is given in sections 95–108.
[93] Part III, "Agricultural Holdings," and Part IV, "Smallholdings," detail these provisions at great length. The Minister must make special provisions for promoting smallholdings—typically considered, in Britain, as more or less the equivalent of the American concept of "the family farm."

dispossessed on the authority of the Minister, etc. The "rules of estate management and good husbandry" are binding also upon the Minister and upon all other departments of national or local government holding land, or managing land under this or any other legislative authority which may be devoted to agricultural purposes.[94]

Thus, so far as the law is concerned, the power of the Minister to guide and direct farming is extraordinary. Under authority of the Minister land holdings which are too small may be combined, and if too large may be broken up; schemes of drainage and water supply may be prescribed; new buildings may be required, or old buildings torn down; crops, systems of crop rotation, all phases of the care of animals and of the care and conduct of crops from planting through cultivation and harvesting must comply with the appropriate standards, etc. For the carrying out of his duties the Minister may call into being elaborate administrative aids. Chief among these is the Agricultural Land Commission which is to be made up of such qualified persons as the Minister may select, and to perform such functions as he may delegate to them.[95] For the adjudication of disputes and other questions requiring arbitration, the Minister is to set up a series of Agricultural Land tribunals, which—though the Minister must refer protests against his orders to them, and must "where such a reference is duly required . . . act in accordance with the report of the Tribunal and not otherwise"[96]—are bound to accept ministerial direction in all important decisions simply because he appoints them, and issues orders for the guidance of their proceedings.[97]

As with the Minister of Town and Country Planning, however, the Minister's most important administrative agencies are to be special local authorities, to be known as County Agricultural Executive com-

---

[94] According to Lord Addison, *op. cit.*, appendix iv, pp. 322–323, land owned by public bodies in the middle thirties totaled somewhat over 3,000,000 acres. A writer in the *Daily Telegraph* estimated the current (1948) total to be over 8,000,000. W. F. Deedes, "State's Grip on over Eight Million Acres," *Daily Telegraph*, Aug. 6, 1948. This figure is disputed by Government spokesmen.

[95] Sections 68–70. There is to be a separate, but in all respects similar, Welsh Agricultural Land Sub-Commission. The Commission must make an annual report to the Minister, and the Minister must lay this report before Parliament. Its first annual *Report* (January 13, 1949) dealt with possible compulsory purchase under the 1947 act of the Romney Marsh area, some 50,000 acres in Kent and East Sussex. *Times*, Jan. 14, 1949.

[96] Sect. 74 (1–4).

[97] According to section 73 (1) the Minister determines "the number of areas . . . as he may consider expedient" for which there are to be Agricultural Land tribunals; section 73 (2) and the ninth schedule empower the Minister to appoint two of the three members of the tribunal (the third, to serve as chairman, is to be appointed by the Lord Chancellor) and all other staff members; and section 73 (3) gives the Minister power "by order" to "make provision for the procedure of Agricultural Land Tribunals" in all important details.

mittees. These are the peacetime surrogates of the wartime County War Agricultural committees referred to above[98] and have substantially the same duties. They are to serve as his agents in the actual supervision of agricultural production within the local areas, are in all respects subject to his instructions, and have as their principal duties taking the necessary measures to see that each larger area, county, and individual farmer makes the best possible contribution toward achieving the national "production targets."

Production "targets," or "goals," or "programmes," are then to be set up by the Minister for all domestic agricultural production—by areas, by types of usage (e.g., acreage under tillage, in permanent grass, or in rough grazing), by crops, and by grades, qualities, or standards of product. Such "targets" are to be given for each successive year, and wherever possible for several years in advance. Ultimately, the targets are to be consistent with the long-run program of Britain's permanently stabilized land-utilization system.[99] Each and every target is to be based on an analysis of domestic needs; costs and prices of domestic production as against the imported product; requirements for machinery, fertilizer, labor, buildings and other plant; and whatever necessary additional aids—ranging from scientific information to direct subsidies—might be required to achieve the desired output.

Avoiding further details—and these seem everywhere consistent with the foregoing sketch—it would seem that the Minister of Agriculture and Fisheries was vested by the Agricultural Act of 1947 with all the authority necessary to plan agricultural production within Britain. Although his obligations and powers stop short when the products leave the farm to pass into the channels of trade to be processed and distributed to the ultimate consumer, the act leaves him with full authority to work out the necessary arrangements with the ministries of Food, Town and Country Planning, Health, etc., whenever the solution of farm production problems is dependent upon action in these other spheres. Up to this point, however, he can control the whole of agricultural production, alter, if need be, owner and tenant relations, and fix the terms of trade which define the degree of prosperity for all cultivators of the soil. He may even—under his authority to dispossess in-

---

[98] P. 467. The Minister may, however, as in the Town and Country Planning Act, combine two or more counties or parts of counties as joint bodies.

[99] For example, the Forestry Commission's "ultimate objective is the establishment in stages over 50 years of 5,000,000 acres of well-managed forest." *Home Affairs Survey*, Aug. 3, 1948. Similarly there is to be—at some time in the future—so much land in grass, so much under tillage, so much devoted to various types of crops, etc.

efficient husbandmen and bad managers—nationalize, in effect, such segments of agricultural land as are, from his interpretation of the relevant facts, not being farmed efficiently.

Actually, so far as may be discovered by examination of the literature put out by the ministry, and from personal questioning of staff members, there exists very little at all by way of a "national plan." The first issue, whether emphasis should be placed upon self-sufficiency or upon enhancement of the export drive, has not been decided upon, nor has Empire policy been determined. Thus far the Minister has not evolved the long-needed national water and land-drainage schemes.[100] Nor have schemes for rural electrification, rural roads, rural housing and the supply of other social needs and cultural amenities been evolved.

With respect to agricultural production itself, the actual conduct of the ministry, under authority of the Agricultural Act of 1947, has been that of an official bargaining agency which must work through the National Farmers' Union (N.F.U.) if it is to achieve any of its targets, and before it can set any of the conditions or supply any of the aids which are subsidiary thereto. The National Farmers' Union, again, is supposed to represent about 80 per cent of the farmers of Britain, and a larger percentage of their product. It is dominated, that is to say, largely if not wholly, by the very squirearchy which provides the most bitter and determined opposition to Labour in and out of Parliament.[101] And it is this same cross-section which "has been the voice of the farmer in negotiations with the Government on agricultural prices and marketing control" in the past—a voice which has been influential in shaping the marketing acts of the thirties, and in giving them the form and content which resulted in the wartime and postwar system of agricultural controls, including, among others, both the establishment of the Ministry of Food and the Agricultural Act of 1947.[102]

[100] See, for example, the listing, "Drainage Schemes Urgently Required" in an early Labour party brochure entitled *How Labour Will Save Agriculture* (1934).

[101] The aristocrat amongst British farm organizations is the Land Union, founded in 1909 "for the purpose of safeguarding the interests in all kinds of landed property, whether agricultural or urban" (Land Union statement in *Farming and Mechanised Agriculture, 1948*, p. 228) largely as a result of the serious inroads made upon landlord prerogatives by the Agricultural Holdings Act of 1908. It sees eye to eye with the National Farmers' Union on the principal point at issue between Labour and the Conservative parties. In a brochure, *Agricultural Reconstruction*, the Land Union quotes from the National Farmers' Union the statement that "The Landlord and Tenant System in British Agriculture has served the industry well in the past and is perfectly capable of continuing to do so." This is quoted as the "farmers' view" in a country where two-thirds of the farmers are tenants!

[102] The N.F.U. was set up in 1908 to protect "the economic and political interests of farmers in all branches of the agricultural industry, and has been the voice of the farmer in

Turning, finally, to this last segment of the British agricultural picture—the agricultural marketing acts—the investigator is left almost wholly in the dark concerning the Labour government's plans and intentions. The only ray of light is shed by the Lucas committee. This committee was set up by Williams in 1946, with the following terms of reference: "To review the working of the Agricultural Marketing Acts; to consider what modifications of the provisions of those Acts for the organisation of producers are desirable in the light of experience before 1939 and of developments since then in Government policy, as it affects food and agriculture; and to make recommendations."[103]

After having reviewed in considerable detail prewar and wartime experiments with the marketing and distribution of agricultural products, the committee based its principal recommendations squarely on the principle that, since "inefficient production and inefficient distribution go hand in hand," the solution of the problems of domestic agriculture must be found in plans which embrace all stages in the path traveled by foodstuffs from the farm to the ultimate consumer. To this end, neither the former commodity boards and commissions nor the wartime measures of the Ministry of Food were adequate. The former failed partly because they vested sole power in the hands of producers and ignored many other interests, and partly because "any scheme of guaranteed prices invited inefficiency" unless coupled to strong incentives to counteract this tendency which were lacking in earlier measures.[104] The latter failed partly because it was a "distributors' Ministry" which was necessarily "distributor minded" and hence suffered from the fault of the prewar producer organizations,[105] and partly because a government department is not "a suitable instrument for disposing of the agricultural produce of this country upon a permanent basis" simply because "the marketing of the crops, meat and milk of Britain

---

negotiating with the Government on agricultural prices and marketing control." (N.F.U. statement in *Farming and Mechanised Agriculture,* 1948, p. 230). It maintains a series of standing committees, a Parliamentary lobby, a series of technical and policy advisory services to farmers, and publishes books, pamphlets, and journals. The latter include: *N.F.U. Record; News Sheet* (weekly) ; *Notes on the Work of the Council; N.F.U. Information Service; Agriculture in the Commonwealth;* and *Commonwealth News-Service.*

[103] *Lucas Report,* p. iv.

[104] *Lucas Report,* pp. 53–57. The allegation that farmers had shown little interest in efficiency once prices were guaranteed has been bitterly resented by the N.F.U.

[105] The term "producer" in this context is decidedly ambiguous. Actually, in most of the prewar commodity boards and commissions (equally with the wartime Ministry of Foods), the dominating interests were food manufacturers, wholesalers, and retailers—represented by their leading trade associations, and dominated within these ranks by large-scale business corporations.

is a huge commercial undertaking, and the very nature of the Civil Service makes it unsuitable for the executive functions of commerce."[106]

Hence a new formula must be found. The committee proposed that, for each major commodity mentioned in the first schedule of the Agricultural Act of 1947, there be set up independent bodies to be known as "Commodity Commissions." These would "have a closer affinity to Public Utility Corporations than to the pre-war commissions" and would "be financed from public funds." The government, for whom they acted, would guarantee "both an outlet and a price," and the "Commodity Commissions should assume ownership of the produce at the point of the price guarantee" by purchase. They would then be "in a position to exercise full proprietary rights in the product from this stage." The commissions would be "jointly appointed by the Agricultural Ministers and the Minister of Food," and should be jointly responsible to them.[107]

The Lucas committee, in effect, recommends sandwiching between farm production and the processing and distribution of farm products a series of autonomous ("independent") government corporations ("commissions"). These corporations would take over physically the whole of the crop or product as it left the farm, and at the guaranteed price. The guaranteed price would already have been negotiated between "the appropriate Agricultural Departments and the National Farmers' Unions"—with the commissions participating—on three levels or stages. First, to secure a "global figure for an appropriate adjustment of the aggregate agricultural income of United Kingdom farmers," second "the allocation of the global figure amongst the various com-

---

[106] "Enterprise and initiative entail willingness to risk mistakes. Civil Servants cannot afford to take these risks. It is of the essence of commerce to win more on the swings than you lose on the roundabout, but if every loss on the roundabouts entails having your Minister pilloried by a Parliamentary Question, then the profits on the swings will be sacrificed to insure against loss on the roundabouts ... efficient agricultural marketing will entail a fairly ruthless cutting of many distributive margins, and the elimination as redundant of many distributive and processing interests. A Government Department is a poor instrument for this purpose. Each and every interest that is subjected to pruning will organize an energetic lobby against it in 500 or 600 constituencies, whilst the tax-payers and farmers who would benefit will be unconscious of these proposals and their defence will probably go by default. A Ministry will therefore always be tempted to let things go on and have a quiet life." *Ibid.*, p. 57. This ignores completely the fact that on its own showing, the establishment and staffing of the Ministry of Food ignored virtually all the sound and well established rules for selecting civil-service personnel. By drawing staff almost entirely from especially interested business circles and allowing them to maintain their former business connections—in many cases, even to remain on business payrolls—the ministry virtually guaranteed divided loyalties in its ranks, and secured the very antithesis of the civil-service attitude of "disinterested devotion to the public welfare" which has so long been the ideal of the British civil service.

[107] All quotation in this context, unless otherwise indicated, are from the *Lucas Report*, pp. 58–68.

modities," and third, the "further breaking down of the commodity allocation into a schedule of prices by making seasonal price variations, quality variations, and so on." The effect would be to divide the national global sum for all agriculture into global sums for each commission, and to divide each of the latter by some appropriate formula among regions and farmers, and by qualities and grades of product. At all stages the commissions would work with and through the appropriate farmers unions or other organizations. The basis for setting prices would be similar to that obtaining under the commodity boards and commissions before the war.

Once in possession of the crop at these prices, these commissions or public corporations would then "normally make full use of the existing channels of processing, manufacture and distribution and sell or direct their produce to private merchants and manufacturers." They would, in other words, work through the existing trade-association machinery and business facilities of food-processing, wholesale, and retail channels. They might, however, by-pass any of these at will should they find them indifferent to methods of securing marketing efficiency. "No tenderness for existing interests," the committee emphasized, "must be allowed to stand in the way of the tax-payer's right to have the produce disposed of by the most efficient organisation possible."

For the farmers the Lucas committee favored applying to all principal crops the prewar device of the commodity boards as they had been set up under the marketing acts of the early thirties. The National Farmers' Union would be the policy coördinating body for the farmers, and would conduct, directly or indirectly through its member organizations, the negotiations with the Ministry of Agriculture.[108] For processing and distribution the wartime habit of dealing with processor and distributor organizations as bodies representative of the whole of the appropriate industries or trades would be continued, along with the tendency to favor combination of these into ever more general peak associations which would coördinate local and specialized associations nationally and coterminous with major commodity lines—wheat and wheat by-products, livestock, meat, and packing by-products, etc. The Ministry of Food would represent the government here.

[108] See, especially, the *Lucas Report*, p. 63, where the committee finds itself convinced that "there is nowadays an eager desire not only to secure as soon as possible the full resumption of marketing schemes now in suspense or partial operation, but also to promote additional schemes . . . there is a sound case for a marketing scheme for virtually every product of British agriculture."

The several commissions, or public utility corporations, would then employ the leverage of their strategic position to encourage implementation of the provisions of the Agricultural Act of 1947 which were designed both to improve farm production and to effect "comprehensive reorganisation and reform of the marketing system." The manner in which these dual purposes might be realized is then illustrated in detail by two examples, one having to do with all stages in the production, processing, and marketing of "fatstock" operating under price guarantees, and the other with hops and horticultural products which are initially to be "non-guaranteed price commodities" until the appropriate machinery can be worked out for applying the basic formulae of the reccomendations to them also. The leverage is to be employed to introduce grades and quality rating, to improve packing, processing, and by-product plants, to divert low-quality raw materials and market surpluses into special manufactured forms, to improve and cheapen storage and transport facilities at all stages of movement, to relocate plants and markets if need be, and in general to rationalize and render efficient all steps, stages, and processes from the farm to the consumer.

How is not indicated. Nor by what means.[109] Yet despite the fact that the Lucas committee recommends—in rather general terms—little more than streamlining prewar and wartime machinery, its suggestions have met with bitter opposition. The Conservatives opposed them because their adoption would set up "monopolistic trading corporations" solely responsible to the state, which would be able to decide policies for all levels of processing and distribution, thus forcing "the whole of British agriculture into one strait-jacket organisation." They favor, instead, "producers' coöperation both through voluntary organisations and through statutory marketing Boards."[110]

A possibly somewhat more potent reason for Conservative opposition was the fear that if the Lucas committee's recommendations were accepted considerable power would be taken from the Ministry of Food, which is now under manufacturer and distributor control so well consolidated that it would be very difficult to loosen without a thorough

[109] In moving the second reading of the new Agricultural Marketing Bill, the Minister of Agriculture (Tom Williams) said it was a comparatively modest measure designed to bring this important part of the agricultural structure into harmony with the major changes brought about in the last few years in food policy and agricultural policy. No position was yet to be taken on the major recommendations of the Lucas report. *Times*, Jan. 20, 1949. Under the new arrangement the marketing boards remain cartel-like bodies as before, modified only by certain residual powers of the Minister of Agriculture to widen and accelerate action along the same general lines.

[110] *Agricultural Charter*, pp. 19–20.

and drastic reorganization of that department—something the Labour government is not at present prepared to carry through—and at the same time considerably strengthen the Ministry of Agriculture. The latter, despite its tendency to cater to the wishes of the powerful National Farmers' Union, has definitely been both more independent of trade-association pressure and more sensitive to the types of programs for agriculture and food distribution which the Labour party has long advocated. There also exists the fear, nowhere clearly expressed, that even though the commissions favored by the Lucas committee might appear as but little more than a new version of the idea underlying the wartime corporations under the control of the Food ministry, nevertheless, in the hands of a Labour government they might once again become the thin edge of a wedge which the Government would use gradually to nationalize or socialize the food industries.

Yet it is also reasonably clear that the Labour government has given way to the Conservative view on this point. Not the Ministry of Agriculture but the Ministry of Food is being strengthened. Despite the conviction, everywhere conceded, that the problems of "efficiency" in one sphere cannot be solved without taking action in the other, the division of function between the two ministries has tended to become more clear-cut and the lack of united policy more pronounced. Finally, the report of the Lucas committee itself seems gradually to have been shelved by the Ministry of Agriculture for having gone too far in proposing future changes. This action of the Labour party cannot be explained on the grounds of opposition to the Lucas recommendations by the powerful coöperatives, since the latter were heard by the committee and have apparently given their general approval to its recommendations, although their own plan received virtually no attention at any stage of the discussions of the committee, nor at any time since the original report was rendered.[111]

[111] Detailed inquiries made in person at the headquarters of the C.W.S. in Manchester received a uniform response on this point. The C.W.S.'s own plan—involving an enormous expansion of the coöperative system—had never been given an adequate hearing in Labour circles. This is particularly surprising in view of the fact that the coöperatives were fully aware that the wartime commodity controls were almost entirely in the hands of representatives of big business combines. On June 26, 1940, a memorandum was submitted by the representatives of the coöperative movement to the National Council of Labour (liaison body on which the coöps were represented) in which they viewed "with grave concern the personnel of the Constitution of the various Government Commodity Control Boards set up since the War. This seriously threatens public interests far beyond the Cooperative Movement. From very similar arrangements Combines and Multiples emerged from the last war enormously increased in trade and power, for example, Levers, Cold Storage, Vestey, Imperial Chemicals, United Dairies . . . That increase gave impetus to vast expansion continuing ever since and providing control over supplies and prices not in the public interest, and, poten-

The over-all effect is that the Labour party has continued into the postwar period the policy of extemporizing and improvising on the agricultural front which characterized the prewar period. Like the issue of "land nationalisation," the "national planning for agriculture," of which Labour spoke so frequently in the past, has either been given up, or postponed. So far as may be told from the literature and the legislation, there seems to be no Labour policy for agriculture which goes very far beyond the makeshifts of the past.

Not only does this seem to be so within the field of agriculture proper and in its relation to the food-processing and distribution industries, but it seems also to be true so far as these problems are joined and integrated with other closely related fields. So far as the visible evidence goes, that is to say, they are not linked to plans for Empire development, which fall in part under the Ministry of Food and in part under the Colonial Office. Again, they are not linked to plans for food imports in general, which fall in part under the Ministry of Food and in part under the Board of Trade. They are not even linked at all closely with plans—such as they are—being formulated by the Ministry of Town and Country Planning. But of special importance, finally, they are not linked with those plans for industrial location and development which must ultimately determine Britain's capacity to effect any significant and sustained postwar recovery at all.

tially, extremely inimical to that interest. Again, for this War, we have the regulation of commodity supplies entrusted to dominant private interests in the trades concerned, which provide most of the directors of commodity controls, particularly under the Ministry of Food." There follows a partial listing of such controls, and the comment, "Under our present competitive system each must have regard to himself and his, and directorships of this kind offer opportunities perfectly fair to the ordinary business mind, but not fair to the consumer. Mostly they will do their best according to their lights, but theirs are not the consumers lights." *Report of the Fortieth Annual Conference of the Labour Party* (London, 1941), p. 9. The gravamen of coöperative complaint, however, seems greatly to be weakened if, as a leading authority in the coöperative headquarters in Manchester put it to the author, the reason for their nonparticipation was because "we found ourselves in the position (during and since the war) when few of our leading men were prepared to relinquish their positions with the coöperative movement to take full-time parts with the ministry. Private trade directors or officials were generally able to make quite attractive arrangements with their own employers or firms" which democratically controlled organizations like the coöperatives could not duplicate. In continuing this system the Labour party, in short, has consolidated the private traders, and in so doing has further weakened the influence of its coöperative supporters in the Labour government.

CHAPTER XII

Industrial Location and Development: National Planning

We cannot...neglect any steps which on the one hand will make our industries more competitive in the markets of the world, and on the other will provide us at home with the best goods at the cheapest price consistent with good conditions for those in the industry. The Government must in one way or another get the best advice it can on what these steps should be. Three conditions are essential; firstly, advice must come from industry itself because that is where all the past experience resides; secondly, employers and workers should be equally represented because both sides not only have a contribution to make but also will have to carry out any plans that may be decided upon; and thirdly, the public and Parliament must be satisfied—whatever the recommendations may be—that they are truly in the national interest and that the two sides of industry have not "ganged up" against the consumer for their own advantage.—Sir Stafford Cripps, October 15, 1945.

THE LABOUR PARTY's outlook is, and has long been, dominated by the social and economic problems of the manufacturing system. Knowledge of this provides the alpha and omega of an adequate understanding of the party's character, biases, and probable courses of action. Sooner or later all its other plans will be found to trace their orbits around this gravitational center and their success or failure will, to Labour, be decided in terms of their relation to it. What happens to industry will determine the future of Britain and the viability of the Labour party as a creative political force.

MANUFACTURING AND LABOUR'S PROGRAM

There are several reasons for this emphasis on the industrial system. First, and most obvious, is the fact that the Labour party is preëminently a trade-union party. Coöperatives, liberals, intellectuals, and miscellaneous middle class groups belong to the party, but the most powerful among them play at best a secondary role. The membership whose interests dominate the Labour party is drawn primarily from persons on factory payrolls. Where this is not so—as in the extractive industries, transport and shipping, and the bulk of the distributive trades—the livelihood of its rank and file is based almost entirely upon the fortunes of the manufacturing industries, and they have long been wont to identify their interests with them. Behind the Labour party, that is to say, and serving almost as its *alter ego*, stands the T.U.C. In the main the T.U.C.

[493]

speaks for the factory employee, reflects his outlook, grapples with his problems, mirrors his values, and programs for his future. In its relation to the Labour party, the T.U.C. is more than the tail that wags the dog; it is the trunk that shakes the head and the driving force that translates creature needs into an inevitable demand for a satisfying course of action.

The strategic importance of the T.U.C. in Labour party councils is heightened by the relative importance which industry plays in British economic life. Relative to the total population, Britain is easily the most highly industrialized major country in the world. More than elsewhere, industry's fortunes determine the level of national well-being, and its illnesses betray the weakness, lame the functioning, and threaten the viability of the social and economic institutions of the whole country. A long line of special inquiries and investigations conducted by various governments in the past has thoroughly established that no plans for any other sector of the economy can long be successful unless they are tied in with plans for industrial location and development. There are no major exceptions; the generalization holds in equal measure for virtually all the sectors nationalized under the Labour government, for town and country planning, for agricultural production and distribution, for health and social security, and it almost completely dominates all planning in foreign trade and empire policy.

There is a third reason why Labour attention should be centered on industry, and that is that Britain came out of the Second World War with an industrial system which was in a very bad condition in comparison with many other segments of her own economic system and with general standards of industrial development among her leading competitors abroad. In some areas, as comparative data—frequently of indifferent quality—will show, British levels of efficiency and planning are high, but these are mostly outside, or at best (with some exceptions) subsidiary to, manufactures proper. British finance and shipping rank with the world's best. Her national and regional power networks represent a *tour de force* of imaginative reconstruction. Her new towns and conurbation planning are setting new standards for the physical reconstruction of urban life among the western countries. In terms of acreage productivity, even her agriculture will rate high in international comparison along several crop lines.

But in industry the picture is different. Despite many bright spots in some of the newer industries—particularly some of those developed during the period of the last war—in the main her industries lag behind. They lag behind best practice on the Continent, and behind the general levels of American production. And they lag behind in many vitally important lines not by small margins but by big ones.

How big it is difficult to say. All such comparisons are likely to possess important theoretical weaknesses. But this does not necessarily invalidate them, although it renders them somewhat imprecise in detail

TABLE 27

OUTPUT PER HEAD IN MAIN INDUSTRIAL GROUPS IN THE UNITED STATES, 1935 AND 1939
(United Kingdom output = 100)

	1935	1939
Average, 32 sample industries....................	211	224
Higher than average U. S. productivity:		
Packing materials (glass containers, tin cans)....	415	423
Durable mass-production consumption goods		
(motor cars, wireless sets).....................	310	312
Machinery.......................................	280	280
Seed crushing, rayon, soap, matches, paper.......	224	225
Less than average U. S. productivity:		
Manufactured food.............................	191	195
Iron and steel..................................	173	174
Clothing..	160	164
Textiles..	155	160
Building materials..............................	113	125

SOURCE: Rostas, *Comparative Productivity in British and American Industry.*

and subject to interpretation in any given case only with considerable caution. The over-all picture, however, seems to show that man-hour productivity in the United States generally ranges from two to three times that in most comparable British lines. Comparative figures have been given for the coal and steel industries.[1] Best known of all are the more comprehensive estimates made by Rostas.[2] These show, for 32 sample industries, that if in the middle thirties British output per worker be represented by 100 the index of American output was 216. Because of the shorter working week in America, "the British worker worked on the average 27 per cent more hours than the American worker." If allowance is made for this, "output per manhour was perhaps 2.8 times as high in the United States as in Britain."[3]

[1] For coal, see chapter iii, and for steel, chapter v.
[2] Laszlo Rostas, *Comparative Productivity in British and American Industry*, Occasional Paper no. XIII (London, National Institute of Economic and Social Research, 1948).
[3] *Economist*, Aug. 14, 1948, p. 274.

Although the results, as shown in table 27, varied widely from one main industrial group to another there was no major class of industries in which American productive superiority was not evident, and in some industries[4] the results were astounding. For tin cans American output per man-hour was 7½ times as high as British; in radio and rubber tires 4 times as high; and in the highly important classification of ma-

TABLE 28

ROUGH ESTIMATE OF CHANGE IN BRITISH OUTPUT PER MAN
BETWEEN 1935 AND 1947

Industry	Production in 1947 compared with 1935 (London–Cambridge index)	Employment June, 1947, compared with June, 1935	Approximate change in output per man
	per cent	per cent	per cent
Textiles............................	−25	−24.5	−0.6
Clothing and leather..................	−12	−22.4	+13.4
Metal production.....................	+33	+48.0	−10.1
Metal using trades....................	+40	+48.4	−5.6
Food, drink, and tobacco..............	+6	−13.0	+21.9
Chemicals...........................	+18	+61.8	−27.0
Building and building materials........	−20	+17.7	−32.0
Fuel and power.......................	+17 [a]	+1.6	+15.2
Coal................................	−14	+5.9	−18.6
Paper and printing....................	−18	−11.8	−7.0
Total (including other trades).......	+9	+14.7	−4.8

SOURCE: *Economist*, Aug. 14, 1948.
[a] This increase marks a fall of 14 per cent in coal, a rise of over one-third in gas and a doubling of electricity output.

chinery 3½ times as high. In only one field, fish curing, where the American index of output per worker was 54, did Britain show a definite superiority.

But that is not the worst of it. While the war brought about something approaching a technical revolution in America, with resulting further increases in worker productivity, in Britain output per man has barely held its own. Data brought together by the London and Cambridge Economic Service suggest a fall of nearly 5 per cent over the 12-year period, 1935–1947. Table 28 gives their figures for 10 industrial groups.[5]

[4] Rostas was criticized by some British economists for his choice of industries, but no evidence that his figures are not representative has been adduced.
[5] For comparable data—worked through at painstaking length—for the prewar period (1907–1935) see Laslo Rostas, *Productivity, Prices and Distribution in Selected British Industries*, Occasional Paper no. XI (London, National Institute of Economic and Social Research, 1948).

That there are occasional exceptions to be found,[6] and that (to repeat) all such estimates—as Rostas has himself pointed out—are of
questionable accuracy at best, does not fundamentally alter the picture.
All the quantitative data are in general agreement, and the qualitative
data support them throughout. Nor, again, is the picture relieved when
one turns to the reason given for the differences. On the contrary. Virtually all analyses of the causes of the low level of British production
show that they cannot be eliminated by piecemeal measures. They are
rooted in the whole British industrial system; in its need for vast new
investment before it can begin to catch up;[7] in the prevalence of small-
scale plant, badly situated with respect to preceding and following
operations, unequipped for modern mass-production methods, and producing a wide variety of unstandardized goods;[8] in relatively low levels
of installed mechanical horsepower;[9] in the well-nigh universal resort
on the part of both management and the worker to practices of a restric-

[6] For example, "it appears that similar ships built in Britain required only two-thirds of
the effort in man-hours needed in America. Technical progress between the wars, the simplification of structural designs, and wartime plant installations, resulted in the average output
per person employed in British yards being 50 to 75 per cent higher than during the years
1914–18." Association of Scientific Workers, *Engineering Reconstruction, the Key to
Britain's Prosperity* (1947), p. 27.

[7] Gross capital formation in Britain was estimated "at £747, £1221, and £1944 million in
1945, 1946, and 1947, respectively" and while the latter figure reached the astonishing total
of roughly 20 per cent of national income, still "the ambitious investment program of the
United Kingdom for 1947, which became the target of criticism, made up only about one-
fifteenth of the deficiency of investment incurred over seven years." Seymour Harris, *The
European Recovery Program* (Cambridge, 1948), pp. 9, 38.

[8] A startling example given by a British automobile engineer personally to the writer
(Summer, 1948), and believed by the narrator to be not at all unusual, was the following:
During the war, army lorry stations on the various British war fronts were typically fitted
out to repair five sizes of trucks (lorries) ranging between one and ten tons carrying
capacity. Each truck has about 2,000 parts. But because of lack of a system of interchangeable
parts, and because of many different makes, and models, each station had to carry not
10,000 parts (with interchangeable parts the sum should be even smaller than this), but
400,000 parts in order to be able to repair any breakdown of this purely utilitarian equipment. While important improvements had been made since then, it was his opinion that the
illustration still reflected the general condition obtaining in the postwar British automobile
industry. One result is that even where, parts plants, or plants processing at one stage for
subsequent further processing, are fully oriented on a mass-output basis, it is still impossible
for them to achieve economy of output because of the supply of unstandardized materials
or the lack of standards in the industries or markets supplied, or both. See, e.g., the letter
of John Ryan, of the Metal Box Company in the *Economist*, Sept. 4, 1948, in which he
maintains, in contrast with the figures of Rostas, that the British tin-box industry would show
productivity as high as or higher than the American industry, were it not that "the British
tin box industry still devotes a great amount of its capacity to the production of highly
decorated non-standard containers, to meet the varied demands of the British manufacturers.
The production of such containers must necessarily show up adversely in terms of output
per man hour."

[9] In 1947, according to the Association of Scientific Workers, *op. cit.*, p. 56, "At the outbreak of war there was approximately 3.5 h.p. at the disposal of every worker in this
country, but in the U.S.A. the figure was 5.5 h.p."

tive character in virtually all lines of industry;[10] possibly in the unnecessarily high ratio of overhead or nonproductive personnel to
productive workers;[11] etc.

All these, and many other, weaknesses are added to any natural
handicaps Britain may possess; for example, the generally low level
of her man–natural-resource ratio, or in the poorer quality of certain
resources, such as iron ore, and the more unfavorable geological conditions under which most of her coal must be mined. Nevertheless, the
very existence of these handicaps is also proof of the need for thoroughgoing and comprehensive overhauling of her industrial structure. Given
such handicaps it is always true that the only way to overcome them is
through a bold and imaginative program which is coextensive with
the boundaries of the problems faced. (The technical reorganization
schemes of the Coal Board are a case in point.) When added to the
foregoing "man-made" shortcomings, these natural weaknesses make
the case for a drastic and far-reaching reconstruction and planning of
postwar industry in Britain well-nigh conclusive, even were there no
further reasons for it.

This backwardness of British industry becomes evident at a moment
when the usual avenues for counteracting its deleterious effects upon
the domestic economy are rapidly closing. Thus Britain can no longer
balance a large excess of vital raw-materials imports by income drawn
from ample and expanding foreign investments. The war narrowed this
stream from a mighty flow to a precarious trickle. Even the Empire has
become an uncertain source of economic strength. Part of it is gone,
and most of what remains—Commonwealth and colonies alike[12]—is no
longer readily, or at least without vast expenditures of effort, to be
coördinated to the needs of a seriously weakened motherland. What
virtually all areas of the Empire need are huge expenditures for new
industrialization and general economic overhaul. They need, in other

---

[10] See, e.g., typical data given by A. S. J. Baster, *op. cit.*, particularly chapter 2, "Producing
Less," and chapter 4, "Working Less."

[11] According to a British industrial consultant, Lewis C. Ord, for every 100 productive
workers in the United States, served by 25 nonproductive personnel, in Britain there were
120 productive workers served by 90 nonproductive personnel. *Secrets of Industry* (London,
1944), p. 118. Ian Mikardo, in a personal letter to the author, states that he believes that
these figures "are phoney" because the necessary data—not to mention classification—do not
exist in Britain, that "management engineers in both countries ... have the *impression* that
the non-productive ratio tends to be higher in the U.S.A., not lower, than in Britain," and
that this very fact may account for higher American productivity. This seems entirely
possible. It all depends entirely upon the nature of the classification "nonproductive," and
the effectiveness—in terms of production—with which such nonproductive man power is
employed.

[12] See chapter xiv.

words, the very resources which Britain lacks most. Without them they are apt to be more of a liability than an asset; yet for Britain to supply them is to risk further crippling of her ability to recover at home.

Thus Britain is thrown back almost entirely upon her capacity to export if she is to secure the vital raw materials she requires for both current needs and reconstruction, and she must do it with a relatively backward industry. So long as there is a world seller's market for manufactured goods, she may be able to postpone the needed reorganization, but the instant competition in international markets becomes keen she faces the gigantic industrial strength of the United States. Here the United States dwarfs Britain in the scale of her production in somewhat the same proportion that Britain outdistanced the rest of the world in the heydey of her industrial might, during the interval from the 1870's to the early 1890's. Furthermore, the United States has an industrial system organized on a mass-production basis—the full productive potentialities of which most British industrial and labor leaders do not appear to understand—which is, at least in the short-run, able to operate with relatively low sunk-capital costs because of the wartime policy of quick write-off, a policy which is, with minor modifications, being extended into the postwar period. The net result is that despite higher American wage levels, as a high-up and pro-British official in the International Fund expressed the matter to the writer in early 1948, there is scarcely an important mass-production line in which the United States could not "in open international competition drive the British to the wall."

But there is still more. Power is interlaced with economics, and economics with power. This is the meaning of British socialism itself—not to mention fascism, sovietism, and the power politics of free-enterprise monopoly capitalism. In the United States, political and military strength has kept step with the swift unfolding of a gigantic industrial system. Internally, its economic system is highly organized, highly concentrated, highly "interest conscious," and politically aware. Hence, there is absolutely no reason whatsoever for believing that export-hungry industries, or industries which may momentarily become export-hungry, will not attempt to dump abroad whenever it is convenient for them to do so; that they will be able to secure some measure or other of political support at home for so doing is almost a foregone conclusion. This is particularly likely to be so if and when the United States has a business depression—however small or large, and whatever its duration. And the United States, it must be kept in mind, is the one major industrial country in the world that has done virtually nothing to escape future depressions, and thus far has nothing beyond the most general and vague plans for ever doing anything to avoid them.

Furthermore, American policy is committed to large-scale reconstruction of Japanese and German industry, both of which excelled British industry in important competitive fields before the war, and in both of which reconstruction with American aid is designed not only to bring them to technological levels of development well above and beyond those of the prewar period, but also to expand heavily export-oriented industries which are bound, for a long time in the future, to operate with very cheap labor. The same holds for American ideas concerning other European countries receiving ERP aid. All of these countries—France, Italy, and the Benelux and Scandinavian countries in particular—have a need for increasing exports which is scarcely less great than that of England. Relative to England, their wage levels are all low, and likely to stay low for a long time.

More than that, these countries can expand their exports only to the very countries to which the British need to sell, virtually all of which are either themselves rapidly industrializing, or being drawn to some significant extent or other behind the so-called "iron curtain"—or both. Industrialization in these areas tends to be at or near the latest technological levels of efficiency, and thus are able to compete on advantageous terms with English goods in their own home markets, and make heavier drafts upon raw materials previously exported to the older manufacturing centers such as England and Germany. One result is to keep high the price of raw materials which Britain must import as a condition to increasing exports. And the other result is to multiply the areas in which Britain must face the same kind of mass-production competition which she receives from America. There is a serious danger, in other words, that short of a veritable *tour de force* in British productive methods, the long-run terms of trade may continue to move against her.

There are other aspects of this picture which need not be gone into here. Suffice it to say that it seems impossible to find a single line of postwar development affecting Britain's problem of recovery which does not continue to underscore with more and deeper lines the necessity for a fundamental reorganization of her entire manufacturing system. So critical is this need, that it is probably not an exaggeration to say that Labour might have neglected all other lines of experimentation in all other fields, and still have gained a tremendous victory had it been successful in this field alone. At any rate, all other plans, in terms of relative importance, are almost of necessity secondary or ancillary to plans for industrial development. It was, of course, necessary to carry through far-reaching improvements in the fuel and power industries, in transport, and in other segments of British economy. But however well carried through, all such plans will come to nought unless her manufacturing industries are thoroughly reorganized—rapidly, comprehensively, and on a huge scale.

Nationalization, Rationalization, and Socialization

Looking through the Labour literature on nationalization—the propaganda and debates, the Parliamentary discussions, the bills, acts, white papers, committee reports and annual reports—one finds a common dominant theme: nationalization will result in higher levels of efficiency; wastes will thereby be avoided, manpower conserved, better use made of resources, overdue integration and coördination of related processes effected, plant better located, and so *ad infinitum*. Other advantages of an economic, social, and cultural character are usually claimed, but—with practically the sole exception of the Bank of England—these claims are almost always secondary to the contention that the proposed change will bring about, directly or indirectly, better and more efficient use of national resources. Nationalization has, in the Labour literature, virtually always stood as a necessary preliminary to rationalization.

But where this identification between national ownership and technical rationalization has not dominated the hopes of Labour, it has been only where it has been subordinated to the belief that nationalization of capitalistically organized business, with its trend toward monopoly, is necessary as a preliminary to the transfer of the power of direction from private owners to the workers. The other line of emphasis, that is to say, has identified nationalization with socialization—or, at least, has considered it as a preliminary to socialization. Given, consequently, inefficient industry which is wastefully competitive or moving steadily and increasingly toward monopolistic types of control—as a host of British writers have been detailing at great length in recent years—the arguments for nationalization of the manufacturing industries would seem to have been overwhelming.

FIRST POSITION: TO RATIONALIZE IS TO NATIONALIZE

On one or another of these two grounds, Labour has included practically all aspects of national economic life on its nationalization lists. In 1901 and again in 1907 the Labour party set as its major objective "creation of an Industrial Commonwealth founded upon the common ownership of land and capital."[13] In 1904 the demand—repeated again in 1905, 1908, 1918, and 1922—was for "institution of a system of Public Ownership of all the means of Production, Distribution, and Exchange."[14] In 1907 it demanded that all "monopolies should be owned and controlled by the community in the interests of the community."[15] In addition to those parts of the economic system listed in the foregoing chapters dealing with nationalization, at one time or another Labour party resolutions have called for the nationalization or public ownership of liquor (1905), hospitals and dispensaries (1909), minerals (1919), all medical services (1932), wholesale and possibly retail handling of milk (1924), sugar beet refining (1935), and some, or if need be—because monopolistically controlled—all of the food industries (1942).[16]

From the early thirties on, the demand for nationalization was increasingly tied up with emphasis upon planning, basic and far-reaching reorganization, efficiency, and rationalization. In 1942 the conference passed a resolution moved by Harold Laski, of the National Executive, proposing "A Planned Economic Democracy." The main body of the resolution stated:

> This Conference affirms that there must be no return after the war to an unplanned competitive society, which inevitably produces economic insecurity, industrial inefficiency and social inequality. It notes that the pressure of war has already necessitated far-reaching Government control of industry, central planning of the nation's economic life, and the subordination of many private interests to the common good, and urges that this process be carried further in order to achieve swift and total victory. It declares that measures of Government control needed for mobilising the national resources in war are no less necessary for securing their best use in peace, and must therefore be maintained after final victory is won. It regards the socialisation of the basic industries and

---

[13] *Report of the First Annual Conference of the Labour Representation Committee* (1901), p. 20.

[14] *Report of the Fourth Annual Conference of the Labour Representation Committee* (1904), p. 52.

[15] *Report of the Seventh Annual Conference of the Labour Representation Committee* (1907), p. 62.

[16] Reference is only to the first year in which the demand was made. Frequently demands of former years were reaffirmed, or appeared in slightly altered form in other resolutions.

services of the country, and the planning of production for community consumption as the only lasting foundation for a just and prosperous economic order in which political democracy and personal liberty can be combined with a reasonable standard of living for all citizens.[17]

This statement is typical of the general emphasis during and after the war. The nationalization of virtually every industry in Britain has come in for Labour party discussion—at the annual conferences, in published literature, or in behind-the-scenes proposals—at one time or another. Thus, all "distribution" has been mentioned as a future "must" on the nationalization list by different groups. The president of the Amalgamated Society of Woodworkers has recently made "an appeal for the nationalization of the building industry."[18] Individual corporations, such as Imperial Chemicals, Unilever, Vickers, and others have been mentioned. "On the agenda for the Margate Conference of 1947 were resolutions calling for the nationalisation of chemicals, motors, cotton, shipbuilding, milk distribution, betting, breweries, water supply, and the land."[19]

In an attempt to clarify for its members the question of what industries are "ripe and over-ripe for public ownership and management in the direct service of the nation," and what small and large industries "can be left to go on with their useful work" or which are "not yet ripe for public ownership,"[20] a Labour-party pamphlet suggests five main tests which should be applied to any proposal for nationalization (or to any proposal for government economic policy short of nationalization).

1. *Does it increase the people's power over their own economic destinies?*
2. *Does it lead to a higher standard of life by enabling industry to perform a better and more economic service to the nation?*
3. *Does it lead to a more equal standard of life?*
4. *Does it lead to a more stable standard of life, i.e. promote full employment?*
5. *Does it open the way to extended industrial democracy?*

The pamphlet says in conclusion:

In the light of the yardsticks suggested by this restatement, a choice should be made from industries which are one, but particularly which are more than one, of the following:

[17] *Report of the Forty-First Annual Conference of the Labour Party* (London, 1942), p. 110.
[18] Strain was reported to have said, "So long as houses were built for profit by private enterprise the building industry would be less a social service than street cleaning ... Nationalization had given the miners a guaranteed week, holidays with full pay, and social amenities, and it could bring those amenities to the building industry." *Times*, June 10, 1948.
[19] *Public Ownership, The Next Step*, Towards Tomorrow Series, no. 2 (Labour Party, 1948), p. 3.
[20] *Let Us Face the Future*, p. 6.

1. BASIC as a supplier of vital raw materials to other industries, to human life, health, or to defence.

2. MONOPOLISED by a large trust or trusts.

3. INEFFICIENT because unable to find finance for capital development, split up into units too small for economic operation, or burdened with particularly low standards of management.

4. INVESTORS of capital on a large scale.

5. Suffering from very bad INDUSTRIAL RELATIONS.[21]

Detailed questioning of Labour spokesmen and of various authorities among Labour's friends and enemies by the author failed to identify a single industry or trade—and, indeed, few individual business corporations—in Britain to which at least two of these "yardsticks" would not apply. Thus, if they are applied, all manufacturing and trade—as well as the great public-utility and service industries—would sooner or later be nationalized. Under socialism in Britain, that is to say, public ownership should in time come to envelop virtually the whole economic system. From this position there has never been any formal or explicit declaration of departure.

SECOND POSITION: TO NATIONALIZE IS TO SOCIALIZE

Labour literature has a long and consistent record of advocating worker control in industry, nationalized and unnationalized alike. Such, in effect, was the central theme of the Webbs' famous early book, *Industrial Democracy*, and such also has been the consistent policy of the Fabian Society from which the Labour party has drawn the essentials of it current program. So clear and unambiguous has this emphasis long been that a single illustration must suffice. In 1919 a resolution was carried instructing the

Executive Committee to consider and report to a further Conference on the arrangements to be introduced into industry in order to provide Labour with facilities to control industry—that is to say, to participate in the promotion of undertakings, the negotiation of contracts, determination of the product, and the selection of markets—and the extent that such control by Labour can be secured or is desirable, on the basis of the private ownership of land and capital. The Executive shall indicate the distinction between conciliatory Labour and Capital and the actual control of industry by the workers, and to that end is instructed to report on:

a. The Industrial Councils and their bearing on the question.

[21] *Public Ownership.* Italics and large type in the original. See also, Bob Edwards, *Chemicals: Servant or Master?* (National Labour Press, 1946); Michael Young, *What is a Socialised Industry?*, Discussion series, no. 4 (Fabian Society, 1947), Young is assistant director of the Research Division of the Labour Party; Ian Mikardo, *The Second Five Years* (Fabian Society, n.d.); and *Labour Believes in Britain*, summarized in chapter xv following.

b. The co-partnership of Labour and Capital.

c. The means to achieve the democratic management of industries in national ownership.

d. How far the representation of Trade Unions, through their Executives, or by ballot of the members, could ensure participation in actual control, and whether for effective control, it is not necesary that the employees in the workshop or the pit shall construct an organisation, integral to any scheme of democratic management.

e. Whether the *sole or partial management by Labour* of industries in national ownership should be confined to the *actual workers therein,* or should include *workers in other occupations.*[22]

The intent of this resolution is entirely clear. The Labour party was to declare itself as being in favor of direct worker control—or at worst, labor participation through its official representatives—at all levels of basic policy formulation, administration, and management of all aspects of business for both nationalized and nonnationalized industries alike. At subsequent annual conferences—with, at first, unobtrusive exceptions—this position was reaffirmed on numerous occasions. The conclusion seems inescapable that Labour's rank and file must have understood that any implementation of Labour policies in industry would of necessity mean outright worker control, or at least worker participation in control, gradually embracing new industries and trades as the Socialist Commonwealth came nearer realization.

ALTERNATIVES TO RATIONALIZATION OR SOCIALIZATION

It is at this point that Labour spokesmen show evidence of not having "thought the problem through" or, indeed, of having rejected the idea that there is any necessity of even attempting to do so. Since the middle thirties, the emphasis on the "practical" as against the "theoretical" or "dogmatic" has come increasingly to dominate discussions by party leaders. "The Labour party," Sir Stafford Cripps told the writer in September, 1948, "has no philosophy and no theory." On the contrary, its approach is practical, "each issue is decided entirely on its own merits." From this point of view, quite obviously, theory comes to mean not clarification, synthesis, and ordering but doctrinaire constriction of movement, and what the theoriest sees as flotsam and jetsam created by sightless muddlers, is to the "clear-eyed realist" the best of all possible constructions.

---

[22] *Report of the Nineteenth Annual Conference of the Labour Party* (Southport, 1919), p. 172.

How then does one "realistically," and without benefit of an ordering theory, approach—even by the methods of Fabian gradualism—a goal, or set of goals, which are unillumined in the larger perspectives and have no philosophic content? Consider the Labour solution. From the middle thirties on, the fraternity of professional economists in Britain, Conservative, Liberal, and Labour alike, came to accept the idea that the *summum bonum* of national economic well-being might be realized by whatever means would be effective in bringing about full employment on an enduring basis. This idea soon came to be most commonly associated with the name of Lord Keynes, who argued—and most of those who disagreed with him on other aspects of his analysis concurred in this—that full employment might be reconciled with the maintenance of the capitalist system in industry. If one planned to maintain full employment, and the successful maintenance of full employment could be viewed as the logical result of economic planning, possibly planning need not then be equated to socialism at all. Rather would it consist of taking a series of detailed steps, many of them very drastic,[23] as need arose and as given circumstances might dictate, all of which would be consistent (in Keynes' view) with the shoring up and reinforcement of capitalism. Then the hope for the future would lie in a virile capitalism which would have two primary objectives—the steady and cumulative improvement of industrial processes and the spreading of the benefits of full employment by redistribution of the social income so that a larger proportion would be received by the lower income ranks, which have a high "propensity to consume"—and not in what Keynes felt must of necessity be a flaccid and dreamy socialism.

Much of this view seems to have been taken over subconsciously by Labour. Though there is no evidence that Labour theorists have accepted the dropping of socialism as the ultimate goal, socialism appears

[23] E.g., the removal of top-policy determining power in national economic affairs from the hands of banking and finance, giving it to those whose interests were centered in industry; the gradual "euthanasia of the rentier" classes as a result of low interest returns on capital resources, when combined with steeply progressive income and inheritance taxes (death duties); the complete reorientation of financial policy away from maintenance of favorable trade terms and bank-reserve ratios to maintenance of full employment; government "deficit spending" on public works to any amount required to prevent unemployment beyond normal turnover levels, etc. All such specific proposals were congruent with Labour's traditional program. Because of this, several efforts have been made by Labour spokesmen to identify Keynes with the "theories" of the party. A. L. Rowse, for example, in a book entitled *Mr. Keynes and the Labour Movement* (Oxford, 1936), finds "little or no divergence between what is implied by Labour policy and by Mr. Keynes" (p. x). While there is much to support this view in *The General Theory of Employment, Interest and Money,* and elsewhere, it certainly does not square with Keynes' own view of his work. See, e.g., Dudley Dillard, *The Economics of J. M. Keynes* (New York, 1948), particularly pp. 310–334.

to have been subtly and significantly redefined. "The Labour Party," says the 1945 party manifesto, *Let Us Face the Future*, "is a Socialist Party, and proud of it. Its ultimate purpose at home is the establishment of the Socialist Commonwealth of Great Britain—free, democratic, efficient, progressive, public-spirited, its material resources organised in the service of the British people." But, at the same time, "the members of the Labour Party, like the British people, are practical-minded men and women, [and] Socialism cannot come overnight." As early as 1935 Hugh Dalton was able to define planning as "a method of trial and error" which was merely an "alternative to the trial and error of Unplanned Capitalism." Planners, he went on to say, "will make mistakes, miscalculate the future, sometimes waste wealth and opportunities, often change direction." But their eyes will be "fixed, not on abstractions, but on realities." Some "central machinery is required to co-ordinate these activities and make them effective" but the "Labour Party . . . has given no dogmatic answer to this question" preferring to "proceed experimentally, guided by the light of experience rather than by any elaborate preconceived theory."[24] Dalton's summary was as valid an interpretation of Labour's view in 1945 as it was in 1935.

In practice this has come to mean two things. On the one hand, definite limitations have been set to immediate nationalization. When its current "program is complete, only 20 per cent of Britain's economy will be under public ownership, while the remaining 80 per cent will remain under private ownership and 'free enterprise.' "[25] On the other hand, both nationalized and nonnationalized sectors are to be coördinated in an effective operational symbiosis by a Central Economic Planning Staff, aided and assisted by an Economic Planning Board which works largely through, and with the aid and advice of a National Production Advisory Council for Industry.

Although the line between the nationalized and nonnationalized sectors of the economy is not to be "drawn haphazardly" nationalization is to be applied only where the industries or services in question seem to have some or all of the following characteristics:

a) They are of key importance to the economy, not only to ensure present production but to guarantee continual full employment, an objective on which all Parties are united.

---

[24] Hugh Dalton, *Practical Socialism for Britain* (London, 1935), pp. 250, 309.
[25] Article entitled "Nationalization"—which states in its heading that "The scope is limited. The aim is economy and efficiency. Compensation is fair"—in *Labour and Industry in Britain*, V (Sept.–Oct., 1947) : 200–212. The 20 per cent figure has been taken from various speeches by Herbert Morrison, Lord President of the Council and a leading Labour spokesman.

b) They have not been fully efficient in the past, and need radical reorganization along the lines of a centrally operated plan. This means monopoly if left to private ownership; and they are therefore taken into public owership.

c) They need large capital expenditure coming to a large extent either from the State or through State guarantee. If the State supplies funds it must be certain that they are spent for public and not private interests.

d) They are already linked so closely with other Government operations that public ownership or control is a logical development.[26]

In view of the current limitation of nationalization to roughly 20 per cent of Britain's economy the line of demarcation is probably meaningless. Not only is it difficult, if not impossible, to determine where and how it is to be drawn but there is also no agreement—even in Labour party circles—on what such a line means. Proof of this is to be found not only in the endless debates within party circles over the question, some of which were briefly summarized above, but also in that the principle has been found almost impossible to adhere to in practice.

An interesting example of the latter difficulty is found in what Sir Walter Benton Jones, chairman of The United Steel Companies, Limited, referred to as industries which are in process of being "silently nationalised" through their connection with other industries brought under formal nationalization measures. His statement, given before an annual meeting of his company, is worth quoting, since it is typical of several similar situations.

While I am talking about coke oven works and the carbonising of coal, it will interest you to be informed of the extent to which in addition to coal gas the other products of coal carbonisation are being silently nationalised. In round figures forty million tons of coal are carbonised annually in the United Kingdom, of which the nationalised gas industry carbonises rather more than 50 per cent., and the nationalised coal mining industry carbonises about 20 per cent., leaving about 30 per cent. in the hands of free enterprise of which the iron and steel industry carbonises more than 20 per cent. If the iron and steel industry were to be nationalised something less than 10 per cent. would be left under free enterprise and nationalised industries would have in their own hands nearly the whole of the products of coal carbonisation, that is the coke, coal gas, fertilisers, motor spirit, tar and many finer chemical products, including bases of dyes and plastics.[27]

Numerous other illustrations might be given of this partial nationalization of industries as a by-product of the main nationalization schemes put through by the Labour government after 1945. Thus, in addition

[26] *Ibid.*

[27] "Statement to the Annual Meeting of The United Steel Companies Ltd.," *Economist*, Nov. 20, 1948, pp. 855–860.

to those mentioned by Jones, the government has nationalized parts of such industries as ordnance, engineering, building materials, hotels, restaurants and catering, wholesaling ("bulk purchase" of cotton and of various overseas supplies through agencies controlled by the Ministry of Food), land, housing, theaters and other places of amusement, etc. Furthermore, most of the nationalization acts contain definite provisions allowing the board or corporation in question to manufacture part or all of the supplies required for its own needs. For the coal, electricity, and gas industries, telecommunications, and the railroad, canal, and docks and harbors sections of transport, this could mean nationalizing, in effect, all of certain lines of supplies. Finally, it is also true that all of the acts give the appropriate Minister powers of interpretation of the authority granted him which could greatly extend the area of any nationalized undertaking without requiring further Parliamentary authorization.

When to such "silent" or "ragged-edge" nationalization is added steel and the large sections of the engineering, metal-finishing, and distributing industries and trades which go with it, it is clear that the 20 per cent limitation on the area to be nationalized has already been exceeded. To this must be added the further difficulty, that the logic of "industrial organization," "interdependence," "coödination," and "integration" which defined the perimeters of the industry to be nationalized can rarely be confined within the borders chosen under the appropriate act. To illustrate: the logic applied to the Bank of England Act would call for nationalizing the joint stock banks; to social security for nationalizing private insurance; to coal for nationalizing coal distribution; to transport for nationalizing coastwise and overseas shipping; to steel for nationalizing virtually all heavy engineering and ordnance; to coal and gas for nationalizing the whole of the petroleum industry and practically all coal and petroleum derivatives.

Since there is no reason for believing that Labour party leaders are in any sense unaware of these facts (quite the contrary is true), it would appear that the 20 per cent limitation has no meaning and is not intended to possess any. Instead of a more or less fixed percentage, the nationalized area has fluid and already expanding frontiers which might well continue to widen incontinently. That is, this is the logical conclusion; but there is much uncertainty as to what Labour leaders mean by "planning." Should it turn out that they interpret "planning" in the more or less purely Keynesian sense, it may very well be that the area of nationalization will not expand in the future, that it is really to be stabilized, or that it might actually shrink. In this event, the Labour party would find itself willy-nilly in the position of shoring up this vast middle area of free enterprise, and the nationalized industries could then be viewed as merely supplying services to business enterprise in direct analogy with the role which municipalized activities—water, gas, sewerage, tramways, etc.—were supposed to play in the decades of the 1880's and 1890's ("Gas and Water Socialism").

The object would be not to destroy capitalism but to salvage it. The task would be, as President Roosevelt frankly understood the purpose of the New Deal in America to be, to "save capitalism despite itself." The object of "socialism" would then be to find a mode of effecting a marriage between "industry working with (instead of against) labor to best serve the people" and "efficiently operated business working under the stimulus of private profit." The shotgun would be in the hands of the Government, but both parties to the covenant—Labor and capital—would see, sooner or later, that the pact into which they had entered was at once best for all parties concerned: best for labor, best for capital, best for the consumer, and best even for "socialism."

There are three reasons why this might seem the more likely interpretation of the general hesitancy of the Labour party to march ahead with further nationalization in the manufacturing field, and why such discussion as it now allows on the subject among its more ardent left-wing membership may be primarily for the purpose of providing a good safety valve for letting off steam.[28] First is the nature of the planning machinery which Labour has called into being. Second is the formulae for labor-capital copartnership which it is now promoting through the device of the independent autonomous public corporation for the nationalized industries, and the development councils for those not nationalized. And finally, there is the new legislation dealing with monopolies which is openly and clearly modeled upon the antitrust machinery of the United States, and which seems to have been placed on the statute books for precisely the same purpose, i.e., correction of the abuses of economic power in the interest of effecting a symbiosis between political democracy and efficient private enterprise.

---

[28] Superficially this isn't borne out by *Labour Believes in Britain*, the 1950 (preëlection) Labour party brochure, which adds to the list of industries which may be nationalized at some time in the future, chemicals, cement, land, iron-ore deposits, suitable minerals, all sugar manufacturing and refining concerns, industrial assurance, and possibly some others. But most of the phraseology is vague and tentative. It appears to be more of a case of "become efficient (or something else) or else," than of a definite commitment to nationalization.

THE NEW PLANNING MACHINERY

THE CENTRAL ECONOMIC PLANNING STAFF

As chart 9 shows, there are three general levels of this planning machinery. At the top is the Central Economic Planning Staff, serving in an advisory role to the Minister of Economic Affairs (Sir Stafford Cripps, also Chancellor of the Exchequer). "Its function is to *initiate* thought and action on general economic matters of vital importance to the nation, and co-ordinate the use of economic resources."[29] Its members are permanent government officials and economists and statisticians from various universities. Its most important publication is the annual *Economic Survey*. "This Survey is at once a report on the whole economy, viewing each major aspect as complementary to the others, and a programme for action in the coming year."[30] In its first annual report it gave its interpretation of planning under socialism:

It is the Government's responsibility to lay down the national tasks, and to use all means at its disposal to ensure that they are accomplished. But the Government cannot achieve them by itself. The tasks are for the nation as a whole, and only the combined efforts of everyone can carry them through. The Government therefore invites the attention of industry and the public to its plans; *it intends to arrange discussion with both sides of each industry of the problems which arise from them;* it will welcome constructive criticism, and it is ready to modify its plans if a case for doing so is made out. There is nothing rigid or final in these plans; they are a working pattern for the nation which will be adapted and modified as conditions require and as experience shows necessary.[31]

Thus the planning staff is a sort of "brain trust" which formulates national economic policy and the strategy and logistics of policy implementation. It is purely advisory and has no executive status. "The Cabinet, Cabinet Committees, Ministers and their Departments continue to be responsible for all actual decisions and for their implementation."[32] Since the creation of the Ministry for Economic Affairs, to which the planning staff was attached, however, this advisory function has been strengthened through the responsibility given Sir Stafford Cripps "for co-ordinating the work of the economic Departments, i.e. the Board of Trade, the Ministries of Food and Supply, the Ministry

---

[29] From a memorandum, *Planning Machinery,* for "the guidance of British Officials" which "must not be ascribed to any official source," but which the author was given permission to quote so long as the latter injunction was observed. It will be referred to hereafter as *Planning Machinery.*

[30] *Ibid.*

[31] *Economic Survey for 1947,* Cmd. 7046, p. 32. Italics mine.

[32] *Planning Machinery.*

SECTION I – GOVERNMENTAL

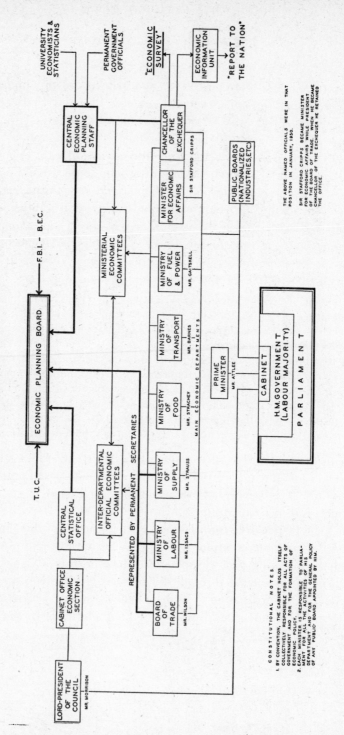

UNIVERSITY ECONOMISTS & STATISTICIANS

PERMANENT GOVERNMENT OFFICIALS

"ECONOMIC SURVEY"

ECONOMIC INFORMATION UNIT

"REPORT TO THE NATION"

CENTRAL ECONOMIC PLANNING STAFF

F.B.I. – B.E.C.

CHANCELLOR OF THE EXCHEQUER

MINISTER FOR ECONOMIC AFFAIRS

SIR STAFFORD CRIPPS

PUBLIC BOARDS (NATIONALIZED INDUSTRIES,ETC)

ECONOMIC PLANNING BOARD

T.U.C.

MINISTERIAL ECONOMIC COMMITTEES

MINISTRY OF FUEL & POWER

MR. GAITSKELL

CENTRAL STATISTICAL OFFICE

CABINET OFFICE ECONOMIC SECTION

INTER-DEPARTMENTAL OFFICIAL ECONOMIC COMMITTEES

REPRESENTED BY PERMANENT SECRETARIES

MINISTRY OF TRANSPORT

MR. BARNES

MINISTRY OF FOOD

MR. STRACHEY

MINISTRY OF SUPPLY

MR. STRAUSS

MINISTRY OF LABOUR

MR. ISAACS

BOARD OF TRADE

MR. WILSON

MAIN ECONOMIC DEPARTMENTS

PRIME MINISTER

MR. ATTLEE

CABINET

H.M. GOVERNMENT (LABOUR MAJORITY)

P A R L I A M E N T

LORD-PRESIDENT OF THE COUNCIL

MR. MORRISON

THE ABOVE NAMED OFFICIALS WERE IN THAT POSITION IN JANUARY, 1950.

SIR STAFFORD CRIPPS BECAME MINISTER FOR ECONOMIC AFFAIRS WHILE PRESIDENT OF THE BOARD OF TRADE, WHEN HE BECAME CHANCELLOR OF THE EXCHEQUER HE RETAINED THE OFFICE.

CONSTITUTIONAL NOTES

1. BY CONVENTION, THE CABINET HOLDS ITSELF COLLECTIVELY RESPONSIBLE FOR ALL ACTS OF GOVERNMENT AND FOR THE FORMATION OF ECONOMIC POLICY.

2. EACH MINISTER IS RESPONSIBLE TO PARLIA-MENT FOR ALL THE ACTIVITIES OF HIS DEPARTMENT AND FOR THE GENERAL POLICY OF ANY PUBLIC BOARD APPOINTED BY HIM.

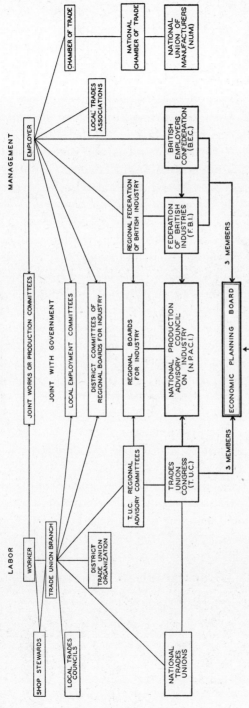

SECTION II - INDUSTRIAL

LABOR

MANAGEMENT

Chart 9. British Machinery for Consultation and Coördination in Economic Affairs.

Source: British government and civil-service officials. Adapted by E. N. Bryant.

of Transport and the Ministry of Fuel and Power."[33] To these powers
were subsequently added those of the Chancellor of the Exchequer.
Hence the planning staff can recommend immediate executive action
in all phases of financial planning, import-export policies, and most
of domestic production.

This planning staff was actually an inheritance from wartime, when
it served as an advisor to the Prime Minister on the mobilization of
British industry. It has been manned, both before and after Labour
came to power, primarily by professional economists from the London
School of Economics, the universities of London, Cambridge, and Oxford. Its policies have been largely dominated by the ideas represented
in current issues of the *Journal of the Royal Economic Society*, edited
jointly by Lord Keynes and Professor E. A. G. Robinson of Cambridge
until the death of Keynes in 1946, and by the latter alone since that
time. While many different lines of thought find expression in the
Journal, the general tenor of its contributions is overwhelmingly in
favor of retention of the main outlines of the capitalist system with
such modifications in detail—the point at which the leading differences
in theory and policy appear—as may be required to insure its continued
viability, not its early demise. The modifications in detail are generally
and almost uniformly of the Keynesian variety, and are primarily
measures of a monetary and fiscal character which are believed necessary to the maintenance of full employment, and which may be further
modified or altered temporarily in order to solve the extraordinary
short-run problems of postwar recovery. This type of general control
planning is now almost as acceptable to Conservatives as it is to
Labour.[34]

The concern of the planning staff is consequently only indirectly and
secondarily with operational planning. It seems almost wholly accurate
to say that operational planning is felt by the Economic Planning Staff
either not to be necessary at all or at best something that will take care

---

[33] *Ibid.* I have been unable to discover whether or not Agriculture and Town and Country
Planning are really excluded or not.

[34] "Almost everybody nowadays (like Mr. Churchill himself) admits the necessity of
planning to the extent that it is necessary to insure an adequate standard of living for every
citizen. The policy of the National Minimum is now so generally accepted that people are
apt to forget how very novel it is. Secondly, there is general agreement that the State must
accept responsibility for striving to avoid the alterations of boom and slump. And thirdly
hardly anybody in these days, when the balance of payments has become a popular spectre,
would refuse to concede that the State must deliberately control the external relationships
of the national economy. Then three agreed objectives of State intervention—social security,
internal stability and external stability—would not satisfy the more ardent planners. But for
most people they are enough to be going on with." *Economist*, Nov. 29, 1947, p. 866.

of itself more or less spontaneously once the proper analyses of needs have been made, the goals have been set, and the appropriate advisory, technical, and (on occasion) monetary aids have been supplied by the government to the otherwise self-initiating entrepreneurial system. Thus the 1947 *Survey* finds that the "five main national needs," consist of ability to (1) man and supply national defense, (2) pay for all imports, (3) provide the necessary capital equipment and maintenance, (4) meet the consumption needs of the population, and (5) provide the necessary public services.[35] A "broad analysis of the national position" is then to be followed by the setting up of economic "budgets . . . for the period under discussion . . . setting out resources and requirements in terms of (i) manpower; (ii) national income and expenditure."[36]

The ensuing "plan" consists of a series of goals ("targets") which are to be reached during the period of reference. They are to be achieved by the striking of a balance between resources and needs for each budget, and a summary or over-all balance between and among these budgets which will define the level of national income for the ensuing period and its relation to the disposition of resources within this period to that in subsequent periods. Thus targets for 1947 included imports totaling £1,450,000,000, and their division among "food and supplies for agriculture" (£725,000,000), "raw materials and supplies for industry" (£525,000,000), "machinery and equipment (including ships)" (£60,000,000), "petroleum products" (£55,000,000), "tobacco" (£50,000,000), and "consumer goods" (£35,000,000). Similar targets were set for exports (a total for the year of 140 per cent of 1938 volume), the "distribution of work on capital equipment and maintenance in 1947," and so on both for each of the primary or "main national needs," and for the several classes of resources required to meet the targets. A summary table in the *Survey* shows how the budgeted "distribution of resources" for the next year will result in an (approximate) "distribution of the national income."[37] (See table 29.)

Subsequent economic surveys are to follow this same general pattern, and will include in each year's report a summary of the degree of "Fulfilment of the Objectives of the Economic Survey" for the preceding year. With a view to achieving the "widest possible understanding of the facts of the situation and the targets laid down," the

[35] *Economic Survey for 1947*, p. 4.
[36] *Ibid.*, p. 6.
[37] *Ibid.*, p. 31.

government supplemented the survey during 1948 with a series of explanatory memoranda on the economic situation. Most important of these were a *Statement on Personal Incomes, Costs and Prices*[38] and a popular adaptation of the *Economic Survey*, profusely illustrated and widely sold over the newsstands, called *The 1948 Short Economic Survey*.

Much of this seems to bear a certain resemblance to the system of control figures used in the Soviet five-year plans. The likeness, how-

TABLE 29

DISTRIBUTION OF NATIONAL INCOME

Expenditure	Percentage of national income		
	1938	1945	1947
Personal consumption..............	78	54	66½
Defence (gross cost)..............	7	49	11
Other public expenditure...........	10	7	13½
Capital equipment and maintenance	16½	6	20
Depreciation....................	−10	− 6	−7
Imports..........................	−18	−10½	−17
Exports and re-exports.............	11½	4½	14
Other net overseas receipts........	5	−4	−1
Total...........................	100	100	100

SOURCE: *Economic Survey for 1947*, p. 31.

ever, is quite superficial and misleading. Underlying Soviet planning is virtually complete state and coöperative ownership, and a centrally directed physical plan for the whole economy. That this is not true for the Labour plan is made quite clear by the 1948 *Economic Survey* which, in summing up, points out the following "Lesson for the Future":

Perhaps the outstanding lesson of the experiment hitherto made in democratic planning in this country, apart from the limitations imposed by dependence on foreign trade, is the importance of the voluntary co-operation of the individual with the plan set by the central authorities. In the matter of industrial productivity, for instance, the Government can encourage, but it cannot compel. Productivity per head is bound to be one of the most important factors in determining the year's results; and it depends on a number of factors such as the

---

[38] Cmd. 7321. Others were: *Employer and Worker:* A Statement on the Economic Considerations Affecting Relations between Employer and Worker, Cmd. 7018; *Capital Investment in 1948:* A Survey to Ascertain What Volume of Work Could be Profitably Undertaken in Each of the Main Sections of the Nation's Economy, Cmd. 7268; and *United Kingdom Balance of Payments 1946 and 1947*, Cmd. 7324.

supply of materials and equipment; improvement of design; redeployment of labour; and efficiency of management. But the skill and effort of the individual are also obviously vital. Much will depend, therefore, on the individual's voluntary response.[39]

To infer from this statement, however, that the Labour government's planning rests wholly on voluntary coöperation is not correct. As pointed out in the 1947 *Economic Survey*, "Over an important part of the national economy, the Government can exercise direct influence. The level of Government expenditure approved by Parliament, and the expenditure of other public authorities, determines the amount of production of a wide range of goods and services, for example, education, public housing, supplies for the Armed Forces; the policies of the socialised industries and services have a substantial effect upon the whole economy, and are ultimately subject to Government control."[40] These direct controls, it must be pointed out, are fiscal controls; they are controls over expenditure, and are not made on the basis of an over-all physical plan. Their purpose is to effect Keynesian balancing, not physical coördination. There is no evidence of the existence of a national physical plan even for those sectors of the economy which are more or less subject to direct fiscal control.

As for the balance of the economy: "The Government's fiscal policy can exert indirect influence over the course of production. There are now a large number of direct controls, the purpose of which is to allocate scarce resources of all kinds between the various applicants for their use—rationing, raw materials controls, building licensing, production controls, import licensing, capital issues control, etc. Other controls again, such as price control, influence the course of production by limiting profit margins."[41] In this area—the vital area which the Lord President of the Council declares constitutes 80 per cent of the British economic system—indirect controls again are fiscal, and direct controls are negative. The effectiveness of the former depends primarily on the exercise of "influence"; that of the latter on such things as the withdrawal of supplies, refusal to issue licenses, the threat of limiting profitability, and other similar methods of adding sanctions of coercion to routines of persuasion.

No positive physical plan covers the functions and duties of the Central Economic Planning Staff. Its area is that of "the general economic

[39] *Economic Survey for 1948*, Cmd. 7344, p. 59.
[40] *Op. cit.*, p. 8.
[41] *Ibid.*

situation," and its function is to "advise" on how to "maintain full employment." Therefore, its duties cease when the application of the necessary and appropriate Keynesian devices has resulted in the characteristic "general equilibrium" of tried and true Marshallian economics which will insure that full employment will persist and not merely occur as a haphazard and occasional limiting case, and bring about a congruence between the resultant general equilibrium at full employment and such redirection of resources as the nature of the more pressing goals set by the government may require. From such a point of view, and with such a manner of procedure, it follows that the Central Economic Planning Staff does not have a physical plan, for the good and sufficient reason that it needs none. Not only does it not need one, but also its "planning" does not need to assume any such a "national physical plan" to exist anywhere else.

THE ECONOMIC PLANNING BOARD

In all the nationalized industries, targets are to be achieved under stimulus of directives issued by the appropriate ministries. But for private business the appropriate method is voluntary coöperation, and copartnership of the "two sides of industry," capital and labor, one with the other and both with the government. In order at once to coördinate on a national basis the stimuli of mutual persuasion, and to spread downward and outward knowledge of the numerous benefactions to all layers of the Socialist-commonwealth-in-becoming which flow from this voluntary coöperation, the Labour government set up in July, 1947, a new agency, the Economic Planning Board, and attached to it in a rather loose manner the wartime regional boards of industry. These boards are tripartite agencies, representative jointly of employers, trade unions, and the government. The functions of the central Economic Planning Board are "to advise His Majesty's Government on the best use of our economic resources, both for the realization of a long-term plan and for the remedial measures against our immediate difficulties."[42] The functions of the regional boards for industry for each of the ten regions into which England and Wales are divided for this purpose are similar to those of the central board (Scotland has its own Scottish Board for Industry).

[42] *Government and Industry, A Survey of Machinery for Consultation and Co-operation* (HSMO, 1948), p. 4. The regional boards were originally set up in 1940 as area boards. They were reconstituted as regional boards in 1942, and as regional boards for industry in 1945. See also appendix 6.

The membership of the Economic Planning Board is made up of three employers, three trade unionists, and several government officials, who include "the Permanent Secretaries of the Government Departments chiefly concerned—the Board of Trade, the Ministry of Labour and National Service, the Ministry of Supply and a Second Secretary at the Treasury," and "expert members of the staff of the Chief Planning Officer and the Director of the Economic Section of the Cabinet Office."[43] The Board is "to act on the analogy of a General Staff and as 'the eyes and ears of the Government' in forming a link with industry."[44] The essence of the innovation wrought by Labour is found in the fact that while "hitherto industrialists and trade union leaders have been *consulted* by the Government on particular problems affecting their special interests," the institution of the planning board represents "a radical departure because it *associates* management and labor continuously with the Government in the considerations of planning problems as a whole. The Government is thus able to receive and take into account in good time the views of industry whilst industry is in a better position to understand the problems confronting Government."[45] In short, a Conservative government concerned with the promotion of a "property owning Democracy" need only consult business and labor, but a Labour government in order to achieve its socialist objectives must associate itself in an active copartnership with the two!

At the regional levels this trinitarian constitution of the boards takes on a more formal character. For each such board there are five labor representatives appointed by the Chancellor of the Exchequer from persons nominated by the Trades Union Congress (T.U.C.), five from nominations made jointly by the Federation of British Industries (F.B.I.) and the British Employers Confederation (B.E.C.), and "senior Regional representatives of a number of Departments," namely, Admiralty, Board of Trade, Labour and National Service, Supply, Fuel and Power, Works, Food, Transport, Town and Country Planning, and the Central Office of Information.[46]

The meetings of the Economic Planning Board are usually on a fortnightly basis; the regional boards meet once a month. "Their main function is to advise upon industrial conditions within their Regions

---

[43] *Ibid.*
[44] *Ibid.*
[45] *Planning Machinery.* Italics mine.
[46] *Government and Industry*, pp. 8–9. For the larger districts there may be six instead of five representatives from the "two sides of industry." There are slight variations on the pattern for Scotland.

and upon steps which may be necessary to bring regional resources in capacity and labour into fuller use. They also provide a link between Central Government and local industry on industrial matters."[47] In the furtherance of their work they may set up subcommittees "to deal with particular questions, such as the Fuel Allocation Committee which deals with the allocation of solid fuel to industry," and district committees similar in constitution to the regional boards and with functions similar "to those of the Regional Boards, but on a smaller scale."

The regional boards have the further distinction of serving as a link between the Economic Planning Board and the partially parallel National Production Advisory Council. This latter body has as its leading purpose the national coördination of the "copartnership of capital and labor," and provides the third link in Labour's postwar "planning" for industry.

THE NATIONAL PRODUCTION ADVISORY COUNCIL ON INDUSTRY

Adapted from an earlier wartime council[48] this body is made up mostly of persons appointed by the Chancellor of the Exchequer from nominations made by the Federation of British Industry, the British Employers Confederation, and the Trades Union Congress; in addition, chairmen of the regional boards for industry are members *ex officio*. The Chancellor presides as chairman. Ministers and senior officers of government departments are present when matters affecting their ministries are under discussion. "Generally there are representatives of the following Departments present" at the usual bimonthly meetings: Admiralty, Board of Trade, Labour and National Service, Supply, and Fuel and Power.[49]

The functions of the NPACI "are to advise Ministers upon industrial conditions and general production questions, and on such subjects as may arise from the proceedings of the Regional Boards for Industry." Although the first category excludes "matters which are normally handled by the joint organizations of employers and trade unions in connection with wages and conditions of employment," these are handled by another national policy-coördinating body, similarly constituted, and responsible to the same central peak associations of business and labor. It is known as the National Joint Advisory Council (NJAC),

---

[47] *Loc. cit.*

[48] It was first set up in 1941 as the Central Joint Advisory Committee; in 1942 it was reconstituted as the National Production Advisory Council; in 1945 it was reconstituted again with the above title.

[49] *Government and Industry*, pp. 8–9.

and has as its function "to advise on matters in which employers and workers have a common interest, and to provide for closer consultation between Government and organized industry. It also provides a channel through which the Government can make available to both sides of industry confidential information concerning Government policy and the national economic position."[50]

From this point on the structure of British advisory and consultative machinery becomes very complex. In broad outline, however, the picture may be summarized as follows.

At the top, and serving as central policy making bodies for labor and business are, respectively, the peak association of labor, the T.U.C., and the peak associations of business enterprise, the F.B.I. and its *alter ego* on labor relations, the B.E.C. All appointments on all consultative and advisory committees are made either directly by these bodies, or indirectly by their subordinate member bodies.

The NPACI and the NJAC are the two top bargaining and consultative agencies bringing the two broad sets of interest—capital and labor (F.B.I. and the T.U.C.)—together under government auspices through the general formula of business-labor copartnership.

Through these two peak and copartnership agencies top-level consultations are held with the Economic Planning Staff, the Economic Planning Board, and the appropriate ministries and departments, and with the regional boards for industry, the various national and industrial consultative bodies, and other special agencies as they may be called into being by the government to solve special industrial problems.

In addition to the regional boards for industry, which operate to coordinate advisory services on regional and local levels, there are a series of functional and industrial consultative bodies operating usually on a national basis and having their own independent regional offices and divisions. The latter again may or may not be further coördinated with the regional boards. There are three important types of these "consultative bodies"—two old and one quite new. The first two may be dealt with briefly here. The innovation, for reasons which will quickly become obvious, must be discussed at more length in the following chapter.

---

[50] *Ibid.*, pp. 8, 10. It was set up in 1939, and reconstituted in 1946. The chairman is the Minister of Labour and National Service. There are 17 members of the B.E.C. (the employer alter ego of the F.B.I.) and 17 members of the T.U.C. It has an executive committee, known as the Joint Consultative Committee, "available for urgent consultations between the meeting of the NJAC."

First are the "Consultative Bodies dealing with a Problem Common to Industry as a whole." Most important of these is the Fuel Efficiency Committee. Others are the National Youth Employment Council, and the National Advisory Council on the Employment of the Disabled. In each there are representatives of employers, trade unions, and the appropriate government officials. The function of each is to "advise, survey, and present information," and otherwise assist government agencies to solve pressing national problems.[51]

Second are the "Consultative Bodies dealing with the Problems of Particular Industries." Thus, in the building and civil engineering industries there is a National Consultative Council, established in 1942, and presided over by the Minister of Works. It is made up of representatives of "employers, operatives and professional institutions," and was established to deal "with broad issues of policy and long-term trends in the building and civil engineering industries, its functions being to advise on the general planning and control of the national building and civil engineering programme, the relationship of the programme to labour and material resources, the use of building materials and the development and use of substitute materials, and the review of the arrangements for licensing building and civil engineering work under Defense Regulation 56A."[52]

In addition this industry has a Building and Civil Engineering Joint Committee, a Building and Civil Engineering Regional Joint Committee, a Building Industry Production Sub-Committee, an Advisory Committee of Specialists and Sub-Contractors, an Advisory Committee on Contractor's Plant, and a Building Apprenticeship and Training Council. A roughly similar pattern holds for the consultative councils of the building materials industries, the engineering industry, the iron and steel industry, and the shipbuilding industry. In all, the secretarial headquarters is in or is "responsible to" one of the ministries, the membership is drawn from the extant central trade union and trade associations within the industry, central policy counciling is combined with some sort of regional breakdown, and the functions are to "consider, observe, review, and advise" both government and industry on how the two should proceed to promote "the best interests" of both.[53]

The third type of consultative council is the development council. This is viewed by the Labour government as one of its most important

[51] For further detail see *Government and Industry*, pp. 12–14.
[52] *Ibid.*, pp. 14–15.
[53] *Ibid.*, pp. 14–23.

planning innovations, and for that reason will be taken up somewhat at length in the following chapter. Here it need only be pointed out that the idea of the development council seems to have been generated in the Board of Trade, which has long served British industry in somewhat the same way as the United States Department of Commerce has served American industry. But in so originating, it also bears the imprimatur of the most powerful leaders of the Labour party, and particularly of Sir Stafford Cripps—once expelled from the Labour party (1938) for an intransigent stand on behalf of socialist objectives (in which he went so far as to favor closer coöperation with the Soviet Union). It is, hence, all the more interesting that this innovation should move comfortably within the channels of the pattern of tripartite organization which had been blazed by wartime planning under the auspices of a Conservative-dominated Coalition government.

Without prejudging the matter—if this be true, what then does the Labour government mean by "planning"? There is a vast miscellany of rather confusing and "wooly" (a favorite expression of the Webbs) literature on the subject. Herbert Morrison, Lord President of the Council, has been the most vocal of the Labour spokesmen on the subject, and his views are probably typical. In an address to the Council of the Institute of Public Administration[54] at the end of Labour's first year in power, he stated his conviction that "planning is a very large and complicated business and Britain is the first great nation to attempt to combine large scale economic and social planning with a full measure of individual rights and liberties." There are "five stages" which this planning must go through. First "is making up one's mind to plan and grasping what planning means." Second "is assembling the necessary facts and forecasts to make sure that the plan can be put on a sound practical basis." Third is to devise "alternative plans" to weight against each other, and to decide "what is to be planned and what is to be left unplanned." Fourth is to make decisions on the third. Last, and "by far the most extensive, is carrying out the plans in practice."

In his subsequent discussion of how all this is to be done so as deliberately to use "the main available resources, in the endeavor to secure the good of the nation as a whole" Morrison mentions none of the planning machinery outlined above,[55] although all but the Economic Planning Board had been established at the time he spoke, and

[54] Released by the Central Office of Information, Oct. 17, 1946.
[55] A partial exception is the National Joint Advisory Council, to which, at one point, he makes parenthetical reference.

even the board was then in process of being worked out as a going concern. The "central piece of machinery" which assists "the Cabinet in planning is the Official Steering Committee representing the key economic Departments together with the Economic Section of the Cabinet Office." It is "assisted by a number of working parties" on manpower, investment, imports, etc.

What Morrison is referring to, of course, is merely the normal machinery for consultation existing within the Cabinet for group consultation, before finally formulating policies and making decisions about the problems which normally come before any national government. He concludes that British planning "as it is taking shape in this country . . . is something new and constructively revolutionary." Guided by "British political sense and British resourcefulness," he said, "After all, planning, though big and complicated, is not much more than applied common-sense."

The real import of this "applied common-sense" for the vital sphere of domestic industrial location and development may possibly be inferred from a more careful examination of the development councils, and of plans supplementary and complementary to them.

CHAPTER XIII

Industrial Location and Development: Copartnership and Monopoly

The only genuinely satisfactory course in some of these instances of monopoly is to socialize them and, I would add, to run them on the lines of a public corporation. In other cases we may be led to find methods of effective management and operation in the public interest without socializing the whole undertaking, at any rate at the outset . . . But . . . the right thing to do in some of these cases may be to enforce competition by legal change.—Herbert Morrison, *Prospects and Policies*, 1944.

THREE PROBLEMS have dominated Labour's discussion and plans for the "80 per cent" of the national economy remaining outside the nationalized sectors. First is the problem of location and relocation of industry. Second is the problem of the type of organization best fitted for achieving most rapidly and effectively the highest possible levels of productive efficiency. And third is the problem of how to control the growing concentration of economic power so as to avoid the evils of monopoly. These three are closely related and must be considered as but different facets of a common problem.

THE DISTRIBUTION AND LOCATION OF INDUSTRIES

One of the last actions of the wartime Coalition government was to pass in June, 1945, the Distribution of Industries Act, "which gave statutory recognition to certain of the proposals contained in the White Paper on Employment Policy (viz: that industrialists intending to open up new factories should first notify the Government of their intention; that the Government should be empowered to purchase land in 'development' areas, i.e., areas which in the past have been unduly dependent on industries specially vulnerable to unemployment, and to render it suitable for industrial purposes; and that financial encouragement should be given both to trading estates and to individual industrialists wishing to start operations in 'development' areas). These provisions, although primarily concerned with forestalling unemployment, opened the way to the extension of State influence over the location of industry along the lines recommended by the Barlow Report."[1]

[1] Central Office of Information, Reference Division, *Town and Country Planning in Britain*, p. 19.

[525]

The Barlow report dealt with two general types of such influence over location of industry. The first was corrective, in the sense that it was concentrated on special measures for dealing with the "distressed areas." The second was developmental, in the sense that it was concerned largely with the dual problems of industrial, occupational, and population balance within and between the major industrial and metropolitan areas of the country. The two kinds of influence overlap, and one rarely excludes the other. Nevertheless, the first is primarily an attempt to deal with an evil heritage of the past, and the second is an attempt to shape the geographic structure of British industry in terms of certain broad objectives to be achieved in the future.

Thus far, the first has almost wholly dominated the planning of industrial location in postwar Britain. But every step taken in this direction has led incontinently to a shift toward the second. And every effort to come to grips with the problem of development has tended to shift attention away from the local area and toward the problem of national physical planning of British industrial location. This is shown most clearly in chapter xii of the Barlow report which deals with the "Problem of the Special and Depressed Areas in Relation to the Balance of Industry Throughout the Country." Here "measures taken in the case of the Special or depressed areas," up to the time of issuing the report, were given in evidence supplied the Ministry of Labour as follows:[2]

a) "Placing" work on the Employment Exchanges;

b) Transference, with financial assistance in various forms, of unemployed, both adults and juveniles, from areas of severe unemployment to more prosperous areas with new openings;

c) Establishment of training centres and instructional centres;

d) Legislation for the four Special Areas:—

  i) West Monmouthshire and the greater part of Glamorgan.

  ii) Tyneside and the greater part of County Durham, etc.

  iii) West Cumberland.

  iv) Middle Industrial Belt of Scotland, excluding Glasgow.

e) The creation of Trading Estates and smaller industrial centres, with financial assistance from the Commissioners for the Special Areas;

f) Land Settlement, also financed by the Commissioners;

g) Location of factories required for the Government's Defence programme;

h) Preference given to areas of heavy unemployment in the allocation of Government contracts;

i) Location of factories established by foreign firms or firms employing foreign labor.

---

[2] *Report of the Royal Commission on the Distribution of the Industrial Population* [*Barlow Report*], Cmd. 6153 (1940), p. 146.

At first glance such a listing might seem to suggest merely a series of *ad hoc* legislative enactments—to be reinforced on occasion by a medley of administrative decisions at the convenience of the appropriate national officials, when properly reminded—dealing with a minor problem. But the problem of the distressed areas was not, and still is not, a minor problem. In 1937 some 4,000,000 people lived in the more seriously distressed areas, and the major industrial regions of Britain which were badly pocked with these areas included some one-third to one-half of her total industrial population; outside of London and the Home Counties, no major industrial region in Britain was entirely free of them. Furthermore, the frequency with which derelict towns and villages were found in these regions suggested that the whole of each region was derelict. Thus not just Jarrow,[3] but the whole of the Tyneside was a distressed area; not just the Rhondda Valley, but the whole of South Wales was in trouble. In general, this also held for the whole of the Scotch Highlands, for the north and west of England in contrast with the south and east, and even for large areas—such as the Black Country west of Birmingham—commonly included in the latter region.

Conditions in the distressed areas have long seemed to include all the possible human miseries that may be imposed on a laboring population by life and labor in industrial centers whose structure and entire mode of existence have been frozen into molds originally shaped in the early days of the industrial system, at a time when that system's masters were most completely indifferent to the welfare of those who toiled within its factory gates. But it required the long-drawn-out condition of chronic unemployment between the two wars, and its special accentuation in the thirties, to show how great was the need for far-reaching reconstruction, and how vast was the scale of the changes required.[4]

The size of the problem alone required a national effort, and careful consideration quickly brought to the fore other aspects which had a tendency enormously to enhance both the gravity of the problem and to underscore the need for national action. Jarrow was left derelict because a single-industry town lost its great steel works, and the Tyneside suffered because industry was moving elsewhere. But in Cumberland, in the vast textile industries of Manchester and the Merseyside, and in South Wales and West Scotland much—if not most—of the

---

[3] For a graphic and highly emotional picture of this derelict town see Ellen Wilkinson, *The Town That Was Murdered: The Life-Story of Jarrow* (London, 1939).

[4] See *e.g.*, Wal Hannington, *The Problem of the Distressed Areas*. With a Preface by Harold J. Laski (London, 1937).

trouble arose because goods produced by the industries which had made these regions famous in the past could no longer compete abroad with those produced in foreign countries. In a sense, the problem of the chronically distressed areas was bound, sooner or later, to become the problem of a chronically distressed Britain.

This was evident for large areas and many lines of industrial activity long before the war. "Durham is finished! South Wales is done for! This area will never be the same!" Such, Hannington wrote in the late thirties, "are the familiar remarks which one hears to-day when the Distressed Areas are mentioned."[5] They can still be heard in the postwar period, but the more persistent and general remark is that "England is finished!" Those among British leaders—and this includes the leaders of the Labour party—who resist this interpretation are, however, now prepared to concede, in principle at least, that the reëstablishment of Britain's position in world economy depends upon the reconstruction and revitalization of her internal economy.

Before this can be done, two conditions must be fulfilled. For both, Labour has declared emphatically in the past, and with rarely a dissenting voice. First is the establishment of a socialist state; second, the evolution of a national physical plan for all British industry. Although Professor Laski's statements rarely have the undivided approval of the Labour party's executive committee, his expressed views on the first point seem almost wholly to echo those of the committee. Speaking, in 1937, of the "problem of the distressed areas" as an "open wound," he wrote, "What causes that wound is capitalism; and there is no way of healing it save by bringing the capitalist system to a close." All measures short of this are "plasters on an open wound," palliatives "each of which founders upon the rock of profit-making."[6] He has reaffirmed this idea in a seemingly endless series of articles, pamphlets, and books since that time. In so doing he has repeated the central theme of the Webb's *Decay of Capitalist Civilization*,[7] countless pamphlets of the Fabian Society, and at least one speech of every well-known Labour government spokesman—Cripps, Attlee, Bevan, Bevin, Dalton, Strachey, and Morrison, to mention only the more highly publicized names.[8]

[5] *Ibid.*, p. 115.
[6] *Ibid.*, p. 9.
[7] Written in 1923 as a sequel to *A Constitution for a Socialist Commonwealth of Great Britain* (1920).
[8] If there is an important dissenter on this point, it is Ernest Bevin, who has, particularly since the Leicester Conference of the Labour Party in 1932, soft-pedalled all talk of socialism, and has usually given majority resolutions favoring more than sentimental support for Socialism at best grudging approval.

Nor has there been much dissent from the general idea underlying the second condition to the achievement of a viable Britain—a physical plan for industrial reconstruction. This is the theme of the Webb's famous *Constitution for a Socialist Commonwealth of Great Britain,* written in 1920, and it was the idea behind the Labour party pamphlet, *Labour and the New Social Order,* which was issued about the same time. Furthermore, this idea runs as a central thread through the recommendations of the Barlow and Scott reports, the Town and Country Planning Act, the New Towns Act, and the various reports—most notably those on the London and Birmingham areas—of special commissions set up to handle problems of replanning the great conurbations and the relationships of the agricultural countryside with industrial and trading urban centers. Virtually all British plans for population relocation and reconstruction frankly and explicitly depend primarily upon industrial location and development, and they concur, as with a single voice, in the view that this latter cannot be solved on any basis short of a national program. Without such a global frame of reference—particularly in a country possessing such a high developed, intricate, complex, and interdependent industrial system—piecemeal changes, expansions, contractions, and new combinations of industries and occupations within and between regions, may very well worsen rather than better the over-all industrial situation. And until an answer has been found for each major question raised about each plant's location and its future within such a framework, there is little possibility of solving any of the more ordinary economic, social, and cultural problems of country, town, and metropolitan planning.

And yet one will search in vain for any such national frame of reference for planning the industrial future of Britain under Labour auspices. Nor is there any indication within Labour circles that such a plan is in the process of development, or that there is felt to be any real need—the foregoing to the contrary notwithstanding—for evolving one for the future. So far as location alone is concerned, the various bits and pieces which Labour inherited from the recent Conservative and Coalition governments constitute the sum total of its machinery for dealing with the problem. Thus it is continuing with the wartime area-development work, the wartime allocation and distribution of scarce raw materials, the wartime discussion of forward planning in agriculture and town and country development and it is being quite active in the further promotion of a considerable number of local trading-estate developments.[9] But in separate details such as these its visible program of action comes to rest—there is no planned coördination.

This is true despite the fact that, general though the Distribution of Industries Act may appear to be at first glance, the government possesses, under its authority, power to do virtually anything which such a national physical plan would call for. Yet, as the white paper on employment policy[10] makes unmistakably clear, these powers are interpreted solely in terms of relief to the distressed areas—more recently better known as "development areas" or "special areas." In a foreword "by the Rt. Hon. Hugh Dalton, M.P., Late Chancellor of the Exchequer," to a pamphlet which purports to summarize Government proposals and measures for meeting the problem of industrial location, comments are confined exclusively to the development areas, and subsequent summaries of the Distribution of Industries Act and those sections of the white paper on employment policy devoted to "Balanced Distribution of Industry and Labour," have no thought for problems of location outside these areas.[11]

This is also true despite the fact that much, if not indeed all, of the basic information which is needed for the purpose of formulating a national plan for industrial location has been gathered and is readily available. One need mention only the extensive work of the Nuffield College Social Reconstruction Survey, begun in 1941 on the initiative of the Coalition government, which has given rise to a series of definitive studies. Particularly important is the exhaustive survey by Fogarty, *Prospects of the Industrial Areas of Great Britain.*[12] This study, in turn, was based upon "some fifty regional reports submitted to the Government between 1941 and 1943" which were not in any significant sense restricted, or even primarily concerned, with the special problems of the development areas. Meanwhile the Ministry of Town and Country Planning has assembled an enormous mass of basic industrial data in the process of evolving plans for the new towns and conurbation developments. When added to what other ministries—Board of Trade, Supply, Fuel and Power, Transport, etc.—possess in their files, or have means for obtaining with little additional effort, the basic raw materials for the drafting boards and policy discussions must be ample indeed.

---

[9] For a good and quite compact description of sample trading estates see the *Barlow Report*, pp. 283–288.

[10] Cmd. 6527, chapter 3.

[11] Walter Scott Elliot, *The Location of Industry*, Report no. 15 (National News-Letter, 1947), pp. ii–iii, 39–45.

[12] M. P. Fogarty, *Prospects of the Industrial Areas of Great Britain* (London, 1944).

Nor, finally, has there been any explicit Labour government declaration in opposition to using this data as the foundation for the formulation of a national plan for industrial location. It has given no voice to the belief that "planning for full employment" can neglect this sector entirely or for long. On this point, however else he may be in disagreement with the Government on other questions, G. D. H. Cole would appear to have correctly summarized at least the past position of the Labour party when he said, "It is simply out of the question, if full employment is to be successfully maintained, to leave it to employers to put their new factories or extensions where they please; nor is it enough simply to try to entice them into areas in which additional industries are needed ... Planning for full employment and planning for correct location of industry necessarily go together; and both depend on key decisions in the field of international economic policy as well as on a correct dovetailing of the public and private sectors of home policy."[13]

It is possible, of course, to take the position that the solution of the problem of industrial location must necessarily wait upon plans for overhauling each of Britain's major industries. Such plans might then be coördinated one with the other in such a way as to produce a pattern which might show the way to a solution of the related problems of differentiation and balance of industry both within and among the separate regions and subsidiary areas, and at the same time outline the general path of industrial development which Britain was to follow in the future. Such might be the interpretation placed upon one of the less publicized, but most extraordinary, programs of the Labour government; the setting up of investigating working parties whose reports are intended to provide the basis for the establishment of industry-wide and semigovernmental development councils.

THE WORKING PARTIES

In October, 1945, Sir Stafford Cripps, recently appointed President of the Board of Trade under the new Labour government, established the first working party, to report on cotton, with the following terms of reference: "to examine and enquire into the various schemes and suggestions put forward for improvements of organisation, production and distribution methods and processes in the Cotton Industry, and to report as to the steps which should be adopted in the national interest

---

[13] *Ibid.*, "Introduction," pp. xxxii–xxxiii.

to strengthen the industry and render it more stable and more capable of meeting competition in the home and foreign markets."[14]

Subsequently the Board of Trade has set up sixteen additional working parties with similar terms of reference,[15] and other ministries have begun to adopt the device. The working parties are all tripartite bodies, being made up of approximately equal numbers of employers, trade unionists, and independent specialists—engineers, economists, management experts, designers, etc. All members are appointed by the President of the Board of Trade and their final report is made to him. They may organize their activity more or less as they see fit, they may appoint any number of special investigating committees and subcommittees, and they may coöpt other specialists as occasion requires and the Board of Trade permits. Their recommendations are purely advisory, and are intended to inform both the government and the industry of conditions and to suggest lines of policy to both regarding future development.

No particular reason has been given for selecting the particular industries for which the first working parties were set up. All of them, with the partial exception of the jute industry, are primarily consumer-goods industries, and nearly half of them are textile industries. Two (cotton and wool) are industries of major importance; the balance are mostly medium-sized or small. Most of them are, relative to size, heavy contributors to Britain's export trade, and all but three (china clay, domestic glassware, and pottery) are heavily dependent on imported raw materials. No reason has ever been given for regarding them as generally representative of conditions as they existed in postwar Britain, although officers of the Board of Trade have expressed the belief that such may very well be so. The terms of reference did not include certain types of problems, most notably that of wage incentives—though they do not exclude this subject—and their concern was primarily with long-run problems.

The reports of the working parties vary greatly in length and the quality of their findings. Some, notably cotton and wool, are quite exhaustive and careful; others yield relatively little new information about the industry. In all reports the lack of adequate statistical information on the most important problems under investigation proved a

---

[14] *Working Party Reports: Cotton* (HMSO, 1946). (Subsequently referred to as *WPR: Cotton*.)

[15] Boots and Shoes, Carpets, China Clay, Heavy Clothing, Light Clothing, Rubber Proof Clothing, Cutlery, Furniture, Domestic Glassware, Hosiery, Jewelry and Silverware, Lace, Linoleum, Pottery, Wool, and Jute.

major handicap, with the general result that analysis was mostly of a qualitative character. Where quantitative data existed they were usually not broken down in such a way as to make readily possible adequate measurements of the separate elements entering into the central problem of productivity.[16] Some reports contained comparative data on similar industries in other countries, though differences in the make-up of industries compared, in the time and mode of gathering the data, and in many other aspects made comparison frequently difficult when not, on occasion, downright misleading.

There are many other qualifications and reservations to be kept in mind in using the findings of the working party reports, but in spite of this the general picture which they present is astounding. In six reports (wool, boots and shoes, heavy clothing, linoleum, furniture, and cotton) where quantitative comparisons between Britain and the United States were possible, "productivity is estimated to be 50% to 100% higher in America" and in the four reports (wool, boots and shoes, heavy clothing, and furniture) where comparisons of productivity could be made among British firms, "the scope for improvement between the worst and the best firm ranges from 30% to 100% even in the relatively small samples of firms which are considered."[17]

An analysis of no one industry can illumine precisely the problems of any other, but in a broad sense the things which were found to be wrong with the British cotton-textile industry illustrate the results to date of all the working party reports, and give some inkling of the problems of Britain's whole industrial system. The cotton report illustrates these problems only in a perhaps somewhat acute and aggravated form.

The troubles of the British cotton industry alone, as shown in the report, must have critically depressed the terms of life over all of the huge area which it had long so completely dominated. In this industry, rated as approximately fifth in size among British industries, the number of workers in the Lancashire area alone had declined by 116,000 between 1923 and 1937.[18] Since Lancashire employs more than 90 per

---

[16] "There is much qualitative analysis in the Reports, interspersed with numerical information of an unsystematic nature. The reason for this failure lies chiefly in the lack of statistical information ... Most noticeable in the Working Party Reports is the failure to break down productivity measurements into their constituent elements: in other words, failure to assess the contribution of various factors to a productivity difference." C. Gordon and D. Evans, *The Working Party Reports and Productivity* (Board of Trade, n.d.). Mimeographed circular.

[17] *Ibid.*

[18] The number of insured workers aged 16–64 declined, according to Fogarty, *op. cit.*, p. 204, from 449,340 in July, 1923, to 333,210 in July, 1937, or by 26 per cent. 1923 and 1937 are roughly comparable years (in terms of general level of business activity in Britain).

cent of all cotton operatives,[19] and since, even after the great decline between 1923 and 1937, it still accounted for 18.2 per cent of the total insured persons in the Lancashire area, it is evident that cotton plays a decisive role in this vast industrial district. Furthermore, the number of persons employed in industries in this area which were directly or primarily dependent upon the fortunes of cotton must have been equal to that directly employed in cotton itself. Thus when cotton was sick, nearly 40 per cent of the population of Lancashire must have suffered, and when 40 per cent of the income and future of any industrial area are in jeopardy, the whole must soon become a distressed area.

What was the matter with cotton? Virtually everything. A primary difficulty was loss of foreign markets. Here, wholly dependent upon imported raw materials as she was and only a little less heavily dependent upon foreign markets for sale of her finished goods, the trends, for one reason or another, had long been moving disastrously against Britain. The cotton report minces no words on the matter.

The main facts [it pointed out] are familiar. Everyone knows how exports to India dropped from over 3,000 million yards in 1913 to under 300 million in 1938. Everyone knows that we were driven out of other markets by a fierce competitive onslaught from Japan—based on a combination of "rice-standard" wages, modern machinery and a national policy determined to have exports at all costs. But it is not so generally appreciated that other countries, too, adopted policies which had damaging effects on Lancashire on a smaller but still very substantial scale. For example, as a result of a tremendous tariff increase, British exports of piece-goods to the U.S.A. fell from 163 million square yards in 1924 to 11 million in 1931. Brazil was another country whose tariff policy killed our trade, exports dropping from an average of 63.5 million square yards in the years 1925–27 to less than 3 million in 1932. Lancashire was in fact hit by blows from all sides. Roughly speaking, two thirds of her export losses were due to development by her former customers of their own industries, and one-third was captured by Japan. Right up to 1939 the industry was fighting a retreating rearguard action. It had been unable to consolidate itself on a new position. When the second World War came, it was still unbalanced, unstable and unprofitable.[20]

The world market situation so far as Britain was concerned had changed only for the worse since the outbreak of the war,[21] and the

---

[19] "In October, 1939, over 95 per cent. of the operatives engaged in cotton spinning and 90 per cent. of those engaged in cotton weaving were employed in Lancashire and adjacent parts of Cheshire, Derbyshire and Yorkshire. Over 97 per cent. of the spinning spindles and 93 per cent. of the cotton looms were in what may be termed the Lancashire area. Finishing is rather more widely scattered, but probably at least two-thirds of those engaged in plants which process cotton were in Lancashire and the West Riding." *WPR: Cotton*, p. v.

[20] *Ibid.*, p. 5.

[21] For example, while world exports of cotton piece goods had declined between 1937 and 1942 from 2,289,000,000 to 2,175,000,000 square yards, British exports had declined from

prospects of regaining lost ground were not any too bright. For one thing, growth of textile industries in raw-materials-producing countries was cutting down the volume of finished goods in international trade. Thus, while world consumption of raw cotton increased by 36 per cent from 1913 to 1937, the volume of international trade in cotton goods declined by 38 per cent.[21] In India, for example, home production of piece goods had increased from an average of 1,141,000,000 square

TABLE 30

PRODUCTION OF COTTON PIECE GOODS IN VARIOUS COUNTRIES
(million square yards)

	1937	1942	Per cent increase
Brazil............................	900	1400	55
Mexico...........................	370	500	35
Canada...........................	245	300	22
Argentina........................	152	300	97
Peru.............................	50	100	100
Columbia.........................	30	100	233
Venezuela........................	15	45	200
Egypt............................	77	370	250
Persia...........................	150	240	60
Syria............................	...	50	...
Palestine........................	3	36	1100
Australia........................	9	30	230

SOURCE: *Working Party Reports: Cotton* (1946).

yards in 1909–1913 to 4,250,000,000 (estimated) in 1938, and imports had decreased from 2,741,000,000 to 724,000,000 square yards. Between 1937 and 1942 Indian exports increased by 700 per cent (from 120,000,000 to 940,000,000 square yards) while British exports declined by 75 per cent (from 1,921,000,000 to 485,000,000 square yards).

A like trend was everywhere observable. Table 30 gives a picture which does not require elaboration.[23] All of these countries except Canada grew part or all of the cotton to meet their own domestic manufacturing requirements. There is no reason whatsoever for believing that this trend will not continue. And although there is every reason for believing that world demand for finished cotton goods will continue to

---

1,921,000,000 to 485,000,000 square yards, or by nearly 75 per cent. Meanwhile her production had dropped by half. *Ibid.*, table 42, p. 121.

[22] *Ibid.*, p. 119.

[23] Compiled from data given in tables 42 and 43, *ibid.*, p. 121.

rise indefinitely, more of that demand is bound, on this showing, to be met from manufactures in countries which grow their own cotton or import it to be manufactured at home to meet their own domestic needs.

Output in the United States has continued to rise. Between 1937 and 1942 the American production of piece goods increased by 23 per cent (from 9,321,000,000 to 12,000,000,000 square yards) and exports approximately doubled. Japanese and German competition, of course, have been temporarily eliminated. This might at first blush seem to hold bright prospects for Lancashire. Between 1928–29 and 1937–38 Japanese exports of cotton cloth had increased as a percentage of world trade from 19 to 39 while the British percentage was dropping from 44 to 21. But the results of war may not favor Britain long for the simple reason that there seems to be quite clear evidence that the strenuous efforts of Lancashire to limit Japanese production to 3,500,000 spindles[24] will meet with strong American opposition. Cotton textiles was one of Japan's leading prewar exports, and if this country is effectively to be rebuilt as a so-called American bastion in the Far East, the interests of Lancashire in the curtailment of the new and technically modern Japanese cotton-textile industry are quite likely to be ignored. The same, under ERP, will surely hold for the revival of German and other Continental textile industries.

Furthermore, there is no very strong reason for believing that the near future will witness any great change in the nationalistic outlook which led in the past to the establishment of protective tariffs and other governmental aids in both old and new textile-manufacturing countries with which Britain must compete—rather the reverse seems to be true[25]— and in most of these countries the new industries have, in the main, the most modern and up-to-date equipment which money can buy and are

[24] See, "Cotton Industry's Plans," *Times Review of Industry*, June, 1948, p. 48. Of total Japanese exports of £27,500,000 to the sterling area between June 30, 1947 and June 30, 1948, £16,000,000, or more than half, "is to consist of cotton textiles." This is several times that which has recently been in force." In the middle of 1947 Japanese exports of cotton cloth had for a short period "risen to as high a level as those from this country ... Production ... has continued to increase and the man-power available in her textile industries has increased likewise. Anglo-American credits seem to be available for the financing of imports of raw cotton." *Times*, November 10, 1948. Before the war three-fifths of Japanese exports were in textiles. Prewar plant capacity is unimpaired. To "rebuild Japan's peaceful economy has ... been the policy of the United States, the dominating Power there." *Times*, Nov. 10, 1948.

[25] Thus, there can be no question but that the new national governments of India, Egypt, Syria, and Palestine will tend to favor home-manufactured textiles by virtually every available means. In addition, of these four countries, all—recent developments (1949) in Syria make the list complete—possess powerful endemic nationalistic movements which are strongly anti-British. In all South American countries the tides of nationalism are running strongly. So far as there exists a telling outside influence, furthermore, it is American and not British.

bound to be manned primarily by very low-cost labor. Although many of them may have high—not to say onerous—investment costs, other factors, including nationalistic sentiment, would appear easily to counteract the handicap.

The greater part of the machinery used in these new overseas industries has been imported from Britain, and it was the opinion of the Cotton working party that, however backward the British cotton industry might be, in the main "the pre-war quality of British spinning machinery compared favourably with that produced by other countries," and that with some exceptions the same held for other branches of the British cotton-textile manufacturing industry. But the significant thing is that it was not used at home; on the contrary, almost all British cotton-textile machinery was exported. For example, between 1932 and 1936 one of the largest textile machinery groups, the Six Amalgamated Companies, exported between 81.5 and 89.3 per cent of all new spinning machinery it produced, while domestic mills continued to use old and less efficient machines. At the time the investigation of the Cotton working party was under way, 90 per cent of all spinning machinery was exported, and makers reported "that for the last 20 years, 95% of new British machinery has been exported." Similar figures for other types of textile machinery were as follows—winding and beaming machinery: warp (cone) winding, 45 per cent export, and weft winding, 27 per cent export; automatic looms, 33 per cent export; and finishing machinery, 75 per cent export.[26]

The wages of the labor which would man these mills in India, the Near Eastern countries, and South America would be, relatively speaking, as much or more below the British level as the British is still below the American. Since American experience in the newer mills in the southern states—not to mention Japanese and Hindu experience—has demonstrated the ability of relatively unskilled (even illiterate) labor to man this new machinery competently and efficiently in a comparatively short period of time so long as it is producing highly standardized lines of output, and since it has also been demonstrated that in these same lines cotton goods made with the more highly paid American operatives can compete on even, or better than even, terms with those produced by cheaper British labor, the newly industrialized overseas countries enjoy a double advantage. They have the new machinery, and their labor is even cheaper than the British.

[26] *Ibid.*, p. 77, and appendix III, p. 266.

They also enjoy additional advantages which, though small in detail, may in their sum come to weigh heavily in the scales. Domestic manufacturers know local markets and consumer needs. They do not have the expense of long shipping hauls which Lancashire must pay. The newer automatic machinery has been developed—as the Cotton working party report points out—to the place where its product is able to compete on a quality basis with many high-priced lines produced by older methods. But perhaps even more important, new cotton industries abroad are certain for a long time to come to enjoy tariff protection from their own governments, and to tariffs may at need be added any one or even all of the various types of aids which the Cotton working party suggests the British government bestow upon its own industry.

Thus the report does not exaggerate in the least when it concludes that "the easy competitive conditions of the last century," which led Britain to stake the "whole livelihood of [its] expanding population on manufacture and trade," are gone, and that the textile industry faces a "great crisis" which requires "a dynamic policy" and "a new outlook."[27] It seems impossible to avoid the conclusion that in order to compete in world markets, the British cotton-textile industry must not only be technically and otherwise as good, but a lot better than its leading competitors.

As the report points out, the reverse is true. The average plant and firm is small. Despite a shrinkage from around 60,000,000 spindles in 1912 to around 39,000,000 in 1940, it was still true that 55 per cent of the mills had less than 90,000 mule-equivalent spindles each, and 249 out of 280 spinning firms had less than 200,000 spindles each—a figure judged by the working party to be less than half the minimum size required to maintain maximum efficiency (500,000 spindles per firm). In weaving, only 69 units (unit = one firm's operations in a weaving shed) out of 1,410 had 1,000 looms or over, and 885 firms had less than 800 looms each. In finishing (1939), 422 out of 593 factories and 333 out of 444 firms had less than 100 operatives each.[28]

There are relatively few mills which have carried vertical integration—from spinning to weaving[29]—very far.

---

[27] *Ibid.*, p. 127. In addition to factors mentioned above it is also true that Britain has lost much, if not all, of the market on the other side of the "iron curtain," and all cotton textiles face the competition of rayon, nylon, and other types of synthetic fibers for the production of which Britain, once again, does not have adequate quantities of the necessary domestic raw materials.

[28] *Ibid.*, tables 16, 17, 19, 20, 23, and 24, pp. 38–43.

[29] The four main processes are: "*Spinning* raw cotton, waste or other fibre into yarn. *Doubling* or twisting together two or more strands of yarn into a single thread. (For

Among spinners (excluding waste spinners) there are 253 separate firms or groups of firms, and ... of these just over a half (131) neither double nor weave. These 131 firms possess 48 per cent of the total spindles (measured in mule equivalents). They have a much larger proportion (63 per cent) of the total mule spindles than of the total ring spindles (26 per cent). A third of the total spinning capacity and more than a half of the doubling capacity are owned by firms which combine spinning and doubling, but do no weaving. A further 14 per cent of the spinning plant and 12 per cent of the doubling plant are owned by firms who weave as well. In all there are 232 firms which double. Of these almost a half are doublers only, most of whom are small firms, owning between them less than a third of the total doubling spindles. There are 1,062 weaving firms, of which 922 neither spin nor double; they own more than three-quarters of the total looms. The general picture is that, while spinning and doubling are closely connected, less than a quarter of the looms are owned by firms which both spin and weave.[30]

Firms are thus organized primarily on a horizontal basis. In a similar fashion production "is for the most part detached from distribution." Related processes are frequently conducted in widely scattered plants. "Spinning, weaving and finishing concerns are in most cases separated from one another by considerable distances." The spinning mills of Oldham, for example, are separated from the weaving sheds of Burnley by some twenty miles. "Finishing works are widely scattered and are often situated in somewhat remote valleys where there is abundant water supply."

The level of technical development is low. Citing conclusions of the Platt mission to the United States,[31] the working party summarized the picture of British technical retardation in cotton textiles as follows:

i) That for spinning, the Lancashire industry is still equipped predominantly with mule spindles, a type which no other country retains on an appreciable scale and which textile machinery makers in general have ceased normally to manufacture.

ii) That for weaving ... automatic looms in Great Britain cover no more than 5 per cent of the industry, whilst in the U.S.A. they cover 95 per cent.

iii) That a substantial proportion of the machinery now in place is ... not only old in type but beyond its efficient working life.[32]

On the last point the report continues, "A partial investigation made in 1930 showed that for most classes of machinery about two-thirds to

---

statistical purposes doubling is often treated as part of the spinning section). *Weaving* yarn into cloth. *Finishing* the cloth by bleaching, dyeing, printing, etc. The bleaching, dyeing, etc. of yarns are also commonly included among the 'finishing' processes." *Ibid.*, p. 36.

[30] *Ibid.*, p. 37.
[31] *Report of the Cotton Textile Mission* [Platt Mission] *to the U.S.A.* (London, 1944).
[32] *Ibid.*, p. 66.

three-quarters of the plant investigated was then more than 20 years old. Re-equipment since then has not been on a large scale." A wartime survey "brought out that the percentages of buildings built mainly before 1900 were: in the spinning section, 67 per cent (representing 61 per cent of the total floor space), and, in the weaving section, 69 per cent. (representing 69 per cent of the total floor space)."[33] A considerable percentage of these buildings would have to be drastically altered before new machinery could be installed and flow methods of production employed; in many they could not be used at all. Such conditions mean a relatively high ratio of plant to production. "A very rough comparison" based on 1937 data, for example, shows that the "spindles in place per bale of cotton consumed were about 13 in the U.K. and 3.1 in the U.S.A. The number of looms per 100 bales of cotton consumed were 15 in the U.K. compared with 6.3 in the U.S.A. The figures for India (and in the case of spindles for Japan) were very close to those of the U.S.A. Similar comparisons with Germany and France indicate that the spindles in place per bale consumed were about two-thirds of the U.K. proportion, but that the looms per 100 bales were almost exactly the same as for the U.K."[34]

It is not necessary to cite further detail in order to demonstrate how seriously the British cotton-textile industry was in arrears. From re-equipment alone, the Platt mission, on the basis of 1937 data, estimated that "for the whole group of coarse, medium and fine yarns of cloth" the saving in numbers of labor force "required, if U.S.A. methods had been employed, would have been as follows: spinning and doubling, 38 per cent; winding and beaming, 80 per cent; weaving, 62 per cent." For the total labor force the savings would have been about 52½ per cent. Roughly, therefore, the labor requirements would have been halved, "allowing for a 48-hour week." On the basis of "a 40-hour week, the saving would be 40 per cent."[35] A study by the Shirley Institute yields similar results. For "two cloths" the number of "operative hours per 100 lb. of loom-state cloth" under British methods was 25.75, and under American methods 11.55. For the coarse cloth "the American method thus shows a saving of 14.20 operative hours (55 per cent) which is made up of 2.01 hours (32 per cent) in spinning, 3.63 hours (81 per cent) in winding and beaming, and 8.56 hours (57 per cent) in weaving. For the medium cloth the total operative hours are 60.17 under the British method and 22.90 under the Ameri-

[33] *Loc. cit.*   [34] *Ibid.*, p. 67.   [35] *Ibid.*, p. 87.

can method, showing therefore a saving of 37.27 hours (62 per cent) for the American method. Of this total 9.04 hours (47 per cent) are accounted for on spinning, 6.11 hours (81 per cent) on winding and beaming, and 22.12 hours (66 per cent) on weaving."[36]

At this point, however, the working party came up against another serious difficulty. Modernization which carried with it the prospect of eliminating half of the man-hours employed in production would mean wholesale loss of jobs unless the output of the industry was to be correspondingly expanded—a prospect which neither the working party nor any other private or public authority anticipates. Relocation would mean the total elimination of many small and scattered plants, virtually the only source of income for a considerable number of small towns and villages. Over the industry, largely because British cotton textiles are generally high-quality fabrics which require highly skilled and specialized labor, it would mean not only loss of jobs, but also loss of alternative lines of employment in which the old skills could be used.

While normal wastage within the industry might take care of this problem in time, there are additional difficulties to be faced. The decline of the industry has been so widespread and continuous that the number of unemployed attached to it has been chronically large. Between 1912 and 1935 the average number of persons employed in "cotton spinning, doubling and weaving industries" decreased more or less continuously from 621,516 to 349,319. By 1945 the number of insured persons had declined to 209,160. Between 1924 and 1938 there was full-time work for no more than half of all persons attached to the industry. If the most optimistic estimate of postwar markets for British cotton textiles is taken,[37] modernization which would reduce man-hour requirements to the American level would decrease employment in the cotton-textile industry to about 160,000 persons.[38]

[36] *Ibid.*, pp. 88–89. Statistical details from the Platt mission are given in appendix IV, p. 269, and from the Shirley Institute in appendix V, pp. 270–271.

[37] The Cotton Board has made three estimates: (1) "assumes the maintenance of the pre-war status quo in overseas markets," (2) "assumes changes which will prove disadvantageous to our competitive position" and (3) "assumes a new state of affairs as favourable as the more optimistic of our consultants could prudently regard as possible," and all three assume an increase of about 5 per cent in the home market. On the basis of the first assumption there would be a decrease in postwar trade, from that of 1937, for spun yarn of 12 per cent and for woven goods of 14 per cent. The comparable percentages for assumption (2) are decreases of 27 per cent and 29 per cent respectively, and for (3) increases of 10 per cent and 9 per cent respectively. Computed from data presented on p. 117, *ibid.*

[38] In 1937 there were 359,703 persons employed in spinning, doubling, and weaving (*Ibid.*, table 30, p. 52); halving man-hour requirements on the same work week would give the above figure. Cutting the work week to 40 hours would increase the figure to a maximum of around 180,000 persons.

In face of this situation, resistance to technical modernization among operatives is likely to be very strong. This could be overcome only if the consequent net shrinkage in textile employment and the drastic geographic reshuffling of these plants were accompanied by large-scale, comprehensive, and detailed plans for new industries and new jobs in the affected area. In contrast with American workmen, as both American and British observers are fond of pointing out, the British worker does not readily change either his residence or his occupation. The very tenacity with which he clings to both means that plans for textile modernization will have to pay extraordinarily close attention to these details, and that the incentives to change will have to be unusually attractive.

On the basis of past Labour party discussions of problems of this order it would follow that from the very scale—in terms of direct investment in the overhauled textile industries and other consequent changes, in terms of the extent of the territory and the size of the population affected, and in terms of the range of the aspects of work and living (housing, town replanning, amenities, etc.) necessarily involved—on which such a reorganization would have to be carried out, instrumentation would require at once a regional plan of industrial location which is at least coextensive with the Lancashire industrial area and an industrial plan which is coextensive with all phases of the national cotton-textile industry. Neither could be effected alone, and there could be no assurance that any important change of detail in one was taking the right direction unless it was linked up at all important stages of development to the other.

Against such a background of conditions, facts, opinions, and problems, what did the Cotton working party propose be done? *"There must be,"* they said, *"a concerted programme and a recognition that the national interest is involved in a manner which, while it may justify a claim for special action by the Government, also puts upon all individual interests in the industry an obligation to collaborate in a joint effort to secure the maximum benefit for the industry as a whole."*[39] As this statement makes clear, "a major transformation" is necessary, overdue, and "inevitable." Four earlier reports and recommendations are reviewed in some detail. Of these, only the report issued in 1943 by the Legislative Council of the United Textile Factory Workers Association—the one group which, it is said, voted solidly for the Labour

---

[39] *Ibid.*, p. 164. Italicized in the report.

party in 1945—advocated socialization of the industry, and this is the one recommendation in all the reports[40] that does not receive any consideration by the Cotton working party.

On the contrary, while the first of the governing conceptions which guided the working party in shaping its "Objectives and Recommendations" was the maintenance of cotton as a major industry, the second main feature was contained in, and determined by, the terms of reference under which Sir Stafford Cripps, the Labour President of the Board of Trade, had appointed the working party. "These make it clear," the report states, "that we are required to submit proposals *based on maintaining the system of private enterprise.*"[41] This of necessity means that its recommendations must aim "to create conditions in which private enterprise can work successfully," and this in turn requires that "that system must be given a basis for confidence and reasonable opportunity and facilities to make good." The central goal for both the industry and the Government thereby becomes that of "maintaining a sound and efficient system of private enterprise operating in the national interest."

How this shoring-up of the cotton-textile industry in private hands may be accomplished the working party then proceeds to spell out in great detail. Their recommendations may, however, be readily summarized under three main headings:[42] (1) technical modernization, (2) adequate provision for the "human factor," and (3) organization of the industry. It is interesting to note that in recommending technical modernization prior consideration is given to the working out of "some plan for, or positive assurance of concerted action" throughout the whole industry. Given this, reëquipment and reorganization become feasible and plant can more adequately be surveyed. A schedule of alterations and of methods of financing them as they are made is to be worked out. Plant and firm amalgamations are to be promoted. Cost accounting systems are to be installed. Marketing and distribution are to be made more efficient. Marketing, textile, and other lines of re-

---

[40] The other three were: The Clynes committee report of 1930 (Committee of the Economic Advisory Council) ; the report of the Cotton Board made to the President of the Board of Trade in January 1944; and the report of the Platt mission. For their recommendations see *WPR: Cotton*, pp. 151–156.

[41] *Ibid.*, p. 157. Italics mine.

[42] There are thirty-four recommendations—many of them detailed under numerous subheadings—divided into four main divisions: "Operating Methods," pp. 168–194; "The Human Factor," pp. 195–197; "External Conditions and Government Action," pp. 198–202; and "Organisation," pp. 203–212; There are also four "Memoranda of Dissent," explanations, and a supplementary note thereto made by different members of the working party.

search of importance to the textile industry are greatly to be enhanced. Plans for plant specialization and for standardization of product are to be carried out. Model "yardstick" or pilot plants are to be set up under central administration, and arrangements are to be made to see that "at least one completely modernised mill or weaving shed" will be found "in each important centre." Other recommendations on modernization are in a similar vein.

To deal with the "human factor," a special effort is to be made to get younger and better trained managerial and expert staff, wage systems are to be reviewed, special efforts are to be made to promote "collaboration between employers, managerial staff and trade unions in increasing productive output,"[43] and such subjects as labor relations, wages, and working conditions—"while specifically excluded from the scope of our inquiry"—should nevertheless be competently and comprehensively reviewed.

The problems of organization are centered around the proposal to create "a Central Body for the industry, to be called 'The Cotton Council,' which would be appointed by the President of the Board of Trade and consist of an independent Chairman and ordinary members of whom one-third should be independent members, one-third persons with knowledge of the various sections of production and marketing, and one-third from the Trade Unions."[44] It would be its function, working within the framework of "a broadly defined strategic objective . . . accepted by the industry and approved by the Government," to supervise changes in the industry on the assumption that "a very wide discretion in working out the tactical methods for attaining it should be left to the industry." It would focus "the general opinion of the industry on matters of policy," see that developments "are proceeding in accordance with national interests," prepare reports for the information of the government and Parliament, and serve as a channel for the two-way flow of opinion and advice between industry and government and for the issuance of "general directives to the industry" by the government.

At all stages and levels of this program, the government should be prepared to stand by with the necessary assistance. Thus it should promote and subsidize both further technical research and modernization programs, expand training facilities for managers and skilled crafts, assist the industry in closing-down and abandonment of obsolete

---

[43] Recommendation XXI, *ibid.*, p. 197.
[44] Recommendation XXX, *ibid.*, p. 204.

plant by making special tax allowances, increase depreciation allowances, aid in the expansion of foreign markets, etc. In most of these relations the government would operate largely, if not entirely, through the medium of the Cotton Council, just as the industry would, in its turn, when dealing with any phase or aspect of law or government policy and control. Although there was some dissent on various recommendations, it was the majority report which the government was prepared to accept.

At the top is a tripartite body, appointed by and generally responsible to the President of the Board of Trade, called the Cotton Council. Since it may "set up any bodies which it considers necessary" for further "assisting the cotton industry" it may establish various subordinate bodies to which it will delegate various functions. Thus it will own and supervise the various "yardstick" mills, take over—in effect—the Shirley Institute (technical research institute serving the industry), possibly establish at some central location a design center, etc. But its overwhelmingly important function is to encourage, aid, guide, and generally supervise plant and firm amalgamations.

Here the idea of a corporatively organized industry, whose powers of policy formation and general direction are coextensive with industry frontiers, finds its fullest expression. Both the establishment of the necessary machinery and the existence of a general will to effect a genuine congruence between national objectives and the interests of the industry operating under private ownership, and between industry-wide associations of capital and labor is assumed. The council's function is to be to determine and interpret general policy directives and to provide over-all aids for ready compliance. These will be implemented through a small number of large combinations (amalgamated by the normal process of business concentration) whose directing authorities will naturally be of a single mind in promoting industrial efficiency, and who will take the necessary steps to see that it is achieved. But should they hesitate, the government—acting through the Cotton Council—will assist the industry at the faltering point with an assorted display of special aids. If serious difficulties arise, or should the industry become irresponsibly recalcitrant, then the enticements of the "carrot" variety are to be supplemented by what Stephen Leacock, speaking of Ajax in the Trojan War, referred to as "propulsion from behind."

In this picture the initiative in policy formation lies in the government and the Cotton Council; the initiative in implementation lies in the hands of the individual business entrepreneurs in command of huge amalgamations which among them will envelop the whole industry. At all levels of policy formation, and at all levels of implementation, there is a possible, if not indeed an existing, congruence of interest between all parties—government, business, labor, and the consuming public— and it is the special function of all responsible parties to see that the proper formulae are found. These formulae will supply at need, and at the necessary point of application, the special devices which may be required to reshape and reorganize, and these in turn will in time combine to evolve a modernized industry.

Such in general also is the picture given of conditions and of the required therapeutic measures for meeting these conditions in the other industries covered by the working party reports. Appendix 7 summarizes roughly the recommendations of the working parties reporting to the Board of Trade. Other working parties established by other ministries[45] are similarly constituted, and have somewhat the same general objectives. So pleased has the Labour government been with the working-party device that special legislation has been passed to promote its application over widening areas of the British industrial system, with a view to the establishment of permanent organizations for carrying their recommendations into effect. This was the purpose of the Industrial Organization and Development Act.

THE DEVELOPMENT COUNCILS

On July 31, 1947, there was passed into law an act known as the Industrial Organization and Development Act[46] having as its general object the granting of power to establish development councils (by

---

[45] Other working parties are being set up from time to time. Among them, are the following: Ministry of Education, working party to report on the establishment of a National Council of Technology; Ministry of Works, working party on building operation; Ministry of Health, Midwifery working party. Similar are the private working committee set up by the Federation of British Industries, "representing advertisers, agents and media owners" to work out means "to reduce the pressure of demand for scarce and luxury goods" which has been accepted by the Chancellor of the Exchequer as a substitute for his proposed tax on advertising, and the committee of enquiry set up by the Lord President of the Council, Herbert Morrison, to look "into the future of the British Film Institute." (This survey is now completed, and the Film Institute set up as a development council.) There are many others.

[46] The full title read: "An Act to provide for the establishment of development councils to exercise functions for improving or developing the service rendered to the community by industries and for other purposes in relation thereto, for making funds available for certain purposes in relation to industries for which there is no development council, for the disposal of any surplus of funds levied under emergency provision for encouragement of exports, for the making of grants to bodies established for the improvement of design, and for purposes connected therewith and consequential thereon." 10 & 11, Geo. 6, Chap. 40.

"development council order") by any of the following ministries: Board of Trade, Agriculture and Fisheries, Supply, Food, Works, and Fuel and Power; the Admiralty; and the Secretary of State.[47] They are to be constituted after the tripartite pattern of the working parties, and are to perform any or all of the functions assigned to them by the appointing authority. These are given in the first schedule of the act.

FUNCTIONS WHICH MAY BE ASSIGNED TO DEVELOPMENT COUNCILS

1. Promoting or undertaking scientific research.

2. Promoting or undertaking inquiry as to materials and equipment and as to methods of production, management and labour utilisation, including the discovery and development of new materials, equipment and methods and of improvements in those already in use, the assessing of the advantages of different alternatives, and the conduct of experimental establishments and of tests on a commercial scale.

3. Promoting or undertaking research into matters affecting industrial psychology.

4. Promoting or undertaking measures for the improvement of design, including promoting or undertaking the establishment and operation of design centres.

5. Promoting the production and marketing of standard products.

6. Promoting the better definition of trade descriptions and consistency in the use thereof.

7. Undertaking the certification of products, the registration of certification trade marks, and the functions of proprietors of such marks.

8. Promoting the training of persons engaged or proposing engagements in the industry, and their education in technical or artistic subjects relevant thereto.

9. Promoting the adoption of measures for securing safer and better working conditions, and the provision and improvement of amenities for persons employed, and promoting or undertaking inquiry as to such measures.

10. Promoting or undertaking research into the incidence, prevention and cure of industrial disease.

11. Promoting or undertaking arrangements for encouraging the entry of persons into the industry.

12. Promoting or undertaking research for improving arrangements for marketing and distributing products.

13. Promoting or undertaking research into matters relating to the consumption or use of goods and services supplied by the industry.

14. Promoting arrangements for co-operative organisations for supplying materials and equipment, for co-ordinating production, and for marketing and distributing products.

15. Promoting the development of export trade, including promoting or undertaking arrangements for publicity overseas.

---

[47] *Act*, Section 1 (2).

16. Promoting or undertaking arrangements for better acquainting the public in the United Kingdom with the goods and services supplied by the industry and methods of using them.

17. Promoting the improvement of accounting and costing practices and uniformity therein, including in particular the formulation of standard costings.

18. Promoting or undertaking the collection and formulation of statistics.

19. Advising on any matters relating to the industry (other than remuneration or conditions of employment) as to which the Board or Minister concerned may request the council to advise, and undertaking inquiry for the purpose of enabling the council so to advise.

20. Undertaking arrangements for making available information obtained, and for advising, on matters with which the council are concerned in the exercise of any of their functions.

As inspection will show, seven of these specified functions are for "promoting or undertaking" research of one sort or another; six (4, 5, 6, 7, 15, and 16) are primarily marketing aids; three (8, 9, and 11) relate to personnel; two (19 and 20) relate primarily to the conduct of business within the councils; and one each is devoted to better organization of the industry (14), and to improving cost accounting methods (17). Thus the development council is to be an agency primarily devoted to providing and pooling aids ("service") to the industry. Though it is to be "a body corporate"[48] appointed by the Minister, its membership is to be either technical or "capable of representing the interests or persons" carrying on business or employed in the industry. In sum, it is to be a corporate body which can gather information, but which has no compulsive powers beyond levying certain small charges required for the conduct of its activities. It has no power to modernize, regroup, relocate, amalgamate, abandon, or otherwise alter conditions or policies relating to either physical plant or business practices. Nor can it prohibit price fixing, patent pooling, production restriction, or any of the other more common types of cartel and monopoly controls.

The first development council established under the act was the Cotton Board, 1948.[49] A definition of its functions, "to which no powers of compulsion are attached," lists ten. These are identical with one-half of those listed in the first schedule of the act, cited above (namely, nos. 2, 3, 8, 9, 10, 11, 17, 18, 19, and 20). It is made up of four employer representatives, four labor representatives, and three "independent

---

[48] "A development council shall be by virtue of this Act a body corporate, by such name as may be specified in the development council order." Section 2 (1).

[49] January 5, 1948, in a white paper and draft order. See *Home Affairs Survey*, Jan. 13, 1948, pp. 17–18.

members." It is to finance its operations with a levy not to exceed £250,000 a year, and it may borrow up to £20,000. Aside from general advice and counsel on how "to increase the efficiency and productivity of the industry"—for which under the authority of the act it has power to collect the desired information from the industry—its special function is to administer a government subsidy for new machinery, but not buildings, up to 25 per cent of the approved cost. Approval of the board is required before the subsidy may be had, and the board's approval is supposed to be withheld unless the company in question has so managed its plans for expansion that the board is satisfied that the net result will be in line with the long-run objectives designated in the act. In practice this has meant primarily insistence that amalgamation of plants and firms be carried through to the point where the result is at least a unit of the minimum size adjudged necessary to efficient operation. Amalgamation, again, has meant primarily firm concentration, and this may be accomplished by the usual means of merger, the establishment of a holding company, or the exchange of shares.

The actual procedure appears to be somewhat as follows:[50] Except on personnel matters, all reorganization plans must come from business management. Manufacturers then come to the Cotton Board, 1948, with proposals for new construction, installation of new machinery, amalgamation of companies, or any other matter of statutory interest to the board. They need not come unless they wish to do so, and they are not prevented from taking the steps proposed if the board disapproves. But if the board approves, they are then entitled to subsidy from the government up to 25 per cent of the new machinery cost, and possibly some additional tax concessions. To qualify "as a satisfactory group" for the purpose they must be of the minimum required size, and their "plans must be accepted as adequate for the effective modernisation of their mills."[51] Although they must submit data to the board, approval of the

---

[50] Based on confidential materials supplied to the author by the Board of Trade, and upon interviews with members of the staff of the Cotton Board, 1948, at Manchester in the summer of 1948.

[51] According to a letter from the President of the Board of Trade to Sir R. Streat, chairman of the Cotton Board, on September 28, 1947 (as abstracted by *Home Affairs Survey*, July 6, 1947), the procedure of qualifying for the subsidy involves "four main essentials: (*a*) The Government grant will be payable in respect of equipment but not buildings. (*b*) If necessary, special steps will be taken to assist grouped firms to obtain the cotton spinning (and preparatory) machinery for the carrying out of approved modernisation schemes put forward under these general arrangements. (*c*) Applications for Government grant must be examined from two points of view, first, can the applicants be regarded as a satisfactory group for the present purpose, and secondly, can their plans be accepted as adequate for the effective modernisation of their mills. They will then be asked to submit detailed schedules of their modernisation plans with estimates of costs, in order that the Cotton Board may advise

plan by the board is not prefaced by an independent investigation of the facts presented or by direct field examination of any physical changes which have already been brought about and for which subsidy is requested.

All this applies, however, only to the spinning section of the industry. The subsidy grant is administered by the board under authority of the Cotton Spinning (Re-equipment Subsidy) Act of 1948. Originally the bill was to require that "groups of mills" applying for the subsidy must have "a capacity of 500,000 spindles" in order to qualify for modernization grants. This was changed, under industry pressure, to 400,000. But where vertical combines were involved, the government announced that it would adopt a "flexible attitude" and would "accept around 250,000 spindles as qualification for the subsidy."[52] From this it would seem to follow that it was not the size of the mill or mills, their location, the degree of plant specialization, product, the nature of the horizontal combination or vertical integration, or even the resort to double-shift production—which it has been estimated could reduce new machine requirements by as much as 60 per cent for a given output—which was required in order to qualify, but rather that new capital be laid out for machinery, and that the ownership or management unit be large scale. If new machinery could be justified on the grounds that it increased efficiency of production at the point of installation, it would qualify. And if any unit was large enough to meet the minimum requirement it would not matter where plant was located, how many plants or of what vintage they might be, or, indeed, whether all the plants whose spindles were added into the totals submitted were even in current operation. For these reasons the industry—and individual members of the Cotton Board, 1948, shared this view—argued that the size limitation was meaningless. Mechanical reëquipment without fundamental reorganization, including relocation, of horizontally and vertically related plant over very wide areas could well mean only additions to capital costs. It

on whether the plans can be accepted as embodying satisfactory modernisation. When the plans have been accepted, payment of the subsidy will be made on presentation of the receipted invoices from the suppliers. As has already been announced, the scheme is being extended to cover deliveries made since V.J. Day (August 16, 1945). (d) The Chancellor of the Exchequer announced in Parliament on 15th April his intention of reducing to half the standard rate the Income Tax charged when, as a result of the formation of approved amalgamations, machinery or plant is sold for more than its written-down value."

[52] *Financial Times*, May 1, 1948. Subsequently, 1,200 weaving units, totaling 450,000 looms, have received questionnaires from the Cotton Board as the first step toward a survey of existing plant complementary to those of the spinning and waste sections. *Times*, Sept. 3, 1948.

would follow from considerations such as these that the government might find that reëquipment would move at a snail's pace. And so it has.[53]

From practically every point of view the Cotton Board, 1948, must appear at first examination to be a most extraordinarily weak reed to support such a heavy program as the government hopes to lay on it. When it is recalled that the cotton working party report, and, for that matter, all earlier reports, stressed in measured and wholly unmistakable terms the necessity for major changes, and for reorganization of the entire industry, one is apt to be completely mystified by the parental pride shown for this curiously pallid progeny produced by the passing marriage of Labour socialism to political power. Not minor changes but drastic reorganization was called for. Not the shoring up of profit margins by special concessions to the backward and weak—which might render them powerful but leave them still backward[54]—but the viability of the industry as a whole and the promotion of the national welfare in one of its most vitally weakened sectors was the problem to be faced. And it was a problem to be faced by a "Socialist Government."

Nevertheless, it cannot be assumed that this Government is ignorant of the facts relating to this huge industry. Quite the contrary seems to be true; further information may be needed, but as it comes in—already in great quantities—it is robed in the same hues. There must, consequently, have been reasons which seem good and sufficient for choosing the device of the development council for the 80 per cent of British industry which Morrison announced was to be left outside the nationalization program. That once having chosen the device the Labour government shows no sign of weakening in support of its choice, reinforces this impression. It has set up other development councils, modeled after the new Cotton Board, and its spokesmen seem in the main to be satisfied that worthwhile results will come from their activities. For this Labour confidence in what seems a rather extreme form of "voluntarism" there are many different lines of explanation.

[53] Harold Wilson, President of the Board of Trade, in winding up debate on the Subsidy Bill complained that while "spinners were already 20 to 30 years behind the world" they "were still not ordering new machinery." *Loc. cit.* Nor have sales picked up very heavily since passage of the act.

[54] Profits of the Lancashire Cotton Corporation on ordinary capital increased from 17.7 per cent in 1945–46 to 27½ per cent in 1946–47 as a result of "its modernisation programme." A review of 73 cotton spinning mills for the year 1947 has shown that the average profit "has been £14,058 per company compared with an average of £9,812 for 68 companies in 1946. The average dividend in 1947 for 108 concerns was 14.71 per cent compared with 12.56 the year before." *Economist,* Jan. 3, 1948.

They are not mutually exclusive, and it seems wholly impossible at present to tell how they are being combined in the minds of the leading supporters of the development-council idea. Some of their explanations may be summarized briefly.

1. *If "voluntary coöperation" fails, the government may nationalize.* This issue is of overriding importance; all other lines of explanation are necessarily subsidiary to it. That this is so may easily be shown. Speaking of certain proposals of the wartime Cotton Board, a Fabian publication comments,[55] "Provided the industry takes the steps necessary to make its operations efficient it has the word of Sir Stafford Cripps, President of the Board of Trade, that it need not fear early nationalization." This is certainly an ambiguous way of putting the matter. On the supposition that it reflects more or less accurately the official position, two questions quite naturally arise. First, if the industry takes the necessary steps to make the industry efficient, is nationalization to be postponed so long as efficiency is maintained? And second, if the industry is not to be nationalized early, then is it to be nationalized eventually?

If the first is answered in the affirmative, then the development council is merely a friendly, but nevertheless a determined, "propulsion from behind"—duly accompanied with the reminder that it is a matter of "get along with the job or else!" In this event, the threat of nationalization might very well have a salutary effect upon private business. But if the second interpretation is the valid one, then nationalization is a sword of Damocles hanging over business, but the traditional version of the Syracusean fable must be modified by the dead certainty that the slender hair that sustains the sword will eventually part under the strain. There may then very well be a general effort by present owners to bleed the industry while the bleeding is good, and this would most certainly not lead to "cooperation in order to make its operations efficient." The threat of nationalization would literally be a boomerang. It is possible that this may account for the failure of the industry to respond to the threat with much enthusiasm. And the same result would obtain in any other industry where a similar position was taken.

[55] *Cotton: A Working Policy*, by a Fabian Research Group, Research Series No. 104 (London, 1945), p. 8. The fact that this pamphlet was written mostly before the elections which brought Labour to power suggests that it may have been penned with fewer inhibitions, for, despite the usual and necessary disclaimers to the contrary, the Fabian Society came about as close to representing the official position of the Labour party as if the pamphlet had been issued by the party itself—in which event, incidentally, it would have been mostly written by the very same people.

In the absence of any definite statement by the Labour party as to which of these two alternatives it has in mind, it is necessary to assume that it is the latter. This conclusion is reinforced by various earlier statements in Labour literature and by reports of current discussions of "what industries are now ripe or overripe" for nationalization issuing from Transport House and various allied propaganda centers. There are many other reasons why business should draw this conclusion. Three such reasons directly connected with the development-council idea will illustrate the point: (1) The setting up of a central policy-forming body for entire industries suggests the possibiltiy of siphoning off from individual businesses more and more of the power to make significant policy decisions. As this occurs the industry begins to take on a public-utility or natural-monopoly character, and both have been declared by Labour spokesmen to define ripeness for nationalization. (2) Clearly, a major—perhaps primary—object of the development councils is to promote concentration of ownership and control. Labour doctrine regards such concentration as an inevitable process within capitalism anyway, and one which merely prepares the way for being taken over by a socialist commonwealth. (3) It has been a fixed tenet in this same propaganda that voluntary action by business enterprise leads to collusion against public and labor interests, and that its natural result is restrictive practices, not promotion of efficiency. Is it possible that the development councils, to change the figure again, are merely devices for feeding out plenty of rope with which to let industry hang itself?

If, in short, the development council is either a sword of Damocles or a hangman's noose, the reaction of industry is likely to be the reverse of that hoped for. Even if it was not intended to be either of these things, so long as the belief exists that it may be, business coöperation is apt to be tentative, slow, and hostile. Yet clearly there is no way of knowing which of these alternatives the Government has in mind. British business spokesmen consulted by the writer were wholly agreed on one thing: although business did not know the answer and hence was uncertain, it generally took the view that Labour sought for voluntary coöperation only to provide it with a breathing space before it took the next step toward a fully socialized economy. If so, the development councils are doomed to failure, irrespective of Labour hopes.

2. *The development councils will be adequate to the tasks placed before them because complementary machinery and controls for im-*

plementing desired action already exist. In addition to the bait of direct subsidy[56] (thus far limited to the cotton industry) there are the usual controls over allocation of raw materials, machinery, investment funds, and man power; price controls of some sort or other over both domestic (most rigid for utility goods) and exported products; tax policy, etc. None of these controls, whether of wartime origin or not, need be relaxed until the government is prepared to do so. If they should be relaxed they can always be reimposed. There are also attractive offers of special scientific assistance from the Department of Scientific and Industrial Research (DSIR).[57] In cotton, there is also the "bulk buying scheme" under which the Liverpool Futures Market (Cotton Commodity Exchange) was closed in the early part of the war, and all raw cotton was purchased by the Cotton Control. Put on a permanent basis by the Cotton (Centralized Buying) Bill, the Raw Cotton Commission has power to adjust prices of the basic raw material and to allocate supplies.[58]

The very existence of the Raw Cotton Commission, of course, represents partial nationalization of the cotton industry. But its greater significance lies in the power it has to force recalcitrant members of the industry to accept the government's decisions. There is nothing to prevent similar control of raw materials in any other field. In fact, bulk buying is still the dominant form of control exercised over imported food supplies by the Ministry of Foods. The establishment of two permanent government boards "to buy and market cocoa in the Gold Coast and Nigeria"[59] suggests a willingness to extend the device as circumstances may dictate.

Such an interpretation of the Government's reliance upon the development council would indicate that voluntary coöperation was to dominate all those parts of the industry in which it seems to be effective, with supplementary controls and additional regulatory machinery

---

[56] For rather complicated reasons, partly psychological, partly political, and partly business (the manner in which the tax laws are drawn up and administered), many textile concerns are not even asking for the subsidy available to them at all. There is also no particular reason for believing other development councils will offer so much, and seemingly such attractive, bait as this.

[57] For details on the organization and functioning of the DSIR see chart 10, p. 646.

[58] "The primary functions of the Commission will be—(1) Buying, importing into the United Kingdom, holding, and distributing of all raw cotton required for the cotton industry, and the re-export trade of the United Kingdom. (2) The selling of cotton, 'at prices best calculated to further the public interest.' " *Economic Record*, British Information Services, No. 36, Nov. 13, 1947.

[59] The purpose: "to protect native farmers in colonial territories against ruinous fluctuations in the prices at which they can sell the commodities they grow." *Loc. cit.*

being improvised to bolster the weaker sectors at need, but only for the duration of the weakness. The boundary lines between nationalization, regulation, and control would then become very flexible; advancing as voluntary coöperation fails to get results; receding as it comes through with what the government has a legitimate right to expect of it. This explanation seems distinctly plausible, and it can be made to square with most of the facts.

3. *Self-government in industry can really be made to work in the national interest.* There are many reasons for believing, strange as it may seem, that the Labour government seriously accepts this view. For one thing, so far as it genuinely believes in the voluntary coöperation which is embodied in the development council idea, it has but little alternative to accepting the basic formula of self-government in industry. British industry is already organized into a vast and complex trade-association network, most of which is to some degree or other of a combined cartel-like and general policy-determining character, and nearly all of it is combined into peak associations which possess considerable capacity to influence business policies throughout British economy.[60]

During the war this web of private-business organization continued to spread under direct encouragement of the Coalition government, and the interlacing of its numerous strands and those of the government offices dealing with industry became so close and intimate that it seemed impossible to tell where one began and the other left off.[61] Furthermore, in making plans for the postwar period, organized British business has generally favored a continuation of these programs. One of its outstanding spokesmen, Lord McGowan of Imperial Chemicals, has declared that cartels are a good thing. Their purpose, he wrote in a highly publicized statement, is "to regulate but not to abolish competition. Such agreements can lead to a more ordered organization of production and can check wasteful and excessive competition. They can help to stabilize prices at a reasonable level," improve technique, spread the benefits of invention, lower prices to consumers, etc.[62] The alternative

---

[60] For a summary of these prewar and early wartime controls see Robert A. Brady, *Business as a System of Power* (New York, 1943), chapter v on Britain's "Feudalistic System of Cartel Controls," pp. 153–188. See also, A. F. Lucas, *Industrial Reconstruction and the Control of Competition* (London, 1937); Herman Levy, *Monopolies, Cartels and Trusts in British Industry* (London, 1927).

[61] See, for example, the very interesting detail in this connection in "The Economic Front," *Economist*, Dec. 9, 1939.

[62] *Hansard* (Lords), Vol. 132, cols. 683–684.

to "unrestricted competition" as the "basis for our economy," states an article in *The Sunday Times,* is "cooperation and agreement."[63]

Such coöperation and agreement means, as the Federation of British Industries has put it in a special memorandum addressed to this subject, that industry should "provide associations with collective representation and responsibility to which the Government could delegate the detailed work involved," and which would be "capable of formulating general production and commercial policies for the sections of industry which they cover."[64] These trade associations would then "act as the official channels of communication between government administrators and industry."[65] A widely circulated statement by 120 leading British industrialists in 1942 states the position clearly. "It appears to us," they said, "to be an essential condition of progress that *the relations between firms, between different industries and between Industry as a whole and Government should be more fully and comprehensively organised in some form of permanent association.* Otherwise there will continue to be loss and friction through forms of competition which are wasteful and uneconomic."[66]

Thus organized at home, the Federation of British Industries would extend this pattern of coöperation and agreement until it was worldwide in order to insure that the "jungle law [of the] free play of market forces [would] be replaced by planning designed to raise world prosperity by orderly methods." Its chosen instrument would be an International Economic Council which "could: (1) do useful work in estimating . . . the requirements and possibilities of supply of the different countries in the principal commodities of international trade; (2) guide international trade into the channels where it would be most beneficial to both producer and consumer; (3) act as the co-ordinating body . . . for the purpose of raising . . . [the] standard of life [in countries needing assistance] or expanding their industrial and commercial activities."[67] A similar proposal calling for a world trade alliance was proposed by Sir Edgar R. Jones, a leading British steel magnate.[68]

---

[63] Cited by George W. Stocking and Myron W. Watkins, *Cartels or Competition* (New York, 1948), p. 357.

[64] *The Organisation of British Industry: Report of the Federation of British Industries Organisation of Industry Committee* (London, 1944), cited *ibid.,* p. 358.

[65] *Loc. cit.*

[66] *A National Policy for Industry* (London, 1942). Cited *ibid.,* p. 359, with the comment, "The italicized portion is in bold type in the original."

[67] Cited, *loc. cit.*

[68] Of this plan Stocking and Watkins, *ibid.,* p. 361, footnote 39, comment: "The plan was to broaden and unify the cartel system so as to make the World Trade Alliance the sole

Although there has been some notable dissent from these proposals in British business circles,[69] it has come from a dwindling minority, and it is wholly out of keeping with trends in British business organization. The general public relations expression of this program is found in the phrase, "self-government in business." This was the formula under which the American National Recovery Administration (NRA) program was launched in 1933. The ideas which shape its organizational patterns underlie the agricultural marketing controls in both contemporary Britain and the United States. It was the same rubric under which both Fascist Italy and Nazi Germany sought to justify their corporative systems. It is an idea which appeals to centralized bodies for coördinating business policies, such as the Federation of British Industries and the American National Association of Manufacturers, wherever they are found, and pretty much in proportion as the business world for which they speak is centralized, amalgamated, cartelized, and monopolized.

Why, then, is British Labour opening its arms to self-government in business in the form of the development council—almost as though the latter were the materialization of a long-lost lover? Searching through Labour literature of the past, one is hard put to find a single case in which advancing monopolistic controls, when left to their own devices, have not been regarded by Labour spokesmen as a terror and an abomination. One might be led, on the contrary, to the certain conclusion that Labour, since time out of mind, has felt that it had barely enough time in which to win the strategic political victory which would begin the rout of its enemies, before the swiftly multiplying strength of the latter had engulfed and destroyed the last vestiges of the very political democracy which was naturally and necessarily both the canonical enemy of reaction and the condition to the birth of the socialist commonwealth of the future.[70]

---

regulator of all international trade. Each industry would be organised first on a national basis and then on an international basis, with the power to fix output and prices and regulate the flow of trade. Although the plan provided for supervision by intergovernmental agencies, the contemplated Alliance was one of businessmen rather than of bureaucrats."

[69] Most notably in such publications as the *Economist* and the *Manchester Guardian*, within business circles generally attached to the Liberal party, and in certain circles to the right represented by the Tory Reform Committee.

[70] Such, for example, is the theme of *Tory M.P.*, by Simon Haxey and of *"National" Capitalism*, by Ernest Davies. Both these books were circulated widely by the Left Book Club at a time when John Strachey, now Minister of Food in the Labour government, and Harold Laski, then and now a member of the National Executive of the Labour party, were two of its three directors. Davies also is a prominent Labour M.P.

The mystery deepens when it is found that nowhere in the literature on the development council is there any intimation that the process of cartelization, amalgamation, and centralization of British business is either disapproved of by the Labour government or seriously and at any point to be inhibited by the growth of this new device. On the contrary, the development councils, like the NRA codes, are predicated on the existence of industry-wide business organization which, after the general patterns of monopoly and cartels, is prepared effectively to regulate almost any aspect of the normal conduct of business as circumstances may dictate.

But as dawn, in the adage, follows almost immediately upon the deepest darkness of the night, so the mystery tends to lighten as soon as one examines certain features of the Labour rationale for the development council. The idea is not self-government in business by business alone, but self-government under the principle of copartnership with government. Given this, it would appear that Labour believes that then the malignant evil contained in former trends can alchemically be transmuted into its veritable opposite, and cartelization can forthwith proceed uninhibited to lead Labour, not to the precipice, but to the promised land. Given copartnership, that is to say, self-government in business can really be made to work—but for ends other and quite different from those envisaged by business.

4. *Alternatively, then, copartnership in industry can succeed in making self-government work.* That this might be the heart of the Labour case for the device of the development council is indicated partly by the nature of the statements made on its behalf by party spokesmen—particularly by Sir Stafford Cripps—and partly by the opposition expressed in various business quarters.[71] Speaking of the private, nonnationalized sector of the British economy for which the development council is his chosen device, Cripps had this to say at the 1948 T.U.C. congress at Margate:

In all the most successful cases (where production has been increased) there has been a close working cooperation and exchange of ideas and information between the management and the operatives ... This is the quickest way to increase our productivity and our production. It is simply applying to all our production the practice of the best ... I regard this as the most urgent next stage in the recovery of our pre-war standards of living, and I have discussed it with

---

[71] "I believe the true explanation of extreme voluntarism to be 80% your (3) and 20% your (4). A lot of businessmen talk about the inhibiting effects of the threat—nationalization—but I've not seen a single case of such inhibition in practice." Ian Mikardo, in a personal letter to the author.

the F.B.I. and T.U.C. as representing the two industrial partners. I believe this is a matter which can best be dealt with by the two partners in industry, and I am glad to know that they are now taking in hand the question of organising parallel and coordinated action to bring about as speedily as possible the widest practicable improvement of productivity.

[These matters] each of the two partners can best tackle in its own way, [but to extract the maximum advantage] from the work of each . . . they should proceed on the basis of mutual understanding . . . both partners have expressed themselves as in agreement with this course of action. [The role of the government will be] to continue to provide all the help and facilities they can, [and thus] seek to create a clearer and wider appreciation among all sections of the public of the general nature of the measures for which the national situation calls.[72]

In this picture, the F.B.I. and the T.U.C. are partners on the national level. The member bodies, trade associations, and trade unions are partners on the industrial or trade level. And at the bottom, the individual business firms and the union locals are partners on the works or plant level. Now this is all very well as a statement of sentiment and an expression of hope, but it is most extraordinarily difficult to square with the facts. Virtually all of the evidence—from statements of policy of both trade associations and trade unions, national and local; from their literature, and the discussions at their conferences and congresses; from interviews with their competent spokesmen at varying levels; and from their behavior in sample cases since the advent of Labour to power—points to the conclusion that copartnership has made practically no headway at all. Such increases in production as have been realized are almost entirely a result of increased labor recruitment, and one is hard put to find a detailed example of increase of labor productivity which is not a result of either technical modernization, or mere return to prewar "normalcy." At the same time, evidence abounds on every side that restrictive policies are still adhered to by both business and labor, and that each considers the exhortations of the other on behalf of increased productivity as but the self-evident hypocrisy of an accuser who is already guilty of knowingly committing the very crime for which he invidiously damns his opponent with seeming self-righteousness.

A leading British management expert, long familiar with best practices both in Britain and abroad along the lines traced out by the concept of copartnership, refers privately to the F.B.I. as the "Federation for Burying Initiative," and a colleague speaks of the T.U.C. as the

[72] *Times,* Sept. 4, 1948.

"Taskforce for Unconditional Ca'canny." To each organization the characterization applied to itself is an unspeakable canard, but each also feels that such a characterization of the other accurately describes its point of view and its effect upon production. From personal interviews with leaders in both camps—interviews which yielded facts and opinions entirely congruent with the run of comment in the daily papers—the following would seem to sum up the situation to data: At the top or national level, agreement between the F.B.I. and the T.U.C. on the need for increased production is an expression of competitive patriotic sentiment, and has little, if anything at all, to do with instrumentation. On all other issues, they remain at swords' points. At the intermediate, or development-council level, copartnership was an idea forced on business by the government, and business will have none of it except under protest and even then with the minimum of coöperation. This, for example, is the record of the cotton-textile working party and its subsequent development council. Virtually all the initiative lies in the hands of the employer, as does also the ability to supply most of the basic facts concerning the possibilities for which the initiative is taken.

And at the bottom or factory level, where actual instrumentation must occur, there is nothing being done of moment to instrument copartnership, nor is there any prospect of a much more favorable outlook in the foreseeable future. Barring the occasional exception—such as Renolds and Cadburys[73]—and most of these are of long standing, copartnership between capital and labor is a figment of the imagination. How then, is one to account for this Labour emphasis on copartnership as though it provided a veritable open-sesame to the most vexing and critical of all British postwar problems, the increase in productive efficiency? There seem to be two possible explanations.

The first, and most probable, is found in the decline within British Labour circles of the syndicalist program and the rise, in its place, of Burnham's thesis of the managerial state. Syndicalism, or the idea that workers should own and control the factories in which they labor, had—as the history of the T.U.C. and the Labour party demonstrates at length—a long and tenacious hold on the trade-union rank and file. In a rather subdued form it still provides a basis for the principal and increasingly more serious complaints made by union representatives against the government corporations set up under the various nationali-

[73] See, e.g., L. Urwick and E. F. L. Breck, *The Making of Scientific Management*, Vol. I, "Thirteen Pioneers" (London, 1945).

zation acts, where the principle has been adopted that boards and staff are to be manned entirely by "competent experts," and at no point by "representatives of interests," labor or otherwise.

At one time, mainly just before and after the First World War, syndicalism was strongly represented in top Labour party circles; particularly among the adherents of Guild Socialism. G. D. H. Cole insisted that "the actual administration of the various industries and services ought to be placed mainly in the hands of the organised workers themselves." While the "sovereignty of the State is an essential point of Guild doctrine," still "the management of industry ought to be placed in the hands of the functional organisations of producers" and "ultimate control ought to be shared between these organisations and 'neighborhood' organisations representing men as consumers and users."[74] In this view "State Socialism or Collectivism, as a creed capable of inspiring idealism among decent people is dead and buried," the "State has become thoroughly unpopular,"[75] and, as Orage put it, "the British Trade Unions are the hope of the world."[76] What is needed in modern industry if it is not to be strangled to death by the general and growing hostility of labor to the profits system, and if political democracy is not to become a sacrificial lamb to economic autocracy, is that labor should have a sense of pride and workmanship in the job. This means a "sense of participation," and a sense of participation is impossible without labor ownership and labor control over the policies of the place where it works.

It seems impossible to read the mass of resolutions coming before the T.U.C. and the Labour party conferences without coming to the conclusion that the rank and file still holds to some variation or other of this syndicalist thesis.[77] Nevertheless, in top Labour circles it no longer has any standing at all. The first major break came with the formal statement on "Public Control and Regulation of Industry" at the Hastings conference in 1933, at which the Labour party, while appearing to accept the principle, actually rejected it. "In discussions in the Trade

---

[74] G. D. H. Cole, *Self Government in Industry* (London, 1920), pp. 2–3, 5, 7. There is an immense literature on Guild Socialism, but practically all of it antedates the middle twenties.

[75] *Ibid.*, p. 7.

[76] A. R. Orage, *National Guilds, An Inquiry into the Wage System and the Way Out* (London, 1914), p. 364. This is one of the classics of Guild Socialist literature.

[77] Ian Mikardo comments in a letter to the author: "No: Syndicalist resolutions have been heavily defeated at the last three Annual Conferences." This is true, but seems largely to be the result of the rigidity of the control exercised by the party executive over the big trade union delegations and a wide and possibly growing belief that the labour-relations formula of the nationalized industries is a snare and a delusion. This last appears to be the real Achilles' heel of the nationalized industries.

Union and Labour Movement following the Newcastle Congress and the Leicester Conference," the report said, "it has been made clear there is a strong desire that the Trade Union should, by statute, be given an adequate place on the Board of Management responsible for the general control and direction of each socialised industry or service."[78] But actually "it will be recalled that a Report which was presented to the Trades Union Congress, and to our own Conference in Leicester last year, provided for appointment on the ground of ability only; it refrained from registering the workers' claim to be appointed as representatives of a particular interest."[79] At Leicester, in other words, the decision was made to renounce not only worker control but also trade-union representation—a position which Citrine, president of the T.U.C., would have resisted but for "the strong representations made by the Executive of the Labour Party."[80] The clinching argument was advanced by Ernest Bevin,[81] president of the powerful Transport and General Workers' Union. Significantly enough, since the Leicester conference and down to the present time—despite even his preoccupation with the duties of his office as Minister of Foreign Affairs—"Ernie Bevin" has been the dominating figure in T.U.C. circles, and he has wielded a power in the Labour party which rides roughshod over all opposition.

From the position which Bevin championed in 1933 the Labour party has never retreated. The converging influences have been Herbert Morrison's rather academic concept of the "independent autonomous public corporation," and Bevin's conciliatory and hard-bargaining business unionism. But the rationale that has been evolved in defense of the position is the Labour concept of the "expert." Now this "expert" is a sort of emotionally disembodied ideological eunuch whose formal training and professional outlook tend unwittingly to make of him at once the scientifically ideal organizer and guardian of the common welfare, and define for him a disinterested role which, elevated above and removed beyond the hurly-burly of politics, stands in the sharpest contrast to the tendentious and emotion-clouded outlook of the partisans of special interests and causes who go to make up the rank and file that treads the hurried streets. The latter, strange as it may seem, include the partisans of the particularistic interests of organized labor. Hence

---

[78] *Report of the Thirty-Third Annual Conference of the Labour Party* (Hastings, 1933), p. 14.
[79] *Ibid.*, comments of George Latham of the National Executive, p. 204.
[80] Discussion by Charles Duke, *ibid.*, p. 205.
[81] *Ibid.*, p. 209.

the rule in the nationalized industries is that any trade-union member appointed to any position of responsibility in any of these industries must first sever his connection with the union. Only then is he able to act independently, and on behalf of the larger public interest. Not all organized labor seems happy about this retreat from a time-honored principle.[82]

This view, it is necessary to keep in mind, is advanced on behalf of a party whose goal is the achievement of a socialist commonwealth in which there are to be no able-bodied "drones." All adults capable of work, that is to say, will be workers, and the public interest must needs be coextensive with the interests of all workers in general. So corrected in each specific instance (factory, trade, occupation, etc.) as to be made congruent with the larger interest, the two would completely harmonize. This position is very hard to reconcile with the position that the worker *qua* worker should have no voice in the determination of policy.

But, more paradoxical still, the "experts" are at present to be found primarily, if not indeed solely, in business ranks. Here the thesis of Burnham's *Managerial Revolution* seems to have been taken over by Labour spokesmen and theoreticians, lock, stock, and barrel. References to Burnham are scattered through Labour literature, and find their way into Labour speeches on the floors of Parliament. One would gather from these references that businessmen in Britain are being led, as though by the unseen hand of some technological logos, to encompass broad social ends which are not only no part of, but are actually contrary to, the narrow objectives of their early entrepreneurial intentions. As "experts," insensibly and through use and wont acquiring the intellectual stigmata of the "professional outlook," it follows— as in the traditional picture of the civil service—that they will work for one master as competently and conscientiously as for another. Not always, but as a rule. Not without many and important exceptions, but increasingly and in the majority of cases.

[82] Believing that it was "basic that controlling boards should be elected by the Workers," a conference—followed by similar conferences in Manchester, Tyneside, and Nottingham— was called by the London Committee for Workers' Control. "Among the signatories to a letter calling the conference are Mr. J. Tanner, president of the Amalgamated Engineering Union, Mr. W. Padley, president of the Union of Shop, Distributive and Allied Workers, acting in his personal capacity, Mr. Edwards, general secretary of the Chemical Workers' Union, and Mr. H. Knight, general secretary of the Association of Supervisory Staffs, Executives and Technicians. Mr. F. Andrews, former editor of the Union of Post Office Workers' paper, the *Post*, and Mr. T. Ashcroft, editor of the National Union of Railwaymen's paper, the *Railway Review*, will introduce discussions. Mr. A. Hemstock, secretary of the Cooperative Productive Federation, is also associated with the movement." *Times*, Nov. 1, 1948.

Hence, when a national productive effort is to be made, or when an industry is to be nationalized, or when a nonnationalized industry is to be overhauled, the necessary "know how" and even the will to effect the called-for changes is already to be found in the top offices of business enterprise. It is as though the magic wand of Moses need only strike the obdurate rock of reaction for the life-giving waters of progress to pour forth in abundant measure. Thus when Herbert Morrison, as Lord President of the Council, appointed the Economic Planning Board, he placed on it four leading businessmen, three labor representatives, and seven civil servants. The three labor representatives were nominated by the T.U.C., now dominated by Bevin's business unionism, and the civil servants were mostly drawn from the Conservative-dominated Coalition government. Thus the body whose "primary task . . . will be to advise His Majesty's Government on the best use of our economic resources, both for the realisation of a long-term plan and for remedial measures against our immediate difficulties" is selected from circles which in the past Labour has sworn to liquidate.[83]

The same has been true of most personnel appointed to run the nationalized industries (the outstanding exception is that of Citrine, now head of the BBC). Thus the chairman of the Coal Board is Lord Hyndley, formerly a leading figure in the largest colliery company in Britain. Most of the regional, district, and even colliery directors and managers under the Coal Board represent also "the same old faces," as the miners have so frequently expressed it. A like picture holds for the other nationalized industries. Leading officials of the British Gas Council gave it as their opinion that if the gas industry were nationalized—as it has been—by the Labour government, it would still be the British Gas Council, manned with substantially the same industry-minded personnel, which would continue to run the industry. A similar

---

[83] The chairman of the board is Sir Edwin Plowden, director of the big chemical company of C. Tennant, Sons and Co., Ltd., with many foreign branches, director of Commercial Union Assurance, "one of Britain's top insurance companies," and director of the large and rapidly growing British Aluminium Company. Chemicals, insurance, and aluminum are all among the industries which have been included in past Labour discussions of "industries ripe for nationalization." Of the three other business representatives on the Board, nominated by the violently anti-Labour F.B.I. and B.E.C. (British Employers Confederation), Sir William Henry Coates is a deputy chairman of Imperial Chemicals, Sir Graham Cunningham, chairman of Triplex Safety Glass Co., and Verdon-Smith, a director of Bristol Aeroplane Company. Of the labor representatives, nominated by the T.U.C., one, Andrew Naesmith, is general secretary of the Amalgamated Weavers' Association, another, J. Tanner, is president of the Amalgamated Engineering Union (one of the "Big Three Bevin Unions"), and the third, H. V. Tewson, is general secretary of the T.U.C. and is virtually a personal representatives of Bevin. Of the members drawn from the civil service, three are permanent secretaries and all are drawn from wartime offices, to which they were appointed by Conservative or Coalition governments.

sentiment was expressed by spokesmen for the British Iron and Steel Federation when pondering the possibility of nationalization of the British iron and steel industry. Most of the government corporations operating under auspices of the food industry have drawn their personnel from the leading private corporations, and many of them remain on private corporation payrolls. Both the Ministry of Food and the Board of Trade are heavily manned at top policy-making levels by personnel drawn from leading business concerns. So also are most of the other economic ministries brought under the general direction of the coördinative Ministry of Economic Affairs.

What personnel is not drawn from business circles comes mostly from the upper levels of the permanent civil service. Toward this civil service the Labour party attitude is the same. This personnel is selected for its competence, and not for its loyalties, Labour spokesmen will tell the inquirer, and on the job it will be loyal to the job, not to the party. Therefore party affiliations, interests, and outlook of civil service employees are no matter of concern to the Labour government. (Unless, that is to say, they be suspected of being not reactionaries, but "Communists.")

Labour does not confine this interpretation to nationalized undertakings but extends it to private business. Here, businessmen, so long as they speak as "experts" and once they understand the situation, can be relied upon to do whatever is required of them on behalf of the common welfare, despite the diverting pressure of personal or vested interests. So also may labor's representatives. Hence, each may trust the other, coöperate with him freely, and the device of the development council serves merely to tap well-springs of spontaneous individual and group initiative which could not be reached by any other source. The old syndicalist idea is then found to be wrong on two counts. One, it is not necessary for labor to own and operate business outside the general "public utility" field, and two, the enmities which divided capital and labor in the past can be overcome in the eventual symbiosis of interest which leads the businessman to adopt the professional outlook, and labor to adopt an attitude of confidence in the "expertise" of the reborn entrepreneur. Not, to repeat, necessarily and always, but typically and generally.

But this sounds ridiculous. It seems wholly out of keeping with labor's history, and it cannot easily be reconciled with what the Opposition, publicly, privately, and with the benefit of a bitter, frequently brilliant, and always unmistakable innuendo, has said and continues to say about the policies of the Labour party. There seems not to be the slightest doubt that the Tories would expel the Labour party and its adherents from every office they now hold, were it possible for them to do so, and that they would do so with gusto. Nor can there be any doubt that Labour leaders know this to be true.

Are they then proceeding with guile? This is the second possible explanation of Labour support of the copartnership thesis. It has considerable appeal, and a little elaboration and not too much exegesis of the facts of recent history can make it fit the events and explain Labour pronouncements. But it also will not do. Quite aside from the fact that the quality of duplicity necessary to such guile is not to be found in most of the leading personalities within the Labour government—least of all such persons as Sir Stafford Cripps, Herbert Morrison, Clement Attlee, Lord Jowitt, and James Griffiths—there are circumstances which wholly rule it out.

It is a fact, well known to Labour, and frequently offered by its most bitter opposition as the basis for alternatives to various Labour programs, that British business is not necessarily opposed to the idea of copartnership at all. On the contrary, when developed on its own terms, copartnership is its alternative to Labour socialism. The manifesto of the 120 leading British industrialists, *A National Policy for Industry*, puts forward a program which proposes "to organize industry into sectional associations, and together with the Trades Union Congress to elect a Central Council of Industry representing all industry, which would formulate over-all policy. They express the hope that Parliament will compel every business concern to join the appropriate association and authorize sanctions for enforcements of association orders. To safeguard consumer interests, they propose that the decisions of the Central Council be subject to review by an industrial tribunal appointed by the Government."[84]

Now this proposal sounds perilously similar to the Council of Corporations under which Mussolini proposed to convert a loose competitive capitalism into a tightly organized Fascist state, which clearly had no place in it for democratic trade unionism. British Labour leaders are keenly aware of the imminent danger to the labor movement, not to mention the hazard to the "socialist commonwealth of the future," which inheres in such an alliance. This is the plan, spokesmen will

---

[84] Stocking and Watkins, *op. cit.*, footnote 36, p. 359.

hasten to say, which the Opposition proposes for the purpose, not of underwriting, but of destroying, the labor movement. They are not so simple as to be taken in by any such obvious trick as this.

Why, then, did Sir Edgar R. Jones' similar "grandiose scheme for the cartelization of world trade," as the *Manchester Guardian* reports, receive "the blessing of the General Council of the Trades Union Congress" along with "the sympathy of the Federation of British Industries?"[85] The answer is simple: not because copartnership is good and sufficient unto itself, but because, as regulation and control are substituted for "wasteful competition," a Labour government moves in to hold the balance against the monopolist's private interest wherever it oppresses the public, and because there will be a convergence between the self-effected transmutation of the entrepreneur into the public-spirited expert and the self-evident success of the socialist planning program. Enlightened business enterprise will convert and be converted at the same time. Not, however, to contrary ends, but to the same end. And that end is not a capitalist, least of all a fascist, end, but inevitably and necessarily a socialist end.

Copartnership, then, is a sort of Trojan horse, with sides not of opaque wood but of transparent plexiglas, and the soldiers who swarm its interior carry not spears with which to maim but a gospel with which to convert. And what is to prevent the attackers from bending the knee to Priam while Achilles foregoes chasing Hector around the battlements in order to nominate him Captain of the Guard? Nothing. For by this token, and in the fullness of time, Socialist gradualism will have conquered the hearts of the Opposition because it has already convinced their heads. The enemies become friends.

This view has been expressed by Herbert Morrison in unmistakable terms on numerous occasions. Not without humor, and occasionally salted with a mild jeer, but always with the utmost sincerity. It is a view which, in one form or another, is shared by virtually all the leaders of the Labour party with the exception, perhaps, of Aneurin Bevan, John Strachey, and Harold Laski. It is the logical result of the adaptation to twentieth-century conditions of the Utilitarianism of John Stuart Mill by Shaw and the Webbs (though Shaw would probably not accept the modern version). It is consistent with belief in "the inevitability of gradualism" and with firm faith in the existence of an underlying demiurgic force making for a singular, unhurried, and

---

[85] Feb. 8, 1944. Cited by Stocking and Watkins, *op. cit.*, p. 361.

irreversible progress—a progress which moves not by revolutionary stages up a precipitous slope, but by evolutionary means and with quickening steps along an easily negotiated and ever more clearly lighted upward gradient. The light that clarifies as it draws is that of science, clear reason, and earnest conviction.

If any single broad generalization can sum up the dominant Labour attitude in Parliamentary debates since the party's accession to power in 1945, it is that Labour's central endeavor has been to point out patiently and consistently to the Opposition what should be even for them the self-evident truth. Since, as Labour is aware, and occasionally points out, the Opposition is made up of men mostly more learned than they, equally well-intentioned and patriotic, the Labour party is placed in the role of instructress only because at this stage in the unfolding of Western civilization the charisma of history has settled upon it. Ultimately the truth will dawn on the Opposition, and then this truth will make them free—free to support Labour's program, which they will then realize is preëminently the best. In doctrinal terms, Labour is the residuary legatee of a basically sound theory which has passed through a long process of refinement. First the philosophic radicalism of Mill was remodeled by the tender and sensitive conservative meliorism of Alfred Marshall. Then Marshall's work was realistically adapted to fit the stern realities of a world which was less easily coaxed than Marshall had suspected, by the reforming conservatism of Keynes. And finally, the resultant "general equilibrim at full employment" may be steered, with the aid of the coercive mechanism of copartnership, by the Fabian epigoni of the Webbs along the gradualist path toward the inevitable socialist commonwealth.

Copartnership, then, is only in part an emergency device; it is also the agent of an evangelical hope. But suppose the Opposition, significantly and at any major point, remains recalcitrant? Suppose business and industry, in this regulated and monopolistically organized world, continue to put private interest above public benefit? To that the Labour answer is now not necessarily nationalization, but rather control of monopoly. So it happens that the Labour party finds itself supporting legislation modeled directly upon the antitrust acts of the capitalist stronghold of the world, the United States of America. As a brief survey will show, this is not viewed by Labour as an alternative to the development-council idea, but only as a supplementary and complementary measure more fully to instrument and give purpose to copartnership.

THE MONOPOLIES AND RESTRICTIVE PRACTICES ACT

On July 30, 1948, there passed into law a Monopolies and Restrictive Practices (Inquiry and Control) Act, 1948,[86] for the purpose, not necessarily of restoring competition where it has become inoperative, but of confining it to those areas in which it may be more efficient than monopoly, and of preventing the abuse of monopoly power in ways deleterious to the public interest. Thus, while it is modeled on the American antitrust acts, its purpose is—at least ostensibly—somewhat different.

A Monopoly and Restrictive Practices Commission consisting of not less than four nor more than ten persons is to be set up under auspices of the Board of Trade. Any "competent authority" may act on the findings of the Commission;[87] any "body which in the opinion of the Board could properly claim to represent, for the purposes in question legitimate special interests"[88] may lay complaints before the Board of Trade. The references may apply to "(a) the supply of goods of any description; or (b) the application of any process to goods of any description; or (c) exports of goods, of any description from the United Kingdom, either generally or to any particular market."[89] In each at least one-third of the goods produced, traded in, or exported must be involved in, or affected by "agreements and arrangements" effected by "any one person, or by or to any two or more persons, being interconnected bodies corporate, or by or to any such two or more persons . . . who, whether voluntarily or not, and whether by agreement or arrangement or not, so conduct their respective affairs as in any way to prevent or restrict competition in connection with the production or supply of goods of the description in question."[90] Compacts with trade unions affecting purely employer-employee relations of the normal type are excluded.[91]

---

[86] The full title reads: "An Act to make provision for inquiry into the existence and effects of, and for dealing with mischiefs resulting from, or arising in connection with, any conditions of monopoly or restriction or other analogous conditions prevailing as respects the supply of, or the application of any process to, goods, buildings or structures, or as respects exports." 11 & 12 Geo. 6, Chap. 66.

[87] Defined in Section 20 (1) as the Board of Trade, the ministries of Supply, Works, Fuel and Power, Health, Agriculture and Fisheries, and Food, the Admiralty, and the Secretary of State.

[88] Listed in Section 16 (3) as "(a) consumers in Great Britain or a substantial proportion of those consumers; (b) the organised workers of Great Britain; (c) trade in Great Britain; (d) industry in Great Britain; (e) agriculture in England and Wales or in Scotland; and (f) the professional workers of Great Britain, of England and Wales or of Scotland, who are particularly concerned."

[89] Section 2 (1).

[90] Sections 3 (1), 4 (1), and 5 (2) and (3).

[91] Sections 3 (1), 4 (1), 5 (4), and 11 (4).

Only when matters are referred to it does the commission proceed, and it has no power to do more than investigate. Any action following its investigations is limited to the Board of Trade or other competent authority. The orders of the competent authority can enjoin and forbid as unlawful all the actions laid bare by the commission which have had restrictive effects upon production, trade, or exports. First, however, the report of the commission must be laid before Parliament "with or without omissions,"[92] and "no order shall be made . . . unless a draft thereof has been laid before each House of Parliament and approved by resolution of each house."[93] Persons found "guilty of an offense under this Act," or of "refusal or neglect," if convicted, to comply thereafter, are subject to either or both fine and imprisonment, and in corporate organizations this rule holds for all officers of the corporation whose positions entitle them to know of the unlawful action or enable them to connive in it, even though it may be impossible to prove that they were aware of the infraction.[94]

An inspection of the act and of the debates in Parliament in the course of passage of the bill will reveal that despite the talk about competition, there was relatively little real interest displayed in the subject. Among the matters relevant to the reference of cases to the commission, for example, there is no mention whatsoever of competition. The listing speaks of efficiency and economy of the various processes of production and trade, better organization, "fullest use and best distribution of men, materials, and industrial capacity," and technical improvements and expanding markets, but to neither competition nor monopoly.[95] Speaking of the criticism of the Committee on Textile Machinery of "the monopoly which exists in that industry so far as spinning machinery is concerned," Harold Wilson, President of the Board of Trade, found that the monopoly had carried out or was carrying out all the recommendations which had been made for bringing the industry up to date. He then cited with approval the finding of the committee that "whatever the objections to monopolies, it is not practicable, even if it were desirable, to put the clock back."[96] Not monopoly, not even "restriction," was the object of attack, but only practices which redounded against the public interest.[97]

[92] Section 10 (1).
[93] Section 10 (7).
[94] Section 18 (1), (2), (3).
[95] Section 14.
[96] *Hansard*, Vol. 449, col. 2025.
[97] See, e.g., the comments by Wilson, *ibid.*, col. 2038.

Thus it came about that after elaborate, and in the main friendly, exchange of opinions between the Government and the Opposition concerning the evils of various and sundry practices which react against the public interest, Morrison was able to sum up the case for the bill by thanking the "House for the sympathetic reception which has been given to this Bill."[98] Although the Opposition felt that the definition of monopoly aimed at in the bill was stretched to "absurd lengths," and both "restrictive practices by trade unions" and "State Monopolies" merited equally exacting scrutiny, yet they were generally "sympathetic to the objectives of this Bill."[99] The reason for this sympathetic approval was precisely that the bill was merely an adaptation by Labour of the Conservative position as it had been elaborated in a pamphlet by one of its leading spokesmen, Sir David Maxwell-Fyfe.[100] This Wilson acknowledged, including even the statement that parallel legislation be set up to eliminate the very self-same "restrictive practices of trade unions," of which the Opposition complained. Quoting from Sir David,[101] he added simply "we entirely agree . . . and that is our approach to this problem."[102]

The underlying harmony of outlook went very far indeed. Both the Conservative proposal and the Labour bill had favored competition, and attacked restrictive practices, but neither looked upon monopoly *per se* as harmful. The Conservative proposal would have set up a Restrictive Practices Commission, similar to the one proposed in the bill. This Conservative commission would have had investigatory powers, and might have made recommendations. It would have been small. It would have dealt with cases referred to it by the Board of Trade, and would have been administratively responsible to that body. The main difference is that the Conservative proposal would have relied more on publicity to curb restrictive practices laid bare by the commission, and less upon punitive measures. Even this difference of opinion would have been wholly minor, but for the fact—pointed out

[98] *Ibid.*, col. 2124.
[99] *Ibid.*, cols. 2123–2124.
[100] Sir David Maxwell-Fyfe, *Monopoly* (London, Conservative Political Centre, 1948), pp. 49–53 in particular.
[101] Their legislation, Sir David said, would "exclude agreements dealing with wages, hours and conditions of employment. These are excluded not because restrictive labour practices are unimportant but because they cannot be appropriately dealt with by the same methods of legislation as restrictive business practices. The Conservative Party believe, as did the Coalition Government, including its Socialist members, that the two kinds of restrictive practices may equally have adverse effects upon expansion and employment, and they wish to see both types dealt with together by methods appropriate to each type." *Ibid.*, pp. 50–51.
[102] *Hansard*, Vol. 449, col. 2040.

by the Conservatives and ignored by Labour—that the American anti-trust law, on which the Labour proposal was based, had thus far proven almost wholly unable to cope with the problem by punitive measures, and without employing a vast and ever-increasing staff of investigators and lawyers.[103]

To fortify themselves on this point, the Labour government relied on evidence gathered in the United States by a small confidential commission which spent from two to three weeks in Washington. They came back with the picture of highly successful control over monopoly in America, and even used the example of breakup of monopoly in the building trades—one of the outstanding failures of Washington—as an example of antitrust success.[104] That they by-passed, in effect, virtually the whole of the findings of the vast TNEC hearings and reports, and the writings of such highly qualified persons as Walton Hamilton and the former director of the Antitrust Division, Thurmond Arnold, on the inability of antitrust facilities to cope with the problems, goes without saying. The point seems to have been ignored, furthermore, that this relative American failure occurred long after the demise of the American equivalent of the British development councils, the NRA boards, had eliminated an official sanction upon the basis of which growth of monopoly devices had been enormously accelerated. The Labour government, in effect, appears to be devising a far weaker instrument to control a far stronger current.

Thus it seems certain that unless the government is prepared to go far beyond the limits set in the Monopolies and Restrictive Practices Act, monopoly control would be due for virtually total nullification. If anything, British economic life is more highly controlled by monopoly and cartel devices than is American; an instrument as weak as that which the act proposes to set up would scarcely begin to deal with the American problem. If there is to be no more strength than this in the chain with which to hold back depredations of the powerful in the

[103] "I think that in 15 years the Federal Trade Commission in the United States required a staff of 546, with 113 lawyers." Punishment under the Sherman and Clayton acts, following "a series of legal Armageddons" had been confined to minor offenders, and the Antitrust Division's "cease and desist orders have become obsolescent so quickly that the operation of the Act has not received great public approbation." Sir David Maxwell-Fyfe, *ibid.*, col. 2049.

[104] In a series of grand-jury investigations shortly before the war, the Antitrust Division had found restrictive practices in the building industry so general and so pervasive that it would have required virtually its entire staff to deal with this problem alone. To have eliminated these practices would have required them to indict virtually all the leading building-supplies companies of the country, a large and possibly dominant percentage of the building companies, most of the trade unions, and most of the building inspection and control authorities in most of the states, counties, cities, and towns of the United States. So huge was the task that it was solved simply by giving it up entirely.

domain of public interest—the recalcitrant who cannot enter like patriotic Englishmen into the spirit of Labour's combination of co-partnership and self-government—then in order to be effective it will have to be far more deceptively and cunningly contrived than the magic fetters with which the Gods of Valhalla bound the savage Fenris, and even then it would appear that Labour had been induced to stick not its hand but its head into the mouth of the monster as a pledge that the trick was no trick at all.

The Labour spokesmen's reply is that they are most assuredly not so simple as this, and that proof is to be found in their new policy statement, *Labour Believes in Britain.* Here it appears that it is the purpose of the Monopolies Commission to expose "anti-social restrictive practices"[105] as a preliminary to the employment of other and more effective means. Following exposure, the methods employed will depend upon circumstances, including possible resort to public ownership where private monopoly, however efficient it might become, is still "a menace to the democratic State." There are four aspects to "Labour's policy for private industry . . . First, controls needed for economic planning will be permanently retained to ensure that industry serves the public interest, while other controls are pruned and removed. Second, assistance will be given to raise the efficiency of competitive concerns, particularly the small and medium manufacturers who are genuinely striving to increase production. Third, where private industry, even with this assistance, is failing to meet the needs of the nation, new public enterprises will be started. Fourth, monopolies, whose growth is a danger to the community, will be made to conform to the public interest."[106]

The only thing wrong with this statement is that, however admirable the intentions of its authors, it gives few clues as to how Labour's intentions are to be carried out. Or even what those intentions are, except that private industry is to be made to serve the public interest. On this there is not, nor ever has been, any serious dispute between Labour and its Opposition. "The public interest? Everybody supports it!" Obviously, everything rests on what is meant by "public interest," and how private industry is to serve it. In the use of the development councils the Trojan horse seems to be moving backward. In the copartnership

---

[105] "In the past, monopolies have taken care to operate behind closed doors. But now that the Labour Government has established the Monopolies Commission, anti-social restrictive practices will be exposed." *Labour Believes in Britain*, p. 13.

[106] *Loc. cit.*

schemes it is difficult at best to know who is doing what, and with which, and to whom. In the Monopolies and Restrictive Practices Act the government's "private eye" is a far weaker agency for exposing collusion than the development council is for consolidating it.

Even if these are stop-gap measures, they seem at best to cancel each other out. *Labour Believes in Britain* strongly implies that far more is anticipated in the future by way of vigorous action. But this implied action can have meaning only if it comes in the context of some clear-cut planning schemes. And in this very field of industrial location and development, upon which all the other physical plans rest, there is as yet no visible plan at all.

Whether one is to be evolved in the future remains to be seen.

CHAPTER XIV

Empire: Commonwealth
and Colonies

British Labour stands and will forever stand four-square against imperialism...and so when we come to power we shall change the policy of imperialism into one of cooperation and commonwealth.—George Lansbury, *Labour's Way with the Commonwealth*, 1935.

There are four objectives in the economic policy in relation to the Colonies. The first is to restore and improve the capital equipment of the territories so as to provide a firm basis for future development. The second is to promote those types of economic activity, whether primary or industrial production, in which the territories are best fitted to engage, having regard to the balance of their economies, and the advantages of their external trade. The third objective is to raise the living standards of the Colonial peoples as rapidly as the level of their productivity permits. The fourth is to secure the mutual advantage of the United Kingdom and the Colonial territories, having regard to the finance, equipment and skill which the former may be able to provide.—D. R. Rees-Williams, Under-Secretary of State for the Colonies, November 19, 1948.

In 1948, POSTWAR British austerity became Spartan severity at the behest of the Minister of Economic Affairs, Sir Stafford Cripps, who insisted that only through increased production and reduced consumption could the battle for Britain's survival as an independent nation be won. In many respects the results were remarkable. On the weakest sector of the widening battle for economic survival, the export trade, the adverse dollar gap had been reduced within the space of a single year from £630,000,000 to £300,000,000. But at the end of the year, production, although still increasing, was definitely beginning to flatten out. While "a real and remarkable recovery" had taken place, a friendly critic commented, yet it was necessary to "admit that the odds are still against our survival." The Herculean efforts of the preceding twelve months had transformed "the apparent certainty of collapse into a possibility—but only a possibility—of independence."[1]

In this life-and-death struggle, the success of the whole domestic program rests in a single hope: increase in productive efficiency. But if the rate of production begins to taper off all hope is not necessarily lost. In and out of the two great twentieth-century wars for political survival, Britain has always had another string to her bow. This is the Empire. So long as she is able to retain it, she retains that which may

[1] *New Statesman and Nation*, Dec. 25, 1948, p. 561.

make recovery from any domestic crisis possible and which may keep her from being wholly engulfed by the manifold adversities which beset her. The Empire may play a role in the economic crisis of the postwar years as vital for Britain's future as that which it played when the ordeal was by battle alone. If plans for the Empire can supplement, complement, and stimulate the further development of domestic plans, then the Empire's need may at long last become England's opportunity. For the Empire needs virtually everything which a modern industrial nation can supply, and it is the Labour hope that England's ailing industrial system may somehow be modernized and streamlined to become one of the world's best.

But this Empire presents postwar Britain with a double quandary: On one hand a matter of "conscience," on the other a matter of "timing." Britain is now governed by a Labour party whose principles are professedly and confessedly socialistic. But what is Empire to socialism? Can a socialist government even consider governing an Empire? Here is the contemporary equivalent of the ancient question put by the great Athenian advocate of "commonwealth" when he asked, "Can a democracy govern an empire?" Pericles' problem, in principle second in all world history only to Pilate's question, "What is truth?" was not only the political expression of the problem raised by the query of the Roman judge, but also posed a question which is swiftly dividing all contemporary civilizations. Social wars are engulfing the world. Wherever one turns—Indonesia, Indo-China, China, Burma, and Malaya—Empire is the essence of the ideas and systems of control against which the fires of revolutionary ardor are flaming. How then shall a Labour government act? On the way this question is answered—academic as it may seem on first consideration—hangs literally the existence of the British Empire.

Not only, however, the existence of the Empire alone. Failure in foreign affairs, as the bitter debates over Palestine and the revival of Germany illustrate, can divide Labour support more readily and calamitously than anything else. And, in the final analysis, the fortunes of the Empire provide the keystone of the arch of British foreign policy. Here, whether Labour's doctrinal heritage should be sold for a mess of Empire pottage is no longer a question of principle only, it is also a question of cold-blooded Machiavellian politics. To divide the ranks of Labour's supporters much further can only result in loss of political power.

The problem of timing is no less difficult. The trouble with the formula, "Empire need is Britain's opportunity," is that what the Empire needs most Britain doesn't have. The Empire needs investment on an unparalleled scale. It needs industrial equipment; roads, railroads, harbors, internal waterways, airways, and every type of communication facility; town and city construction, educational and cultural amenities, health and hospital facilities; soil conservation and agricultural mechanization; irrigation, hydroelectric and steam-generated power; it needs, in short, everything that industrially backward and undeveloped countries need for development. The need is pressing, insistent, and well-nigh universal throughout all phases of life in all of the colonies, it exists as a vital condition to the ambitious plans for expansion and development in the English-speaking dominions, and its satisfaction is very nearly the only remaining link which can bind the new dominions of India, Ceylon, and Pakistan to the Commonwealth at all.

But there is another and possibly even more difficult problem posed by the necessity for timing. What comes first, political responsibility or economic development? Suppose other colonies choose to follow the path of India, Ceylon, and Burma and demand political self-determination before "they are ready for it?" Suppose they demand their freedom before they are "fit for self-government" by the accepted criteria of education, political organization and experience, knowledge of administration, or by given levels of economic or other development? What then is a Labour government to do? What position is it to take? What shall its policies be if the several dominions choose to follow an independent or even hostile course of action, like Eire during the war or the Malan government in South Africa in 1948?

IMPERIALISM AND EMPIRE

Before the Second World War neither the T.U.C. nor the Labour party had much to say about Empire. In one of the few early references to the subject, the president of the T.U.C. asked in 1875 "whether it would not be noble work for the unionists of Great Britain to assist in obtaining a Factory Act for the Indian Empire."[2] (The audience chanted, "Hear! Hear!") Four years later the congress gave ear to an astonishing proposal by a guest speaker, James Bradshaw, merchant

[2] John Battersby, in the *Report of the Eight Annual Trades' Union Congress* (Glasgow, 1875), p. 7.

in the Manchester trade, for the establishment of a "powerful African trading Corporation" for the unified development of "the vast, long-neglected, dark continent of Africa." The "great continent," he said, "might not only become our chief outlet for manufactures, and a great field for railway and steamship development" but it could also "prove a reservoir for supplying all sorts of raw material for manufacture and our chief ground for food." With this lever, Britain's already chronic trading crisis, a result of rising foreign tariffs (particularly American), could be overcome, and Britain could "compel the civilised world to accept free trade." Truly, "Africa was England's mission."[3]

What could organized British Labour say to this undisguised bid for Labour support of imperial expansion and exploitation which had run its course from the days of the East India Company, Drake and Raleigh, on down to the Pax Brittania of her last great empire builder, Cecil Rhodes? The reaction of the audience is not clear from the record. It cheered the closing remarks, which concluded with a quotation from the great Tory imperialist, Lord Palmerston, who held that if the slave trade could be finally quashed in Africa, "that continent would be a source of wealth, not only to Europe, but to the whole world, to such an extent that the imagination itself could hardly follow it." One delegate who looked upon "all such schemes with the utmost horror" was also cheered, but applause echoed again when the speaker replied that he was not "in favour of warlike methods of advancing commerce and civilization, he was a member of the Peace Society." Naturally, he went on to add, "If his scheme ever saw the light of day he wanted it to have a national stamp, and especially that the working classes should be largely represented on it." Another delegate "moved that the thanks of this Congress be given to Mr. Bradshaw for the able and exhaustive paper . . . such a scheme would improve every trade in the United Kingdom. They would find work for engineers, ironfounders, and every description of workmen imaginable. All the labour required would have to go from this country, and they would get goods in exchange." With the deletion of the words "and exhaustive" the "vote of thanks was unanimously passed."

In 1881 another president of the T.U.C. asked, "What interest have we, workmen, what interests have the people of England, in carrying on war for the sake of Empire?"[4] but the question was not followed

---

[3] *Report of the Twelfth Annual Trades Union Congress* (Edinburgh, 1879), p. 31.
[4] *Report of the Fourteenth Annual Trades Union Congress* (London, 1881), p. 13.

up. Three years later the audience cheered again when another guest speaker, Lord Roseberry, Earl of Aberdeen, told them that "Germany is planting its flag in Africa" and commented, "I am sure we wish all success to Germany in her colonising and civilising efforts." Britain, he lamented, "with an empire which furnishes them with a model, and which excites their envy [is] allowing that empire to drift away from us."[5] Whether the congress shared his fears the record does not make clear.

In another mild flurry of interest the congress in 1905 carried unanimously a resolution moved by John Ward of the Navies Union: "That this Congress views with alarm the rapid exclusion of white workmen from the Rand mines by the importation of Chinese slave labour and considers that the callous attempt of the mineowners, supported by the Balfour Government, to prevent South Africa from becoming a white man's country is a disgraceful episode in imperialist exploitation and a blot upon the previous record of the Country."[6] These references to Empire are typical: with them the subject disappears from the surface of discussion as though it did not exist as a problem of any concern to trade unionists at all.

The same holds for the Labour party. Its first real interest was shown in the subject when a resolution was carried unanimously at the 1921 conference, linking "war and imperialism" as "a danger to international peace," and a distraction from "domestic affairs." Imperialism, it read, "tends to perpetuate the reign of capitalism not only by increasing the power of wealth, but by neglecting the needs of the home market, and leaving the natural resources of our own country undeveloped."[7] In 1926 a resolution proposed by the Teachers' Labour League was carried condemning "the widespread reactionary and imperialistic teaching in the schools, particularly with regard to Empire Day celebrations."[8]

It required, however, the dire emergency of the Second World War—when the Nazi assault on Britain looked as though it might be successful in its deliberate attempt to break up the Empire—finally to compel formulation of a "testament of the principles of the Labour Party as applied to the Government of the Colonies and the status of Colonial

[5] *Report of the Seventeenth Annual Trades Union Congress* (Aberdeen, 1884), p. 32.
[6] *Report of the Thirty-eighth Annual Trades Union Congress* (Hanley, 1905), p. 159.
[7] *Report of the Twenty-First Annual Conference of the Labour Party* (Brighton, 1921), p. 207.
[8] *Report of the Twenty-Sixth Annual Conference of the Labour Party* (Margate, 1926), p. 265.

peoples." The "testament" is a very interesting statement in its own right, but it acquires additional significance from the fact that it appears not as a part of the resolution on "The International Situation and Colonial Policy" put forward by the National Executive of the party, but as an amendment from the floor expressing rank and file sentiment. "Carried without dissent," it read:[9]

This should be a Charter of Freedom for Colonial peoples abolishing all forms of Imperialist exploitation and embodying the following main principles:—

1. All persons who are citizens of the Colonial Commonwealth should be considered to possess and be allowed to enjoy equality of political, economic and social rights in the same way as the citizens of Great Britain.

2. The status of Colony should be abolished and there should be substituted for this that of States named according to the country in which they are situated and having an equal status with the other nations of the Commonwealth.

3. In all Colonial areas there should be organised a system of democratic Government, using the forms of indigenous institutions in order to enable the mass of the people to enter upon self-government by the modification of existing forms of Colonial administration in conformity with these principles.

4. In all Colonial areas, in Africa and elsewhere, where the primitive systems of communal land tenure exists, these systems should be maintained and land should be declared inalienable by private sale or purchase. All natural resources should be declared public property and be developed under public ownership.

5. A Commonwealth Council of Colonial Peoples should be set up on which each former Colonial State should be represented in accordance with the number of its population, but giving also special attention to the representation of national groups within each State.

As a simple examination will show, this "radical" statement simply proposed that the colonies be elevated to the status of self-governing dominions, that British aid be given to insure that each colony's resources are "developed," and that in so doing the social program of the Labour party at home is made basic for the colonies when they acquire their new status. Even this latter is confined to communal ownership of land and national (dominion) ownership of natural resources. Empire as British Commonwealth is the objective. If there were any doubts whatever that this was the meaning of the Labour view of the Empire, the 1943 conference was to set them finally to rest. Quoting from its newly issued pamphlet *The Labour Party and the Future*, which it then presented as part of the Executive Committee's report, the leadership defined the party understanding of the right type

[9] *Report of the Forty-First Annual Conference of the Labour Party* (London, 1942), p. 154.

of empire. Since this statement has remained down to the present as Labour's definitive position on the subject, it is worth quoting at some length:[10]

Let the Colonial Empire now enter upon a period of unprecedented development and progress under the guidance of the Mother Country. Standards of health and well-being must be secured not only by wise administrative measures but by the fostering of strong and expanding economic systems. If money is needed for these purposes it should be laid out—prudently, but in no niggling spirit. If vested interests exploiting native populations stand in the way of progress—and there are many parts of the Empire in which this is certainly the case—they must be properly supervised, made to contribute their due share to social welfare in their territories, and if need be taken over by public concerns. A growing number of the economic functions of these expanding and developing societies must be performed by public agencies.

Everywhere the goal should be political self-government, but the attainment of that goal in many instances cannot be near at hand. We must not be too quick to cut at the roots of those native forms of social organisation in which the life of many undeveloped societies takes its shape and gains should be based upon progressive educational policies helped by our willingness to transfer to the Colonial peoples particular functions of government, local or otherwise, as soon as their ability to assume them grows.

Later, the conference passed a supplementary resolution which expressed appreciation of colonial aid in the war, proposed to make "the terms of the Atlantic Charter and the 'Four Freedoms' . . . active principles in Colonial administration," once again urged the abolition of colonial status and favored the "application of a Socialist policy in the economic organisation of the Colonies." All this was to result in a "genuine partnership between this country and the Colonial peoples" under which "the Government (in consultation with the Colonial peoples) shall press on with the social and economic welfare of their territories, including adequate education, health and nutrition services, and the attainment of political rights not less than those enjoyed or claimed by British democracy."[11]

The colonies, in short, are to remain within the Empire. They are to be made self-governing whenever in the judgment of the "mother

[10] *Report of the Forty-Second Annual Conference of the Labour Party* (London, 1943), p. 3. The statement is based in part on a pamphlet published in 1933 by the Labour Party called *The Colonies*, which was revised and brought up to date in 1943 with the publication of *The Colonies: The Labour Party's Post-War Policy for the African and Pacific Colonies*. Dr. Rita Hinden, Secretary of the Fabian Colonial Bureau, feels that these pamphlets are much more authoritative than party resolutions, which may be sent in by local Labour groups, never properly debated, and automatically passed by the conference. (Letter to the author, Jan. 15, 1949.) They are however, entirely in keeping with the resolution cited. The 1945 campaign manifesto, *Let Us Face the Future*, does not even mention the Empire.

[11] *Ibid.*, p. 207.

country" they are fit for it. During the period of necessary tutelage, and while they are learning to pattern their politics and other aspects of social existence after the more civilized British model, they will receive socialist guidance and socialist aid of the most enlightened kind. Even in the hands of Labour spokesmen, accordingly, there exists a beautifully self-congratulatory version of Britain's Empire mission which the more devout among its adherents can endlessly embroider with unquestionably sincere sentiments, and concerning which they will reject with great indignation any suspicion that they act from any other than the purest and most unselfish motives.

Why not? A naturally beneficent process is thereby set under way. When it has run its duly appointed course, each and every colony will be elevated to the coveted status of the dominions. What then will have happened to the bitter legacies of imperialism—bitter alike to the tongues of the colonists abroad and their Labour defenders at home? They will have disappeared, because Empire will have fled. In the place of Empire will be found a once again enlarged British Commonwealth of Nations. Could anyone wish for more? Where else is there a higher expression of the fine fruits of the long, toilsome democratic process? Socialism is the brotherhood of man; the Good Samaritan nowadays gives more enlightened aid than did his gentle forebear. Succor includes high material standards of living to displace poverty, and enlightenment to displace the meanness of ignorance and the emotional squalors of superstition which have held sway longer than the memories of man. The new freedoms will bring socialism to the colonies, and new strength to the charmed circle of the British Commonwealth of Nations.

What, in the minds of Labour leaders, are the implications of such a program? Are these sentiments merely a socialist version of the time-honored theses of the "White Man's Burden," and necessarily acceptable to the colonial peoples for that reason? Certainly it is true that minus the phraseology of socialism, the outlook and most of the details are borrowed directly from the Opposition. It was Disraeli in a famous speech at the Crystal Palace in 1872 who proposed to conduct Britain down the primrose path of imperialism and social reform.[12] Seven years later he was to counsel Englishmen not to "be beguiled into believing

[12] J. Ramsay Macdonald, in his *Labour and the Empire*, Labour Ideal Series (London, 1907), p. 13, found this a mere concession by Disraeli to the "inner light" of liberalism which even the greatest Liberal of the times, Gladstone, did not understand and could not follow.

that in maintaining their Empire they may forfeit their liberties. One of the greatest of Romans, when asked what were his politics, replied, *Imperium et Libertas.*" And that, said Disraeli, "would not make a bad programme for a British Ministry."[13]

In a very few years Kipling had written a glittering slogan for this program—"The White Man's Burden." It served even better than Cecil Rhodes' ambitious Pax Britannia to show the whole anxious world that the purpose of the new sense of empire was "to seek another's profit, and work another's gain." Every great British imperialist thereafter has echoed these sentiments. It was Lord Milner, long High Commissioner for South Africa, and perhaps the most eloquent British spokesman of the imperial idea, who found that it was a task of the mother country and the dominions "to deal with the dependent Empire, as indeed with all their common interests, on the basis of partnership." In this partnership England's main contribution would be simply to confer upon the colonies the British way of life. "These privileges of British citizenship," he said on one occasion, "are without parallel in history." But on the more practical side, there must, in the course of time, be set up "a real Council of the Empire" to provide the "great straggling body" of the Imperium with "a central brain." This brain would so organize the partnership that all would reap advantages in equal measure. Among other things, this organization called for enormous expenditures for developing the colonies—involving such things as "experimental farms, bacteriological laboratories, afforestation, and bringing men of science—often receiving high salaries—from different parts of the world to give a new impetus to agriculture." So also for all other phases of commercial, industrial, social, and cultural development.[14]

By time of the outbreak of the First World War sentiment and program had converged to formulate the concept of a Third British Empire, or British Commonwealth of Nations, which was to stand for a completely new and revolutionary interpretation of empire. Suitable labors of exegesis soon provided a patriotically adequate historical explanation for this culminating efflorescence of the British genius. For a proper grasp of the Labour philosophy of empire it is important that this rendition of British history be understood. In shorthand fashion

[13] Cited in A. Maurois, *Disraeli: A Picture of the Victorian Age* (London, 1927).

[14] Viscount Milner, *The Nation and the Empire* (London, 1913). See in particular the speeches, "Imperial Unity," pp. 302 320, "The Two Empires," pp. 289–300, "Imperial Organisation," pp. 452–461, and "Crown Colonies," pp. 461–469.

it runs as follows: In the beginning, the First Empire had been founded "in a fit of absence of mind" (Sir John Seeley) by the sixteenth- and seventeenth-century buccaneers of Elizabethan mercantilism, and rounded out by the brilliant successes of the Seven Years War (1756–1763). This Empire was brought to a close by the American Revolution, but the sobering influence of this disastrous loss was also to put an end to the view that empire consisted of colonial outposts whose sole justification for existence was to serve as private national preserves for naked and unabashed exploitation by the home country.

Chastened by this experience, and in a mood shaped partly by indifference and partly by the humanitarian philosophy of her next great Empire builders, the Pitts, Britain reconstituted her Empire on the basis of sea power, and seasoned her spread-eagling controls over the world's sea lanes with the economic philosophy of free trade and the political philosophy of laissez faire. The sea power was her grand inheritance from the Napoleonic wars, and the gospel of free trade was an expression of the new-found interest in world resources and trade which her vast, new, and swiftly growing industrial revolution thrust upon her. Both internal and external policy were based on the philosophy of individualism, and represented the triumph of the ideas of Smith, Ricardo, Mill, Cobden, Bright and their contemporaries. Internally, individualism combined with laissez faire soon brought to the fore the manifold problems of social reform. Externally, free trade encouraged gradual loosening of the bonds of Empire, while presenting energetic British expansionists with the gratifying picture of a world peopled mostly by miserable and unkempt races badly in need of material redemption through purchase of English-made goods, and of spiritual redemption by gift of the Healing Word.

The result was the interval of Humanitarianism and Empire which witnessed an unparalleled series of internal and external social reforms (principally abolition of the slave trade) on the one hand, and near disintegration of the Empire on the other. Cobdenism saw no need for empire at all, and the Christian missionary tended to see in empire merely a black legacy of the past which even his companion in pioneering the new *Völkerwanderung*, the enterprising trader, found of little use. It helped him but little in British dominions where he had no competitors; and the empire outlook frequently proved nothing but an obstacle in the imperial domains of others. Hence, "the entire period from the American Revolution to, approximately, the year 1886, is usually termed an era of anti-imperialism." Colonies were "groomed for independence through grants of self-government, and opposition to the possession of colonies" was "manifested by a majority of the English People."[15] The logical product of this attitude was the device of self-governing dominions. In itself largely a bowing to necessity, "it also pioneered what was eventually to become the keystone in the imperial arch of the Commonwealth of Nations" idea.

It does not matter a great deal for present purposes that much of this picture represents some very inaccurate history. The First Empire—the older and more simple-minded American textbooks to the contrary notwithstanding—was modified in its severity by a prevailing mood in which there was typically more indifference, or even boredom, than consistently brutal acquisitiveness. Conversely, the "humanitarianism" of the Second Empire modified but little the conventional practice of pursuing abroad such adventures as lurid imagination might promote, in virtually total disregard for the rights or interests of native peoples. If the gestation ground for the American Revolution was the First Empire, that of the Irish upheavals was clearly the Second Empire. Nevertheless, it was the policies announced and championed during the First Empire, rather than the practices followed, which fixed the prevailing overseas picture of the intent and purpose of the British Empire for all time, and it was the professed humanitarianism of the Second Empire—associated as it is with the rise of the democratic movement and social reform at home—which seems to have determined the coloring and composition of the popular British picture of England's role overseas.

Consider the latter picture. By hook or by crook—even at times seemingly by accident—the British Empire had come into being.[16] As the homeland could be (and was) slowly democratized and socially reformed, so also could (and would) the Empire be humanized and made a vehicle for the spread of the new amalgam of popular British institutions and social Christianity throughout the Empire. What early Napoleonic success had meant for the forced spread by fire and sword of the French Enlightenment, the opportunity thrust upon England now

[15] Oraville Jane Tuttle, *Humanitarianism and British Imperialism, 1820–1886* (Master's dissertation, University of California, 1937), p. 5.

[16] An interesting summary of this "accident" theory of empire acquisition, brought down to the First World War, is given in a pamphlet written by H. E. Edgerton, Beit Professor of Colonial History at Oxford, called *Is the British Empire the Result of Wholesale Robbery?* (Oxford, 1914). The answer, as is to be expected, is not merely in the negative. The truth, says Edgerton, is that England acquired what others did not want, or would not work or care for, and concerning which the British people have, on the whole, been downright indifferent.

meant for the peaceful and voluntary Diaspora of the disciples of the English Enlightenment. Mixed, however, with a loosely contrived philosophy of individualism, it had lacked driving ardor until the stern realities of the second half of the nineteenth century forced a change of pace.

. These realities came in a combination which soon compelled the closest attention. Among them were such events as the great depressions of 1837, 1857, and 1873, which shook British institutions to their foundations; the events—especially disastrous for the great Lancashire cotton industries—associated with the American Civil War, and the subsequent opening up of the grain lands of the American Middle West (which also ruined the British grain-growing districts); the dramatic rise of Germany as a great world power under the masterful direction of Bismarck and its extraordinary challenge to British industrial supremacy;[17] the growth of other industrial rivals (France, Belgium, and the United States in particular) and the rise within both industrial and nonindustrial countries of nationalistic tariff and similar policies; and all of the other allied events which brought about the last great imperial scramble for colonial holdings in the eighties and the launching of the great armaments race that culminated in the First World War. Out of the growing alarm came, among other things, a changed British attitude which gradually led to the concept of the Third Empire.

The new ideas about empire succeeded, almost insensibly and by slow degrees at first, in fusing the "humanitarianism" of the Second Empire, with its "accident" explanation of past imperial acquisition—which had led up to and graced so beautifully the "blossoming time of laissez faire" (primarily the decade of the sixties)—to a new, very hard-headed, but subtly revised version of the First Empire. Henceforward these two march together in a strange partnership, and step by step.

The myth was believed by the British public; the realities were largely ignored by all except the Empire builders. Both at home and abroad only Cecil Rhodes' great mishap in South Africa, which led to the Boer War, raised any serious doubts as to the validity of the romance that was being spun. But neither this nor the perennial Irish question spoiled the over-all effect. The jingoism of the earlier stages was sometimes crude and hard to reconcile with lofty motives, but after

---

[17] A good picture of the bearing of this competition upon British internal and empire policies is given in a very useful book, Ross J. S. Hoffman, *Great Britain and the German Trade Rivalry, 1875–1914* (Philadelphia, 1933).

the general elections of 1900 even these harsh overtones were subtly woven into the new symphony of Empire. The dropping of free trade and the substitution of Imperial preference became consonant with Disraeli's *Imperium et Libertas*. Colonial development became "partnership and trusteeship." As early as 1871 there was talk of "Imperial Federation" in which Britain would be merely *primus inter pares*. At about the same time the Royal Colonial Institute, shortly to be transmuted into the Royal Empire Society with branches throughout the Empire, began its enormously effective propaganda for drawing the scattered members of the Empire into a vast "family union."[18] By the close of the Victorian era the great Queen had come to epitomize in her person the maternal role which the mother country now saw herself playing both to her self-exiled sons across the sea, and to the myriads of "new-caught, sullen peoples, half-devil and half-child" of whose future education Kipling wrote so rapturously—even though her latter years had been saddened by the ferocious outbreaks attendant upon the African adventures.[19]

Now it was precisely while this vast myth of the Third Empire was being formulated in its most persuasive forms—and set hard as an *idée fixe* by the violent and overshadowing bluster of the brutal German challenge and the growing fear of a coming world war—and while significant new social reform from within was being blended with newfound British patriotism reflecting the pressures from without, that organized labor was beginning to learn to walk as an independent political force. Hence, although in the changing domestic environment they might denounce the capitalists, their radicalism became milder as one grudging reform led to another. And although they continued to castigate the imperialists, the venom of their attacks was slowly drawn as the belief grew and became general that somehow, and despite the never failing criticisms of "British Imperialism" abroad, this Empire was different. More and more of it was becoming Commonwealth—independent, free, adult, democratic, and essentially British—and hence not Empire at all. And what was not yet Commonwealth would

---

[18] See, Avaline Folsom, *The Royal Empire Society; Formative Years* (London, 1933).

[19] A typical expression: "But upon the English race Fate had imposed the further, ecumenical function of Empire: and for all time that we can foresee, great nations in all Continents will look back, for the origins of their polity, and their institutions, to the years when they were first united in freedom, or the hope of freedom, under the sceptre of Victoria." G. M. Young, *Victorian England: Portrait of an Age* (London, 1936), p. 182. A more jejune and parochial misjudgment of history—past, present, and future—than this it would be hard to imagine, yet it is extraordinary how widely it is held in one version or another by many of even the more astute Britishers of various political persuasions.

in time arrive, under the mature guidance and through the tender solicitude of a well-intentioned parent, at a like status. What was happening to Empire, in short, was a mere reflection of what was happening to Britain. It was becoming democratic and free. And who could naturally be expected to express greater and more heartfelt approval of this than British labor?

It is all the more important that this point be stressed because it has generally been supposed that British labor, long so indifferent to what was going on outside the homeland itself, was naturally and inevitably dedicated to the "Little Englander" point of view.[20] Certainly the brilliant and pioneering study of imperialism by Hobson[21] would justify the latter interpretation, and Hobson's general position has been championed ever since by a small group of people close to Labour party circles of whom the most important is Leonard Barnes. Yet it is also true that what Barnes proposes when he gets down to talking in terms of action is largely, if not wholly, consonant with the general outlook of the Commonwealth enthusiasts as expressed, for example, by Alfred Zimmern, the outstanding Liberal academic exponent of the Third Empire.[22]

Thus a Labour program for the Empire in the eyes of this more radical Labour critic of imperialism proposes "independence for India, Burma, Ceylon and the West Indies," beginning first with "adult suf-

[20] This is the conclusion of the only study that exists of the evolution of the Labour attitude towards Empire: Tingfu F. Tsiang *Labor and Empire: A Study of the Reaction of British Labor, Mainly as Represented in Parliament, to British Imperialism since 1880*, Studies in History, Economics, and Public Law, vol. CVI, no. 1 (New York, Columbia University Press, 1923). Yet this study is an interpretation of the logical implications for empire that would come from a shedding of the attitude of indifference and more positive concern with Labour's championship of the rights of colonial peoples. It does not square with subsequent Labour behavior. The earliest of the Fabian tracts on the subject, George Bernard Shaw, ed., *Fabianism and the Empire* (London, 1901), dealt primarily with the Boer War and favored a hands-off policy on the grounds that the Boers were no better than the invading British. As for the Webbs, not until the writing of their *Decay of Capitalist Civilization* in 1923 did they have much to say on the subject. Even then they did not propose to do away with the Empire. On the contrary, what they wanted was genuine reform in place of the existing "cant of humanitarianism." As late as 1935, Sir Robert Hadfield, in a widely circulated booklet proposing the "establishment of an Empire Development Board" was able to include the names of the Right Hon. Lord Passfield (Sidney Webb), Arthur Henderson, and J. H. Thomas—three of contemporary Labour's great leaders—among those expressing "the warmest and full approval" of this Tory plan for Empire economic development. Sir Robert Hadfield, *Empire Development* (London, 1935), p. 11.

[21] J. A. Hobson, *Imperialism* (London, 1902). Republished without substantial alteration in 1938.

[22] Alfred Zimmern, *The Third British Empire* (London, 1934). He finds virtually complete agreement between the Conservative and Liberal parties with respect to the meaning and role of the Commonwealth. To Zimmern the British Commonwealth of Nations is really a League of Nations. The establishment of the actual League of Nations meant merely a widening of the arc of influence of the self-same policies which underlie the organization and development of the Commonwealth.

frage leading rapidly to self-government, and "for tropical Africa, a liberal charter of democratic rights, including (1) compulsory free education, (2) freedom of speech, movement, and association, (3) a minimum level of labour and social provision, (4) popular African representation in the Colonial legislatures."[23] Barnes' program, it will be noted, refers wholly to the colonies. "I had better make it clear," he writes, "that where I speak of Empire or imperialism I am not thinking of Canada, Australia, New Zealand, South Africa, or their relations to this country" for "their powers of self-government are, within limits, real."[24] Since, accordingly, reference is wholly to the areas under "forcible subjection," it might and could follow that the lifting of the colonies to dominion status would entirely solve the problem of "imperial exploitation."

Both Hobson and Barnes are supposed to have been heavily influenced by Marx.[25] Nevertheless it proved possible, as subsequent events were to make clear, to reconcile their views with those of the so-called "humanists," or liberal anti-imperialists. "This humanist school joined in the protests against the evils of imperial domination. The battle was carried forward by devoted Socialists like Lord Olivier [Governor of Jamaica, 1907–1913], Leonard Wolff and Roden Buxton. Dr. Norman Leys and Macgregor Ross championed the Africans against the Europeans in Kenya; Sir John Harris, of the Anti-Slavery Society, combatted the forced labour system; Professor MacMillan, Frank Horrabin, and many others exposed the defects of colonial policy; and the struggle was pursued with gusto by a small group of Labour M.P.'s in the nineteen thirties, who, in and out of Parliament, urged changes on the Government. Of this group Arthur Creech Jones became the most notable."[26]

In this mixture of "Marxism and humanist attitudes" the latter definitely became predominant. Arthur Creech Jones became head of the Fabian Colonial Bureau when it was founded in 1940 for the purpose of securing "a drastic overhaul of policy" in the colonial empire, and remained its director until the Labour victory in 1945. He then became Secretary of State for the Colonies in the Labour government, and the

---

[23] Leonard Barnes, *Empire or Democracy: A Study of the Colonial Problem* (London, 1939), pp. 286–287.

[24] *Ibid.*, "Foreword."

[25] In turn, Hobson's book is supposed to have provided the groundwork for Lenin's better-known tract on imperialism which subsequently became the Communist Bible on this subject.

[26] Rita Hinden, *Socialists and the Empire* (London, Fabian Colonial Bureau, 1946), p. 5.

official spokesman and policy formulator for colonial empire problems. Speaking at the opening session of the United Nations Organization as the official representative of the Labour government, he summarized the new policy with the simple declaration that "Britain's attitude was merely one of service to colonial peoples."[27] It was an old theme;[28] did it have a new content?

Before attempting to answer this question by examination of specific Labour party proposals, it is necessary to note two or three rather obvious facts. First, the problem of Empire has narrowed to the colonies; the self-governing dominions are no longer part of the Empire, but are instead equal partners in the British Commonwealth of Nations. The sole concern of this Commonwealth is to maintain friendly relations between its several members and the mother country. This idea rests on the assumption that because the dominions have reached political adulthood, their internal and external policies will sooner or later, and more or less as a matter of course, become consonant with those of a socialist Britain. Thus, in immediately proceeding, as the Labour party did, to give dominion status to India, Burma, and Ceylon, they saw themselves as "liquidating His Majesty's Empire" in Churchill's flamboyantly expressed sense, only in order to effect the extension and consolidation of the Commonwealth in the "humanist," or Third Empire, sense. It is not possible to read the pronouncements of Labour leaders which accompanied these measures without reaching the conclusion that they felt that the "independence" they were conferring could, and if properly handled would, strengthen rather than loosen the bonds that linked the members of the Commonwealth with each other, and that this result would follow because "independence" carried with it the assurance that the new Government would necessarily pursue internal and external policies consistent with the Commonwealth idea because that idea was consistent with the policies of the Labour government.

They had been duly warned that this result might not follow—both by friends and by political enemies,[29] and by events in Eire during the

---

[27] Cited by J. F. Horrabin, *Short History of the British Empire* (London, 1946), p. 54. This pamphlet was issued by the Socialist Book Centre by arrangement with the National Council of Labour Colleges—set up largely on the urging of the T.U.C. and the Labour party.

[28] Twenty-five years before Lord Halifax had said, "The well-being and development of people not yet able to stand by themselves is a sacred trust of civilization." Cited, *ibid.*

[29] Most notably among friends by J. A. Hobson, *op. cit.*, who warned that there was great danger that the dominions might themselves begin to follow the very type of "imperialist" policy with respect to colonial expansion and exploitation which was currently the gravamen of the Labour charge against the then-existing Government. He warned in particular of

war and in South Africa after the war. In both, dominion status has meant the eventual triumph of violently antidemocratic, antisocialist, and anti-British governments. In Eire it has led finally to throwing off even dominion status. Furthermore, Burma had barely acquired the dominion status conferred on it by Labour before a similar expression of national sentiment began to assert itself.[30] It is quite possible that India may shortly follow suit, though its reasons for doing so may be different.[31]

But there is still another problem relating to the dominions which the Labour government either does not see, or seeing merely chooses to ignore—the question of Canada and Australasia. That Canada is being increasingly viewed in certain circles as a sort of "forty-ninth state" of the United States seems unquestionable, and that New Zealand and Australia exist as outposts of the British Commonwealth because they are protected by American air and naval power seems equally clear. But there are two factors which, in the minds of Government leaders, make this material dependence on the United States of negligible importance. First is the sense of "mystic union" between the British peoples, wherever they may be, which provides a more powerful Empire cement than any mere national considerations. (Aside from the obvious fact that this is the favorite theme of the Conservative Opposition on the subject of the British Commonwealth of Nations[32] it sounds

---

Australia, already beginning to reach out for holdings in New Guinea and other of the South Sea Islands, and South Africa. A similar warning on the possibility of a future Africander movement in South Africa, which would be anti-British and expansionist, was sounded by one of Cecil Rhodes' lieutenants (appointed by Cecil Rhodes as first Administrator of Mashonaland), Archibald R. Colquhoun, in his *The Africander Land* (London, 1906). See in particular Part III, chapter i, "Nationalism and Imperialism."

[30] "Lord Trefgarne has warned us and the Government of the danger of sinking money in a Colony which makes known its intentions of clearing out of the Empire at the earliest possible moment. After what has happened in Burma, I quite see the point of his warning, because Burma has certainly done very well out of its disloyalty to the Crown. It has got out of paying its war damage liabilities; it has expropriated the assets of British companies and, if I may put it this way, it has out-Daltoned the ex-Chancellor of the Exchequer in the terms which it has paid to companies which have been taken over. We have given them £30 million, and now we have loaned them another £2 million of our dollar resources." L. D. Gammans, speaking for the Opposition on the Colonial Loans Bills, in *Hansard*, Vol. 458, col. 770.

[31] During the war India accumulated—largely as a result of supplies furnished from Indian resources to British forces stationed in the Eastern theatres—huge credits against England. An Indian economist who visited Berkeley, California, in the fall of 1947, very frankly stated that it would not be wise for India to throw off dominion status until she "had collected as much of this sum as possible," and that she would "collect all she could of it short of bankrupting England—a foolish thing to do since then she could collect no more!"

[32] E.g. "Let me ask you this. What subtle almost mystic attraction was it that drew the manhood of Canada, Australia, New Zealand, South Africa, thousands of miles across the oceans to fight and suffer for four years in Flanders or at the Dardanelles or in the Balkans or in Palestine, in a quarrel about which, to tell the truth, they had not been formally consulted. What was it? What was this attraction? You could not write it down on paper, or

decidedly odd in the mouths of "socialists" who are supposed to lay such heavy stress on economic determinants.) Second, and by far the more important, is the almost subconscious tendency, shared by many Americans, to include the United States in the new concept of this enlarged, though vaguely conceived, Commonwealth. That the United States is, in the conventional Labour party patois, a capitalist nation par excellence, does not necessarily matter, since it is also true that the prevailing Labour picture of the United States is one in which the country is still largely under the sway of the New Deal philosophy as it was formulated in the colorful language of President Roosevelt, which seems consonant throughout with the underlying objectives of the Labour party.

Thus the prodigal son, so to speak, is not only returning to the bosom of the great Anglo-Saxon family, but the return is in a certain elemental sense forced by parallel lines of growth and change in two countries which stem from basic common traditions, institutions, social philosophies, and even possibly racial traits. American entry into the First and Second World Wars on the side of England fits this thesis. So also do the loan of 1946, the programs for European recovery evolved subsequent to the Marshall Plan—in which England got the lion's share—Anglo-American partnership in the unification of Western Germany, promotion of Western Union, standardization of arms and ordnance, virtual fusing of military staffs, the establishment of a top-level Anglo-American advisory production council, joint action by American and British trade unions in leaving the World Federation of Trade Unions, and so *ad infinitum.* Against this background of growing Anglo-American copartnership, there is more than a passing disposition on the part of Labour party spokesmen in London to feel that American criticisms of such Labour government programs as nationalization—even of steel—or retention of wartime controls in the postwar period are either unimportant, or unrepresentative of popular American sentiments, or possibly based on mere misunderstanding. Where this is not so then the opinion is likely to be expressed that differences exist only because the British, as is usual with them anyway, are only

---

print it in a book. You will not find it in any Acts of Parliament. Search the statute books as you may, it is not there. Nor will you find it in any Constitution or Treaty, in any Agreement, Obligation, or Compact of any kind. But it was there—this attraction, strong, deep, galvanic, irresistible—and it worked all at once and all together in every heart. Some ancestral voice echoing down the ages suddenly called 'Come.' So they all came." Winston Churchill, *Responsibilities of Empire* (London, 1937), p. 22.

a step or two ahead of America in the great Anglo-Saxon parade of progress. When the United States reaches the fence which England has climbed, the old misunderstanding will cease, and any new one taking its place is to be interpreted in the same self-evident light.

That there is a very great danger that any such view will require considerable self-delusion to sustain it is evidenced by the fact that the suggestion that the United States is or might become either im- perialist—as a twentieth-century residuary legatee of the British—or anti-British in pursuit of its own basic interests is likely to be regarded as either nonsensical on the face of it, or, more probably, as communist propaganda. Dissent within Labour circles from this opinion is either wholly quiescent, or at best minor. There is, in short, no American problem—no necessary or fundamental conflict of interests—*vis-a-vis* either Britain or her Commonwealth. Hence American aid to Britain can be continued, and in the future it may freely be widened to include development of both Commonwealth and colonial empire, without any basic hazard to the Labour program. The Labour party seems to have come, in short, to accept Churchill's view of the (at least potential) natural symbiosis of Anglo-American interest—though Churchill, need- less to say, has most emphatically not accepted the Labour view of the terms and conditions on which it can and will be effected any more than they have his.

In general, then, it comes down to this: The Labour party proposes to keep Empire, but to eliminate imperialism. The only place in which imperialism has any meaning is the colonial territories, and there it dies a natural death when for "exploitation" is substituted "develop- ment and welfare" and fulfillment of "the political aim of British colonial policy, which is to teach the peoples of the Colonies to govern themselves."[33] As the lingering simulacra of imperialism disappear like the smile of the Cheshire cat in *Alice in Wonderland*, the new, substantial reality which takes their place—with, it is hoped, but with- out if necessary, some formula of working partnership with the United States—is an expanded Commonwealth of Nations. In Labour litera- ture, this commonwealth is sometimes referred to as the real Third Empire; it has been spoken of, perhaps slyly, as the Socialist Empire. And this empire, to repeat, is no empire at all. It is, rather, a com- monwealth, or community, of free, independent nations united by a

[33] Richard Frost, *The British Commonwealth and the World* (London, Royal Institute of International Affairs, 1945), p. 61.

common democratic (socialist?) outlook, and rendered highly interdependent by a swiftly elaborating web of ever more intricately laced
strands of mutual interests.

It is against the background of such a generally vague and romantic
view that Labour's program for colonial development has been etched.
In this context it becomes relatively easy to outline, but most extraordinarily difficult to understand.

The Labour Program for Colonial Development

"The British Colonial or Dependent Empire of to-day," states a Labour
government handbook on the British Commonwealth and Empire,[34]
"consists of some 63 million people, inhabiting over 50 different territories, almost all of which are situated in tropical or sub-tropical
areas. It is a vast miscellany of communities, including in its range
developed societies of Europeans, cultured Asiatics, and tribes as
primitive as the ancient Britons." It is however, as map 7 shows,
largely African, and colonial development, accordingly, has been
dominated, and hence may be elucidated, by African development.

The potentialities of African development have been dealt with in
the most glowing terms. A Labour M.P., writing in the official Labour
paper, the *Daily Herald*, speaks of the "African Treasure House."[35] A
special correspondent for the same paper who had just returned from
an investigation of trouble on the Gold Coast, spoke of the African
colonies which "contain the tropical treasures for which hard currency
is paid." This year, he added, "the Gold Coast alone will earn
100,000,000 dollars in Canada and the United States. There is gold in
that colony; manganese, mahogany and diamonds as well. But the real
riches of the Gold Coast are in the lush green jungles, where more than
half the world's cocoa is grown."[36] Another writer, able to speak as an
official appointee of the Labour government, commented on "Viscount
Kemsley's call . . . for greater Empire-awareness." He believed that
"never has the need for economic cooperation been more acute than it
is today," and he referred to a conversation in which "Mr. Ernest Bevin
told me recently that a 15 per cent increase in exports from Central
Africa to the Americans would have a profound effect on our Imperial

---

[34] *Origins and Purpose: A Handbook on the British Commonwealth and Empire.* (Origi-
nallly issued by H.M.S.O. in 1944 before the Labour government came into office. "Revised
and re-set in 1946" to "expound present *Purpose* in the light of historical *Origins*."), p. 73.
[35] John Hynd, in the *Daily Herald*, June 14, 1948.
[36] Peter Stursberg, "We Must Know Awumbo," *Daily Herald*, April 15, 1948.

well-being." Central African development on a huge scale is the answer to Britain's dilemma.[37] There has been talk of numerous great hydro-electric developments. A recent example calls for harnessing the White Nile at Owens Falls where a four-fold cataract drops sixty-five feet. In the more distant vistas are projects of the TVA type enveloping vast areas centered around unified development of the great river systems of the Zambesi, Niger, Nile, Congo, and many others—British and non-British alike.

The phraseology with which Labour spokesmen advocate colonial development in Africa and elsewhere is almost indistinguishable from that of the Liberal and Conservative Opposition. The same appears to be true of Labour's actual plans. Of the four basic pieces of legislation specifically devoted to colonial development, two, in fact, are products of the Conservative-dominated Coalition government, and two were passed by the Labour government. Only the Conservative-sponsored legislation specifically gives major attention to problems of social welfare. The Labour-sponsored acts, largely supplementary to those of the Conservatives, are devoted almost exclusively to economic development[38] and where attention is paid to social welfare at all it has been virtually without exception justified on the grounds that it is absolutely essential as a condition to getting more efficient work out of the African natives whom development projects must employ in large numbers. Throughout all the debates on the latter measures there was but little difference of opinion between Labour and the Opposition, and that little

---

[37] Sir Miles Thomas, member of the board of directors of the Colonial Development Corporation, in an article "More Dollars from Africa," Sunday *Times*, May 16, 1948. He went on to say: "The focal point of integration of Central African territories is likely to be along the Kariba-Kafue axis. Here, where Northern and Southern Rhodesia face each other across the Zambezi, is the site for a hydro-electric scheme which, northwards, will bring increased energy to the copper belt, and southwards, will feed the rapidly expanding industrial economy of the high veld of Southern Rhodesia ... The key to increased output from Central Africa today is the provision of more food for the native. At present his energy output is low because for several months of the year he is really half-starved. Native methods of agriculture must give way to modern mechanised husbandry." There must be more mechanization of agriculture, new markets, elimination of "artificial barriers," etc. "Such," he concluded, "is real progress—both humanitarian and economic."

[38] Dr. Rita Hinden suggests that this may give "rather a false impression" because "the 1940 and 1945 Colonial Development and Welfare Acts, were specifically intended to encourage welfare as well as economic development and framed accordingly. It was then found, by all Parties in the House, that Social Services were being built up without economic development to sustain them. There was a complete lack of *enterprise* on which development was bound to depend and the Overseas Resources Bill which set up the Corporations was designed to provide this enterprise. It was a deliberate corrective to the difficulties which were already revealing themselves owing to the stress having all been on welfare. This was said in the Debates and welcomed by everyone. I find it rather misleading to suggest that because of this Conservatives are more interested in welfare than Labour is." (Letter to the author, Jan. 15, 1949.) I agree entirely with this comment, and I had not thought that either the above or the following implied the contrary.

EUROP[E]
Total Population.
Commonwealth...

NORTH AMERICA
Total Population...210,284,000
Commonwealth......16,587,000

GREENLAND

CANADA

UNITED KINGDOM

Atlantic Ocean

UNITED STATES

GIBRALTAR   MALTA   CYP[RUS]

BERMUDA

BAHAMAS

AFRICA

ANGLO-EGYPTIAN
SUDAN

BR. HONDURAS

JAMAICA

TRINIDAD

GAMBIA

SIERRA LEONE

GOLD
COAST

NIGERIA

UGAND[A]

BRITISH GUIANA

TANGANYIK[A]

SOUTH AMERICA

ASCENSION

N. RHODESI[A]

BECHUANALAND

ST. HELENA

SOUTH AMERICA
Total Population...105,285,000
Commonwealth..........393,000

SOUTH-WEST
AFRICA

TRISTAN DA CUNHA

UNION OF
SOUTH AFRICA

Population
World Total.......2,350,866,00[0]
Commonwealth......588,154,00[0]

25.0%

75.0%

FALKLAND IS.

U.K. and Member Natio[ns]

Map 7. The Brit[ish]

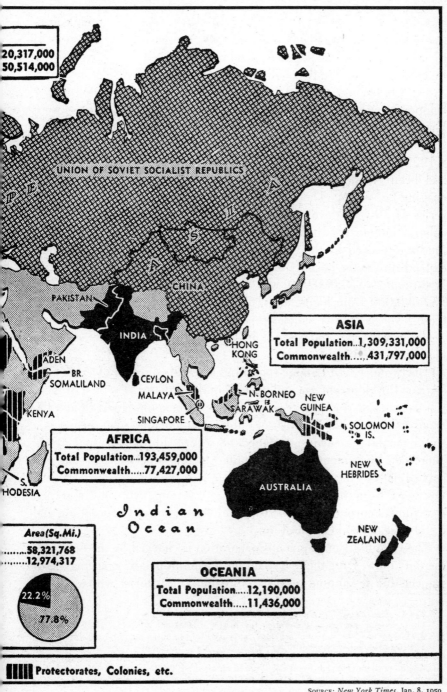

20,317,000
50,514,000

UNION OF SOVIET SOCIALIST REPUBLICS

CHINA

PAKISTAN

INDIA

HONG KONG

ASIA

Total Population...1,309,331,000
Commonwealth......431,797,000

ADEN

BR. SOMALILAND

CEYLON

MALAYA

N. BORNEO
SARAWAK

NEW GUINEA

KENYA

SINGAPORE

SOLOMON IS.

NEW HEBRIDES

AFRICA

Total Population...193,459,000
Commonwealth.....77,427,000

S. RHODESIA

Indian Ocean

AUSTRALIA

NEW ZEALAND

Area(Sq.Mi.)

........58,321,768
........12,974,317

22.2%

77.8%

OCEANIA

Total Population.....12,190,000
Commonwealth.....11,436,000

▥ Protectorates, Colonies, etc.

SOURCE: *New York Times*, Jan. 8, 1950

ommonwealth of Nations

was devoted almost exclusively to administrative and financial questions. Discussion was centered primarily on the prospective gain to Britain from these developments, and was conducted almost exclusively in terms of empire, in the ordinary and conventional sense of the word.

The Coalition-sponsored legislation consisted of two Colonial Development and Welfare acts, passed in 1940 and 1945. These were largely earnests of an attempt to move ahead with the Conservative intentions to promote colonial development which had been embodied in a 1929 Colonial Development Act. Under the 1940 act, £50,000,000 had been "made available . . . for colonial development within the ensuing ten years."[39] The two acts had encouraged the launching of a series of 10-year development programs on the initiative of various colonial authorities. By 1948 some 17 such 10-year programs had been finally approved by the Colonial Office, "and these provide for total expenditure in the period of approximately £180,000,000, of which it is estimated £59,000,000 will come from the British Exchequer, £52,000,000 from loans, and £68,000,000 from revenue."[40] Most of these projects involve much preparatory work of an exploratory and research character, and welfare projects of one sort or another are quite heavily stressed.[41]

The two pieces of Labour-sponsored legislation are the Overseas Resources Development Act and the Colonial Loans Act. The first of these is a measure to accelerate economic development of all sorts under the sponsorship of either British or colonial authorities. The second is a supplementary measure designed to secure additional funds from American investment sources; limited to this purpose, it is entirely subordinate to the first. Passed into law on February 11, 1948, the Overseas Resources Development Act,[42] set up two wholly owned government corporations: the Colonial Development Corporation, and the Overseas Food Corporation.

The Colonial Development Corporation is charged by the act "with the duty of securing the investigation, formulation and carrying out of projects for developing resources of colonial territories with a view to

---

[39] Hinden, *Socialists and the Empire*, p. 8.

[40] *The Colonial Empire, 1947–48*, Cmd. 7433, p. 4.

[41] Thus "Social Services" accounted for nearly £5,000,000 out of slightly less than £12,000,000 for the "development schemes" approved for the fiscal year 1947–48. *Ibid.*, p. 63.

[42] The full title reads: "An Act to Provide for the establishment of a Colonial Development Corporation charged with duties for securing development in colonial territories, and for the establishment of an Overseas Food Corporation charged with duties for securing the production or processing of foodstuffs or other products in places outside the United Kingdom, and the marketing thereof, and for matters connected therewith." 11 Geo. 6.

the expansion of production therein of foodstuffs and raw materials, or for other agricultural, industrial or trade development therein." Specifically, it shall have power:

a) to carry on all activities the carrying on whereof appears to them to be requisite, advantageous or convenient for or in connection with the discharge of their said duty, including the processing and marketing of products;

b) to promote the carrying on of any such activities by other bodies or persons, and for that purpose to establish or expand, or promote the establishment or expansion of, other bodies to carry on any such activities either under the control or partial control of the Corporation or independently, and to give assistance to such bodies or to other bodies or persons appearing to the Corporation to have facilities for the carrying on of any such activities, including financial assistance by the taking up of share or loan capital or by grant, loan or otherwise;

c) to carry on any such activities in association with other bodies or persons (including Governmental authorities) or as managing agents or otherwise on their behalf.[43]

Wholly appointed by and responsible to the Secretary of State for the Colonies, the Colonial Development Corporation may borrow up to £100,000,000 plus an additional £10,000,000 for temporary and emergency purposes. In effect it is to serve as a sort of giant holding company, with detailed operations being conducted through subsidiaries which presumably may serve as either or both operating companies or holding companies for their subsidiary operating companies. By this means capital resources far beyond those mentioned in the act may be placed at the Colonial Office's disposal. Thus an early announcement spoke of setting up five subsidiary corporations, each having a nominal capital as large as that of the parent corporation (£100,000,-000) plus extensive borrowing powers.

Each has the name Colonial Development Corporation, followed by the name of its area in brackets. Areas with headquarters, are:

West Indies.—H.Q. at Kingston; Jamaica, Barbados, British Guiana, British Honduras, Leeward Islands, Trinidad and Tobago, Windward Islands.

West Africa.—H.Q. at Lagos; Gambia, Nigeria, Sierra Leone.

Central Africa.—H.Q. at Lusaka; Basutoland, Bechuanaland, Northern Rhodesia, Nyasaland, Swaziland.

East Africa.—H.Q. at Nairobi; Kenya, Tanganyika Territory, Uganda, Zanzibar.

Far East.—H.Q. at Singapore; Brunei, Hongkong, Malaya, North Borneo, Sarawak, Singapore.

[43] *Ibid.*, Section 1 (1) and (2).

Each subsidiary will have the powers and authorities of the parent company, will be responsible to it, and will receive technical aid and staff from London. A member of the parent Corporation will sit as its chairman.[44]

The Overseas Food Corporation is to be appointed by and be responsible to the Minister of Food. It has power to borrow up to £55,000,000—£50,000,000 plus an additional £5,000,000 for short-run and emergency purposes. It is set up with authority identical with that of the Colonial Development Corporation, but its activities are confined to "projects for the production or processing in places outside the United Kingdom of foodstuffs or agricultural products other than foodstuffs, and the marketing thereof,"[45] and it may operate anywhere in the Empire—colonies or dominions[46]—or possibly even outside the Empire. The "first project" to be carried out by the corporation is that of "securing the large-scale production of groundnuts [peanuts], together with crops rotational therewith or ancillary thereto, in colonial territories in East and Central Africa, and the marketing thereof."[47]

The purpose of both corporations is to set up a three-way copartnership between the British government, the colonial governments, and private enterprise. "I believe," said Creech Jones, Secretary of State for the Colonies, "that by the creation of these two Corporations enormous assistance can be given to enterprise. By collaboration with existing enterprise, by the creation of new enterprises of a public character, by association with peasant production and with co-operative groups, and in a thousand ways, enterprise which previously was impossible can now be launched" with results leading to "a very substantial addition to the wealth of our Colonies and to the happiness of the peoples involved, and we can prove ourselves more worthy of the Empire under our control."[48] More to the point, a concurring spokesman for the Opposition felt that it was now possible to "look forward to a prosperous co-operation between these three partners, the Colonial Governments, the Corporations and private enterprise."[49] John Strachey, Minister of Food, seconded the sentiment with the hope that in the "launching of what is a national series of enterprises . . . we have now . . . a triple instrument for Colonial and overseas development—

[44] *Daily Telegraph*, July 8, 1948.

[45] *Act*, Section 3 (1) (a).

[46] As stated by the Under-Secretary of State for the Colonies, D. R. Rees-Williams, in the House of Commons. *Hansard*, Vol. 446, cols. 65 and 96–97.

[47] *Act*, Section 3 (1) (a).

[48] *Hansard*, Vol. 446, col. 135.

[49] *Ibid.*, col. 139.

the method of the Colonial government acting directly, the method of private enterprise, and now the method of Government Corporations . . . for many years an established part of our national life in this country." All should pull together. "Our national position is really too grave," he said, "to warrant any indulgence in our particular opinions on the methods of overseas development." To obtain "by one means or another, by hook or by crook, the development of primary production of all sorts" everywhere in and outside the Empire is "a life and death matter for the economy of this country."[50]

The makeup of the directorate of the Colonial Development Corporation reflects this three-way partnership idea. Lord Trefgarne, Conservative member of the House of Lords, was made chairman. Sir Frank Stockdale, an old hand and permanent civil servant[51] in the colonial Empire as it had long existed under the guidance of Conservative empire-builders, was made deputy chairman. Other original appointees were "Mr. Tansley, formerly marketing director of the West African Produce Control Board; Sir Miles Thomas, chairman of the Development and Co-ordinating committee of Southern Rhodesia, until recently vice-chairman of Morris Motors Limited; Mr. H. M. Hume, chairman and managing director of Charterhouse Investment Trusts Limited; Mr. H. M. Gibson, who is a director of the C.W.S.; Sir Charles Darwin, director of the National Physical Laboratory; Mr. R. E. Brook, director of the Bank of England; Mr. J. Rosa, a banker who saw war service in the Treasury and the Colonial Office and who was on the Commission of the East African groundnut scheme."[52]

The Overseas Food Corporation was set up specifically for the purpose of taking over the East African Groundnut Scheme from the United African Company, a Unilever subsidiary, on the direct initiative of Frank Samuel, managing director of the United Africa Company. "The proposal submitted by Mr. Samuel [March 28, 1946] provided for the clearance and planting of 73 units of land in Tanganyika, each 35,000 acres in extent, of which three sevenths would be under ground-

---

[50] *Ibid.*, cols. 140–141.
[51] Among the serious "dangers when the Labour Government took office . . . was in the machine itself. Ministers can at best lay down the general lines of policy; the detailed execution has to be left to their officers—the officials in the Colonial Office and the men 'on the spot,' who may have been brought up in a very different school of thought." Hinden, *Socialists and the Empire*, p. 23. There is not a trace of fear of this "danger" in any of the debates on the bill. Labour spokesmen, on the contrary, vied with the Opposition in acknowledging the "great services" of the men "on the spot" and in the Colonial Office. Yet that this confidence was largely unjustified was clearly evidenced in the troubles which ensued in Malaya and the Gold Coast (Accra affair). See pp. 612–614 following.
[52] Creech Jones, in *Hansard*, Vol. 446, col. 136.

nuts, one seventh under an alternative crop, and three sevenths under a grass ley."[53] Pursuant thereto, the Labour government set up a three-man official mission including D. L. Martin, head of the Plantations Department of the United African Company, to make a more detailed investigation of the project, and to report its recommendations.

On September 20, 1946, the mission rendered its report, recommending "the establishment of 107 mechanised units: each unit being 30,000 acres in extent, and the total area 3,210,000 acres. Eighty units are proposed for Tanganyika Territory; 17 for Northern Rhodesia, and 10 for Kenya."[54] The recommendations were taken without serious modification as the basis of the Government proposal, and until the appropriate legislation could be passed the United Africa Company was asked to serve as the managing director for the scheme.

THE GROUNDNUTS SCHEME

Any careful study of the Labour party's plans for Empire development would necessarily have to make a very detailed examination of the Groundnuts Scheme if for no other reason than that it is the first of the many big schemes which the Overseas Resources Development Bill visualized. It appears to be regarded by the Labour government as prototypal for future plans, and as such it has been seen by many as a sort of "Exhibit A" proof that there is nothing to distinguish the Labour program for Empire from that of its Conservative Opposition.

Without an exhaustive investigation—there has been none as yet—it is impossible to judge whether or not the Groundnuts Scheme, as has been charged, can really be taken as an example of old-style imperialism with all its trappings, containing little in the way of social reform beyond minimum concessions of the sort which even the more modest of the "humanitarian imperialists" were demanding before the Labour government took over. Yet Empire unquestionably plays an important part in the Labour government's plans, and cannot be passed by in any effort to determine the scope and implications of its over-all program. Hence, it is necessary to indicate certain rather obvious points, none of which, unfortunately, can be gone into at any considerable length here.

The two Labour bills for colonial development were interpreted quite cynically by the Opposition during the debates on them. They had

---

[53] *A Plan for the Mechanised Production of Groundnuts in East and Central Africa*, Cmd. 7030 (HMSO, 1947), p. 3.

[54] "Report of a Mission to Investigate the Practicability of the Mass Production of Groundnuts in East and Central Africa," *ibid.*, pp. 11–48.

the word of a Labour supporter that it would be "quite premature for anyone on this side of the House to assert that the foundations for a brave new world of Bush Socialism have now been well and truly laid in the heart of Central Africa. I think we shall have to wait a long time yet before 'Let Us Face the Future' has been translated into the language of the drums and the beat of the tom-tom resounds to all its rhythmic cadences." The bill should put to rest "the least vestige of suspicion that anyone connected with the machinery which this Bill initiates"—including the Opposition—would have any interest or intention of lending "himself in the slightest degree to the exploitation of any single native in any of our Colonial possessions."[55]

Other Opposition comment was pitched to a similar key. One, held by Labour supporters to be "a silly man," jibed that the Socialists were now committed to colonial exploitation which "is only another way of saying investing outside capital in a particular colony."[56] The Unilever Company put out a special reprint of a series of *Fortune* articles on the company in which, speaking of Samuel's feat of persuading the Government to undertake the Groundnuts Scheme, it comments that "what the Labor government has found out, ironically, is that Unilever's interests and the British national interests coincide so much of the time lately that it is sometimes difficult to recognize the company as the biggest Octopus in the whole Old World."[57] In accepting the Samuel plan, and asking the United Africa Company "to manage the undertaking until it was in production" Food Minister Strachey, "author of *The Coming Struggle for Power*" had aroused "derisive laughter from the right, and sharp questions from the left, and Strachey could only reply that U.A.C. had the experience and that was that." It was, *Fortune* went on to comment, "almost as if Churchill got up and said he wanted Aneurin Bevan as Prime Minister." A few months later Strachey spoke of the

---

[55] Dr. Segal, in *Hansard*, Vol. 446, col. 152.

[56] L. D. Gammans: "Hon. Members opposite must forgive me if I support this Bill with a certain amount of cynical amusement, because all my life I have listened to Socialists beating their breasts unctuously about what they call Colonial exploitation. Colonial exploitation is only another way of saying investing outside capital in a particular colony. Here we have it in full measure—not merely British money but money which is largely American, capital which has been gained by private enterprise, and also the profit motive. So the circle has turned completely full. The hon. Gentleman is rather like the secretary of a Band of Hope who has been offered a substantial donation by the Licensed Victuallers' Association and wonders whether he should accept it. However, he has wrestled with his conscience and has gone round to the nearest pub and pocketed the cheque. Well, we live and learn; some of us have to live a very long time before we learn." *Hansard*, Vol. 458, col. 767.

[57] Reprinted from issues of *Fortune*, Dec., 1947, Jan. and Feb., 1948, under the title, *Ourselves as Others See Us*, marked "For private circulation within the Unilever organization only," but given out freely by the company's officers as "the best study yet made of the Unilever Company." P. 28.

custodianship by U.A.C. in these terms: "I believe that the U.A.C. and all those who have been officially and unofficially responsible for the very rapid launching of 'Operation Groundnuts' deserve well of the people of Great Britain."[58]

Fortune advanced another reason for accepting the "cynical interpretation"—the "rather interesting charge, sometimes made, that they [Unilever] are running the Labor government." That this charge might seem, so far as Unilever interests are concerned, highly plausible to *Fortune* is evidenced in part by the fact, pointed out in chapter xi above, that the Ministry of Food has properly been described by the Lucas report as a "distributors' organization," and that the Oils and Fats Division of the ministry is almost wholly in the hands of former Unilever employees who still draw their regular pay checks from that Corporation. Furthermore, under Ministry of Food auspices, nearly 95 per cent of the imported edible oils and fats consumed in Britain are processed and distributed by Unilever subsidiaries. Through these employees, lent, so to speak, to the government to run the division whose policies affect it most directly, Unilever gets almost exactly what it wishes in terms of controls. Even if Unilever did run the Labour government, *Fortune* comments, it "wouldn't have to; the government's desire to maintain controls happens to coincide with Unilever's yearning for stability" of prices and markets.[59]

Even more important, the Groundnuts Scheme exactly fits the needs of Unilever. It is universally attested that the trouble with native production is that it is terribly inefficient. Speaking of the experience of the various U.A.C. subsidiaries engaged in tropical African palm-oil production on some 80,000 acres of plantation, *Fortune* comments:

The plantations have proved themselves vastly superior to the native "farm" methods. The forest is cleared and the young palms are planted, and they begin to bear within a few years. Since other trees do not keep the sun from them, they do not grow long trunks, and thus harvesting becomes easier and safer. The trees are more than twice as productive, and the oil is of consistently high quality, being expressed from the pericarp in plants right on the estate. Total cost has been cheaper than the price paid for native produce in all except the deep depression years. And today the finest palm oil can be produced for about half of the £25 a ton that the inferior native product brings. As a result of such differences in cost, the plantation-farmed Netherlands East Indies passed Nigeria in palm-oil exports in 1936 and the Congo is rapidly catching up.[60]

---

[58] Cited, *ibid.*
[59] *Ibid.*
[60] *Ibid.*

The same experience has been reported for the vast nut, rubber, and palm-kernel production of West Africa. As for groundnuts, the special mission sent to Africa estimated that under its recommendations "average cost of production works out at approximately £14 5s. 6d. per ton of groundnuts f.o.b., whereas to-day's cost of purchasing groundnuts in the free market is not less than £32 0s. 0d. per ton, a level likely to be maintained for several years. This margin, of approximately £17 0s. 0d. applied to a crop of 600,000 tons would mean a saving of £10,000,000 per annum in Britain's food bill."[61]

Why, then, should Unilever have been so anxious for the government—particularly a Labour government—to take over such a highly lucrative proposition? Among many explanations four closely related reasons stand out. They are worth brief examination for their obvious bearing on Labour's Empire policy.

1. The scale of investment is gigantic, and possibly beyond the capital resources of Unilever or any other private business enterprise. Not, however, for the reasons given by the corporation, and accepted by the Government, that the estimated direct investment was too high, for it amounted to only £25,000,000. When it is recalled that the U.A.C. alone did an estimated £75,000,000 worth of business (purchases plus sales) in Africa during 1946, and that the Unilever combine as a whole was estimated by *Fortune* to have made sales (including "only its principal products") of £341,036,750[62] in the same year, investment on the scale required to develop the whole of the Groundnut Scheme—particularly when scattered over a ten-year or longer development period—is certainly not very large.

The real reason for Unilever reluctance on this score appears to lie in the concealed or conditional investment costs. A condition to the developments visualized, for example, is elimination of sleeping sickness and this will require destruction of the tsetse fly over immense areas. It is literally an intercolonial problem which requires both international coöperation and huge expenditures of money, man power, and other resources over long periods of time upon which there can never be any direct monetary return.[63] The same holds for the problem of disease

[61] Cmd. 7030, p. 15. The arithmetic is a little bit bad, but these were intended only as rough estimates.

[62] *Fortune, op. cit.*, pp. 20–21, 41.

[63] "Mr. Rees-Williams, Parliamentary Under-Secretary for the Colonies, who last week returned from a tour of Uganda, Tanganyika, and Kenya, has decided that the elimination of the tsetse is the indispensable preliminary to planned development in East Africa. The problem is too big for any one colony to tackle alone. It will demand international action,

in general. "Malaria is chronic in all but a few areas. About half a million cases of leprosy are actually known: probably as many more again are also in existence. All East African territories have reported outbreaks of bubonic plague, which is endemic in Tanganyika. In West Africa estimates of the incidence of veneral disease vary from 50 to 90 per cent of the total population. It has been established, on the basis of a sample survey, that in East Africa over 90 per cent of the population are infected with one or more kinds of worms, while the incidence of yaws and syphilis has been calculated at about 60 per cent. In overcrowded areas and particularly in towns, tuberculosis is already common."[64] Dysentery is general. All the diseases of malnutrition—rickets, beri-beri, dental caries, etc.—flourish over wide areas.

The expenditure necessary to overcome these conditions is colossal. In 1934–35 Great Britain spent £6 per capita on social services (government expenditures) on its home population. Expenditure per capita in 1937 in the African colonies ran from a high of four shillings in Basutoland to a low of less than one shilling in Nigeria (largest of British African colonies).[65] To bring the average of Basutoland up to the British average would require a twenty-four-fold increase; for Nigeria an eighty-fold increase. And the standard in England, on the Labour government's own showing, was disgracefully low in the middle thirties. Worse still, African population is increasing at an extraordinarily rapid rate,—doubling every twenty-five years in East Africa—adding a factor of alarming proportions to the problem. In terms of the native methods of cultivation, vast sections of Africa are seriously overcrowded. One by-product of particular significance for the Groundnuts Scheme is the astonishing rate of soil erosion. The soil is "sick," largely owing to this overcrowding. Something like 300,000 acres of African land are annually removed permanently from cultivation because of this alone.

The low standard of living of the colonial areas has been adumbrated at great length in countless books, brochures, and official reports. The data are in general agreement, and the picture they present is unbe-

---

and the co-operation of Belgium in particular is likely to be sought by the Colonial Office. Plans include spraying from the air with chemical insecticides and the clearance of thousands of acres of bush." *Daily Telegraph*, May 10, 1948. Other tests indicate that appropriate antitoxin may immunize both cattle and men.

[64] Julian Huxley and Phyllis Deane, *The Future of the Colonies*, Target for Tomorrow, no. 8 (London, 1944), p. 34.

[65] Cited, *ibid.*, p. 33, from *Economic Survey of the Colonial Empire, 1937*. At the end of the first year of operation of the health service in Britain medical services alone were running close to £200,000,000 per annum, or £4 per capita.

lievably bad. Income from industrial employments in the reputedly "high wage" area of Northern Rhodesia in 1936 averaged £6 per worker per annum.[66] Speaking of the results of past expenditures, an Opposition supporter of the Overseas Resources Development Bill said that of the "two almost adjacent territories . . . the vast population of Nigeria, numbering something like 23 million, can only claim an income per head of the population of something like 10s. per year, whereas in the Gold Coast, with far richer natural resources, and with a far greater degree of development, the income per head of the population is at least £2 per head."[67] Since income, standards of living, health, the entire native social system in all its complex ramifications and variety, illiteracy, etc., are bound with labor efficiency in an inseparable and indissoluble whole, each of these aspects must be dealt with more or less simultaneously. There appears to be no escape from this dilemma. If this is the legacy of seventy-five years of colonial development, however haphazard it may have been, which involved an estimated investment "up to the end of 1936 no less than £420,000,000 . . . in one form or another in the African colonies,"[68] even the £550,000,000 involved in all overseas measures, Labour and pre-Labour together, spread out over a long-term program—impressive though it may be—looks like only a veritable drop in a gigantic bucket.[69] While it seems impossible satisfactorily to relate the cost of any program of social welfare to a specific project such as the Groundnuts Scheme, it is possible that for at least each of the pioneering ventures it would demand almost as high capital and operating expenditures as the project itself.

2. There are also huge supplementary costs on which there may or may not be any return. Closely related to the inescapable social or conditional costs is the fact that the areas selected for groundnut production are all inland, and that the task of clearing the forest and getting the ground under cultivation requires railroads, highways, dock and harbor construction, warehouses, industrial and other miscellaneous buildings, housing, schools, and a vast miscellany of other facilities.

[66] Rita Hinden, *Plan for Africa*, with a Foreword by Creech Jones (London, 1941), p. 98.
[67] Dr. Segal, in *Hansard*, Vol. 446, col. 151. Wilfred Sendal, in the *Daily Telegraph*, Feb. 18, 1948, estimates average family income in Nigeria to be "somewhere between £5 or £10 a year." Families are large.
[68] Wilfred Sendal, *ibid.*
[69] As given by Ivor Thomas: £50,000,000 Treasury guarantee to Colonial Governments for Development purposes; £350,000,000 Colonial Development Welfare Funds—"when supplemented by local resources"; £150,000,000 "under the Overseas Resources Bill" = £550,000,-000. *Hansard*, Vol. 458, col. 766.

All this, of course, was known to the U.A.C., and yet their estimate of necessary costs appeared, within a year after the Ministry of Food took over, to be almost 50 per cent too small. How this could have happened to the estimates of a company so successful commercially, and so fully aware of all the problems which development on the anticipated scale in tropical climates inevitably raises, is a touchy question which has so far gone unanswered. Furthermore, in the areas selected the soil is predominantly of a friable texture, the slope ranges from near level to gradients as steep as five to seven degrees, and the rainfall cycle consists of torrential downpours interspersed with long dry periods. These are ideal conditions for maximum soil erosion, and from the outset only soil conservation on a heroic scale can provide a stable culture. This means large expenditures for equipment, and all the additional costs associated with practices of contour cultivation, crop rotation based upon special types of ecologically balanced cultivation, a special fertilizer program, etc. But far overshadowing considerations such as these is the simple and elementary fact that the unit of reference in any large-scale and industrialized land-utilization program is the watershed, and watershed control means vast expenditures for developments similar to those of the American Tennessee Valley Authority. The capital outlay and the operating expense for watershed development of any one of the major areas in which the various Groundnuts schemes are now planned would necessarily be several times the direct cost of all these existing schemes combined.

3. Thus the U.A.C. might well shun the Groundnuts schemes on a purely business basis alone. But it is also true that U.A.C. is, and long has been, primarily a trading corporation. Despite the extraordinarily wide variety of projects it has undertaken in the tropical colonies,[70] its interest has been from the beginning purchase and wholesale in both colonial and home markets. It has developed an immense world-wide organization of docks and warehouses, shipping, processing, and by-product plants, and supplementary sales, promotion, and public-relations facilities. As a near-monopolist in its principal lines—both as buyer and as seller of raw materials and finished products—it is interested, as *Fortune* puts it, in "stability." "Stability" has here, as nearly always in the mouths of cartel-minded business spokesmen, the special meaning of stable volume of raw materials, purchased at stable

[70] For a description of these various activities see *Fortune, op. cit.* Considerable detail is also given in the *Annual Report and Statement of Accounts*, Lever Brothers and Unilever Ltd. See, e.g., the *Report* of 1946.

prices and sold at stable prices in stable markets. Thus the government, in taking over the Groundnuts Scheme, is not only saving Unilever vast conditional and supplementary development expenses on which no direct return may be expected, but it is shouldering a supply problem which Unilever simply could not handle on its own—yet one which it has a very great interest in seeing adequately solved on a large scale.

4. There is a special reason, however, why Unilever would not enter this field even if it had the necessary resources and a desire to become a producer as well as a distributor. That is the fact that it is suspect by virtually all natives—as indeed are all large overseas business corporations, British or otherwise, doing business within the colonies—with having a primary, if not sole, interest in exploiting native natural and human resources at the expense of the resident population. It does not matter that natives may exploit each other with equal or greater severity.[71] The outside exploiter is not only resented merely because he is an outsider; he also upsets the whole native social system. If he is a European this is doubly true, for he brings with him a regime which has a direct and vested interest in destroying the native social life, in drawing large and increasing percentages of natives into urban centers and strange specialized employments, in arousing their interest in new ideas, new goods, new outlooks, and generally in unsettling all the settled ways. Even if he pays the accepted wages for hired labor, unavoidably he holds out prospects of a new life, of new wants, new outlooks, new hopes, and soon, unless he is able to substitute or fulfill, new angers, new hostilities, and new despairs. All this, of course, is a very old story.

But under a Labour government there are some new aspects to African development. For one thing, the Labour party is committed—publicly and officially—both to improvement of colonial welfare, and to eventual self-government for the colonies. And, contrary to the Labour

[71] In Africa, from the days of the slave trade to the present, exploitation by local chieftains and local traders has frequently been as severe and unprincipled as that of any outsider. But all the evidence seems to indicate that both native exploited and exploiter unite in their opposition to the outsider. Some can be bought off, but not for long. When Unilever buys cocoa at £75 a ton and sells it in world markets at £250 a ton, the local trader who has forced the native producer to sell his product at a low price tends to side with the man he has fleeced as well as with the overseas purchaser who feels that he is being "held up." According to *Fortune, op. cit.*, p. 32, "to assure every native connected with the fats-and-oils business a decent living by European standards (very low by American standards), soap and margarine would have to sell for £5 a pound." But the company, which pays the native labourer 20 cents a day, also supplies a cocoa to American chocolate producers which brings "howls and laments" from them too. At the same time, Unilever supplies European goods to West African natives at prices higher than those in European markets.

view, advance *per se* does not make Colonial peoples less hostile to out-side well-doers, but more. As an official of the U.A.C. put it, "when they advance that's when they get hard to handle."[72] The Labour gov-ernment, therefore, must advance native welfare and self-government faster than has any previous British government not only because na-tives expect more of it, but also because it must keep at least one step ahead of the perennial native complaints that whatever has been done is still not enough. Each advance increases, in geometric ratio, the need for further advances; for every effort the Labour government makes to shoulder the burden, the already too heavy load becomes heavier still. But this is not all; there are other circumstances which add even more weight.

Any foreign corporation in Africa automatically becomes heir to the residual native hatred of foreigners until it has proved itself different from its predecessors in a manner self-evident to native eyes. To do so its policies must be different from those of the past not by small, but by large—and to the native—qualitatively obvious margins. The point was well put by one of the Opposition during House of Commons de-bate. "There is also the political danger," he said, "which I do not think the Under-Secretary has fully appreciated; here for the first time are His Majesty's Government exploiting a Colonial territory direct. He will have to be extremely eloquent in due course if he can persuade the people of East Africa that this is not being done primarily for the benefit of the people of this country who will want the food which that scheme is going to produce. Up to now, the Colonial Office has always been, as it were, the judge standing in an intermediary position be-tween capital and the people of the country. Now they have become the exploiters themselves. I warn the hon. Gentleman that political agita-tors in a Colony would put a very different interpretation on that form of enterprise from that which the hon. Gentleman would wish."[73] This is not mere carping rhetoric. The Groundnuts Scheme was begun and managed during its infancy by Unilever. The government is also the owner of the British South Africa Company, now functionless, but a company which was founded by Cecil Rhodes—"exploiter" in the grand and ruthless old Empire sense—and hated by virtually every native who has given a thought to the matter. And the initial and primary pur-pose of the Groundnuts Scheme—reiterated on numerous occasions—

---

[72] *Fortune, op. cit.*, p. 30.
[73] Gammans, in *Hansard*, Vol. 458, col. 769.

was to solve Britain's problem of oils and fats shortage[74]—not to elevate and to educate the native. To be sure, welfare measures were provided for, but such provisions were definitely subsidiary to this main consideration and conditional upon it.

Furthermore, the major colonial territories are now heavily seasoned with returned war veterans. However awkward and inadequate the war propaganda which reached them, and however much of it they may have misunderstood, they did bring back two things which augur little for future colonial harmony. First is the knowledge of how to handle arms, simple and complicated alike, and how to conduct guerrilla warfare under central direction, and second, how appropriate propaganda may justify resort to arms whenever and wherever the belief exists that certain "fundamental and basic human rights are invaded." Between a half million and a million native Africans have been competently and efficiently trained in war technology, and many of them are familiar with at least the phraseology of the propaganda; the "fundamental and basic human rights" were spelled out for them by internationally recognized war heroes and in the ringing words of the Atlantic Charter and the Four Freedoms. If, in other words, the native peoples do not find the colonial plans of the Labour government all that they might have hoped for, native unrest may now be quickly and dramatically leavened with hostile programs implemented with the necessary skills for effective and crippling action.

This factor might well be utilized to add enormous strength to the Labour party's social program in the colonies—new freedoms in one area reinforcing those in another. But this potential asset may be turned into an immense and cumulating liability through the disposition on the part of Labour to see any objections to their own well-meant programs and slogans as evidence of "Communist" activity. There are three places in which this has already been true: Burma (shortly after the conferring of a rather specialized dominion status), Malaya, and the Gold Coast (Accra incident). The reasons for trouble were different

[74] E.g., the "Overseas Food Corporation . . . was established to undertake schemes for the production overseas of foodstuffs to meet United Kingdom needs." *The Colonial Empire*, Cmd. 7433. *The Report of the African Mission*, p. 15, begins with the words: "The world is to-day suffering from a critical shortage of oils and fats, the annual shortfall in the case of Britain alone amounting to the equivalent of 1½ million tons of groundnuts." In all cases there is talk of "welfare" and of "native participation" in control *later* on in the discussion, and *later* on in the development of the project—when, that is to say, the natives are *prepared* to take over. This may be proper and unavoidable, but it is also difficult to square with the idea that colonial development exists to promote first "the interests of the inhabitants," as argued in the Labour party pamphlet, *The Colonies*, p. 12.

in each, and the government's policy toward them varied also, but in all three Labour government spokesmen immediately described the troubles as "Communist"—using as synonyms, "rebels," "gangsters," "terrorists," "murderers," and the like. "The trouble in Malaya is due to world-wide Communism," said Rees-Williams, Under-secretary of State for the Colonies.[75] Not all of Labour's loyal followers accepted this interpretation, even in Malaya, where there was the most evidence of "Communist activity." "It is not Communism in the main," said Harold Davies, "which is the cause of the trouble in Malaya and South East Asia; it is shortage of rice and other foods, and political groups have taken the opportunity of exploiting this shortage. The repeated assertion that it is Communism all the time which is the cause of the trouble is now growing nauseating, and is not in strict accordance with the real economic facts of that country . . . The tragedies and troubles in Malaya have been largely caused by the low price of rubber."[76]

Perhaps even more important is the fact that, precisely at a time when the primary concern of the postwar Labour government is solution of the problem of dollar shortage, Malaya is far and away the most important net earner of dollars within the sterling bloc.[77] Thus rubber and tin seem to account for British policy in Malaya, and "Communism" is at best probably a mere by-product of inability (or unwillingness) to do anything effective about "rice and other foods" and the "price of rubber." But if there is any doubt here, the irrelevance of the Labour government's shout of "Communist" at the first indication of labor unrest in the colonies should be put to rest by the Accra affair.

In its report on this affair—centered around the shooting of a number of African ex-servicemen, carrying a petition for redress of grievances, at a crossroads near the Government House in the town of Accra—the Commission of Enquiry into Disturbances in the Gold Coast,

[75] *Hansard*, Vol. 458, col. 756.

[76] *Ibid.*, cols. 771–773. Dr. Rita Hinden comments on this paragraph as follows: "I don't think you would get anyone here—except Communists—to agree that the trouble in Malaya is *not* Communist-inspired. I agree that there is too much readiness to blame all troubles on Communists, but what is happening in Malaya is beyond all doubt." (Letter to the author.) This may be so (But Davies is *not* a Communist!), but it is also true that in the whole postwar world there has been no Communist success where conditions could be described as reasonably satisfactory by Labour party standards. Communism results primarily from "condition," not from inspiration.

[77] In 1936–1938 imports to the United States from British Malaya were $174,400,000, and exports to Malaya from the United States were only $7,600,000. Thus, excluding the United Kingdom and Canada—which between them had a trade deficit with the United States of $434,200,000—Br. Malaya had a trade surplus with the United States of $166,800,000. All other British countries put together had a trade deficit with the United States of $434,200,-000. British Information Services, Reference Division, *British Commonwealth Trade* (1947), table vi, p. 8.

1948, included among its "approximate underlying causes" no reference to communism at all. When, in turn, it came to examine the actual incident it found an organization of ex-servicemen whose policies may have been strategically influenced at one point by a lone "Communist."

The basic causes of the trouble include an amazing cross-section of the maladies of empire, and at the risk of being tedious, are worth reproducing in full:[78]

A. POLITICAL

i) The large number of African soldiers returning from service with the Forces, where they had lived under different and better conditions, made for a general communicable state of unrest. Such Africans by reason of their contacts with other peoples including Europeans had developed a *political and national consciousness*. The fact that they were disappointed at Conditions on their return, either from specious promises made before demobilisation or a general expectancy of a *golden age for heroes*, made them the natural focal point for any general *movement against authority*.

ii) A feeling of *political frustration among the educated Africans* who saw no prospect of ever experiencing political power under existing conditions and who regarded the *1946 Constitution as mere window-dressing designed to cover but not to advance their natural aspirations*.

iii) A failure of the Government to realise that, with the *spread of liberal ideas, increasing literacy* and a *closer contact with political developments in other parts of the world,* the star of rule through the Chiefs was on the wane. *The achievement of self-government in India, Burma and Ceylon had not passed unnoticed in the Gold Coast.*

iv) A *universal feeling* that *Africanisation was merely a promise* and not a driving force in Government policy, coupled with the suspicion that education had been slowed up and directed in such a way as to impeded Africanisation.

v) A *general suspicion of Government measures and intentions* reinforced by a hostile Press and heightened by the general failure of the Administration in the field of Public Relations.

vi) Increasing resentment at the *growing concentration* of certain trades in the hands of foreigners, particularly at the increase in the number of Syrian merchants.

B. ECONOMIC

i) The announcement by the Government that it would *remain neutral in the dispute* which had arisen between the traders and the people of the Gold Coast over high prices of imported goods which led to the organised boycott of January–February, 1948.

ii) The continuance of *war-time control of imports,* and the *shortage and high prices of consumer goods* which were widely attributed to the machinations of European importers.

---

[78] *Report of the Commission of Inquiry into Disturbances in the Gold Coast,* Colonial no. 231 (London, HMSO, 1948), pp. 7–8. Italics mine.

iii) The alleged unfair allocation and distribution of goods in short supply by the importing firms.

iv) The Government's acceptance of the scientist's finding that the only cure for Swollen Shoot disease of cocoa was to cut out diseased trees, and their adoption of that policy combined with allegations of improper methods of carrying it out.

v) The degree of *control in the Cocoa Marketing Board* which limited the powers of the farmers' representatives to control the vast reserves which are accumulating under the Board's policy.

vi) The feeling that the *Government had not formulated any plans for the future of industry and agriculture* and that indeed, *it was lukewarm about any development apart from production for export.*

C. SOCIAL

i) The *alleged slow development of educational facilities* in spite of a growing demand, and the almost complete failure to provide any technical or vocational training.

ii) The shortage of housing, particularly in the towns, and the *low standards of houses for Africans compared with those provided for Europeans.*

iii) The fear of *wholesale alienation of tribal lands* leaving a landless peasantry.

iv) Inadequacy of the legal powers of government necessary to deal with speeches designed to arouse disorder and violence.

The italicized sections indicate what appear to have been the more important factors contributing to the general unrest within the colony and which bear most directly upon the long-run program of colonial development formulated by the Labour government. The report outlines conditions existing in the Gold Coast under each of these headings, and suggests the necessary corrective measures. Since, in the main, conditions in the Gold Coast were, if anything, somewhat better than in any other African colony, the meaning of the commission's proposals for the future conduct of Empire are wholly unmistakable. What they call for, in effect, is a rapid, large-scale revolution in the political, economic, and social life of the colony, to raise it quickly to levels above and beyond reach of the communist appeal.

The dilemma which faces Britain at this point inheres in three simple, closely related facts. (1) Such a program for this one colony alone would require resources—financial and technological—which the Labour government cannot possibly supply for many years to come, and yet clearly solution of the problem cannot be postponed. (2) Even if it could spare the resources for one colony, it is very difficult from a political point of view to favor for long one section of the African continent, or, indeed, one section of the Empire, at the apparent expense of others. What is done to improve one, must soon be done to improve all. Britain's inability to supply the necessary resources at any given weak spot is a compound factor. (3) All such plans, on whatever scale and however timed, necessarily depend upon the coöperation of such local governments as exist—and these exist in some form or other in most of the British colonies—and yet it seems also clear that the existing local governments cannot, even if they desire, coöperate on any such terms as those which the Labour government is almost certainly bound to offer.

If, as seems probable, the Government is unable, in consequence of factors such as these, to carry through the necessary reforms and developments, it is faced with another dilemma. Should it attempt to put down uprisings and to quash other evidence of militant colonial feeling by the usual police methods on the grounds that they are "Communistic" and hence outside the pale of a reasonable approach, then the tendency—if there is any lesson to be learned from the experiences of the British in Malaya, the Dutch in Indonesia, and the French in Viet Nam—would be not to achieve the objective but rather to push native opposition into the arms of the "Communists." Obviously, so to proceed is self-defeating. If, on the other hand, they do nothing about it, the Empire drifts to pieces—something, to repeat, which the Labour party will certainly soon come to feel that it cannot afford if Britain is to continue to have any significant influence in the world, or the Labour government is to survive.

So far as it seems possible to be at all sure of the nature of the Labour diagnosis of colonial problems—and this is frequently very difficult indeed—there appear to be two possible ways out of this dilemma. The first is some form of close coöperation with the local colonial governments which would have as one of its major objectives preparation for self-government at the earliest possible date. The second is to call in outside aid. What are the possibilities of each?

The success of all the various colonial development and welfare schemes—including the Groundnuts Scheme—is postulated on the assumption that coöperation with colonial governments is necessary, inescapable, and (hopefully) desirable. Yet in most of the colonial governments, perhaps most notably in East Africa, the white settlers have a dominating influence, and as such have long been, and are continuing to be, as a general rule, vigorously and bitterly opposed to racial equality. Officials of the British Colonial Office almost unanimously agree that the problem of what to do about the intransigence of the white settler is one of the most important factors to be considered in formulating any plan of action. The Groundnuts Scheme has already run into this difficulty in the colonies of Northern Rhodesia and Kenya—even though in Kenya the percentage of white settlers is extremely low. It is faced wherever white settlers are to be found.

There are two reasons why this problem threatens to become more difficult rather than easier to solve. First: the rise to power of the Malan government in 1948, as representative of the Africander movement of South Africa, which completely repudiated Labour party guidance and adopted a policy of rigorous race segregation which postulates a permanently servile condition for the numerically proponderating blacks (more than 8,000,000 out of a population of slightly over 10,000,000 are negro). The repudiation of the Labour party's program along these lines is complete, and includes political rights, social welfare, and economic conditions. That the Malan program has stiffened the backs of white proponents of segregation everywhere in Africa is almost unquestionable. The bloody Zulu riots in the winter of 1948–49 are a by-product of this policy; all observers agree that these are a mere foretaste of what must follow in all of the African colonies unless the segregation policy ceases.

Progress towards colonial self-government wherever whites have settled in considerable numbers, in other words, now runs the very serious risk of being progress on the white colonials' terms, not on those of the Labour government. This situation is not likely to be changed for the better by the second reason referred to above: the growing interest in England in large-scale migration to overseas dominions and colonies. Fear of Eastern encroachments—first of Japanese and now of communist—has led Australia to invite white settlers en masse in the hope of quickly doubling her population of some ten millions. For analogous reasons migration to African and other overseas colonies is being encouraged. There is, in fact, a large and growing literature, not taken very seriously by the Labour government, which views such migration as Britain's only hope of salvaging the Empire at all. Such propaganda, furthermore, is especially designed to appeal to British Conservatives and Liberals; to convince them that by migrating they can find immense opportunities for personal advancement and new opportunities for "free enterprise" now being denied to them at home by a "Socialistic" government, and at the same time sow more widely throughout the Empire the "seed" of British blood without which the Empire cannot be held together.[79]

That this is not mere idle speculation nobody familiar with British business circles can doubt. Rumors persist everywhere that despite the rigor of exchange controls large amounts of capital are actually being transferred abroad in defiance of government regulations.[80] Literature circulating quite widely in Britain describes the opportunities open to the enterprising pioneer in the colonies in most glowing terms.[81] If such considerations are stimulating migration to the colonies of persons (and capital) basically opposed to Labour policies both at home and in the Empire, then "cooperation with the Colonial Governments" will increasingly become translated into giving aid to undermine the very program which Labour has committed itself to advancing. Not in any vague and general sense, but in precisely those phases and aspects of the Labour program—social welfare and political self-government— which a Labour government must of necessity stress heavily, and without which it has no chance at all of effecting the economic development that has become, willy-nilly, its immediate objective.

Since the general attitude of white colonial settlers is well known to the Labour government, what about the other possibility, that of relying ever more heavily upon outside aid—principally the United States? Much of the equipment necessary for the success of the Groundnuts Scheme—tractors, bulldozers, and other heavy equipment for clearing "the bush" and otherwise preparing the land for cultivation—will have to come from America. Trained negro scientists, engineers, and other technicians will have to be recruited mostly from American schools.[82] But that is only the beginning. If, as seems probable, the success of the

---

[79] See, e.g., an early statement, R. A. Piddington, *The Next British Empire: A Population Policy for Home Amenity and Empire Defence* (London, 1938).

[80] This is not necessarily confined to the sterling area—leakages to the dollar area also occur. In an attempt to track such rumors down, I ran across an example of "how it was done" in the summer of 1948, and personally witnessed the transfer to a "hard-currency" area of several thousand pounds without benefit of either government approval or knowledge of any of the transactions. I was able personally to verify the fact of the transaction, and was informed by parties thereto that "hundreds or thousands of similar transactions were going on all the time." As one person put it: without its being known to the public, Britain is literally "bleeding at every pore." How much truth or how much venal gossip there is in such an opinion it is impossible to say.

[81] There are countless examples to be found in such magazines as *Cavalcade* and *British Africa Monthly*.

[82] "The Colonial Office now asked the United States Economic Cooperation Administration whether a number of American scientists and technicians can be found to undertake work in the Colonies which is essential to plans for economic development." *Daily Telegraph*, April 11, 1948.

individual projects depends eventually both on TVA types of water-shed development, and a steady and large-scale new construction of supplementary plants and other facilities which could and should be developed for exploiting other natural resources in the same areas, then the scale of capital requirements will make absolutely necessary heavy and cumulating drafts on American capital resources.

Much the same might then be true for most of the other types of over-seas development visualized in the Overseas Resources Development Act. In the debates in Commons on the Colonial Loans Bill it was frankly recognized that the purpose of the bill was to tap American financial resources for colonial development purposes. "There is only one source at the present time," said Ivor Thomas, "from which . . . capital investment in the Colonies can come. If we face the facts we know that that source must be the United States of America."[83] Lord Winterton for the Opposition believed that "the hon. Gentleman will agree that we as a Nation welcome American participation in the de-velopment of British Colonies" and "this Bill is the one means of obtaining it."[84] Sir Arthur Salter hoped that "Governmental loans of this nature" would soon be "supplemented by the resumption of private lending and private enterprise," and he trusted that, with the tempo-rary restoration of equilibrium in "the world balance of payments" through the assistance of "such measures as Marshall Aid," finally "American private investors should find the Colonies an attractive field for the investment of their money."[85]

What did the Labour government think? What were its intentions? What did it see in the more distant perspectives of Empire develop-ment? Here it was sponsoring a bill to promote assistance from capital-ist America—which, particularly since the introduction of the Steel Bill, was showing less and less evidence of approval of the socialism of the Labour party—for colonial governments which were already pre-disposed to attempt the defeat of those very aspects of Labour's Empire policy which in any way differentiate its colonial program from that of its bitterest opposition. Was Labour being shrewd in beginning a tactical maneuver the meaning of which only the expertise of the insider could decode? Or, was it merely being gullible? There seems at first practically nothing on which to base answers to questions such as these.

Consider briefly the over-all picture. The Colonial Loans Bill came

---

[83] *Hansard*, Vol. 458, col. 764.
[84] *Ibid.*, col. 756.
[85] *Ibid.*, col. 780.

after, not before, the South African triumph of Malan's Africander party which champions the political domination of white minorities in overwhelmingly black territories, and whose rise to power was greeted in British Labour circles with gloom and apprehension. The bill comes after, not before, the Malayan and Accra affairs, different in kind, but alike in that they helped to serve notice in most unmistakable terms—on the Labour government's own finding—that increasing native participation in colonial government is one of the inescapable preconditions to native coöperation in British colonial development schemes. In general, the bravura of hopeful words and sentiments surrounding all British colonial development schemes since the war has woven its irridiscent patterns for a brave new world of Third Empire rejuvenation after, not before, proof of Britain's inability to comply with the requirements of even the milder "humanitarian" Labour programs for colonial welfare has been so heavily underscored by the bitter struggle for survival through the "battle of the exchanges" that all who run may read.

Nor is that all. The Labour plans for the Empire have been unfolded in face of growing evidence that neither the American government nor the dominant private groups which help to shape its overseas economic policies show the slightest tendency to leave for their greatly weakened British compatriots exclusive rights to markets or new investments in any part of the world. On the contrary. One of Britain's greatest and most honored American friends, President Roosevelt, speaking in 1944 of the problem of postwar prosperity, said, "I intend to find jobs for 60,000,000 Americans by trebling our exports."[86] In a similar vein, the first big British loan and Marshall Plan aid both have frequently been referred to abroad—not by opponents alone—as "the export of American depression."

In short, there is no current version of American plans for the future which give the British government any reason for believing that American interest in rising exports and export surpluses is going to decline for a long time to come. The accumulation of American export surpluses will make it necessary for the United States to do either or both of two things: (1) Force entrance into markets by means and with

[86] Quoted by L. S. Amery, *The Washington Loan Agreements; A Critical Study of American Economic Foreign Policy* (London, 1946), p. x. The debates in the American Congress in the summer of 1949 over the renewal of the Marshall Plan have shown how strong is the sentiment to use this leverage on behalf of American business whenever it is faced with faltering domestic demands.

resources which no country so weak in resources as contemporary Britain can possibly counteract. (2) Increase investment of the consequent capital surpluses in developments abroad.

The implications of such a posture of affairs cannot be gone into here. For present purposes one conclusion only seems merited: the role which Empire is to play in Labour's program for recovering Britain's place in world affairs cannot be determined by examination of either contemporary British statements on colonial policy, nor from the acts and projects which have been inaugurated for colonial development. The more time and effort one devotes to such study, the more it becomes evident that this procedure is like looking through the wrong end of a telescope. It may be possible that if the telescope is reversed, the picture will begin to take on quite different outlines, and many of the crosscurrents and confusion of the microcosm begin to fit into some sort of an intelligible pattern. An examination of what has actually been done may permit generalizations to be made which will give a clearer picture of Labour's colonial policy than can be found in any statements of the party's spokesmen.

ELEMENTS WHICH CONDITION LABOUR'S EMPIRE POLICY

By one means or another the colonial empires of the western European countries are, in effect, to be pooled. This will be true at least where they are contiguous one with another, particularly in Africa, and may be the most important immediate result of Western Union. At any rate, the Western European colonial powers have discussed this subject at some length since the war, and it seems quite evident that something in the nature of an effective pooling of Empire holdings for purposes of joint exploitation is slowly shaping up. Two illustrations must suffice.

On February 17, 1948, an "Anglo-French technical conference on Africa was opened . . . at the Quai d'Orsay by M. Paul Coste-Floret, Minister for Overseas France"; the British delegation was headed by Sir Oliver Harvey, British Ambassador to France. The first statement given out by the French Foreign Ministry was designed to correct "an impression that the talks embraced political questions." It read:

The talks are simply a natural development of conversations and conferences which have been taking place continually during the past three years between the French and British in France and in Africa regarding African economic questions and the life of the local populations, namely: Hygiene, health, agriculture, soil, teaching, nutrition, labour, communications, and the fight against animal diseases.

To-day's conversations are aimed at co-ordinating and extending this activity by examining the possibiity of a wider co-operation in four determined spheres:

1. Improvement of communications and ports.
2. Inter-African trade.
3. Development plans.
4. Price policy.

These questions will be examined in West Africa where British and French territories are particularly concerned.[87]

Details of plans under discussion followed expected lines. Nigerian coal is to be shipped to French areas, and French salt is to be produced for the "benefit of British colonies." A new railway is to be constructed to connect British Togoland with the French port of Lome. Efforts are to be made to secure, by joint action, "fair prices for the products of West African territories." Prices are to be "stabilized," etc.[88] Similar discussions extending the areas covered and the range of joint action were anticipated in the future.

In June of the same year, an informal series of discussions conducted by "a mixed bag of professors, politicians, high-officials and ex-officials"[89] representative broadly of the five colonial powers of Western Europe—Britain, France, Belgium, the Netherlands, and Portugal—addressed themselves to the "impact of Western Union upon the Overseas Territories." There was general agreement that "main emphasis" should be "laid on the mutual advantages of the maintenance of ties between the Western Metropolitan Powers and their Overseas Territories." Talk and plans should treat of the latter not "as dependencies but of all of us as interdependencies." Today "neither the free peoples nor the peoples who are on the road to freedom can afford, economically, strategically and culturally to live unto themselves, or by themselves alone." Future techniques, hence, "must be based on a frank avowal of inter-dependency re-interpreted on the basis of partnership" with the "cement of the whole edifice" being "a realization of mutual advantage applied with the trowel of mutual understanding." With this "Imperialism in the old sense, or anyhow in the sense which it connotes to the Overseas Territories," may be declared "dead," and "grave responsibilities" reconciled with "questions of self interest."[90]

---

[87] *Daily Telegraph*, Feb. 18, 1948.
[88] *Daily Telegraph*, Feb. 21, 1948.
[89] There were some important names, nevertheless. Papers leading off these separate sessions were "read by Mr. Ivor Thomas, MP, until recently Under-Secretary for the Colonies, Monsieur P. M. Henry, Administrator of Colonies in the *Ministère de la France, d'Outre Mer*, and Professor de Vries, Head of the Economic Division of the corresponding Netherlands Ministry." *Time and Tide*, June 26, 1948, p. 658.
[90] *Ibid.*

A similar meeting in Portugal was planned for the ensuing year. All delegates spoke as individuals, and not as representatives of any government or party. Yet these may be most significant straws in the wind. Similar conversations—official and unofficial alike—are going on constantly among the Western European powers. In detail and at large they point to the possibility of the creation of a vast pool of overseas territories for the development of which there might then be increasingly close coöperation among the colonial powers.[91]

The *self-governing British dominions are apparently to be encouraged to share freely in colonial development plans.* The structure of Imperial preference, and other types of economic, political, and similar links whose purpose is to bind the Commonwealth more closely together may be generally widened to include the colonial territories. The whole, in effect, would then become a vast free-trade area, in which all of the members of the sterling bloc could freely participate. So far as this is paralleled by Empire "cooperative development" by the Western European powers, this obviously could mean dominion participation in at least certain lines of important trade and general development in French, Dutch, Belgian, and Portuguese colonial holdings as well. And vice versa.

A possible precondition is the consolidation of colonial holdings on a regional basis. Both the French and the British have been working toward this solution. Proposals for union of West Africa, Central Africa, and East Africa have been made, and much of the preliminary machinery has already been worked out. Such federations have to be made on the terms of the coöperating colonial governments, and this appears to mean that wherever many white settlers are to be found they will make a strenuous effort to achieve complete domination—even when the principle of equal representation by racial blocs is accepted on Labour government insistence.[92] The pattern, in other words, runs

[91] Dr. Rita Hinden believes that the "idea that we intend pooling the Colonies with the other West European Powers has no concrete reality. There has been a lot of discussion on international cooperation, but there is no suggestion of pooling." (Letter to the author.)

[92] For example, in East Africa the territories of Kenya, Uganda, and Tanganyika have gradually evolved "certain common services—transport, customs, posts, defence" which "cross the political boundaries and during the war a complicated network of inter-territorial boards and committees has taken shape. The Government has now decided to give this a constitutional basis, and proposals have just been published to set up an East African High Commission" which is to have a central legislature meeting at Nairobi "composed of 12 officials and 24 non-official members. Among the non-official the three racial groups—European, Indians and Africans—will be represented in exactly equal numbers." *New Statesman and Nation*, Dec. 22, 1945, p. 418. According to the *Handbook on the British Commonwealth and Empire*, pp. 131–132, these three colonies in 1948 had a population made up of 12,086,204 "natives," 92,413 "Asiatics" and 30,429 "Europeans." Thus for 1 European

the risk of becoming only a slight variation of the one which has become triumphant in South Africa under the Malan government. This does not, however, necessarily preclude emphasis upon either the welfare or the self-government aspects of colonial development. But the reason why this is true seems only in part to be because of the capacity—or will—of the Labour government to insist upon its "humanitarian" programs; it may also depend on the quite different and very special nature of the new and potentially very important American influence.

The United States may come to participate freely in European colonial development, and be able to make up the major part of the existing shortage of investment resources. This is a conclusion which no representative of the Labour government has been able to bring himself to draw publicly, although it is freely discussed in American circles—when not, indeed, taken as a matter of course. The British Opposition has not been so reticent. Speaking of the American loan to Britain in 1946, L. S. Amery, former Secretary of State for India and Burma, found that while he liked "the robust buccaneering spirit of modern American economic imperialism" he could see absolutely no reason why "it should be exercised at the expense of the British Empire."

It is [he said] against the British Empire, above all, that this policy is directed. That is why there is this insistence on our abandonment of Empire Preference, the least restrictive of all tariff arrangements in the whole world. That is the reason for the determination to break up the sterling system. The British Empire is the oyster which this loan is to prise open. Each part of it, deprived of the mutual support of Empire Preference, is to be swallowed separately, to become a field for American industrial exploitation, a tributary of American finance, and, in the end, an American dependency." He coud not "see the slightest chance, under the conditions of the proposed commercial agreement, of this country, deprived of preference, deprived of the bargaining power of our consumers' market, deprived of the expansionist effect of the sterling system on all its members, ever being able to pay its way, let alone paying back the loan."[93]

---

there were 3 Asiatics and 400 Africans." The Europeans (less than one-quarter of 1 per cent of the population) had 12 official and 8 nonofficial representatives, or 55 per cent of the total number; the Asiatics (roughly three-quarters of 1 per cent of the population) had 8 nonofficial representatives or 27½ per cent; and the natives (more than 99 per cent of the population) also had 27½ per cent of the nonofficial representatives. The *New Statesman and Nation* felt that this was real progress towards racial equality, and it may be. But both the natives, who are "suspicious of the settler's influence," and the Europeans are protesting. The former for obvious reasons, and the latter because "they discern here a sinister move on the part of the Labour Government to use constitutional arrangements 'as a cloak for the introduction of political principles, especially that of equality of racial capacity and responsibility' for which, they claim, the other races are unprepared." *Ibid.*

[93] Amery, *The Washington Loan Agreements*, p. xi.

Amery sees a common design running through the economic clauses of the Atlantic Charter, the lend-lease (mutual-aid) agreement, the financial agreement of 1946 (lending Britain $3,750,000,000) the Bretton Woods agreement, and the first preliminary agreement forecasting ECA under the Marshall Plan. All of these agreements carried provisions calling for world free trade, the absence of tariff barriers and preferential systems, equal access to raw materials, equal opportunities for expansion of trade and investment, and in general for equal rights of participation in all territories possessed by the parties to these agreements. There has subsequently been no retreat from this position. It runs through the International Trade Organization, the world food agreement, and the European Economic agreement.[94]

Persuasive, however, as the argument presented by Amery may be, and however impressively it may be supported by reference to American statements and compacts of one sort or another made between the United States and other parts of the world, it would seem that it must, to some extent or other, be out of focus. Were Amery's thesis correct British Labour could not expect to rely so heavily on American support as both a corollary and a condition to colonial development within the Empire.

Although there can be no certainty on any given point, the Labour view of Empire–United States relations may probably, with some faults of omission, be summarized about as follows: American aid can freely be accepted, and American private investment can freely be allowed, both within the Western European countries and their holdings, because American interest in promoting reconstruction and development in such areas in order to prevent the spread of communism is at least as great as is that of those countries themselves. Thus Britain has something to give which can hold occasional excessive American economic aggression in check, namely, the will to coöperate in what lies closest to American hearts. Otherwise, and more generally, the mutuality of interest that binds these countries and their empires together, and all of these with the United States, will necessarily override conflicts resulting from the national interests of the compacting parties. Hence Europe's need is America's opportunity—to save itself by saving Europe and Europe's imperial holdings.

The ideological part of this thesis is clearly a correct interpretation of the American attitude. The economic corollary seems merely naïve.

---

[94] For the appropriate passages in each of these agreements see appendix 8.

As economic determinists, American politicians and businessmen yield second place to few (their closest rivals might be the City and the Kremlin). A catalog of "American penetration" into Europe and her colonies will show that this is economic expansion old style, with no holds barred.[95] The attitude of the informed American private investor, trader, and searcher for new business outlets, resources, and opportunities abroad appears simply to be that of a person who consciously sees himself as the "senior partner" in whatever undertaking he wishes to go into. Not, however, because of egomania or for any abstruse reasons, but simply because he knows that he has the financial resources which the "junior partner" lacks. If, in addition, he feels that he has more technical knowledge and more of the necessary plant, machinery, equipment, and other developmental resources—which the American typically does—then he is doubly reassured of the role that he should play.

To the conservative Briton there is nothing in such an attitude that should, or which apparently does, surprise him. The attitude is merely an American version of the role which English business abroad pioneered, and which the American upstart has learned at the English knee. American belief in world free trade, with its corollary of equal access for Americans in all territories, domestic and imperial alike, of the Western European countries, is a more or less precise twentieth-century equivalent of the doctrines which Britain championed for itself throughout the nineteenth century. If it seems arrogant at times to the British, it will only be because of resentment that another should have come to play, with respect to them, the role which they have long taken to be their own in their relations with the rest of the world. The whip hand which is given to American expansion by the Marshall Plan and its corollary of preponderating strength in the military bloc which is being built up in Western Europe is no more nor less than an American equivalent of the whip hand which British capital has received for the past two centuries from Britain's control of the sea.

But why should Labour, too, accept American leadership with such apparent equanimity? There is, of course, a strong element of bowing to necessity. But the more basic answer seems to lie in Labour's acceptance of the interpretation of American policy which combines the Churchillian "mystic" of Anglo-Saxon world mission—in which the United States has now become the principal bearer of the oecumenical

[95] For a necessarily incomplete, but illustrative, listing, see appendix 9.

charisma—with a belief that American policy is of an essentially Rooseveltian New Deal hue. It is common practice in British Labour circles to compare British socialism with New Deal liberalism. (The Atlantic Charter and the Four Freedoms came from the discussions of Churchill and Roosevelt, but to Labour leaders they might have come just as well from the mouths of Cripps and Truman. There is no *idée fixe* regarding things American so strong as this in Labour circles.) In this general view, England has pioneered most reform and change, and America has followed. But occasionally, as for example, in monopoly control and national-resources planning, the United States has led the way. In some policies, such as the conferring of dominion status upon the colonies and the grant of political independence to the Philippines, the methods differ, but the underlying ideas are the same. So also is the general formula for maintaining economic stability. What the Labour party has proposed in its development councils is paralleled by the program of the American Committee for Economic Development, and the "planning" of the Minister of Economic Affairs in Britain finds its equivalent—in general outline and in basic theory—in the American President's Council of Economic Advisers. Keynes, Beveridge, Hansen—the transmitters of the tablets are the same.

There is no need to cite further examples. Not only does the idea exist that the similarities in philosophy and outlook override differences in application and phraseology, but it has been sedulously promoted by every propaganda means at the disposal of the Labour government. It has been generally concurred in by a large and growing number of both Americans and Britons; trade unionists most emphatically of all. Differences are generally treated as though they were of negligible importance, and at worst as the faults which are the usual accompaniment of first enthusiasms or of an immaturity which experience and time will ultimately correct.

The significance of this general attitude—represented in its clearest and strongest expression in the utterances and policies of Ernest Bevin—for Labour's Empire programs is not hard to decipher. In the generally accepted American view, one does not need to put colonial welfare first, since improved conditions and standards of life follow naturally in the wake of economic development. Thus, if American capital comes into the British colonies, social welfare need not be underscored heavily, since the economic development of the colonies will almost certainly carry with it the solutions to problems of disease, bad housing, malnutrition, and the like:[96] consider American policies in the Panama Canal Zone, Puerto Rico, and the Hawaiian Islands. The left wing of the British Labour party could not, of course, accept this view. But the right does, and it is the right wing of the Labour party which is shaping colonial policy.

There is only one large fly in this particular jar of ointment—the problem of race. What about the American attitude toward the Negro in the South? Can this be transplanted to Empire, and how can the Labour party tolerate American enterprise if it carries such policies with it? British Labourites answer this by saying that the joint Anglo-American statements made in the course of the war declared, directly and indirectly, for race freedom and equality. Furthermore, the FEPC movement in America has been watched both in London and in the Empire, and President Truman's attitude toward it carefully noted. And finally there is the fact—grudgingly conceded in Labour circles, but a fact which, once conceded, adds further weight to the case for American participation—that however bad American domestic policies towards the Negro may have been, their past overseas record in dealing with native peoples is incomparably better than that of Britain.

Out of elements such as these has gradually evolved a Labour rationale for Empire collaboration with America in which misgivings—

[96] This view has been stated so clearly by Louis Hacker in an inaugural address before the University of Oxford as the visiting Harmsworth Professor of American History that it requires no elaboration: "On the question of capital movements, Professor Hacker said that instead of constituting a malevolent force—as Lenin had it—they were one of the great civilizing agencies of the modern world. If used to effect the change-over from primary to secondary and tertiary production—to convert primitive agricultural societies into manufacturing economies; to inaugurate hydro-electric projects, erect steel furnaces, build railways, improve harbours, establish branch banks—capital movements in the process raised standards of living and made welfare realizable. The misery of the East was not due to the foreign capital that shattered its idyllic content; its misery continued because the West never had enough surplus funds to invest in this area where such a large part of the world's population was to be found.

"The whole theory of imperialistic exploitation could be disposed of easily enough by an examination of the experiences of Great Britain and the United States. In 1914 the long-term British investments oversea came to about £4,000m.; all but £300m. were publicly issued securities, or portfolio investments. Not much more than 30 per cent. of these holdings were to be found in regions of the earth where the exploitation of native peoples—because of political domination or interference—was possible. Nearly 70 per cent. of British portfolio investments were to be found in politically independent lands—where the investor entered at his own risk, and where standards of living were high rather than low. British capital had helped to raise those standards. The record of the United States had been similar.

"Capital formation—in the nineteenth and a part of the twentieth centuries—in still underdeveloped countries was helped through capital movements. That was one of the great roles England performed for more than 100 years; the United States, since World War I, had been seeking to follow in England's footsteps. Capital movements took place as a result of private initiative and the willingness to assume risks. With capital went engineers and chemists, physicians and teachers, periodicals and books; and the values of a civilization dedicated to the preservation of human freedom and individual integrity. These values Americans cherished and many knew that they came to flower in England." *Times*, Nov. 9, 1948.

although many still exist; some with bitter overtones—seem slowly to be yielding pride of place to assurances and a mild, if rather sad-eyed, new hope. The United States becomes the senior partner, and since it pays the piper it calls the tune. The efforts of the junior partner to achieve a viable future can succeed only with American aid both in the Empire and at home. The more successful these efforts the better the bargaining position of Britain within this new, greatly enlarged, and American-dominated Commonwealth of Nations. The pleasant surface of things remains unruffled; all the richly hued panoply of Imperial etiquette and the sentimental expressions of national sovereignty are maintained—at points reinforced. The British "meddling" which Robert Briffault, in his gleeful *Decline and Fall of the British Empire*,[97] expected to find increasing everywhere, may become more and more the hushed expression of a junior partner's interest in matters of mutual concern. But what of it? The result is a new symbiosis of reformed private enterprise (purged of monopoly), political democracy, and the Christian ethic. Toynbee—or at least Sir Stafford Cripps—is right after all!

At least, such appears to be the general position as it has gradually taken shape under the ambiguous guidance of Ernest Bevin, who is commonly and currently regarded (so the Scripps-Howard press has recently proclaimed) as "America's best friend." Lord Beaverbrook may object to what is happening for one reason, the British Communists for another, the Mosleyites for a third, and Labour's own left wing for a different reason still, but it appears to be happening nevertheless. This somewhat revised version of the Third Empire may possibly be able to retain more of real Empire than could otherwise be saved—and with it salvage at least some of the conscience of the erstwhile British Labour reformer. But it is also highly possible that the last historical paradigm of Empire-minded John Bull may be a man at least physically built for the part, Ernest Bevin, whose labors will succeed in avoiding the "liquidation of His Majesty's Empire" only the better to smooth the way for the United States to take it over. Perhaps the United States might do so with gusto, possibly with some reluctance, but most certainly not without strong opposition from within Labour and liberal American ranks. But take it over they might.

What then of the natives? Are they to be merely pawns in a new version of "big league" power politics? The Labour intentions are

[97] (New York, 1938.)

high-minded and their answer is clearly "no." But the picture is complicated, and the *Realpolitik* confused. "On political matters, there is an enormous amount of consultation going on—note the present constitutional discussions in Nigeria. In the working out of the ten-year development plans, many Colonies have drawn in Committee after Committee of local people to advise them (see the British Guiana ten-year plan). The point is made in every debate in Parliament; and in the individual 'community-development' plans in different parts of Africa consultation has gone down to the lowest levels. It is mainly in the big Development Corporation schemes—such as ground-nuts—that consultation has been entirely lacking, and there has been no lack of criticism on this point."[98] There can be no question that Labour takes its humanitarian mission in the Empire very seriously. It is pledged to consult with the natives not merely in minor things—as so frequently in the past—but on all major policies relating to native cultures and civilizations. But—as may very well happen, especially if the Colonial Office adopts the policies of the Foreign Office—should the time come when neither the ability nor the will to give consideration to the needs of the natives any longer exists, then the hoped-for development which might have saved the badly crippled homeland will be conditioned upon plans for native welfare made, not by Britons, but by persons— Americans, natives, or others—who have different objectives in mind.

---

[98] Dr. Rita Hinden in a letter to the author.

CHAPTER XV

Achievements and Prospects

This is the fourth year of our Labour Government. They have been four years of hard work and of solid achievements. We can look back with pride on the work we have done. We have battled courageously with the immense problems that are the aftermath of war. We have brought to fruition a splendid programme of social advancement. We have begun the tasks of laying the foundations of the new Britain. By the end of this year we shall be able to claim that we have implemented the programme upon which we were elected in 1945 ... The major task now confronting us is that of winning the fight for economic recovery ... When 1950 comes we shall be entitled to claim that we have been faithful to our trust.—James Griffiths, Labour Party Chairman (1948–49) and Minister of National Insurance, in a New Year Message to the Labour Movement, "The Challenge of 1949–1950," January, 1949.

BY THE MIDDLE of 1949 the attention of the Labour party was shifting from the records and achievements of its first five years in office to the political issues of the general elections of 1950, and with this to prospects and plans for another five years in which to build further on the foundations already laid. But to speak of "foundations" may be to employ a misleading figure, for the term has implications which it is difficult to reconcile with certain facts. If, for example, it is taken to mean a significant new social orientation, then it is the social security acts which Labour feels most clearly express the socialist outlook. Yet the central tenets underlying the new measures were not socialist in origin, nor do they involve any change in direction which must necessarily seriously divide the Labour party from its Liberal and Conservative opposition.

On the contrary, the main features of the several social security acts, as well as those of most of the other supporting social legislation, such as indicated in the Town and Country Planning Act, were based on reports and recommendations in the formulation of which leading members of the Opposition had participated, which had been supported and promoted by Conservative-dominated governments, and which had, like the American New Deal under President Roosevelt, been advocated not because they were seen as steps in the direction of socialism, but as buttresses to strengthen capitalist society against socialist attack. If we except steel, a parallel generalization holds for the other nationalization measures. All parties were agreed that there was no issue of principle involved in the nationalization of the Bank of England which had any important bearing upon the form or type of government, or which challenged the central theses underlying the cultural outlook of the contemporary British economic and social order. With minor exceptions, the same holds for the nationalization of the "natural-monopoly public utilities" of inland transport, overseas airways, cable and wireless, and the gas and electric industries.

In all, public ownership and operation had precedents both in Britain and abroad, and these precedents were not correlated with any given form of government or any specific party doctrine.[1] In coal the situation is somewhat less clear, but here the Labour government advanced no well-defined plan of its own. It dealt with what all parties agreed was a most extraordinarily critical emergency situation, but it acted on the basis of data supplied by the Conservative-minded Reid report and with a view to carrying out policies outlined in it. It also had before it the precedent of the nationalization of coal royalties which the Tories had decided upon in 1938. For coal, in short, a good—though not necessarily watertight—case could be made for saying that, when all factors were included, there seemed literally no alternative to nationalization if the needed and long-overdue reorganization of the industry was to be effected within the time limitations of the postwar recovery program. At least no other workable plan was forthcoming, and clearly without this quick recovery a viable future for Britain seemed out of the question. Furthermore, when the proposal for nationalizing coal was advanced, it was supported at few points by argument based on the more definitely socialist principles of public ownership of basic natural resources. As with land, which it was decided not to nationalize, rules of expediency, not principles, shaped the policies and divided the parties.

Such, however, was not true of steel. At least on the surface, nationalization of iron and steel looked entirely different, and it was the Labour government's announced determination to transfer this industry to public ownership which did most to strengthen the hostility of the more determined members of the Opposition to Labour's other nationalization measures. Yet at this point a number of elements bring the nature

---

[1] This is not to imply that the Opposition approved of the action taken, nor that if in power they would have moved in favor of the nationalization measures sponsored by the Labour government. But it is to say that they might have done so—the Central Electricity Board, the British Broadcasting Corporation, and the London Passenger Transport Board were all nationalized by Conservative governments—without involving any crucial question of principle or social doctrine which was in dispute between and among leading British political parties. For precedents in each case see the relevant foregoing chapters.

of the Labour government's intentions into question. While this and other nationalization measures were being proposed and carried through Parliament, Herbert Morrison—shortly supported by Sir Stafford Cripps and other Labour spokesmen—was giving wide currency to the idea that modern economic activity more or less naturally divided itself into two major segments, public and private. The former was to consist of roughly 20 per cent of the economic activity previously left to private enterprise, and private enterprise was to remain in indefinite—possibly permanent—possession of the balance. The former was the area of the "public utility" and the "natural monopoly," and it could be enlarged only by government initiation of a limited range of vitally necessary and common social services, such as health, social security, and town and country planning, which were not or could not adequately be supplied by private enterprise, or by nationalization of other "artificial monopolies" or nonmonopolized business activities, whenever these remained obdurately resistant, or unable for one reason or other (e.g., lack of the necessary capital resources) adequately to respond to the national need for enhanced production, or whenever they persisted, despite all efforts to dissuade them, in the pursuit of wage, price, or other policies that were clearly inimical to the public interest.

Under such conditions, the public sector might encroach upon the private sector, but only after the offending segment of the latter had plainly been warned that its continued existence was dependent upon its adoption of measures designed to extirpate the offense. These measures are clearly consonant with those assumed to govern business according to the accepted principles of the very same conventional economic theory[2] which so frequently appear to critics as mere apologia for the property and class sanctions that underlie capitalistic society as a whole. Furthermore, several of the most highly advertised sections of the Labour government's general program appear to be simple extensions of the position that apparently treats of nationalization as a mere last resort, and not as a facet of socialist principle at all. This is true of the Anti-Monopoly Bill; of such stuff is the concept underlying the whole development council plan and the various projects for overseas developments. A similar notion provides the *raison d'être* for the sup-

---

[2] As argued, for example, by J. E. Meade in his *Planning and the Price Mechanism* (London, 1948), in which he bases his position—which he describes as "Liberal-Socialist"— upon the experience of the American Antitrust Division. In this connection see also Corwin D. Edwards, *Maintaining Competition* (New York, 1949).

plementary finance corporations (originated by Conservative governments) set up under the auspices of the Bank of England, encourages the vast expansion of such special aids to private business as those given in the field of industrial research by the Department of Scientific and Industrial Research,[3] and even goes so far as to paralyze any desire on the part of the Labour government to encourage the extension of the coöperatives—or, for that matter, any other form of effective rationalization—in the overmanned, chaotic, and highly inefficient distributive trades.

It is against the background of such policies that the one major economic heresy of the Labour government, the nationalization of the iron and steel industry, must be examined, weighed, and appraised. The proposal appears to visualize a plan for reorganization of the industry, but no such plan accompanied the bill, nor has any subsequently been offered. At the very time when debaters in Parliament were denouncing the Iron and Steel Federation as a "monopoly" and a "cartel," strong efforts were being made to convert other large industries (most notably the cotton industry) into government-sponsored, cartel-like, monopolistic groupings. These latter plans, furthermore, were being promoted against a background of lethargy towards effective technical modernization which stood in sharp contrast to the plans of the iron and steel industry for modernization and rationalization. Although much emphasis was placed on the industry's lack of capital—which it was said the industry could not raise on its own initiative—to carry through its reorganization schemes, by the time the argument was advanced the industry was able to declare that it had the necessary resources in sight. Labour urged nationalization on the grounds that the government was already heavily subsidizing the industry out of public funds, yet at the same time it was offering an outright gift of one-quarter of the cost of all new machinery installations to the wholly private cotton textile industry.

There is, in short, ample paradox in this, and many other Labour government programs, to confound both supporters and opponents, and to confuse the outside observer. But it remains true, nevertheless, that the Opposition stayed no less suspicious and no less determined to resist any further "Labour advance." Part of this suspicion is occasioned by past and current professions of Labour leaders (outlined briefly in the first chapter of this book). Part arises from certain "logi-

---

[3] See chart 10.

cal" implications for further advance inherent in schemes already proposed for most of the nationalized and nonnationalized industries (sketched in previous chapters), and is further promoted by circumstances which appear to compel Labour to make some early and tentative efforts to proceed along past lines in the solution of certain of these problems. But most of it inheres in the nature of the achievements which Labour now feels it may chalk up to its credit as it nears the close of its first five years in office, and in the conditions and circumstances upon which depend future successes. And, strange and more paradoxical still, all of it tends less to be quieted than strengthened by Labour's announced program for the next five years—mild and half apologetic as that program may seem at first glance.

A brief summing up of achievements and further plans may aid in interpreting what has already been done.

First Objective: To Close the Import-Export Gap

Because this short-run, immediate, postwar, emergency problem came quickly to be seen as *the* precondition not only to the continued existence of Britain under any form of government, but also and especially, to the successful pursuit of any long-range change-over to a socialist society, it must be dealt with first. Here the statistical data are ample, comprehensive, and in many respects quite definitive. Furthermore, they are widely available to experts, and much of the material has been popularized in such a way as to reach large audiences both at home and abroad.[4] A few of the more important data have been condensed in tabular form, and appear in tables 1 to 10 in appendix 10 following.

The purpose of the long-term program, said the government's report on *European Co-operation,*[5] was to "detail the policies which the United Kingdom proposes to follow in order to 'achieve and maintain a satisfactory level of economic activity without extraordinary outside assistance' by 1952–53." This involved four major features: (1) expansion of the volume of exports (by value) to the equivalent of 150 per cent of the 1938 figure while holding imports to 15 per cent or less;[6] (2) in-

---

[4] Especially valuable are the annual *Economic Surveys*, for 1947 (Cmd. 7046), 1948 (Cmd. 7344), and 1949 (Cmd. 7647); the annual *Budget Statements*, and especially the reports of the Parliamentary debates, on budget proposals and the economic situation inaugurated in 1948—the 1949 debates on the 1949–50 budget ran over four days in the House of Commons, and take up 559 columns of *Hansard*; and the "four-year plan" incorporated in the memorandum, *European Co-operation, Memoranda Submitted to the Organization for European Economic Co-operation relating to Economic Affairs in the period 1949 to 1953* (Cmd. 7572)—also reproduced in the *Report of the E.C.A. Mission to the United Kingdom.*

[5] Cmd. 7572, p. 1.

[6] *Ibid.*, pp. 12, 41.

crease of the level of net invisible earnings to "much the same in value as they were in 1938" but with "their buying power in terms of imports" being "little more than one-third of that of 1938";[7] (3) general redirection of imports and exports away from dependence upon the Western "hard-currency" or "dollar-bloc" countries, and back to the "sterling area"; and (4) most important of all, such a reintegration of Britain into the postwar structure of world economy that she will be free to devote primary attention to domestic social reform and raising the home standard of living, and to take the leadership in the orderly development of her Imperial holdings.

The achievements and prospects along each of these lines seem to be about as follows. Exports at the end of 1948 were already running at the level of 147 per cent of 1938, and the target for the end of 1949 was set at roughly 160 per cent in terms of 1948 prices.[8] For the whole year they "were 25 per cent. above 1947 and were in volume the largest since 1929." Imports were up by some 4 per cent.[9] Thus exports were somewhat ahead of schedule, and imports were moving slightly in a direction opposite that planned. Favorable as this picture appears, yet as the subsequent devaluation demonstrated, the net outlook was distinctly not bright. For one thing, as previously mentioned, the "terms of trade" were continuing to move against Britain, being reckoned for the year at about 5 per cent, an amount equal to a worsening of the "balance on current account by some £100 million in a year."[10]

Although there were some reasons for believing that raw-materials prices abroad might continue to drop—like those of foodstuffs in North America—yet such factors as the combined westward and eastward expansion of the "iron curtain," which seems bound to curtail free access to Asiatic sources of raw materials,[11] industrialization of overseas territories (South American, African, Australasian, etc.) which favor home

---

[7] Including return on investments. *Ibid.*, p. 40.

[8] Cmd. 7647, table 8, p. 17.

[9] *Ibid.*, p. 4.

[10] *Ibid.*, p. 20. Decrease in the physical volume of imports and corresponding increase in the physical volume of exports more than counteracted the adverse terms of trade during this interval, converting a deficit of £150,000,000 for the first half of 1948 into a surplus of £30,000,000 for the second half of the year. *Ibid.*, p. 16.

[11] There has been, on the other hand, considerable revival of British sponsored east-west trade. Thus an agreement signed December, 1947, with the Soviet Union called for an exchange of 750,000 tons of grains for £20,000,000 worth of manufactured goods. A five-year agreement signed with Poland, January, 1949, provides for exchange of goods to the value of £150,000,000 by 1953—making Britain Poland's major customer. Similar agreements have been entered into with Finland (March, 1948,—£11,000,000) and other countries behind the "iron curtain." The leading difficulties in further extending these agreements appear to be prices and delivery terms—not ideological factors. "The Gap in the Curtain," *Fact: The Labour Party Bulletin*, March, 1949, pp. 34–35.

manufacture of home-produced raw materials, growing need of other Western European powers for these same raw materials and hence enhanced competition from them, and so on, were certain to prevent much further fall. In general, the world faces a long-run shortage of raw materials, not a surplus, and the more heavily a country is oriented to imports, the greater the chance of continuing adverse terms of trade so far as raw materials are concerned.

On the other side of the ledger, the *Economic Survey* for 1949[12] finds that "The limitations on exports in 1949 fall into three categories. First, there are difficulties of supply on our own part which prevent, in particular, any great expansion in the export of cotton goods, pottery, coal and metal goods. These difficulties derive generally either from manpower scarcity, e.g., in the cotton and pottery industries or from the rival claims of the home market. Secondly, there are the restrictions which other countries in balance of payments difficulties continue to place on the entry of a wide range of consumers' goods which form an important element in United Kingdom exports. Finally, there are the difficulties of finding buyers at our present selling prices." Of these three factors, the second shows little sign of decrease, but under any circumstances, correction lies beyond British control. This is not true of the first and the last. Here the problem is one of efficient production, and little further is to be expected along that line in the near future. It is, however, absolutely critical, and hence must be considered more at length later.

For invisible items, tables 1, *a* and *b*, appendix 10, show that although Britain's net surplus of £232,000,000 in 1938 had dropped to a deficit of £189,000,000 in 1947, the direction had been reversed in 1948, and it was anticipated that 1949 would bring a comfortable surplus of £35,000,000. Encouraging as this may seem, there is nothing either in the record or in any of the qualitative analysis which accompanies it which indicates the slightest hope of achieving the four-year plan objective of one-third (in terms of 1938 purchasing power) of the 1938 net invisible earnings of roughly £77,000,000. So long as world social unrest continues, there is no reason for believing that the spectacular overseas military expenditures will fall, and the very considerable offset from "war disposals and settlements" cannot continue much longer. Although some decline is to be anticipated in the smaller items of postwar relief, sums released here cannot begin to equal the

---

[12] Cmd. 7647, p. 18.

necessary expenditures for colonial welfare activities. Furthermore, revived imperial interest in Egypt, the Sudan, in holding Malaya and Hong-Kong, and in other overseas military adventures promise much expansion of nonrevenue items. There is increasing competition from foreign shipping interests, and Britain's temporary advantage here is rapidly melting away. So far as travel is concerned, British disbursements have always exceeded receipts and the debit balance is bound to increase for some time to come.[13] The outlook for further aid from the category of invisibles is depressing indeed.

With respect to the long-term program for achieving independence from the "hard currency" countries, on "the short run the problem of financing our essential dollar expenditure is solved with United States and Canadian help," and here the net deficit has been cut down some £600,000,000 within a year, or from a total of £1,024,000,000 in 1947 to £423,000,000 in 1948, and it was planned to further reduce it to under £400,000,000 in 1949.[14] "For the present," the *Economic Survey* goes on to warn, "but only for the present, E.R.P. aid and the Canadian credit enable us to meet this deficit, and to cover the other calls on our gold and dollar holdings, such as the requirements of countries in the rest of the sterling area, and the payments which we have to make to certain countries in Europe and elsewhere."[15]

This obligation, owed mostly on war account to Ireland, Egypt, India, Pakistan, and Ceylon, led to "unrequited exports" of $844,000,000 during 1948, a sum only slightly less than that which Britain received under ECA. The net effect is "that E.C.A. aid is funneled through the British economy to outside recipients and are an important part of the explanation why the expansion of British exports since the war has been so much towards the sterling area and so little, in comparison, towards the dollar area."[16]

Furthermore, ECA aid declined from $1,263,000,000 in 1948–49 to $940,000,000 in 1949–50, and to anybody familiar with the general trend of thinking in the American Congress it is evident that further curtailment may be even more severe.

---

[13] Primarily for two reasons: (a) the internal pressure for increased travel allowances for Britishers is already proving to be politically irresistible, and (b) any large-scale expansion of tourist traffic in Britain is doomed so long as hotel accomodations and food remain generally dismal, costly, and are tendered with indifference or even hostility—in sharp and growing contrast to conditions on the Continent.

[14] *Ibid..* p. 28, and table 16 (reproduced as table 5, appendix 10 following).

[15] *Ibid.*, p. 18. Italicized in the original.

[16] John H. Williams, "The British Crisis," *Foreign Affairs*, Oct., 1949.

But even should it be made available, the real problem for Britain is to decrease imports from the hard-currency area, while correspondingly increasing its exports. The percentage decline in imports has been marked, the "total payments for imports" from the Western Hemisphere dropping from 46 per cent in 1947 to roughly 33 per cent in 1948, and a further drop to 28 per cent was anticipated for 1949.[17] Contrariwise, the "Volume of Exports of United Kingdom Produce" to the United States has been upped from an index figure (1938 = 100) of 94 for 1947 to 139 for the latter half of 1948. A further rise to 150 was forecast for the first half of 1949.[18]

These plans were overoptimistic. By mid-summer of 1949 it was evident that the international seller's market had disappeared. British sales in the United States were rendered more difficult by the growing domestic competition of American manufacturers who were already being faced with falling prices for important products, and rising unemployment. Simultaneous weakening of the pound's position, which led to its devaluation in September, 1949, offered some short-run stimulus for British sales in America, but the increased dollar deficit also encouraged the launching of a British policy for cutting imports from America 25 per cent or more. It seems highly doubtful that American manufacturers will stand idly by (particularly as long as the United States is granting such large sums under the ERP recovery program) while Britain employs these seemingly inescapable stratagems for improving her trade position in the dollar area. This is true even though the devaluation was apparently forced by American pressure. An augury of American sentiment on this score was to be found in the negotiations over the renewal of American film contracts, and the resentment aroused by the acute depression in the American film industry which British curtailment of film imports has helped to bring about. There have been other straws in the wind, chief among which is Hoffman's desire to reconsider the conditions under which ERP aid is extended with a view to promoting further markets for American products in the sterling area.

But far more serious is the British belief that in the face of this situation they can continue to find expanding markets for their products in the United States and Canada. Not, however, serious merely because of British restriction of American imports, but also because of the pro-

---

[17] *Ibid.*, table 12, p. 21 (reproduced as table 6, appendix 10, following).
[18] *Ibid.*, table 10, p. 19 (reproduced as table 2, appendix 10, following).

hibitively high prices of British products, which must meet the competition of American mass-produced goods. As pointed out in chapter xiv, the British are at a large and apparently growing disadvantage not only in domestic American markets, but in any markets in which they must compete with mass-produced goods from America, Germany, Japan, and other modern industrial countries. High American tariffs and import restrictions, which there seems to be no disposition to remove, further worsen the prospect for British sales in the United States. It seems necessary to conclude that prospects for success of this third point in the long-term program are not very bright; that here again they rest largely on Britain's capacity to lower prices by greatly improving her industrial efficiency.

Finally, the reintegration of Britain's economy with world economic development in order that attention can be turned to raising and improving domestic standards of living, and, as a partial corollary at least, to beginning large-scale economic and social developments in the colonial empire, depends upon her capacity to solve the other problems sketched out above—particularly so long as she remains committed to multilateralism in international trade.[19] Should she renounce this movement towards ultimate free trade in favor of bilateral trade agreements—and there has been considerable internal pressure for doing precisely this on the grounds that "free trade" is a good policy for the strong, but a poor one for the weak—then the situation would be greatly altered.

As for Empire development, it is not necessary to recapitulate the argument of the preceding chapter. Suffice it to say that under the Organization for European Economic Cooperation, and other understandings, e.g., the Bermuda agreement on telecommunication, the United States is gaining equal rights in Empire development at precisely the time when Britain lacks, and the United States possesses, an abundance

---

[19] "How fast the United Kingdom will be able to modify its own trading and financial policies in the direction of a more complete multilateralism depends upon a number of factors outside its control. No multilateral system can work while large disequilibria exist in important trading countries' balance of payments either in the creditor or debtor sense. The necessary structural changes have to be made in each country's pattern of production, consumption and trade before a sound multilateral system can be firmly established." Cmd. 7472, p. 14. Thus even solution of the problem of low-cost production may not help Britain to improve its import-export situation at all, for its over-all impact might be simply to create other "disequilibria," such as the highly publicized British policy of pushing sales of her exports in France while curtailing French imports to the maximum—a policy tending to worsen the French import-export balance, and to strengthen the tendency to take retaliatory measures—or at any rate to promote autarchic policies in areas attempting newly to industrialize—both in raw materials supply areas (e.g. the Argentine) and among industrial competitors.

of the vitally necessary resources required to launch development in these areas, and that Britain may be able to spare capital resources for the needed developments only if she can solve the problems previously discussed in such a way as to provide the necessary surpluses. However important Empire development may be to British recovery, Britain must first produce the capital surpluses needed for that development, and this necessarily means production at such high levels of efficiency that she can earn her way in international markets against the competition of American and other industrial systems more or less fully oriented on a mass-output basis. Furthermore, however much the British may protest that they are being asked to sign a pact with "Uncle Shylock," it seems clearly evident that no important American resources will be placed at Britain's disposal for development purposes unless adequate political guarantee of both principal and interest can be given. This guarantee cannot be given for the more important colonies, and the aid, accordingly, is not forthcoming—President Truman's "bold new program" to the contrary notwithstanding, American investment in the colonies is not expanding and gives no prospect of doing so in the near future.

To summarize: whatever else Britain must do to insure a viable future, she must solve the problem of productive efficiency before the import-export gap can be closed. It does not follow that if this problem alone were solved satisfactorily the future would be assured (e.g., it would not solve the problem of the dollar gap) but it does seem certain that without its solution satisfactory resolution of all other problems will still leave her situation beyond repair. In this sense, the problem of production is absolutely critical, and upon its solution all other questions of recovery and future progress necessarily rest.

SECOND OBJECTIVE: TO SOLVE THE PROBLEM OF PRODUCTION

From a technical and economic point of view, the key to this problem would appear to lie in the rate of gross capital formation. The four-year program places the yearly national figure "at current prices at about $8,500 millions of fixed investment" at home, which, together with "the claims of overseas investment for colonial and other development within the sterling area . . . will account for 20 per cent. of the gross national product."[20] Although, as pointed out above, much of this represents repair of war damage, and compensation for low levels of

[20] Cmd. 7572, p. 32.

prewar and wartime investment, still the rate is nominally very high, and it was intended to adapt the utilization of these resources to a pattern of national economic development which would greatly enhance Britain's competitive position. The intention was to concentrate on the following purposes:[21]

 a) the expansion of home agriculture and fisheries;

 b) the development of basic industries, particularly steel, coal, oil, basic chemicals and cement, in order to make possible the unfettered expansion of industrial production;

 c) the strengthening of the public utility services where necessary, particularly electricity, transport and port services, in order to support the expanding level of industrial activity;

 d) the modernization of industrial equipment so as to increase the volume and reduce the cost of production;

 e) the development of new raw materials and alternative sources of supply for existing raw materials at home, in the Colonies and elsewhere overseas;

 f) the removal of shortages of widely used basic products, such as ball bearings, precision chain, refractories;

 g) the stimulation of industrial research;

 h) the provision of essential services, such as housing, and of basic social services, such as water, health services and education (particularly on the technical side), which contribute to the nation's economic strength.

In pursuance of these objectives, and "excluding ordinary maintenance of houses and miscellaneous small works" the available investment resources were to be distributed, over the four-year period, about as follows:

Investment	Per cent
Fuel and Power	15
Transport and Communication	18
Agriculture	6
Industry (including Iron and Steel and Shipbuilding)	33
Housing	16
Social Services (Water Supplies, Health, Education, etc.)	7
Defense and Public Administration	5
Total	100

Thus roughly one-half (48 per cent) was to be spent on industrial modernization, 6 per cent on the promotion of a higher degree of agricultural self-sufficiency, 18 per cent on transport and communication

---
[21] *Loc. cit.*

modernization, and 28 per cent on what might be regarded as the "social overhead." Excluding the last—which will be dealt with in the following section—the problem is not merely whether the actual amounts to be spent are adequate, but whether the expenditures will be of such a character as materially to raise man-power productivity. A very high percentage of this investment is directly subject to government guidance, yet in speaking of current expenditures the government's official estimates paint a very gloomy picture. Despite gross capital formation at the record-breaking level of 20 per cent of national income, the increased productivity anticipated for the budget year 1949–50 had already dropped to $2\frac{1}{2}$ per cent over the preceding year—from an estimated 12 per cent for 1947–48[22]—and this $2\frac{1}{2}$ per cent is roughly the estimated annual rate of secular long-run growth in British output before the Second World War. This long-run figure includes some of the years of Britain's industrial heyday, but also many years of slowly creeping economic stagnation and industrial paralysis. If it can be taken to forecast the rate of growth of productivity, British production will clearly be no more able to meet the demands of the future than it is those of the present.

But estimates and generalities such as these prove little. What is generally lacking, and is urgently required, is detailed and exhaustive examination of the current status and future prospects of British industry in terms of potential contribution to productive efficiency from each of four principal factors: (1) *Research,* which determines the scale, quality, and use of the "cutting edge" of industrial change and improving efficiency. (2) *Standardization,* which may supply the most important single precondition to the orientation of raw materials supply, processes of manufacture (plant specialization, flow production, automatic machinery, etc.), and products on a thoroughgoing mass-output basis. (3) *Scientific management,* which should explore the possibilities of organizing personnel in mass-output industry in keeping with sound psychological laws, and at the same time galvanizing interest and arousing a positive enthusiasm throughout all layers of working cadres, from top echelons to bottom ranks, in problems of production and the more efficient use of severely limited domestic

---

[22] It seems impossible to discover just how these figures are arrived at. There appears to be no well-established index upon which they are based, and no clear-cut explanation of how the estimates are computed has ever been made public. When this question was raised in the House of Commons by Captain Lyttelton for the Opposition, no explanation was forthcoming. See *Hansard,* Vol. 463, col. 2670. For the distribution of total capital investment by source (government and private) see table 5, appendix 10, following.

natural resources. (4) *Industrial location and development,* under which plans for reorganization of given industries, and the entire range of industries over given areas, can be worked out in such a way that they permit and promote the maximum degree of plant specialization consonant with a minimum of cross-hauling while maintaining appropriate local, regional, and national industrial balances. Plans must also make provision for coördination and unification of industrial development at each stage and in each area with plans for housing, town and country planning, provision of necessary social services, and so on.

Of these four modes of attack on industrial arteriosclerosis, the current British record on research is clearly the best, quite possibly because research meets few obstacles which increased expenditures may not overcome. But even here there was much to be done.

A report of the Parliamentary and Scientific Committee,[23] estimated the expenditure on research in the United States to be ten times that of the United Kingdom. Viscount Samuel drew attention in the House of Lords[24] to the National Research Council's figure of 2,200 laboratories in American industry employing 70,000 scientists at an annual cost of £60 millions. British industry on the other hand, according to the report of the Federation of British Industries' Industrial Research Committee[25] was employing in 1928 some 5,000 scientists at an annual cost of £5½ millions. This same report pointed out the imposing record of British research achievement and that the majority of industries upon which modern civilization rests were originated in this country. H. M. Tory, in an address to the Canadian Club in Ottawa in 1943, estimated Russian Annual expenditure on research at between £75 millions and £125 millions in 1934. Bernal[26] set the United States expenditure at £75 millions in 1935, and the Association of Scientific Workers,[27] gave the British expenditure as £7½ millions in 1934.[28]

On a per capita basis, Sir Harold Hartly[29] in 1943 "quoted Russian expenditure on scientific research at 1.0 per cent. of the national income, American at 0.3 per cent. and British at 0.1 per cent."

Expenditures, however, are not only a qualitatively "poor guide to the output of research," but frequently the manner in which research is organized makes it virtually impossible to estimate the actual outlays for this purpose. A further difficulty in the present connection is that

---

[23] *Scientific Research and the Universities in Post-War Britain,* Oct., 1943.
[24] July 15, 1943.
[25] *Industry and Research,* Oct., 1943.
[26] *The Social Function of Science* (London, 1939).
[27] *Proceedings,* Jan., 1943.
[28] Douglas W. Hill, *Co-operative Research in Industry* (London, 1946). The footnote references in this passage are Hill's.
[29] *Are you Research Minded,* cited *ibid.*

such data as exist have not been brought up to date and it is therefore difficult to evaluate the role of research in Labour's program. In general, however, it is certainly true to say that the war gave an immense impetus to industrial research, and that the range and variety of organized research now under way in Great Britain[30] indicates a vivid appreciation of its role in the economic life of the country and a determination on the part of the present Government greatly to expand efforts along this line.

Among other things, this intention is evidenced by attempts to expand and correlate government-financed research, by the giving of special aid and assistance to promote research in private industry, and by the setting up of the Anglo-American Council on Productivity. Government financed research is applied and promoted "through three main organizations, the Department of Scientific and Industrial Research, the Medical Research Council and the Agricultural Research Council. A growing amount of research related to specific and practical problems is done by or under the auspices of particular departments such as the Ministry of Works, the Ministry of Food and the Ministry of Supply."[31] Most of the ministries now have scientific advisory services which work very closely with the three main organizations. Each of the latter has a most comprehensive coverage of facilities, laboratories, and subject matter; works in close coöperation with universities and other research facilities, public and private; issues a wide range of technical and scientific magazines, brochures, tracts, specialized reports, etc.

Under the Labour government there was set up in January, 1947, the advisory Council on Scientific Policy, shortly reinforced by the Committee on Industrial Productivity. The council was charged with the broad task of promoting and correlating scientific work throughout Great Britain,[32] and is directly responsible to the Lord President of the

[30] See, e.g., the comprehensive manual and handbook, Percy Dunsheath, ed., *Industrial Research* (London, 1948), covering government, university, special-endowment, trade-association and private industrial and other laboratories for the whole of Great Britain. This manual is reissued annually, and is an indispensable source of information. Also useful are the books, *Science and the Nation* (London, Pelican, 1947), *DSIR, A Description of the Work of the Department of Scientific and Industrial Research,* (HMSO, 1946), and *Scientific and Technical Research in British Industry, A Statistical Survey by the FBI Industrial Research Secretariat* (Federation of British Industries, 1947).

[31] *Home Affairs Survey,* July 20, 1948, p. 43.

[32] Specifically, it was charged with the duties of effecting an appropriate organization, and making due arrangements for "scientific research within the Government with special reference to research on building and on fuel and power; an adequate flow of scientific manpower to meet the needs both of Government and of industry; the appropriate form of research effort to assist the maximum increase in national productivity during the coming decade"; and especially to promote oceanographic research. *Ibid.*

Council, Herbert Morrison. The same holds for the Committee on Industrial Productivity.[33] Of the agencies with which they work, the DSIR is the most important, and through this department—established during the First World War—they are brought into direct contact with industrial research throughout the entire country. Much of this research is directly subsidized by the DSIR. Some of it has been brought into close contact with the special working-party investigations of various industries undertaken under the auspices of the Board of Trade and other departments. Here, as with the Anglo-American Council on Productivity, the only thing that can be said at present is that interest in the bearing of this research on problems of productivity is running fairly high, and that the use of methods of international comparisons, and of pooling of industrial knowledge is very definitely encouraging.[34]

Nevertheless it remains true that in all this, "something," as the Lord President said rather sorrowfully when reviewing the first annual report of the Advisory Council, "is still badly wrong. The trouble is not with British science, which by and large still leads the world, but with our understanding and use of science."[35] The difficulty, he felt, was lack of "trained men . . . to translate scientific discoveries from something in the laboratory into something which you and I can use by pressing a button or pulling a lever." But this places too great emphasis on a minor part of the problem. The difficulty is only to a small extent lack of personnel; on the record the major obstacles are the indifference, even resistance, shown by both government and industry to the adoption of new techniques, and the failure to comprehend the requirements and implications of mass production methods.

At the forefront stands the problem of standardization. Since an extended discussion of this very important problem is not possible here, it will suffice to point out that although Britain has the oldest and one of the best and most comprehensive central standards-formulating or-

[33] "The Committee, set up under Sir Henry Tizard, was asked to tell the Government how research and its application could most quickly increase productivity so as to decrease imports and raise exports. The main work of the Committee has been done through four panels—on technology and operational research, imports, substitution, human factors affecting industrial productivity, and technical information services." Summary of the committee's first annual report, *Home Affairs Survey*, April 4, 1949, p. 14.

[34] It is anticipated that some fifty teams from various industries would visit the United States during the first six-months operation of the plan. Workers and employers are both to be represented. Each team is to consist of a technical group, a supervisory group, a workshop group, and a secretary. Each team program will last about three and a half months and consist of approximately two weeks preliminary visiting of British factories, two weeks oceanic travel, six weeks in the United States, and four weeks subsequent discussion. *Ibid.*

[35] *Home Affairs Survey*, July 27, 1948, p. 39.

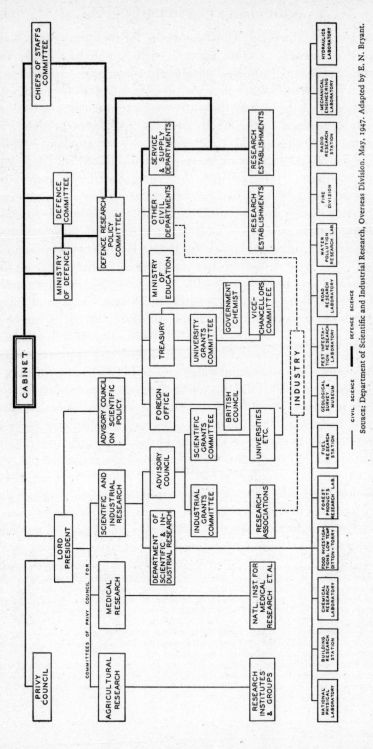

Chart 10. Official Scientific Organization in the United Kingdom.

Source: Department of Scientific and Industrial Research, Overseas Division. May, 1947. Adapted by E. N. Bryant.

ganizations in the world in her British Standards Institution,[36] she still lags far behind in the actual application of standards to many important lines of manufacturing, particularly in the consumers' goods field.

There are many reasons for this, and most come to focus in the fact that it has long been true that "as compared with other countries, especially with the United States and Germany, the size of undertaking in many branches of English industry is relatively small."[37] According to the Central Statistical Office,[38] the last census figures (1935) on "Size of Establishments in Factory Trades" showed 132,338 out of 181,282 establishments, or 73 per cent, with 10 employees and under. They employed 536,600 out of 5,694,200, or a little over 10 per cent of all persons attached to the "Factory Trades." Conversely, there were only 533, or roughly 0.3 per cent, of the total number of establishments with 1,000 or more employees, although they engaged 1,105,900, or roughly 20 per cent, of the total number of persons employed. When small size is combined with low horsepower consumption per worker, we have a picture of industry dominated by handicraft, or semihandicraft plants, practices, and habits.[39] Although wartime concentration schemes of one sort or another[40] did a great deal to improve this situation in a number of lines of production, improvement was largely confined to a scattered fringe of consumer industries,[41] and its over-all effect upon

---

[36] It is impossible in short space, adequately to summarize even the broad outlines of its operation. A good, though to the layman largely unintelligible, beginning is to glance through any recent *Yearbook on British Standards*, published by the British Standards Institution.

[37] Hermann Levy, *Monopolies, Cartels, and Trusts in British Industry* (London, 1927), p. 207.

[38] *Annual Abstract of Statistics*, No. 84, 1935–46, table 145, p. 123.

[39] I am indebted to Professor Sargent Florence (letter to the author, September 19, 1949) for the following comment: "It is the horse-power per man that differs and not the number of men per plant. You say that 10 per cent of all persons are employed in England in establishments of 10 and under. Unfortunately, the American and British censuses use different size intervals, but they coincide in taking workers per plant as the class limit. If we use this as a criterion, the American census gives about 30 per cent of workers in plants employing 100 and less, British census 35 per cent." There are no comprehensive postwar data on horsepower per worker. Using prewar data, Rostas found that "factory trades" in Britain used 2.83 units of installed horsepower per worker in 1930, while the comparable American figure for 1929 was 4.91 per worker. For these same years, furthermore, 66.2 per cent of the power was applied electrically in Britain and about 79 per cent fell into this classification in the United States. Postwar data, such as it is, would seem to indicate a still greater disparity. See Rostas, *op. cit.*, pp. 52–55.

[40] A fairly complete résumé of these schemes is given in *Concentration of Consumer Industries and Trade in Britain* (British Information Service, 1943). The situation remained substantially unaltered thereafter.

[41] As may be seen from the record. Applied to some 50 industries, it released by the middle of 1943 some 270,000 workers, and resulted in the closing down of some 3,000 plants. *Home Front Handbook* (1943), p. 14. Roughly 50 per cent of British war production came out of plants employing 50 persons or less.

postwar production methods—aside from the highly important, but narrowly limited, range of utility goods—must have been comparatively slight.

Though the effect of a lack of standards on distribution is mostly indirect, and though it may be overshadowed by other factors, yet small-scale, specialized manufacturing in Britain is paralleled by similar fractioning of the retail trades into a vast and bewildering variety of small, local, man-power absorbing, and relatively high-cost and low-efficiency retail shops, which favor endless product differentiation. Ministry of Labor data in 1939 listed some two million insured workers in the distributive trades, but these figures do not include noninsured groups, nor the commercial staffs of manufacturing establishments. Thus in 1931 the total number of persons engaged in distribution was estimated at some 5,375,000, or more than 25 per cent of the 21,075,000 total labor force.[42] It is not believed that either the depression or the war materially or significantly thinned these ranks.

The practices that attend this general lack of standards are generally and almost uniformly wasteful of man power and raw materials, and frequently affect both the quality and usability of the product itself.[43] Furthermore, they consolidate into the normal functioning of the economic system a vast range of useless activities, many of which may be classed, to employ one of Ruskin's phrases, not as "wealth, but as 'illth.' "[44] But however great the need for expanding the scope of the

---

[42] Distribution, The Case for a National Census, Fabian Publications, Research Series No. 108 (London, 1946), p. 9

[43] It is part of the generally accepted British commercial idiom that standards mean uniformity, lack of aesthetically desirable variety, etc., but this position involves, nevertheless, a total misunderstanding of the meaning, scope, intent, and implications of a properly conceived system of standards—which has as its central functions (a) to orient all subthreshold-of-taste output on a low-cost and efficient mass-production footing, (b) to go into the area where taste and discrimination count only by way of submitting possibilities of command and control (aesthetic, etc.) over materials otherwise wholly unattainable, and (c) to relate the structure of supply, through techniques of specification drafting, to the structure of clearly defined use. The over-all effect is to pull down costs, and not only not to destroy variety, but to make expansion of variety possible on an intelligible and functional basis—including all phases of consumer preferences.

[44] For example, a 1946 report by the National Institute of Social and Economic Research for the Advertising Association, The Statistics of Advertising, found that manufacturers' expenditures for advertising ranged as a percentage of sales between 3 and 60 per cent in the following typical lines: tobacco, household stores, entertainment, vehicles, and accessories. In the "toilet and medical groups manufacturers' advertising amounted in many cases to about half the value of sales," and "in the case of medical goods advertising appeared to represent about a quarter of the value of the consumers' purchases." Economic Record, November 13 and 23, 1946. Supply in all of these fields is short. The advertising data was almost wholly confusing, irrelevant, or downright misleading. Hence advertising here is merely idle overhead for the community as a whole under even the best of circumstances. But in the field of patent drugs, nostrums, and quackeries—which enjoy a huge home market, despite the medical program—this is mostly little more than mere "illth." Yet it absorbs man power, materials (billboards, newspaper space, etc.) on a very large scale.

work of the British Standards Institution,[45] an equally, and possibly even greater shortcoming in the current British production effort—notwithstanding notable exceptions—is the general, pervasive, and well-nigh uniform neglect of most of the central and generally accepted canons and practices of scientific management.

This is true despite the fact that "by 1935 Great Britain was equipped with professional or semi-professional institutions covering every aspect and function of modern management,"[46] and despite the existence of a considerable number of British firms whose practices will compare with the best[47] and the tendency to lay heavy stress on management during the war. Here again, the problem is coincident with the smallness of the typical manufacturing and retail unit, but it is by no means restricted to small operations. The neglect is general even within the newly nationalized industries, where there is frequently—as in the Coal Board—a pronounced tendency to scoff at the whole problem, nor does the import of what is at stake appear to be understood by top Labour government officials except in the vaguest and most general sense of the term. There was little direct reference to scientific management in most of the reports of the working parties set up under auspices of the Board of Trade to inquire into the ways and means of modernizing British industries, and it is only with difficulty that an investigator can bring the typical British businessman to discuss the subject at all.

The Labour government has made one promising gesture in this direction by the establishment in 1947 of a British Institute of Management,[48] but it has almost wholly neglected the Institute thereafter. When visited in the summer of 1948, it was found to possess a small, competent, but badly discouraged skeleton staff, to be proceeding without benefit of operationally meaningful directives, and to be, in effect, without duties, functions, or obligations of moment which extended beyond making an annual report. Yet not a little, but a very great deal indeed, needs to be done. The working-party report on cotton textiles, in summarizing conditions in the industry, said,[49] "As a result of these

---

[45] See, e.g., the suggestions to this effect in the speech by Ian Mikardo during the 1949 budget debates, *Hansard*, Vol. 463, cols. 2718–2719.

[46] L. Urwick, *The Development of Scientific Management in Great Britain*. A Report prepared for the British Management Council, June 7, 1938.

[47] For a recent, and quite comprehensive review, see L. Urwick and E. F. J. Brech, *The Making of Scientific Management* (London, 1945). 2 vols.

[48] Based upon "The Report of a Committee appointed by the President of the Board of Trade in November, 1945, to formulate detailed proposals for setting up a Central Institute for all questions connected with Management," entitled, *A Central Institute of Management* (HMSO, 1946).

[49] Reference is also made to this conclusion by Mikardo, in *Hansard*, Vol. 463, cols. 2719–2720.

studies we were led to the conclusion that the first need was not for new or improved equipment, nor for further technical research, but rather for a concerted effort to apply the principles of good organization and deployment of labour over an increasing range of firms." The *Economic Survey for 1949* added the solemn warning that *"Our recovery will never be complete unless we can develop a keen and adventurous spirit in management and a readiness to welcome new and improved methods by labour."*[50]

The whole range of problems involved in scientific management are closely and intimately interlaced with the problem of industrial location and development. It will not be necessary to add much to what has been said on this point in several previous chapters. So far as industry in general is concerned, the iron and steel industry and the cotton textile industry are probably typical. In these industries there is (along with a host of other difficulties) little vertical integration and relatively little modern plant specialization,[51] and they lack many other of those features which characterize a scientifically laid out complex of interdependent industrial plants.

The problems of these two industries are directly or indirectly related (1) to location of plants within the region, (2) to the location and distribution of housing, transport facilities, social amenities, etc., for all regions, large and small, and (3) to whatever scheme exists, or which at some remove or other must exist, to relate industries, populations, and facilities of localities to regions, and of regions to the nation. Virtually no broad, national planning, and little regional planning, for industrial location has been done in Britain. What plans exist are badly confused. Nearly all tangible and workmanlike plans like those for the trading estates in the development areas—have strictly local applications. But, as pointed out in previous chapters, for all transportation, for most major industries, and for many minor industries, the local problem of industrial location cannot be solved in its restricted frame

[50] *Op. cit.*, p. 44. Italics in the original.
[51] That is, plant specialization that is integrated with preceding and following operations, such regard being had for location of raw materials and markets as to permit a maximum of free, continuous, flow on a mechanized, or semimechanized basis throughout all stages, and that the unit—plant, stage, or machine—is at all points, at or near "optimum size." This latter is never wholly clear-cut, being a compound of various elements—physical size, proportioning of factors, structure of policies lying behind factor prices, etc.—which may change rapidly from time to time. Nevertheless these are the general terms which give meaning to mass production, and which leave most of even the specialized modern British industrial plants in a state of arrears. Such, e.g., is the condition of the otherwise very advanced British machine tool industry, as may be seen by examining the recent (1949) special survey published by the London *Times*.

of reference with any expectation that detailed and separately arrived-at local decisions will add up to an industrial structure which is capable of meeting the needs of the nation. The benign demiurge whose pervasive influence, *hinter den Kulissen* of the atomistically organized society, bent the individual and self-seeking will to subserve, willy-nilly, the larger interest of the community, has long abandoned his former calling, and is not to be induced to return to old haunts merely because society needs a helmsman to guide local committees through the intricacies of Robert's Rules of Order.

This is not to imply, of course, that it is not highly desirable to arouse a sense of local participation, and to stimulate a capacity for taking the initiative at the "grass roots." Quite the contrary. But it is to say that solution on a local basis—with most of the detailed decisions being worked out primarily with reference either to strictly local considerations or to the problems of individual industries (as contemplated in the various working-party reports)—is no solution at all, and on the current showing seems bound to add further to the confusion, misproportion, and general inefficiency of the British industrial system. So far, also, as most of the other factors making for industrial and commercial efficiency are dependent upon solution of the problem of location, they too rest upon the existence of some over-all national plan and in the absence of such a plan are likely to add little or nothing to the improvement of the existing situation. Yet there is no evidence at all of the existence of any such national plan. It seems wholly gratuitous to comment that aspirations and hopes—even the setting of "targets," when implemented by no more than adjectival benefit of clergy—do not constitute planning, and where objectives are pursued with the aid of no more than uncorrelated and unrelated encouragements or negative controls the most prodigious labors may yield little more by way of tangible achievements than did the endless tribulations of the Danaïdes.

In short, the outlook for achieving the second major objective of the Labour government's postwar program—the solution of the problem of production—does not appear on present showing to be very bright. That is, it is not now, and it is not likely to be, bright unless and until there occurs a drastic change of attitude among Labour leaders and their following toward the key production problems which beset postwar Britain. Until this happens, and until there occurs with it a drastic shift in emphasis, followed by a vigorous, sustained, interstitially well-balanced, and—in larger outlines at least and especially in the initial stages—centrally directed program of action which is carried out on a national basis, and of such a character that it is capable of arousing popular enthusiasm for widespread participation at all levels, the leaden pace of the current effort will surely remain unaltered. And unless it is soon altered, it will almost surely be found that the present rapid and encouraging (though actually in large part illusory) gross capital formation may, so far as significant rationalization of British productive methods are concerned, mean only that water has been poured down a bottomless well.

Much, possibly the greater part, of this new investment represents compensation for underinvestment, or even downright disinvestment, in the past. This is unavoidable. But, also, most of what is being spent— as for example, in the cotton and steel industries—comes out of high early depreciation allowances, and is being used to apply patchwork to worn-out, or obsolescent, or badly located, or vertically unintegrated, or otherwise technologically and economically bad plants. Most of it, consequently, can provide no more than "shots in the arm" with which to revive momentarily an industry already caught in the vicelike grip of production-inhibiting control and cartel-like policies[52]—for which the new antimonopoly legislation is a weak antidote indeed. Yet so far as research in general, and so far as standardization in important lines of heavy production are concerned, the situation is relatively favorable, and the potenial gains from further extension of both are surely very great, and should not require the expenditure of much additional money and effort.

But—in spite of notable exceptions—the situation with respect to standardization of consumers' goods,[53] the extension of scientific management, and the problems of industrial location and development, is distinctly bad. In the main, it is as bad in the newly nationalized industries as in those left under private management—and only in part because of the physical heritage, although this in itself was certainly

---

[52] "—British industry has grown very rigid and is kept in its present form and structure, which is in many ways quite unsuitable for the new trading position of the country, by a conspiracy of controls and regulations, cartels and trade associations, trade union practices and general prejudices against enterprise and change. So long as these obstacles to change persist productivity will remain low and the nation will be working with one arm in a sling." *British Industry in 1948: A Manchester Guardian Survey.* (Reprinted from the *Manchester Guardian*, March, 1948.)

[53] Perhaps the outstanding example of successful standardization in this field is the production of various lines of utility goods. Unfortunately, although many designs are quite good and a fair amount of variety has been introduced, the general tendency has been to associate such standardization with emergency conditions, goods scarcity, uniformity, lack of aesthetic qualities, etc.

enough of an incubus to stay the hand of all but the most stout-hearted. It is bad primarily because of the failure to see; or seeing, because of the failure to plan; or planning, because of the failure to do so in terms of some of the most important parameters of the problem of industrial development and balance.

Among these parameters, however, are a number which are indissolubly linked with the necessity for solving the social problem. And here one faces a triple paradox: first, that although it is here that Labour has recorded its major achievements and scored its most important successes, it is also here that its program is the least original, and divides it least from its most determined Opposition; second, that although it is precisely in Labour's answer to the "social question" that one would expect to find the most unambiguous expression of the long view, it is the one place in which expediency appears most clearly to rule, and where one will search in vain for any expression of something bordering on a clear-cut social philosophy as a guide for appraising intentions and tracing implications; and third, that critical as the role of social reform may be in the Labour program, it is also the area in which the failure to break new paths may do most to defeat the very productive effort without which all else is sooner or later bound to come to nought.

Third Objective: To Introduce a "Socialist Society"

The central idea of this Labour "socialism in becoming" appears to be most aptly expressed in the frequently employed phrase, the "welfare state." The welfare state is viewed by Labour as the legal heir to what is left of the Tory social reformism of the early and middle nineteenth century, and the Liberal reformism of the late nineteenth and early twentieth century. As has been pointed out earlier, the British idea of such a state was developed by the Webbs, and found its first expression in the minimum program of the minority report of the Poor Law Commission of 1909. The legislation which that report called for, considerably amplified in scope and content, became the social security legislation of the first three years of the Labour government. To it, meanwhile, were added the supplementary programs which have found expression in other Labour legislation, most notably the Town and Country Planning Act.

Nothing need be added here to what has been written above about these acts and programs. Contrary to impressions commonly held abroad, health and social security legislation has been immensely popular with the British people, and opposition on all except a limited range of general inconsequential issues has definitely been negligible. This is less true of the town and country planning program, though the basic legislation called down the wrath of few except the bitter-enders in Tory circles. Aside from certain weaknesses—most notable in town and country planning—in the planning and direction of these programs, which do not, however, affect their general popularity, there is no questioning their worth to the Labour government in arousing interest and support in labor and nonlabor circles alike.

The same holds for those other planks in the program of the welfare state which provide further aids to education and wide-ranging government promotion of popular interest in the sciences and the arts. "An approximate total for all forms of direct Government expenditure on the promotion of the Arts, including scientific institutions, is estimated for 1949–50 at £10,869,188"[54] and it runs the gamut of literature, architecture, pictorial arts, music, drama, films, industrial arts, rural crafts, museums, special recreational and occupational training of youths,[55] national parks and playgrounds, etc.

In all this, however, Labour advanced no new principles of action; all of it appears as a more or less straight-line projection, modified by considerable widening at points, of plans and programs long accepted, both in principle and in practice, by previous parties and Governments of unequivocal nonsocialist presuasions. It is not here that fundamental differences may be joined. Basic disagreements within the Labour party, and between Labour and its Opposition, arise only when one turns to the time-honored controversies over the sanctions which provide the basis for the capitalist system itself. Since the Labour government has made a rather general case for fundamental changes in these sanctions, it is important to ask what it has achieved along these lines, for theoretically its general position is based on the premise that without drastic changes here the future of both socialism and Britain cannot be assured on an enduring basis.

Broadly speaking, the Labour program adds to the general concept of the welfare state the objectives of greater equalization of wealth and income and a basic shift in ownership and control of productive re-

---

[54] Home Affairs Survey, April 12, 1949. Appendix 10, table 6, gives a tabular summary of these expenditures for the three years, 1946–47—1949–50.

[55] See, e.g., "The Organization of Youth—Leisure Time," Home Affairs Survey, July 6, 1949, pp. 45–47.

sources. So far as it seems accurate to say that the nub of the Labour solution of the "social question" lies in this area, it is important to note briefly the nature and implications of its accomplishments, and to see what results it may claim from the steps already taken.

According to data cited from the *Economist*, "up to the end of 1947, the effective purchasing power of the wage earner had increased by 16 per cent. over that of 1938; that of the salary earner was down by about 19 per cent.; and that of the dividend drawer and *rentier* was down by 4 per cent. These trends were certainly not reversed during 1948, and this represent a very important move towards greater equality of income in this country."[56] Part of this appears to be due to factors associated with relatively full employment, part to price stabilization—reinforced by a continuation of rationing of certain foodstuffs and by subsidies—and part to the structure and incidence of taxation.

None of these, however, is in any significant sense new. With the partial exception of taxes, all factors accounting for redistribution of income downward come from continuation into the postwar period of policies and practices of wartime, and are regarded by the Labour government as temporary extensions of emergency controls. Thus much of the rationing has already been abandoned, and all of what remains is scheduled for a similar fate as soon as "supplies become adequate to meet the demand." Subsidies amounted to £485,000,000 in 1948, and the decision not to continue to offset price increases by subsidies already indicates a possible decline in the real purchasing power of the workman's income.[57] Since total elimination of the subsidies system "would add 13 points to the Retail Price Index," an amount equal to "about 3s. 6d. per head per week"[58] for every man, woman, and child in Britain, it represents—depending upon the incidence of the tax burden—a very considerable source of "free income."

Although it is expected that this "free income" will be reduced as conditions return to "normal," the reverse is anticipated for expenditures for social services. The cost of these services increased from £498,200,000 in 1947–48, to £747,400,000 in 1948–49, and are to

---

[56] Jenkins, in *Hansard*, Vol. 463, col. 2250.

[57] On the basis of current estimates, Sir Stafford Cripps believed that with prices remaining constant and food imports increasing, total subsidies at the end of the fiscal year 1949–50 would amount to £568,000,000. The decision to stabilize the total amount of these subsidies at the figure of £465,000,000 involved "a rise in the Cost of Living figure on the All-Items Index of rather less than two points," but one that forecast, nevertheless, the implications of gradual abandonment of the whole food subsidy system. *Ibid.*, cols. 2093–2094.

[58] Douglas Jay, *ibid.*, cols. 2656–2657.

be further increased to £845,500,000 in 1949–50.[59] On a per capita basis, this represents an increase from roughly £15 per head per annum in 1947–48 to £17 in 1949–50. Combined with food subsidies, the total of "free income" is more than 10 per cent of the national income, which was estimated at roughly £10,900,000,000 for the fiscal year 1949–50.[60]

Before turning to the incidence of taxes which provide this "free income," it may be relevant to point out that the statistical data indicate some fairly important qualitative changes in the makeup of the average real income, but that these more or less balance out. For example, the health service and the housing program represent vast extensions— even with the limited resources available—of the real income of the lower brackets. So also do certain changes brought about in food consumption—consumption of milk solids, for example, has increased from a yearly average of 38.3 pounds per capita in the prewar period to 48.0 pounds in 1947–48. Less favorable are a number of other changes, such as the decrease from 109.6 pounds of meat per capita per annum to 74.8 pounds during the same interval.[61] By and large, however, the real income of the lower income brackets appears to be decidedly higher than it was before the war, not only because of significant per capita improvements, but because rationing and price controls have greatly improved the relative position of the working classes on basic standard-of-living items.

Quite aside from theoretical considerations concerning the shifting of the burden of taxation, the tax structure has not been greatly changed from that obtaining in wartime, but even this represents a drastic shift from prewar conditions. Thus, while at 1946–47 rates the "proportion of income before tax retained after deduction of taxes" for incomes under £250 per annum was 98.9 per cent as against 98.8 per cent at the 1938–39 rates, the comparable percentages for incomes of £10,000 and over were 23.6 and 45.9 per cent, respectively. At the extremes of the scale, in other words, the amount retained by the lower brackets was only slightly less, while in the higher bracket it was roughly one-half. This is not, of course, the whole story. Price controls and dividend limitation have reduced the number of persons in the upper brackets, and lower minimum-wage rates and full employment have raised both

[59] See table 7, appendix 10.
[60] See table 8, appendix 10.
[61] Table 9, appendix 10.

the level of the lower bracket income and the number paying at higher rates. Nevertheless, broadly speaking, the shift is large-scale and[62] very significant.

The picture is less clear when one turns to "indirect taxes on consumption," where the total amount has increased from £611,000,000 or 12.5 per cent of total national "personal income," in 1938, to £1,685,000,000 or 18.4 per cent, in 1947.[63] It is somewhat difficult to determine accurately how this burden is distributed by income classes. In the 1949–50 budget debates in the House of Commons, the Parliamentary Secretary to the Treasury argued that it was borne by the "ordinary householder," whose income was expended mainly for necessities, only to a very limited extent.

The Purchase Tax [he said] after last year's concessions, is far more a tax on less essentials, including luxuries, than seems to be realized. Of course, many common household goods which all sections of the people have to buy are taxed, though at the lower rate. But the bulk of the actual Purchase Tax revenue is in fact raised from the following main items: Non-utility clothing, non-utility footwear, non-utility furniture, motor vehicles, stationery and toilet preparations. These items account for over £140 million, or about half the whole Purchase Tax revenue. At the same time, a much higher percentage of clothing and footwear production is now utility, and therefore free of Purchase Tax, than seems to be realized. For instance, of the present output of woven woollen garments, some 73 per cent. is now utility; of woven cotton garments, 68 per cent.; of knitted garments, 95 per cent.; and of boots and shoes 87 per cent. Thus, it is quite clear that the Purchase Tax is not, to the extent that people seem to think, a tax on the ordinary wage-earning household.[64]

Jay concluded that, although the gross tax burden amounted to some 40 per cent of the national income, the British "economy can sustain this measure of redistributive taxation much more easily than we had thought,"[65] partly because there was no evidence of impairment of private savings,[66] and partly because so large a part of it was mere transfer

---

[62] For further details see the *Report of the ECA Mission*, vol. ii, table B, "Distribution of Private Incomes," p. 179.

[63] *Ibid.*, vol. iii, table 72, "Taxes as percent of Personal Income," p. 65.

[64] Douglas Jay, in *Hansard*, Vol. 463, col. 2659.

[65] *Ibid.*, col. 2660.

[66] "Now that we have this high level of direct taxation and this high depreciation allowance, we have these long piled-up order books. The fact is, for instance, that one cannot get delivery of a boiler—and a boiler is a very good index because all industries, or practically all industries, need boilers,—in under two years. There is some machinery in some trades which one can obtain, but one cannot obtain machinery for the woollen industry or pasteurising machinery for milk under two years delivery date. Many manufacturers are refusing to take any more orders because they have so many orders piled up. When this is so it cannot be true that industry cannot find the money to re-equip itself. Obviously, it is finding the money—and finding it without any difficulty." Mikardo, *ibid.*, col. 2722.

income.[67] The question remains as to what has happened to the distribution of incomes before taxation. Here the data are inadequate to support any very precise evaluations, but in general, wages and rents have been stabilized at or near wartime levels (rents had previously been stabilized early in the war), some dividends have been stabilized on a voluntary basis, and profits have risen rapidly.

It would lead too far afield to attempt to sift and weigh the highly conflicting data and arguments which surround this subject in contemporary Britain. Complaints of excessive taxation of business have arisen partly because of the excess-profits tax, partly because of the "Once For All" capital levy imposed in 1948, and partly because of the belief that when due allowance is made for proper depreciation deductions there is comparatively little real net addition being made to productive capital resources—despite the high nominal rate of gross capital formation.[68] Labour complaints are based on a still extremely "austere" standard of living,[69] countless evidence of high living in the more fashionable restaurants, hotels, stores, and resorts,[70] and what the daily papers continue to show as high and mounting profit returns.[71] The long and the short of the controversy over income distribution before

[67] "We know exactly what the real burden of taxation is, and it is nothing like 40 per cent. According to the White Paper on National Income and Expenditure, in 1948 the gross national income was £10,600 million. The actual expenditure of central and local government upon goods and services was £1,914 million. That is not 40 per cent. It is barely 18 per cent of the national income . . . Twenty-two per cent of the taxation rate is paid back in the form of increased income to somebody or other." G. Benson, *ibid.*, col. 2242.

[68] Thus the *Economist* believes that, despite high "depreciation provisions allowed for tax purposes (owing to the initial allowance of 25 per cent on new machinery and plant under the Income Tax Act of 1945) and also in undistributed company profits" yet "it is virtually certain that industry as a whole has not put aside sufficient out of its apparent profits to keep its real resources intact—much less increase them. For several years past, industry has been distributing to the tax collector and its shareholders more than the real profits it was earning." June 12, 1949, p. 977.

[69] Captain Hewitson, whose "main occupation is national industrial officer for the second largest trade union in Britain" presented data based on information concerning "a list of industries numbering 151" in 122 of which "95s. or less is the average weekly basic wage." In a typical case, for a statistical family of 3.73 persons, after making no allowance for spending money, drinks, smokes, sweets, cinemas—"nothing on pleasure" and only one "extravagance" on ration points—"1 lb. of sausage and sixpenny worth of bones"—the total bill at lowest prices prevailing in the area was £4 19s. 3d. (99s. 3d.) *ibid.*, cols. 2278–2280.

[70] E.g.: "Here are just a few examples . . . The Government issue papers appealing to the workers in the Lancashire area; they are appealing to the Lancashire cotton operatives to increase output, to boost output. . . . Then one comes across this—one fur coat priced at £1,450 and another at £3,310. So one can go on. Everyone knows that that does not apply only to fur coats. These are the people who have the Rolls-Bentleys, these are the people who have the Humber 'Snipes,' these are the people whom that standard of living represents who are skimming off the cream in this way." Smith, *ibid.*, col. 2296.

[71] Referring to white paper data, Colonel Wigg pointed out that "undistributed profits in 1947 were £405 million; in 1948 £540 million; and in 1949 £575 million. So that in two years we get an increase of almost 50 per cent in undistributed profits. To what does this point? It points to the fact that profit margins are far too high." *Ibid.*, cols. 2161–2162.

taxes would seem to be that there has been remarkable little real change. What "redistribution of wealth" has taken place has been achieved through continuation of the wartime tax structure in the post-war period of full employment and by a highly complex system of price, cost, and other controls and aids whose precise effects upon income distribution are difficult to trace, and which probably do not represent any very large net scaling down of income distribution *before* paying taxes.

Nor does this picture seem greatly altered when one turns from income distribution to ownership and control. So far as the nationalized industries are concerned, the government now owns properties for which it has generally paid former owners somewhat less than they wanted, but in securities—government bonds or their equivalents—upon which return is steady and secure. Excepting the Bank of England and parts of the gas and electricity industries, most of these properties were badly run down, or badly organized, or underdeveloped and in need of new investment, or suffering from other difficulties and shortcomings. State ownership has not altered the general structure of ownership of securities, or of income claims on the community's real resources except, possibly, somewhat to improve the status of the rentier.

What has been substituted for private capitalism in this sphere is state capitalism, with the result that labor tends to find itself in a relationship with its new employer—the government and its representatives—much similar to that with which it had long been familiar before the changeover was made. There is no official labor representation on the boards, and it is proving to be very hard indeed to instill a sense of participation in labor, even at the lower levels. Outside of the nationalized industries, some results are said to have been attained from the propaganda on behalf of copartnership schemes, but most turn out on investigation either to be illusory or definitely unimportant.

The principal gains are claimed from "redeployment"—moving workers from unproductive or unnecessary jobs to useful, strategic, or productive ones. The daily papers carry numerous references to this subject, and a number of the working-party reports have offered suggestions for widespread changes. Here again, however, the net changes seem to be relatively unimportant. Aside from some rather loosely managed shifts in employment through the employment exchanges, after two years of application the only recorded data showed less than a hundred persons purposefully "redeployed" by the government. This seems particularly unfortunate in the face of the vast potentialities inherent in "redeployment" which would be open to the Government if it were willing to attack the major problems facing Britain's over-all occupational structure. According to the *Economic Survey* for 1949, agriculture, despite a decline in acreage cultivated, some significant decreases in crop output, and—most important—despite a very large scale extension of farm mechanization, .still absorbed 45,000 more workers in 1948 than it did in 1946. The already vastly overloaded and disorganized field of distribution employed 97,000 more persons (in a seller's market) and "consumer services" employed 136,000 more persons. Although these data show decreases from prewar figures (except in agriculture), they also show an unchecked tendency to creep back to the old levels.[72]

Far more serious, however, is the large and possibly very strategic statistical *terra incognita* of the occupations associated with Britain's still relatively well-knit and status-minded social system. According to published estimates[73] there were, in 1948, no less than 644,000 persons engaged in private domestic service; some 763,000 were occupied in the catering trade; there were 95,000 fully employed persons in the sports and betting services; and some 808,000 were in the armed services. These four classifications alone account for 12 per cent of all gainfully employed or occupied persons in Britain. How much of this may be regarded as dispensable or redundant? Leaving out the armed services, possibly from one-third to one-half, or approximately the same number of persons as are employed in coal mining.

It does not follow that satisfactory transfers to more useful activities could easily and quickly be made by all these persons or that, for many, transfer would be possible. But it does follow that concealed in the nooks and crannies of the British economic, social, and political system is a huge supply of available man power which is largely or wholly unproductive; a large part of this is now absorbed in catering to the whims of the wealthy, and lacks social and economic justification except in terms of keeping up appearances and making good in the books of etiquette,[74] and an even larger part exists largely because the work on

---

[72] See table 10, appendix 10.
[73] Appendix 1.
[74] In one large area in southern England—sometimes referred to as the "brokers' paradise"—an old resident estimated that the country houses or estates employing servants maintained staffs of from three to eleven persons engaged solely in personal and household service, and that this represented anywhere from a 25 to 50 per cent decrease from prewar conditions.

which it is currently employed is badly and inefficiently conducted. Generally speaking, postwar Britain contrasts sharply with Weimar Germany, with which she is not infrequently compared, in that neither the servant class nor the petty bourgeoise have decreased very greatly in numbers.

Speaking of the reintroduction of wartime distribution-of-man-power controls in 1947, the *New Statesman and Nation*[75] feared that it might mean no more than "planning by paralysis." This statement forecast the actual development so accurately that it is worth quoting at length:

The steps so far announced by Mr. Isaacs for correcting by "direction the maldistribution of Britain's manpower" are gingerly. The eels and butterflies, the spivs and drones, will still tread their primrose path to the black market; men and women released from the Forces will still be free to drift into unessential occupations; and it is not apparently intended to conduct any comb-out of persons actually employed no matter how ill-adapted to the crisis their employment may be. Direction is to apply only to men between 18 and 50 and childless women between 19 and 40 who go to a Labour Exchange for a "wage-earning" job. They may be directed for a minimum period of six months to an essential occupation; but only single men and unmarried women between the ages of 20 and 40 will normally be directed to any work outside the range of daily travelling distances from their home. This will limit considerably the extent to which unemployed labour can effectively be redeployed. First, however, labour has got to become unemployed; and, as a means of creating unemployment, unessential trades will be denied priority in allocations of fuel and raw materials. In other words, manpower is to be redistributed by inducing, over a not yet clearly defined sector of industry, a species of creeping paralysis. This will be a slow-acting process. From its results essential industries are unlikely to gain many useful recruits in the near future. Against this, application of this "limited direction" is likely to cause a good deal of resentment. The minority— and unless the Board of Trade is surprisingly ruthless in allocations of raw materials it will be a small minority—who will be affected by direction will undoubtedly protest that they are being called upon to make sacrifices of convenience, if not of money, while large numbers of persons employed in uneconomic occupations not dependent on any raw material—to say nothing of the whole class of persons living on rentier incomes—make no contribution whatever towards meeting the national crisis.

Two years later this forecast has been borne out virtually to the letter. Little if any progress toward the solution of the "social problem" has been made at the points where it impinges most directly on the production problems of the postwar economic crisis. The general structure of British society has not been seriously altered. In a few respects,

[75] September 27, 1947, p. 243.

primarily where long, slow disintegration of the old order had been evident since before the First World War, various measures of the Labour government may somewhat have hastened the process. But aside from this midwifery, it has done relatively little in general to alter the structure, to redistribute the burdens, or so to galvanize interest as to secure the active, positive, creative support and participation of labor and its other following in the supremely necessary national productive effort. What has been done on this social sector has been as piecemeal, as patchy, as hesitant, as tentative, as disorganized and unorganized, and—in many respects—as amateurish as have its efforts at industrial reorganization and development for nationalized and nonnationalized industries alike.

The idea that Britain badly needs a cleansing of her Augean stables is strongly supported by some of the more ominous signs of unrest on the horizon. Demands for wage increases have paralleled the rise in cost of living forecast in the 1949–50 budget, and there is a growing readiness to resort to strikes or other means of direct action to implement the demand.[76] Lethargy, apathy, and what Durkheim called *anomie*—a sense of planlessness—continue to lead many to high and sustained expenditures for tobacco, alcohol, and gambling. Resolutions at trade-union and other conventions are definitely more strident. The large, and once-again expanding military budget is arousing increasing apprehension.[77] The rosy optimism which accompanied the production increases of 1948 has given way to uneasy dismay at the "standstill budget" of 1949–50. Because of his tranquil call for further extension of a confessedly sodden, when not downright grim, postwar "austerity," Sir Stafford Cripps has been referred to by a mocking Opposition as the "Iron Chancellor." But the more fundamental trouble is that the immediate future holds out no brighter prospects, and it is in the immediate future—by testament of all the most widely circulated, most widely understood, and most convincing arguments of the Labour party—that Britain's capacity to survive as a great and prosperous industrial nation must and will be determined.

Unless Labour soon finds a solution to the problem of production in which closely interrelated social, and within limits, cultural issues

---

[76] Between 1945 and 1949, according to the most widely accepted indexes (1938 = 100), retail prices rose 21 per cent (from 148 to 179) ; wholesale prices 37 per cent (from 166.7 to 228.6) ; and wages 25 per cent (from 154 to 193). See, Lionel Robbins, "The Sterling Problem," *Lloyd's Bank Review*, Oct., 1949.

[77] E.g., statements by J. R. Robinson and Mrs. B. A. Castle, in *Hansard*, Vol. 463, cols. 2707, 2752–2753.

are dealt with as basic parameters of the fundamental question, and unless these matters are taken in hand with benefit of more than the time-honored belief that a benign deity will surely see that a gratuitous "through" is added to "muddling," then Britain is surely finished. Others in their time, as Gilbert Murray pointed out for the Hellenistic world, have suffered a "loss of nerve," while living on the trappings of past greatness. The combination of sanity, superficiality, and general incapacity to act which Bernard Shaw has so brilliantly caricatured in the personality of Stephen Underschaft in his *Major Barbara,* is a luxury Britain can no longer afford. The price of timidity in times of crisis is usually defeat, and if postwar Britain fails on the production front the failure may very well be the result of timidity in grappling with the "social problem" in her hour of supreme need.

But there may be an answer to all this after all. "Socialism" in Britain consists of reform on the installment plan. There is, of course, nothing in its hire-purchase contract to prevent an upping of the payment schedule, and the necessity for paying each successive installment on time may provide a needed stimulus to more productive effort. One of Labour's most articulate literary spokesmen, R. H. S. Crossman, holds that Fabian Socialism is no philosophy at all, but rather "a series of *ad hoc* proposals dealing with *ad hoc* problems," and that these have now all been worked out. The problem now is one of power."[78] But since the retention of power by Labour rests—as it would for any other political party in Britain today—upon a solution to the problem of production, Labour must formulate a program which will deal with every aspect of national life which has a significant bearing upon it, and this program must be backed by a will to effect a veritable *tour de force.*

LABOUR PLANS FOR THE SECOND FIVE YEARS

In April, 1949, the Labour party issued a pamphlet called *Labour Believes in Britain.* It was designed to play in the 1950 election campaign the role assigned *Let Us Face the Future* at the time of the 1945 elections. Slightly modified by resolutions of the subsequent annual conference held at Blackpool,[79] and by occasional supplementary statements on minor points, *Labour Believes in Britain* is both a summing up of the achievements of Labour's first five years of office and a prospectus of further changes to come.

---

[78] In the symposium *Ideas and Beliefs of the Victorians* (London, 1949), p. 443.
[79] *Report of the Forty-eighth Annual Conference of the Labour Party* (Blackpool, 1949).

The manifesto, as an attempt to rally support for the party in the elections, may perhaps be pardoned for singing a paean of praise to the Government for its achievements. Certainly there is no intimation of any general, or even partial, failure at any significant point. There is no intimation of a decrease in exports, already apparent at the time the pamphlet was being drafted, nor of the forthcoming devaluation, which was even then being anticipated. Nothing is said about the tapering off of production, the once-again-evident increase in inflationary pressures, growing trade-union pressure for wage increases, the virtually total failure of the development councils, the nearly complete disaster of the Groundnuts Scheme, the inability to cope adequately with rising unrest in the colonies—particularly in the Gold Coast, Nigeria, and Malaya—the well-nigh complete collapse of British foreign policy in Germany, Palestine, Greece, and the Far East, and the total failure to achieve anything at all by way of an integration of British and Continental economic systems.

But if such omissions may be excused on the grounds that the *noblesse oblige* of political maneuver does not make mandatory resort to the public confessional, yet the new manifesto should surely make clear the obstacles that still remain to be overcome. This *Labour Believes in Britain* does not do. Instead, against a background of apparent general successes, it proposes future action along lines laid out in the recent past for the achievement of further successes in pursuit of the same goals. Exports are to be further expanded; productive efficiency is to be enhanced; economic planning is to be further promoted; "both public and private enterprise shall serve the public interest . . . be enterprising with plenty of room for vision, energy and initiative . . .";[80] such devices as development councils, joint production committees, pit committees and works councils are to increase in "importance in our industrial life"; investment is to be controlled—particularly in the socialised industries—"in order to prevent any slump developing";[81] business entrepreneurs are to become "trustees responsible to the nation," freed "from the heavy hand of financiers" and prevented from resorting to restrictive and monopolistic practices;[82] the costs of distribution are to be reduced and "an independent and publicly financed

[80] *Labour Believes in Britain*, p. 6.
[81] *Ibid.*, p. 8.
[82] *Ibid.*, p. 10.

Consumer Advice Centre will . . . be set up";[83] social services, which already add to the normal income of a family of five "at least £2 15s. a week in the form of social benefits,"[84] will be increased; Britain will continue to work for world peace, a task becoming increasingly difficult because "Russia Blocks the Road," scorning "the path of co-operation" trod so heavily by Bevin;[85] and the advance of the Commonwealth and Empire is to proceed apace. Sometime in 1950 there is to be a Golden Jubilee of the British Labour party, when all its past achievements, "unmatched by any socialist party in the world," will give pride to celebrate "the conscientious care with which we framed our election programme for 1945 and . . . the democratic vigour and efficiency with which the Labour Government has kept trust with the people by carrying that programme through.[86]

There is little indication of how all this is to be made to achieve tangible results. Although the general position has been that the second five years in office would be mostly spent in consolidation "of past gains," there is some nationalization to be done. In general, if and when "private enterprise fails to act in the public interest," Labour "makes three proposals. First and foremost, the Government should have the power, wherever the need is clearly shown, to start up new public enterprises. Second, the existing power to take over inefficient concerns which are woefully failing the nation should be continued. Third, the Government should be prepared to acquire suitable existing concerns where these are willingly offered for sale."[87] This would permit the government to nationalize virtually any enterprise in any industry at will. In a similar vein, the government may further extend "its power to take land into public ownership and put it in charge of the Agricultural Land Commission for expert management."[88] Further extensions of subsidy to housing and the social services may be made at will.

---

[83] *Ibid.*, pp. 15–16. The Consumer Advice Centre "will conduct expert tests and examinations of the various consumer goods on the market. It will issue buying guides, indicating the relative merits and demerits of the products tested, and how far each is reasonable value for money." The model is the Consumers Union of New York, but how the libel laws of Britain are to be handled is not indicated, though these now effectively prevent any such type of consumer counseling even of a private sort. There is also to be a "free Legal Aid and Advice scheme." (P. 29.)

[84] *Ibid.*, p. 18. This figure seems unduly high. I have been unable to check it.

[85] *Ibid.*, pp. 24–27.

[86] *Ibid.*, p. 30.

[87] *Ibid.*, p. 12.

[88] *Ibid.*, p. 14.

More specifically, "a further step forward" will be taken "by placing all suitable minerals in public ownership";[89] some or all of both
slaughterhouses and cold storage plants will be placed under some
form of public ownership;[90] "all the sugar manufacturing and refining
concerns" will be transferred to public ownership;[91] local governments
will be encouraged further to extend public entertainment and other
services catering to leisure hours; since "splitting off industrial assurance from the remaining business of the companies would lead to confusion and inefficiency . . . all the industrial assurance companies, the
biggest being the Prudential and the Pearl, and the larger collecting
societies, should be taken over as they stand";[92] the cement industry
will be taken over;[93] and the chemical industry "will be carefully examined" to see if it also deserves a similar nationalization.[94]

Nationalization is throughout dealt with as though it automatically
implied increased efficiency; this equation is considered axiomatic, but
there is no evidence submitted that nationalization has raised efficiency
in the past. The same holds for other programs affecting production.
On one estimate, productivity per worker between October, 1947, and
October, 1948, increased by only about 1 per cent in the national economy as a whole.[95] Meanwhile the "large . . . unproductive middle class
of brass-buttoned doormen and redundant bank clerks left over from
her great commercial past"[96] had not been combed out. Inflation was
once again on the rise; the seller's market had disappeared; exports
were falling; and, with a widening dollar gap, devaluation with its
consequent cuts in social security and other domestic expenditures was
just around the corner. There had been very little by way of planned
redirection of either investment or man power, and very little—if, indeed, anything of moment at all—in new redirection of sales by private
business away from the sterling and towards the dollar area. To cap

[89] *Ibid.*, p. 15.
[90] *Ibid.*, p. 16. At the Blackpool conference, Dr. Edith Summerskill of the Ministry of
Foods, member of the National Executive of the Labour party, stated that "the time has
come when we must . . . take over the whole of the meat wholesale and importing business
and administer it under public control." Again, "We have built 48 new stores and the nation
now owns a fifth of the total cold storage." *Report of the Forty-eighth Annual Conference*,
p. 186.
[91] *Labour Believes in Britain*, p. 17.
[92] *Ibid.*, p. 20. This was later modified from a proposal for nationalization to one for compulsory mutualization.
[93] *Ibid.*, p. 22.
[94] *Ibid.*, p. 13.
[95] *Manchester Guardian*, Dec. 14, 1948. Subsequently Sir Stafford Cripps issued figures
showing a slightly higher rate of increase, but a rate which was still astonishingly low.
[96] Howard K. Smith, *The State of Europe* (New York, 1949), chapter 2, "The Fallen
Bastion," p. 36.

the climax, British foreign policy, particularly the recognition of Communist China (January 11, 1950) threatened to produce drastic curtailment of Marshall Plan aid.

* * * * * * * * *

It is not necessary further to detail the record. What it shows is a series of partial successes offset by partial failures, and little by way of an enduring solution of the fundamental problems which might make possible a viable future. This in itself is unfortunate, but not hopeless. What makes future prospects seem very dim indeed is the Government's failure to see that nothing less than a revolutionary replanning of all the factors bearing on the problems of improving British productive methods is required at home, and that a drastic reorientation of both colonial and foreign policy is needed abroad. Should it continue to remain complacent about domestic problems, and to follow traditional patterns overseas, then, on the available evidence to date, Britain needs only a Gibbon to write her chronicle. The Labour party alone is not to blame. So far as platform and public utterances bear witness, it has done as well, and possibly far better, than would its Opposition had it been in power.[97]

But it is true, nevertheless, that Britain has been living on borrowed time. There may still be just barely enough time left for a last Herculean effort to turn the tide, but the sands in the hourglass are running exceeding low.

[97] One of the most severe critics of the Labour movement, Professor Lionel Robbins, of the London School of Economics, in *Lloyds Bank Review*, Oct., 1949, p. 12, writes, "The fact is that since the War the majority of the community, whether Conservative, Liberal or Labour, have been living in a fool's paradise concerning what we can afford; and the majority of their leaders, whether Conservative, Liberal or Labour, have done little to correct the delusion."

Appendixes

APPENDIX 1

TABLE 1

ESTIMATED NUMBER OF INSURED EMPLOYEES IN SELECTED SERVICE
TRADES IN THE UNITED KINGDOM IN JULY, 1948

(In thousands)

	Male	Female	Total
Insurance, banking and finance.............	275	151	426
Professional services			
Accountancy.............................	37	22	59
Education..............................	159	321	480
Law..................................	24	38	62
Medical and dental......................	124	313	437
Religion...............................	15	13	28
Other.................................	71	48	119
Other services			
Theaters, cinemas, etc...................	69	75	144
Sport, betting, etc......................	51	44	95
Catering..............................	238	525	763
Laundries.............................	33	123	156
Cleaning and dyeing....................	12	30	42
Hairdressing...........................	25	43	68
Private domestic service (resident)........	17	202	219
Private domestic service (nonresident)....	48	277	325
Other.................................	91	75	166
Total................................	1289	2300	3589

SOURCE: Dudley Sears, University of Oxford, Institute of Statistics.

[671]

TABLE 2
(Appendix 1)

ESTIMATED NUMBER OF WORKERS WHO WILL BE EMPLOYED BY PUBLIC
CONCERNS IN 1950

(Figures from official sources)

Public concern	Estimated workers	Date of estimate
Transport		
Railways	590,356	March, 1945
Railways, ancillary	32,013	March, 1945
Tramway and omnibus	239,800	October, 1946
Other road passenger services	23,400	October, 1946
Goods by road	50,000	October, 1946
Port transport	106,500	October, 1946
Harbour, river, canal	26,080	October, 1946
Total	1,068,149	
Armed forces	1,170,000	December, 1947
Post office	350,901	January, 1947
Other civil service	677,099	January, 1947
Civil defence, NFS, police	89,000	January, 1947
Education	200,000	January, 1949
Health services	380,000	December, 1947
Gas, water, electricity	260,000	January, 1947
Other local government services	588,000	March, 1947
Coal mining	770,000	December, 1947
Pig iron, smelting, rolling	213,620	January, 1947
Cables	4,471	December, 1946
BBC	10,927	December, 1946
Civil aviation	18,065	December, 1946
Coöperative movement	327,962	End 1945
	6,040,194	

SOURCE: John Parker, *Labour Marches On*, p. 211.

APPENDIX 2

RELATIONSHIP OF LABOUR PARTY MEMBERSHIP TO TRADE UNION
AND COÖPERATIVE MEMBERSHIPS

End of year	Labor party membership			Trade union membership			Coöperative membership		
	Total	Trade union membership	Per cent	Total	Affiliated to the T.U.C.	Per cent	Consumers societies	Coöperative party membership	Per cent
1913	....	....	..	4,135,000	2,232,466	54	2,878,296	....	..
1914	1,612,147	1,572,391	97	4,145,000	....	..	3,053,770	....	..
1915	2,093,365	2,053,735	98	4,359,000	2,682,357	61	3,264,211	....	..
1916	2,219,764	2,170,782	98	4,644,000	2,850,547	61	3,520,227	....	..
1917	2,465,131	2,415,383	98	5,499,000	3,082,352	56	3,788,490	....	..
1918	3,013,129	2,960,409	98	6,533,000	4,582,085	70	3,846,531	....	..
1919	3,511,290	3,464,020	99	7,926,000	5,283,676	67	4,131,477	....	..
1920	4,359,807	4,317,537	99	8,346,000	6,505,482	78	4,504,852	....	..
1921	4,010,361	3,973,558	99	6,631,000	6,417,910	97	4,548,557	....	..
1926	3,388,286	3,352,347	99	5,218,000	4,365,319	84	5,186,728	2,009,240	39
1931	2,358,066	2,024,216	86	4,624,000	3,719,401	80	6,590,020	3,522,566	53
1936	2,444,357	1,968,538	80	5,295,000	3,614,551	68	7,807,942	5,250,000	67
1937	2,527,672	2,097,071	83	5,842,000	4,008,647	69	8,084,990	5,340,000	66
1938	2,630,256	2,158,076	82	6,053,000	4,460,617	74	8,404,688	5,656,698	66
1939	2,663,067	2,214,070	83	6,244,000	4,669,186	75	8,643,233	5,883,082	68
1940	2,571,163	2,226,575	87	6,558,000	4,886,711	75	8,716,894	6,161,875	71
1941	2,485,306	2,230,576	90	7,109,000	5,432,644	77	8,772,255	6,305,017	72
1942	2,453,392	2,206,209	90	7,810,000	6,024,411	77	8,924,868	6,773,443	76
1943	2,503,240	2,237,307	89	8,117,000	6,642,000	82	9,082,218	7,071,225	78
1944	2,672,845	2,375,381	88	8,026,000	6,576,000	82	9,217,739	7,392,242	80
1945	3,038,697	2,510,369	82	7,803,000	6,671,120	85	9,400,000	7,511,072	80

SOURCE: N. Barou, *British Trade Unions* (London, 1947), p. 258.

APPENDIX 3

TABLE 1

Aggregate Number of Working Days Lost from Work Stoppages in Great Britain (1934–1948)

Year	Number of stoppages beginning in year	Number of workers involved in stoppages			Aggregate number of working days lost in year in stoppages	
		Beginning in year		In progress in year (thousands)	Beginning in year (thousands)	In progress in year (thousands)
		Direct (thousands)	Indirect (thousands)			
1934.......	471	109	25	134	955	959
1935.......	553	230	41	279	1,849	1,955
1936.......	818	241	75	322	1,726	1,829
1937.......	1,129	388	209	610	3,132	3,413
1938.......	875	211	63	275	1,329	1,334
1939.......	940	246	91	337	1,352	1,356
1940.......	922	225	74	299	938	940
1941.......	1,251	297	63	361	1,076	1,079
1942.......	1,303	349	107	457	1,527	1,527
1943.......	1,785	454	103	559	1,805	1,808
1944.......	2,194	716	105	826	3,687	3,714
1945.......	2,293	447	84	532	2,827	2,835
1946.......	2,205	405	121	529	2,138	2,158
1947.......	1,721	489	131	623	2,389	2,433
1948.......	1,758	322	100	423	1,935	1,944

Source: *Home Affairs Survey*, Feb. 22, 1949, p. 27.

TABLE 2
(Appendix 3)
AGGREGATE NUMBER OF WORKING DAYS LOST FROM WORK STOPPAGES IN GREAT BRITAIN BY INDUSTRY GROUP (1947–1948)

Industry group	Number of stoppages beginning in year		Number of workers involved in all stoppages in year (thousands)		Aggregate number of working days lost through all stoppages in progress in year (thousands)	
	1947	1948	1947	1948	1947	1948
Coal mining.................	1,053	1,115	307.9	186.6	912	464
Other mining and quarrying...	13	9	.8	.9	3	9
Brick, pottery, glass, chemicals, etc....................	24	28	2.2	3.0	8	12
Engineering..................	79	88	27.6	48.2	211	131
Shipbuilding.................	114	78	67.4	20.1	324	237
Iron and steel and other metal	98	100	16.0	39.3	44	531
Textile......................	25	40	4.4	14.6	13	56
Clothing.....................	22	26	3.5	6.6	15	26
Food, drink and tobacco......	23	26	3.9	4.2	17	20
Woodworking, furniture, etc....	18	19	1.6	1.5	7	7
Paper, printing, etc...........	10	10	1.6	3.5	10	26
Building, etc.................	35	36	5.2	7.3	24	27
Gas, water, and electric supply.	5	8	.7	1.1	1	2
Transport....................	119	111	140.2	73.1	628	347
Public administration services.	12	12	4.9	2.5	61	12
Distribution, commerce, etc....	22	17	19.8	3.7	73	12
Other industries and services..	49	35	15.3	6.8	82	25
Total......................	1,721	1,758	623	423	2,433	1,944

SOURCE: *Home Affairs Survey*, Feb. 22, 1949, p. 26.

APPENDIX 4

The arrow (→) indicates direction of transfers permitted without the necessity of individual approval by the United Kingdom Control, between different categories of sterling accounts. All other transfers require separate approval.

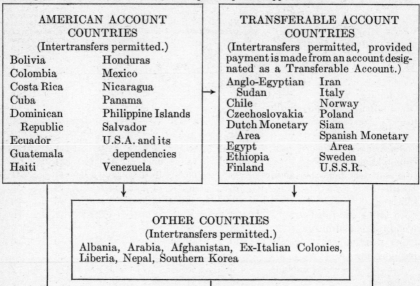

AMERICAN ACCOUNT COUNTRIES
(Intertransfers permitted.)

Bolivia	Honduras
Colombia	Mexico
Costa Rica	Nicaragua
Cuba	Panama
Dominican	Philippine Islands
Republic	Salvador
Ecuador	U.S.A. and its
Guatemala	dependencies
Haiti	Venezuela

TRANSFERABLE ACCOUNT COUNTRIES
(Intertransfers permitted, provided payment is made from an account designated as a Transferable Account.)

Anglo-Egyptian	Iran
Sudan	Italy
Chile	Norway
Czechoslovakia	Poland
Dutch Monetary	Siam
Area	Spanish Monetary
Egypt	Area
Ethiopia	Sweden
Finland	U.S.S.R.

OTHER COUNTRIES
(Intertransfers permitted.)

Albania, Arabia, Afghanistan, Ex-Italian Colonies, Liberia, Nepal, Southern Korea

SCHEDULED TERRITORIES: "STERLING AREA"
(Broadly speaking, intertransfers are freely permitted; but some limitations are imposed by local controls, e.g., South Africa, Fiji, Hongkong, India, and Australia.)
British Commonwealth and Empire except Canada and Newfoundland
British Mandated Territories of Cameroons, Nauru, New Guinea, South West Africa, Tanganyika, Togoland, and Western Samoa
British Protectorates and Protected States: Burma, Iceland, Iraq

BILATERAL COUNTRIES
(Intertransfers not permitted unless specifically authorized by U.K. Control.)

Argentina	Palestine
Austria	Paraguay
Belgian Monetary Area	Peru
Brazil	Portuguese Monetary Area
Bulgaria	Roumania
Canada and Newfoundland	Switzerland
China	Syria
Denmark (including Faroe Islands and Greenland)	Tangier
	Transjordan
France and French Monetary Area	Turkey
Germany (Bizonia, French and Russian Zones)	Uruguay
Greece	Vatican City
Hungary	Yugoslavia
Japan	

SOURCE: *Midland Bank Review.* Feb., 1949.

APPENDIX 5

LOCAL AUTHORITIES' POWERS: CHANGES UNDER RECENT
LEGISLATION

(From *Home Affairs Survey*, March 1, 1945)

The Minister of Health, Mr. Aneurin Bevan, on February 22nd (1949), in answer to a question made a statement on the powers which have been added to, and taken from county councils, county boroughs, municipal borough, and district councils, respectively, by legislation passed in the present Parliament.

POWERS ADDED TO COUNTY COUNCILS

Town and country planning (Town and Country Planning Act, 1947)
Fire services (Fire Services Act, 1947)
Miscellaneous powers for prevention and treatment of illness (National Health Service Act, 1946)
Provision of Entertainments (Local Government Act, 1948)
Power to supply information and publicity with regard to local government services (Local Government Act, 1948)
Provision for financial loss of members, and enlarged power to provide for their expenses (Local Government Act, 1948)
In some areas, police (Police Act, 1946)
In some areas, child life protection (Children Act, 1948), maternity and child welfare, and midwifery services (National Health Services Act, 1946)

POWERS TAKEN FROM COUNTY COUNCILS

Provision of hospital and maternity homes (National Health Services Act, 1946)
Relief of the poor except for provision of residential accommodation (National Assistance Act, 1948)

POWERS ADDED TO COUNTY BOROUGHS

Fire services
Provision of entertainments
Power to supply information and publicity with regard to local government services
Provision of civic restaurants—wartime powers replaced by permanent legislation (Civic Restaurants Bill)
Powers in connection with rent control of furnished dwellings where Tribunals have been established—keeping registers of rents fixed, referring cases to tribunals, instituting proceedings for offences (Furnished Houses Rent Control Act, 1946)
Provision for financial loss of members

POWERS TAKEN FROM COUNTY BOROUGHS

Provision of hospitals and maternity homes
Relief of the poor, except for provision of residential accommodation
In some areas, supply of electricity (Electricity Act)
In some areas, supply of gas (Gas Act)

POWERS ADDED TO MUNICIPAL BOROUGHS

With the exception of fire services, these are the same as the powers added to county boroughs.

POWERS TAKEN FROM MUNICIPAL BOROUGHS

Town and country planning
Miscellaneous powers for prevention and treatment of illness
In some areas, child life protection, provision of maternity homes, maternity and child welfare and midwifery services.
Provision of ambulance services
In some areas, police
In some areas, supply of electricity and supply of gas

POWERS ADDED TO METROPOLITAN BOROUGHS

With the exception of fire services and civic restaurants, these are the same as those added to county boroughs.

POWERS TAKEN AWAY FROM METROPOLITAN BOROUGHS

Miscellaneous powers for prevention and treatment of illness

POWERS ADDED TO DISTRICT COUNCILS

These are the same as those added to county boroughs, with the exception of fire services; and with the addition of power to pay an allowance to the chairman, and in rural districts of provision for traveling and subsistence expenses of members.

POWERS TAKEN FROM DISTRICT COUNCILS

Town and country planning
Miscellaneous powers for prevention and treatment of illness
Provision of ambulance services
In some areas (mainly urban districts), child life protection, provision of maternity homes, maternity and child welfare, and midwifery services
In some areas (mainly urban districts), supply of electricity and supply of gas

APPENDIX 6

TRIPARTITE INDUSTRIAL AND CONSULTATIVE BODIES

(From *Home Affairs Survey*, August 1, 1948)

Industry	Name of body	Year founded	Composition	Frequency of meetings	Purpose
Building and civil engineering	National Consultative Council	1942	Representatives of employers, operatives and professional institutions under the Minister of Works	Two to three monthly	Advise on joint planning and control within the industry
	Building and Civil Engineering Joint Committee	1942	Representatives of five principal organizations of employers and workers under Parliamentary Secretary to the Ministry of Works	Monthly	Advise on detailed execution of plans including labor and welfare matters and work of the Regional Joint Committees
	Building and Civil Engineering Joint Committees (Regional)	1946	Representatives of employers and workers organizations under Regional Director of Ministry of Works	Monthly	Regional counterparts of the Joint Committee above
	Building Industry Production Sub-Committee	1946	Subcommittee constituted from the Joint Committee	Monthly	To advise on production policy and its execution
	Advisory Committee of specialists and subcontractors	1945	Specialists and subcontractors under Deputy Secretary to Ministry of Works	Bi-monthly	To advise on matters affecting specialists and subcontractors apart from wages and conditions of employment
	Building Apprenticeship and Training Council	1943	Representatives of employers, operatives, professional institutions, educational organizations, and government departments	Six monthly or as required	To advise on recruitment, education, and training

TRIPARTITE INDUSTRIAL AND CONSULTATIVE BODIES (*Continued*)

Industry	Name of body	Year founded	Composition	Frequency of meetings	Purpose
Building materials industries	National Brick Advisory Council	1942	Both sides of industry, British Refractories Research Association, and Department of Scientific and Industrial Research	As required	To advise on all matters connected with the industry, particularly prices, supplies, and research
	Area Brick Committee	1942	Representatives of local manufacturers under Ministry of Works Regional Director	Monthly	To advise on carrying out National Council's decisions and on all local problems
Engineering industry	Engineering Advisory Council	1947	Both sides of industry, Board of Trade, Ministry of Fuel and Power, Admiralty, Ministry of Labour, and Lord President's Office	Monthly	Improvements of general concern in the engineering field
	Engineering Industry Advisory Panel	1947	Ten representatives of both sides of industry under the Minister of Labour	Monthly	Special labor problems
	National Advisory Council on the Motor Industry	1946	Both sides of industry, Ministry of Transport, Board of Trade, Ministry of Supply, one independent member	Monthly	To advise on all matters affecting the efficiency of the motor industry
	Heavy Electrical Plant Committee	1947	Both sides of industry, Central Electricity Board, the Scottish Hydroelectric Board, and the department concerned under the Minister of Supply	Monthly	Estimation of supply and demand, planning to meet the demand, production efficiency

TRIPARTITE INDUSTRIAL AND CONSULTATIVE BODIES (*Continued*)

Industry	Name of body	Year founded	Composition	Frequency of meetings	Purpose
Iron and Steel	Iron and Steel Board	1946	Three representatives of industry, two of trades unions, a Treasury official and an independent chairman who works wholetime with a permanent secretariat	At frequent intervals	Development policy, current policy especially in regard to supplies, controls, and prices
	Labour Supply (Iron and Steel) Committees	1941	Both sides of industry under Regional Controllers of Ministry of Labour which provides secretariat	When necessary	Regional labor problems
Shipbuilding Industry	Shipbuilding Advisory Committee	1941	Both sides of shipbuilding and shipping industries, Ministry of Transport, Ministry of Labour, Admiralty, under independent chairman responsible to Admiralty and Ministry of Transport	Bimonthly	Efficiency and stability of shipbuilding industry, its requirements on grounds of national security
Agriculture	County Agricultural Executive Committees	1939 (Reconstituted 1947)	Seven representatives of both sides of the industry, five persons appointed by Minister of Agriculture	Very frequently	Application of policy of Minister of Agriculture. Executive action to secure good husbandry
	District * Executive Committees	1939 (Reconstituted 1947)	Appointed at discretion of County Committees	Very frequently	Similar to County Committees but on district level
	Scottish Agricultural Executive Committees	1947	Appointed by Secretary of State for Scotland after consulting representative organizations	Very frequently	Scottish equivalent to County Agricultural Executive Committees

TRIPARTITE INDUSTRIAL AND CONSULTATIVE BODIES (*Concluded*)

Industry	Name of body	Year founded	Composition	Frequency of meetings	Purpose
Agriculture (*Continued*)	Agricultural Improvement Council	1941 (Reconstituted 1944)	Scientists and prominent farmers and growers		To advise on application of research results to farming practice
	Agricultural Advisory Council for Scotland	1947	Both sides of industry; technical and advisory experts		Scottish parallel to Agricultural Improvement Council
	Horticultural Liaison Group	1945	National Farmers' Union, Horticultural Trades Association, Ministry of Agriculture and Fisheries	Monthly	To advise on horticultural matters
	Hill Farming Advisory Committee for England, Wales, and Northern Ireland	1947	Hill farmers, land owners, and scientific interests		To advise on action under Hill Farming Act 1946

APPENDIX 7

GENERALIZED SUMMARY OF WORKING PARTY REPORT
RECOMMENDATIONS

By EDWARD N. BRYANT

The seventeen working parties, whose reported recommendations are summarized below, were appointed by the President of the Board of Trade with these terms of reference:

to examine and enquire into the various schemes and suggestions put forward for improvement of organisation, production and distribution methods and processes in the ———— industry, and to report as to the steps which should be adopted in the national interest to strengthen the industry and to render it more stable and more capable of meeting competition in the home and foreign markets.

The number of members of the working parties, including the chairman, secretary, and assistant secretary, varied from 11 (China Clay and Light Clothing) to 20 (Heavy Clothing), with an average membership of 15. In addition several of the working parties coöpted unofficial members into subcommittees for special studies. Typical of the composition of working parties is the Boot and Shoe working party, which has a chairman, secretary, assistant secretary, five representatives each of management and labor in the industry, three technical and engineering representatives, one representative of the Board of Trade, and one economist.

Several of the working parties sent delegations abroad to study foreign industry. Seven members of the Lace working party visited France and eight members of the Heavy Clothing group traveled in America visiting factories from New York to California.

Owing, in part, to the varying natures of the industries studied and also to the different degrees to which each industry was investigated by its working party, the reports vary considerably as to the breadth of their findings and the detail of their recommendations. The most extensive report (Cotton) consists of 278 pages, lists 34 recommendations, and mentions 97 meetings of the working party. The report on Furniture mentions 90 meetings, with the Lace report citing 29. Several of the reports make many detailed recommendations which are later subsumed in a few general recommendations, e.g., the report on Lace reduces 67 to 21, while the Hosiery report condenses more than 80 to 17. The report of the Linoleum working party has only 48 pages but makes 24 recommendations.

The generalized summary of the 17 working party reports in the following table does not contain all recommendations of all reports, but includes the major recommendations and in particular those that are common to most of the reports. Some reports cite the specific implementing agency for each recommendation; others assume a designation such as "Industry" to mean both management and labor. In any case, for most of the industries concerned, implementing the recommendations would be the joint function of labor, management, and government, since all but three working parties (Carpets, Lace, and Linoleum) recommended tripartite development councils for over-all control of the industry studied.

WORKING PARTY REPORT RECOMMENDATIONS
GENERALIZED SUMMARY

PART I. ORGANIZATION OF INDUSTRY—PRODUCTION, ETC.

(*Appendix 7*)

Generalized recommendations	Boots and shoes	Carpets	China clay	Clothing—heavy	Clothing—light	Clothing—rubber proof	Cotton	Cutlery	Furniture	Glassware—domestic	Hosiery	Jewelry and silverware	Jute	Lace	Linoleum	Pottery	Wool
Long-term planning																	
Development councils	x	−	x	x	x	x	x	x	x	x	x	x	x	−	−	x	x
Trade associations:																	
Unify and increase scope	x	x	−	x	x	−	−	x	x	x	−	x	x	−	x	−	x
Registration of members	x	−	−	x	−	x	−	x	x	−	−	x	−	−	−	−	−
Levy on members	x	−	−	−	−	−	−	x	−	x	x	x	−	x	x	x	x
Centralize																	
Statistics	x	−	x	x	−	x	x	x	x	x	x	x	x	−	x	x	x
Research	x	−	x	−	−	x	x	x	x	x	x	x	x	x	x	x	x
Design	x	x	−	x	x	x	−	x	x	x	x	x	−	x	x	x	x
Standardize																	
Size	x	−	−	x	x	x	−	−	−	−	−	−	x	−	−	x	−
Quality	x	−	−	x	x	x	−	x	x	x	x	x	x	−	−	x	−
Manufacturing																	
methods	−	−	−	x	x	x	−	x	−	x	−	−	−	−	−	−	−
Cost accounting	x	−	−	−	x	x	x	x	−	x	x	x	x	−	x	x	x
Unit capacity policy																	
Concentrate	−	−	x	−	−	−	x	x	−	−	−	−	x	−	−	x	−
Free entry	−	−	−	x	−	−	−	−	−	−	−	−	−	−	−	−	−
Expand	−	x	−	−	−	−	−	−	−	x	x	−	x	−	−	−	−
Control or reduce	−	−	−	−	x	x	x	x	−	−	−	−	−	−	−	x	−
Raw material supply																	
Control	x	−	−	x	−	−	x	−	−	x	x	−	−	−	x	−	x
Consultation or survey	−	x	x	−	x	−	−	x	x	x	x	−	−	x	x	x	x
Standardize	−	−	x	−	−	−	−	x	−	−	x	−	−	−	−	x	−
Pool	−	−	x	−	−	−	x	−	−	−	x	−	−	x	−	−	−
Equipment suppliers (domestic):																	
Control	x	x	−	−	−	−	x	−	−	x	−	x	−	−	−	−	−
Expedite	x	x	x	−	x	x	x	x	x	x	x	x	x	−	x	−	−
Government aid	x	−	−	−	−	−	−	−	−	x	x	−	−	−	x	−	−
Rationalization and reëquipment via:																	
Tax relief	x	x	−	x	−	x	x	−	−	−	−	−	x	x	−	x	x
Trade levy	−	−	−	−	−	−	x	−	−	−	−	−	−	x	−	−	−
Government loan	−	−	−	−	−	−	x	x	−	x	−	−	−	−	x	−	−
Price increase	−	−	−	−	−	−	x	−	−	−	−	−	−	−	−	−	−
Long-term production policy:																	
Divide for specialization	−	x	−	−	−	−	x	−	x	−	−	−	−	−	−	−	x
Stretch or shorttime	x	−	x	−	x	x	−	−	−	−	−	x	−	−	x	−	−
Control outworkers	x	−	−	−	x	x	−	x	−	−	−	x	−	−	−	−	−

PART II. DISTRIBUTION—MARKETING

(Appendix 7)

Generalized recommendations	Working party report																
	Boots and shoes	Carpets	China clay	Clothing—heavy	Clothing—light	Clothing—rubber proof	Cotton	Cutlery	Furniture	Glassware—domestic	Hosiery	Jewelry and silverware	Jute	Lace	Linoleum	Pottery	Wool
Central agency for:																	
Export	x	–	–	–	–	x	x	–	x	–	x	x	–	x	x	x	x
Market expansion or sales	–	–	–	–	–	x	x	x	–	x	x	x	–	x	–	–	–
Publicity and information	–	–	–	x	x	–	–	x	x	x	x	x	x	–	x	x	–
Price fixing	–	–	–	–	–	–	–	x	–	–	–	–	–	–	x	–	–
Codes	–	–	–	–	–	–	–	x	x	–	x	–	–	–	x	x	–
Consumer and market research	x	–	–	x	x	x	x	x	x	x	–	x	x	x	–	x	–
Quality inspection	–	–	–	x	–	x	–	x	x	x	–	x	–	–	–	–	–
Foreign markets:																	
Protective tariff	x	x	–	–	–	–	–	–	–	–	x	–	x	–	x	–	–
Minimum standard imports	x	–	–	–	x	–	–	–	–	–	x	–	–	–	–	–	–
Agreement with	–	–	–	–	–	–	–	–	–	–	–	–	–	–	x	–	–
Develop permanent	–	x	–	x	–	–	–	–	–	–	x	x	–	–	–	–	x
Minimum standard exports	–	–	–	–	–	x	–	x	x	–	–	–	–	–	–	–	–
Retail and distribution:																	
Stabilize sales	x	–	–	x	x	x	–	x	–	–	x	–	–	x	–	–	–
Cost survey	–	x	–	–	–	–	x	–	x	–	x	–	–	–	–	–	–
Price increase	–	–	–	x	x	–	–	x	–	–	–	–	–	–	–	–	–
Eliminate cost-plus	–	–	–	–	x	x	–	–	–	–	–	–	–	–	–	–	–
Standardize price	–	–	–	–	x	x	–	x	–	–	x	–	–	–	x	–	–

PART III. INDUSTRIAL RELATIONS

(*Appendix 7*)

Generalized recommendations	Working party report																
	Boots and shoes	Carpets	China clay	Clothing—heavy	Clothing—light	Clothing—rubber proof	Cotton	Cutlery	Furniture	Glassware—domestic	Hosiery	Jewelry and silverware	Jute	Lace	Linoleum	Pottery	Wool
Joint consultation																	
Works committees..	x	x	x	–	–	x	–	x	–	–	–	x	–	–	x	–	x
Industry wide......	–	–	–	–	x	x	–	x	–	–	x	–	x	–	–	x	x
Employment and recruiting																	
Disperse and/or diversify.........	x	x	–	–	–	x	–	–	x	–	x	–	–	–	–	–	x
Stabilize...........	x	–	–	x	x	x	–	–	–	–	x	–	–	–	–	–	–
Increase...........	–	–	x	–	–	–	x	x	–	x	x	–	–	x	–	–	x
Women, part-time..	x	x	–	–	–	–	–	–	–	–	–	–	–	x	–	–	x
Juvenile............	–	–	–	–	–	x	–	x	–	x	x	–	–	x	–	x	x
Training																	
T.W.I. schemes.....	x	x	–	–	–	–	–	–	–	–	–	–	–	–	x	–	–
Supervisory........	x	x	–	–	x	x	x	x	x	–	x	–	–	–	x	–	–
Worker............	x	x	x	x	x	x	–	x	–	x	x	x	–	x	–	x	–
Increase apprenticeship.............	–	–	–	–	x	–	–	x	–	x	x	–	–	–	–	x	–
Decrease apprenticeship..........	–	–	–	x	–	x	–	–	–	–	–	–	–	–	–	–	–
Schools............	x	x	–	–	–	–	–	–	x	x	–	x	x	x	–	x	x
Welfare																	
Enforce factory acts	x	–	x	x	x	x	–	x	x	–	–	–	–	–	–	x	–
Industrial psychology study........	–	–	–	x	–	x	x	x	–	–	–	x	–	–	–	–	x
Improve...........	–	x	x	–	x	–	x	x	x	x	x	x	x	x	x	–	–
Incentives and efficiency																	
T.W.I. schemes.....	x	x	–	–	–	–	–	–	–	–	–	–	–	–	x	–	–
Piece-rate study....	–	–	–	x	–	x	–	–	–	–	–	–	–	–	–	–	–
Comparative productivity study...	x	–	–	x	x	–	–	–	–	–	x	–	x	–	x	–	x
Scholarships.......	x	–	x	–	–	x	–	–	–	–	x	–	–	–	x	–	–
Modify P.A.Y.E....	–	–	–	–	x	–	–	–	–	–	–	–	–	–	–	–	–
Time and motion study............	x	–	–	x	x	x	–	x	–	–	x	–	x	–	–	–	–
Advisory experts...	–	x	–	–	x	–	–	x	–	–	–	–	–	–	–	x	–
Personnel manager.	x	–	–	–	x	x	–	x	x	–	x	–	–	–	–	x	–

APPENDIX 8

"Equal Rights of Economic Participation" Terms in Major Agreements Signed by Great Britain and the United States since 1941

Atlantic Charter[1]

The President of the United States and the Prime Minister Mr. Churchill, representing His Majesty's Government in the United Kingdom, being met together, deem it right to make known certain common principles in the national policies of their respective countries on which they base their hopes for a better future for the world.

First, their countries seek no aggrandisement, territorial or other.

Second, they desire to see no territorial changes that do not accord with the freely expressed wishes of the people concerned.

Third, they respect the right of all peoples to choose the form of Government under which they will live; and they wish to see sovereign rights and self-government restored to those who have been forcibly deprived of them.

Fourth, they will endeavour, with due respect for their existing obligations, to further the enjoyment by all States, great or small, victor or vanquished, *of access, on equal terms, to the trade and to the raw materials of the world which are needed for their economic prosperity.*[2]

Fifth, they desire to bring about the fullest collaboration between all nations in the economic field, with the object of securing for all improved labour standards, economic advancement and social security.

Sixth, after the final destruction of Nazi tyranny, they hope to see established a peace which will afford to all nations the means of dwelling in safety within their own boundaries, and which will afford assurance that all the men in all the lands may live out their lives in freedom from fear and want.

Seventh, such a peace would enable all men to traverse the high seas and oceans without hindrance.

Eighth, they believe all of the nations of the world, for realistic as well as spiritual reasons, must come to the abandonment of the use of force. Since no future peace can be maintained if land, sea or air armaments continue to be employed by nations which threaten, or may threaten, aggression outside of their frontiers, they believe, pending the establishment of a wider and permanent system of general security, that the disarmament of such nations is essential. They will likewise aid and encourage all other practicable measures which will lighten for peace-loving peoples the crushing burden of armaments.

[1] *Joint Declaration by the President of the United States of America and Mr. Winston Churchill, representing His Majesty's Government in the United Kingdom, known as the Atlantic Charter, August 14, 1941,* Cmd. 6321.

[2] Italics appearing in the text of agreements cited in this appendix are the author's.

Lend-Lease[3]

Article 7.—In the final determination of the benefits to be provided to the United States of America by the Government of the United Kingdom in return for aid furnished under the Act of Congress of the 11th March, 1941, the terms and conditions thereof shall be such as not to burden commerce between the two countries, but to promote mutually advantageous economic relations between them and the betterment of world-wide economic relations. To that end they shall include provision for agreed action by the United States of America and the United Kingdom, open to participation by all other countries of like mind, directed to the expansion, by appropriate international and domestic measures, of production, employment, and the exchange and consumption of goods, which are the material foundations of the liberty and welfare of all peoples; *to the elimination of all forms of discriminatory treatment in international commerce*, and to the reduction of tariffs and other trade barriers; and, in general, to the attainment of all the economic objectives set forth in the Joint Declaration [Atlantic Charter] made on the 12th August, 1941 by the President of the United States of America and the Prime Minister of the United Kingdom.

At an early convenient date conversations shall be begun between the two governments with a view to determining, in the light of governing economic conditions, the best means of attaining the above-stated objectives by their own agreed action and of seeking the agreed action of other like-minded Governments.

Bretton Woods

THE INTERNATIONAL MONETARY FUND[4]

Article I: Purposes.—The Purposes of the International Monetary Fund are:

(i) To promote international monetary cooperation through a permanent institution which provides the machinery for consultation and collaboration on international monetary problems.

(ii) To facilitate the expansion and balanced growth of international trade, and to contribute thereby to the promotion and maintenance of high levels of employment and real income and to the development of the productive resources of all members as primary objectives of economic policy.

(iii) To promote exchange stability, to maintain orderly exchange arrangements among members, and *to avoid competitive exchange depreciation.*

---

[3] *Agreement between the Governments of the United Kingdom and the United States of America on the Principles applying to Mutual Aid in the Prosecution of the War against Aggression, Washington, February 23, 1942,* Cmd. 6341.

[4] "Articles of Agreement of the International Monetary Fund," in *Proceedings and Documents of the United Nations Monetary and Financial Conference, Bretton Woods, New Hampshire, July 1-22, 1944,* vol. I, annex A, p. 942 ff.

(iv) To assist in the establishment of a multilateral system of payments in respect of current transactions between members and in *the elimination of foreign exchange restrictions* which hamper the growth of world trade.

(v) To give confidence to members by making the Fund's resources available to them under adequate safeguards, thus providing them with opportunity to correct maladjustments in their balance of payments without resorting to measures destructive of national or international prosperity.

(vi) In accordance with the above, to shorten the duration and lessen the degree of disequilibrium in the international balances of payments of members.

The Fund shall be guided in all its decisions by the purposes set forth in this Article.

THE INTERNATIONAL BANK[5]

Article I: Purposes.—The purposes of the Bank are:

(i) To assist in the reconstruction and development of territories of members by facilitating the investment of capital for productive purposes, including the restoration of economies destroyed or disrupted by war, the reconversion of productive facilities to peacetime needs and the encouragement of the development of productive facilities and resources in less developed countries.

(ii) *To promote private foreign investment by means of guarantees or participations in loans and other investments made by private investors;* and when private capital is not available on reasonable terms, to supplement private investment by providing, on suitable conditions, finance for productive purposes out of its own capital, funds raised by it and its other resources.

(iii) To promote the long-range balanced growth of international trade and the maintenance of equilibrium in balances of payments by encouraging international investment for the development of the productive resources of members, thereby assisting in raising productivity, the standard of living and conditions of labor in their territories.

(iv) To arrange the loans made or guaranteed by it in relation to international loans through other channels so that the more useful and urgent projects, large and small alike, will be dealt with first.

(v) To conduct its operations with due regard to the effect of international investment on business conditions in the territories of members and, in the immediate post-war years, to assist in bringing about a smooth transition from a wartime to a peacetime economy.

The Bank shall be guided in all its decisions by the purposes set forth above.

[Lord Keynes, chairman of the United Kingdom Delegation, was chosen to make the final address at the closing session of the conference.][6]

---

[5] "Articles of Agreement of the International Bank for Reconstruction and Development," *ibid.*, p. 984 ff.

[6] *Ibid*, vol. II, p. 1240 ff.

Mr. President: I feel it a signal honor that I am asked to move the acceptance of the Final Act at this memorable Conference.

We, the Delegates of this Conference, Mr. President, have been trying to accomplish something very difficult to accomplish. We have not been trying, each one to please himself, and to find the solution most acceptable in our own particular situation. That would have been easy. It has been our task to find a common measure, a common standard, a common rule applicable to each and not irksome to any. . . .

And I make bold to say, Mr. President, that under your wise and kindly guidance we have been successful. . . . I am certain that no similar Conference within memory has achieved such a bulk of lucid, solid construction. . . .

Finally, we have perhaps accomplished here in Bretton Woods something more significant than what is embodied in this Final Act. We have shown that a concourse of 44 nations are actually able to work together at a constructive task in amity and unbroken concord. . . . We have been learning to work together. If we can so continue, this nightmare, in which most of us here present have spent too much of our lives, will be over. The brotherhood of man will have become more than a phrase.

Mr. President, I move to accept the Final Act.

World Food Agreement[7]

Preamble.—The Nations accepting this Constitution, being determined to promote the common welfare by furthering separate and collective action on their part for the purposes of

raising the levels of nutrition and standards of living of the peoples under their jurisdictions,

securing improvements in the efficiency of the production and distribution of all food and agricultural products,

bettering the condition of rural populations, and thus contributing toward an expanding world economy,

hereby establish the Food and Agriculture Organization of the United Nations . . .

Article I: Functions of the Organization.—

1. The Organization shall collect, analyze, interpret, and disseminate information relating to nutrition, food and agriculture.

2. The Organization shall promote and, where appropriate, shall recommend national and international action with respect to

(*a*) scientific, technical, social, and economic research relating to nutrition, food and agriculture

(*b*) . . .

---

[7] Food and Agriculture Organization of the United Nations, *Constitution Rules and Regulations* (Washington, 1949).

(c) the conservation of natural resources and the adoption of improved methods of agricultural production

(d) the improvement of processing, marketing, and distribution of food and agricultural products;

(e) adoption of policies for the provision of adequate agricultural credit, national and international;

(f) the adoption of international policies with respect to agricultural commodity arrangements.

3. It shall also be the function of the Organization

(a) to furnish such technical assistance as governments may request;

(b) to organize, in cooperation with the governments concerned, such missions as may be needed to assist them to fulfill the obligations arising from their acceptance of the recommendations of the United Nations Conference on Food and Agriculture; and

(c) generally to take all necessary and appropriate action to implement the purpose of the Organization as set forth in the Preamble.

Washington Loan Agreement[8]

Article 7: Sterling Area Exchange Arrangements.—The Government of the United Kingdom will complete arrangements as early as practicable and in any case not later than one year after the effective date of this Agreement, unless in exceptional cases a later date is agreed upon after consultation, under which immediately after the completion of such arrangements the sterling receipts from current transactions of all sterling area countries (apart from any receipts arising out of military expenditure by the Government of the United Kingdom prior to December 31, 1948, to the extent to which they are treated by agreement with the countries concerned on the same basis as the balances accumulated during the war) *will be freely available for current transactions in any currency area without discrimination; with the result that any discrimination arising from the so-called sterling area dollar pool will be entirely removed and that each member of the sterling area will have its current sterling and dollar receipts at its free disposition for current transactions anywhere.*

Article 8: Other Exchange Arrangements.—(i) *The Government of the United Kingdom agrees that after the effective date of this Agreement it will not apply exchange controls in such a manner as to restrict (a) payments or transfers in respect of products of the United States permitted to be imported into the United Kingdom or other current transactions between the two countries or (b) the use of sterling balances to the credit of residents of the United States arising out of current transactions.* Nothing in this paragraph (i) shall affect the provisions

[8] *Financial Agreement between the United States of America and the United Kingdom, Signed at Washington December 6, 1945, Effective July 15, 1946,* Department of State, Treaties and other International Acts Series 1545 (Washington, 1946).

of Article VII of the Articles of Agreement of the International Monetary Fund when those Articles have come into force.

(ii) The Governments of the United States and the United Kingdom agree that not later than one year after the effective date of this Agreement, unless in exceptional cases a later date is agreed upon after consultation, *they will impose no restrictions on payments and transfers for current transactions.* The obligations of this paragraph (ii) shall not apply:

(*a*) to balances of third countries and their nationals accumulated before this paragraph (ii) becomes effective; or

(*b*) to restrictions imposed in conformity with the Articles of Agreement of the International Monetary Fund, provided that the Governments of the United Kingdom and the United States will not continue to invoke the provisions of Article XIV, Section 2 of those Articles after this paragraph (ii) becomes effective, unless in exceptional cases after consultation they agree otherwise; or

(*c*) to restrictions imposed in connection with measures designed to uncover and dispose of assets of Germany and Japan.

(iii) This section and section 9, *which are in anticipation of more comprehensive arrangements by multilateral agreement,* shall operate until December 31, 1951.

Article 9: Import Arrangement.—If either the Government of the United States or the Government of the United Kingdom imposes or maintains quantitative import restrictions, such restrictions shall be administered on a basis which does not discriminate against imports from the other country in respect of any product; provided that this undertaking shall not apply in cases in which (*a*) its application would have the effect of preventing the country imposing such restrictions from utilizing, for the purchase of needed imports, inconvertible currencies accumulated up to December 31, 1946, or (*b*) there may be special necessity for the country imposing such restrictions to assist, by measures not involving a substantial departure from the general rule of non-discrimination, a country whose economy has been disrupted by war, or (*c*) either government imposes quantitative restrictions having equivalent effect to any exchange restrictions which that government is authorized to impose in conformity with Article VII of the Articles of Agreement of the International Monetary Fund. The provisions of this section shall become effective as soon as practicable but not later than December 31, 1946.

Havana Charter[9]

SUMMARY OF CHARTER PROVISIONS

Key Provisions.—The Charter of the International Trade Organization (ITO) has *one over-all purpose* which should be borne in mind in any study

---

[9] *Havana Charter for an International Trade Organization, March 24, 1948, Including a guide to the study of the Charter,* Department of State (Washington, 1948), p. 3 ff.

of the provisions of this document: *to establish and maintain by mutual agreement, an "open" or multilateral system of trade relations between members of the organization, and to expand on businesslike principles the trade of each member with all other members.* The opposite state of affairs calls for numerous "closed" economies, each of which conducts foreign trade under strict governmental control in accordance with short-term agreements based on planned "barter" with politically selected countries. . . .

The purpose of the Charter is reflected in three "key" provisions of chapter IV in which members agree to grant equal treatment to each other with respect to tariff and other foreign trade matters (article 16); *to reduce tariffs on a selective basis* (article 17); and *to refrain from using quantitative restrictions, i.e. quotas, on imports or exports to protect particular industries from competition* or for other purposes detrimental to international trade (article 20). A study of the Charter may, accordingly, begin with a summary of these provisions.

I. Article 16: Equal Treatment (Non-discrimination).—In this article each member agrees to apply, in its import and export trade with every other member, the same customs duties and the same laws and regulations concerning customhouse procedures generally. No special privileges can be given in the future and existing discriminations must be abolished, except as to tariff rates on certain products based on historic agreements. Most important are those agreements between countries of the British Empire and between the United States on the one hand and Cuba and the Phillippines on the other. However these tariff rate differentials cannot be increased, and they are subject to reduction in the future in accordance with the selective bargaining procedures of article 17.

II. Article 17: Reduction of Tariffs and Elimination of Preferences.—In article 17, members undertake to enter into and carry out negotiations with each other directed to the substantial reduction of tariffs and the elimination of preferences. The procedures contemplated are similar to those under the Trade Agreements Act which has been in force in the United States since 1934. Tariff cuts are not made by reducing all existing rates by some uniform percentage. Instead, a country bargains individually with other countries, one at a time, concerning tariff reductions on those articles of which each country is the chief or an important supplier of the other and which each elects to put up for bargaining. In effect, countries agree to "swap" tariff concessions on a "product-by-product" basis.

This procedure was actually carried out on a large scale at Geneva in 1947 when the United States negotiated tariff reductions with 22 other countries, and many of these countries likewise negotiated with each other. The resulting tariff rates were then incorporated into one inclusive document known as the "General Agreement on Tariffs and Trade."

At this point article 17 ties in closely with article 16 which obliges each member to extend to all other members its lowest tariff rates including all tariff concessions negotiated in trade agreements. The members who participated in Geneva negotiations must extend to all other countries joining ITO the same reduced tariff rates on every product included in the General Agreement. However article 17 requires that if these other countries are to continue to be entitled to receive "bargain" rates, they must also, within two years, negotiate tariff reductions with countries now parties to the General Agreement.

III. Article 20: General Elimination of Quantitative Restrictions (Quotas).— This article concerns quantitative restrictions, trade barriers that consist of governmental regulations specifying the amounts of any product that can enter or leave the country during a certain period of time. Article 20 lays down the general rule that members shall not use quantitative restrictions to regulate the import or export of any product, save under exceptional circumstances.

The chief exception to the rule against export restrictions in this article relates to the case of a critical shortage of foodstuffs or other essential products. The chief exception to the rule against import restrictions in the article relates to agricultural products, where the domestic supply is also subject to governmental restrictions. When used in conjunction with such domestic programs, however, quantitative restrictions on imports cannot be used as a protective device to increase the share of domestic producers in their national market.

The basic rules of the Charter with regard to equal treatment, the reduction of tariffs, and the elimination of quantitative restrictions are directly involved in some related articles. Approximately half of these articles may be regarded as supporting or extending the basic provisions, while the remainder may be considered as qualifying them. . . .

Marshall Aid[10]

Preamble: The Governments of the United States of America and of the United Kingdom of Great Britain and Northern Ireland:

Recognising that the restoration or maintenance in European countries of principles of individual liberty, free institutions, and genuine independence rests largely upon the establishment of sound economic conditions, stable international economic relationships, and the achievement by the countries of Europe of a healthy economy independent of outside assistance;

Recognising that a strong and prosperous European economy is essential for the attainment of the purposes of the United Nations;

[10] *Economic Cooperation Agreements Between the United States of America and The United Kingdom: First Report to Congress of the Economic Cooperation Administration, June 30, 1948; Supplement* (Washington, 1948), pp. 185–197.

Considering that the achievement of such conditions calls for a European recovery plan of self-help and mutual co-operation, open to all nations which co-operate in such a plan, based upon a strong production effort, the expansion of foreign trade, the creation or maintenance of internal financial stability and the development of economic cooperation, including all possible steps to establish amd maintain valid rates of exchange and to reduce trade barriers; . . .

Article II, Section 3.—The Government of the United Kingdom will take the measures which it deems appropriate, and will co-operate with other participating countries, to prevent, on the part of private or public commercial enterprises, *business practices or business arrangements affecting international trade which restrain competition, limit access to markets or foster monopolistic control* whenever such practices or arrangements have the effect of interfering with the achievement of the joint programme of European recovery.

[An interpretation of this agreement as far as it affects the investment of private American capital in the British colonies, is given in the following passage from the *First Report*,[11] section entitled "Strategic Materials."]

Promoting the Security of the United States.—The Act contains certain provisions designed to promote the security of the United States. These deal with means for increasing our stockpile of materials in which we are deficient or potentially deficient and with the scrutiny and control of exports.

Materials Needed by the United States.—In compliance with section 115 of the Act, the bilateral agreements have included provisions for the participating governments to negotiate arrangements designed to insure the delivery—from their own sources or their colonies and dependencies—of a fair share of materials needed by the United States, *to give suitable protection to the rights of American Citizens who invest in the development of productive facilities for such materials,* and to schedule, where practicable, an increase in their output. Some of the materials in which there are deficiencies or potential deficiencies in the United States are manganese, lead, tin, copper, graphite, industrial diamonds, palm oil, and coconut oil.

The Appropriation Act provides, as noted before, that withdrawals may be made from the counterpart local currency funds deposited by the participating countries for the purpose of financing the procurement of materials needed by the United States. Furthermore, to promote increased output of such materials the Administration may supply funds for the purchase of special equipment *and extend guarantees of convertibility to American Citizens or enterprises investing in projects designed to increase production of such items abroad.* Plans were made during the quarter for negotiations with the participating countries to stimulate the procurement and increased output of these vital materials.

[11] *Ibid.*, pp. 18–19.

APPENDIX 9

Private United States Direct Investments Abroad

(An abridgment of an article with the same title, by Milton Abelson, in the *Survey of Current Business*, November 1949. Mr. Abelson is a member of the International Economics Division, Office of Business Economics, U. S. Department of Commerce.)

Private long-term American investments abroad rose rapidly during the twenties from $6.5 billion at the end of 1919 to a peak of $16.8 billion by the end of 1929.[1] The depression brought a sharp reduction in the value of overseas assets . . . and by the end of 1940 they amounted to $10.1 billion. . . . However, foreign direct investments declined less sharply than domestic net capital expenditures in 1931 due to the incentive to invest in the British Empire and produce behind tariff walls. On the other hand, when domestic investment recovered in 1936 and 1937, economic and political factors abroad were not conducive to new investment. . . . However, since the end of World War II they have again expanded rapidly, and at the end of 1948 had an estimated value of $15.3 billion. Most of this capital at the end of 1948—$11.4 billion—was in direct investments. . . . With the end of hostilities and the conversion of industry in general to production of more usual products, investments in directly-controlled enterprises abroad were resumed. The net movement of such funds as shown in Table 1 was over $1.6 billion during 1946–48. [A further breakdown of these data by area and year is shown in Table 2, and Table 3 shows the capital movement data for a number of countries.] In addition to these net investments reported in the balance of payments in 1946–48, a considerable amount of American capital was invested abroad out of the undistributed earnings of foreign subsidiaries. . . . Such reinvested earnings totaled about $1,260 million during 1946–48. Total investment during the three postwar years, therefore, was $2.9 billions, or an average of almost $1.0 billion a year. The previous high mark was $602 million in 1929—also including reinvested earnings. These outflows represented the first sizable exports of American equity capital since the early thirties. . . .

United States residents earned an estimated $1,552 million in 1948, after foreign taxes, on direct investments abroad [largely equity capital] with an

---

[1] The movement of American private long-term investments is generally divided into two major components, namely, portfolio and direct investments. Portfolio investments consist of real property, estates and trusts, and the holdings of miscellaneous foreign securities—including dollar bonds—which do not involve any controlling interest on the part of the American investor. Direct investments, on the other hand, represent the extension of American business into foreign countries and consist largely of foreign branches and subsidiaries of American companies. . . . The value of the excluded long-term portfolio investments was approximately as follows (in billions): 1919: .0; 1929: 1.2; 1940: 1.2; 1940: 1.2; 1948: 1.5.

approximate value of $10 billion at the end of 1947.[2] Returns for major American direct-investment industries abroad ranged from 2.4 percent on public utility investments to 25.6 percent for petroleum. Returns for other industries included 17.6 percent for manufacturing, 14.7 percent for distribution, 11.9 percent for agriculture, and 10.6 percent for mining and smelting. . . .

The composition of private postwar investments differed materially in character from that of the 1920's and early 1930's. In the decade ending with 1929, 60 percent of American foreign investments consisted of publicly offered foreign dollar bonds, which were purchased in relatively small amounts by a large number of individual and corporate investors. In 1947, by contrast, $717 million or 90 percent of the net private outflow (excluding undistributed foreign subsidiary earnings) consisted of direct investments— almost entirely by corporations and very largely for the expansion of existing enterprises. . . . Over 75 percent of the net outflow of American direct-investment capital in 1947 was accounted for by 10 of the approximately 2,500 American companies with foreign branches and subsidiaries.

The bulk of the postwar investments was made with funds obtained largely from internal sources of the investing companies, chiefly undistributed profits. In the twenties, by contrast, almost half of new direct investments was apparently made with funds obtained from security sales to the general public. Another difference in the two periods was the distribution of direct-investment outlays over a larger number of industries and countries in the twenties. . . .

The United States Government has attempted to stimulate the flow of private investments abroad by reducing or eliminating risks peculiar to such investments and which, therefore, have deterred investors from participating in enterprises in many foreign countries. Among the measures undertaken have been investment guaranties, treaties of friendship with foreign countries, the reciprocal trade agreements program, and other measures aimed at establishing a better balance in international accounts.

The Economic Cooperation Act of 1948 contained provisions for a guaranty fund to stimulate the establishment of direct investments in countries participating in the ERP. Under its terms, dollars were to be available over a 14-year period to remit earnings from such investments if foreign-exchange difficulties abroad prevented transfers. The same applied to invested capital, in the event of liquidations.

More recently, the President requested the Congress to authorize an experimental program for the guaranty of newly invested private capital in undeveloped countries. The capital would have to contribute to the

---

[2] If the value of direct investments in countries such as in Eastern Europe, Germany, and Japan, to which there was no free access, is eliminated, the overall rate of return is increased from 15.6 per cent to 17.1 per cent for 1948.

economic development of such areas and would be guaranteed against risks related to foreign investments, other than ordinary business risks. Outstanding among such risks proposed for a program of Government guarantees are risks of (1) nonconvertibility of returns derived from the investment, including capital, and (2) loss through seizure, confiscation, or expropriation, without prompt, adequate and effective compensation. . . . Treaties of Friendship, Commerce, and Navigation are currently under negotiation with a large number of countries, and contain more comprehensive provisions for protection of investments than did earlier treaties.

TABLE 1

(*Appendix 9*)

FACTORS AFFECTING VALUE OF UNITED STATES DIRECT INVESTMENTS ABROAD BY PRIVATE CAPITAL, 1945–48

(Millions of dollars; capital inflow [−])

Industry	Value, end of 1945	1946–48			Value, end of 1948
		Capital movements	Reinvested earnings	Other factors[a]	
All industries....................	8,370	1,650	1,259	100	11,379
Manufacturing.................	2,671	162	714	56	3,603
Distribution..................	672	118	131	10	931
Agriculture and fishing..........	518	54	55	...	627
Mining and smelting............	1,063	44	23	16	1,147
Petroleum.....................	1,538	1,205	301	3	3,047
Public utilities.................	1,357	−88	13	5	1,287
Miscellaneous.................	551	155	21	10	737

SOURCE: U. S. Department of Commerce, Office of Business Economics.
[a] Other factors affecting the change in value include some allowance for revaluation of assets because of fluctuations in foreign exchange rates during 1946.
NOTE.—Capital movements represent the net of known new investments less liquidations. Reinvested earnings are the undistributed portion of the net earnings of foreign subsidiaries. Value is the American equity in direct investments abroad and includes expropriated property for which compensation has not yet been received and properties in Germany and Japan. No allowance has been made for war damage.

TABLE 2
(Appendix 9)
VALUE OF PRIVATE AMERICAN DIRECT INVESTMENTS ABROAD, BY AREA AND INDUSTRY, 1945–1948
(Millions of dollars)

Area and end of year	Manu-factur-ing	Distri-bution	Agricul-ture[a]	Mining and smelting	Petro-leum	Public utilities	Miscel-laneous	Total
All areas:								
1945................	2,671	672	518	1,063	1,538	1,357	551	8,370
1946................	2,904	752	544	1,078	1,760	1,283	592	8,913
1947................	3,205	836	578	1,111	2,364	1,275	648	10,017
1948................	3,603	939	627	1,147	3,047	1,287	737	11,379
Canada:								
1945................	1,145	141	13	451	160	383	234	2,527
1946................	1,257	163	14	479	181	383	263	2,740
1947................	1,362	167	14	498	229	350	253	2,873
1948................	1,573	198	14	501	278	353	270	3,187
American republics:								
1945................	433	146	420	412	645	898	46	3,000
1946................	487	166	445	397	769	822	59	3,145
1947................	595	211	474	410	1,089	847	97	3,723
1948................	676	267	503	433	1,376	852	104	4,211
ERP countries:								
1945................	832	265	4	64	299	20	205	1,689
1946................	885	281	4	64	309	20	202	1,765
1947................	949	295	4	64	337	20	216	1,885
1948................	1,035	291	4	65	369	20	237	2,021
ERP dependencies:								
1945................	12	17	56	40	127	5	7	264
1946................	12	19	55	40	151	5	7	289
1947................	13	21	56	38	249	5	7	389
1948................	17	22	56	42	391	5	7	540
Other Europe:								
1945................	105	39	2	85	64	10	24	329
1946................	107	40	2	85	64	10	25	333
1947................	111	40	2	83	65	10	26	337
1948................	113	42	2	82	68	11	25	343
All other countries:								
1945................	144	64	23	11	243	41	35	561
1946................	156	83	24	13	286	43	36	641
1947................	175	102	28	18	395	43	49	810
1948................	189	111	48	24	565	46	94	1,077

SOURCE: U. S. Department of Commerce, Office of Business Economics.
a Includes fishing.
NOTE.—For an explanation of value, see table 1, appendix 9.

TABLE 3
(*Appendix 9*)

UNITED STATES PRIVATE DIRECT-INVESTMENT CAPITAL MOVEMENTS
BY SELECTED COUNTRIES, 1945-1948

(Millions of dollars; capital inflow [−])

Country	1945	1946	1947	1948
American republics.....................	140	56	460	318
Argentina......................	1	−86	43	15
Brazil.........................	2	23	72	25
Chile.........................	−1	4	6	−3
Colombia......................	7	18	3	4
Costa Rica....................	20	4	9	5
Cuba, Dominican Republic, and Haiti.....	−6	−8	2	−11
Ecuador.......................	4	1	−3	2
Guatemala.....................	14	3	1	13
Honduras......................	13	7	14	5
Mexico........................	6	−2	21	16
Panama........................	a	24	121	37
Paraguay......................	1	2	3	3
Peru..........................	8	a	9	−7
Uruguay.......................	9	1	a	2
Venezuela.....................	59	60	157	213
Other countries...............	2	5	2	−1
ERP countries.....................	−7	15	48	41
United Kingdom................	7	1	21	11
Belgium.......................	a	2	7	3
Denmark.......................	a	3	−1	3
France........................	2	1	1	13
Germany.......................	a	−2	1	4
Italy.........................	a	1	1	4
Netherlands...................	−1	3	3	6
Portugal......................	−1	1	3	a
Sweden........................	1	4	6	−2
Switzerland...................	a	a	2	1
Other countries...............	−14	1	3	−2
ERP Dependencies..................	−16	4	52	114
British West Indies...........	1	a	5	2
Netherlands East Indies.......	a	4	29	1
Hong Kong, Malaya, and Straits Settlements..	...	4	4	5
Dependencies in Africa b......	a	3	5	10
Other dependencies............	−17	−7	9	96
Other Europe......................	−87	1	1	3
Spain.........................	−87	1	2	2
Other countries...............	a	a	−1	1
All other countries..............	31	49	153	226
Australia.....................	−3	3	21	3
China.........................	2	8	5	1
Egypt.........................	−1	3	7	17
India, Ceylon, and Pakistan...	a	4	−1	1
New Zealand...................	a	1	3	2
Republic of the Philippines...	a	14	25	20
Union of South Africa.........	−3	5	16	16
Other countries...............	35	12	77	167

SOURCE: U. S. Department of Commerce, Office of Business Economics.
a Less than $500,000.
b Includes Algeria, Belgian Congo, British East and West Africa, Eritrea, French West Africa, Morocco, Portuguese East Africa, and Tunisia.
NOTE.—For explanation of capital movements, see table 1, appendix 9.

APPENDIX 10

TABLE 1, *a*

INVISIBLE PAYMENTS AND RECEIPTS

(Millions of pounds)

	1938	1947	1948 Jan.-June	1948 July-Dec. (provisional)	1949 Jan.-June (forecast)
PAYMENTS					
Government overseas expenditure:					
(a) Military....................	...	197	64	50	117 [a]
(b) Relief and rehabilitation....	...	58	13	2	6
(c) Germany..................	...	80	12	11	7
(d) Administrative, diplomatic, etc......................	...	37	22	19	21
(e) War disposals and settlements...................	...	−121	−28	−59 [b]	−65 [c]
(f) Other government (net).....	...	−44	−1	4	10
Total (net)...................	16	207	82	27	96
Shipping.......................	80	181	94	96	98
Interest, profits, and dividends....	30	106	56	56	56
Films (net).....................	7	14	7	3	2
Travel.........................	40	80	27	43	30
Total payments..............	173	588	266	225	282
RECEIPTS					
Shipping.......................	100	205	123	127	134
Interest, profits, and dividends....	205	153	78	84	81
Travel.........................	28	21	15	20	17
Other (net).....................	72	20	66	76	85
Total receipts................	405	399	282	307	317
Surplus or deficit.................	232	−189	16	82	35

SOURCE: *Economic Survey for 1949*, Cmd. 7647, p. 23.
[a] Includes £55,000,000 paid under Indian settlement.
[b] Includes £45,000,000 received under Indian settlement.
[c] Includes £55,000,000 received under Indian settlement.

TABLE 1, *b*

(*Appendix 10*)

BALANCE OF PAYMENTS ON CURRENT ACCOUNT BY AREAS

(Millions of pounds)

	1947	1948		1949 Jan.-June forecast
		Jan.-June	July-Dec. provisional	
Western Hemisphere:				
Imports (f.o.b.)	717	293	276	270
Exports and re-exports (f.o.b.)	173	119	145	160
Invisibles (net)	−111	−26	−9	−5
Deficit	−655	−200	−140	−115
Sterling Area:				
Imports (f.o.b.)	504	337	323	360
Exports and re-exports (f.o.b.)	562	350	392	435
Invisibles (net)	−3	52	91	55
Surplus	55	65	160	130
O.E.E.C. Countries:				
Imports (f.o.b.)	233	156	167	202
Exports and re-exports (f.o.b.)	268	180	200	220
Invisibles (net)	−60	11	12	17
Surplus or deficit	−25	35	45	35
Other Countries:				
Imports (f.o.b.)	87	110	106	128
Exports and re-exports (f.o.b.)	97	81	83	95
Invisibles (net)	−15	−21	−12	−32
Deficit	−5	−50	−35	−65
Total:				
Imports (f.o.b.)	1,541	896	872	960
Exports and re-exports (f.o.b.)	1,100	730	820	910
Invisibles (net)	−189	16	82	35
Surplus or deficit	−630	−150	30	−15

SOURCE: *Economic Survey for 1949*, Cmd. 7647, p. 25.

TABLE 2
(*Appendix 10*)
UNITED KINGDOM BALANCE OF PAYMENTS: CAPITAL ACCOUNT
(Millions of pounds)

	1947	1948 Jan.–June	1948 July–Dec. provisional	1949 Jan.–June forecast
Net gold and dollar deficit				
United Kingdom................	655	186	125	130
Rest of sterling area............	202	17	9	15
Whole sterling area: net gold and dollar payments to nondollar countries.....................	167	51	35	50
	1,024	254	169	195
Net reduction in United Kingdom external capital assets				
Nonsterling area................	−73	57	43	
Sterling area....................	−179	−142	−50	
	−252	−85	−7	−180
Net increase in sterling liabilities				
Nonsterling area................	3	−138	−108	
Sterling area....................	−145	119	−84	
	−142	−19	−192	
Net overseas disinvestment........	630	150	−30	15

SOURCE: *Economic Survey for 1949*, Cmd. 7647, p. 27.

TABLE 3
(*Appendix 10*)
DISTRIBUTION OF TOTAL PAYMENTS FOR IMPORTS BY SOURCES [a]
(Percentages)

Source	1938	1947	1948 Jan.–June	1948 July–Dec. provisional	1949 Jan.–June forecast
Western Hemisphere.........	32	46	33	32	28
Sterling area [b]...............	31	33	38	37	38
O.E.E.C. countries..........	23	15	17	19	21
Other countries..............	14	6	12	12	13
Total....................	100	100	100	100	100

SOURCE: *Economic Survey for 1949*, Cmd. 7647, p. 21.
[a] The percentages for 1947, 1948, and first half of 1949 relate to f.o.b. payments. The 1938 percentages relate to c.i.f. values of imports from the Trade and Navigation Accounts.
[b] Approximate figures for the Colonies only are: 1938, 6; 1947, 9; 1948, 11.

TABLE 4, *a*

(*Appendix 10*)

VOLUME OF EXPORTS OF UNITED KINGDOM PRODUCE BY DESTINATIONS

(Volume indices, 1938 = 100)

Destination	1947	1948 Jan.–June	1948 July–Dec.	1949 Jan.–June forecast
Western Hemisphere	94	125	139	150
Sterling area [a]	117	143	157	165
O.E.E.C. countries [b]	102	121	136	138
Other countries [c]	107	113	111	118
Total	109	130	143	150

SOURCE: *Economic Survey for 1949*, Cmd. 7647, p. 19.
[a] Approximate figures for the Colonies only are: 1947, 130; 1948, 190.
[b] "O.E.E.C. Countries," here and elsewhere in this section, means nonsterling members of the Organisation for European Economic Cooperation together with their dependent overseas territories. It excludes Eire and Iceland which are included in the sterling area.
[c] Includes Egypt, Sudan, Palestine, and Transjordan throughout.

TABLE 4, *b*

(*Appendix 10*)

EXPORTS OF UNITED KINGDOM PRODUCE, 1947 TO 1949, BY COMMODITY GROUPS

(Volume indices, 1938 = 100)

	1947	1948 Jan.–June	1948 July–Dec.	1949 Jan.–June forecast
Machinery	158	186	200	220
Vehicles	189	254	278	290
Electrical goods and apparatus	164	209	225	235
Iron and steel	107	112	124	135
Other metal goods	177	206	242	235
Textiles and clothing	73	86	100	104
Chemicals	140	152	160	170
Pottery, glass, abrasives, etc	154	200	206	215
Coal	3	21	36	38
All other exports	91	102	106	108
Total	109	130	143	150

SOURCE: *Economic Survey for 1949*, Cmd. 7647, p. 19.

TABLE 5
(Appendix 10)

CAPITAL INVESTMENT

A. INVESTMENT WHOLLY AT THE DISCRETION OF THE NATIONAL OR OF LOCAL
GOVERNMENTS BECAUSE GOVERNMENTALLY OWNED AND OPERATED
(AS OF JULY 1, 1949)

(Millions of pounds)

	1947	1948	1949
Coal..	16.4	25.3	27.6
Electricity..	70.3	85.8	114.7
Gas..	28.0	32.0	37.0
Transport and communication......................	133.0	161.0	170.0
Roads..	46.4	42.6	51.7
Road vehicles (for public transportation)............	19.0	33.0	29.0
Ports and inland waterways........................	9.7	11.0	15.5
Civil aviation.....................................	20.0	18.2	24.5
Post office..	32.0	37.0	42.0
Education...	13.7	28.2	47.0
Health services...................................	13.4	17.3	24.4
Water supply and sewerage.........................	12.8	17.5	25.5
Services administered by home departments..........	1.8	2.3	5.4
BBC..	0.3	0.6	1.6
Defense and administration:			
Service departments (military)....................	18.5	19.0	26.0
Ministry of supply..............................	11.5	15.0	19.5
Government buildings............................	17.3	24.3	26.4
Northern Ireland (public construction)..............	.....	.....	18.0
Total..	464.1	570.1	705.8

TABLE 5 (*Continued*)
(*Appendix 10*)

B. INVESTMENT WHICH IS PARTLY OR PREDOMINANTLY MADE BY THE
NATIONAL OR BY LOCAL GOVERNMENTS

(Millions of pounds)

	1947	1948	1949
Coke ovens..	3.5	4.1	6.6
Petroleum...	73.0	92.0	115.0
Road haulage (vehicles).............................	56.0	50.0	35.0
Forestry..	4.1	6.8	7.2
Housing...	461.0	477.0	421.0
Total...	597.6	629.9	584.8

C. INVESTMENT MADE WHOLLY (OR ALMOST ENTIRELY) BY PRIVATE ENTERPRISE

(Millions of pounds)

	1947	1948	1949
Shipping..	152.0	175.0	154.0
Agriculture and fisheries............................	67.9	85.2	91.8
Iron and steel......................................	27.0	34.0	50.0
Other manufacturing................................	340.0	370.0	400.0
Northern Ireland (private construction)..............	.....	.....	9.0
Total...	586.9	664.2	704.8

SOURCE: Compiled from "Appendix on Capital Investment in 1949," *Economic Survey for 1949*, Cmd. 7647 pp. 48–63.

TABLE 6
(Appendix 10)

ESTIMATE OF GOVERNMENT EXPENDITURES ON THE ENCOURAGEMENT OF THE ARTS

(Pounds)

	1947–48	1948–49	1949–50	Departmental vote
ENGLAND				
Arts and science buildings...	721,390	869,905	2,507,650	Common Services
Royal parks and pleasure gardens..................	533,725	531,530	662,000	Common Services
Historic monuments........	41,055	44,605	60,090	Common Services
Ancient monuments........	165,630	173,155	210,450	Common Services
National building record...	11,000	11,000	11,000	Common Services
British council.............	2,913,000	2,570,000	2,551,000	(Foreign Office: Colonial and Commonwealth)
Council of industrial design.	164,000	164,000	231,500	Board of Trade
Royal college of art........	26,536	31,284	....	Education
Victoria and Albert museum	242,550	188,006	330,394	Education
Science museum............	102,891	132,443	144,091	Education
Bethnal Green museum.....	10,034	10,741	11,250	Education
British museum............	250,353	283,927	275,712	Education
Natural history museum....	178,386	197,649	215,315	Education
Imperial war museum......	38,183	26,904	32,723	Education
London museum...........	10,882	12,305	13,862	Education
National gallery (including Tate)....................	64,248	67,676	77,377	Education
National maritime museum.	20,475	21,906	22,078	Education
National portrait gallery...	15,559	17,876	17,876	Education
Wallace collection..........	21,463	22,230	24,202	Education
Grants for science and the arts[a]....................	1,805,585	2,409,164	3,370,868	Education
SCOTLAND				
National galleries..........	24,982	25,467	27,505	Education
National library...........	7,998	11,097	13,468	Education
Royal Scottish museum....	41,210	43,928	48,586	Education
Edinburgh observatory....	5,860	8,915	10,091	Education
Total..................	7,416,995	7,875,713	10,869,188	

SOURCE: *Home Affairs Survey*, April 12, 1949, p. 2.
[a] Includes further breakdowns on grants for science and the arts not reproduced here.

TABLE 7

(Appendix 10)

COST OF SOCIAL SERVICES

(Millions of pounds)

	1947–8	1948–9	1949–50
Education and physical training[a].....................	168.2	198.1	225.3
Housing...	56.0	70.0	66.3
National health service............................	2.1	203.6	249.3
Health services: aid to local services................	10.6	12.5	14.0
Government contributions to national insurance and pension schemes and noncontributory:			
Health insurance funds.............................	14.2	4.2	.....
Unemployment fund................................	27.5	7.8	.....
Contributory pensions accounts.....................	117.0	31.9	.....
National insurance fund............................	.....	97.5	141.0
National insurance (industrial injuries) fund..........	.....	4.0	6.0
National assistance etc............................	14.9	30.1	55.7
Old age pensions (noncontributory)..................	26.7	28.2	27.7
Family allowances.................................	61.0	59.5	60.2
Total...	498.2	747.4	845.5

SOURCE: British Information Service, Reference Division, I.D. 829. (1949), p. 9.
a Including teachers' pensions.
NOTE.—The Budget estimates that "Health, Housing, Town Planning, Labor and National Insurance, etc." will cost £725,000,000 in 1949–50.

TABLE 8
(Appendix 10)

NATIONAL RESOURCES AND EXPENDITURE
(Millions of pounds)

	1947	1948	Forecast for 1949 at end 1948 prices
RESOURCES			
National income of the United Kingdom.....	8,725	9,675	10,000
Provision for depreciation and maintenance..	750	825	900
Net loans and gifts from abroad and sales of foreign assets.............................	630	120	......
Total resources available for use at home..	10,105	10,620	10,900
EXPENDITURE			
Domestic expenditure on goods and services at market prices:			
Personal.................................	7,465	8,004	8,200
Government.............................	2,069	1,914	2,040
Gross capital formation...................	2,040	2,352	2,330
Total.................................	11,574	12,270	12,570
Subsidies.................................	434	515	515
Less indirect taxes........................	−1,903	−2,165	−2,185
Total resources available for use at home....	10,105	10,620	10,900

SOURCE: *Economic Survey for 1949*, Cmd. 7647, p. 35.

TABLE 9
(Appendix 10)

FOOD CONSUMPTION IN THE UNITED KINGDOM

	Pre-war	1947–48	1948–49 partly forecast
AVERAGE DAILY INTAKE PER HEAD			
Protein			
Animal (gms.)..........................	42.7	41.0	41.0
Vegetable (gms.)........................	37.2	46.1	47.9
Total (gms.)...........................	79.9	87.1	88.9
Fat (from all sources) (gms.)..............	130.2	104.8	110.0
Visible fat (butter, margarine, lard, etc., fat content) (gms.)........................	56.2	44.4	49.9
Total energy value (calories)...............	3,000	2,860	2,990
ANNUAL CONSUMPTION IN LBS. PER HEAD [a]			
Dairy products (milk solids)...............	38.3	48.0	50.1
Meat (edible weight).....................	109.6	74.8	70.8
Fish, game, poultry, etc. (edible weight)....	32.8	37.7	38.0
Eggs and egg products (shell egg equivalent)..	24.0	21.3	22.3
Oils and fats (fat content).................	45.3	35.6	40.0
Sugar and syrups (sugar content)...........	109.9	88.0	91.6
Potatoes................................	176.0	257.8	280.1
Pulses and nuts..........................	9.6	6.0	6.3
Tomatoes and fruit (fresh equivalent).......	141.5	138.4	143.3
Vegetables..............................	107.4	111.8	118.0
Grain products...........................	210.1	242.7	252.8
Beverages...............................	14.7	14.5	14.6

SOURCE: *Economic Survey for 1949*, Cmd. 7647, p. 37.

[a] The method used for arriving at consumption per head makes allowance for exports and changes of stocks and includes estimates for home produced food consumed on farms and obtained from gardens and allotments, but no allowance is made for wastage in the home and consumption by domestic animals.

TABLE 10
(Appendix 10)
DISTRIBUTION OF MAN POWER IN GREAT BRITAIN, 1939–1948
(Thousands)

	Mid 1939	End 1946	End 1947	End 1948 Economic survey	End 1948 Actual
AVAILABLE MAN POWER					
Total working population...............	19,750	20,435	20,430	20,100	20,327
Less strength of Armed Forces.........	480	1,461	1,119	730	808
Less ex-service men and women on release leave.......................	......	300	123	50	18
Total industrial population.............	19,270	18,674	19,188	19,320	19,501
Men................................	14,176	12,983	13,476	13,720	13,772
Women............................	5,094	5,691	5,712	5,600	5,729
DISTRIBUTION BY INDUSTRY OR OCCUPATION					
Coal.................................	773	730	758	790	766
Other mining and quarrying............	100	71	73	75	74
Public utilities.......................	242	264	270	280	279
Transport and shipping................	1,233	1,384	1,438	1,460	1,461
Agriculture...........................	910	1,046	1,055	1,110	1,091
Fishing..............................	40	35	35	37	35
Building and civil engineering..........	1,310	1,289	1,364	1,200	1,357
Manufactures					
Building materials...................	567	574	590	575	585
Metals and engineering..............	2,267	2,822	2,876	2,900	2,908
Cotton............................	344	255	267	325	287
Wool..............................	210	167	178	200	186
Other textiles......................	244	193	207	235	217
Clothing...........................	1,005	807	831	800	839
Food, drink, and tobacco............	654	599	623	600	642
Chemicals..........................	266	321	336	335	343
Other manufactures.................	1,258	1,268	1,343	1,355	1,337
Distribution..........................	2,887	2,309	2,351	2,320	2,406
Consumer services.....................	2,225	1,984	2,120	2,123	2,110
Public service—					
Civil service.......................	397	711	680	715	707
Other national government...........	222	395	388	360	377
Local government...................	846	1,052	1,105	1,075	1,146
Total employed........................	18,000	18,276	18,888	18,870	19,153
Unemployed..........................	1,270	398	300	450	348

SOURCE: *Economic Survey for 1949,* Cmd. 7647.

TABLE 11
(Appendix 10)

GOVERNMENT EXPENDITURES AND RECEIPTS FOR FOUR SELECTED YEARS

A. CENTRAL GOVERNMENT EXPENDITURE

(Millions of pounds)

	1907–08	1924–25	1933–34	1949–50[a]
Interest and management of national debt....	21	312	216	485
Other consolidated fund services.............	2	22	36	42
Supply services:				
Defence...............................	58	115	108	760
Civil...................................	41	240	338	1,983
Customs, excise and inland revenue..........	3	11	12	31
Post Office (excess of expenditure over revenue)...............................	...	...	...	7
Total "ordinary expenditure".............	126	700	711	3,308
Expenditure of borrowed funds.............	3	10	7	456

B. EXPENDITURE ON CIVIL SUPPLY SERVICES

(Millions of pounds)

	1913–14	1924–25	1933–34	1949–50[a]
Central government and finance.............	1	2	2	12
Foreign and Imperial......................	2	8	8	52
Home department, law and justice...........	3	11	16	55
Education and broadcasting................	17	48	51	244
Health, housing, town planning, labour and national insurance.......................	14	65	151	668
Trade, industry and transport..............	1	4	9	169
Common services (works, stationery, etc.)...	4	8	8	82
Non-effective charges (pensions)...........	1	71	49	95
Exchequer contributions to local revenues...	...	...	45	57
Supply, food and miscellaneous services......	...	...	...	548

[a] Budget estimates.

TABLE 11 (*Continued*)
(*Appendix 10*)

C. CENTRAL GOVERNMENT REVENUE

(Millions of pounds)

	1907–08	1924–25	1933–34	1949–50[a]
Customs..................................	32	99	179	830
Excise....................................	36	135	107	664
Inland revenue:				
Income taxes[b]...........................	32	337	282	1,595
Death duties.............................	19	59	85	176
Stamps..................................	8	23	23	48
Profits tax and EPT.....................	...	19	2	240
Special contribution.....................	...	...	...	25
Other...................................	3	1	1	1
Motor vehicle duties......................	...	16	31	54
Post Office (excess of revenue over expenditure)...................................	5	5	13	...
Sundries.................................	4	54	28	145
Total.................................	139	749	750	3,778

SOURCE: *Midland Bank Review*, May, 1949, p. 2.
 [a] Budget estimates.
 [b] Standard rates of income tax respectively 1*s.*, 4*s.* 6*d.*, 5*s.* and 9*s.*

Index

INDEX

Abercrombie report (London), 430

Accra affair, 19, 611, 612

Addison, Lord, 451, 471

Africa: unrest in, 19, 612; Accra affair, 19, 611, 612; Barnes' proposal for, 589–590; development potentialities, 594–595; health, 605–606; overpopulation, 606, 607; soil erosion, 606, 608; investment in, 607; Labour's commitments for welfare and self-government, 609 ff.; attitude of natives toward foreign corporations, 610; veterans, 611, 613; Communism(?), 611–612; basic causes of trouble, 613–614; Labour's program and dilemma, 614–615; coöperation with local governments, 615, 629; problems of race, 616 ff., 627; Africander party, 616, 619; Anglo-French technical conference, 620–621; welfare follows economic development, 626–627. *See also* Colonial policy; Groundnuts Scheme; Malan government; U.A.C.

Agricultural Act of 1947, 475 ff.; guaranteed prices and assured markets, 476, 482, 490; rules for good estate management and good husbandry, 476, 483; no nationalization plan, 476; no correlation with various ministries, 476–477; no national physical plan for agriculture, 477; possible interpretations, 480–482; power of Minister, 484–485

Agricultural Marketing acts: Lucas committee reviews, 453–454, 487; purpose, 454–455; lack of organized grading and standardization, 454; compulsory cartels, 455; prewar marketing schemes, 455; special commissions, 456; plan for organization, 457–458; subsidy system, 458–459; Lucas committee recommends commodity commissions, 488–490, and Conservative opposition to, 490–491

Agricultural Mortgage Corporation, 72–73, 453, 475 ff.

Agriculture: land lost to, 403–405, and average decline, 449; lack of national policy, 446, 451–452, 471 ff., 480, 482, 486, 492; food imports, 446 ff.; prewar conditions, 449 ff.; import policy, 450; competition of foreign producers, 450–451; no organization, 454; prewar legislation, 453 ff.; wartime changes, 459 ff.; change-over from permanent grass to tillage, 468–469; postwar survey, 469; self-sufficiency(?)

469, 470; Cripps Four-Year Plan, 471; Conservative program, 471, 480–481; nationalization or land planning(?), 471 ff.; Scott committee report, 477–479

Agriculture, Ministry of: control over production, 459, 460, 467, 485; wartime powers, 466–467; determines acreage cultivated, 467, 468; standards for land usage and crop management, 467, 468, 483–484; subsidiary to Ministry of Food, 481, 491; annual reviews, 482–483; powers under Agricultural Act, 484–485; Agricultural land commissions and tribunals, 484; local authorities, 484–485; goals, 485; works through N.F.U., 486. *See also* Food, Ministry of

Airways: nationalization of overseas, 275 ff.; Civil Aviation Act, 275, 277; three government corporations, 275, 278, coördinated through Ministry of Civil Aviation, 281; B.O.A.C., 275, 276, 278, 279; Conservatives' Overseas Airways Act of 1939, 276; government subsidies, 276–277; intergovernmental aids to navigation, 277; Swinton Plan, 279

Approved societies: and industrial assurance, 320 ff.; under National Health Insurance Act of 1911, 320; types, 320–321; purposes, 320, 321; weaknesses, 321–322, 324; 1947 act because inadequate, 322; Labour government takes over, 327; Beveridge committee opposes, 328; Labour's solution, 328–329, 330; election pledge, 329–330; exist for supplementary benefits, 329, 349; virtual dissolution, 329, 349; differences between friendly societies and, 329, 330; assets from partial liquidation, 339

Arts, government expenditure on, 654

Assistance Act, National: purpose, 318–319, 320; no contributions, 340; state grants increased by administrative action, 340

Atlantic Charter, 308, 581, 611, 624, 626, App. 8

Bank of England; MacMillan report, 41, 65; Dalton proposes public ownership, 43–44, 45, and Pethick-Lawrence, 45–47; arguments for nationalization, 44, 47–49; charges against, 47–50; and "Big Five" commercial banks, 48; credit policy, 49; relation with Treasury, 49–50, 57, 58, 431;